P9-CIT-873

BALANCE OF POWER

BALANCE OF POWER

*Presidents and Congress from the Era of
McCarthy to the Age of Gingrich*

JIM WRIGHT

TURNER PUBLISHING, INC.
ATLANTA

Library of Congress Cataloging-in-Publication
    Balance of power: presidents and congress from the era of McCarthy to the age of Gingrich / by Jim Wright.
      p. cm.
   ISBN 1-57036-278-5 (alk. paper)
    1. United States—Politics and government—1946–1989. 2. United States—Politics and government—1989– 3. Presidents—United States—History—20th Century. 4. United States. Congress—History—20th Century. I. Title.
E839.5.W75 1996
320.973—dc20   95-44193
                                                    CIP

Published by Turner Publishing, Inc.
A Subsidiary of Turner Broadcasting System, Inc.
1050 Techwood Drive, NW
Atlanta, Georgia 30318

First Edition
10 9 8 7 6 5 4 3 2 1

Printed in the United States.

This book is dedicated to Betty Hay Wright,
my wife and my inspiration;

To Mary Nelle and Betty Lee;

To Jimmy, Ginger, Kay, and Lisa;

To Christopher, Erik, Kevin, Stephen, and John;

AND TO

Parker Stephen Wright,
my son for a little time,
like his father, imperfect,
now, like his mother, sublime.

BALANCE OF POWER

PREFACE

This is the story of Congress and nine American presidents—Dwight D. Eisenhower through Bill Clinton—the fascinatingly different personalities of these chief executives, their widely differing approaches to our nation's problems, and their respective efforts to deal with that colorful collection of opinionated individualists known as Congress. The Constitution makes presidents and Congress interdependent. They are, at once, both partners and adversaries. Neither can accomplish much without some help from the other. That's what our founding fathers deliberately designed: a *balance of power*.

The American presidency is the world's most demanding job. Also the most fateful. Jefferson called it a "splendid misery." Truman said "the buck stops here." Lyndon Johnson said it "has made every man who occupied it, no matter how small, bigger than he was; and however big, not big enough for its demands." I have watched each of the presidents with whom I worked age visibly while in office. The White House is a pressure cooker.

Our story spans three presidential generations. When I first went to Congress, as a first-term member from Texas in 1954, President Eisenhower was precisely the age of my father. As I became House Majority Leader in 1976, President Carter was approximately my own age. Now, President Bill Clinton is the age of my eldest child. Hoping to be around when we have a president who is now the age of one of my five grandsons, I find myself secretly wishing that it will never be one of them. What the public and the national media have come to demand of our chief executive is more than any reasonable person should expect or any normal human being can deliver.

This is also a story of Congress, that amorphous collection of ordinary men and women called upon to grapple with such extraordinary problems. The House, in which I served for thirty-four years, is of all our institutions of government closest to the people. Subject to their moods, it mirrors their strengths and weaknesses.

I don't pretend that this is an objective book. I'm not sure there is any such thing. Nobody views events with the mechanical detachment of a camera, but all of us through the prisms of our personal experiences. I can only promise that I'll tell you the truth—as I saw it—about people and events that contributed to the major national decisions of the past forty years.

We'll focus here upon the peculiarly American, and often intensely personal, interplay between Congress and presidents. At times, they worked together; sometimes at tense cross-purposes. These four decades have seen periods of great productive cooperation and moments of bitter confrontation, with both sides thinking they were right. For twenty-six of those forty years, five Republican presidents served while at least one house of the legislative branch was in the hands of the Democratic majority. For the past two years, Democratic President Bill Clinton has had to deal with a Republican majority in both houses. This struggle to accommodate diverse philosophies and strong, conflicting personalities is the dynamic business of our democracy.

Great changes have swept the country in the span of these four decades. We've conquered space, put a man on the moon, engineered a revolution in race relations, discovered our debt to the environment, ended the Cold War, plunged into world trade, flirted with cyberspace. On the darker side, we've seen the diminution of civility, the rise of drugs and crime, the growth of adversary journalism, a loss of comity in our political structures, a mean-spirited magnification of negative campaigning, and the galloping dependence upon big money in our political system.

People sometimes ask which of the nine presidents I thought was the best. That's a hard call. Each had strengths, and each was human. Eisenhower may have been the most widely respected. Kennedy was the most inspiring. Johnson was the most personally persuasive, got the most from Congress, achieved the most social progress. Nixon did more for world peace than he gets credit for. Carter, I think, was the most painfully honest, Reagan the most gifted in mass communication. Bush was strong in foreign affairs. Bill Clinton is, in my view, smarter than most give him credit for being. I am convinced that every one of the nine, without exception, has very earnestly wanted to do the right thing for our country.

My perspective on all of this is that of a participant, not an onlooker. Through these four decades, I was one of those trying to make a difference. It's been an exciting journey. Sometimes I did make a difference. And so can you.

CHAPTER ONE

WELCOME TO WASHINGTON

"That's the man whose gavel is going to end the power of Joe McCarthy," Lyndon Johnson told me as mild-mannered Senator Arthur Watkins left his office that hot summer day. It was August of 1954, only my second trip to our nation's capital.

The Senate Minority Leader's statement astounded me.

I had arrived in Washington that week, midway through President Eisenhower's first term, a newly chosen Democratic nominee for Congress. In my part of Texas, the Democratic nomination was equivalent to election. I liked Senator Johnson. Twice I had been his local campaign manager. As president of the Texas Municipal League the previous December, I had seen to it that he was featured at the state convention of mayors and city officials. I admired his work and trusted his political judgment. But now, I wondered at the bold prediction Johnson had just made. McCarthy's power ending? His hypnotic spell broken?

For all my faith in Lyndon's sagacity, I had trouble comprehending that prophesy. During four miserable years, the Wisconsin firebrand had terrorized and intimidated the nation with bullying attacks on the patriotism of all who had the temerity to oppose him. While I had canvassed my district for votes, the Army-McCarthy hearings dominated daytime television coverage. Everywhere I went, the Wisconsin senator's bold charges about Communist infiltration in our armed services captivated the public's attention. His reckless accusations had already broken the faith of many Americans in our State Department. Politicians were afraid to cross him. Nobody wanted to be a target of his vitriol. Now, seated in the Minority Leader's high-ceilinged office off the Senate floor, I pressed my friend and mentor to justify the conclusion to which he had given voice. I wanted to believe him, but caution tugged at my mind like a bridle. Fear, after all, is a virulent germ.

"How is Senator Watkins going to stop Joe McCarthy when nobody else has been able to?" I asked.

"The Senate is going to censure him," Johnson replied. "I have felt it for two weeks. Arthur Watkins, whom you just met, is chairman of the committee of inquiry. He and Ralph Flanders will get a majority of the Republicans, and I believe I can get all of the Democrats. We've given that man enough rope, and he's hanging himself."

Senator Ralph E. Flanders of Vermont, a rock-ribbed Republican of flinty moral honesty and blunt Yankee directness, had introduced a resolution to expel the freewheeling Wisconsin witch hunter from the Senate, and another to censure him. Watkins, Johnson told me, was a Republican of unimpeachable credentials and a solid Mormon reputation for fairness. He and Johnson had been discussing the case when I arrived for our appointment.

"Ev Dirksen will stick by McCarthy. As Majority Leader, he thinks he has to," Lyndon continued. "But more and more Republicans are fed up with McCarthy. His blowhard charges against administration people are becoming an embarrassment to them. Ike doesn't like him. Arthur Watkins says we'll have the votes, and I believe him."

Still, I was unconvinced. McCarthy didn't invent the Red scare, but he had institutionalized it. Brazenly and effectively, he exploited it. Several senators, among them Millard Tydings of Maryland and William Benton of Connecticut, had met defeat at the polls after openly opposing the Wisconsin senator. Tydings had been the victim of a last minute smear, a doctored photograph circulated throughout his state portraying him flanked by suspected Communists. Before the photo could be exposed as a phony, it did its damage. In California, Vice President Richard Nixon had profited, both in his 1946 election to the House and in his Senate victory over Helen Gahagan Douglas in 1950, from the tactics of innuendo and guilt-by-association. Nixon's 1950 campaign literature attacked a "statewide conspiracy" of a "subversive clique" and accused Mrs. Douglas of voting 353 times with ultra left-wing Congressman Vito Marcantonio of New York. Not mentioned was the fact that, on most of those votes, a majority of all members had voted with Mrs. Douglas and the outspoken fellow traveler. McCarthy appeared personally in 1950 on Nixon's behalf via regional network from Los Angeles. In that speech, he cried treason, demanded the resignation of Secretary of State Dean Acheson, and referred to the president's political party as the "Commicrat Party of Betrayal." Nixon won handily.

Senator Claude Pepper lost in the Florida Democratic primary that same year, bombarded by Red-baiting and disgraceful scare tactics, victimized by deliberately planted rumors, publicly advertised by his opponent as "Red Pepper." Little wonder that Senate colleagues had found it prudent not to cross McCarthy publicly. Now, McCarthy was saying that seventy-three-year-old Senator Flanders, in filing the motion to censure him, was acting out of "senility." Having intimidated the State Department, the U.S. Information Service, and the Commerce Department with charges of Communist infiltration, McCarthy as chairman of the Senate Permanent Investigation subcommittee, finally had taken on Secretary of the Army Robert T. Stevens and the Pentagon. He charged they were engaged in a conspiracy to cover up Soviet sympathizers in the military.

To be sure, some voices rose in protest. Edward R. Murrow took on McCarthy frontally in a televised broadcast, pointing to the outrageous reign of error fueled by McCarthy's unsubstantiated claims. Arthur Miller wrote a play in 1953 titled *The Crucible*. Built around the Salem witch trials, the powerful drama was recognized as an allegory of the climate of smear and fear that McCarthy and others like him had fueled. Lyndon Johnson aide Harry McPherson would write years later that he went to law school expressly hoping to defend victims wrongly accused by McCarthyism. But broadcasting networks and Hollywood studios, wary of being tainted or accused of harboring fellow travelers, shied away even from respected professionals like Murrow. Blacklisting agencies arose to comb the background of actors and artists. Accusations abounded in an atmosphere that too often tilted toward an assumption of guilt.

One man who never wavered in his opposition to McCarthy was Harry Truman. In 1950, he vetoed the Internal Security Act, which would have made a civil service employee's political beliefs reason for dismissal, calling it a "mockery of the Bill of Rights." Later, in response to Merle Miller's oral questions in *Plain Speaking*, Truman looked back upon that period of hysteria. Responding to a pointed query about Joe McCarthy, the former president said, "Oh, yes, and I've told you he was just a no-good son of a bitch."

But this was summer, 1954. Two years earlier, the Republicans, with popular Dwight D. Eisenhower as standard-bearer, had romped to electoral victory, seizing both House and Senate. Behind the facade of dignity the former general gave to the ticket, the theme in many successful congressional races had been "crime, Korea, and corruption." Sometimes it degenerated to a cruder "crime, *communism*, and corruption."

"Supposing the Senate *does* vote to censure Joe McCarthy for his behavior," I asked Johnson. "How is that going to change things? How will it reduce his power over public opinion?"

I told Lyndon I had just encountered a rag-tag group of demonstrators on the Capitol steps. Their hand-made signs proclaimed their faith in McCarthy. "The people who believe him think he's God!" I said.

"After the Senate officially censures him," Johnson replied evenly, "this god won't be God anymore. The news media that fawn over him today and give front page headlines to every preposterous exaggeration he utters will ignore him. He'll be last week's news. Discredited. He'll make a speech and get a brief story below the fold on page eight. That'll destroy him. And I'm working," said the skilled parliamentarian, "to see that this happens this year—while there's a Republican majority in the Senate. That'll take all partisanship out of it. He'll be repudiated by a Republican Senate."

Johnson's eyes narrowed. I thought they had a new sparkle. "I think we've got a good chance, Jim, to win back both the House and Senate come November."

In the 1954 general election, for which both parties were tuning up as I talked with Senator Johnson, McCarthy would charge previous Democratic administrations with "twenty years of treason." Attorney General Herbert Brownell would state that Truman had knowingly promoted a Communist.

President Eisenhower did not approve of such comments. Privately, he made his opinion known to top Republicans. But not even the president could control zealous professional campaign hucksters. The Republican congressional committee would distribute a series of strident radio tapes for spot political advertisements on local stations. One of them followed this text:

> *Crier: Oyez! Oyez! Oyez! Listen to the record of the Fair Deal, and the*
> *New Deal, the Double Deal!*
> *Different Voices: Communists and spies infiltrated the top spots in*
> *our government!*
> *Voice B: Traitors stole the secrets of the A bomb and gave them to*
> *Russia!*
> *Voice C: Traitors stole the secrets of the H bomb and gave them to*
> *Russia! . . .*
> *Announcer: Yes, this is the record of twenty years of Double Deal—a*
> *record of communism and corruption. It must not happen again!*
> *America's future is at stake. Vote Ike a Republican Congress and*
> *endorse his crusade against communism and corruption. Vote*
> *Republican in November!*

This would permanently offend Speaker Sam Rayburn. In aroused indignation, he'd tell the House: "I can stand charges of crime and corruption, but charges implying treason are unforgivable."

That August evening, after my visit with Senator Johnson, I went to dinner with Speaker Rayburn. The venerable icon of Texas political culture made no secret of his pleasure at my primary victory over incumbent Wingate Lucas, whom Rayburn considered gratuitously troublesome. Lucas once had told the Speaker that if his Fort Worth constituency knew he so much as talked with Rayburn, they'd turn him out of office. My win, with 60 percent of the vote in our fairly conservative district, gave the lie to that unfortuitous claim. I was known as a devoted friend and admirer of the Speaker. I had rallied to his call for volunteers, given three days a week to the 1952 Adlai Stevenson campaign when Governor Alan Shivers, Senator Price Daniel, and the entire State Democratic Executive Committee abandoned ship and endorsed Eisenhower.

"It doesn't make any difference how smart or gifted a man may be," Rayburn opined that night. "Without loyalty, you haven't got a starting place."

We ate, along with several Texas congressmen—Frank Ikard, Homer Thornberry, and Paul Kilday—in a small private dining room at Hall's Seafood Restaurant, then housed in an old frame building on a corner in the heart of Washington's dilapidated southwest quadrant. It was the Speaker's favorite eating place. The group had gathered beforehand, at Rayburn's invitation, for a touch of bourbon and branch water in the Speaker's private hide-away office on the first floor of the Capitol, directly below the House chamber. I discovered that members referred privately to this room as the "Board of Education." After a few drinks and about an hour's friendly conversation in the unpretentious little room, we drove separately to Hall's, where we gathered for dinner. Without a car, I was invited to ride with Speaker Rayburn in his commodious black limousine. I observed that gray-haired driver George Donovan, to whom Mr. Rayburn introduced me, took pains to ease the car along at an unhurried pace. I had a feeling that the Speaker was sizing me up, taking my measure.

"I noticed that you had only one drink and nursed it through the whole conversation," said Rayburn. I was surprised at his directness. "Is that your general habit?" he asked.

"I'm trying to keep my wits about me," I replied, smiling. "There's a lot for me to learn."

Rayburn laughed. "You keep that attitude, and there's no limit to how far you can go."

At dinner, I noticed the deference everyone paid the Speaker. He didn't seem to demand it. He didn't have to. He was friendly, as relaxed as he ever got. His courtly demeanor seemed as inseparable a part of him as the dark-blue suits he always wore, the short Camel cigarettes he smoked, and the pince-nez glasses he fished out of the handkerchief pocket of his coat whenever confronted with something he had to read.

I would learn that the impromptu stag dinner with a few chosen male friends was a trademark of Rayburn's life-style and an informal tool of his leadership. Product of an earlier time, he was unfailingly courteous to women, but slightly uncomfortable in their presence, at least where business was being discussed. His habit of inviting colleagues on the spur of the moment, I learned, was something congressional wives came to expect and accept.

Following dinner, the Speaker asked George Donovan to drive him first to his private quarters on Capitol Hill and then take me to the Washington Hotel, where I was staying that week. Part of my mission was to find a house for my wife, Mab, and our three children, Jimmy, Ginger, and Kay. I had no doubt of being elected in the fall. As if by habit or prior arrangement, Donovan drove up Fourteenth Street to the Mall, just east of the Washington Monument, and turned right between the picturesque buildings of the Smithsonian. The west front of the Capitol, at the crest of a gentle promontory, loomed ahead of us, the dome bathed in soft light.

"Jim," remarked the Speaker, "that's the most inspiring sight in the world!"

Riding thus beside Sam Rayburn, I could not know that I'd one day occupy his office, nor that I would be the one to trade in the sleek black limousine for a standard sedan, nor that I would cite to a future generation of new congressmen Rayburn's awe, after all his years of familiarity, at the vista of the lighted Capitol dome.

I could not know then that each of Lyndon Johnson's predictions would come true, that the Senate by a vote of 67 to 22 on December 2 that year would condemn Joseph McCarthy for his irresponsible abuse of colleagues and the institutions of our government. I couldn't know that this would, indeed, break his grip on the public and bury his public statements back with the classified ads. Nor that Johnson's prophesy of a Democratic House and Senate would be fulfilled. I most surely couldn't know that the House, of which I was about to become a part, would continue in the hands of my political party for the next forty years—four decades, during which I'd work with nine presidents and participate in cataclysmic change, book-ended between the downfall of Joe McCarthy and the emergence of Newt Gingrich. The latter, then a boy of eleven, would become Speaker of the House in 1995 and, from that post, exhort corporations to withhold advertising dollars from newspapers he charged with harboring "socialists" on their editorial boards. *Déjà vu.*

But I'm getting ahead of the story. There was a lot that I didn't know. I was thirty-one and had a great deal to learn.

CHAPTER TWO

PRAIRIE ROOTS

"What makes a fellow want to run for Congress in the first place?" I've often been asked. "Just what does the average one of you guys really expect to accomplish?" There might be 535 answers to those questions at any given time, one for each member of the House and Senate. No two of us are exactly alike. We all are the bent and molded products of our individual histories. All I can tell you is why I, a fellow of fairly average endowments from a fairly average American background, decided at an early age to seek a political career and stayed on to spend a major part of my life in the Congress of the United States.

The two great national events of my youth were the Great Depression and World War II. They shaped my view of the world and influenced the largely unconscious set of values I'd bring to Washington in 1954 at age thirty-one. During my public school years, our family lived in seven different Texas and Oklahoma towns, and in twelve different houses, none of which we owned. There were my mother and father, two younger sisters, and I. We went where Dad could make the best living for us. We never had a lot of money in those days. But in many ways we were rich.

Marie Lyster Wright was a lady. In a day before political correctness rearranged the language, that noun was my mother's perfect predicate nominative. It fit her like a pair of hose, and she wore it like a tiara. No boy she raised would fail to respect and appreciate womanhood or what it meant to be a gentleman. The manners on which Mother insisted—like holding a door for women, removing one's hat in the presence of a lady or rising when one enters the room, making sure never to malign another's motives, or seeing to it that nobody takes advantage of the small and less fortunate—may seem quaint today. But social graces were important to Mother. She called them marks of breeding.

It wasn't that my mother lived a sheltered life or was unacquainted with toil. She was born in 1894 in the New Mexico Territory. When she was only eighteen months old, her father died. He, a civil engineer born in Australia and graduated from Heidelberg University, came down with a fever while surveying a route for the railroad to the West Coast. Her widowed mother, then barely twenty and hundreds of miles from home with an infant to raise, took a job running a retail store. Later, the two returned to Weatherford, Texas, the family's ancestral home, where my grandmother managed a hotel owned by an aunt. Among the recurring guests were troupes of actors and actresses who came four times a year to perform plays at the local Opera House. At an early age, Mother developed a strong yen to be an actress. Her very proper family squelched that ambition. Their objections did not extend to being a teacher, however, even if she spent her hours teaching the acting arts to others. So, after completing school, Mother taught drama, poetry, reading, and English literature until her marriage.

Memories of her evoke images of three objects. One was her sewing machine, from which she made many of my younger sisters' dresses, usually prettier and more stylish than they could have bought at a boutique. Another was the family piano, around which we'd all gather and sing to Mother's accompaniment. The third was her enormous collection of books, many of which she publicly reviewed for women's clubs and other civic organizations.

She and my father married in 1916 in Valentine, Texas, near the Mexican border. Dad commanded a company of the Texas National Guard, sent there by President Wilson to protect the border from incursions by Pancho Villa's forces. The marriage was an attraction of opposites. She was, by training and practice, aristocratic; Dad was egalitarian. He had been a professional boxer—the quickest route in those days for a strong and agile Texas farm boy to put aside some money, until he saved up enough to buy a business in Weatherford. He was a captain in World War I, commander of an infantry company in France. A stray piece of shrapnel gave him a permanent dimple in his cheek.

Both Mother and Dad were, however, bibliophiles, sharing a love of language and a penchant for poetry, which they encouraged their children to recite at the dinner table. They had a marvelous bond of mutual rein-forcement. My mother's praise of him made me regard my father as a hero, and he told me repeatedly how fortunate we were to have her example. Largely self-educated and a voracious reader, Dad burned with determina-tion to give his children the formal benefits he had been denied. In the process of doing that, he challenged us to the peak of our capacities. "Not good enough to do just as well as I've done," he'd say. "Unless each generation can make some improvement on the one before, there's not much point to posterity."

James Claude Wright was born in 1890, the youngest of four brothers. His father soon died and his mother was stricken with polio, confined to a wheelchair. Dad had to leave school and find work at about age ten, chopping cotton and firing a brick kiln. Yet he never felt sorry for himself. Gifted with self-confidence and a sense of humor, my father had a way with words that made ideas embed themselves in my mind inextricably. Dad exalted ambition. He believed emphatically in self-improvement and in America's limitless promise. "You can do anything in the world you want to do," he would tell me, "if you want to do it strongly enough and are willing to pay the price." What a relentless admonition for a boy!

My father's first effort to create a nationwide company ended in failure. That was 1931, remembered thereafter in wry family jest as "the year we ate the piano." We ate the car, too. We wouldn't own another until 1937. But that didn't discourage his ambition.

The political philosophy I would carry with me to Congress must have begun taking shape, I think, in 1932, when I was nine years old. My grandfather, then sixty-three, lost the job he'd held for twenty-three years, two years shy of a promised retirement annuity. Jobs were almost nonexistent in that Depression year. My family moved from Weatherford to Fort Worth to rent an apartment in my grandparents' house. The purpose was to provide income for them to meet mortgage payments and avoid losing their home. Even today, when I read of layoffs and unemployment, I don't see statistics. I think of human dramas. My mind returns to that time in my youth and to a man I grew to love.

William Dee Walker was not really my grandfather, but that's how I thought of him. He had married my grandmother, then a young widow, when my mother was a child of seven. I recall his erect bearing and pervading dignity. He carved a turkey with the precision of a surgeon and the flair of a symphony conductor. He sharpened my pencils to symmetrical perfection: "Anything worth doing, Jimmy, is worth doing well."

His exemplary demeanor belied the stories I would hear later about his hedonistic youth. The scion of a land-wealthy Brazos River family, Willie Walker had tired of schooling after one year in a military college. His youthful passions, according to those who knew him then, were fast horses, hunting dogs, and saloons. He was best remembered among his aging contemporaries, whose stories I would hear with near disbelief, for getting tanked up in a saloon and lighting cigars with five-dollar bills.

"Still, you gotta remember, that was before Willie Dee got religion," Charlie McMahon would cackle. "And religion in his case was Lena!"

That was my grandmother, Lenora Crowder Lyster Walker, a woman of strong convictions, widowed at age twenty with an eighteen-month-old infant. When Will Walker proposed to her five years later, my grandmother told him absolutely not. "You'd have to be a different person," she said. "You'd have to be a person who did not drink, nor smoke, nor gamble, and who worked steadily at a productive pursuit. And you cannot be such a person, Mr. Walker."

He became such a person. From that day until his death almost a half-century later, Will Walker refused to wager so much as a penny. Liquor never passed his lips. He never again lighted a cigar, although he'd hold an unlighted one in his mouth, sometimes for hours. And he worked productively. Central to his character was the belief that "a gentlemen keeps his word." The only time I ever heard him speak contemptuously of anyone, it was of a man who had given his hand on a pledge and not kept it. "A promise made is a debt unpaid," my grandfather told me.

Suddenly, in the depth of the Depression when he was sixty-three, the national company for which he worked fired all employees with twenty years or more of seniority. Upon completing twenty-five years, according to their contract, an employee could retire with a comfortable pension. It was this commitment on which my grandparents had relied for twenty-three years. Now, cut adrift with only two years to go, the retirement pension denied them and no other income, they felt betrayed. Mr. Walker searched doggedly for another job. There was no such thing as Social Security then. No such thing as vested pension rights. No Medicare. No unemployment compensation. And there were no jobs in 1932 for a sixty-three-year-old man. But there were five years of unrelenting mortgage payments remaining on their home.

My grandfather plowed the bottom third of their block-long lot, planted a vegetable garden and an orchard. He physically built a small rent house on the property. He fenced in the middle third of the lot and built hen houses. My grandmother sold enough eggs to pay the utility bills. It was in those years that I knew him best. He would read the help wanted ads in the *Fort Worth Star-Telegram* every day, eagerly call for appointments, walk the streets in search of a prospective employer, only to be told repeatedly that he was too old.

Now I saw the hope slowly drain from this brave man's eyes, fleetingly rekindled only to be extinguished again. As month after unemployed month wore on, I watched the deterioration of the pride that had been the steel girder of his erect posture. His physical dimensions seemed to shrink. Fifteen million others, also suddenly out of work, faced their own personal traumas.

In later years, I'd hear the smug judgment that anybody who really wants a job can find one. That may have been true in the 1960s. It was not in the 1930s. It isn't exactly true today. Times are less severe now. There are cushions to absorb the shock, to soften the adjustment, to relieve the hopelessness. Thank God for Social Security. For Medicare and Medicaid. For unemployment compensation. Even so, the loss of a job is a great blow to the nervous system. As a youth, I saw it at close range. That experience helped shape my sense of social right and wrong. It came to me, a kid of nine and ten, that in a just world something ought to be done to prevent depressions and to vanquish unemployment.

Two years later we went to Duncan, Oklahoma, where my father had been hired as manager of the Chamber of Commerce. My parents sent something every month to my grandparents. I saw the struggle of small town America and its retail merchants to claw a foothold on the "road to recovery." Franklin D. Roosevelt was president, and we had faith in him. The New Deal developed a Home Owners Loan Corporation, which helped millions like my grandparents save their homes from foreclosure. Every Saturday morning in Duncan, now age eleven, I would spend delivering circulars, for twenty-five cents, to the large rural crowds that came into Duncan weekly. A dime of that quarter gained admission to a Saturday afternoon movie, a nickel bought a hamburger. Afterward, I would visit the city's biggest newsstand, peruse all the out-of-town Sunday papers for the one with the most extensive collection of comic strips and take it home.

For two dollars Dad bought me a slightly used 22-caliber rifle that year and taught me its use and care. I raised bantam chickens and had two dogs, went out for football, sewed two large pieces of canvas into a punching bag, filled it with cottonseed meal, and hung it from a large tree limb in the backyard. Every Sunday morning our family went to the Presbyterian Church. On Sunday evenings, Dad and I would sample the other churches and discuss the sermon on the way home, comparing the various preachers' philosophies and oratorical styles.

My father was an ecumenist before I ever heard that word. He once asked me to draw a picture of a wagon wheel. He compared the world's religions to the spokes in the wheel, with God as the hub. "Suppose you and I are two red ants on separate spokes," he suggested. "Notice that the farther we are from God, out here on the rim, the farther we are from each other. And the nearer we are to one another, the closer we are to God." Dad believed in tolerance. Returning from World War I, he actively opposed efforts to revive the Ku Klux Klan in Texas. Exposed to the wider world, he said he had observed that all the races and religions were composed of people who "wanted the same things, felt the same hurts, and bled the same color." Those were the days of segregation. Dad asked me once to imagine just how I'd feel if red haired boys, like me, were required to use separate water fountains and restrooms.

Once, I said Pentecostal religionists were "crazy" because they thought they heard God talking to them.

"What makes you so certain they do not?" my father asked.

"Gee, Dad, I was there. If God had said anything, I'd have heard him for sure!"

Dad switched on a radio set. A vocalist was singing. "Hear that?" he asked. I said I did. As abruptly, he turned it off. "Hear it now?" I admitted I could not. "Do you think he's quit singing?" I realized from this the folly of hastening to criticize the religious convictions of others. I just might not be tuned into their frequency.

After about a year, we moved to Seminole, another Oklahoma town, where the local Chamber offered Dad a higher salary than he was making in Duncan. Seminole had recently enjoyed an oil boom, but it had gone bust. The merchants needed business. My father organized goodwill tours to the surrounding areas and perfected a program he called "Appreciation Day." Every Wednesday the merchants would contribute toward a treasure chest from which they gave cash awards. This drew large mid-week crowds and produced the economic impact of two Saturdays a week. Dad began systematically developing and expanding Seminole's trade territory. Soon, other Oklahoma towns were calling my father for advice on how to revive their retail business and expand their trade radiuses. My dad formed a national company to help small towns and small-town merchants cope with the competition from big cities, the national chains, and the mail-order houses. His second try at building a nationwide company became a success. That company was to last for a generation and ultimately to serve more than 100,000 merchants in almost 3,000 different communities throughout 42 states. This, no doubt, biased me to the side of the small independent businessman and in opposition to interstate chains and monopolies of various types.

We moved to Dallas in 1936. At age thirteen I had skipped two grades in school and was entering the sophomore year. That summer, Dad gave me the complete works of O. Henry. "Read these short stories with a pencil in your hand," he instructed. "Each time you come upon a new word, underline it. When you've finished the story, look up the unfamiliar words. Then use each one at least five times in sentences during the next week. That way you'll own those words. They will be part of your arsenal!" Today, a septuagenarian, I'm still looking up words.

Throughout my school career, I was a good student, but never the very best in the class. I made good grades, As and Bs, and never failed a subject, but

I had discovered in all our peregrinations from city to city and school to school, that the poorest route to peer acceptance was for a new kid to come in and start showing up the others, acting as though he thought himself smarter. I concentrated instead on being like the other guys, doing the things they liked and admired. I played football, boxed, mastered a harmonica, rode horses, never cut in on another's steady date. Having skipped grades along the way, I was younger than most others in the class and desperately eager that they not discover this fact. In an effort to please my dad, I became good at boxing, developed footwork and a fast left jab. I came to enjoy the sport, winning all my bouts, but I would never have been a great boxer. I lacked the "killer" instinct. I never wanted to hurt or embarrass an opponent, just outpoint him. Dad didn't quite understand this trait, but Mother did. "He'd rather have a friend than a victim," she explained to my father.

In the fall of 1937, the apex of my ambition was to be a football coach. That was the model my crowd most admired. In my hip pocket, I carried a little notebook, each sheet containing the diagram of a football play. I was forever inventing new ones. Early in that season, a high school junior, I suffered a chipped cartilage in my right knee. The sliver embedded itself in the joint, rupturing blood vessels when I put weight upon it. Unwilling to be sidelined, I kept playing. The knee swelled and had to be lanced to drain the fluid off. Then it was put in a cast for most of the season.

The coach, a man named Bob Harris, sympathized. Sensing my disappointment, he turned me in a new direction. "What we really need, even more than a good halfback," he said, "is somebody to represent our school in debate. You're the best prospect we've got." Maybe it was a nice way of telling me, I reflected much later, that I wasn't likely to become All-American, even all-conference, halfback. I wasn't big enough not to be faster, nor fast enough not to be bigger. About all I had going for me was superior desire. I ran harder. That's how I busted up my knee.

Buoyed by Coach Harris's confidence, I plunged with equal vigor into new ambitions, to win debate tournaments for the school and make top grades in Harris's world history class. In adolescent non sequitur, I thought if my hand was the first raised in response to every question, he'd let me start all the games in my senior year. In the process, I got hooked on history. It was powerfully seductive. Studying the period of World War I, I was seized by the conviction that the Senate had bungled it badly for all of us by rejecting the League of Nations. If nations could talk out their problems, I reasoned, we wouldn't have to kill each other. I began to read Woodrow Wilson's speeches.

In 1920, Wilson had warned that rejection of the League would result in another, more devastating war in twenty years. In that spring of 1938, I could see Wilson's prophecy reaching fiendish fulfillment. The world was not "safe for Democracy;" the "war to end wars" had not. This realization became a major turning point in my life.

Clearly, to my mind, President Wilson had been right. Isolationists in the Senate had been tragically wrong. Because of their folly, my generation would have to perform anew the task undertaken by my father and his contemporaries of World War I. Pondering this, I came to believe there was something even better than being a football coach: to go to Congress and help build the bases for a peaceful world. That ambition, from this point, never really changed. I was an aspiring politician. I organized the "Progressive Club" to influence school elections, and launched along with another ambitious young fellow named Joe Bailey Irwin a thing called the Future Democrats of Texas. I volunteered to help in political campaigns. Voraciously, I studied history, government, economics. Journalism fascinated me.

Upon my graduation from high school in 1939, the family moved back to Weatherford, our old hometown. Dad's business was doing well. Since his clients lived and did business in small towns throughout America, he reasoned, the home office of his firm should be located in one. Best of all, from my point of view, we bought a fine, old two-story Victorian home with a wide wrap-around front and side porch. It was the first time in my life that we'd owned a home, and that made me indescribably proud. Weatherford College, which I entered as a freshman that year, was an affiliate of the Methodist Church. The official atmosphere was sedate, religious, conformist. Part of this I set out to change. Elected editor of the college paper, I crusaded for some things of doubtful popularity—popular with students perhaps; not with the faculty, whose jobs depended on the smile of the regents.

As Congress was voting in 1940 for the first peace-time draft, I took the opposite editorial position. Although hating Hitler and the Japanese war lords, I called the draft a "step toward militarism" and "an insult to the patriotism of American youth." I argued that if the country were ever attacked, we'd volunteer in such overwhelming numbers that the recruiting offices would have trouble handling us all. Some on the college board didn't like that editorial, or another I'd written advocating the church-affiliated school sponsor student dances. I was absolutely wrong, of course, in my view of the draft. Hindsight confirms that the draft saved us. But I did mean what I said about volunteering, and when the time came, I didn't wait to be drafted. The First Amendment and the decent intercession of faculty journalism professor Sam Householder kept me from being kicked out of my job as editor. I was developing a reverence for freedom of expression, enjoying the editor's job, and was picking up some pocket money by covering sports and occasional other stories for the *Fort Worth Star-Telegram*.

Finishing Weatherford College, I went to the University of Texas, then a single Austin campus of about 13,000 students. Scarcely more than a month before the attack on Pearl Harbor, in November of 1941, a classmate named Edgar Shelton and I represented the University of Texas debating team before the student body at Baylor University. We argued the affirmative side of the subject, *Resolved that the United States should declare war on the Axis powers.* I boldly declared in my presentation that Germany and Japan were plotting an attack on our country. Little did I dream that they really were.

Immediately following our entry into World War II, before the month of December 1941 ended, I left the university to enlist in the Army Air Corps, where my first full month's pay as a private was twenty-one dollars. A year later, December 12, 1942—ten days before my twentieth birthday—I got my flier's wings and a second lieutenant's commission at Williams Field, Arizona. Within two weeks, I was married—on Christmas day in Tucson—to my college sweetheart, Mab Lemons. Four months later, I was bound for Australia and the Fifth Air Force.

My unit flew bombing missions over the South Pacific jungles in B-24 Liberators, attacking Japanese shipping and air bases on Timor, the Celebes, New Guinea, even Java and Sumatra. In August of 1943, we set a record for the longest bombing mission ever flown to that date—2,700 miles to Balikpapan, Borneo, and back. We blew up the oil refineries there, thought by the Japanese to be beyond reach of our aircraft. In 1944, I was rotated back stateside and assigned to training air crews in Lincoln, Nebraska. As one of the earlier returnees from overseas combat duty, I was also assigned by the Community Base Relations office to fill numerous speaking requests from local civic groups in and around Lincoln. Two local businesses made fairly attractive career offers if I'd stay in Lincoln after the war, but I figured my future was in Texas.

That fall of 1944, I got in trouble on a free speech question at the Nebraska State Fair Grounds. To the crowd assembled at the race track one afternoon when I was in attendance, the Fair Committee presented Republican Congressman Dewey Short of Missouri to speak for Thomas E. Dewey's presidential candidacy. When nobody was offered to speak for Mr. Roosevelt, then seeking his fourth term, I demanded to know why. The races had begun by the time I could find and consult anyone in the management, but I introduced myself and promised I'd be back the next day. If they didn't have someone to speak for President Roosevelt, I said I'd be glad in the interest of equal time to do so myself.

The next morning I got a surprise. I was called before the Commanding Officer of the base, given twenty-four-hour duty as officer of the day—which kept me physically confined to the air base—and ordered not to appear at the

Fair Grounds. "The military do not mess in politics," the General said. "Yes, Sir!" I responded. "But you know, Sir, I'm a citizen first. Free speech is one of those things we're fighting for." His response: "I don't think you understood me, Lieutenant."

The General won, of course.

That year, 1944, marked the first time in American history that men in uniform were even permitted to vote. I cast my first ballot for FDR. During those war years, I read more than two hundred books, even subscribing to the *Southwest Reporter*, a digest of Supreme Court cases. I bristled on reading the case involving the incarceration of Americans of Japanese ancestry on the West Coast, upheld as constitutional by the Supreme Court in 1944. This was racism, pure and simple. The ruling was wrong, I decided, and vowed to do something about it. Forty years later, I was to have that opportunity.

The war over, I returned to Weatherford with a wife and a five-month-old infant son, Jimmy. My first civilian job was selling memberships for the National Federation of Small Business. In that job I traveled an area in North Texas, meeting small businessmen, learning of their problems, and earning a satisfactory living. I also joined with others in reorganizing the then-defunct Young Democrats of Texas, became its National Committeeman, and was elected in 1946 to the State Legislature. There I soon gained a reputation as something of a radical. I advocated abolishing the poll tax, lowering the voting age to eighteen, imposing a severance tax on natural gas, letting women serve on juries, passing a lobby registration law, increasing the pay of school teachers, and admitting black students to the University of Texas Law School. All these things have long since been done, and none is considered radical anymore. But each was frightening to the conservative power establishment of our state in 1947.

To make matters worse, I had joined the call for academic freedom at the University of Texas and had supported the gubernatorial candidacy of deposed University of Texas president, Homer P. Rainey. On behalf of dairy farmers I caused the State Attorney General to file suit against the big milk distributors for conspiracy in restraint of trade when five of these companies simultaneously reduced the price to the farmer from $5.30 per hundred weight of milk to $3.20. The establishment saw me as a prairie populist and a radical one at that.

In the 1948 election, I was opposed by two men. One, Eugene Miller, was a former state senator, a gifted orator and negative campaigner; the other, Floyd Bradshaw, a clean-cut school teacher. Miller would attack me as a radical on the stump, while Bradshaw ran a colorless and inoffensive campaign. The strategy was clear: Miller was to shake the tree and Bradshaw was to catch the apples in his basket. It was a ploy that had been used before in other races, but I was leading, buoyed by support from the dairy farmers and plain folks. A few days before the election, someone shot Eugene Miller. Told of the shooting, I went immediately to the hospital and donated blood for a transfusion, but Miller died. This traumatic event, coupled with the rumors of "radicalism," proved enough to defeat me by a thirty-nine-vote margin. People didn't think I had been involved in the shooting, but there were whispers that the foul deed might have been performed by some of my "radical" friends or "socialist henchmen." (We never discovered who did it.)

Crushed by these events, Mab wanted to move elsewhere. I said no, we'd stay and prove by the way we lived that we were not the kind of people whom some apparently thought we were. I plunged into business, having borrowed from the bank on a GI business loan to purchase a one-fourth interest in my father's firm. For the first time, I wondered if maybe politics was just not my thing. I began to make money and found some satisfaction in teaching Sunday school class, being a scout master, and coaching the local Golden Gloves team. One of my boxing protégés was Larry Hagman, later to star in the long-running television series, *Dallas*. Life was good in Weatherford in 1949. Our first daughter, Ginger, arrived. She was a delight. I was making more money than I'd ever expected. Yet somehow this didn't satisfy me. I began to ponder the church as a vocation—at least a parttime one. I enrolled in theology courses at TCU's evening college and, at the urging of the Presbyterian Church, conducted services twice monthly at a small pastorless church in the nearby town of Granbury.

As it turned out, I couldn't abandon politics and make it stick. In November of 1949, the mayor of Weatherford resigned. A special election was called, and I was drafted to run. In the special election of January 1950, I won an easy victory and embarked upon a gratifying avocation. Still actively involved in business, I divided my days into halves. Until noon I was a businessman. In the afternoon I was mayor. Our third child, Kay, came in 1951. The business was doing well. Soon the city was, too. We completed a municipal swimming pool and a series of community playgrounds and parks, paved city streets and extended sewer lines. I negotiated with the Texas & Pacific Railroad for a small lake to give Weatherford an auxiliary water supply. We passed a bond issue by 9-1 for a new waste treatment plant.

During the winter of 1951, there was a heating crisis on Weatherford's north side when the narrow gas lines could not carry enough fuel to warm the houses. Appliance jets, many in poorly insulated homes, gave forth no more than a candle's faint flicker of warmth. I took up the cudgel for these shivering residents, badgering the gas company into emergency line replacements by threatening to pull the company's franchise. A parching seven-year drought smote Texas during the early 1950s. We went for months at a time without a drop of rain. Ultimately, Weatherford had to ration water. Only those with private wells could legally water their lawns in the severest throes of the shortage. Finally, at my urging, we built a new city lake of adequate size.

I was learning to pick my fights more carefully and to present my case in terms that others could embrace. When I became mayor, the black students in our town had no locally available school beyond the eighth grade. For most, therefore, education stopped at that point. To pursue even high school, they'd have to go to Fort Worth, thirty miles away, and practically none could do it. Most of their families did not own cars. Parents who did needed them for work. It had been this way for generations. That fact gnawed at me. One day in 1952, I told the city council, "We've got trouble, Fellas." I said I had a tip from some people in Fort Worth that the NAACP was talking of filing suit against the Weatherford School System to make us open Weatherford High School to black students. "They have some studies showing that hardly any of the Negro children can get transportation to attend high school in Fort Worth," I said. That was only a slight exaggeration. The "studies" were my own observation, confirmed by talking with parents in Weatherford's black community. Everyone on the council knew it was true. "This could be really embarrassing," I cautioned. "Shouldn't we strike first by buying a couple more school buses and offering daily transportation for all our colored young-sters who want to go to high school in Fort Worth?" It was an easy sale. Although there still was a remnant of local citizens who insisted that, "educa-tion'll only ruin 'em," the City Council wanted no part of a public embarrassment like being hauled into court.

The specter of a lawsuit was largely imaginary. I had supposed it theoreti-cally possible, but did not really expect any such thing. Politics was and is the art of the possible. Sometimes, I discovered, the only way to get the right thing done was by giving the wrong reason. Little did I dream the Supreme Court, just two years later in *Brown* v. *Board of Education*, would provide the exact result of which I had warned.

There also was a prolonged rate fight with Southwestern Bell Telephone Company during my tenure as mayor. We finally agreed to higher business rates, but I held out successfully for a lower rate at the bottom and on party line service, so as not to price telephone needs out of the range of the poor, elderly, and sick. The Texas Municipal League, impressed by some of the things we were doing in Weatherford, elected me State President in 1953. There were lots of speaking engagements, and I took all I could get—particu-larly in Fort Worth. The time was coming soon when I'd run for Congress.

In 1954, the 12th Congressional District contained five counties, but the city of Fort Worth made up about 75 percent of the population. To win, I knew I'd have to carry the four rural counties overwhelmingly and get at least a close-to-even split in Fort Worth. Almost everybody in Weatherford (population 12,000) was eager to help—even those who thought it couldn't be done. The difficulty was Amon G. Carter, kingmaker and owner of the dominant newspaper, the *Fort Worth Star-Telegram*. Carter led what was then called the Seventh Street establishment. As long as anyone could remember, that small group had dictated the selection of congressmen and most other officials in Tarrant County. Its members tended to political conservatism, and Amon Carter was *el papacito* to the group, indisputably the most influential man in Fort Worth. Wingate Lucas, the incumbent congressman, had been handpicked by Mr. Carter eight years earlier and had done nothing to offend him. He voted frequently with a Dixiecrat-GOP coalition and repeatedly outraged organized labor. But labor union members and their families accounted for less than 20 percent of the district's vote.

My strategy consisted of three elements: mobilize all my friends; maintain an intensely active physical schedule of fourteen-hour days, handshaking, and personal appearances; and television. There was only one TV station in the district. It, like the *Star-Telegram*, was owned by Mr. Carter. While he ran a hands-on editorial policy for the paper, however, he did not touch programming on the television or radio stations that he owned. I'd counted: Three out of five farm houses in the district sprouted television antennas. My official campaign opener was broadcast live on radio from the cattle barn at the Fort Worth rodeo grounds. We packed in about 1,200 people at $1 apiece for a barbecue dinner. It was the largest political event in the town's recent recollection and was covered by *Star-Telegram* reporter Bill Haworth. The next morning's edition of the paper, however, ignored it—totally.

If the paper won't take note of me, I decided, I'll have to go directly to the people by television. Programming was more relaxed in those days, and affordable. I bought 5-minute, 15-minute, and 30-minute programs, looking straight into the camera and talking directly to people in their living rooms in prime time. I could buy thirty minutes at 7:30 P.M. for $520. The strategy worked—magnificently. After the first program, I knew immediately that this was the formula. Suddenly I was known. Everywhere I went, strangers recognized and approached me to remark upon my televised message. Mr. Amon Carter had not reckoned with that. Going into the last two weeks, I knew I was gaining ground. The incumbent began attacking me, a fact that only gave me encouragement. I knew I had him worried.

Unexpectedly, a political bombshell exploded. Two weeks before the election, the U.S. Post Office Department announced an investigation of the company owned by my father and me, charged internally with using the mails to promote a lottery. Never mind that the firm had been in the business for twenty years, with clients in some 2,000 towns, their merchant groups conducting our programs in the most public places available. I answered directly on television. We traced the complaint to a Republican former colleague of Congressman Wingate Lucas. The public resented the unfairness, and the dirty tricks boomeranged. Public feeling became so high, in fact, that on two evenings during the last week of the campaign—at the Fort Worth baseball park and at the Weatherford football field—Lucas was lustily booed by the crowd. The reaction embarrassed me; after all, Congressman Lucas was a guest in our hometown. I stood up and raised my hands to get the crowd quiet, lecturing them gently about the respect we owe to the office and the courtesy we always show to visitors. The crowd silenced, Lucas continued—albeit halfheartedly.

On Thursday afternoon before Saturday's primary election, the *Star-Telegram* ran a front page editorial endorsing Lucas. Its theme was that Lucas was a proven quantity, I an unknown. The editorial asked, in effect, "Who knows anything about this young fellow from Weatherford or anything he stands for?" It was fortunate for me that I picked up an early edition of the afternoon paper. Searing with outrage that the area's dominant journal had deliberately ignored my stated campaign positions and now faulted me for their being unknown, I sat down immediately and wrote an *Open Letter to Amon G. Carter and the Fort Worth Star-Telegram*. Then I called the newspaper's advertising department, reserving the better part of a full page for the next morning's edition. A friend hand-carried my typed copy along with my personal check for $974.40, the price for enough space to dominate a page. As I would learn later, the copy editors, upon reading it, took the ad to Carter personally, asking whether to use it. By the eyewitness account I received, the colorful old patriarch read the ad, raised his eyebrows, and asked, "Do you think his check is good?" Assured that it was, Carter said, "Run it!"

In that ad, which would be a conversation piece for years in Texas political circles, I began with a quote from Kipling: "If *all* men count with you, but *none* too much!" The message was bold, "brassy," some would say. I briefly recounted my position on the issues, predicted my election, and told Mr. Carter I'd work *with* him but not *for* him, would be *his* congressman as well as *everybody's*, but not his *personal, private* congressman. I'd be a congressman for *all* the people. Maybe the strongest line was, "you have at last met a man, Mr. Carter, who will not come running at your beck and call like a simpering pup." The people loved it. I was going to win, anyhow. The ad was the frosting on the cake. Mr. Carter, too big for petty grudges, told associates he admired my spunk. In later years, Carter's son Amon Jr. and I would become very good friends.

I was nominated with 60 percent of the vote in 1954. In those days, victory in the Democratic primary meant election. The race had cost about $32,000, half of which I paid personally. I observed a strict rule in those days—to accept no contribution larger than $100 from any source. The average contribution, in fact, was more like $10.

So that's who I was, warts and all, when I arrived in Washington in 1954, ready to take the oath of office as a freshman member of the U.S. House of Representatives. Along the way I had picked up a habit of championing the underdog—the dispossessed, the oppressed, the powerless. Maybe I thought God had given me more than I'd earned, and I owed some dues to the less fortunate. At times I had been audacious, probably even arrogant. I'd made waves, rocked boats, more than once taken on the Establishment. Sometimes I won; sometimes I got crushed. Now I would discover how very much I had yet to learn in the ceaselessly fascinating arena of American politics.

CHAPTER THREE

LEARNING
THE ROPES

I n the middle 1950s when I first came to Congress, Washington was settling into its new role as undeclared capital of the world. These were the
salad days of our postwar epoch. The reassuring Eisenhower presence
spread an atmosphere of well-being across the land. In the Congress,
Johnson and Rayburn kept things running with almost machinelike precision. While they dispatched pesky difficulties, the Eisenhower grin dispelled
doubts. America believed in itself. There was almost a renaissance of manifest
destiny, but without the territorial acquisitiveness. When Red China rattled
sabers and flexed its muscles across the straits from Taiwan, Congress passed
the Formosa Resolution. It said we'd defend Taiwan against attack. And that
was that! The bellicose fever in the mainland Chinese dissipated. When
Colonel Nasser overmatched himself and was pushed back from the Suez
Canal by British and Israeli forces, Eisenhower and John Foster Dulles
benignly asked our friends to desist from crushing the strutting Egyptian and
demolishing his forces. They promptly did desist, though not without mut-
terings and sputterings. It meant the end of a long and distinguished career
for British Prime Minister Anthony Eden who had ordered the action. But
the British suffered that price, and swallowed their pride. Nobody was prepared to question, let alone cross the wisdom of Washington.

For a new congressman from small-town Texas, the city itself presented
new experiences almost daily. Mab and I rented a town house on Klingle
Road just one-half block from the Cathedral grounds and only two blocks off
Massachusetts Avenue. A block away began the spacious grounds of the
Marjorie Merriweather Post mansion. Foreign embassies lined Massachusetts

Avenue on either side. When we arrived in late December of 1954, a handsome Muslim mosque—the only one in our country—was under construction just four blocks from our residence. The daily sight of foreigners in their turbans or other native attire gave strength to the illusion of Washington as a sort of new worldwide mecca.

The house we occupied was four stories high, counting the basement. It was joined on either side by other dwellings. For me, from the wide open spaces, this was a baffling phenomenon. "Suppose someone wanted to move his house to another lot?" I asked. "To which house would the wall belong?" Apparently the question had never arisen.

Ginger was five, and we enrolled her in public school kindergarten at a schoolhouse only two blocks from our residence. It was the same school attended by Jimmy, then in the fourth grade. On the first morning, before walking the two youngsters to school, I supposed a word of caution would be desirable, since the racially integrated Washington school would be a different experience for our two offspring.

"There may be some little colored children in your class," I began, with the intention of assuaging concern. "That's all right. Don't worry about that at all."

"Well, you certainly wouldn't want to say anything about it, Daddy," said Ginger. "It might hurt their feelings."

They were way ahead of me.

The first formal event to which we were invited, before the convening of Congress, was a reception at the White House for new members of the House and Senate. The handsome invitation card contained in its lower corner two words I'd never before seen on an invitation: "white tie." Not supposing I'd have enough formal invitations to warrant buying a set of tails, I rented all the accoutrements from a Washington haberdasher. Admiring the unaccustomed attire, I laid the pleated shirt with the empty neck-place for the detachable collar upon the bedspread prior to adorning it. It occurred to me that our two little girls would enjoy seeing such a garment, and I called them in to ogle it.

"I wish you girls would look at that shirt!" I declared.

Our elder daughter's eyes grew wide with horror.

"I didn't do it, Daddy, honest! I haven't had the scissors all day!"

My first look at a president up close was a startling experience. Dwight D. Eisenhower, with his wife Mamie in the receiving line, reminded me uncannily of my father. They were the same height, the same size, the same physical build. Eisenhower had the same pink glow of complexion as my father and just about the same amount of hair. Several of his mannerisms were the same. Perhaps it should not have been so surprising to me. Both were born in Texas, just a few days apart, in October of 1890. Indeed, Eisenhower was a father figure to the whole country, a Daddy Warbucks. He had seen our country safely through World War II. He had gone personally to Korea and there negotiated a settlement. He was steeped in American tradition, polite and profoundly respectful to women. He was by nature nonpartisan. His instincts were basically good.

Three personalities dominated the Washington scene during the latter half of the 1950s. They were President Eisenhower, House Speaker Sam Rayburn, and Senate Majority Leader Lyndon B. Johnson. Although sometimes disagreeing on issues of public policy, they developed a comity born of mutual respect and a set of overriding goals on which all agreed. They never sought to embarrass one another. It was an entirely different ambiance than the one which would be ushered in with the arrival of Ronald Reagan twenty-five years later. Eisenhower was not out to destroy the social gains of the New Deal. He merely wanted to slow things down a bit. And somebody undertook to chide Sam Rayburn, pointing out that the veteran Speaker had supported approximately 70 percent of the president's recommendations. "I'm surprised he didn't say 85 percent," replied Mr. Rayburn with a chuckle. "Fully 85 percent of the executive requests have been for the extension of programs begun under Democrats!"

Rayburn never missed a chance to say in any public forum that he liked the president. Only in private, in small groups he trusted, would he occasionally fulminate over some minor personal difference. He liked pointing out that Eisenhower had been born in Denison, Texas. "He's bound to be a good man," the Speaker would say jauntily. "After all, he was born in my district!" When the inevitable chuckles from listeners subsided, Rayburn would add: "And those who knew him then say he was a good baby!"

On fifty-eight occasions during those early Eisenhower years, Democrats under Rayburn saved key White House legislative proposals when members of the president's own party defected. Even in 1953, when Ike's party enjoyed a majority in the House, the president once called Rayburn, then Minority Leader, appealing for his help to put down a strong push among conservatives to kill the excess profits tax as it applied to corporations. Rayburn rallied Democrats and supplied the votes to suppress the uprising.

Sam Rayburn was personally fond of many House Republicans, I discovered. He had a soft spot for Dan Reed and John Taber of New York, who had been there longer than any of the others. He liked Tom Jenkins of Ohio, Clifford Hope of Kansas, and George Dondero of Michigan. He once told me, "as long as Oklahoma has to have one Republican, they couldn't have a finer man than Page Belcher!" But the Speaker enjoyed a very special relationship with Joe Martin of Massachusetts. In Congress since 1935, Martin was the House Republican leader. In 1946 and again in 1952, when Republican majorities temporarily swept the Democrats out of power, Martin became Speaker. Rayburn and Martin had changed Capitol offices on those two occasions, switching back in 1948, when Truman and the Democrats surged back into power. Now, Martin's party once again in the minority role following the 1954 election, Joe Martin wearily prepared to pack up all his belongings and move again from the spacious Speaker's office, which looked out upon the Mall, the monuments, and the Tidal Basin, to the green upward tilt of Virginia countryside that is Arlington National Cemetery. Sensing his old friend's despondent mood, Rayburn called Martin to the side. "Joe, I am tired of all this moving around," he said. "Why don't we just stay where we are?" Martin never forgot that personal kindness.

Relations between Ike and the Rayburn-Johnson leadership axis were strained briefly during the 1954 congressional campaign. The president, at his party's urging, made a speech in which he warned that a Democratic congress would bring on "a cold war of partisan politics." Rayburn and Johnson jointly sent Eisenhower a telegram reminding him of the many key occasions on which they had bailed out his programs, tersely stating that if there were to be any "cold war," he and not they would be the aggressor. Chastened, the president called the Texas duo, and invited them to come by the White House for a little private talk about "foreign policy and some other things."

One of my most memorable early impressions came on January 6, 1955. It was State of the Union day. In those years before presidents discovered prime-time evening television, the presidential appearance before Congress occurred in early afternoon.

Veteran doorkeeper William "Fishbait" Miller alternately announced the arrival of different groups into the chamber. "Mr. Speaker," Miller intoned with gusto, "the Vice President of the United States and Members of the United States Senate!" Senators streamed down the center aisle to take their seats on either side in front rows reserved for their occupancy. Vice President Nixon walked up to the podium, shook hands with Speaker Rayburn, and took a seat in the tall chair beside the Speaker's. I noticed that Rayburn nodded curtly, politely. He barely smiled. Nixon in the 1954 election had made some reference to the Democrats as "the party of treason." Mr. Rayburn never truly forgave him that remark.

Supreme Court Justices, announced in the same stentorian tone by Fishbait Miller, strode to seats assigned on the front row, clad in black robes. "Ambassadors Plenipotentiary!" formed a colorful procession as they entered the chamber, some wearing native regalia of their countries. Then a door opened in the president's gallery, and Mrs. Eisenhower entered, taking her seat beside the aisle in the gallery's front row. It was a sign that the president was prepared to enter.

"Mr. Speaker, the President of the United States!"

Suddenly, explosive applause rose in waves as President Eisenhower, looking tanned and rested, strode down the center aisle, nodding, smiling, waving. He mounted the rostrum and stood before the single podium in the center, grinning that famous Eisenhower grin. Every person in the huge chamber was on his feet. All were applauding. It would be impossible, unless you knew where they sat, to distinguish a Democrat from a Republican.

Then, at the beginning of his presentation, the president turned aside from his prepared script to take note that it was the seventy-second birthday of Sam Rayburn. Half turning to look up at the Speaker on the higher platform behind him, the president smiled, extended his hand, and wished Mr. Sam many happy returns of the day. Once again, the audience was on its feet, whistling, cheering. The second ovation matched the first. Mr. Rayburn blushed at this show of affection, which had greeted his name. A flush of color rose to the top of his gleaming bald head. Finally, he scowled that businesslike scowl, rapped the gavel, and restored order.

Many times I would think of that spectacle. What a wondrous thing, to live in a country and work in a system where these two men, who represented the rival political parties and the sometimes rival branches of our government, did nevertheless respect one another professionally and actually liked one another personally.

One other episode acted out on the House floor in my first year would leave a lasting impression upon me. The Reciprocal Trade Agreements act was up for extension. The subject provoked strong sentiments on both sides. Some members represented districts that produced goods sold on world markets. These areas benefited from international trade. Others came from sections where old and inefficient factories were already beginning to find their goods displaced on American shelves by upstart foreign products. Such a one was Cleve Bailey of West Virginia. Out to scuttle the trade bill by any means available, Bailey worked with several others to perfect an amendment requiring trade negotiators to give greater consideration to the effects of competition on domestic businesses.

Debate on the Bailey amendment was intense. The roll-call vote was close. The lead shifted back and forth as members, polled alphabetically, called out "aye" or "no" in response to their names. Finally, the list of names had been called twice. Members whose votes had not been recorded crowded into the "well" of the House, that area directly in front of the Speaker and the tally clerks, so they could be recognized and their votes counted. The rules provided that *if a member was in the chamber* and listening, but failed to hear or be heard when his name was called, then he or she could come to the front of the chamber at the end of the roll call and vote. One of those who came to the front that day was Chet Holifield of California. Holifield voted no on Bailey's amendment.

Immediately, Bailey was on his feet. "Point of order! Point of order, Mr. Speaker!" Cleve Bailey's face was the color of a ripe tomato.

"The gentleman will state his point of order," said Rayburn from the chair.

"The gentleman from California, Mr. Holifield," he blurted out. "That gentleman was *not* on the floor when his name was called. He's not entitled to vote!"

Speaker Rayburn's brow furrowed. His face flushed.

"The Chair *always* takes the word of a member!" Rayburn declared. His gavel fell. That was the end of it. Holifield's vote would stand.

The chair always takes the word of a member. There was something precious in that. All members are presumed honorable, and that assumption was part of the very oxygen of the chamber in Sam Rayburn's day.

Because I was sitting directly behind Cleve Bailey, I saw and heard other members come by to remonstrate with him. "That was a *terrible* thing to do, Cleve," said one. Another insisted, "That's not like you, old friend." A third, shaking his head in sadness, told Bailey he probably had hurt Chet Holifield's feelings.

Cleve Bailey stood and sought recognition to speak. Before his colleagues, he apologized publicly and abjectly to the one whose honor he had offended. His voice trembled. There were real tears in the crusty old West Virginian's eyes.

Quaint? Perhaps. A trifle maudlin? Maybe so. But it was the mutual assumption of honor that, in those days, distinguished the U.S. House of Representatives from most other institutions. Like an epoxy glue, it held things together.

There always has been some demagoguery in American political life. I suppose there always will be. But its practitioners, in the long run, almost always self-destruct. Very early in my legislative career I was introduced to what in those days was defined as the Congressman's eleventh commandment: *Thou shalt not demagogue against thy colleagues.* This dictum was recited frequently in the 1950s. In fact, an important part of any serious lawmaker's duty, I soon learned, was to meet, cultivate, and assist one's fellow congressmen. Mr. Rayburn often would say: "Each member has two constituencies—the people he serves at home, and the people he works with here." Conceivably, a politician of glib tongue and sparkling personality might succeed in palming himself off as something he wasn't to constituents at home, who see him maybe only once every two years, "but you don't deceive your colleagues!" Rayburn would insist.

To help colleagues in the Texas delegation—and folks back home in the Fort Worth area—was in fact the consideration that led me to accept appointment in my first term to the Public Works Committee. No Texan at that moment served on this panel, which had jurisdiction over all the dams, highways, waterway developments, and public buildings. Texas needed a friend in court.

Everybody who comes to Congress is motivated by one thing or another. We come, bringing our dreams and our baggage. Two events had shaped my philosophy and formed my life's driving ambition. They were the great Depression of the 1930s and World War II. A world without war and without depression. That vision never faded. It had taken me the next sixteen years to go to college, fight a war, build a career and make some money—all with the single purpose of getting to Congress. Now I was here. My real interest, I thought at the time, was foreign affairs. My personal preference would have been assignment to the Foreign Affairs Committee, where I somewhat naively supposed I could make major contributions to world peace. But Speaker Rayburn and my Texas colleagues asked me to consider Public Works instead. As a favor to them, and to our state, I did. I never regretted it.

CHAPTER FOUR

TEXANS AND BIG DREAMS

"**M**ake no little plans," wrote Danish astronomer Tycho Brahe. "They have no magic to stir men's blood." As a youth I embraced that philosophy. Now I was learning that most big victories were merely culminations of a thousand minor triumphs, and the best a new congressman could expect was to be a small part of a big effort. At the start of my second term, I had the option of staying on the Public Works Committee or taking a berth on Foreign Affairs. By then, I'd discovered two things: the limited jurisdiction of the Foreign Affairs Committee in the House, and the advantages of being a team player who could make things happen in Congress for folks back home.

"Any jackass can kick down a barn," Sam Rayburn was fond of saying, "but it takes a skilled carpenter to build one." He used that homey analogy in extolling to me the virtues of public works. "One of the first acts of the Continental Congress was to authorize a system of post roads and trails," he reminded me, "and it is this kind of thing that has tied America together ever since."

Emblazoned on the wall high above the Speaker's dais in the House of Representatives' chamber are these words of Daniel Webster: *Let us develop the resources of our land, call forth its powers, build up its institutions, promote all its great interests and see whether we also in our day and generation may not perform something worthy to be remembered.* I saw those words every day. They silently confirmed my committee choice, summing up the mission of worthwhile public construction projects.

When I was mayor of Weatherford in my twenties, these had been the warp and woof of my existence. We paved miles of dirt streets, replaced hundreds of outhouses and septic tanks with sanitary sewer lines, brought the boon of piped water to previously unserved outskirts. I had actively promoted a bond issue for a modern sewage disposal plant, opened five neighborhood parks, and replaced the city dump with a sanitary landfill. Our town in the choking throes of a seven-year drought, I had negotiated purchase of a small lake from the Texas Pacific Railroad and begun work on a large city reservoir. The first time I heard someone refer snidely to projects of this kind as "pork barrel," I was dumbfounded. "Pork, hell!" I stammered. "That's bread and butter!"

A congressman, I discovered, had to be a tripartite personality. He was a personal intercessor for literally thousands of private citizens, a grantsman and regional advocate for the civic interests of his own area, and simultaneously a statesman. He had to balance these parochial concerns with, and sometimes subordinate them to, the national interest. To be effective, any lawmaker must network with others. Most of us found that our closest continuous ties would be with others from across the country who served on our committees of choice, those who entered Congress in the same year we did, and the members of our own state delegations. For Texans, this relationship was pervasive.

The Texas delegation was one of the most cohesive in Congress. Every Wednesday at noontime when Congress was in session, its members came together for lunch in the Speaker's dining room. By general understanding, every member owes help to other Texans whose districts have matters of importance pending before his committee. This bond of loyalty served the state effectively. It gave the newest and least influential member the presumption of a court advocate for his major local projects. That particular bond transcends ideology. The delegation always has numbered liberals, conservatives and moderates in its ranks, along with some colorful and unpredictable individualists who defy categorization.

Other state and regional groupings could summons up a similar cohesion on one or two issues during a given year. But no other, I think, commanded quite the same camaraderie and sense of shared mission. This tendency to close ranks on things of parochial interest often created both envy and resentment. Congressman Frank Ikard of Wichita Falls was an indefatigable booster for the products of his district. One of these interests was cattle. In fact, it was one of Frank's forebears who'd introduced the white-faced Hereford to the region. During one congressional recess, Ikard placed a cattlemen's association sticker on the rear windshield of his car. *Texans Eat BEEF Every Day,* the sticker proclaimed.

The word BEEF stood out in boldface letters printed in red ink, while the rest of the slogan was in blue. The hot West Texas sun scorched and faded the red coloring completely away, leaving the following blue-inked words clearly legible: "Texans Eat . . . Every Day."

Back in Washington, a passerby stared in mild astonishment at the sign on Frank's auto, shook his head, and muttered to a companion, "Those damn Texans! You never know what they'll be braggin' about next."

Somebody once asked Rayburn why Texas always seemed to have so much influence in Congress. In typical brevity the old man replied, "We pick 'em young, we pick 'em honest, we send 'em there, and we keep 'em there." This formula explained our state's extraordinary number of committee and sub-committee chairmanships. These came by seniority. The member of the majority party with longest service on each committee was chairman.

A chairman in those days was very nearly supreme in his realm. His was an office of power. Speaker "Tip" O'Neill in the 1980s would refer to House committee chairs as the "College of Cardinals." To me, in my early congressional years, they seemed more like medieval barons, invulnerable in their fiefdoms.

Paul Kilday of San Antonio approached me in friendly banter one day. "Jim, I don't suppose you care much for this seniority system, do you?"

"Well, no, Paul," I confessed. "To tell you the truth, I don't see a whole lot of logic in it."

"Just take my word for it," he said with a broad wink. "You'll come to appreciate it more every year you're here."

The wry comedy of that assurance gave me scant comfort. I had big dreams. Ambition's hot blade had not yet been tempered by the slow fires of experience. I couldn't see myself marking time for decades waiting to be a chairman.

Three of my Texas colleagues, exhibiting Job-like patience, were nearing that apex of power. All had worked and waited for what seemed to me an inordinately long time. They were Wright Patman of Texarkana, a gutsy old populist, from the pine tree country in our state's northeast corner abutting Arkansas; tall and lanky George Mahon of Lubbock and the south plains; and crusty, scholarly W. R. (Bob) Poage from Waco in Central Texas. Each twitched anxiously in second ranking of seniority on an important House committee. Patman, after twenty-six years in the House and a long apprenticeship on the Banking Committee, maintained stoic deference to Chairman Brent Spence of Kentucky, with whom Patman often disagreed over monetary policy. Spence, at eighty-two, feeble, nearly deaf and sight-impaired, thought Patman a dangerous radical. George Mahon, in Congress since 1935 and an acknowledged authority on defense expenditures, sometimes carried papers and briefcase for cantankerous old Clarence Cannon of

Missouri, solicitously inquiring after the latter's health. Not until Cannon chose to resign could Mahon accede to the powerful Appropriation chairmanship. Likewise, Bob Poage, Congress's most knowledgeable member on Agriculture, waited twenty years to become Agriculture Committee chairman when Harold Cooley of North Carolina retired.

For each of these men, a House chairmanship represented the zenith of his political ambitions. But it wasn't power for its own sake. Each had brought with him a dream. For Patman, who came to Congress in 1929, it was to disperse and broaden the base of economic power, whose concentration in too few hands he saw as a major cause of the Great Depression. In his youth a crusading district attorney who prosecuted the Ku Klux Klan, Patman opposed bullies throughout his life. Part of his dream was to keep interest rates low to let "the little fellow" get a toehold on the path of upward mobility. George Mahon lived in the little west Texas town of Colorado City when first elected to Congress in 1934. It was hard-scrabble, sandy country that spawned a special breed of independence. Senator "Pitchfork" Ben Tillman of South Carolina once said of Mahon's flat plains that "you can look farther and see less than anywhere else in the world." That country also breeds more military volunteers per capita than almost any other region of the country. Part of Mahon's vision was to amass enough military strength to make another attack upon the United States of the Pearl Harbor type unthinkable. As number two on the Appropriations Committee, he was in a good position to promote his dream. Bob Poage, from the dry cotton country of central Texas, wanted to keep small family farms viable in our increasingly urbanized culture. Poage specialized in legal incentives for crop rotation, upstream dams and terraces to save the country's thinning layer of topsoil. He farmed and understood farming.

One advantage of the seniority system was a degree of stability. It had come into being as a liberating reform, a sort of noblemen's *Magna Carta*, in 1910. It broke the sometimes abusive powers of Speaker Joe "Boss" Cannon, who unilaterally appointed his own henchmen to committee chairs. Not only that, he appointed all members, including minority members of all committees. Cannon often used this leverage to block consideration of popular reforms. But the most obvious effect of the seniority rule in the 1950s was to insure an *ad hoc* Southern dominance of congressional committees. The Rules Committee, which cleared bills before they came to the House floor, was ruled by "Judge" Howard Smith of Virginia. Graham Barden of North Carolina ran Education and Labor. The tax-writing Ways and Means Committee answered to Jere Cooper of Tennessee. Percy Priest of Tennessee headed Commerce. When he left, he'd be succeeded by Oren Harris of Arkansas. Armed Services was chaired by Carl Vinson of Georgia, who stayed in Congress for fifty years. All these men, and others like them, were products of the long-standing one-party system that spread across the South from Virginia to Texas. Southerners identified as Democrats. An aspiring politician with any hope of winning election would call himself a Democrat. Our party spanned the spectrum. This built seniority in Congress not through any intense party organization, but through individual public loyalties assiduously and personally cultivated by political office holders. Since there was no real Democratic organization, each had been forced to win his seat in Congress by route of a primary election, often vigorously contested by many candidates. In so doing, each had built his own intense personal following through prodigious campaigning. Once in Congress, he maintained it by often superb constituent service.

Two Texans headed committees when I arrived in Congress. Olin Teague was chairman of Veterans Affairs, and Omar Burleson chaired House Administration. Poage, Patman, and Mahon would make it, after long waits, to the zenith of their respective committee pyramids. Mahon and Albert Thomas of Houston already led important Appropriation subcommittees. But the nexus of our state's extraordinary influence was the Rayburn-Johnson partnership.

Rayburn and Johnson, in spite of a symbiotic relationship that made them a formidable team, were utterly unalike. The Speaker's office functioned in old-fashioned simplicity. Rayburn operated no "robotypers," sent out no newsletters, maintained no card files. His long-time assistant, Miss Alla Clary, told me Rayburn never allowed one of his staff, on answering the telephone, to ask "who's calling?" Every caller, high or low, was put directly through. If Speaker Rayburn was out, calls were answered in the order of their receipt. Johnson's office, by contrast, was an outpost of modern efficiency. It featured the latest time-saving and rapid duplicating devices available. Productive aides rolled out a constant volume of correspondence, most of it signed by auto-pen, that would have overwhelmed the capacity of an average small-town post office. Lyndon was the first person on Capitol Hill to install a mobile telephone in his automobile. His opposite number, Senate Republican Leader Everett Dirksen of Illinois, followed suit as soon as he learned of the innovation.

Riding in to the Capitol on the first morning that his own car phone was operable, Dirksen wasted no time in dialing Johnson's mobile number.

When the Texan answered, Dirksen said, "Lyndon, I just wanted to call you from my new car phone and tell you that you're not the only—" At this, Johnson interrupted. "Excuse me, Ev, my other phone's ringing."

Lyndon Johnson dreamed bigger than any of us. I believe I instinctively felt the first time I had a lengthy conversation with him, back in 1947 while he was still a member of the House, that he was headed for the White House. And that was fine with me. I had seen him come within a tissue paper's width of winning a Senate seat over W. Lee O'Daniel in 1941 and had helped him triumph in the photo finish against Coke Stevenson in 1948. He had vision and courage.

Lyndon pushed his staff to near exhaustion, but he demanded even more of himself. Driving his lanky frame at a whirlwind pace without a pause for breath for as long as I knew him, Johnson dared fate. Finally, his heart gave way to the strain. At a July 4 weekend outing with a passel of Texas friends at a horse farm in Middleburg, Virginia, Johnson became nauseated. He asked to sit, then wanted to lie down. This was so unlike him that it alarmed the rest of us. Hurried to the Bethesda Naval Hospital, Lyndon Johnson was diagnosed with a heart attack. Doctors said it could have been fatal.

When medics first told the intense, hard-driving man that he had to quit smoking and alter his lifestyle, the big fellow knotted his brow. "Gee, Doc," he drawled. "I'd rather give up my seniority than my cigarettes."

But Lyndon Johnson devoted himself to the job of getting well with the same single-minded determination that he'd given to every other pursuit in his adult life. And get well he did.

Like every new member of Congress since the republic's early days, no doubt, I struggled to carve out a bigger niche for myself. Impatient like others before me to break out of the cocoon of anonymity, I yearned to be the author of major legislation. For a new member, alas, it wasn't easy. Texas and much of the Southwest were suffering the last scorching days of a seven-year drought. Unable to grow feed, cattlemen were selling off their breeding stock. Dallasites, their city forced to pipe brackish water from Lake Texoma, one hundred miles to the north, were buying bottled water to drink. Most towns forbade the watering of lawns. Then, when the skies opened up and poured forth torrents in the spring of 1957, rivers overran their banks and flooded towns all the way from Kansas to Central Texas. Boldly I introduced a bill to cope with both kinds of crisis. We would create a National Water Transport Authority. It would build pipelines and aqueducts, bringing water from areas of recurrent overabundance to the sections of chronic scarcity. We'd retire the cost by selling the precious fluid to communities in the drought-prone areas. My bill was duly referred to the Committee on Banking and Currency.

And there it lay. It got nowhere. A junior member of Congress simply did not father major legislation, I discovered.

In the fall of 1957, the Russians hurled Sputnik into orbit. America was stunned that our scientific supremacy had been challenged. Russia was ahead of us, and there was a nervous national consensus that we must catch up. I introduced a bill to assist America's schools in scientific studies, to buy modern laboratory equipment for our far-flung educational system, to finance college scholarships for promising students of the sciences, and to create a nationwide organization of Future Scientists of America. The far-ranging bill was referred to the House Committee on Education and Labor. I gained permission to appear and testify.

There I discovered an important axiom. Major bills bear the imprimatur of subcommittee chairmen, not of junior members who do not even belong to the committee of jurisdiction. Most of the things I'd put in my bill were incorporated into a successful piece of legislation entitled the National Defense Education Act. Its author, however, was not Jim Wright but Carl Elliott of Alabama, the chairman of the subcommittee. This was simply the way things worked. To a large extent, they still do. I got some vicarious satisfaction out of seeing some of my suggestions engraved into law. Junior members have been gaining the same satisfaction ever since. One small feature of the bill was left, by Carl Elliott's indulgence, to my authorship, the chartering of an organization called Future Scientists.

A member of Congress, in his first few terms, is lucky indeed if he can manage a minor coup here and there to benefit his own constituency. And I *was* lucky. From my junior berth on the Public Works Committee, I was able to enact a Survey Resolution directing the Corps of Engineers to develop plans to cope with the flooding of Big Fossil Creek and an appropriation to complete the Fort Worth floodway. I also passed a little bill to modify the law that created the Benbrook Reservoir, letting Fort Worth and other communities buy water on an emergency basis in times of drought. I argued with mixed success before the Civil Aeronautics Board for more flights to Amon Carter Field, the airport constructed at considerable expense mid-way between Dallas and Fort Worth to serve our community. Within a few years, I would be able to influence the purchase of more B-58s and the awarding of the TFX ("tri-service" aircraft) contract to the Fort Worth manufacturer, General Dynamics. I got a new post office for Arlington and started the wheels in motion for building the Fort Worth Federal Center, which stanched the flow of federal offices and employees to Dallas. These things were important to my constituency. They should have been enough to satisfy me.

The older bulls of Congress seemed like giants. Their power was formidable. There was crusty old Graham Barden of North Carolina, Chairman of the Committee on Education and Labor. Once, after repeated unanswered entreaties by mail, I mustered the courage to ask him in person when I might expect to get some action on one of my bills in his committee. He favored me with only the briefest glance. "When you start voting right," he rumbled.

"Right," by his yardstick, meant more conservatively. I had been one of only five from below the Mason-Dixon line who refused to sign the "Southern Manifesto," denouncing the Supreme Court decision on school integration. That, along with several of my votes, had not escaped the attention of the North Carolina titan.

By far the biggest domestic landmark of the Eisenhower administration was the Interstate Highway Program. It was, in fact, the costliest and most extensive public works project in the history of nations. Following years of wartime and post-war neglect, many of our country's best highways had fallen into disrepair. President Eisenhower wanted a system of superhighways to connect every American city of 100,000 people and more. It was a boldly ambitious plan. The initial draft drawn up by a presidential commission headed by General Lucius D. Clay called for 40,000 miles of concrete highways, built to a minimum standard of six lanes, with median separations between the traffic heading in opposite directions. This ambitious plan came to the Public Works Committee, but the Clay panel dodged the most critical issue: Who would pay for the roads? The commission settled for simply floating thirty-year tax bonds for the enormous project, estimated initially at $25 billion, but soon recalculated at $35 billion. Let future congresses wrestle with how to pay off the bonds! Interest alone would have added about 60 percent to the cost of the highways over the thirty-year period. I didn't like that arrangement. I didn't want to yoke another generation with the burden of paying for roads we'd be wearing out before some of its members reached tax-paying age. Several others on the committee felt as I did. Fred Schwengel, a new Republican member from Iowa, and I began agitating for a pay-as-we-go plan. It would be fairer, we stressed, and cheaper in the long run. Our comments were picked up by several newspapers. Soon other members were joining our ranks.

When General Clay testified before the committee, he tried to defend the bonding proposal. It would not require voting an increase in the national debt *limit*, he said, since the bonds would be distinct from bonds sold to finance the general debt. Committee member Brady Gentry, a former state highway commissioner, bore in on the General. "You're not trying to say this would not increase the national *indebtedness*, are you?" General Clay had to admit that his argument was mainly semantic. The nation's debt *would* increase by $35 billion or more.

Fred Schwengel and I went to see Speaker Rayburn, who agreed with us. "The time to pay is when you buy," he said. "In time of war or depression, we *have* to go into debt, but not now! I think you boys are right." Rayburn suggested that those of us on the committee who felt strongly about it should call for an appointment with President Eisenhower, since the whole idea was "his baby," and try to convince him that we ought to pay for the roads with current taxes.

It was my first real conversation with a president. I felt like a hot dog on a stick! I gulped and began.

"Mr. President, we think the highway program is a wonderful idea, and we want to help, but we believe there is a better, more straightforward way to finance the roads. We think people are patriotic enough to pay for them up front. And people are tired of going into debt. Let's not give the next generation another legacy of debt. Let's give them a legacy of safe, modern highways, completed and paid for!"

The president was listening. "How would you do that?" he asked. Encouraged, I continued.

"Let's build a highway trust fund, made up of road-user taxes. Two or three pennies on each gallon of gasoline, a couple of dollars on big commercial truck tires, things like that. Those who benefit most from the roads will pay the most into the fund. We'll not spend a penny more in a given year than the fund takes in, and we'll not let a penny go from the fund for any other purpose. We'll raise enough to complete the program on schedule, and we won't add a dime to the national debt!"

Others of our group elaborated on that theme. Finally, President Eisenhower cleared his throat. We all fell silent.

"Gentlemen, if you think you can sell that to the American people, you have my blessing. More power to you!"

The result was a magnificent investment in America. Every dollar spent on the roads has generated between thirty-five and forty dollars in private investments in job-creating enterprises—factories, office buildings, hotels, and service institutions of all kinds—along the routes of the Interstate. The program, which passed in 1956, has paid for itself many times over: in lives, in money, in convenience, in jobs. Nobody tried to deceive people into thinking it could be done on the cheap or that it wasn't going to cost them something. The public, seeing the tangible results of their taxes, did not complain. People are fairer than some give them credit for being. A generation later, I would ache and hunger for that kind of simple, unfeigned candor in the White House over fiscal matters.

On several issues I disagreed with the Eisenhower administration and said so. At the insistence of John Blatnik of Minnesota, the Public Works Committee in 1956 launched the nation's first real attack on water pollution. The bill provided $50 million a year to help cities build needed waste-water treatment plants. This was a matching fund. Half must be awarded to cities with fewer than 125,000 persons. The federal contribution could be no more than one-third of the cost. Even so—and modest as it would seem by later standards—the bill ran into opposition from the White House. Bill Cramer, a young Florida Republican, argued on the floor that water pollution was a problem for cities to handle without federal help, but Blatnik and I, along with others, called the growing contamination of our streams a "national disgrace." We stressed the unfair health hazards inflicted upon innocent downstream citizens by upstream polluters. My attitude was influenced strongly by my experience as mayor of Weatherford.

In the end, the bill passed by a large margin. Eisenhower turned his back on nay-sayers in the administration and signed the bill. The fact that it originated in Congress, without his recommendation, did not faze him. He was not looking for fights with Congress. We passed an omnibus water resources bill, however, which did draw his ire. It was one of those triennial authorizations that packed more than a hundred individual projects into one bill. One of the items approved was completion of the Fort Worth floodway. Having seen the suffering that came in the wake of a major flood, I felt strongly about the bill. President Eisenhower, egged on by a claque of critics who insisted on equating water resources with "pork barrel," vetoed the bill. In the ensuing fight, Congress handed Ike his first override. Quizzed by Texas reporters on the day before that vote, I said the president just really didn't comprehend the gravity of the problem in human terms.

"If he'd spend a little less time on the golf course and a little more time visiting communities afflicted by natural disasters, he would understand why this is so important to people," I said.

The next day, Texas newswoman Sarah McClendon arose in Mr. Eisenhower's news conference. "Mr. President, Wright says you ought to spend less time on the golf course and more time visiting flood victims," she bluntly announced.

Those present said the president flushed noticeably. "Well, I don't know who Wright is, but I'll tell you this: I've seen more floods than he has!"

As a matter of fact, he undoubtedly was right. For all my presumed authority, I was only thirty-three. Mr. Eisenhower was sixty-six. While the incident made me a sort of momentary folk hero among recent flood victims on the home front, I wished I hadn't said what I did. Underneath it all, I really did like the man.

Two events, little noticed at the time, bracketed my first congressional year like a set of parentheses. Each would cast long shadows into our collective future. Early that year, on February 23, 1955, President Eisenhower sent a small force of military advisers to help an embattled anticommunist government in South

Vietnam, a country about which most Americans then knew practically nothing. Toward year's end, on December 1, a forty-three-year-old black woman named Rosa Parks boarded a city bus in Montgomery, Alabama, and took a seat at the front. Refusing to move to the back of the bus, she was arrested. The travail and triumph these two events set in motion could not be guessed at the time. Each began an ineluctable chain of agonizing decisions for presidents and Congresses to come.

CHAPTER FIVE

RACE, RAYBURN, RECESSION

T he volatile issue of race took center stage beginning in 1956. The Supreme Court ruling in *Brown v. Board of Education*, after two years, was only beginning to force its changes. When President Eisenhower sent troops to enforce a federal court order admitting a handful of African American children to previously segregated Little Rock, Arkansas, public schools in 1956, he stirred a hive of angry, frightened, and occasionally violent opposition.

In my own congressional district, throngs assembled at the schoolyard in Mansfield, Texas, to protest the admission of African Americans. Former Texas governor and U.S. Senator W. Lee O'Daniel showed up with a soundtruck to harangue the crowd with anti-integration rhetoric. Several southern Legislatures passed resolutions of "interposition," giving a patina of self-assumed respectability to die-hard segregationists. *Impeach Earl Warren!* billboards sprouted across the South. In Congress, members from segregated states sought signatures for a document protesting the assumption of power by the Supreme Court. It was called *The Southern Manifesto* and questioned the right of the "Warren Court" to rule in matters involving state school policies. I was one of only five members from states below the Mason-Dixon line who refused to sign the document. Three others were Texans.

At the height of the controversy, in the Texas town of Mansfield, I was asked to come and speak to the Parent Teachers Association. I went with trepidation. I talked about schools, their central role in the life of a community, their mission in preserving a free society. I quoted Mirabeau B. Lamar, second president of the Republic of Texas: "The cultivated mind is the guardian genius of democracy." I opened the floor to questions.

"What about these niggers?" asked a red-faced woman in the front row.

"Well, I think I have to agree with the Apostle Paul, who said God created of one blood all the nations on the face of the earth. Remember that line from the song we learned as children in Sunday school? 'Red and yellow, black and white, all are precious in His sight.' I guess I take that literally."

"I don't mean that!" she replied. "What are we going to do about these niggers in our schools?"

I answered slowly and as calmly as I could: "This is a nation of laws," I said. "Civilized society must abide by laws. Ours is a government of law, not a government of men. That's why it has lasted for two hundred years. That's the price we pay for our freedom. We respect and abide by the law, even if we disagree with it. That's the only way we can have a free society. The Supreme Court in our system of government is the final arbiter of what is and is not constitutional. The court has ruled, and I think we must comply with its ruling."

There was long silence. Finally, someone asked who I thought would win the Southwest Conference football title. I shouted "TCU!"—naming the hometown favorite. Many in the audience cheered loudly, as relieved as I to get past the tense moment.

Waves of anger, fear and resentment coursed through much of the South, including Texas. Defending school segregation, agitators often demanded: "Just tell me this: Would you want your daughter to marry a nigger?" The fear of change that always reinforces conservatism was heightened by a paranoia that breeds in economically stagnant communities. Always at the base of the economic pyramid were the unskilled and marginally employed white workers who earned barely enough to subsist. They felt with poignant intensity a fear of job competition if blacks gained better education.

Once, as I drove the family on a Sunday afternoon outing through rural Virginia, we observed in one small community an uncommon predominance of racially mixed people, ranging from youngsters to middle-aged. "You really have to admire these unreconstructed rebels," Mab commented sardonically. "They may cohabit with blacks, but they have principles against going to school with them!"

Yet it was no laughing matter. The House worked itself into a lather in June of 1956 as New York Congressman Adam Clayton Powell offered an amendment to deny all federal funds of any sort to any school district that had not integrated its classes. Chicago's veteran black congressman Bill Dawson spoke against the motion, arguing that schools and communities needed help, not threats, to overcome their prejudices. The amendment was defeated, but the debate exposed the volatile race issue in all its naked ugliness.

Bitterness intensified as Senate Majority Leader Lyndon Johnson performed the unexpected. For the first time since reconstruction days, the Senate passed a civil rights bill. Always before, even when a majority of Senators favored such a measure, a militant Southern minority would mount a filibuster and halt all Senate business until the offending bill was dropped from the calendar. This time, Johnson, with patient persuasion, mustered enough votes for cloture, breaking the filibuster and passing the bill. The legislation was mild compared to the rhetorical bombast that assailed and defended it, but the symbolism was profound. It broke with the past and set the nation on a course of systematic removal of the overt and subtle barriers that, ever since the Civil War, had held black citizens back.

When this bill broke out of the Senate and headed for action on the House floor, it unleashed a stampede of emotional mail to House members. Their old ways threatened, people in turn threatened congressmen whose loyalty to their basic racial concepts was in any way suspect. One week I counted 648 letters, telegrams, and postcards on the subject of the Senate bill. All but eleven were against it. In the vortex of this storm, Speaker Sam Rayburn taught me a valuable lesson in leadership. People, I knew, could be motivated by appealing either to their better instincts and nobler impulses or to their baser motives, their prejudices and fears. Sam Rayburn appealed to the better side.

On the day the civil rights bill was called up on the floor, Mr. Rayburn sent a page to find me and ask me to come up to the speaker's dais. Sam Rayburn put it this way: "Jim, I think you want to vote for this bill. I'm sure you have been receiving a lot of angry, bitter mail threatening you with all sorts of dire consequences, including political defeat, if you support it. But I believe you are strong enough to do so, and I know that in future years you will be proud that you did."

As it turns out, I *did* want to vote for the bill. I *was* being threatened politically. I *did* withstand that opposition. And I *am* proud of having done so. All these years later, I honor Sam Rayburn's memory for having believed the best about me and appealing to me in a way that brought out the best.

Mr. Rayburn was a man of basic simplicity. He never wasted words. He could reduce the complexities of an issue to a single sentence. Several times I sat in on conferences where members would be haggling around the perimeter of a question. Mr. Rayburn would listen for awhile, then sum it all up in one sentence of such uncomplicated clarity that everyone must have felt, "That's just what I was trying to say."

The veteran Speaker liked to take new members under his wing, when they'd let him. He felt a particular affinity for Texans, but was always on the lookout for young men of promise whose careers he could help advance. Hale

Boggs of Louisiana and Dick Bolling of Missouri were two non-Texans to whom he obviously had taken a liking. Rayburn was a patriot in the old-fashioned sense, and a man of strong likes and dislikes. He believed he could judge character in another's face. As noted earlier, he never forgave Dick Nixon, then vice president, for the "party of treason" comment made during the 1954 congressional elections. Another to whom the Speaker took a strong dislike was Bruce Alger, a handsome, athletic member from Dallas. Elected in 1954 and a freshman along with me, Alger then was one of only three Republicans sent to Congress from Texas since Reconstruction days. After his maiden visit with the Speaker, Alger committed the indiscretion of saying to the press that he thought Rayburn cared more about his party than about his country. Mr. Rayburn took a dim view of that.

During Wednesday luncheons, the Texas delegation often would hash out our problems in private. Free from prying eyes and ears, each member could say what was on his mind or report arcane intelligence to the group without fear of being quoted outside the familial confines of the delegation. Alger apparently didn't understand—or didn't care to abide by—this unspoken rule. Twice he went to the press with reports of what members had said in the presumed sanctuary of the private meeting. It was, to Rayburn, an unforgivable breach. About midway through my first year, I was standing with Mr. Rayburn outside his office when a reporter tried to get him to comment on some statement Alger had made. "Mr. Speaker," the reporter began, "what do you think about Bruce Alger—" That was a far as he got.

"I *don't* think about him," exclaimed Rayburn. "He is a shit ass."

With that, the old man turned on his heel and walked away. End of interview.

Undeviating Democrat that he was, Sam Rayburn's code of likes and dislikes was thoroughly bipartisan. He indulged a particular fondness, as earlier mentioned, for Joe Martin, his opposite number. Rayburn never tolerated a critical word about the Massachusetts Republican in his presence. "If Joe Martin tells you something, you can count on it," Mr. Rayburn would say. "If he promises you he'll do a thing, you don't have to write it down and remember it. *He'll* remember it, and he'll do it." That was one more clue to the Rayburn character. He put a strong reliance on a colleague's word. "If you tell the truth the *first* time, you don't have to remember what you said." That was the heart of one of his favorite lectures.

Mr. Rayburn was a voracious reader. His favorite literary form was biography. When he came to the hundredth page of a book he was reading, he'd sign his name on that page. The Rayburn Library in Bonham is filled with volumes bearing the famous signature on that particular page. The old gentlemen loved to talk with young people. Frequently I heard him counseling them to get interested in history. "But don't read it like you're taking a dose of medicine," he'd say. "Read it like it's fun, because it *is* fun. It's the only real truth in the world. The way to understand history, and the way to enjoy it, is to read biographies. You'll learn history best through the lives of people who lived it."

Sam Rayburn was kind to me, brash and bumptious as I surely was in those early years. When the annual Democratic fund-raising dinner was held in Washington that first year, I hadn't sold any tickets. They were $100 apiece, and I had bought a couple, but I just frankly didn't have any friends of whom I felt free to ask that much money for tickets to a dinner they probably couldn't attend in any case. Mr. Rayburn had been looking over the list of ticket sellers. Apparently, he wanted me to get off to the right start with the national party. Without even consulting me, he called Bob Windfohr, a wealthy Fort Worth attorney, and sold him a $1,000 table in my name. Rayburn gave me the tickets to disburse in any way I desired. (That, incidentally, was the dinner at which the Speaker got off one of his best quips. "The Democratic Party has some amiable idiots," he said, "but we don't have any old fogies—or what's worse, young fogies!")

A lot of people had the wrong idea about Mr. Rayburn. They'd see him on TV, presiding over the national Democratic conventions. Many would mistake his irate manner when the sessions were slow to come to order for the irascibility of an "old fogey." It wasn't that. Sam Rayburn had an absolute reverence for democratic procedures. He was accustomed to presiding in a body where the gentle rap of his gavel brought instant order. At the conventions, he often faced a roiling sea of disorder. It was an offense to the old gentleman's well-developed sense of propriety. The lack of respect for the democratic process offended him. For the same reason, he didn't like for a member to appear on the House floor in an oddly matching ensemble. "Look at that fellow!" he once said to me, indicating one of our colleagues. "He's got on a coat of one color and britches of another. Looks like he's worn out the britches to his coat and gone and got him some other britches!" He made J. T. Rutherford of El Paso take off his cowboy boots and buy himself a pair of shoes for wear on the House floor. Ken Gray of Illinois was given to flamboyant attire. Rayburn once told him, "Ken, if I ever see you properly dressed, I'll let you preside over the House." The next day Ken Gray wore a dark blue suit, and Rayburn installed the Illinois freshman in the Speaker's chair during the routine business session.

For all his quaint individualities, Sam Rayburn must rank as the greatest lawmaker in the history of our country. More truly significant laws bear the stamp of Rayburn's authorship than that of any other man. He served longer in Congress than any other person in the first two hundred years of our nationhood. He presided over the House longer than any other Speaker in history, twice as long as any predecessor in that office. Laws guided and shaped by Sam Rayburn led the United States out of its worst depression, to victory in World War II and to the pinnacle of power our country achieved in the postwar years. Presidents inspired us and occasionally stirred us with their oratory, but this short, bald, unpretentious man from Bonham, Texas, performed much of the heavy lifting.

He was, in so many ways, a simple man. He never traveled but once outside the United States. Until he was almost seventy, he never flew in an airplane. The place nearest his heart was Bonham. He loved his home town, he said, "because people know it when you're sick, and they care when you die."

Sam Rayburn was a man of direct action. He felt impatience and contempt for ceremonious delays. Once, when Omar Burleson was chairman of the House Administration Committee, he brought to the Speaker a resolution he wanted to introduce, authorizing a study of the need for a third House office building. "Would authorize a—what?" Rayburn asked. "A *study*, Mr. Speaker," said Burleson. "That's the way it's done, you know. We authorize a study, then fund the study, then complete the study, and, if worthy, we then authorize money for planning and eventually construct the facility."

"Study, hell!" replied Rayburn impatiently. "Everybody knows we need that building. Don't *study* it! *Build* it!"

Sam Rayburn may have been an anachronism in the television age. He was a throwback to a time when political contributions were made in cash, appeals for votes were made in person, and a man's word was his bond. He had contempt for any congressman who was, in Rayburn's words, "afraid of his district." He told me more than once that "any congressman worth his salt can *lead* his district."

Mr. Rayburn lived in a house built for his parents, and he never had much money. He was content with a bachelor's life. He was wed to the U.S. Congress as surely as a Roman Catholic priest is wed to the church. He died childless, but his protégés were legion, and his intellectual offspring—those influenced by his uncomplicated traits of honesty, straightforwardness, absolute dependability, sympathy for the underdog, and undeviating love of country—are beyond our capacity to number.

In 1958, Congress seized the economic initiative from a largely complacent administration. Spurred to action by Speaker Rayburn and Senate Majority Leader Lyndon Johnson, legislative committees sprang forward quickly with a well-timed package of anti-recession measures to cope with an alarming downturn in the nation's economy. As the year began, Commerce

Department and Federal Reserve statistics were revealing a host of gathering economic woes. More Americans were out of work than at any time since 1941. Industrial production fell in January for the fifth consecutive month. Automobile sales dropped sharply. More than 14,000 small businesses had turned belly up in 1957, the highest rate of failures for any year since 1939. The initial response from the White House was to deny the seriousness of the problem. It seemed to me that most members of the president's cabinet were more economically conservative and less socially conscious than Eisenhower himself. Treasury Secretary George M. Humphrey probably did not mean to sound elitist when he said, "What's good for General Motors is good for the country." And Charles E. Wilson, recruited from General Electric to serve as Secretary of Defense, rubbed a lot of people wrong when he compared those who worried about unemployed workers to "lap dogs." If they were more like "bird dogs," Wilson opined, they'd go out and find work.

President Eisenhower, sensing that something should be done, suggested we embark upon a $2 billion post office building program. This hardly amounted to a comprehensive anti-recession program, and the General Services Administration wanted to do it on the cuff with a lease-purchase plan. Private builders would finance construction by private lease-purchase plan borrowing. The government would lease the buildings from the builders and acquire them after twenty or thirty years at a guaranteed profit to the builders. In thirty years, the public would have paid out about twice the construction value of the properties. Congress was cool to the plan.

By the end of March, the economic situation had tightened grimly. Unemployment hovered above five million, at just about eight percent of the job force. Yet Eisenhower continued to express the conviction that we'd seen the worst, that an upturn was in sight.

One weekend, I traveled with a colleague named Pat Jennings to western Virginia, where the coal mines had been laying people off for months. As I listened to newly unemployed, middle-aged people in Marion, Virginia, my mind drifted back twenty-six years to 1932, when I was nine years old, and I thought of my grandfather, William Dee Walker, who searched so long and doggedly for a job, any job.

In response to the 1958 recession, stimulants to business and employment began to flow in a stream from Congress. The Senate passed a bill to speed up the rate of construction of the interstate highway building program. The House initiated an emergency $177 million appropriation to start actual work immediately on a backlog of needed public buildings. Congress passed a housing bill to make $1.8 billion available for Federal support of home mortgages. Another committee provided low-cost loans to cities and towns for local public works improvements.

Goaded, the executive branch began to join the parade. The army announced that, as a boon to the sick auto industry, it would let $100 million in military truck and trailer contracts during the next month. The president was preparing to ask Congress for action to help states extend jobless benefits up to thirty-six weeks. The maximum then varied from sixteen weeks in Florida to thirty weeks in Pennsylvania. The Agriculture Department announced in April it would make surplus foods available from Commodity Credit Corporation inventories for eligible welfare recipients.

President Eisenhower signed, with some misgiving, the $1.8 billion highway construction speed-up—it was expected to create about 88,000 additional jobs during 1958—but he vetoed a $1.5 billion water resources authorization of new works stretching over a period of several years. Congress overrode the veto. I enjoyed this display of legislative assertiveness. It got the economy moving again. But in the big, broad world, Ike was still supreme.

CHAPTER SIX

IKE
AND THE
WORLD

Even as Democrats in Congress seized the initiative from the president on questions of the domestic economy, our leaders were giving him forceful support on international fronts. Eisenhower had made a decisive break from the discredited isolationism of earlier Republican presidents, and most Democrats agreed with his foreign policy. Nobody wanted to gain partisan advantage from a foreign policy failure. On more than one occasion, it was Democrats who pulled Ike's foreign policy chestnuts out of the fire. When he asked legislative support for a show of strength in the Formosa Straits, in Lebanon, in the islands of Quemoy and Matsu off the China mainland, his requests were reinforced by immediate statements of ungrudging support from Democratic congressional leaders.

The president believed in the absolute need for foreign military and economic aid. His administration invented the term "Mutual Security" to make the package more salable to the public. When the initial undertaking began in 1947 as the Marshall Plan, it was something altogether new in world diplomacy. The effort saved Western Europe, crushed by six years of war, from financial ruin. Winston Churchill called it the "most unsordid" political act in history. Now, the Eisenhower administration was using a mix of economic and military aid to buy time for newly emerging democracies in the developing world. Wanting to shore up domestic political support for the effort, Ike scheduled a huge White House conference for newspaper editors and political writers. After day-long State Department briefings, the president spoke personally at a large dinner in a downtown Washington hotel. Lindy Boggs, wife of Louisiana Democrat Hale Boggs, organized a group of young congressional wives to serve as hostesses to the visiting newsmen. Along with other invited congressmen, I attended.

As soon as she spotted me, Lindy Boggs came hurriedly. "Do you know a man named John Ellis?" she asked.

"John Ellis? Sure! Editor of the *Fort Worth Star-Telegram*. Good friend of mine."

"Well, he's over there to the left, Jim. He can't find his seat. He, along with some other western editors, think the best seats have been gobbled up by the eastern press, and they're unhappy about it."

I spotted John, hailed him, insisted that he and his colleagues sit with me. We exchanged a lot of stories over dinner. I kept stressing how important it was for all of us to close ranks and support President Eisenhower's foreign policy. But I don't think I ever got any of them to call it "mutual security." They were hooked on "foreign aid."

When Republican Senator John Bricker of Ohio seemed to be making headway with an America-firstish Constitutional amendment, which Eisenhower opposed on foreign policy grounds, it was Democrats who stalled it. House Judiciary Chairman Emanuel Celler of New York, taunted by the press to say how he stood on the Bricker measure, replied with disarming candor: "I don't stand on it," he said. "I'm *sitting* on it. It rests four square under my fanny, and it will never see the light of day."

One day in 1960, as the presidential campaigns were warming up, I got unexpectedly drawn into the effort to save one sensitive item of the president's foreign policy. Assistant Secretary of State Roy R. Rubottom was on the telephone. His plea was urgent. "President Eisenhower has a very serious problem on the House floor today," Rubottom insisted, "and we really do hope you can help us." I had met Rubottom and liked him. "The president invited the countries of our hemisphere to establish headquarters for the Pan American Health Organization here in Washington," he explained, "and they voted to accept. The president promised them we'd build a complex to house the effort. It's very important to all of Latin America."

"I know it is, Mr. Secretary," I said. "It has done great work to wipe out malaria and pellagra. What's the problem? How can I help?"

A bill authorizing the construction was scheduled for a House vote under suspension of the rules that very afternoon. This meant only forty minutes of debate, with a two-thirds vote required to suspend rules and pass the bill. This procedure was usually reserved for relatively non-controversial items.

It was Monday. Over the weekend, a crazy coalition had been forming against the bill. Eager to attack anything that sounded remotely like "foreign aid," an isolationist remnant of Republicans, joined by partisan Democrats simply anxious to embarrass the administration in that election year, had been building opposition to the authorizing legislation. If the bill went down, it would be deeply embarrassing to President Eisenhower—also, obviously, hurtful to our relations with Latin America.

At the Secretary's urging, I dropped everything else and spent a very busy day on the telephone, persuading as many colleagues as I could reach to support the bill. Committee chairman Tom Morgan, told by Rubottom of my interest, asked me to take three minutes in debate on the House floor. As I groped for an adequate summary, I knew I'd have to dispel election year-mania. This thought came to me: "Although I did not personally vote for this president, I want everyone in this House to know that he is my president. If he is embarrassed, then I am embarrassed—because my country is embarrassed." In those days, that kind of simple appeal could quell partisanship. The bill passed handsomely.

In May of 1958, after Vice President Richard Nixon was beset by angry, violent mobs in Peru and Venezuela, Democratic congressmen and staffers joined Republican counterparts to help swell a welcoming crowd at the airport for Nixon's return. It wasn't that we admired him or necessarily agreed with what he had been saying. We wanted to give the world a showing of solidarity and thus diminish the sting of the anti–U.S. demonstrations. When Nixon came to Fort Worth that fall to speak for Republican candidates, I personally called on him at Hotel Texas to welcome him to our city. It seemed the appropriate thing to do. My courtesy call was wholly unexpected. I hoped it pleased the vice president, given his party mission, even more than it surprised him. It was like the old army maxim about senior officers: "If you don't like the man, salute the uniform."

Successful statehood drives for Alaska and Hawaii in 1958 and '59 made those years memorable for many of us. Eisenhower endorsed statehood, Rayburn and most Texas members were doubtful, but I became emotionally and intellectually involved. Shortly after my first primary election in 1954, I'd been contacted by a friendly, persistent New Orleans man named George Lehleitner. The compelling logic of his arguments for Hawaii, where he'd seen World War II naval duty, made me a statehood disciple. Shortly after coming to Washington in 1955, I'd met Ernest Gruening and learned of the passionate pride with which Alaskans wanted to end their territorial status and share full citizenship. In that year, I had voted for a bill to make states of both territories at once. That bill had gone down in a ludicrous political irony. Many Republicans opposed it out of fear that Alaska would send Democrats to Congress, while members of my party were voting "no" in the clear apprehension that Hawaii would be represented by Republicans.

After the defeat of that bill, Gruening, the former territorial governor, masterminded a bold stratagem. At his urging, Alaskans called a constitutional convention, audaciously declared themselves a state, and elected two Senators and one Representative. These three came to Washington and formally presented their credentials. The maneuver was patterned upon a similar gambit by Tennessee in 1796. It was successful. Gruening and E. L. (Bob) Bartlett, picked as two of Alaska's choices to serve them in Congress, first had to work out an arrangement with John Burns, Hawaii's territorial delegate. Burns was implored to stand aside, delay Hawaii's bid until the following year, and give first right of passage to Alaska. It was not easy for John Burns to consent to this scenario. But we'd seen the hazard of trying to force both through simultaneously. While there was no guarantee that Hawaii's suit would be honored even if Alaska's succeeded, as a matter of tactics they had to be pursued separately. John Burns ultimately agreed. He discussed his dilemma with me. He knew his judgment would be misunderstood and bitterly assaulted by many back in Hawaii. He wasn't even sure Islanders, disappointed in being relegated to the next train, would reelect him as their delegate, but he felt strongly that he was doing the right thing.

In my own scale of values, statehood for both territories was a matter of principle, a chance to reaffirm our own ideals. To reject Alaska's and Hawaii's claims again, I believed, would be to renege shamelessly upon the most fundamental beliefs we professed to cherish. Americans had fought the Revolutionary War to gain for ourselves the very rights we were denying them. "Taxation without representation," we'd said, "is tyranny." That was a central point, I believed, which had potential worldwide implications. There was a subtle racial undertone to the arguments against statehood, often expressed as a conclusion that inhabitants of the two territories were "not ready" for full citizenship. Why not? Because they were Polynesian, Asian, Aleutian? Did the "taxation without representation" doctrine apply only to Caucasians? And if someone suggested that Alaska didn't have enough people to be a state, I pointed out that at least twenty-eight of our states had fewer people when Congress admitted them. Most of the Texas delegation voted against Alaska statehood for another reason—actually a non-reason. Privately, they confessed a simple unwillingness to sanction a state larger than Texas. They thought constituents would resent it. "You're selling your constituents short," I told them.

When the Alaska statehood bill came up for a vote in the last week of May 1958, I spoke for the bill. I said it could be the "most historically significant" choice to confront us:

> *There are two ways by which a nation may grow . . . by military conquest or by the willing attachment of others to it. The first is*

*anathema to us. . . . The latter is the route of Statehood, the manner
in which we grew throughout the nineteenth century and the early
years of the twentieth, while our example inspired mankind and popular people's movements throughout the world were seeking to model
new governments after our own . . .*

*What an example it could be to the uncommitted peoples of the
world, now wavering between our way and that of the communist
ideology. What a contrast to the method by which Communism has
expanded its sphere. Where they have achieved growth by the route of
subversion and military conquest, we can be expanding by the voluntary method, by peoples coming to us, as Alaska has come, and asking
to be united with us in the whole enjoyment of our freedoms.*

The House, which three years before had rejected the combined bills, passed
Alaskan statehood by 208–166. The Senate acted affirmatively, and our
forty-ninth state became a reality. Now it was time to redeem our tacit pledge
to John Burns and Hawaii.

Burns called me one night in October of 1958 from Hawaii. Lyndon
Johnson, then Senate Majority Leader, was to make a speech the next day on the
West Coast. Could I ask Johnson to pledge in that speech that the Senate would
schedule and pass the Hawaii statehood bill in the coming year? If Johnson
could just make an unequivocal commitment, it would go a long way to quiet-
ing the noisy clamor swirling around Burns's head. A lean former police officer
with prematurely white hair and an invalid wife to whom he was devoted,
Burns had done a statesmanlike thing, for which he now was about to be pun-
ished. Standing aside and helping Alaska attain its goal was undoubtedly the
best way to help fulfill Hawaii's ambition, but a lot of his fellow islanders were
having a tough time understanding this. Luckily, I got hold of Lyndon before
his speech. "How would you like to do a 100 percent decent thing and also
make sure that the state of Hawaii sends Democrats to Congress?" I asked.

"Sounds fine to me," Johnson replied in high good humor. "What miracle
do I have to perform?"

I told him. "Just promise to bring the statehood bill to a vote next year and say
you'll support it." He made the commitment to Hawaii in the speech that day.

The Cold War dominated and in some ways distorted our whole national
outlook throughout the 1950s and beyond. The interstate highway program,
our biggest domestic investment, was officially labeled the Interstate *and
National Defense* Highway system. When Congress moved to stimulate
higher education, it named its laudable effort the *National Defense* Education
Act. The most often heard argument for its passage was not the need to

improve learning opportunities for the sake of our kids but the fear that Soviet technology was getting ahead of us and Russian schools were doing a better job than ours in preparing their youth for the space age.

America put an enormous amount of money into military and space hardware. Defense spending mounted up to about 63 percent of our annual appropriations. It seemed to me that the arms and space race could be self-defeating for both the United States *and* the Soviet Union. It was soaking up an enormous lot of treasure, which both we and our ideological adversaries could put to much better use in a peaceful competition to improve living standards on both sides of the Iron Curtain. On December 22, three days before Christmas in 1958, I reread the Christmas story from Luke's gospel, then I looked out my office window upon Washington, turned to my typewriter, and began to peck out a whimsical letter to a mythical Russian named Ivan. "Dear Ivan," I began . . .

My Christmas letter attracted newspaper attention. Lyndon Johnson saw it and inserted a copy, with his comments, in the *Congressional Record*. I reproduced it and sent it to the several thousand people who by then had asked to be included on my weekly newsletter list. The letter offered a simple proposition that both the U.S. and the USSR reduce annual military weapons expenditures by 10 percent a year for five years and put the savings in a common fund to feed the hungry and eradicate disease:

> *Want to help mankind, Ivan? Well, here's your chance. Here's your chance to help mankind and get rid of our fears at the same time. You like five year plans, so I'll make you a five year plan. Let's keep this up . . . and we'll have put a total of 81 billion dollars. . . . We could make an 81 billion dollar gift to humanity, Ivan.*
>
> *Do you know how much 81 billion dollars is? Well, it would build and equip a brand new two million dollar hospital for every city of 10,000 or more in the world. Or medical experts say that with four and a half billion they could absolutely eradicate malaria, typhoid, smallpox, yellow fever and leprosy from the face of the earth. It would build and stock 250,000 first-class libraries and it would provide 20 million four-year college scholarships. It would build 20 million modern homes to replace the world's infested slums. It would build almost a million miles of modern roads . . . enough to circle the earth several times . . .*
>
> *Then, after five years we could slack off. We could reduce our contributions to the Christmas fund and give some tax relief to the folks who have been carrying the burden for so many years . . . yours as well as ours.*

Nothing much happened that I could measure. Probably nobody in Russia saw my letter. Nikita Khrushchev seemed only slightly less hostile than his predecessors in the Kremlin. He would tour the U.S. the following year, creating a brief thaw in superpower relations, which would freeze again in the 1962 Cuban missile crisis. More than twenty-eight years after writing this letter to an unknown Russian, I would hand a copy of it in 1987 to Soviet President Mikhail Gorbachev in the Kremlin. After reading it, Gorbachev invited me to speak to the people of his nation by television. There is nothing more indestructible than an idea.

The Eisenhower years, known to alliterative commentators as the "fabulous fifties," came to a close with the election of John F. Kennedy. The old soldier had been a stabilizing influence. He had produced an ambience of well-being. There'd been a minimum of partisan rancor. Ike was not the best, the strongest, the most eloquent, or most innovative president of the century. He may have been, however, the most universally respected.

His generation's most renowned soldier, he was at heart a man of peace. He proposed an "open skies" policy thirty years before Russia was prepared to accept one. He participated with Canada and Great Britain in opening the St. Lawrence Seaway. If the foreign policy theme of his years was more *anticommunism* than *pro-democracy*, he kept the world's uneasy peace from shattering into war.

His farewell speech was an expression of the essential man. The speech surprised a lot of people who expected platitudes and pap. The phrase that stood out came in his warning against the acquisition of ever-greater power by the "military-industrial complex." But Eisenhower said a lot more than that. He was genuinely concerned about the spiraling arms race, its dreadful waste, the emotionally satisfying jingoism and self-serving economic interest that would make it so wickedly hard to stop or even slow down. His insights into the moral problem of priorities and the brutish economics of displacement were acute. Years earlier, in the descending shadow of World War II, General Eisenhower had said: "Every gun that is made, every warship launched, every rocket fired signifies, in the final sense, a theft from those who hunger and are not fed, those who are cold and not clothed. This world in arms is not spending money alone; it is spending the sweat of its laborers, the genius of its scientists, the hopes of its children." And his farewell speech ended with a prayer that "all peoples will come together in peace guaranteed by mutual respect and love." I have no doubt that he meant it sincerely.

CHAPTER SEVEN

HIGH
HOPES

To me, as to hundreds of thousands of my generation, John F. Kennedy was a major inspiration. Never mind the obsession among revisionist historians with his romantic peccadilloes. I neither knew of them at the time, nor do I care now. The important thing to me is that John F. Kennedy stood for so many of the right things, expressed them with incomparable eloquence, and made people my age want to do something for America. He helped Americans identify with their government as an instrument of their own highest ideals.

My first personal encounter with John F. Kennedy came during my first term in Congress. I'd read his book *Profiles in Courage* and was impressed by it. In those days, I hosted a weekly television interview for each of the two Fort Worth–based stations. Needing interesting subjects for two different programs every week, I was alert to all sorts of possibilities. The Kennedy book was so intriguing that I guessed its author would be a fascinating interview. He was. Readily assenting to my invitation, Senator John Kennedy enriched the fifteen-minute program with sparkling good humor. Conscious of the Texas audience, he talked a lot about Sam Houston, subject of one of the chapters in his book. At the end of the interview, I offered a copy of Kennedy's book, personally inscribed by the author, to any college student or high school senior who would send me a 500-word essay on his own favorite character in American history. Almost a hundred young people in the television audience responded. Senator Kennedy signed each of the books with a personal inscription to the recipient and let me purchase them from him at the author's price—as I recall, $2.30 per copy. I liked the book so well that I bought extra copies and had Senator Kennedy autograph them in his almost illegible longhand for a score or more of personal friends and relatives. Thirty years later, an archivist appraising the library of my friends Edgar and Edith Deen of Fort Worth assessed the book's value at five hundred dollars.

John Fitzgerald Kennedy then was virtually unknown to the national audience. In the next four years, he became a hot property. Trying to help capture the Democratic presidential nomination for my friend Lyndon Johnson in 1960, I repeatedly encountered the Kennedy magic on the campaign trail. I was awed by the Massachusetts senator's winsome way with people and his almost never failing Irish humor. It was at the Kansas state convention in the spring of 1960 that I first sensed the compelling magnetism of what came to be called the Kennedy *mystique*. I was representing Lyndon Johnson. A colleague, Representative Charlie Brown of Missouri, appeared for Senator Stuart Symington. Hubert Humphrey and Kennedy sent word that they would personally attend the event. Rumor had it that a Kennedy emissary had been talking coyly with Kansas Governor Docking about the possible need for an attractive young midwestern governor to fill the second spot on a Kennedy ticket. I would encounter similar rumors in Oklahoma and North Carolina involving Governors Howard Edmondson and Terry Sanford. Kansas, I thought, would be a "natural" for Johnson. He had more in common with most of the convention delegates than any of the others. As much as I liked John Kennedy personally, I couldn't imagine his coming across in a warm enough way to make Kansans identify closely with him. How mistaken I was!

Speeches for all four of the candidates were to follow a banquet for all the delegates. The order of appearance was determined by lot. Humphrey's name was drawn first, Symington's second, Johnson's third, and Kennedy's last. Humphrey was outside the banquet hall shaking hands with stray delegates when this set of rules was announced. His followers had planned a triumphal entry procession for the Minnesota senator, to an accompaniment of horns, balloons, and confetti. When introduced from the podium to make the first speech, Hubert Humphrey entered the hall from the rear, smiling and waving and shaking hands as he proceeded toward the microphone at the head table, his followers trying to make the demonstration last as long as possible. Nobody told the loquacious Minnesotan of the twenty-minute time limit that had been imposed, and he spoke for fifty minutes. Toward the end, the crowd began to squirm.

Charlie Brown held his recommendation of Symington to fifteen minutes, calling him "the best darn vote getter the midwest has ever produced." I knew people must be growing weary after sixty-five minutes of speaking and cut my pro-Johnson remarks to twelve minutes of what I thought were impelling reasons to support the Senate Majority Leader. I was well received, but not wildly. Less than one minute into Jack Kennedy's wrap-up speech, I knew he had the entire audience in the palm of his hand. Eight minutes after he began, he sat down to thunderous applause. That, I would learn, was a Kennedy trademark: a short speech. Always leave them wanting more!

Throughout the spring and early summer of that campaign year, John Kennedy racked up a growing mass of committed delegates in state after state. Early that year, believing we could capture the presidential nomination for Johnson, I had suggested to Lyndon that Kennedy might be a very attractive vice presidential nominee. But when someone raised that possibility in an interview on the campaign trail, Kennedy grinned and said, "Let's not talk about *vice*. I'm against vice in any form."

When the Wisconsin primary went for Kennedy over that state's Minnesota neighbor Hubert Humphrey, everyone realized Jack Kennedy was a contender. A few weeks later, the Boston Irishman dealt a crushing *coup* to the Minnesota senator's aspirations by trouncing him in the West Virginia primary. If the downtrodden dirt farmers and unemployed coal miners of that hard-bitten rural state could identify with a wealthy Boston politician, everyone sensed that Jack Kennedy had a real chance to capture the nomination. At one stop in a little West Virginia mountain town, Kennedy confessed that he'd never been poor, but believed he could identify with the problems of poverty nevertheless. A grizzled miner, shaking the senator's hand after the speech, sought to console him. "That stuff about not ever being poor—don't let that worry you none, Senator. Just take it from me: You ain't missed a damn thing!"

Many were the jokes, both good humored and snide, about the enormous wealth of the senator's father, Joseph P. Kennedy. At a Washington Gridiron Club dinner, the skits teased Kennedy about his father's lavish spending on behalf of his bid for the nomination. On stage, an actor portrayed the senator singing, "Just send the bill to daddy." Jack Kennedy's quick Irish wit saved the day for him. Recognized for remarks immediately following the skit, Kennedy began with this quip: "I have just received the following telegram from my generous daddy: 'Dear Jack: Don't buy a single vote more than necessary. I'll be damned if I'm going to pay for a landslide!'"

By the time convention delegates assembled in Los Angeles, the Massachusetts senator had garnered almost but not quite enough votes to sew up the nomination. Johnson was the only other candidate with even a slim chance to reverse the momentum. Those of us in the Johnson camp took assignments and visited uncommitted delegations in the Texas Senator's behalf. In a last-ditch move to derail the runaway train, Johnson publicly invited Kennedy to appear with him in a nationally televised debate. Before Kennedy could respond, Johnson reserved a small amphitheater in the Biltmore Hotel, set a specific time for the event that very afternoon, and invited the Texas and Massachusetts delegations along with a huge battery of news media personnel covering the convention.

Texans filed into the small auditorium thirty minutes in advance, feeling very smug about our candidate's maneuver. "Lyndon has bear-trapped him," said my friend George Nokes of Waco. Kennedy faced a dilemma: If he showed up, he would dignify Johnson's candidacy and run the greater risk of losing support to the wily Texan if he didn't perform well in the debate. But if he failed to appear, people would say he was afraid of the one-on-one comparison. Either way he chose, he had nothing to gain, everything to lose.

Two minutes before the scheduled hour for the televised debate, a door opened at the rear of the room, and a smiling Jack Kennedy walked in, accompanied by only two or three others. Where was the Massachusetts delegation? I thought about the old story of the Texas Ranger who appeared all alone in a strange town to put down a riot. Asked why there weren't more Rangers, he said: "There's only one riot, isn't there?" Somehow we had to admire Jack Kennedy for his boldness. He walked into the camp of the enemy almost alone and smiled at us broadly, as though we were his enthusiastic supporters. Truth to tell, we soon would be.

Lyndon spoke first. In polite accepted style, he refrained from mentioning his opponent's name, but everyone knew exactly whom he meant. "When the people gave to each of the two of us on this platform their solemn trust by sending us to the United States Senate, they had every right to expect us to take that trust seriously. Surely they expected us to value their trust by attending to the duties of the office they gave us before seeking another. Most surely they expected us to be present and voting in their behalf when issues of the greatest importance to our nation were being decided. Surely they did not expect us to abandon our duties on the Senate floor simply to seek another office any more than they would expect a soldier to abandon his post of duty.

"Certainly the American people do not expect to give the most fatefully responsible job on earth to someone who, given one responsibility to the people, was *absent* and not voting on seventy-six of the last seventy-nine roll-call votes in the Senate!"

It was powerful stuff. Everyone knew Johnson was making a telling argument. He had stayed at his post of duty and managed the affairs of state. His opponent had spent full-time seeking delegate votes while important issues were being decided in the Senate.

Then it was John Kennedy's time to speak. He walked to the podium, flashed that infectious grin, and began with this wry remark: "Since Lyndon mentioned no names, I'm sure nobody was talking about me." Caught completely off-guard by the humor and the sheer audacity of our guest, the Texans roared with laughter. The spell of Johnson's logic was broken.

Kennedy spoke for about seven or eight minutes. He talked about our country and our party and our opportunity to "get things moving again in America." He complimented Lyndon. He said absolutely nothing about his own record of Senate absenteeism. When he finished, he waved and walked out of the room to our applause. He had faced the Johnson challenge. He had not won our votes for the nomination, but he'd won our admiration. He had made some new friends.

Kennedy won the nomination, of course, and the election. One of the proudest moments of my life was the evening I spent in Houston as John F. Kennedy made his testament of religious freedom before an assemblage of Protestant ministers. It was a major turning point in the campaign. Never before had a Catholic candidate openly faced the unthinking criticisms of America's Protestant majority and answered them with such clinical precision. Watching the performance, I was reminded of the bad old days of the Ku Klux Klan with its wicked invocations of religious prejudice to which so many in the Protestant clergy were innocent heirs. As John F. Kennedy walked into that room filled with religious practitioners steeped in the traditions and still lingering prejudices of Protestantism, I could not help but think of Daniel in the lion's den. With great self-confidence and in high good humor, he faced their barbs and their heavy bombardment. He did not apologize for his Catholicism. He spoke instead of the American tradition—religious freedom, the Jeffersonian advocacy of religious toleration, the right of each to worship God in his own way. Jack Kennedy lanced the boil, and America has not again been the same.

In the week preceding that November Tuesday's general election, vice presidential nominee Lyndon Johnson and his wife began a tour of his pivotal home domain of Texas. They appeared in five major localities in our electorally important state. The first was Dallas, where in the preceding week a noontime downtown audience had greeted a Kennedy motorcade with deadpan silence and a notable lack of civil welcome. I was with Kennedy that day following his speech in Fort Worth. On the following week, I accompanied Lyndon and Lady Bird Johnson as we arrived at the Baker Hotel, diagonally across from the Adolphus at which he would speak an hour later. Bruce Alger, Republican Congressman from Dallas, had assembled a self-satisfied and self-righteous group of rich young women to protest the Johnson appearance. He called it a "tag day." I never understood what the term meant. Approximately two hundred young women from upwardly mobile homes, clad in socially impeccable attire, converged at the intersection of Commerce and Akard streets in Dallas to assert their belief in *laissez-faire* economics and the divine right of the upper class to be freed from the mundane pursuits of American government.

As our motorcade arrived at the west door of the Baker, vice presidential nominee Johnson and his wife were surrounded by an assemblage of well-dressed young Dallas women chanting a cacophony of epithets. Cries of "Socialists!" and "Pinko!" rang out in shrill soprano voices as the U.S. Senate Majority Leader and his wife disembarked to enter the west door to the lobby of the Baker Hotel. Johnson, who probably had encountered as much criticism as anyone in American life at that point, paused at the hotel's door to address the chanting mob. He signaled for silence. "I recognize that many of you are Republicans," he said, "and you have every right to be. I have many friends who are sincere and committed Republicans."

"Louder!" shouted someone from the crowd. "Louder and funnier!" rejoined another. Catcalls rang out in shrill voices. Each time Senator Johnson began to say something, the voices joined in a raucous and discordant medley of mindless noise. Finally, the Senator and Mrs. Johnson despaired of being heard. They entered the hotel and repaired to their rooms. Johnson was to speak at a noon luncheon in the Adolphus, at the opposite corner of the intersection from the Baker. Lady Bird, offended by the unprecedented rudeness, vowed that she would not cross the street.

"Yes, we will," said Lyndon calmly. "We will walk straight through the shouting crowd. We will contrast their boorishness with our civility. And I do *not* want a police escort. If it has come to the point in America where a citizen cannot walk across a public street with his lady without being accosted by noisy and unthinking mobs, I want to know that fact."

We exited the Baker to walk slowly and deliberately amid catcalls and insults, to the hotel on the diagonal side of the intersection. Johnson wore the enigmatic smile of a Mona Lisa as he strode slowly and silently across the intersection, refusing to acknowledge the mindless screaming epithets of the well-dressed crowd. How little they *looked* like hoodlums, I thought, yet how perfectly they mimed the hoodlum culture!

Once inside the Adolphus, Johnson with Lady Bird at his side moved at a painstaking pace through the hubbub that filled the hotel lobby. At one point, John Tower, the Republican nominee for senator, approached Johnson to issue a challenge to a public debate. Johnson, smiling, merely shook his head in a gesture of noncomprehension as he moved in agonizing slowness across the noisy, crowded lobby. Once inside the banquet hall, the vice presidential nominee delivered a recitation of his and his family's opposition to racial and religious bigotry. His father, Johnson reminded the audience, had opposed the Ku Klux Klan and efforts to denigrate American citizens of German ancestry during World War I.

Outside the Commerce Street entrance to the Adolphus, I was surrounded by a gaggle of newsmen as Dallas's Republican Representative Bruce Alger accosted me. "We sure showed Lyndon what we think of him!" Alger crowed.

"Don't you think that demonstration was needlessly rude?" I asked.

"I don't think it's rude to tell a socialist and a traitor what you think of him!" retorted Alger hotly.

The 1960 election was a classic contest between the old and the new, between religious bigotry and toleration, between two fundamental philosophies of society. Texas went for Kennedy and Johnson, and the nation did as well.

The New Frontier was ushered in on January 20, 1961, amid an avalanche of snowflakes. So much snow fell on the preceding day that some of us who lived in Virginia could not make it across the bridges and had to spend the night in the capital city. I slept on a cot in the gymnasium of the House Office Building.

Riding in the inaugural parade was a group from west Texas known as the Fisher County Sheriff's Posse. It was a matter of pride to me that I had been able to engineer an invitation for the group. This was one of those obligations we sometimes thoughtlessly build for ourselves. During the 1960 campaign, I had spoken in the little towns of Roby and Rotan, about 150 miles west of my district, on behalf of the Kennedy-Johnson ticket. The sheriff's posse had met me at the county line with a handsome palomino mount and invited me to ride into town with them. As I began my speech, I commented upon the hospitality of the posse and remarked offhandedly what a great thing it would be for them to represent our state in the Kennedy-Johnson inaugural parade! It was the kind of spur-of-the-moment remark a campaign orator sometimes makes. The crowd applauded wildly. I had not considered my offhand comment as a formal invitation. In fact, I hadn't considered the matter at all. But the people of Fisher County would not let me forget it.

When our team won, that community sent an emissary to see me in Fort Worth, asking when and where their posse was supposed to appear for the parade. Only then did I discover what a coveted plum I had committed. No group could participate in the parade except by official formal invitation of the Inaugural Committee. I must have been either very persuasive or very frantic: "You *have* to make room for them," I insisted to the committee. "I've already invited them!"

The Kennedy inaugural speech set a tone for the next three years. Kennedy, the first president born in the twentieth century and the youngest ever elected, sparked the imagination of America's youth when he noted that

"The torch has been passed to a new generation of Americans." Invoking the ancient command of Isaiah to "undo the heavy burdens and let the oppressed go free," he promised to our sister republics in Latin America "a new alliance for progress, to assist free men and free governments in casting off the chains of poverty." To the Soviet Union, he offered both a warning and an olive branch, an invitation to "explore what problems unite us instead of laboring those problems which divide us." And to his fellow Americans, he threw out the best remembered challenge of all: "Ask not what your country can do for you: Ask what you can do for your country."

In the words of the popular show tune that Kennedy had adopted as his campaign theme song, Americans entered the new decade with "High Hopes." Craving to be a more active, intimate part of this administration with which I so instinctively identified, I announced immediately as a candidate for Vice President Johnson's unexpired term in the Senate. I made my announcement before anyone else could do so, foolishly thinking that I would be so formidable that my candidacy would scare others out of the race. As it happens, exactly seventy other candidates followed my example—the greatest number ever to have their names on a ballot for the same office in the history of our state, perhaps any state. I would jokingly console myself later by insisting that this made me a "leader of men."

From the beginning, I knew I'd be underfinanced. I had no idea where or how I'd raise enough money for a statewide race in Texas. It was a blind leap of faith. I vowed that I would get up earlier, go to bed later, travel more miles, shake more hands, make more speeches, and expend more energy than anyone else in the race. I am convinced that I did all of these things. In a state as large as Texas with only four months to campaign, I might as well have been trying to siphon all the water out of the Gulf of Mexico with an eyedropper! If I'd been able to raise enough money for television exposure, I might have pulled it off. As it turned out, I received only $264,000 in total contributions. I'd pledged to myself that I would spend no money I hadn't raised. Unknown to me, well-meaning volunteer supporters in Houston and San Antonio ran up some $90,000 in bills to local vendors—of which I was blissfully unaware. In the early returns on election eve, I was leading, but my lead began to fade as votes from Dallas and Houston came in. In the end, I ran a close third after Republican John Tower and Dallas businessman Bill Blakley, but close didn't count. Oh, well! If I were tempted to feel bad about the two who had run ahead of me, I just thought about those sixty-seven who had run behind me. There *was* one problem: Those $90,000 in unpaid bills. I hadn't even been aware that these debts were being made, but vendors in good faith had extended credit to my local campaign committees for a campaign in my name, and I was not going to let them suffer. I went to the bank and borrowed the money on my own name and paid the bills. The cumulative debt would hound me for the next sixteen years. I would learn only later that not even wealthy candidates paid campaign debts personally—and I wasn't wealthy. I was, in the best and worst senses of the term, proud—also, maybe, stupid.

The Kennedy legislative program faced a bizarre hurdle in the House. The Rules Committee, under Chairman Howard Smith of Virginia, had a strangle hold on the flow of legislation. Several times in the preceding Congress the tight little group of hardheaded conservatives that dominated the committee under Smith's leadership had simply turned on the red light and walked away, leaving bills destined for floor consideration to stack up like traffic on a freeway in the wake of an accident. Twice in 1960 the Rules Committee had flatly refused to allow members to vote on Conference Committee reports necessary for passage for bills that had been approved by large majorities in both houses. Once, toward the end of the previous session, Smith had arbitrarily adjourned the committee *sine die* and gone home to his farm in Virginia, frustrating the House leadership in its effort to move the legislative program.

Speaker Sam Rayburn's patience with the crafty Virginian had worn thin. Rayburn was determined that President Kennedy's program would not be stymied by these tactics. In a Democratic caucus at the beginning of the session in 1961, the Speaker sponsored a proposed rules change giving him authority to appoint two additional Democratic members to the Rules panel. Republicans, as the minority party, would get one additional member, but this change would tilt the balance against Smith and open the gates once more, so that the full membership of the House could work its will on major legislation. No longer would members be deprived of the opportunity to vote by a tight-fisted little coterie of six men (four Republicans and two Democrats) on the Rules Committee. The fight that ensued in the caucus was fierce and intensely personal. I left the campaign trail in January long enough to return to Washington and cast my vote in the caucus on the Speaker's side. I felt I was voting on the side of democracy. In the end, Rayburn prevailed and the first obstacle to a successful Kennedy presidency was overcome.

On March 1, Kennedy began putting the New Frontier into place by signing an Executive Order launching the Peace Corps, which trained volunteers to work directly with citizens in the less developed countries. Volunteers of all ages were invited to apply. The government paid only for their transportation and living expenses. The lofty purpose of the mission, in the president's words, was to help "liberate independent nations from the bonds of hunger, ignorance, and poverty."

Congress voted an appropriation to carry out the world-wide effort and thousands of volunteers, mostly recent college graduates, flocked to register. At a signing ceremony in the White House, Edwin Willis, a tough Louisiana member from the cajun country, confronted Kennedy. "Mr. President," he said in a deep Louisiana drawl, "I voted for youah Peace Corps. But the fust time some innocent young blond-haired girl from Louisiana gets put in a pot and eaten up by a bunch of those gooks or Ghanarians, I want *you* to promise to come down to the Bayou Country and *explain* that to the people for me!" There was resistance to the program from some quarters. John Tower, newly elected to the Senate over Bill Blakley in the Texas special runoff, disparaged the idea as "a bunch of starry-eyed liberals wandering around the world apologizing for the United States." But the Peace Corps turned out to be an almost unqualified success, perhaps the most popular of all Kennedy's programs and our best received international initiative.

The new president's momentum suffered a major setback in April with the ill-fated Bay of Pigs invasion. The secret plan, it turned out, had been put into motion during the preceding administration, months before Kennedy took office. Eisenhower formally broke off diplomatic relations with Cuba in January before leaving the presidency, but the young president did not attempt to avoid responsibility or place blame on anyone but himself. "There's an old saying that victory has a hundred fathers and defeat is an orphan," Kennedy observed. "I am president, and I am responsible." It was the low point of the Kennedy presidency.

The next month, building upon another effort begun in his predecessor's term, Kennedy dispatched one hundred military advisors and four hundred "Green Beret" army troops to help the government of South Vietnam in its effort to throw back the Communist invaders from the North. The goal was to win a victory for the South without committing U.S. fighting units. The goal soon would be seen as unattainable.

We didn't linger long in the doldrums of the Bay of Pigs. The president knew how to challenge the national imagination with new and exciting dreams. John F. Kennedy thought big. He opted for boldness over timidity. I still remember the thrill that coursed through me, as I sat in the House chamber on May 25 and heard him say: "I believe this nation should commit itself to achieving the goal, before this decade is out, of landing a man on the moon and returning him safely to earth." There was something about the sheer audacity of the scheme that commanded my enthusiasm and that of most of my colleagues. Most of us hadn't the faintest idea how such a feat would be accomplished. But John F. Kennedy made us believe it could be done. On May 5, thirty-seven-year old astronaut Alan Shepard became the first

American in space, hurtled 115 miles over the Atlantic in a Mercury capsule and parachuted into the ocean just fifteen minutes later. President Kennedy was celebrating this achievement in a ceremony on Capitol Hill when he threw out the moon landing challenge. Shepard's accomplishment would be duplicated in July by Virgil "Gus" Grissom.

On February 20, 1962, John Glenn orbited the globe three times in a twelve-hour flight before splashing down in the Atlantic seven hundred miles southeast of his Cape Canaveral launching site. Our scientific community fully mobilized, we were closing the technology gap with the Russians. John Kennedy didn't live to see fruition of the vision he invoked of a man on the moon, but it was he, and his inspiration, that set it in motion.

There were tussles with Congress. I was affected directly by some of them. From Ford Motor Company, Kennedy recruited a bright, young, no-nonsense executive named Robert S. McNamara to be his Secretary of Defense. McNamara began as though his specific assignment were to alienate Congress. One of his first acts was to abolish the reserve military units that met weekly on Capitol Hill. For years, Air Force, Army, Navy, and Marine components had been conducting briefings and drills to allow lawmakers and staffers who held reserve affiliations to maintain and upgrade their proficiency. One of these units was the 9999th Air Force Squadron under the command of General Barry Goldwater, to which I and other Air Force reservists belonged. Some of my colleagues took angry umbrage. Joe Kilgore of Texas, who had finished World War II as a colonel and been active enough in the Reserve to warrant promotion to the rank of brigadier general, was irate. "If I'm forced to choose between my Air Force commission and staying in Congress," Joe complained to some of us, "I'll just leave Congress!"

McNamara's explanation for his precipitate action was that it violated the separation-of-powers doctrine for people in the legislative branch to have a proprietary interest in military units. Technically, he may have been right. But it ruffled a lot of feathers. Next, when McNamara signed off on his departmental budget request for fiscal 1962, it quickly became evident that he was trying to cut out manned bombers entirely. Since World War II, we had worked diligently and spent many billions to develop a "triad." Our long-range strike force consisted of bombers, submarines, and land-based missiles. The latter were largely untested, their reliability still unproven. Now Secretary McNamara apparently wanted entirely to substitute them for bombers.

Aside from what it did to orthodox defense planning, the Secretary's new doctrine interfered brutally with the Fort Worth economy. The General Dynamics plant in my district was building the B-58 Hustler, a sleek supersonic delta-winged bomber designed to replace the already-aging fleet of subsonic B-52s. The B-58 was the first aircraft capable of flying twice the speed of sound. Smaller in size and manned by a crew of only three, it reflected a much lower "profile" on enemy radar screens. In almost any conflict, its survival rate would have been much higher than the massive B-52. Moreover, its production provided payroll for 18,000 families in my part of Texas. To drop from the budget all money for bomber production would terminate this program abruptly, casting these people adrift with no economic life raft.

As soon as I learned of this, I went to work as a self-appointed one-man sales force to restore bomber money to the military budget. First, I went to the House Armed Services Committee. There I stressed the obsolescence of the B-52s. I pointed out that bombers can do a lot of things that missiles cannot. They carry people who can see and communicate. Bombers can change directions when the need arises, turn around in flight in case the original alert turns out to be a false alarm. Once committed, a missile is irrevocable. The committee, impressed, was shocked that McNamara had zeroed out all money for our bomber fleet. I took the same message to the Senate Armed Services Committee and to the Appropriations committees of both houses. The upshot was that Congress put up $525 million for continued bomber production in the coming fiscal year.

But that action wasn't enough. The administration didn't have to *spend* the money. George Troutman, a former Air Force colonel now working with General Dynamics, picked up a rumor that Air Force Chief of Staff Curtis E. LeMay did not intend to ask for a dime of that money for B-58s. If it were forced on him, he'd spend it instead for some more of the old B-52s. LeMay, Troutman reported, had a prejudice against the B-58 configuration, in which the three-member crew rode in tandem, one behind the other. The General wanted pilot and co-pilot to sit abreast of one another. Beyond that, for reasons I never did fathom, LeMay reportedly had his stinger out for General Dynamics. He favored Boeing, the Seattle manufacturer that built the B-52s.

The only thing left was to go over LeMay's head. I got an appointment to talk with Secretary of the Air Force Eugene M. Zuckert. After I made my argument, Zuckert seemed impressed but hesitant. "If you can get General LeMay and General Power to tell me what you've just told me," said Zuckert, "I'll spend every penny you've given us for B-58s." (General Thomas S. Power was Commander of the Strategic Air Command. He and LeMay held equal military rank, but LeMay, as Chief of Staff, was his senior in the hierarchy.) There was nothing to do now but see LeMay.

Before calling for that appointment, I went by to see my old friend, Vice President Johnson. If anyone could give a clue to approaching the crotchety general, surely Lyndon could. The conversation was disappointing. "Jim, I wish you well," said Lyndon. "But if you're able to reach him, you'll do better than I've done." Johnson told of being with LeMay and a group of others a few days previously aboard the presidential yacht *Sequoia*. "I spent so much time with him on this very subject that Lady Bird complained I was ignoring the other guests."

"How far did you get?" I asked.

"I fanned out," said Lyndon.

My heart sank. If Lyndon Johnson can't budge him, I thought, nobody can.

"What is his basic objection?" I probed.

"He doesn't say," Johnson replied. "He just says 'I don't agree with you.' About all I know is that he has been invited repeatedly to fly in the B-58 and has consistently refused to do so."

Prior to seeing the general, I wanted to fly in the plane. Maybe I could get some hint of his reasons for negativism. Better, I might have some positive observations that I could report to LeMay. It wasn't hard to get an invitation from General Dynamics. They were needing every bit of help they could get and eagerly jumped at the chance to have me, as an old Air Force officer, experience in person the enormous advances in the state of the art that this aircraft represented. Accompanied by two active duty Air Force fliers, I mounted the ladder to the triple cockpits and took my place in the middle cubicle. We'd communicate only by radio phones built into our headgear. As the plane zoomed off the runway, I looked out to the side and suddenly realized how fast we were moving. It was strikingly apparently in the swift retreat of the landscape. I'd never traveled that fast. "Mach one!" came the crisp report from the lead pilot. In what seemed like much too little time, the second report announced, "Mach two!" We were moving at twice the speed of sound. We went past Waco, one hundred miles to the south, performed some maneuvers, and returned to make a hot landing on the Carswell strip from which we'd taken off. We'd done the whole thing in about twenty minutes.

General Curtis LeMay sat in his Pentagon office, scowling. He seemed annoyed that I had asked to see him. I talked briefly about the "triad." Surely he'd agree with that! Then I told him of my flight in the B-58.

"I think Boeing makes better planes than General Dynamics," he announced.

"I understand, General," I said. "It's natural to have preferences. Most of the fellows with whom I attended cadet school wanted to be assigned to B-17s. That Flying Fortress was one attractive plane!"

He nodded, as if to say get-on-with-it.

"Instead, to our mild disappointment, some of us were sent to join B-24 outfits. We didn't much like it at first, but that old flyin' boxcar was mighty reliable. When that Davis wing kept bringing us back safely, even with lots of machine-gun holes in the fuselage, we developed an enormous amount of confidence in the B-24."

"I don't care what you say," LeMay replied. "I still say Boeing makes better planes that G.D."

LeMay seemed fixated on the comparison. As I drew my breath to begin in another direction, he interrupted.

"Listen, Congressman, I could sit here and talk all day with you about this if I thought you had the intelligence to absorb it."

The retort was in character with the man's fabled personality. For some reason, it amused rather than offended me, but I got the uneasy feeling that, like Lyndon, I was "fanning out." I tried to recover. *Treat him gently, Jim.*

"I hope I may explain one or two points of the thinking in our congressional committees on this subject, General. I'm sure you don't have a closed mind on the matter," I began.

"Oh, yes, I do," snapped LeMay.

I *had* fanned out.

CHAPTER EIGHT

AIRPLANES
AND
IDEALS

G eneral LeMay's decision not to spend the money Congress had appropriated for more B-58s hung like a storm cloud over my hometown. Since World War II, the old frontier community had come to depend more and more upon military contracts, especially upon the General Dynamics plant, and to a slightly lesser extent upon a Bell helicopter factory. A succession of Air Force contracts had kept employment high at General Dynamics, the area's largest employer, for two decades. Building the B-24 wartime Liberators, the globe-girdling six-engined B-36s, and the B-58s, had revved up the local economy. Now, in spite of my successful efforts to secure $525 million in procurement funds, the General Dynamics pipeline started to dry up in the wake of LeMay's order. During the first eight months of 1962, about twelve thousand family breadwinners drove out the gates with termination slips in their hands. Shockwaves reverberated through the business community. Hardly a retail establishment, big or small, was impervious to the job shrinkage.

Frank Davis, General Manager at the Fort Worth bomber plant, asked me to come out and visit with him. There was, he hoped, a chance to recover. Defense Secretary McNamara had cast out the net for contractors to compete on an entirely new concept—a tri-service airplane which somebody labeled the TFX. General Dynamics engineers had been working around the clock to perfect a design. McNamara wanted a supersonic fighter-bomber, which would be an all-services plane, small enough to fly off aircraft carriers and capable of short take offs and landings for hastily built Army and Air Force landing strips in hostile terrain. The new plane also should be able to perform low-level penetration and to fly under enemy radar. This project was the only thing on the horizon that could save the Fort Worth plant from possibly fatal shrinkage. Frank Davis asked me to seek an appointment for the two of us to visit personally with Secretary McNamara.

We went by the Secretary's office and had a long talk. McNamara was anxious for assurances that his ambitious design goals could be met. Some generals and admirals were resisting. They didn't *want* one all-services aircraft. Each was jealous of his own turf. Frank Davis opened his briefcase and pulled out a model, only about eighteen inches long. It had a revolutionary wing design. They would sweep back and lie alongside the body like a duck's wings in the water; then they'd spread out full length on take-off for maximum airlift. At supersonic speeds, Frank explained, they'd fold back into the fuselage to cut wind resistance and maximize speed. McNamara's eyes sparkled with interest. We had our foot in the door.

But at least a dozen other companies, including Boeing, would like to build that plane. LeMay was cozy with Boeing. He had told me as much. General Powell, Commanding officer of the Strategic Air Command, liked the B-58. He might like our TFX design also, but he answered to LeMay. For all his independence, McNamara would surely pay some attention to the generals. Above all, I wanted to pre-empt another arbitrary decision like the one by which LeMay had sounded the B-58's death knell. It was apparent that we'd have to go over LeMay's head, maybe even McNamara's, too. I discussed our dilemma with Vice President Johnson, who suggested I talk personally with President Kennedy. The president liked me, he said, had been impressed by some of the things I'd said in my race for the Senate. He knew and appreciated my active support for the Peace Corps, the space program, the Alliance for Progress. Johnson agreed to set up a meeting for me to meet with the president. I'd talk about our country's need to keep the Fort Worth plant in operation.

It was a cold, clear January morning when I drove to the White House for the scheduled meeting with President Kennedy. Little remnants of snow were melting slowly in the sunlight. Riding with me was Graham Purcell, the newest member of the Texas delegation and a Kennedy Democrat. Congressman Frank Ikard had retired to accept a lucrative administrator's job with the American Petroleum Institute, and Purcell, a former State District Judge, had just been elected to fill the vacancy. Purcell had never met the president. I thought Kennedy would enjoy welcoming the newest Democrat in Congress.

A Cabinet meeting was in progress when we arrived, and we were ushered into the Oval Office. Johnson had told me we'd have about twenty minutes of Kennedy's time following the Cabinet meeting. Suddenly Purcell gazed in wonderment as a comfortably-clad figure walked along the porch past the room's east window and into the Rose Garden.

"Is that who I think it is?" Graham asked. Jacqueline Kennedy was dressed in dungarees, sloppy boots, and what looked like a leather jacket, carrying a trowel in one hand and a potting plant in the other. Even in that casual attire, she managed to look fashionable. I assured my colleague that he had indeed just seen the First Lady.

The cabinet meeting ended, Kennedy and Johnson came into the Oval Office together. The president greeted Purcell warmly. The president listened attentively, not interrupting, as I made my earnest spiel. I had rehearsed it carefully. No need to dwell on how vital it was to our local economy. I spoke instead from the national standpoint—of the enormous investment all tax-payers had in the huge factory that stretched almost a mile in length. Officially titled Air Force Plant No. 4, it was owned by the public, and leased to General Dynamics. With the premature termination of the B-58 program, I reported, its corridors were already half vacant—a costly national asset, idled, wanting utilization. Next, I talked of the sophisticated management-manpower-technology team with such an outstanding record. What a national loss it would be to dismantle this team, force its engineers and aero-dynamicists, metallurgists and machinists to disperse in search of other work. Boeing, I pointed out, already had plenty of other work to occupy its hands and stay intact against a future hour of need. Fort Worth's plant, with its trea-sure of capabilities, on the other hand, needed the TFX contract if it were to survive. I had talked eight minutes.

"Thank you, Jim. You've made a good case," the president said. "I would imagine, if the price is in the ballpark, that the Fort Worth plant will get the job."

That was all I needed to hear. Lyndon Johnson smiled broadly. We thanked President Kennedy and left.

The incident has a sequel. By early fall, the list of bidders was narrowed down to two—Boeing and General Dynamics. I kept hearing that Senator Henry M. Jackson of Washington state was spending time courting Secretary McNamara. "Scoop" Jackson was a formidable adversary. He was a depend-able Democrat with unimpeachable credentials, a strong defense supporter. Stories began to appear suggesting that Jackson felt confident of the contract for Seattle's Boeing plant. Lyndon Johnson was closer to the president, of course, but, as vice president, he had to be outwardly impartial. One day in late October, back in my home office during the adjournment for the 1962 Congressional elections, I got an urgent call from Johnson. "You'd better get up here as quickly as you can," the vice president told me. "Somebody needs to touch base at the White House again right away and renew our commit-ment on the TFX." I was on the next plane to Washington.

Twice, I learned, a recommendation had come over to the White House from the Secretary's office suggesting the selection of Boeing for the contract. The first had been returned to McNamara with a JFK notation requesting a careful review and a second opinion. Now, the review apparently completed, McNamara again had sent his private recommendation, once more favoring the Seattle manufacturer. I went to see President Kennedy's right-hand man, Kenny O'Donnell, and asked for an audience to discuss this matter again with the president.

"What are you worrying about, Jim?" O'Donnell asked. "You heard what the man said last January. The plane will be built in Fort Worth."

I told the President's trusted lieutenant what I had learned. McNamara's office had recommended Boeing for the second time. O'Donnell simply picked up the telephone and asked to be connected with Secretary McNamara.

"Mr. Secretary, Kenny O'Donnell," he began. "I'm calling about the TFX contract." There was a long pause while McNamara responded. O'Donnell resumed with this brief instruction: "Apparently you didn't understand, Mr. Secretary. We said we wanted *another* recommendation."

A few weeks later, just shortly after the election, I got the word officially at my home in Fort Worth. The White House called to say we had won the contract. I called the General Dynamics switchboard and asked for Frank Davis.

"Who is calling?" the operator wanted to know.

I identified myself.

Excitedly she asked, "Did we get it?"

I said yes. She let out a whoop and left the line. I thought I had been cut off. The switchboard operator just couldn't restrain herself from spreading the glad tidings to all within earshot. Finally, she returned, connected me with the general manager, and we shared congratulations.

I learned two things from that experience. The first was that you could count on this president and his inner team. When they gave their word, they kept it. The second thing was a lesson in economics. Immediately after the news was out, Fort Worth's economy improved visibly. Throughout all of this, it did not occur to me to wonder for a moment whether the Fort Worth plant would give the government our best effort and its best value. I took that for granted. I believed in the scientists, the engineers, and the work force. I knew them. They were my friends. I could count on them to deliver.

It did bother me that the nation had to spend as much as we did on military readiness. There were so many legitimate human needs that a portion of this money could address. The spirit of my "Letter to Ivan" was deeply imbedded in my consciousness, and President Eisenhower's farewell statement frequently recurred to my mind, but I knew that, for the time being at least, our national security and ultimate hope for a lasting peace lay in a superiority of arms. Most congressmen of both political parties felt as I did. Each year when the House voted on the annual military spending authorization bill, venerable old Chairman Carl Vinson of Georgia would demand a recorded vote. The clerk would solemnly toll each name alphabetically until the list had been called twice. Year after year, the vote would be unanimous— not a single "nay." Once I asked Chairman Vinson, out of curiosity, why he insisted on a recorded vote when the outcome was never in doubt. "There are two reasons," Vinson said in his slow, nasal drawl. "First, I want every member to be able to show his constituents that he supports our national defense. Second, and more important, I want the Kremlin to know that there's no division among us."

But John F. Kennedy was working, too, on the *positive* side of international relations. Still in my thirties, I was proud to identify as a spear carrier in the New Frontier. President Kennedy appointed Michigan Governor G. Mennen Williams as a special ambassador to Africa. We were beginning to learn that freedom is contagious. It is like a genie that, having breathed free, resists being stuffed back into the bottle. Nowhere was this more evident than on the African continent. A new awakening stirred discontent among native populations in Kenya, the Belgian Congo, Rhodesia, and South Africa. Leaders like Jomo Kenyatta and Nelson Mandela sent chills through the bloodstreams of the European gentry. Many in the United States looked upon them as dangerous radicals. Shortly after his arrival, Ambassador Williams made a statement to the effect that Africa should be for the Africans. That remark, widely quoted in the U.S. press, stirred hostility. Some thought Williams was encouraging social upheaval. "Africa for the Africans!" was hurled at Kennedy in a televised presidential press conference. The president replied calmly, "I don't know who else Africa should be for." I liked that.

As the Peace Corps began to come into shape under the guidance of the president's brother-in-law, Sargent Shriver, I invested some time trying to help that dream to become a reality. I had worked the floor for the project, pulling some reluctant Southerners and Southwesterners along with me when the House passed the authorizing legislation. At Shriver's invitation, I went over to Baltimore and talked with the first batch of volunteers. Then I invited Shriver to come and speak in Fort Worth. The Peace Corps Director made a big hit. He told of the reaction of one South American citizen. "I became convinced that the United States really is a democratic country," the benighted South American told Shriver, "when I heard that your country had picked a mere *sergeant* to head up such a big and important program!"

The Alliance for Progress likewise stirred my imagination. It swept in a tide of hope, idealism and economic reforms throughout the southern half of our hemisphere. Financial aid from the United States was to trigger self-help actions by the nineteen participating nations. Latin Republics pledged to raise ten dollars of their own resources for every dollar of U.S. aid. They agreed to respect and abide by civil elections and to reform unfair and regressive tax laws, which so long had favored an exclusive aristocracy. Too often in the past, our own country had been identified with the oligarchies that ran things. Most of our southern neighbors admired the more egalitarian opportunity for economic and social advancement they associated with the United States. Here, they knew, a person could start from humble beginnings and make it to the top of the ladder. They wanted to be more like us in that respect, but they did not want us telling them how to do it.

People south of our borders, I discovered, felt deep admiration for two American presidents—Abraham Lincoln and Franklin D. Roosevelt. Now the name of John F. Kennedy was being added to that list. A decade later, in the mid 1970s, in the heart of the primitive Darien jungle, I would encounter a native wearing a Kennedy half-dollar on a chain strung around his neck as a talisman. In several private homes, from Mexico to Colombia, I now observed a striking coincidence of two photographs adorning walls. They were the pictures of Pope John XXIII and President John F. Kennedy.

In response to the newly awakened interest in our southern neighbors, Congress created a bipartisan delegation to meet annually with a similar group from the Mexican congress. Assigned to this delegation by Speaker John McCormack, I enlisted in early morning Spanish classes at the State Department's Foreign Service Institute and began a dialogue with Mexican lawmakers, which I would continue for almost twenty years. Because of my earlier visits to Panama, I became an intermediary for Panamanian leaders who wanted the new administration to allow U.S. Ambassador Joseph Farland, appointed by Eisenhower, to remain in service rather than being replaced by a new Kennedy appointee. Admiring Farland for his shirtsleeve diplomacy, I passed on this request to Larry O'Brien, Kennedy's Chief of Congressional Liaison. The administration agreed to let Farland stay for a time.

A veritable horde of idealistic young political practitioners, inspired by the Kennedy mystique, began pounding at the gates of public service. References to Camelot were apropos. A host of aspiring knights began volunteering for service at the Round Table. Almost every time I went home to Fort Worth, bright and highly motivated young men and women would clamor for appointments to ask how they could get more involved with our government's efforts. It struck me as peculiarly significant that a number of seminarians studying at Southwest Baptist, Texas Christian, and Southern Methodist seminaries were reconsidering their vocations, wondering if they

might make a more meaningful contribution to mankind in diplomacy or
social service.

My administrative assistant, Craig Raupe, came to me one day saying he
wanted to join the Agency for International Development. He wanted to get
personally involved in what we all saw as the worldwide struggle for the
minds and hearts of newly emergent people's movements in the less developed countries, where almost 80 percent of the earth's population lived.
Loathe to lose Craig's help on which I had grown dependent, I nevertheless
encouraged him. After a year in Indonesia, Craig was assigned to the
Washington AID headquarters and began recruiting contemporaries to serve
the Kennedy administration in missions abroad. He enlisted, among others
Jim Boren, a young activist college professor who had served as Senator Ralph
Yarborough's campaign manager and whose first cousin, David Boren, would
come some years later to the U.S. Senate, and Ed Brooks, the brother of my
Texas colleague, Congressman Jack Brooks. Soon there grew a new genre of
jokes about Kennedy's "Irish Mafia" being infiltrated by a "Texas Mafia."
Caught up in the spirit, I began wondering if I couldn't make a bigger impact
by leaving Congress and signing up for a post on the president's inner team. I
formed warm friendships with DeLessups Morrison, whom the president
appointed as our ambassador to the Organization of the American States, and
with Teodoro Moscoso, selected to head the Alliance for Progress.

I liked "Shep" Morrison the first time I saw him. It was at his confirmation
hearing. Under fire by critics, the former New Orleans mayor with the heavy
Louisiana accent won the day with wit and charm. One senator asked how
someone ingrained in the traditions of the deep South could expect to be welcomed by the citizenry in Latin America. "That's easy," replied Morrison with
a disarming smile. "If anyone starts chanting, 'Yankee go home!' I'll just tell
myself, 'they sure can't be talking about *me*.'" Moscoso was similarly impressive, and I invited both Morrison and Moscoso to fill speaking engagements
in Fort Worth. We made a lot of converts to New Frontier causes among the
local business community.

"You will hear me use the word *revolution*," Moscoso told a gathering
sponsored by the Fort Worth Chamber of Commerce. "It is not a word of
which any American need be afraid." He described what he had in mind as a
revolution against poverty, illiteracy, and human despair. It did not have to be
bloody, he said. But one way or the other, it had to come. "The Communists
can only seize and pervert these revolutionary forces if we in the United
States, and the real democrats in Latin America, abdicate our responsibilities
and our traditions."

On one Sunday, when Lyndon Johnson invited my wife and me to spend
the afternoon and evening at The Elms with him and Lady Bird, I decided to

broach the possibility of joining the administration. Sunning on the spacious patio after a swim, I asked the vice president if he felt I would have a chance at a cabinet position or an ambassadorship to some Spanish speaking country. Lyndon looked at me quizzically. "Why do you ask that, Jim?"

"Well," I said. "I am getting frustrated. I believe in what you and President Kennedy are trying to do, and I am trying to help. But I just don't think I'm making a big enough contribution."

"Did you say you were frustrated?" he asked. "Do you think *I'm* not frustrated? And who do you think is the most frustrated man in Washington?"

"You're going to say Jack Kennedy, aren't you?"

Johnson's eyes narrowed, and he looked at me intently. "That's right; I am. Yes, we could get you a spot in the cabinet or certainly the sub-cabinet. But do you think you'd be happy there? Do you think you'd make policy there? Do you think an ambassador makes policy? He just carries out the policy that is passed on to him from Washington. When that changes, he has to change."

I remembered the words I had heard four years earlier from Whiting Willauer, then our Ambassador to Costa Rica. "I'd like to pick your brain. I'm thinking about running for Congress," Willauer had told me. "That's where the power is!"

Now Johnson pressed that same theme. "I could do this for you, Jim, but you wouldn't be happy. John Connally has not been happy. We made him Secretary of the Navy, and a year later he is back in Texas, running for governor."

"Jim, I have seen all the jobs in Washington. The best jobs—the two best, the two most influential—in this town are in the House and the Senate. If you want to make a contribution, that's the place to be."

That Sunday afternoon in 1962 was critical. Later, when Shep Morrison decided to retire from his post as ambassador to the OAS, he called to tell me he'd like to recommend me as his successor. A few months earlier, I would have leaped at the opportunity. Now, I thanked him and politely declined. I would stay in Congress.

CHAPTER NINE

CAMELOT

I am glad I lived during the presidency of John F. Kennedy. It was a time when a man could have heroes and be unapologetic. Many years later, in one of her rare interviews, Jacqueline Kennedy would say of her husband: "But then I realized history made Jack what he was. You must think of him as this little boy, sick so much of the time, reading in bed, reading history, reading the Knights of the Round Table, reading Marlborough. For Jack, history was full of heroes. And if it made him this way, maybe other little boys will see. Men are such a combination of good and bad. Jack had this hero idea of history, this idealistic view."

The spirit of the New Frontier was contagious. On those rare occasions when I disagreed with President Kennedy, I still admired him. Politics was fun, exciting things were happening, the Vietnam war had not yet split the country into angry camps, *government* had not yet become a dirty word, and political rivals did not so snarlingly rip apart one another's personal reputations. Those few who did were often scorned by voters.

Progress came on many fronts at once. As we fought to improve conditions abroad through the Peace Corps and the Alliance for Progress, we were striving for excellence at home. Newton Minnow, new chairman of the Federal Communication's Commission, shocked a lot of people when he challenged television networks to improve the quality of their programming, calling the current video fare "a vast wasteland." Indeed, "We can do better" was a theme that echoed with resonating vibrancy. President Kennedy called on the public schools to improve not only the mental but physical capacities of the nation's schoolchildren. In one of the boldest moves of all, the president in April of 1962 challenged collusive price increases announced almost simultaneously by the nation's big steel companies. The inflationary threat of the sudden industry-wide price hike sent waves of apprehension through the country. Kennedy wasted no time. His brother, Attorney General Robert Kennedy, immediately launched a grand jury investigation into the apparent anti-trust violation. Senator Albert Gore Sr. of Tennessee introduced a series of bills empowering courts to act more swiftly to break up monopoly prac- tices. The president publicly accused company management of pursuing "private power and profit" at the nation's expense. He had earlier asked labor unions to keep a tight rein on wage demands. Noting that labor had cooper- ated, Kennedy now lashed out at the irresponsibility of the big steel companies. He said it was not patriotic policy for "a tiny handful of steel exec- utives" to demonstrate such "utter contempt" for the American people.

Suddenly, two of the large companies, Bethlehem Steel and Inland Steel, rescinded increases announced the day before. Then U.S. Steel, feeling the sting of public disfavor, caved in. On April 13, basic steel prices went back down to the level of April 10. Presidential critics inveighed against what they called "jawboning," but the president's quick initiative had worked. As 1962 came to a close, it was apparent that New Frontier economic policies were holding inflation in check, while the economic growth rate was humming forward at a robust 6 percent.

Back home in Fort Worth, 1,200 miles from Washington, we felt the change and participated in it. Office holders became less timid. Tarrant County District Attorney Doug Crouch, approximately my own age, became the first local office holder since Reconstruction to employ African Americans to perform professional tasks in his courthouse office. State Senator Don Kennard, asked by the press to explain how he and I each polled between 90 and 98 percent of the votes in our city's black precincts, refused to be put on the defensive. Smiling broadly, Kennard said, "I think black is beautiful." A year or two earlier, such a jaunty statement would have been not only politically inexpedient, but shocking.

On another occasion, Fort Worth native Bill Newbold was home on leave from his United States Information Agency job in Cambodia. Newbold extolled the flora and fauna of that faraway country. "The little ocelots are beautiful!" Bill exclaimed. "When I get back to Cambodia I'm going to get a pair sent to the Fort Worth zoo."

"Ocelots!" Don Kennard exploded in mock contempt. "That's the trouble with Fort Worth! We think too small. Don't send ocelots. Send elephants! Send something big enough to challenge our imagination!"

I filed that comment away. After a couple of months, with Newbold back in the Far East, I conspired with a friend in the customs service to send a bogus message to Kennard: "Your elephant in hand. $1,273 owing. Please remit. Give instructions for shipment to you."

Doug Crouch and I supposed Kennard would throw up his hands in horror. His house occupied a small city lot. But our mirth was cut short when we picked up the next day's *Fort Worth Star-Telegram*. Senator Kennard had publicly announced his good fortune. He owned a Cambodian elephant and would have it shipped immediately to Fort Worth, he proclaimed.

The senator called me later that morning to share this glorious news. "I've always wanted an elephant!" he exulted. He said he'd ask advice from Lawrence Curtis, then curator of the Fort Worth zoo, on care and feeding.

The only problem: there was no elephant.

Frantically I called Curtis. "Whatever you do, talk him out of taking delivery! There *isn't* any elephant. Tell him how much trouble they are, what a mess they make, how much it costs to feed one!"

Curtis owed me favors. I had sprung some zoo-bound penguins from quarantine in Peru and had talked Australian authorities into sending the zoo some rare lung-fish, called "living fossils." Surely the zookeeper could dissuade Kennard from wanting the non-existent elephant.

What I failed to reckon with was Curtis's appetite for a practical joke. The next headline trumpeted: "Kennard Gives Elephant to Fort Worth Zoo."

Now, I was really on the spot. But where to find an elephant? I feverishly called zoos and circuses. Nobody had one to spare. My phony customs source sent messages of delay, quarantine, red tape. Time was running out.

Finally, our ambassador to India, Chester Bowles, came through for me. The raja of Kollengode had a baby elephant and was trying to give it to our ambassador as a token of international goodwill. Unlike Kennard, Bowles had no yen for a pet pachyderm. He convinced the raja to give it to the children of Fort Worth instead. American Airlines sent a freight plane. The raja's son, who had always wanted to visit America, accompanied the young animal as *mahout*, or caretaker. With much fanfare, a presentation was made at the zoo. The mahout stayed on for six weeks as Kennard's house guest, and, as the saying goes, a good time was had by all.

In Washington, my old friend Craig Raupe, back from Indonesia and working in the AID agency, enjoyed a close rapport with the bright group of young practitioners with whom Kennedy had staffed key jobs in his administration. Craig's home in Falls Church was a scene of frequent gatherings, at which he made a conscious effort to meld a closer understanding between appointed New Frontiersmen and members of Congress from Texas and other southwestern states. I was always invited to these gatherings. During 1962, Mab and the kids back in Fort Worth, I spent many evenings talking, eating, drinking and laughing with the eager young crowd which had come to be known as "the Irish Mafia." Unlike the Arthur Schlesingers and Robert McNamaras, who tended to make up the intellectual elite of the administration, these fellows understood practical politics. There was a special delight for me in learning more about the way things worked in places like Boston and Chicago, and I got the feeling that our northern counterparts were often amused and occasionally enlightened by our recounting of events in Texas. Craig and I joked that we were manufacturing the "axle grease" for the "Boston-Austin axis."

My favorites in the White House crowd were Larry O'Brien, Kenny O'Donnell, and Henry Hall Wilson. The latter, unlike the predominantly Boston-based crew, hailed from North Carolina. He worked directly with O'Brien in rounding up votes on the Hill for Kennedy's legislative program. Wilson and I formed a working alliance. Several times I helped him count votes and promote support among southern members. Twice I was asked to come along for an impromptu session at Hickory Hill, Bobby and Ethel Kennedy's residence in McLean. Not that I was a member of that inner circle. Nobody seemed quite sure enough of my camaraderie, for example, to shove me, fully dressed, into the swimming pool—a commonly remarked practice among family insiders. Bobby didn't wholly trust me because of my long-standing friendship with Lyndon Johnson. It was common gossip that Bobby resented Lyndon and didn't want the Texan's allies to get too close to the decision-making process. He had, of course, tried unsuccessfully to keep Johnson off the ticket in 1960. I never was able to resolve this unspoken tension. I was for sure Lyndon's friend, would have come down on his side in any imaginable showdown, but indulged the probably foolish fantasy that I might somehow help build a bridge of better understanding between the two.

In the fall of 1962, the ancient race issue arose in all its brooding fury to interrupt our idyll and bring us back to harsh reality. A twenty-nine-year-old black former Air Force sergeant named James Meredith flouted a historic taboo when he insisted upon enrolling as a student at the University of Mississippi. Meredith's actions set off several days of rioting by a sometimes violent white supremacist mob numbering in the thousands. President Kennedy dispatched U.S. troops and federal marshals, twenty-eight of whom were wounded by gunshots. Two people died and more than two hundred protestors were arrested. When the smoke cleared, the campus was littered with bombed-out automobiles, broken glass, and spent tear-gas canisters, but Meredith, accompanied by U.S. marshals, was legally enrolled. He graduated in May of the following year. Throughout the ordeal, President Kennedy stood firm. He and his brother, Bobby, appealed by telephone to Mississippi

Governor Ross Barnett, who remained implacable. As the riot raged into the night, Kennedy went on television, personally pleading for order. In the end, Governor Barnett yielded. The following June, the scene was reenacted less violently in Alabama. Governor George Wallace stood "in the school house door," in visual protest, but offered no physical resistance as two black students entered the auditorium of the University of Alabama, escorted by National Guardsmen, and registered for classes. Segregation at American state universities was ended.

Clearly, a social ferment was working through our society. We felt it in Fort Worth, too. Politicians, at least Democrats, began actively cultivating voter registration among minority citizens. Practically all blacks and Hispanics in Fort Worth supported me, and in national elections, they voted Democratic when they voted. During my first race for Congress in 1954, I had created a precedent by purposefully inviting African Americans and Hispanics to every public dinner over whose invitation list I had any control. I wanted them to know they were welcome, to feel included. But I had done this unobtrusively, blowing no loud trumpet to announce to the community the inauguration of a new policy. Now, I struggled with an inner conflict. I remembered with clarity the sharp awakening I had experienced when, at about age twelve, in the time of separate rest rooms and drinking fountains, my father had asked me to imagine how I might feel if there were a sign saying "no redheaded boys can drink at this fountain." Deep down, I believed the ideal for which we should be striving was a *color-blind* society. On the way to its achievement, I began to sense the creation of a more *color-conscious* society. In all my speeches and public appearances before black audiences, I intentionally avoided any reference to race. I talked exactly as I would to an all-white audience, thinking this the best preserver of everyone's dignity. Now, this too was changing. My friend Senator Don Kennard and others were making specific references to race in the effort to stimulate a pride in voting. True enough, in talking with Hispanic audiences, I often had lapsed into Spanish. The local Mexican-American community always invited me to speak and crown the queen at their annual September 16 celebration on Fort Worth's North Side. Now, I joined their leaders in broadcast appeals over the local Spanish-language radio station, encouraging voter registration. We also held meetings aimed directly at cultivating this awareness in what had been known as "colored" precincts.

At least, that's what we *had* called them. In my youth, "colored" was the term of polite usage. It conveyed respect. Now, even the terminology was changing. Black citizens of social awareness preferred being called Negroes. Once, following a talk with a group of Negro civic leaders, I felt a tug at my sleeve. A popular local black minister whispered in my ear and pressed a folded piece of paper in my right hand. "Put it in your pocket, and read it when you have a chance," he said with a confiding wink. Opening the paper later, I discovered that my helpful friend had penned this hand-written note: "The preferred pronunciation sounds like KNEE-grow."

At a gathering in Como, a local black neighborhood, a tradition took root. A friend of mine named Don Woodard told a story involving a recent trip he had made to Washington with his wife, Wanda, who had complimented my necktie. With a flourish, I had taken it off and presented it to her. No sooner did Woodard finish this story than one of the women present announced how much *she* liked the tie I had on at the moment. There was nothing to do, of course, but take it off ceremoniously and make a public presentation of it to her then and there. For years thereafter, almost every time I visited one of Fort Worth's black neighborhoods, some woman or other would come forward with a mischievous twinkle in her eye, would feign ecstasy over my necktie, and of course it would be hers. I'm convinced that more than one made a collection of my ties for private display. All of this was part of the spirit of anxiety as well as wonderful camaraderie that grew up in and around the New Frontier.

One night I discussed the broad groundswell of social change with Bobby Kennedy. We were riding down the Potomac on the president's yacht, the *Honey Fitz*, named for Kennedy's maternal grandfather. I remarked that the decision to hold the Mississippi and Alabama governors' feet to the fire must have been a tortuous experience.

"It wasn't hard. It's nothing but right!" said Bobby. He was more a moral absolutist than his brother, I decided, probably less tolerant of opposing convictions.

I said higher education had to be the main key to broad-scale economic advancement for members of our nation's long denied racial minorities. Bobby warmed to that subject and expressed some curiosity about the long-standing nature of southern traditions and why they hadn't yielded to swifter change. He seemed incredulous that segregation had been so long tolerated in the South. I told Bobby I had understood from things told me by Speaker McCormack and my Massachusetts colleague, Torbert Macdonald, that de facto segregation was still common in South Boston. Bobby shook his head. "It shouldn't be," he said.

In coming years, as I got closer to Tip O'Neill, I would learn that segregation had indeed imbedded itself in Boston's culture. As recently as a generation earlier, Tip told me, his own father had led the fight to open the ballot box to Boston's Irish voters and other predominately wage-earning families. Prior to that struggle, Tip told me, working-class Bostonians of whatever ethnicity had been deliberately frozen out of real participation in local elections by opening the polls at 10 A.M. and closing them at 4 P.M.

Not always did I vote with President Kennedy. I was neither a real insider nor a wholly uncritical down-the-line supporter. So wrapped up had I become in my zeal to begin paying off the national debt, even by tiny increments, I just couldn't bring myself—in spite of a personal call from President Kennedy—to support a proposed 1962 increase in the national debt ceiling. Nor did I give any help to a White House request for the creation of a new cabinet-level Department of Urban Affairs. To the argument that such a department was necessary since more Americans now lived in cities than in rural sections, I responded, "that's like saying we need a department of women's affairs, just because the country has more women than men." This country boy remark probably didn't endear me to either big city dwellers or women.

But on most things I was a member of the Kennedy team. When the president called the signals, I usually ran the play. As a member of the Public Works Committee, I worked to help shape up the president's public works acceleration bill and get it passed. When Kennedy, concerned with an international trade deficit, asked for an Office of International Trade and Tourism within the Department of Commerce, I helped defend the bill on the House floor. That plan set in motion a new program to stimulate and encourage travel to our country by foreigners, and the balance of payments, though still a problem, began to show signs of improvement. A new era of confidence was in the making.

And things were going well for Fort Worth, too. I had succeeded in getting appropriations to renovate the Fort Worth General Army Depot and to build a new chapel at Carswell Air Force Base. We had established a customs office for Fort Worth. Working closely with the Corps of Engineers, I had gotten the bureaucrats to shave four years off the normal time drag in completing flood control projects for Sunset Acres and Fossil Creek. In a televised report on the evening of October 9, 1962, I unveiled an architect's sketch of a downtown federal building to be constructed on a lot adjacent to city hall. This was a major coup. Officials in the Eisenhower General Services Administration had come to Congress three years earlier with plans for a large regional federal office building and center in Dallas. None was planned, I discovered, for Fort Worth. A mental alarm sounded. I could anticipate a drain of federal offices and jobs from my hometown as soon as the Dallas building was completed. Courting support from colleagues on the House Public Works Committee, I sent back a reply to the GSA that a Dallas building would be authorized only after one was first approved for Fort Worth. Seeing our determination, the administration relented, and I kept my word. Once our Fort Worth office center was fully launched, I pitched in and helped get one for our neighboring community.

But the biggest ten strike of the year, judged from my district's parochial interest, was a decision I persuaded members of the Civil Aeronautics Board to make. At my urging, backed by statistics of growing airline passenger travel in our metroplex, the Board voted to order an official investigation into the need for a single regional airport to serve the twin cities. Twelve years later, in 1974, we would dedicate the world's most modern civilian airport on a site exactly half way between Fort Worth and Dallas. No longer would local citizens have to drive to Dallas for commercial airline service.

Each of these prideful plums caused momentary local celebration. They all faded from the public spotlight in late October of 1962, however, overshadowed suddenly by the most threatening military confrontation of the Cold War period. On October 16, just one week after my Federal Office Center announcement, photographs from an American reconnaissance flight revealed the incontestable presence of nuclear missile sites, nearing completion, in Cuba. President Kennedy huddled immediately with his key advisors. On October 22, all the nation's lawmakers—Congress then in recess for the upcoming 1962 elections—were suddenly summoned to assemble informally in each of several regional locations throughout the country. My friend Craig helped engineer the selection of the site for southwestern legislators as the Texas and Pacific Building in Fort Worth. Members flew into my city from Oklahoma, Arkansas, Louisiana, New Mexico, and other parts of Texas to listen together to a televised report by President Kennedy.

The president revealed the inescapable facts, described the absolute unacceptability of offensive missile bases within striking distance of American cities, and announced his plan of action. First, he ordered a strict and immediate quarantine of "all offensive military equipment" under shipment by sea to Cuba, a complete U.S. naval blockade. He mobilized military reserve units, put active forces on alert, evacuated dependents from our base at Guantanamo, reinforced that installation militarily, and called upon the Organization of American States to recognize the approach of Soviet missiles, then known to be en route by Soviet ships destined for Cuba, as a "threat to hemispheric security." He also called for an immediate emergency session of the United Nations Security Council to order the prompt dismantling and withdrawal of offensive weapons already in Cuba, to be supervised by U.N. observers.

The world had been brought to the brink of nuclear confrontation by a terrible miscalculation of one man in his personal assessment of another. Nikita Khrushchev had underestimated John F. Kennedy. The two had met at Vienna in June of 1961. At that encounter, they had parried and thrust verbally. Khrushchev tried a bit of clumsy humor, asserting that Kennedy owed him his 1960 election. If the Russians had released American spy plane pilot Gary Powers just before that election, Khrushchev claimed, Nixon would have won. "Don't spread that story around," Kennedy retorted. "If you tell everybody that you like me better than Nixon, I'll be ruined at home."

Later in the meeting, the American president had curiously asked the Soviet leader to identify a prominent medal he was wearing. Khrushchev said it was the Lenin Peace Medal. "I hope you keep it," Kennedy quipped.

Khrushchev may have been misled in the meeting by Kennedy's buoyant manner, easy humor, and youthful charm. Now, in the crucial showdown, he was shocked by the hard metal of Kennedy's response to his Cuban missile gambit.

Khrushchev's first reaction was to order Soviet vessels, laden with the actual missiles, to refuse boarding, crash the U.S. Navy's quarantine line, and hastily assemble the missiles in place, capable of actual launching within twenty-four hours. On the morning of October 24, with Soviet ships then less than one hour away from our own naval forces, the world was perilously close to war.

At the last minute, learning that Kennedy had put our Strategic Air Command on continuous airborne alert—fifty-seven bombers, with nuclear missiles, and sixty-one refueling tankers airborne every minute of the day and night—Khrushchev had a change of heart. He ordered the Soviet ships to turn around. On October 26, the Russian leader offered a settlement to the crisis, proposing the removal of the Russian missiles already on Cuban soil, dismantling the sites, and promising to deliver no more offensive weapons. In exchange, he secured an American pledge never to invade Cuba. By the morning of October 27, Khrushchev added a new stipulation to his settlement terms: If Soviet missiles were removed from Cuba, the United States should remove NATO Jupiter missiles from Turkey.

Kennedy knew that this would create complications of almost impossible complexity. Under the NATO agreement, only the nuclear warheads were in U.S. custody. The Jupiter missiles themselves were under the absolute jurisdiction of the Turks. Recognizing that he must do something very quickly to avoid the collapse of the settlement before it could be implemented, President Kennedy moved with lightning speed. He formally announced U.S. acceptance of Khrushchev's first offer and totally ignored the second, that concerning Turkey, as though he had never heard it. Kennedy had no illusions about the desperation of the situation and the fact that there could be no turning back if our position were rejected. He swiftly sent his brother Robert to the USSR embassy in Washington to deliver an urgent "statement of fact" to Khrushchev via Soviet Ambassador Anatoly Dobrynin. The brief message stated that Khrushchev had twenty-four hours to agree to the terms of the American letter or the United States would move militarily against Cuba.

Now intensely aware of the young president's unmistakable resolve, the Soviet premier accepted the terms of the Kennedy letter. From his dacha thirty miles outside Moscow, Khrushchev rushed by car a conciliatory reply for immediate transmission over Radio Moscow. He ordered Soviet forces in Cuba to begin physically dismantling the missile sites. Feeling that Castro was spoiling for a war that nobody could win, Khrushchev could only hope his message would reach the American president in time.

Lyndon Johnson put it in his own words the next day: "Khrushchev and Kennedy stood eyeball to eyeball, and Khrushchev blinked."

CHAPTER TEN

NEVER
YOUNG AGAIN

There is no ideal arrangement for congressional parents with school-age children. During those first eight years in Congress, I was haunted by a recurring dread—that someday I'd awaken to discover our children grown and strangers to me. My happiest memories were of the precious times I had been able to steal from the insatiable demands of political activism to take a pack of youngsters horseback riding on Ginger's birthday, to attend a father-daughter Bluebird dinner with Kay, to go on a Saturday Scouting trip with Jimmy or drive him on his Sunday morning paper route, so he could be finished in time for Sunday School. Rare and wonderful were the cross-country trips we had taken between Texas and Washington, together in the family station wagon, in those 1950s days, when Congress adjourned at a respectable date in late summer or early fall. We had tried all three of the available options for school schedules. Twice we had enrolled the kids in Weatherford's public schools for the fall semester, transferring them to Northern Virginia schools at mid-term. This posed problems when the courses of study didn't mesh. In 1959 and 1960, we had started them in school in Virginia so they could have a full year's continuity, while I went alone back to Texas, when Congress adjourned for the fall, to keep in touch with the constituency. During whatever weeks remained before the January reconvening, I'd cram a schedule chock-full with appointments at the home-district office, interspersed by speeches to luncheon clubs and civic audiences, never fewer than two and sometimes three or even four a day. I missed the family.

In September of 1961, Mab announced that she wanted to take the girls back to Texas. Jimmy was a high school sophomore that year. His grades in Washington & Lee High School had been disappointing—far short of his potential. On the advice of Roland Murray, Weatherford's Presbyterian minister, we had enrolled him in Schreiner Institute, a church-related military school in the Texas hill country near Kerrville. Throughout 1962, I fretted over my absence from the family. I roomed alone in the small Coronet Hotel on Capitol Hill. God, it was lonely. On two, sometimes three weekends each month I'd fly back home on Friday afternoon for a Saturday with Mab and our three daughters. Then back to Washington on Sunday. Twice that school year I drove 250 miles southwest to Schreiner to see Jimmy. Once, on semester break, Jimmy came to Washington, stayed for a week with me at the Coronet. Members of the House Gymnasium Committee celebrated an annual feast with money left over from our unspent dues. I took Jimmy with me. As we approached the festive area, an unaccustomed excitement, visible and audible in people's faces and voices, sent an unmistakable signal. Just as Jimmy and I approached the crowd's periphery, an avenue opened and President Kennedy walked out from the inner circle. A sometime habitué of the gym during his own House days, the president had come by to pay his impromptu respects. Beaming with parental pride, I introduced my son. Kennedy asked Jimmy a couple of questions, talked for a minute or so, and was gone. I was imagining the indescribable thrill I would have felt, at fourteen, if I had been unexpectedly introduced to the president of the United States.

"Well! What did you think of that?" I exulted.

Thoughtfully, my son replied: "He's skinnier than I thought he was."

The frequent airline commutes were wearing a big hole in my pocket book. In those days, members had to pay personally for any travel to and from their home districts, except for one publicly financed round-trip each year. Frequent travel was simply not an effective way to retire the big campaign debt I had assumed from the 1961 senatorial race. Mab and I discussed our dilemma. We decided on two courses of action. I'd sell my four hundred-acre ranch in the hill country and apply most of the proceeds to campaign debt retirement. Mab would shop around for a house in the Yorktown High School district in North Arlington, Virginia. She and the girls would move back and live year around in the Washington area while Jimmy finished Schreiner. We'd keep the Fort Worth home, but rent it out to cover mortgage payments. All of life is a compromise. The Virginia house, once owned by Kate Smith's family, had twenty-one dogwood trees on a nice corner lot. But, at $42,000—twice what it cost to build our Weatherford home—it cost much more than I had ever imagined paying for a house.

The night we agreed to the purchase, the two of us were invited to have dinner with Vice President and Mrs. Johnson at The Elms, their residence in northwest Washington. We talked about the '62 elections and plans for the coming year. One of the television networks was carrying a thirty-minute special that night on the career of Richard Nixon. We watched it together. The former vice president had just been defeated by Pat Brown in his race for California's governorship. Bitterly, Nixon had pronounced what everyone took as his political valediction. "You won't have Richard Nixon to kick around anymore."

When the program ended, I asked Vice President Johnson's opinion of it. His answer surprised me. "I thought it was unnecessarily harsh," he said. "Needlessly prejudicial. Unfair in spots. Meaner to Nixon than it ought to have been. He really isn't as bad a man as they make him out to be," said Johnson. "I don't agree with him politically, of course. That's another matter."

As well as I thought I knew him, I was always being surprised by some aspect of Lyndon Johnson's personality. I'd see yet another facet that evening: his natural, earthy informality. After the four of us had visited following dinner, Mab and I were preparing to leave. Suddenly, the vice president said, "Come upstairs with me, Jim. There's something I want to show you." We left Lady Bird and Mab sitting in the dining room.

In Johnson's bedroom was a folder containing a study his staff had just prepared on the meaning of electoral results throughout the South. Johnson was particularly interested in southern receptivity to social change. The voters' message was mixed. In Arkansas, for example, Governor Faubus, outspoken foe of integration, and Senator Fulbright, regarded as a social moderate, had each won by better than two-to-one margins. But in Alabama, liberal southern Senator Lister Hill won with less than 51 percent of the vote, while George Wallace, running without Republican opposition, garnered 96 percent.

As I studied the paper, Lyndon was undressing and putting on his pajamas. "I don't have to be *asleep* by 9:30," he explained. "Stay and talk for a little. I just promised the doctor I'd be in *bed* by 9:30." He crawled beneath the covers, propped himself up with three pillows, and prepared to continue the conversation. I figured it was time to take my leave. "We both need to be up early," I said.

"Tell Mab goodnight for me," he smiled.

Results of the 1962 congressional elections put new energy and enthusiasm into the Kennedy administration. The president's party traditionally loses numbers in off-year contests, but in 1962 the Democratic Senate majority actually grew by four, while House Republicans were held to a meager net gain of two seats. Texas races confirmed the national trend, although our victory margins were generally larger. I won reelection by 61 percent to 39 percent over my Republican opponent, Del Barron. I led the ticket, and that was satisfying, but I felt a pang of sympathy for my classmate, J. T. Rutherford, who lost in the El Paso district to a Republican named Ed Foreman.

Two new Democrats, Birch Bayh of Indiana and George McGovern of South Dakota, joined the Senate with tissue-thin margins of less than one-half of a percentage point. McGovern's victory, narrow though it was, came as a surprise. Pundits had expected him to lose in the conservative prairie state. Having spent several days campaigning in South Dakota with George in his first House reelection four years earlier, I was elated. He and I were good friends in those days, about the same age and of similar backgrounds. In the 1950s, when we worked closely together, McGovern was the only Democrat in his state's congressional delegation. Folks joked that the state Democratic headquarters consisted of George's station wagon.

In 1961, President Kennedy tapped my midwestern friend to serve as Food For Peace director. His Senate win now was taken as an endorsement of Kennedy's foreign policies. Under McGovern's brief guidance, the Food For Peace program had soared like a butterfly liberated from its confining cocoon. Having exported only twelve million tons of surplus food and fiber in the previous two and a half years, that program sent abroad, in 1961 alone, thirty-three million tons from America's farms, not counting special emergency shipments for famine-stricken lands. In the anti-communist fervor that dominated American politics, Food For Peace brought together the best of both worlds. On an altruistic level, it carried out the biblical mandate to feed the hungry. It also became a tool by which timely distribution of needed provender helped prop up friendly regimes abroad and built resistance to native Communists' appeals.

In fact, McGovern had some internecine quarrels with other international agencies over the fundamental Food For Peace mission. In one long talk with him, I discovered that he was personally embarrassed over the way in which a few public officials in southeast Asian countries, while maintaining a pro–U.S. stance, had manipulated American food deliveries for their own political and financial gain. This apparently had happened with full knowledge of CIA officials. George McGovern was furious, but intensely loyal to President Kennedy, and he put the blame on shadowy operators in the intelligence agencies. He resented the use of food to maintain corrupt leaders, even staunch anti-communists.

It was inevitable, no doubt, that, in a vision as broad and multi-faceted as that which the New Frontier unleashed, there would be clashes and compromises between the mortals charged with carrying it out. Perhaps if we hadn't been so keenly aware of our intensely competitive ongoing contest with

Russia for the allegiance of the less developed world, we wouldn't have cared much about the Third World.

Maybe the greatest day of Kennedy's presidency came on June 26, 1963, when he stood on the balcony of Berlin's city hall, 110 miles deep in Communist territory, and set off a thunderous demonstration with his ringing declaration, "Ich bin ein Berliner." No symbol of the Cold War was as enduring, or as defining, as the Berlin Wall. Nor, from the Soviet standpoint, as self-defeating. President Kennedy's appearance in Berlin dramatized the differences between the two sides more strongly than anything else he had done or would do.

A few days earlier, on June 11, Attorney General Nicholas Katzenbach escorted two black students into the University of Alabama, walking past Governor George Wallace, who'd vowed to "stand in the schoolhouse doors" to protest court-ordered integration. In August, James Meredith, grandson of a slave, became the first black to graduate from the University of Mississippi.

Later that summer, on August 28, more than 200,000 demonstrators assembled jubilantly but peacefully along Washington's grand grassy Mall, facing and surrounding the Lincoln Memorial, as Doctor Martin Luther King, Jr. held them, and a national television audience, spellbound. A long subdued impulse to gender equality also began to find its voice that year as a forty-two-year-old housewife, Betty Friedan, published *The Feminine Mystique*, which dissected the boredom and long-subdued personal identity of many American women. Her book called for a liberating life plan that would glorify the expression of their human individualities. Unconsciously for the most part, I was a male chauvinist. I had been all my life. Quite naturally and unquestioning, that state of mind pervaded my background, the culture in which I had been reared. As though taking a distasteful draught of medicine, I resolutely read Ms. Friedan's book, mentally resisting her conclusions, but reluctantly reexamining my matrix of biases.

All this was part of the intellectual ferment that bubbled up during those brief three years. America was, for the moment, young, unfettered by the cynicism that would creep upon us. The vitality of the historic moment held me in its grip the day Vice President Johnson asked me to help him organize a tour of personal appearances in Texas in November for President Kennedy.

From the moment the presidential trip was suggested to me, it commanded my enthusiastic attention. As envisioned by Johnson, the two-day tour would touch down in our state's four biggest cities—Houston, Dallas, San Antonio, and Fort Worth—and end with a statewide dinner in Austin. I talked with Governor John Connally. Always a little more pragmatic than I, he focused on the fundraising potential of an Austin dinner. My instinctive emphasis was on crowd building—exposing people to Kennedy and his message—but I promised Connally I'd try to help him sell $100,000 worth of tickets in Fort Worth and environs, including parts of West Texas. But it wasn't enough to expose John Kennedy to our community's elite, its civic, political, and business leadership. I wanted plain citizens to have a chance to see and hear their president. Against resistance from some of the itinerary's planners, I held out for a very early, pre-breakfast public appearance on a huge parking lot, which filled the city block adjacent to that occupied by the Fort Worth hotel where the breakfast would be held. I knew there were thousands of working people who loved the president and couldn't attend the breakfast even if invited, since most of them had to punch in for work at 8:00 A.M. But they would show up eagerly for a 7:00 A.M. chance to see Mr. Kennedy in person. There was one hitch. The whole city block, including the parking lot, was owned by William A. Moncrief, a colorful independent oilman and philanthropist, an early pioneer of the Texas petroleum industry—and hardly a Kennedy supporter. His first reaction was to decline the request, but John Connally and I both worked on him, appealing to his sense of civic duty. "Monty," as he was affectionately known, finally relented.

This much nailed down, I turned to the fund-raising chore I had taken on at John Connally's request. Tickets to the Austin dinner were $100 each, and I was out to raise $100,000. This translated to 1,000 paid tickets. First, I assembled a fair cross-section of Fort Worth's business and professional community. About a hundred or so showed up.

Then I got together the labor leadership of our area, and with the help of David and Marjorie Belew (she was our State Democratic Executive Committeewoman) and Committeeman Garrett Morris, I assembled all our Democratic precinct chairman for individual ticket sales. Next, I got on the telephone and called friends in nearby Central and West Texas counties—as far away as Brownwood, 130 miles distant. In all, I got pledges exceeding my ticket sale commitment and saw checks totaling about $78,000. Fundraising was never my forte, but it was and is, as Boston mayor James Michael Curley succinctly described it, the mother's milk of politics.

The first day of the president's Texas trip was a tour de force. The entire series of speeches was an elaboration upon the New Frontier theme. In San Antonio, Kennedy dedicated his remarks to the twin frontiers of space and medical science. At Houston that afternoon, he spoke to a state convention of the League of United Latin American Citizens (LULAC). His message addressed the Alliance for Progress. Jacqueline Kennedy followed with a few words spoken to the group in Spanish. The two of them wowed the Hispanic crowd. That evening, in Houston's spacious coliseum, the Chief Executive addressed a dinner honoring veteran Congressman Albert Thomas, first elected in 1936 when, as Kennedy pointed out, Houston had fewer than 200,000 people. But there, as elsewhere, the president's focus was on the future. By 1990, Kennedy anticipated, America would need three times as much electric power and four times as much water. This look ahead justified the list of specifically enumerated Texas water and power development projects being authorized that year by Congress, including desalination plants. We also would need by 1990, he prophesied, the capacity to serve three times as many college students, and airports to accommodate five times as many passenger miles. He predicted a $2 trillion economy "in this century."

The speech was a sign of the times. We believed everything would be bigger and better, and we could help make it that way. Exhilaration kept us from exhaustion as the traveling party flew to Fort Worth. It was after ten o'clock when the big presidential plane touched down at Carswell Air Force Base in my home town. But a large official welcoming party awaited. Mrs. David Belew presented Jacqueline Kennedy a huge bouquet of yellow roses. Then the president spotted a large number of airmen and their families, roped off from the runway apron by a chain-link fence. They were applauding lustily.

"Take me over to the fence, Jim, and introduce me to some of these good people," he said. But their exuberant cheers as we walked toward them and passed along the fence shaking hands drowned out any attempt I might have made at an introduction. They wanted to touch him. I marveled again at his energy. But by now we all were tired. It was almost midnight. Tomorrow would be November 22.

On that Friday morning, which today seems an eternity ago, it would have been hard not to feel that the nation and this man who so perfectly symbolized it were in their finest hour.

The events of November 22, 1963, burned themselves indelibly into my memory. No sitting president had visited Fort Worth since 1936, when Franklin Roosevelt rode in an open touring car down Main Street. The lilting joy of hosting my president and presenting him that morning to my people in my hometown would give way only hours later to the stark trauma of the assassination in Dallas and the unutterable pathos that followed. But I didn't know this as I stood, so early, looking out the window, waiting expectantly for dawn.

The day began to the patter of raindrops on the streets outside Fort Worth's Hotel Texas, where the president and his party were billeted. The rain had begun during the night, and I had been unable to sleep, worrying about its effect upon our first scheduled event, the 7:00 A.M. outdoor appearance on which I had personally and so doggedly insisted. A damp crowd was already assembling, some in rain gear. Then, at 6:40, the rain stopped, and the sky began to clear. "The luck of the Irish," I thought, with an enormous sigh of relief.

I walked to the elevator, rode up five floors, spoke to my boyhood friend and then city detective, Harvey McMahan, who stood in the corridor. I knocked at the door of the president's suite. He was ready.

The crowd outside was tumultuous with joy. In that inimitable way in which he gave himself, John Kennedy walked past the flat-bed trailer rigged for a speaker's platform and directly into the assembled crowd of people. He obviously enjoyed going among them, shaking their hands, feeling the press of their hopes and aspirations. The little group accompanying the president onto the trailer consisted of Vice President Lyndon Johnson and Texas Governor John Connally, State Senator Don Kennard, Committeewoman Marjorie Belew, and Chamber president Raymond Buck.

"Where's Jackie?" somebody shouted.

"It takes Jackie a little longer to get herself together," the president answered. "But, then, she's prettier than we are. After all, nobody ever asks what Lyndon and I were wearing."

As he talked, another crowd was gathering at the breakfast. But he would not bring himself to leave, so hungry were the people assembled on the rain-soaked asphalt lot to hear him and to clasp to themselves forever the imprint of his personality. Almost whimsically, I thought of the words of that last stanza of his favorite poem:

> But I have promises to keep,
> And miles to go before I sleep,
> And miles to go before I sleep.

The breakfast was a great success. Kennedy spoke of national defense, of Fort Worth's historic contribution since its inception as a cavalry outpost in 1849 (I had given speechwriter Ted Sorenson that background; was pleased the president used it), and of our role in the world. Kennedy went out of his way to pay me personal praise: "I am glad to be here in Jim Wright's city. . . . He speaks for Fort Worth, and he speaks for his country, and I don't know any city that is better represented in the Congress of the United States than Fort Worth." At this, my friends set off a loud stampede of applause that lasted too long. I didn't even have the grace to be embarrassed. Everybody was in an ebullient mood.

En route from Carswell Air Force Base to Dallas Love Field aboard Air Force One, I talked with President Kennedy. Someone had shown him a copy of the *Dallas Morning News*, which contained a scurrilous display advertisement accusing the president of treason. What a boorishly rude and inhospitable thing! Any self-respecting newspaper, I thought, would have rejected such a vulgar advertisement on the day the president of the United States was visiting the city. Kennedy was puzzled by the extreme right-wing fanaticism that seemed to pervade the upper echelons of Dallas. What made the twin cities, Fort Worth and Dallas, so different? he asked.

I suggested that the right-wing viewpoint so rampant in Dallas was instilled and cultivated by daily exposure to the very newspaper that published this singularly offensive ad. John Connally attributed the city's extremism to economic causes. Large banks and insurance companies, not factories, provided the bulk of Dallas employment. The work force was white collar, non-unionized, he explained. President Kennedy was intrigued with the question, said he'd like to discuss it further, maybe en route to Austin later in the day.

We arrived in Dallas. The sun shone brightly. The president deliberately chose to ride in an open convertible with the top down, rejecting the official limousine with a protective bulletproof bubble top, which the Secret Service was recommending. Jack Kennedy wanted to show his identity with the people and his faith in them. He wanted to see their faces and for them to see his. Jack Brooks, Dallas Congressman Earl Cabell, and I rode in the fifth or sixth car, separated from the presidential and vice presidential vehicles by several cars of media representatives.

What a contrast to that day three years earlier when Kennedy, then a candidate, had last ridden through the downtown Dallas streets! On that day in 1960, the noontime crowds in the Dallas business district stood in stony silence, neither smiling nor applauding with any vigor. This November day in 1963, they waved lustily and cheered heartily as the presidential car rode slowly past them.

The motorcade now inched its way through downtown Dallas. The president's car was approaching a grassy knoll filled with people. The vehicle in which I rode had rounded the corner past the old courthouse and was heading north toward the Texas School Book Depository warehouse when the first shot rang out. We were startled, suddenly alert. Then a second crack from the same rifle, its echo reverberating. I thought, "How foolish! Someone's trying to fire a twenty-one-gun salute with a rifle." Then the third shot, the cadence slightly off. I knew quite suddenly that this was no salute. Something was wrong!

There were three clearly audible shots. Of that I am absolutely certain. They all were from the same rifle. If any other shots were fired, they would have had to come from a weapon with a silencer. A witness named Howard Brennan within minutes told police that he had seen a young white male firing a rifle from a corner window on the sixth floor of the Book Depository.

Congressman Cabell's wife, Dearie, also reported seeing the gunman at the window.

We were turning west at the intersection below that depository window as we saw a scene of pandemonium in the president's open vehicle. Jacqueline Kennedy, inexplicably, was facing backward, looking to the rear, her fashionably clad torso leaning over the back seat of the convertible. Then the car suddenly lurched forward and speeded up the ramp of the Stemmons Freeway. Vice President Johnson's car followed in swift pursuit.

Now we passed the grassy knoll. The crowd was stunned. In people's faces was a look of sheer horror. Some were crying. What they had witnessed held them traumatized. I saw a uniformed policeman running uphill, as if trying to find the gunman.

Short minutes later we arrived at Parkland Hospital as the president was being carried inside. The back seat of the car in which he rode was stained with great quantities of fresh blood. We feared the worst as we entered the hospital behind the group accompanying President Kennedy. It soon was confirmed. John F. Kennedy was pronounced dead at one o'clock P.M.

Connally, riding in the seat directly in front of the president, had been grievously wounded but would recover. Nobody knew at this moment if the killing had been the work of a lone madman or part of a well-organized conspiracy. Someone suggested there might be a team of assassins. Jack Brooks broke the silence. "Lyndon, we need to get you out of here as soon as possible. Nobody knows where a gunman may be hiding." Secret Service men quickly agreed.

"But first," insisted Jack, "you need to be sworn in."

Lyndon, stunned at the thought, seemed about to demur.

"This is no time to hesitate, Mr. President," said one of the Secret Service.

Someone asked who could administer the oath. Brooks never lost his presence of mind. He was cooler in that crisis moment than I. He suggested Federal Judge Sarah T. Hughes. Called by telephone, she agreed to meet the presidential party at Air Force One, standing by at Love Field. There Lyndon B. Johnson took the oath of office, Lady Bird Johnson and Jacqueline Kennedy at his side.

To describe the depth of sadness that engulfed us that day defies the vocabulary. In Washington, one of the New Frontiersmen said to Larry O'Brien, "We'll never laugh again." Kennedy's chief apostle replied, "Yes, we'll laugh again. But we'll never be young again."

For several days most of us moved about in a cloud. The trip back to Washington . . . long queues of people, which streamed through the Capitol all Saturday night and into Sunday to pay respect at the casket as it lay in state in the rotunda . . . the little boy, John, unaware of the finality of what had happened to his father, saluting the flag . . . the long, slow march to Arlington Cemetery . . . all this burned itself into our memories.

Was there a conspiracy? Conceivably. Lyndon Johnson, in fact, felt that there was one. He believed, at least for a time, that the assassination was somehow the work of Castro, upon whose life an unsuccessful attempt had been made by people reportedly traceable to U.S. intelligence. It is at least possible that, at this stage of the Cold War, zealous agents from the communist bloc, either in Europe, Asia, or Latin America, could have been involved somehow. But I emphatically do not believe that the Warren Commission or any of its members engaged in a deliberate cover-up. Whatever shortcomings may be seen in their product are, in my firm judgment, honest errors. I knew four of the members personally, and they were honest men.

Now we look back after all these years and seek meaning. How unreal it seems. How beyond our capacity to fathom. How incongruous and paradoxical that, in the cosmic fitness of things, so premature an end to so fine a life would come at such a time and in such a seemingly senseless way. Yet as deathless as immortality are some of the things he said and did. After a hundred years, perhaps, the children of this land may still recite and apply to their lives the timeless challenge of that inaugural address: *Ask not what your country can do for you—Ask what you can do for your country.* Men and women of compassion may find enduring confirmation in Kennedy's 1962 message to Congress: *We are not developing the Nation's wealth for its own sake. Wealth is the means—and people are the ends. All our material riches will avail us little if we do not use them to expand the opportunities of our people.* And just perhaps it may not be forgot: *If a free society cannot help the many who are poor, it cannot save the few who are rich.* These, I think, are among the things John F. Kennedy would have us remember.

CHAPTER ELEVEN

JOHNSON
ASCENDS

L yndon Johnson was bigger than life, a compulsive overachiever, always racing both the clock and the calendar to nail "another coonskin on the wall," as he once impulsively boasted at a bill-signing ceremony during the heyday of Great Society legislation. If Eisenhower was the most respected of the eight presidents with whom I served, and Kennedy the most inspirational, Lyndon Johnson was the busiest. I also believe he was the smartest—not the most polished, nor the most intellectual. His was not the graceful patina of academia. After the lilting prose of the Kennedy years, Lyndon's formal speeches seemed almost labored at times. But in sheer brainpower, in the ability to read other people and stay two steps ahead of an adversary, Lyndon Johnson was without peer. Like many other good friends and admirers, I harbored the sometimes disquieting feeling that "this guy could outsmart me if he wanted to." Johnson had an uncanny ability to know what other people were thinking and to say something—often offhand and totally disarming in its informality—that would set their minds at rest, quiet their apprehensions, play to their own predilections, and enlist them as allies in his effort.

When Chief Justice Earl Warren first expressed reservations about heading the commission to investigate the Kennedy assassination, Johnson played unabashedly to Warren's sense of duty. "The President of the United States is asking you to do this for the good of our country," Johnson pressed. In the end, Warren assented.

Television was not his forte. I always thought it might have been, if the speech doctors and other gurus could simply let Lyndon be himself. Instead, they tried to tame his natural mannerisms and filter the Texas twang out of his voice. They tried to make him over and it didn't quite take. But, wow! Get Lyndon Johnson in a room with twenty-five or thirty people—or 250, sometimes—and he was dynamite. Forgetting formalities, being himself, tying his shoelaces, or scratching his ear as he talked, Lyndon Johnson could be as rough as a corncob or as smooth as a baby's bottom—whichever the situation required. He had a kind of magic.

As he talked, he would be studying his audience. He'd know instinctively what one person wanted, what another feared, what a third hoped for. He would be saying some particular thing to appeal to each of us in that room. Thirty minutes later we'd walk out in mental lock-step, each of us eager to do whatever it was Lyndon wanted done.

But there was another side to Lyndon Johnson. He was what Sam Rayburn called "a big-brained man." Lyndon had a dream—or, better maybe, a barrel of dreams. He wanted to be the instrument of major beneficial change. Conscious of his powers of persuasion and hounded by his self-imposed goals, he was painfully aware of his own mortality and in a hurry to get things done before the sands in his hour glass ran out. "All the men in my family have died young," he remarked to me on two different occasions. As if in justification for his frantic haste to remake the landscape of life for the less fortunate in our society, he'd quote his father's prodding. "Lyndon, get up," his dad would tell him. "Every other boy in town has an hour's start on you!"

There is no question that Lyndon Johnson wanted to make life better for plain people. As a teacher, he had seen the plight of rural Hispanic children in the hard-scrabble country of southwest Texas. In his job as administrator of the National Youth Administration, he'd gotten a thrill from helping thousands of improvident youths to get through college. As a young congressman, he had insisted that agricultural programs be extended to black farm families. When a little town in South Texas refused burial for the body of a young Mexican-American slain in World War II, Johnson arranged for the remains to be buried with honors at Arlington National Cemetery.

Robert Caro, in the first two volumes of his biography, seems unconscious of the central belief systems that drove and motivated our thirty-sixth president. Caro stresses the manipulative skills and self-promotion stratagems that propelled Johnson in his rise to power. But the writer didn't know Johnson. He ignores the most important ingredient: *why* Johnson wanted power. Let me here simply relate my own experiences with President Johnson and tell you how he seemed to me.

The spring of 1956 was a crucial point in Johnson's career. Only a year before, he had suffered a near-fatal coronary attack, which had caused many to conclude that his political future was all behind him. Now his mentor, confidant, and longtime personal friend, Sam Rayburn, had pushed him out into the arena of statewide combat to wrench from the hands of Governor Alan Shivers the leadership of the Democratic Party in Texas. Four years earlier, Shivers had led a successful bolt away from the party and helped put Texas into the Republican column in the presidential election. Now, still governor and titular head of the party, Shivers seemed intent on leading the state's delegation to the national convention for the purpose of once more bolting and again handing the state machinery over to the hands of the opposition. From the Democratic Party point of view, someone had to stop him. Clearly there was only one person who might have the statewide following to do so: Senator Lyndon B. Johnson. He had not sought the role of gladiator in this conflict. He had considerable personal respect for the governor and for his ability, and he would not deliberately have picked the fight. Johnson often seemed happiest when serving in the function of peacemaker. The passage of scripture he most frequently quoted is from Isaiah: "Come, let us reason together." Yet there he was in the middle of the ring. Without directly consulting Lyndon, Sam Rayburn had publicly announced him as his personal choice for leader of the Texas delegation to the national convention. The gauntlet had been thrown down.

Johnson asked several of us in the House delegation to help him round up support in our areas. At his request, I joined him and Lady Bird in a quick week-end flight. I would stop off in Fort Worth; they would go on to Austin. George Reedy, Johnson's press aide, also was aboard. As he flew down on the airplane to our home state, Senator Johnson knew it would be a bitter fight. In his briefcase were the latest newspaper clippings from over the state. Shivers had been traveling Texas, speaking at rallies, grabbing all the headlines. His technique was to identify Johnson with Washington powers intent on snuffing out "states' rights." With a broad brush, the governor was tarring the Senate majority leader with an alphabet of unpopular causes, allying him with "the ADA, the CIO-PAC and the NAACP!" Indignantly, Shivers accused Johnson of conspiring "radical outside influences" in a plot to take over Texas and manipulate it from the banks of the Potomac.

There was something else, too: the explosive race issue. Ugly and brooding, it had festered just beneath the surface of Texas political decisions for two years. Since the 1954 Supreme Court ruling on school integration, smoldering hates and fears had been threatening to break into a flame. The state legislature, reflecting what it believed to be the public sentiment, passed a series of harsh anti-integration bills for the courts to knock down.

Now, seated beside the senator and reading the news clippings, I could see the pattern of the duel emerging. With increasing frequency, Shivers was sounding the bugle for a fight on the integration issue. Since the battle would turn on which of the two could get more of his partisans out to participate in the precinct conventions, the race issue seemed ready-made for the governor's purposes. Johnson was being portrayed by his antagonists as a turncoat, a traitor to the southern cause, a tool of the NAACP. Even among moderate Texans, this organization in 1956 carried a stigma of disaffection. If people could be led to believe that their senator was playing up to such a group or doing its bidding, they would have rejected him. If he remained silent in the face of the charge, what would people believe?

"What are you going to do about this accusation?" someone on the aircraft asked the majority leader. "Don't you think you'll have to deny it?"

"No," Lyndon Johnson replied. "I'm not going to demagogue on that issue. If I have to try to prove that I hate Negroes in order to win, then I'll just not win."

He mused for a brief moment, then continued. "There's a little colored girl named Helen, who brings my coffee to the majority leader's office every morning. I'm not going to have to look away, when she comes in, for being ashamed of something I've said."

Then, turning to me, Senator Johnson said, almost in a reverie, "When I lay there in that hospital bed, I thought of a lot of things. A man doesn't occupy this earth forever. I don't know when I'll die, and I hope it won't be soon. But I'm not going to die with *that* on my conscience."

Ultimately, he met the issue head on. In San Antonio, Johnson said: "I didn't come back to Texas to divide class against class, or race against race, or section against section."

He won, all right. He won big and led the delegation to the national convention. It was the beginning of his comeback from a premature political demise to which many had consigned him. It was the beginning of something else, too. It was the beginning of a more enlightened policy in Texas on this particular issue. It gave encouragement to a new breed of Texas politicians. No longer was it necessary to mouth the old political shibboleths of "white supremacy" in order to win elections in the Lone Star State. One man had blazed the trail.

Eight years later, when President Johnson so effectively pleaded for the Civil Rights Act of 1964, certain cynical and slightly jaded political observers commented, tongue in cheek, that Lyndon was "smart" to give the nation an "image" of a "national figure" who had "outgrown his parochialism." Poor, silly, clever fellows. They thought it was expediency. I knew better. I knew it was *conviction*.

"Complex" is the word most often used to describe Lyndon Johnson's personality. He was a mixture of many things: prudence and daring, sophistication and simplicity, gravity and humor, frugality and extravagant generosity. As a politician he was both cautious and bold. The first time I ever saw Lyndon was in 1941. Then a young congressman, he was running along with twelve others to fill the U.S. Senate vacancy created by the death of Senator Morris Sheppard. Johnson came within an inch of winning that contest, barely nosed out by the sitting governor, W. Lee O'Daniel. Although I was trying to help Attorney General Gerald Mann in that race, a lot of my friends were for Lyndon. Intrigued, I went to hear him one night at a rally. He was preaching the New Deal gospel. I instinctively liked a lot of the things he was saying. I was eighteen at the time.

The thing that struck me like a thunderbolt was this audacious pledge, hurled out at a climatic point in the campaign speech: "On the day that it should ever become necessary for Congress to vote to send young American men to do battle for our country overseas, on that day Lyndon B. Johnson will leave his seat in the United States Senate and go with them!" Two friends of mine, Joe Kilgore and Sidney Reagan, worked for Johnson in that campaign. They confessed to me years later that they would separate, one going into the heart of the crowd at the candidate's right and the other among listeners on the speaker's left. When Johnson would intone this ringing pledge, each of them would let out a loud war whoop of approval. It never failed to set off a stampede of applause.

Gaudy showmanship?

Lyndon did not win that race and was not in the Senate, six months later, when Congress declared war on Japan and the other Axis powers. But he was in the House, and, true to his word, Lyndon Johnson was the very first of a fairly large group of his colleagues to shed their Congressional togas for a military uniform. He won the Silver Star in the South Pacific.

Both the promise and the deed were Johnson at his boldest. But he also could be cautious. He was not a *Kamikaze* liberal, forever daring political demise. In a one-party state, where the more conservative of the Democratic finalists invariably won the gubernatorial nomination, Johnson knew the danger of being *too* progressive, *too* outspoken, *too* far ahead of the pack. He cultivated a casual folksiness and gave a homey, good ol' boy rationale for each of the liberal positions he took. He vigorously championed the state's principal economic interests—oil, cattle, cotton—and cultivated some of the state's well-heeled entrepreneurs such as George and Herman Brown of Houston. These were among the dues he paid for voting more liberal than others of the state's elected leaders.

Now, as president, he moved deftly. His first defining acts were symbolic as well as practical. He went around turning off White House lights to demon-strate concern for the taxpayer's dollar. Subordinating his own agenda to that of the fallen president, Johnson asked every member of the Kennedy cabinet to continue to serve. He and Lady Bird invited Jacqueline Kennedy and her children to stay on in the White House as long as she wished.

Johnson's cost-cutting spree, aside from the obvious merit of eliminating waste, served three practical ends. It quickly established presidential control of the bureaucracy. It fixed Johnson in the public eye as a fiscally prudent leader. It paved the way and eased the pain for the social spending he'd be ask-ing for. And Johnson's economies amounted to more than just tokenism, as doubters soon discovered. Less than a week in office, Johnson called the joint chiefs of staff and told them he wanted reductions in military expenses. "Cut all the fat but leave the muscle." On November 30, he sent memos to all gov-ernment departments and agencies, demanding reports on cost reductions in the past year and eliciting ideas for tightening up in the year to come. On December 1, he wrote approximately 7,500 defense contractors, urging internal belt tightening. He instructed Defense Secretary Robert S. McNamara to consider each contractor's cost-cutting performance in evalu-ating future bids for defense business. The next day, he ordered top military personnel to pass the word that cost-conscious performance would be studied in evaluating career militarists for future promotion. Johnson personally tele-phoned the chairmen of four Congressional committees, asking that their investigative panels be alert to administrative duplication and over-staffing. Not even the space program, in many ways Johnson's brain child and consid-ered by some his pet among the agencies, was left unscathed. On December 5, at the president's urging, NASA administrators ordered a halt to the hiring of personnel at twenty-four companies engaged in manned space flight pro-grams. The freeze was to give NASA time to reassess its ambitious undertakings in light of new budget strictures.

On Christmas Eve, Johnson revealed from his ranch that he had reviewed budget requests from all departments for the coming fiscal year and had reduced military askings by $9 billion and those from civilian agencies by $10 billion. Johnson's critics often had tarred him as a "big spender." Within a month after assuming office, he had established solid credentials as a cost-cutter.

On the seventh day following the assassination and his oath of office, Johnson announced the appointment of a blue-ribbon, bipartisan President's Commission on the Assassination of President Kennedy. The tumultuous events of that fateful week had the nation reeling. The slaying of the president and the wounding of Governor Connally, the killing of Dallas Patrolman J. D. Tippit, the arrest of Lee Harvey Oswald and his own gunning down two days later by Jack Ruby in the clear sight of millions of television viewers unleashed a phantasmagoria of wild rumors. President Johnson knew the only way to restore calm was for the nation to be reassured that the truth would be found and fully disclosed by an apolitical panel with unimpeachable credentials. The Warren Commission would take testimony under oath from 552 witnesses and publish an 816-page report, with 63 additional pages of footnotes. It concluded that Oswald was indeed the assassin and that he acted alone.

Since Oswald was from Fort Worth, we searched our own files in my Congressional office to see if we had ever heard from him or any of his family. Sure enough, on March 6, 1960, his mother had written to me, asking if I could help her locate her son. She believed him to be somewhere in Russia and had not heard from him for many weeks. I'd forwarded her inquiry to our State Department, which in turn had sent it to our embassy in Moscow. That embassy had replied that it had no record of any contact with Oswald since November of 1959, at which time he was threatening to renounce his U.S. citizenship. Our trail ended there, and we gave this information to the Commission.

Johnson's first speech to Congress as president was eloquent and quietly forceful. "The greatest leader of our time has been struck down by the foulest deed of our time," he began. He pledged his total energies to carrying out the uncompleted work of President Kennedy. In the first nine months of Johnson's presidency, it became apparent that he was putting more of John F. Kennedy's program on the law books than the charismatic Kennedy had been able to do in almost three years. The Kennedy tax cut, featuring tax credits for investments to modernize America's aging industrial plant, sailed through. The major poverty bill (called the Economic Opportunity Act of 1964) attacked the root causes of poverty—poor health, poor education, inadequate housing. The civil rights bill forbade merchants and hotel and restaurant keepers from denying service to any because of race. Five big education bills helped colleges build facilities, provided money for fellowships, grants and loans for college students, and trained workers in new skills. More than thirty conservation measures produced dozens of new national parks and four national seashores, as well as a far-reaching research program for the desalination of water. Several bills targeted public health, attacked air pollution, helped families with mentally retarded children, trained nurses and doctors, and financed massive research to seek cures for such imposing problems as cancer and coronary disease. Congress, at Johnson's urging, launched the food stamp program. The list of achievements included a treaty banning nuclear tests in the atmosphere. Through it all, Lyndon Johnson continued to credit his predecessor with the initiatives that produced this stunning agenda. There would be time enough, after his landslide election in 1964, to embroider his own initials into the historic tapestry of the Kennedy-Johnson years.

President Johnson took the starchiness out of White House receptions. He gave them an air of warm, personal informality. They also became, for the first time, forums for genuinely productive conversation. Under previous presidents, there had been one big reception each year for the 535 Members of Congress and their wives. Through the Eisenhower years, these were appallingly formal affairs. During President Kennedy's administration, the receptions became less formal—members wore tuxes instead of tails, Kennedy did not stand in a receiving line but circulated among the crowd. The Johnson technique was less formal still. There were more gatherings, and they were smaller. Johnson divided the House and Senate membership into ten groups and scheduled ten separate receptions. This made for a maximum of individual attention. At one point in the evening, the spouses would go upstairs with Mrs. Johnson for a tour of the living quarters. The members would accompany the president into the Gold Room for informal talks. Usually, Secretary of Defense McNamara and Secretary of State Rusk would speak briefly about the world situation. Then they and the president would answer questions. Following this session, an orchestra would tune up for a ball in the big East Room. President Johnson made it a point to do a turn around the floor with each of the wives. As the evening ended, the President and Mrs. Johnson would shake hands again and have a parting word for each congressman and spouse.

While vice president, Johnson almost always had managed to get away on Wednesday noons for a trip to the Capitol, where he'd join the Texas delegation at its weekly luncheon. Now, as president, these occasions became fewer and fewer, but he compensated by inviting selected groups of us to the White House on Sunday evenings. Often we'd ride over to the Anacostia River dock and board the president's yacht, *Sequoia*, for a leisurely ride down the Potomac past Mount Vernon. During dinner aboard the yacht, the president lobbied us gently in behalf of his current projects.

Twice, wanting my help with a bill in the Public Works Committee, he asked me to come and join him for a swim in the big pool, which Franklin Roosevelt had installed in the White House basement. We'd swim awhile and talk awhile. Swimming and walking were the two exercises in which Johnson indulged regularly. Once, walking around the south White House lawn with four of us early in his presidency, the big Texan ambled informally over to the fence to shake hands with some tourists, who had called out to him from the sidewalk. While engaging in friendly banter, we heard the shrill screech of brakes. We looked up to observe a rear-end collision. The driver of one auto-mobile, excited to get such a close glimpse of the president, had turned his head to gawk and had not noticed that the car in front of him was slowing down, so that its driver could get a better look at the chief executive, too. Lyndon Johnson vowed he never would go within sight of the street again.

The presidency wrought one major change in Johnson's demeanor. He became much more cautious, even secretive about his movements and travel plans. The Kennedy assassination profoundly transformed Johnson's attitude toward the Secret Service. As vice president, he sometimes had chafed at their presence. After that dreadful day in Dallas, his attitude underwent a meta-morphosis. Lyndon was particularly devoted to Rufus Youngblood, the young Georgian who rode with him on that day. Youngblood was in the front seat of the vice president's limousine, with a clear view of the president's lim-ousine ahead. At the sound of the first shot, Youngblood immediately vaulted across the front seat, shoved the vice president to the floor, and shielded Johnson's body with his own. On December 4, less than two weeks after the tragic incident, President Johnson presented a rare Exceptional Service Award to Youngblood in a moving private ceremony at the White House. At his gen-erous best, the president said: "There is no more heroic act than offering your life to save another, and in that awful moment of confusion, when all about him were losing their heads, Rufus Youngblood never lost his. Without hesi-tation, he volunteered his life to save mine."

One reason for the president's great caution in that first year was that the office of vice president was vacant. Speaker John McCormack, then in his seventies, would have become president if anything had happened to Johnson. Not only did McCormack have absolutely no desire to be president; he had no patience with the requirement that, as next in line, he be accompa-nied at all times by the Secret Service. Politely, the dignified Speaker would simply dismiss the agents assigned to him. "Young man," he would say, "I know you are only trying to do your job, but I have no need of your services. As you can see, I am constantly on the move, and there is no place for you to sit. Furthermore, members might not feel free to confide in me if someone else were standing around. So, you see, there is just no need for you here."

Not easily daunted, Secret Service Chief James Rowley arranged to place an agent in the room next to McCormack's apartment in the Washington Hotel. Knowing the Speaker's devout Catholicism and wanting the agent to work his way into McCormack's confidence, Rowley had his man don the vestments of a Roman Catholic priest. On his first evening in this assign-ment, the disguised agent scored. Speaker McCormack spotted the young "priest" sitting alone at the table next to the one he and Mrs. McCormack invariably occupied in the hotel's upstairs dining room. The Speaker invited the young stranger to join him and his wife for dinner. The two very soon became friends. They began to join for dinner every evening. Strangely, each morning when Speaker McCormack left his room to go downstairs, the make-believe clergyman would be leaving his adjacent room at just the same moment. They would ride the elevator together and often remark at the singularity of their apparently identical schedules. Outside the lobby, McCormack would enter his limousine while the "priest" entered a taxi for his daily ride, presumably to Georgetown University where he'd told the Speaker he was doing a sabbatical.

One day, Speaker McCormack was unexpectedly delayed at the hotel door by a colleague. Walking to his car, he noticed that the taxi his young friend had entered was still immobile. Its driver seemed to be waiting for McCormack's limousine to depart. Once under way, McCormack watched and discovered that the taxi was following his limousine at a discreet distance. The "priest" was not going where he'd said. Suddenly, it dawned on the old man exactly what was happening. He ordered his driver to stop, got out, and motioned the cab forward. With great dignity, he addressed the younger man whom he'd befriended.

"You've been deceiving me, haven't you? You have betrayed our friendship by not being truthful with me, and that makes me very sad. But much worse than that, you have impersonated a priest. And if that is not a mortal sin, it surely is a sacrilege." On such beliefs arose the hierarchy of values in the life of John McCormack. He was a man of towering decency, but not cut out to be president in the world of the 1960s.

Mindful of the constitutional void, Johnson urged Congress to amend the procedure of almost two hundred years by arranging a methodology to fill future vacancies in the office of vice president. Upon nomination by the president, a new vice president may be elected by Congress. The new provision was to be activated, twice in the next ten years, in the selection of both Gerald R. Ford and Nelson Rockefeller.

Johnson's war on poverty and his educational initiatives thrilled me. They fulfilled my concept of what government was all about—spreading the base of prosperity to share more of the good things of life with those to whom they'd been too long denied. In April, the House passed the Food Stamp Bill by a vote of 229 to 189. For the first time, the helping hand would be open not only to people on public assistance rolls. States would establish standards of eligibility, and grocers wishing to participate would agree to abide by the program's terms. Other paving stones in the road to the Great Society would be put into place month by month. There was stubborn resistance, even some determined attempts at obstruction. In the House Public Works Committee, where I was helping to get the Appalachian initiative on track after many weeks of sub-committee hearings, Republican members employed a rare tactic in their effort to derail the package. On the third Friday in July, they boycotted the committee en masse. They simply failed to show up for the "mark up" session we'd scheduled. Deprived of a quorum, the committee could not proceed, and the bill was temporarily stalled. Old timers on the Committee were stunned. They vowed such a thing had never happened before.

We would pass the Appalachian program, but not without a fight. The Republican resistance in my committee slowed down the 1964 adjournment. Speaker McCormack had said that the House could call it quits for the year only when it disposed of the pending anti-poverty bills. This was not the first nor would it be the last time for election year maneuvering to clog the legislative machinery.

Nobody exactly defended poverty, of course. Even President Hoover in his first presidential campaign in 1928 grandly prophesied a day "When poverty will be banished from this nation." Now that elusive goal and national dream seemed actually capable of accomplishment, almost within sight. On balance, our nation had never been richer. The gross national product for 1964 was expected to hit an incredible $623 billion. It was understandable that Johnson's effort to bring everyone into the promised land would be greeted by hoots and sneers in some quarters. For one thing, most Americans in their day-to-day lives did not see glaring signs of poverty in 1964. Most folks just didn't come into direct contact with the "other America" of squalor and ragged clothes, of hunger, hopelessness, and despair.

By far the largest, most deeply rooted pocket of poverty was Appalachia, the mountainous region lying between the thriving Eastern seaboard and the prosperous industrial Middle West, an area of 165,000 square miles—ten times the size of Switzerland, stretching through ten states, from northern Pennsylvania to northern Alabama. It was home to fifteen million people, where one family in every three lived on less than $3,000 a year. Kennedy had promised a new approach to Appalachia's problems. Johnson was determined to make good on the pledge.

These mountain people, like others in underdeveloped areas across our nation, were poor because they were not equipped to make a useful contribution to our modern economy. Crops and industries on which they formerly depended had been made obsolete by the onward rush of technology. Until they could be given the training and opportunity they needed to fit themselves into the new national economy, they would continue to be left out, no matter how fast the economy grew. Those at the bottom must be equipped with the education and skills necessary to lift themselves, to make their own contribution to our country.

In September, the House debated the first appropriation of money for the antipoverty program. Advocates recited the stark statistics of grisly want in the midst of affluence. Democratic spokesmen rhapsodized upon our unrivaled opportunity to "heal the gaping sores of economic denial" and "banish poverty from our land!" Then Joel Broyhill, Republican Congressman from Virginia's Tenth District, entered the debate. His speech ripped into some of my most cherished assumptions. Broyhill denounced the antipoverty program as the "most flagrant, unabashed vote-buying scheme I have seen in all my years in Congress." Others in the House elaborated upon the Broyhill theme. Some expressed deep concern over the increasingly popular fallacy that "the world owes me a living." One gave voice to the view that anyone who really wants to work can find a job, and another hinted darkly that too easy access to goods without work was "destroying the moral fiber" of the American people. Someone charged that multiple welfare payments were encouraging illegitimate births. A southern Democrat, leaning on the back railing of the House chamber, peered over his glasses and grunted to a colleague: "The Bible says, if you don't work you don't eat!"

Most of these nay-sayers were my friends. We had disagreed before. From my earliest days I had tried consciously to cultivate the art of disagreeing without being disagreeable. This time, the self-righteous tone of some of the opposition was beginning to get under my skin. The use of Scripture, so widely at variance with my own interpretation, disturbed me. I knew that men of good will often disagree. I knew this could happen without either being a demagogue or a rascal. "There's too much name-calling and self-righteousness on both sides of this issue," I fumed to my family. In truth, I probably was as guilty as any of the others. In the war against poverty, I was a true believer.

Johnson's Economic Opportunity Act covered a wide range of programs. It launched the Job Corps, giving some 450,000 young high school dropouts practical training for a marketable skill. It gave loans and technical help to farm families, and financial encouragement to people who would hire the handicapped and the unemployed. Its cost for the first year was estimated at nearly $1 billion. In 1964 that was a lot of money. But less than one-fiftieth the amount we were spending that year on national defense. I realized with a twinge of personal poignancy that the $1 billion to fight poverty was actually less than one-eighth of the total earmarked to be spent within a few years on one weapons system, the TFX, which I had fought successfully to get built in Fort Worth. Under these comparisons, I thought it morally indefensible to let millions of people go hungry while, as Senator George McGovern pointed out, our country was producing six hundred tons of food per minute, and a lot of it was going to waste.

Another big victory for Johnson was the Civil Rights Act of 1964. It passed the House in February and became law in July. The bill attacked the denial of human rights on a broad front. It sped up school desegregation, broadened the powers of the Civil Rights Commission, outlawed discrimination in employment and in labor union memberships. The sticking point for a lot of people was the "public accommodations" section. It presented me with one of the most difficult choices of all my years in Congress. Looking back later, I've often wished that I had chosen differently.

The bill required businesses holding themselves out to the public to serve all of the public. Specifically targeted were restaurants, hotels, and other service establishments. Not only in the South, but across the country, many establishments restricted their clientele to whites only. It would not be out of character for me to break ranks from the great column of members from my region. I had done that before. While in the legislature I had favored opening the University of Texas law school to black students. When that was not done, I voted to build a law school expressly for them. As mayor of Weatherford, I had taken the initiative to bus black students to high school. I had joined only two others from our delegation in refusing to sign the "Southern Manifesto" protesting school desegregation. I had voted for other civil rights bills.

Yet this one bothered me. I thought about all those thousands of small businessmen in small towns across America with whom I had worked in business, and I worried about the government's right to tell them whom they must or must not serve. There is a difference, I thought, between publicly owned facilities and privately owned facilities. I pondered in my mind the distinction between a right and a convenience. In tax-supported institutions, the same rights surely must be accorded to all of our citizens. Schools, highways, parks and playgrounds, libraries, public hospitals—all tax-supported things belong to all of us together. But my neighbor's store, like his home, does not belong to me, nor to the public generally. It belongs to him, I reasoned. I enter his door only at his pleasure.

I was wrong. I was viewing the matter, I later came to believe, too legalistically. I knew that I would have found it offensive to be turned away from a business establishment whose premises I had entered—but that never had happened to me. I doubt that I *could* know how deeply repugnant the experience would be. I should have voted for the bill. Instead, captive of my past and limited in vision by my own experiences, I voted as the others did throughout my part of the country. Only four Texans out of twenty-three in the House supported the bill. They were Jack Brooks, Henry Gonzalez, Jake Pickle, and Albert Thomas. I wish I had been with them.

The first Johnson years were, on balance, very good ones for me. The country prospered, and the projects I had launched for my district flourished. Assembly lines hummed at General Dynamics, winner of the TFX award, at Bell Helicopter, and at LTV Aircraft Corporation. Things were looking up nationally, too. In the 1964 Democratic primary, I was opposed for the first time. I'd had opponents in the general elections, but not in the primaries. My opponent was a popular city councilman named Tommy Thompson. I carried every precinct and won renomination with a better than 10 to 1 margin. That fall I would triumph over Republican challenger Fred Dielman with 68.5 percent of the vote. I had popularity to spare, I thought. I *could* have voted for that public accommodations bill.

Something else was happening, too. In the first week of August 1964, in a faraway body of water called the Tonkin Gulf, several PT boats under the North Vietnamese military command fired upon one of our destroyers, the USS *Maddox*. Later speculation would raise a question of whether the commanders of these boats, thinking our ship was in their territorial waters, might have fired warning shots. Whatever they thought will never be known. On the order of President Johnson, our navy counteracted swiftly and decisively. Our warships not only drove off the attackers, they sank them. After a second wave approached, navy planes flew out to destroy the remaining PT boats, their bases, and fuel supplies.

President Johnson wasted no time on stilted words of stuffy protests conveyed through diplomatic channels. He let our actions speak. Anxious that America should present a united front, President Johnson immediately called Senator Barry Goldwater, whom the Republicans had nominated as their candidate to oppose him in the November election. Before news media could report the retaliatory attack, Johnson personally advised Goldwater of his decision. Knowing that the Arizona Republican would be called upon for a public comment, Johnson reached him first. Goldwater issued a statement supporting the president's action.

Although Johnson's role in this crisis would be widely criticized later, it was vastly popular at the time. Calmly and reassuringly, the president recited the details of the skirmish in the Tonkin Gulf to a nationwide television audience. As always, the people rallied. It is an unfailing phenomenon. In the immediate aftermath of an unexpected military engagement with any foreign adversary, the people instinctively close ranks. I have observed the reaction in more than a dozen situations over a period of more than fifty years. But, as we discovered in Korea and, to our lasting confoundment, in Vietnam, the public's expectation is for victory, and its patience evaporates easily. Presidents Reagan and Bush would play adroitly to this trait in the American character as they pursued the swift destruction of lesser foes in Grenada in 1983, in the bombing of Khadafi's headquarters in Libya in 1986, in the swift sack of Panama in 1989, and in the pulverizing bombardment of Iraq in 1991.

President Johnson immediately asked Congress for a resolution of unity and support. He reminded Congress that our commitments in Southeast Asia had been made ten years before by President Eisenhower and upheld by President Kennedy. With absolute predictability, Congress gave him what he wanted, and the open-ended Gulf of Tonkin Resolution authorized the president "to take all necessary measures to repel any armed attack against the forces of the United States and to prevent further aggression." A federal court would later equate this with a declaration of war.

Polls gave President Johnson approval ratings in the eighties. Noting that our country was entering three months of political campaigning, Johnson held up the shield of public opinion as a warning to the world. "Hostile nations must understand," he said, "that in such a period the United States will continue to protect its national interests, and that in these matters there is no division among us. . . . As I have repeatedly made clear, the United States intends no rashness, and seeks no wider war. We must make it clear to all that the United States is united in its determination to bring about the end of Communist subversion and aggression in the area."

The protest movement was not yet under way. Patriotism was rampant. My nineteen-year-old son, Jimmy, wanted to be a part of the struggle for freedom. A year earlier, when he had wanted to go into the Peace Corps, I'd persuaded him to stay in college. "There'll be plenty of time for the Peace Corps if you want to do it later," I'd assured him. Now, in his second year at Texas Wesleyan College in Fort Worth, Jimmy told me he'd made a decision. "A lot of kids can't go to college, Dad," he said. "They're being drafted and being sent to Vietnam. It isn't fair. Some fellows are just prolonging college and dragging it on to avoid serving the country. I don't feel any sense of purpose here. You left college and went to war when you were my age, and you've always been proud you did. I have decided I want to do exactly the same thing. In fact, I have enlisted in the navy."

There was a lump in my throat and a shiver up my spine. I tried lamely to dissuade him, but what could I say? I tried to convince him to get at least another year of college under his belt first and think about it carefully. But he had already made a decision. I had to honor it—and be prouder of him than I could express in words. At that point, both he and I believed that what our country was doing in Vietnam was just and right and noble.

Lyndon Johnson romped to victory that November. Johnson, who had won all his previous political battles by putting together a coalition of the left and the middle, now drew support also from many rank-and-file people who considered themselves "conservative." Barry Goldwater's stark conservatism was seen as harsh, radical, extreme.

In the ensuing campaign, I ignored my own Republican rival to campaign throughout Texas for the ticket and to make appearances at the invitation of colleagues in six other states. Dan Blocker, the big genial Texan who played the Hoss Cartwright character in the *Bonanza* television series, joined us one day at the Johnson ranch and accompanied me in three public appearances on behalf of the Democratic ticket. Friendly as a big Saint Bernard dog, "Hoss" drew fantastic crowds. He'd tell of his boyhood on a dry West Texas farm and end his peroration with this laconic comment: "These Republicans say we've been goin' down hill ever since Franklin D. Roosevelt came into office. If that's really the direction we're slidin' in, I just cain't hardly wait to get to the bottom!"

In the Johnson landslide that November, precedents were shattered like window glass in the wake of a sonic boom. His popular majority topped FDR's stunning 1936 reelection win—and Johnson's coattails were almost as broad. The Democratic majority in the new Congress was a little better than 2 to 1 over the GOP—68 of the 100 Senators, and 295 of the 435 member House.

On inauguration eve, Mab and I invited the whole Texas contingent—two busloads of more than a hundred people—to our house in northern Virginia for a buffet dinner. We had intended for one busload of passengers to come from seven to eight and the other from eight until nine o'clock. But the seven o'clock crowd stayed on. Everyone was in a festive mood. An arctic cold gripped the Washington area, and nobody seemed to want to brave the icy air for a walk to the bus, sitting outside with its engine running. We encased the screened-in porch with a makeshift layer of isinglass to give one extra room for the crowd to spill into. It was wall-to-wall guests, but nobody seemed to mind. A Texan had been *elected* president!

Happy though I was to be host to such a magnificent celebration, there was an aching void somewhere inside me. My son Jimmy would be twenty in one more month. He would have enjoyed these festivities. I wished he could be here. But he was at the Memphis Naval Air Station, soon to see service on an aircraft carrier in the South China Sea. Across the land, other young men were gearing up for military service. This fact would loom like a dark storm cloud on the horizon of President Johnson's upcoming term. It would dump a sorrowful cargo of sleety rain upon his—upon our—parade.

CHAPTER TWELVE

GREAT SOCIETY

Beginning one's sixth term in Congress, a member can feel invincible, like an athlete in his prime. Behind are the early frustrations of the seniority system, the years of waiting to be recognized by one's colleagues, the condescension of older members. In 1965, spurred by the electoral victories in which I'd so recently participated, I was determined to make a broader mark in the legislative arena. Already I had carved out a leadership role in the delayed Appalachian bill. I would move this year with the Trinity River Development Plan, after ten years of grooming it and shepherding it through the exhaustive Corps of Engineers studies. I would take a major hand in expanding the Clean Water Program. These were the goals I was mulling in my mind as the victorious Democrats convened for our presession caucus. I did not know at the time that I would get caught up in the fights for Medicare, the Voting Rights Act, and Highway Beautification. I also would grow more deeply involved in the struggles of Latin America and grope for a handle to a door to peace in Vietnam.

House Republicans, discouraged by their losses, overturned their leadership. They replaced Minority Leader Charlie Halleck of Indiana with Gerald Ford of Michigan. I wrote in a newsletter at the time that Ford's most apparent advantage over Halleck was that he'd look better on TV. Halleck was pudgy with heavy jowls. He also was a more vigorous debater than Ford and more prone to pick partisan quarrels. Ford presented a more "moderate" image. Republican dismay over the election's outcome was evident in a comment by New York Rep. John Lindsay. Admonished not to rock the GOP boat, Lindsay replied: "How can you rock a boat that is already sunk?"

In 1965, I became a sub-committee chairman, appointed to head the Public Works panel on watershed development. I was beginning a book manuscript on the nation's clean water problems. In recognition of my growing status in Congress, I was invited along with Republican House members John Anderson and Ross Adair and a handful of Senators, including Foreign Relations Chairman William Fulbright, to spend a week in discussions with British parliamentarians at an old English country estate called Ditchley. That trip coincided with Winston Churchill's funeral. I observed the procession from a window of the British foreign office and felt a strong affinity. From the first solemn pealing of the bells at Westminster to the soft falling of twilight over the quiet old churchyard at Bladon, the funeral was a pageant reenacting the history of the century. Churchill's life, like the central refrain of a musical composition, had threaded its way subjectively through most of the major events of my lifetime.

For the four days following the funeral, the American congressional delegation met with some of England's leaders—Lord Mountbatten, Selwyn Lloyd, and others—in a discussion of our mutual problems. The similarities were notorious. East of Suez, we seemed to be fighting the same holding action against leftist expansion: Britain in Malaysia, the U.S. in Vietnam.

Back in Washington, I pushed deeply into the fight for the Appalachian Regional Development Act. Over the past ten years, I had been to the region many times with West Virginia Senators Robert Byrd and Jennings Randolph and with House colleagues Bob Mollohan and Pat Jennings. I had driven its winding country roads, stopped at crossroads mountain towns, eased my way into conversations with the people. Most of the inhabitants, I learned, lived on hillside farms and in little "ribbon towns," which meander among the hollows and valleys of the mountain range, largely isolated from the world and from one another. Yesterdays of neglect had left their stain. Family income for the sixteen million Americans who inhabited its mountains lagged a full 35 percent behind the rest of the nation. Coal, timber, and marginal farming, the three historic pillars of the economy, had all deteriorated as fonts of income. The remote inaccessibility of the vast rural interior long had discouraged industry.

The Appalachian bill was the result of more than four years of intensive planning. Former President Kennedy, shocked by the deprivations he witnessed there in 1960, began a crusade for a coordinated attack upon the causes of economic paralysis. The congressional committee, on which I served, and its companion in the Senate, after months of hearings, finished drafting and perfecting the legislative package in the summer of 1964. More essential than any other thing was a system of roads to bridge the hills and span the valleys. Only this could open up the hidden wealth of latent water, mineral and recreational resources to profitable job-creating private investments. So the lion's share—$840 million of the financial authorization—was dedicated to highways. Next, in order to convert thousands of welfare recipients into productive taxpayers, we proposed to establish vocational schools to train the youth in new technologies and to reequip with useful skills the legions who'd lost their only livelihood when the coal mines closed. Agriculture, the only remaining staple of the economy, was centered historically on family farms. Generations of erosion and rapacious timber and coal exploitation had left hillsides barren. A program of hillside terracing, contour planting, intelligent reforestation, and sealing of coal voids would help small landowners to hold and improve what they had.

The Appalachian bill sailed through the Senate on February 1 by 62 to 22. In early March we took it to the House floor. I was chairman of the task force to round up votes. In arguing for the bill in speeches and individual appeals to members, I stressed a theme I would use for the rest of my congressional career: *Not a handout, but a hand.* This had been the philosophy behind other strictly regional approaches, I recalled—including the Tennessee Valley Authority and the Great Plains Conservation Act of the 1930s. Experience demonstrated that the approach could work. To westerners, I pointed out that the reclamation program, designed for seventeen underdeveloped western states, by utilizing water resources for irrigation farming in erstwhile deserts, had transformed a formerly backward region into one of the nation's most progressive. I would remind fellow Texans that, ten years earlier, our state's drought-stricken ranchers had received massive federal relief. Without it, many would have been out of business, forced to liquidate their breeding stock. Now they had recovered sufficiently to pay back into the Treasury more than enough taxes to compensate for their benefits. I discovered that, as early as 1785, in our republic's infancy, the Northwest Land Ordinance called upon citizens of the eastern seaboard to share of their bounty with fellow Americans trying to grub out a living north and west of the Ohio River. What we were trying to do for Appalachia was as American as biscuits and gravy. The opposition was vigorous and vocal, but we outnumbered them. After three days of debate, the bill passed by a vote of 257 to 165.

A month later came the Medicare bill, a centerpiece of the Johnson years. The idea of federal aid to help people cope with rising medical costs had been the subject of public debate for decades. Thirty years earlier, when I was a junior high school student in Seminole, Oklahoma, it was the official Interscholastic League debate subject. In all the intervening years, the medical profession and conservative ideologues had quaked in fear of any modicum of governmental assistance, equating any such effort with "socialized medicine." Chairman Wilbur Mills of the House Ways and Means Committee, working with Oklahoma Senator Robert S. Kerr, extracted much of the venom from the opposition. Patiently, Mills called opponents who had spoken out when the idea first surfaced. He asked them to appear before his committee, listened carefully to their objections, worked tirelessly to find areas of accommodation. The finished product was a rare example of congressional creativity. It embodied the better features of President Johnson's proposal along with safeguards suggested by the doctors in a milder "eldercare" plan they were offering as an alternative. Mills also incorporated suggestions advanced by the private insurance industry.

The Medicare bill provided a four-pronged attack on the problem of providing health care for older citizens:

1. A basic *hospital insurance* program, available to everyone over sixty-five.
2. A supplementary *voluntary health insurance* program for those who want it.
3. An expanded Kerr-Mills medical assistance program to extend Federal matching grants to the states for all medically indigent.
4. A 7 percent increase in Social Security benefits.

The private doctor-patient relationship was guaranteed. Physicians would not deal with the government, but with private insurance companies under the optional plan. Each individual was free to select his own doctor or hospital. This pulled the teeth of the medical lobby. The bill passed the house by 313 to 115. One aged legislator, sprawling in an overstuffed chair in the private members-only cloakroom behind the House chamber, took a sip from a coffee cup and commented whimsically: "I've been making campaign speeches in favor of this bill for the past twenty years! I almost hate to see the problem solved. It's been such a fine thing to talk about."

In 1965, Coward-McCann published my first book. It was about the Congress, the thing I knew best. The title was *You and Your Congressman.* It was not an exposé. I didn't try to scandalize the institution with lurid tales of corruption. As a matter of fact, I didn't know any. I was, to the contrary, in love with the Congress. It was my life, and I wanted to share it. In the preface, I laid out my own sentiments in these words: "The Congress of the United States is probably the most fascinating human institution in the world. It is, beyond question, the most criticized legislative assembly on earth and still the most honored. It can rise to heights of sparkling statesmanship and, on occasion, sink to levels of crass mediocrity. In both postures it is always interesting—because it's human. The story of Congress is the story of people."

The book got encouraging critical acclaim while not making a great deal of money. I didn't care. It was a labor of love, and already I was collecting material for the book on the national water crisis. We Presbyterians had always gone in for sprinkling. ("You haven't been baptized; you've just been dry cleaned!" a Baptist friend sometimes chided me.) By now I was being "totally immersed" in the subject of water. From my spot on the Public Works Committee, I was taking on more and more responsibility for the nation's water programs. As a child of Texas, I had seen its effect in feast and famine, the sudden disaster of floods, the slow devastation of drought. Now I was fascinated by the human capacity to overcome the ancient challenge. For the moment, I concentrated on helping to perfect the water quality effort so tentatively undertaken a few years earlier. Our government's pilot program in eight years had encouraged the building of 5,994 modern sewage treatment plants in communities throughout the country. About $500 million in federal grants had stimulated local investments of more than $3 billion in water purity. Impressive though this was, it wasn't nearly enough. The problem, I saw, was outpacing our solutions. Thousands of *local* crises were merging into a *national* crisis.

We passed a bill that spring to expand the existing law to speed the clean up of the nation's waters. The bill increased the matching-grant program to $150 million a year and raised the arbitrary ceiling on individual grants, so that big metropolitan cities, where most of the pollution originates, could participate. We put up money for research grants to find new ways of treating toxic wastes. We encouraged the states to get into the act. There had been opposition when the federal government got into the fight against pollution in 1956. Nine years later, this broader bill passed by 395 to zero. Our enlightened culture was taking notice of the most basic demand of all.

The sources of our growing affluence were also the sources of our growing pollution problems. Our band of true believers in Congress were out to help Lyndon Johnson convert this increasingly affluent society into a "Great Society." For shock effect, I consented to let my New York publishers title my new book *The Coming Water Famine*. An artist painted a scene of cracked dry earth for the dust jacket. New York City, where more books are purchased than anywhere else in our country, was undergoing a terrible drought. Waiters were forbidden to bring a glass of water to the table at restaurants except upon demand. Tiffany's patriotically replaced the water with gin in its window fountain display. Observing all this, my agent gleefully foresaw widespread sales for my book in the Big Apple.

Just before the book went on sale, the rains came. It rained so much, in fact, that New Yorkers began talking about flood relief. Scarcely anybody bought my book. Never mind. I was establishing credentials as a congressional authority on the nation's water problems. I was part of making things better.

Another milestone came with passage of the Voting Rights Act. I threw myself into the effort and spoke for the bill on the House floor, although my help was scarcely needed, as it turned out. To me the act represented an important affirmation of what America should symbolize. A briar patch of superficial tests, devices, and artful subterfuges still denied large segments of our people the right to vote. In some states, arbitrary and hypertechnical "tests" and deliberate delays were employed in a determined design to prevent otherwise qualified African American citizens from voting. The question was whether we were ready, a full century after the Emancipation Proclamation, to trust the descendants of former slaves with the most elemental right of citizenship. As the vote approached, I thought about the late Adlai Stevenson, whom I had so greatly admired. "Trust the people," Stevenson once said. "Trust their good sense, their decency, their fortitude, their faith. Trust them with the facts, trust them with the great decisions." This, I decided, should be our text.

After so many years of subtle and not-so-subtle denial, the act passed the House by a tally of 333 to 85 and the Senate by 77 to 19. Linda Chavez, writing twenty-six years later in the June 24, 1991 *New Republic,* would call this bill "the most radical piece of civil rights legislation ever enacted—and the most effective."

As one after another of the Great Society reforms passed Congress, I took increasing if vicarious satisfaction in Lyndon Johnson's success. Many others in Congress must have felt the same. Lyndon Johnson was *leading* the nation.

Devoted though I was to the president, we sometimes clashed. For ten long years, ever since assignment to the Public Works Committee in my first month, I had been laying the foundation for the major effort I now was ready to launch. Trinity River navigation had been my dream. It was the legacy I wanted to leave to Texas posterity. Every Corps of Engineers dam built on the upper tributaries of the Trinity—at little towns like Benbrook, Grapevine, Lewisville—contained a legal reserve of stored water committed to the long-sought goal of navigation. By bringing barge traffic upstream from the Gulf of Mexico to Fort Worth, we'd get cheaper freight rates. Wheat farmers on the high plains, and cotton farmers as far west as Lubbock would benefit. Gravel and brick and clay producers all over the Trinity basin would be able to get their goods to market more cheaply. The long-neglected small towns in the middle stretch of the river from Houston to Dallas would boom with new industry.

For a decade, I had courted members of the Public Works Committee and others in Congress who could be helpful in achieving the ambitious goal. I had assembled reams of statistics in support of each of the arguments for Trinity development. I had hosted a bipartisan delegation of strategically placed colleagues on a three-day helicopter trip from the point where the Trinity spills into the Gulf of Mexico upstream to the Fort Worth–Dallas metroplex. Now, in mid-1965, the Corps of Army Engineers had completed its decade-long study and reported a favorable economic outlook for Trinity development. But this analysis was hung up in the Bureau of the Budget. Charles Schultze, Johnson's director of BOB, was dragging his feet. The Bureau had not made an *unfavorable* report; it simply had delayed reporting. And time was critical. I had talked with Charlie Schultze on several occasions previously and discovered what I regarded as a general bias against public works per se. Charlie seemed to think they were inflationary, stimulating economic activity long after the need for stimulus had passed. Times were booming, and prices were holding stable, but Schultze worried that the rapid buildup in the Vietnam War effort would unleash inflationary pressures. I went to see him again.

"The engineering study gives it a positive benefit-to-cost ratio," I pointed out. "We need to move on it this year, Charlie. It'll be three more years before another omnibus bill comes along."

"The Army Engineers are always trying to promote water developments," Schultze said. "I'm not sure that I trust their figures."

With that I grew impatient. "History tells a different story, Charlie," I pointed out. "When the Gulf-Intracoastal Canal was authorized between New Orleans and Corpus Christi, the army engineers said it might ultimately carry as much as seven million tons a year. Last year it carried more than fifty million tons! The Ohio River hauls eight or nine times as much tonnage as the engineers forecast!"

In the end, Schultze was unmoved. For some reason, Schultze and the Budget Bureau were trying to protect the president against big expenditures. This one would cost about one billion dollars. I made up my mind I'd talk with President Johnson. The BOB worked for him, after all.

By the time Johnson ushered me into a seat beside his, in a little room on the White House ground floor, I had carefully rehearsed my speech. A few days earlier, I'd signed a discharge petition to bring District of Columbia home rule to the House floor for a vote. To my great surprise President Johnson had called to thank me and ask if there were anything he could do for me. Now I was about to tell him.

"Mr. President, I've always been fascinated by your stories of the frustrations you encountered in trying to develop the lower Colorado River electrification program," I began. "As a young congressman, you turned to the one man you admired the most. You went to Franklin D. Roosevelt, and he countermanded the bureaucratic underlings who were frustrating your efforts. He helped you do for your people the thing they were counting on you to get done."

I thought I'd made a good beginning. I tried to read Lyndon's eyes. I could not discern a response to my opening. I plunged ahead.

"Well, I'm in that same predicament today, and I need your help. As you know, I've spent ten years working on the Trinity River canal project, which you and John Connally and every other Texas leader with any vision have endorsed."

I thought I noticed a twitch of impatience tug at Johnson's face.

"Jim, my BOB people tell me that project is not economically justified," Johnson stated.

"I know that, Mr. President. I've talked with Charlie Schultze. The Corps of Engineers says it *is* justified. It has as good a benefit-to-cost ratio as the Tombigbee in Alabama or the Arkansas River project that Bob Kerr got approved all the way up to Tulsa. I have been collecting the facts for several years, and I believe I can show you—"

President Johnson cut me off. "Jim, I sat and listened to John Connally and Charlie Schultze debate that issue in my presence for thirty minutes last week. When they were finished, no man in his right mind would have sided with John's argument."

Connally was closer to Johnson than I was. If he had failed to move his old boss, I began to wonder what was on Lyndon's mind to make him want to oppose a project he had publicly supported in the past. Could it be a disinclination to appear greedy for his home state? Did the president fear being accused of "pork barrel" politics while the war was going on in Vietnam? His expression told me nothing.

Finally I said, "We both know, of course, that the law does not require Congress to have the permission of the BOB. The Corps of Engineers report is favorable. We have included items in omnibus bills previously with only Corps approval. I've worked on this project too long to drop it, and I don't want to wait for another three years. I believe I can get it passed with or without the BOB sanction, but I surely would like to have your personal blessing."

The president scoffed. "Jim, they'd laugh us both off the House floor if you tried to pass that bill over the Bureau's objection!"

"I don't care if they laugh, Lyndon," I blurted. "I can pass the bill with them laughing."

"*I* do," Johnson replied. "I care."

At that moment, the drone of helicopter engines sounded above the south lawn. A group of governors was arriving for a conference with the president. Our conversation was ended.

As soon as I left the White House, I called Ben Carpenter, who was staying at the Sheraton-Carlton Hotel. Ben was one of the principal leaders of the Trinity booster group in Texas. He'd heard about the problems with the Bureau of the Budget and had flown to Washington to be in town when I talked with the president.

"I feel lower than a snake's belly," Ben moaned when I told him of my conversation with Johnson. "We've put too much effort into this to let it die," he groaned, "but I'm afraid it's dead for now."

"No, it isn't, Ben," I said. "This makes it harder, but I can still pass the bill in Congress."

Like Amon Carter, Jr. in Fort Worth, Ben Carpenter of Dallas was the son of a father who had spearheaded the drive for a navigable waterway a full generation earlier. Too many hopes and dreams had gone into this project over too long a time for me to let it fail.

During that summer, I paraded representatives of some seventy Texas cities before the committee in Washington. They explained that state, local, and private funds of more than $269 million already had gone into taming the sometimes unruly stream and putting its waters to work. They pledged to raise $256 million more to complete the comprehensive plan, which included navigation. In August, 281 Texans crowded into the committee hearing room in support of the Trinity project. "Almost as many people live in this river valley as live in all of Appalachia," I pointedly reminded my colleagues.

In the first week of September, the Rivers and Harbors Subcommittee approved the project by a vote of 13 to 2, and the full committee formally ratified that action on the following day. When the omnibus bill came to the floor, I had so many members lined up from so many parts of the country to speak in behalf of the Trinity Project that nobody even offered a serious effort to amend it from the bill, notwithstanding the Bureau of the Budget's failure to give its approval. The House bill sailed through the Senate with the help of Senator Ralph Yarborough, the Trinity provision intact. President Johnson signed the omnibus bill without a negative murmur. So far as I could learn, nobody spoke a word of criticism against the administration for the Texas project. President Johnson quietly gave me a White House pen he used in signing the omnibus bill.

Mine was, as it turned out almost eight years later, an empty victory. A bond issue for $150 million had to be passed in Texas to guarantee the local share in order to qualify for the more than one billion dollars in federal expenditures. Along with most of the Trinity's supporters, I thought the bond issue would carry easily. It went down in 1973, sunk largely by a big negative vote in Dallas.

In the wake of this victory in 1965, I was riding the crest of a popular wave back home. A lot of people up and down the Trinity Valley and scattered throughout the rest of the state were urging me to run again for the U.S. Senate. John Tower would be up for reelection in 1966. Some of the knee-jerk liberals who had voted for him over Blakley in 1961 were ready to reverse that action now. Yellow dog Democrats of the old school were outraged at a Republican representing our state in the Senate. Some who thought I could not win in 1961, now regretting their lack of support, were ready to make it up to me this time. But I was still deeply in debt from the '61 effort. I had borrowed money personally to pay off all the campaign vendors and even sold my ranch in the country to reduce the debt, but I still owed a very substantial amount. My private source of income from the family business in Weatherford had almost completely dried up. I was not prepared to jeopardize my children's college by taking another costly plunge into statewide politics without evidence of ample financial support.

Importuned by friends and bludgeoned by conscience, I hit upon a scheme. I would make a statewide television broadcast and candidly put my dilemma in the hands of the audience. I would explain exactly how much it cost to rent billboards, how much one statewide mailing would cost. I'd tell the public exactly how much the broadcast itself was costing me. I'd candidly confess my own financial status, explain my unwillingness to beg money from the lobbies or even accept it in big chunks from wealthy private donors. Somewhat arbitrarily, I decided that if as many as twenty-five thousand Texans thought well enough of my running for the Senate to send me ten dollars apiece for the campaign, that would yield a quarter of a million dollars and be enough for openers. If that happened, I'd take the plunge and depend on faith to raise the rest.

It cost right at $10,000 for thirty minutes at 7:30 in the evening of December 16, 1965, on seventeen stations across our state. I tried to get one in each media market. There was a lot of newspaper speculation as to what I would say, and therefore a reasonably broad listening audience. I laid it out as plainly as I could. For the first twenty minutes I described my vision of America and its role in the world. Then I talked frankly about the cost of a statewide race and the need for a lot of small contributions from a very great many people to make it possible for me to run. I said if as many as twenty-five thousand Texans would mail ten dollars each, I'd do it.

There was a broad response. By some measurements it would be counted excellent. More than eight thousand people wrote to send money and urge my candidacy. Their letters were heart-warming. but the numbers fell short of the goal I had explicitly set. After two weeks, I figured I had the bulk of the responses. I held a press conference, announced the results, declared that I would not be a candidate, and sent each of the contributions back with a letter of earnest appreciation to the donor.

Fate has a way of dealing with individual ambitions. Several times earlier in my life it had happened to me. A knee injury in high school had closed the door to one career and turned me toward another. Classmates in college had selected another for president of the student body and made me editor of the college newspaper. Voters in Parker County had rejected me for a second term in the state legislature and eighteen months later elected me mayor of Weatherford. In every case the door that opened was more rewarding to me than the one destiny shut. It would be that way this time, too.

The war in Vietnam was taking its toll. Each time the number of combat troops increased, the decibel level of protest rose. Congress was still support-ive, but, increasingly, members reported hostility on the home front. In early 1966, Congress approved a $4.8 billion supplementary authorization for the war. Only four members in the House and two in the Senate voted against the bill. Some of us hoped that overwhelming vote might dampen propaganda abroad, but this was not to be. Interrogators of captured Vietcong reported that almost all had been intensely indoctrinated to believe that the American people were becoming weary of the struggle, and, like the French before them, would soon withdraw.

The commitment of American troops to Vietnam stood at about 200,000 men in early 1966, already as many as had gone to Korea, but combat deaths were fewer—only about one-eighth the loss rate in the Korean war. Eco-nomically the nation was much better prepared to sustain a prolonged effort than it had been in the early 1950s. Taxes were relatively much lower than at the time of Korea. A measure of affluence had reached many more American families. One of President Johnson's proud achievements of his first two years in office had been a smaller budget deficit each year than forecast. This came about through the rising tide of prosperity which brought heavier than expected tax receipts. In Johnson's third year the steady movement toward a balanced budget fell victim to the rising price tag of the Vietnam effort.

Johnson *was* making peace overtures. He broadcast a speech from Johns Hopkins University in Baltimore, tacitly pledging financial aid to the Ho Chi Minh government in North Vietnam if it would cease its invasion of the South. The bid got no response. Hanoi and Peking seemed frozen like blocks of ice in the rigid demand for our complete military withdrawal as a precon-dition to discussions in any form.

More of us now were getting letters from sons abroad. Mine wrote that he was well, but lonesome for home. Lyndon Johnson later would tell Doris Kearns, the Harvard professor who worked with him on his autobiography, that the war had done him in, had robbed him of his dream. "The kids were right. I blew it," he would say. "I knew from the start that if I left the woman I really loved—the Great Society—in order to fight that bitch of a war . . . then I would lose everything at home."

Johnson kept trying for peace. I watched via television as he received the Freedom Award on February 23, 1966, at a black-tie ceremony in New York. The audience interrupted Johnson's speech repeatedly with applause, but each time a wave of applause came, the cameras homed in on Bobby Kennedy, stone-faced and unapplauding. I remembered a Robert Kennedy speech during the term of his late brother, in which Bobby promised the South Vietnamese we'd not abandon them until we won the final victory. Now he withheld applause from his brother's successor. I wondered if he knew the cameras were focused on him.

At one point President Johnson said: "Men ask who has a right to rule in South Vietnam. Our answer there is what it has been here for two hundred years: The people must have this right—the South Vietnamese people—and no one else. . . . We stand for self-determination—for free elections—and we will honor their result." That set me to thinking. This had to be the key. It might explain why the South Vietnamese seemed so vulnerable to Vietcong propaganda. Maybe one reason they fought no harder in their own defense was the dismal fact that, for the twelve years of its independent status, South Vietnam had *not* elected its national leaders! The country had labored under ten premiers in the past two years, and not one of them was chosen by the people. Little wonder they'd showed such limited enthusiasm for defending their "freedom."

A peace plan began to come into shape in my mind. I couldn't shake it. Whatever else I turned my thoughts to, they'd return to this core of an idea. What a dramatic thing it would be, I decided, if President Johnson could go before the United Nations and there present to the world a clear-cut peace plan based upon that one simple keystone: the will of the people. To begin, he could call for a free election to be held in South Vietnam—not next year but this year—in which the people could chose by ballots, not bullets, just what sort of government they wanted and whom they wanted for their leaders. Our president could propose that these elections be supervised by the U.N., to avoid being rigged by either side, and preceded by a U.N.–supervised six weeks truce to provide a proper atmosphere for their conduct. Both sides would be asked to agree in advance to respect and abide by the results of the elections. On what defensible basis could Hanoi or the Vietcong refuse? A turndown would expose as fraud their pretense at representing the popular will.

As a second stage, under my scenario, the president would submit a concrete proposal for similar free elections, perhaps two years later, in which all the people of North and South Vietnam could vote on unification as decreed in the Geneva Accords of 1954. Spokesmen for both North and South were professing to want reunification—but each on its own terms. The Geneva agreement specified that nationwide elections would be conducted in July 1956 for this purpose. South Vietnamese leaders were suspicious that free balloting would be subverted in the Northern zone, and the solemn agreement was never kept. Much of the bitterness that provoked the war stemmed from that failure—a fact many Americans did not realize.

Thinking I had a worthwhile idea, I put it in memorandum form and began trying it out on various people. I asked for an appointment with President Johnson and broached the idea. I took with me a copy of our joint declaration with Great Britain, made in Washington on June 20, 1954. It read: "In cases of nations now divided against their will, we shall continue to seek unity through free elections, supervised by the United Nations to insure that they are conducted fairly."

"So, Mr. President," I said to Johnson. "We've really said these things before at different times and places." At worst, I argued, a clear proposal like this coming from the president would put Hanoi on the psychological defensive. If the overture failed, I argued, then all the world would know we really had tried, and everybody would have a clearer idea just what we were fighting for. And if Hanoi should accept, it might pave the way to the conference table and an honorable settlement.

The president seemed tired. When I finished telling him of my suggestion, he sighed. "Jim, everything you say makes sense to me, but what makes sense to us doesn't make sense to them. I'd be glad to talk, but they don't want to talk." He shook his head sadly. "All they want to do is fight and die."

For the first time since I'd known him, I suddenly felt sorry for Lyndon Johnson, this man whom I admired so much.

"Tell you what I'd like for you to do, Jim," he said. "Go and talk this all over with Walt Rostow. He is putting together some thoughts for me on this, and he'd like to ponder this idea you have brought to me. Maybe we can do something like that, and if not right now, maybe later on."

So I talked with Walt Rostow, who seemed almost as frustrated as the president over the implacable attitude of the Ho Chi Minh government. He sent me to see Abe Fortas, whom Johnson had nominated to the Supreme Court. "Abe Fortas has President Johnson's ear. If anyone can show him a new approach, it would be Abe." I had a visit with Mr. Fortas, whom I'd met only four or five times casually. Abe Fortas was convinced that the only thing Hanoi would ever understand was force. "They will never come to the table willingly," he said. "The only thing we can do is to make the war cost them more than they're willing to pay."

My peace plan died aborning.

But I was up to my eyebrows in the Great Society.

CHAPTER THIRTEEN

THAT BITCH
OF A WAR

"**G**eorge," said the president, "the Senate passed the Highway Beautification Bill last night. If you can get it through your committee before the end of this week, I think I can get the Speaker to schedule it for the House floor next week!"

It was Lyndon Johnson at his persuasive best. He was talking with George Fallon, chairman of the House Public Works Committee. At issue was Mrs. Johnson's pet project, Highway Beautification. People already had taken to referring to it as "The Lady Bird Bill."

"Mr. President," Congressman Fallon stammered, "We're going to do all we can to pass your bill, but I don't see how we could possibly do it that fast. There is a certain amount of opposition on the House side, and—"

"The longer you delay, the stronger the opposition will get," insisted the president. "Move now, and they won't have a lot of time to get organized!"

"Mr. President, a lot of members have already notified me that they'll have amendments to offer in committee. We haven't even begun the mark-up yet. It may take a full week to consider these amendments and report the bill from our committee."

"Why don't you just take the Senate bill?" Johnson persisted. "They've already considered all those amendments!"

"We don't even have a copy of the Senate bill yet." The urbane chairman was feeling unaccustomed pressure. "There probably won't be an engrossed copy of the Senate's final bill for two or three more days, anyway. And our own members want—"

"That's a poor excuse, George. I can get you a copy in five minutes. All you have to do is clip the language of each amendment out of today's *Congressional Record* and paste it up on a piece of paper!"

George Fallon of Maryland was an easy-going man. He caught the train for Baltimore every afternoon at five o'clock and enjoyed a leisurely drink in the club car. He usually arrived at his office on Tuesdays through Thursdays just in time to chair a ten o'clock meeting of the full Public Works Committee. Now, Fallon tried to explain to the dynamo in the White House all the trouble he'd have if he even suggested bypassing the orderly procedure. Sitting in a big blue leather chair not more than four feet from the Chairman in the comfortable little ante-room adjacent to the committee chamber, I grinned. I knew how insistent Lyndon Johnson could be, and I knew how determined he was to pass this particular bill as a present to his wife.

"He's in a big hurry for this one, isn't he?" I said.

"Jim, I've never heard anybody so much in a hurry. Is he always like that? He thinks I can pass that bill just by banging the gavel out there in the committee room. He doesn't have any idea how hard it's going to be to get that bill through the House in any form at all, let alone the way the Senate passed it."

"He doesn't care, George. This one's for Lady Bird. I'll try to help you, but I think we're going to have to take some sweetening amendments."

For the next two weeks, we struggled our way through the committee mark-up sessions. There was plenty of opposition and a lot of earnest debate.

Several White House operatives led by Larry O'Brien haunted our committee meetings. At one point Republicans on the committee made a point of order about their presence in the room.

"This is an executive session, Mr. Chairman," said Republican Bill Cramer of Florida. "That means members of the committee only, doesn't it?"

The White House emissaries retired to the ante-room, where they'd call the White House each time an amendment was offered and send word in to some of their friends that the amendment was not "acceptable." I was one of their "friends," but I soon grew weary with their efforts to micro-manage the bill. It was as though I were a base-runner, and they had to coach me from the sidelines whether to stop on third or try for home. By the time we got the Highway Beautification Bill through our committee a lot of resentment had arisen over the White House tactics. Even some members who wanted to beautify the highways considered the administration's position high-handed and arbitrary.

The bill had three basic parts: billboard control, screening of junkyards from the public view, and scenic enhancement of the highway rights-of-way through planting and landscaping. It was the first that drew most of the heat. In many locations along the busiest thoroughfares, outdoor signs had become cluttered, crowded, and garish, an eyesore. On the other hand, travelers on our interstate highways wanted a certain amount of information available primarily through billboards. They wanted to know where to stop for a bite of lunch or a cold drink, what brand of gasoline was being sold around the next bend, what overnight accommodations provided a swimming pool or a bar or a dining facility. Advertising was a legitimate American enterprise, after all. Billboards were located on private property. They yielded a modicum of extra revenue to farmers and ranchers. Those who drafted the original bill for the White House were in favor of encouraging states to use police power to take down offending billboards. They wanted to remove all the signs from the Interstate Highways immediately. Both Democrats and Republicans in the House fretted that we were being swept along too fast. They worried that tearing down a person's billboard, a thing of intrinsic value, amounted to confiscation of property without cause.

On the day we took the bill to the floor, a few of us met in Speaker McCormack's office for a preliminary discussion. Fallon had asked me to be floor leader for the bill. Majority Leader Carl Albert reported widespread disenchantment among House Democrats. "Isn't there some way we can sweeten this up, at least with some guarantees against arbitrary abuse of power?" he asked.

Larry O'Brien spoke up immediately: "I don't have authority to agree to any changes. If you want any change, I'll have to call the White House and get their approval."

"It's too late for that now, Larry," I told him. "When the bell rings, we are going to have to go out there on the House floor and make our own judgments. If I think an amendment will help us pass the bill, and if it's reasonable, I'm going to accept it. You fellows will just have to go and sit in the gallery and leave the judgments to members of the House."

We took two amendments that were offered by a new member from Georgia named Russell Tuten. One provided that no lawfully existent property could be taken without the government's paying "just compensation" to its owner. The other decreed that size and space limitations on advertising signs within incorporated cities would leave something to the discretion of the local governing bodies. They'd follow "customary usage" in each town. A third provision, to which we agreed, protected the right of any business person to have a sign on his own place of business identifying it to the public. Thus fortified, the Highway Beautification Bill passed the House.

Lyndon Johnson demanded a lot of himself and a great deal of his associates. He insisted on results. He reminded Clark Clifford of "a powerful old-fashioned locomotive roaring unstoppably down the track." He sometimes bullied and intimidated his underlings. But then, realizing his excesses, he could be suddenly sensitive and so spontaneously generous that he won their undeviating loyalty. It is only natural, given his temperament and his impatience with failure, that Johnson's appointees sometimes stretched the limits of their legal authority to carry out policies in ways they thought would please him. Sometimes they ignored clear provisions of laws written by Congress. Highly allergic to this tendency in the executive branch, Congress began to itch in various parts of its anatomy, as with a case of poison ivy.

The housing committees set up a howl over the way the Rent Supplement Act was being run. Congress made it clear in passing this program initially that benefits must be confined to "low income" families. The first draft of administrative guidelines to carry out the law would let families earning as much as fifteen thousand dollars a year get help from the rest of the taxpayers. In the mid-1960s, that was a substantial income. Congress blew the whistle. Next, the House Commerce Committee scheduled hearings into the use of wiretaps by the Internal Revenue Service. The Communications Act of 1934 provided that "no person" would be allowed to "intercept and divulge" telephone conversations. The Supreme Court, as early as 1939, ruled that federal agents may not legally tap telephones. Now IRS agents were discovered breaking into homes and offices, in clear violation of law, to plant tiny radio transmitters and other bugging devices.

Another discovery raised the hackles of my committee. The Public Works Committee wrote the Economic Development Act of 1965, and I supported it. It allowed grants for roads and utilities to attract various commercial enterprises to small backwater communities and urban pockets of poverty. The law also authorized government loans to start viable new businesses in these neglected areas. But we had carefully required that no government loans should be used to finance any new enterprise where the present demand for its goods or services was "not sufficient . . . to employ efficient capacity of *existing* competitive commercial or industrial enterprises." In spite of this injunction, we found that people administering this program had okayed taxpayer loans that in some cases set up direct competition for existing firms. A new clay pipe manufacturing company sprang up in Oklahoma with the help of such a loan and took business from existing plants as far away as Texas and Kansas. Those plants had to lay off workers. Congress bridles at any attempt by an executive agent to ignore the written mandates of the legislative branch.

The evidences of runaway bureaucracy were putting me on an uncomfortable spot. The Highway Beautification Act became a case in point. The law expressly decreed that standards on size, spacing, and lighting of billboards would comply with "customary usage." Hideous, outsized or abnormally cluttered signboards along the highways inside city limits would come down, but the others would stay. The federal bureau charged with carrying out the program utterly ignored that requirement. It promulgated standards which, if followed, would destroy approximately 80 percent of all the properties owned by legitimate outdoor advertising firms. This would throw thousands of people out of work and cost the government an estimated $2.9 billion. Even after the effect of these administrative dicta was called to the attention of the regulators by those who actually wrote the law, the Bureau persisted. Faced with growing complaints from colleagues whom I had implored to vote for some of these programs, I vented my frustrations in a newsletter on April 28, 1967: "As everybody knows, I am a Johnson man. I have supported the president actively and enthusiastically in each of his political campaigns. . . . But, the . . . president needs to tighten the screws on his appointed administrators and tell them that Congress still makes the laws. He spent twenty-five years of his life on Capitol Hill. He should know this better than anyone."

President Johnson read my newsletter and was horrified. At his next cabinet meeting, Johnson passed around copies of my newsletter and lectured the top lieutenants of the Great Society to keep their administrators and regulators within the boundaries set forth by Congress. I was prouder than ever of our president.

Exciting results began to surface from some of the Great Society experiments. In my home town of Fort Worth, an African American educator named Dr. John Barnett conducted a trail-blazing effort among ghetto children. It was his mission, along with other pioneers in a handful of America's inner-cities, to develop and validate a curriculum of directed learning experiences for "culturally deprived" preschool children. His school, located in Fort Worth's economically backward North Side, admitted only youngsters from homes where neither parent was available during the day. Most were one-parent homes. At Barnett's invitation I visited his school and became a disciple. He was achieving infinitely more than I had imagined possible. Dr. Barnett proudly showed me scores from nationally recognized testing systems. Many of his daytime charges doubled their I.Q. measurements in the school's first year.

The Job Corps was beginning to chalk up an impressive record in reclaiming dropouts for useful, taxpaying roles in society by giving them marketable skills. I invited Sargent Shriver, initial director of the Peace Corps and now head of the Job Corps, to speak to a dinner I arranged in Fort Worth. Eight hundred civic leaders were impressed with the performance he reported to us.

Julius Truelson, Superintendent of the Fort Worth school district, was ecstatic over gains we were beginning to see in English language proficiency among youngsters from Spanish-speaking homes. "Give our schools one generation of continued support, and we'll wipe out poverty," he once boasted to me. "Absolutely wipe it out!"

But inspiring as this record of social progress was, the darkening cloud of Vietnam hovered ever more ominously. Waves of antiwar protests spread across the country. My eldest daughter, Ginger, graduated from Yorktown High School in suburban northern Virginia that spring. Ginger was popular, head cheerleader and Homecoming Queen in her senior year. Our house was a frequent gathering place for students. Most of them were friendly, polite, respectful. Imagine my shock when the salutatorian, a young man whom I'd met several times, launched into a formal diatribe before students and assembled parents against the "power structure." He claimed parents, leaders, authority figures of all types were both insensitive and stupid. Slightly embarrassed by the lad's bad taste, I burned in amazement as the students greeted his monologue with wild applause.

The protests began to take on racial overtones. Johnson had been concerned that they might. All of his heartfelt solicitude over racial deprivation could not alter the fact that blacks represented a disproportionate share of the young Americans serving in combat. The president favored military deferments to let serious students finish college. He meant this for students of every race, but the social reality was that it deferred induction for a greater percentage of white youths than for those of racial minorities. Seizing upon this fact, Harlem's congressman, Adam Clayton Powell, compared our policies to those of Hitler. Martin Luther King, quite possibly the nation's most respected black leader, gradually expanded his cries for racial equality to embrace an antiwar position. In doing so he rejected personal pleas from the president who had done so much to relieve racial injustice.

In the hot July of 1967, Detroit suffered a week of rioting in which thirty-eight people died. A few days later, black-power advocate H. Rap Brown called on blacks to "wage guerrilla war on the honkie white man." In Cambridge, Maryland, fires broke out after Brown urged a crowd of young blacks to "burn this town down." Michigan's Republican Governor George Romney, in an outrageous attempt to turn political capital from the rioting, blamed President Johnson, saying his Great Society programs had raised "false hopes" among blacks.

Protests were hardly confined to the black community. More and more, the issue of the war divided families. Most often, the division line was generational. My son, now in Vietnam by his own choosing, was expressing second thoughts about our military presence there. My sister Mary became so vociferous in her antiwar convictions that it was no longer pleasant for me to be in her company. As intensely as I had searched for an honorable solution, I believed we now had no choice but to see it through. Our public display of disunity, I felt, was quite certainly prolonging the war.

In the last week of September 1967, President Johnson signed a $70 billion military appropriations bill. Never before in our 177 year history—not even during World War II—had Congress passed so large an appropriation for any purpose. Our military personnel commitment to Vietnam escalated to 525,000. Johnson tirelessly probed for some way to bring the conflict to an end. Hanoi remained intractable. So did the critics at home.

At the other end of the spectrum from the peace demonstrators were the hard-liners, who wanted us to use nuclear weapons on North Vietnam. This sentiment surfaced one night at the White House. Fifty or so members had gathered after dinner in the East Room. Secretary of State Dean Rusk and Defense Secretary Robert McNamara briefed the group on the latest military and diplomatic initiatives. Then it was time for questions. Basil Whitener, a tall, slow-talking representative from North Carolina gained recognition. "Mr. President, let me tell you what my folks back home are saying," he drawled. "My folks are saying we ought to drop the big bomb on Hanoi and get it over with. They also think we ought to blow up all those ships coming into Haiphong, trading with our enemy!"

The room grew silent. Johnson answered slowly and very calmly.

"Is that your opinion?" the president asked.

"Yes, Mr. President, it is," responded Whitener.

"Well, you see," said Johnson, "there's a basic difference between an *opinion* and a *decision.* You're certainly entitled to your opinion. But I can't be content with just an opinion. I have to make a decision."

He let that sink in, then continued.

"I could very easily do what you suggest. I could order the Air Force to drop the 'big bomb,' as you call it, on Hanoi tonight. We could reduce the whole city to a rubble of radioactive ashes. We could put a bomb down the smokestack of every ship in Haiphong harbor—all those Chinese ships, and Russian ships, and British ships . . ."

He paused again.

"But, then, tomorrow," the president continued, "tomorrow, if bombs were falling on Washington, you could call me up on the phone—if you and I were both still here—and you could say: 'Mr. President, that's not just exactly what I had in mind.'"

"That bitch of a war"—a war he felt he had inherited—kept robbing Lyndon Johnson of the victories he'd worked so hard to attain. As 1967 wound down, it became increasingly evident that the war protest movement was taking a toll of our people's capacity to communicate in civil discourse. We hurled words past one another's ears, but the meanings did not connect.

No man could have tried harder than Lyndon Johnson. Few if any could have done more. He declared war on poverty and dealt it powerful blows. He passionately worked to help the poor. His was the leadership that abolished the poll tax, launched the Model Cities program, created the Department of Housing and Urban Development, lifted immigration quotas and opened the nation's arms to persecuted foreigners, gave food to hungry kids so they could learn more in school, provided grants and student loans that opened college doors for hundreds of thousands of young people otherwise denied.

Marches, chants, and slogans became the stuff of public expression. On October 21, capping a week of protests in several cities, tens of thousands of antiwar demonstrators gathered in Washington and marched on the Pentagon, vowing to "shut it down." Carrying Vietcong flags and "Dump Johnson" banners, the mob, led by radicals David Dellinger and Jerry Rubin, screamed epithets at guards massed in front of the building bearing rifles and tear gas grenades. A small group actually worked its way into the building before being forcefully expelled.

On November 29, Secretary of Defense Robert S. McNamara resigned his post to take a less prestigious job as president of the World Bank. This set in motion a wave of speculation. A year earlier, McNamara had warned that our massive bombing was not moving Hanoi any closer to the peace table. Wearied by the frustrations of seeking signs of hope in the dreary landscape of war, he now looked forward to helping less developed nations through the World Bank. On the following day, Senator Eugene McCarthy of Minnesota, an outspoken war critic, announced that he would challenge President Johnson in several Democratic primaries for the presidential nomination.

In the third week of 1968, twenty thousand North Vietnamese troops surrounded five thousand American marines at Khesanh and cut them off from allied supply lines. Then, at the beginning of the Tet religious holiday, North Vietnamese and Vietcong launched a massive offensive, their largest and most determined of the war. They targeted all the cities of South Vietnam. A suicide squad blew a large hole in the wall of the American Embassy in Saigon. North Vietnamese forces actually took over our embassy grounds for five hours. They did not relinquish the yard until all of them had been killed.

For all its titanic terror, the Tet offensive was a military failure. Communist forces suffered more than four times the fatality rate of allied personnel. But it was a propaganda success. Most Americans, reading the daily news accounts and seeing the stretchers of dead and wounded vividly paraded on nightly television, believed Hanoi had scored a major victory.

In the March 11 New Hampshire primary, Senator Eugene McCarthy received 42 percent of the vote to Lyndon Johnson's 58 percent. Under other circumstances this might have been described as a landslide for Johnson. But McCarthy's campaign had captured the fancy of the media. News commentaries were referring to the 42 percent showing as McCarthy's "surprise win." More significantly, the public was increasingly weary with the war. The Gallup poll showed that while heavy majorities supported President Johnson's domestic program, only 26 percent now favored his handling of the war.

Then, on March 31, Johnson announced over television that he would not be a candidate for reelection. The Vietnam conflict, he declared, had created a deepening "division in the American house." The president had billed the speech as a report on the war. "Tonight," he began, "I want to speak to you of peace in Vietnam and Southeast Asia." He recited our government's repeated overtures to a peaceful settlement and announced a new peace offensive. He offered to stop the bombardment of North Vietnam and asked Hanoi to sit down with us for talks on peace. As a token of good faith, he announced a substantial reduction in our military activities. We would halt our attacks in areas that included 90 percent of North Vietnam's people and in the food producing areas. Johnson appealed to President Ho Chi Minh to respond "positively, and favorably, to this new step toward peace."

The president's speech was almost over when he dropped the bombshell:

> With America's sons in the fields far away, with America's future under challenge right here at home, with our hopes and the world's hopes for peace in the balance every day, I do not believe that I should devote an hour or a day of my time to any personal partisan causes or to any duties other than the awesome duties of this office—the Presidency of your country.
>
> Accordingly, I shall not seek, and I will not accept, the nomination of my party for another term as your president.

A few days later, the president called. "Jim, I have nine months left in office," he said. "I want you to tell me what I can do for you in that time to show how much I appreciate all the wonderful things you've done for me over the years."

Accustomed as I was to Lyndon Johnson's notorious unpredictabilities, the impulsive generosity of this gesture took me by surprise. No doubt he was making similar calls to others. That did not diminish the genuineness of his offer. Critics called him crude, and he could be that. He also knew how to be gracious.

"There's one thing I think of, Mr. President," I replied. "Come out to Fort Worth this June and speak at the TCU commencement. That will be the greatest thrill of those students' lives. And let me have a public reception for you where you can say whatever you'd like to all the folks out there who love you so much."

It was at the graduation ceremony for Texas Christian University that year that President Johnson first called for lowering the voting age to eighteen. I couldn't help thinking, as I listened, of all those eighteen-year-old kids in Vietnam and others getting ready to go. I thought of my son, Jimmy. Could I, and should I, have dissuaded him from enlisting? Would I ever forgive myself if he were wounded? Or worse? I couldn't bring my mind to form the word.

Was it my example, something I had done or failed to do, that made Jimmy leave college and enlist? Olin "Tiger" Teague and I, so far as I was aware, were the only congressional parents with sons in the war. Had I glorified patriotism excessively? Had I shown undue contempt for those who avoid duty to country? Who, though rich, do not pay taxes? Who, though strong, do not . . . ? Was my son trying to please me?

Lyndon Johnson was ending his speech. The eighteen-year-old vote was so much an extension of everything else he'd said and done. It was a broadening of participation, a widening of opportunity, an inclusion of those left out. He wanted to spread out all the good things of life so everybody could have some. That was the thrust of his career.

The bitterness and polarization of the time stood in contrast to Johnson's mission. Martin Luther King was murdered on April 4. He was thirty-nine. His death touched off an angry wave of riots in stunning contradistinction to his lifelong preachment of non-violence. On June 6 Robert Kennedy died from point-blank gunshot wounds inflicted by a crazed immigrant named Sirhan Sirhan. "Good Lord, what is this all about?" exclaimed New York's Cardinal Cushing. "We could continue our prayers that it would never happen again, but we did that before."

On May 10, the United States and the North Vietnamese began peace talks in Paris. Johnson's appeal had stimulated a modicum of movement.

Johnson having withdrawn from the presidential race, I threw myself into the Hubert Humphrey campaign. The vice president and I had begun a personal friendship. I liked his candor, his spirit, his genuine friendliness for people of all sorts. Hubert Humphrey was warm, imaginative, enthusiastic, and tireless. He also was loyal. People tried to goad him into distancing himself from Johnson, but he would not do so. Senators Walter Mondale of Minnesota and Fred Harris of Oklahoma headed up Humphrey's preconvention bid for the nomination. The vice president asked two of us from the House, Jim O'Hara of Michigan and me, to represent his interest on the Rules and Credentials committees.

The Chicago convention was a maelstrom. It was as though some powerful lens had gathered all the piercing gleams of hatred, anger, and frustration from throughout the country and focused them in one mighty beam upon the city. Outside the Hilton Hotel, streets roiled with unrest. Antiwar demonstrators occupied Grant Park across the street from the headquarters hotel and massed in front of buses carrying delegates to the convention center, impeding their progress. A few delegates were frightened. Many were angry. Some applauded the demonstrators. The mood on both sides grew tense and ugly.

Whenever delegates left the security of the hotel lobby to venture into the streets, some would be surrounded by mobs of mostly young people screaming slogans. "Dump the Hump!" was one of their favorites. Looking into the eyes of some of these agitated youths, I wondered how many of them knew of Hubert Humphrey's beginnings. How many knew his career had its genesis in the reform movement? How many had any awareness of his successful battles for human rights, for social progress?

No doubt most of the peace demonstrators were motivated by idealistic purpose. The large majority wanted to influence the elected delegates by non-violent means. One huge banner proclaimed: "WARS WILL CEASE WHEN MEN REFUSE TO FIGHT." But a remnant agitated for physical confrontation. They got it. After three days of remarkable restraint, in which police had stood impassive under orders, the police responded with all the passion of pent-up fury. They arrested 650. Leaving Grant Park, demonstrators headed southward through the city for an announced march on the amphitheater where delegates were conducting convention business. Under orders to protect the proceedings, police turned back the marchers. Clubs and rocks flew as news cameras rolled, recording the ugly scene. This, apparently, was what the more militant of the protesters had wanted. "The whole world's watching! The whole world's watching!" they chanted. In the end, some seven hundred demonstrators and eighty police reported injuries.

Inside the convention, McCarthy and McGovern delegates were pushing for a resolution condemning America's involvement in the Vietnam war. Hubert Humphrey asked me to speak against the effort in the Resolutions Committee. Shirley Maclane and Paul Newman appeared and made arguments for it. I argued that a public repudiation of our country's position would send exactly the wrong message to Hanoi, now that North Vietnam's leaders had finally agreed to peace talks at President Johnson's urging. The antiwar resolution was defeated in the committee and on the floor of the convention. Humphrey was nominated.

The first nationwide poll showed Humphrey trailing sixteen points behind Republican nominee Richard Nixon. I sent telegrams to several hundred Democratic activists throughout Texas and invited them to join me in Fort Worth to plan a campaign. We met there in early September. Will Davis of Waco, Bob Strauss of Dallas, and I led the effort. Bob undertook the difficult chore of fund raising among the party's relatively few big contributors. I went to Austin and opened a headquarters there in the Commodore Perry Hotel. For the six weeks until election day, I did not return to Washington except for an occasional flight in and out, usually on the same day. I buried myself in the Humphrey campaign. In October we organized a speaking tour through the state for vice presidential nominee Edmund Muskie, and on the next week brought Humphrey in for a six-city tour. I hosted a luncheon for him in Fort Worth, where we featured remarks from both Governor John Connally and Senator Ralph Yarborough. For several years the two had feuded publicly. Their joint appearance and sharing of the head table were heralded as a peace-making miracle. Bob Strauss and I met privately with Vice President Humphrey before the luncheon. Strauss commented about my "brass" in asking the two political heavyweights to share the podium. "Wright has all the pride and reticence of a whore," he quipped.

"I think he means that as a compliment, Mr. Vice President," I offered somewhat lamely.

On the eve of the Humphrey trip, I sat at my typewriter and wrote a twenty-eight-minute television script. I hired a professional camera crew to accompany the entourage across the state for video footage. I had raised enough money for one statewide TV broadcast and booked time for the evening of the day following Humphrey's departure from the state. With only twenty-four hours to view the film and marry it to my script, I embarked upon what might have been the most frantic twenty-four hours of my life. The crew had shot reel upon reel of footage, most of which did not correspond to the script as I'd written it. I had to do a lot of rewriting and pasting. We couldn't postpone the show. With the patient help of veteran television producer Jett Jamison, I finally finished gluing the patchwork together into one twenty-eight-minute tape just twenty minutes before air time. Not trusting the homemade script to unfamiliar eyes, I narrated the piece myself. It was the only statewide television program the Texas Humphrey campaign had been able to afford up to that point. There were just about ten days to go.

On the Sunday before Tuesday's election, Texas Democrats packed Houston's Astrodome. President Johnson spoke, warmly endorsing Humphrey. We carried Texas, and it turned out to be the only presidential election since 1924 in which a Texas majority went differently from the nation. As we eked out a Texas victory for Humphrey, the nation was going narrowly for Nixon.

Richard Nixon would tell of seeing a sign in a crowd which triggered his imagination. The sign read: "PLEASE BRING US TOGETHER AGAIN." That, said Richard Nixon, was what he would like to do.

Damn shame, I thought. That's what Lyndon wanted to do, too.

CHAPTER FOURTEEN

BRING US
TOGETHER

R ichard Milhous Nixon was a remarkable man, little understood
and insufficiently appreciated for his contributions to world
peace. He was gleefully demonized by some in my party. Unlike
more gregarious predecessors in office, Nixon often withdrew
behind an almost glacial reserve. Even some who worked closely with him
considered him as enigmatic as a cross between the Sphinx and Whistler's
Mother. Yet I developed a feeling that, behind the facade of controlled emotions and sometimes contrived conviviality, there lived a warm person eager
to be known but almost afraid to be.

Nixon's political career was a collection of paradoxes. It began when he
answered a newspaper ad seeking a young war veteran to oppose incumbent
Congressman Jerry Voorhies; soared to a level of professionalism seldom
matched; and ended twenty-eight years later in his gut-wrenching resignation
from the presidency. Catapulted up the political ladder by appeals to the
nation's fear of Communism, Nixon actually did more than any other
post–World War II president to thaw relations with the Soviet Union and
China and to set into motion the end to the Cold War.

At the outset of Nixon's term in office, I was highly skeptical. Like many in
my party, I had bought off on the "Tricky Dick" image. I saw Nixon as intelligent, articulate, and verbally persuasive, but lacking in sincerity and warmth.
The first time I heard him speak was at a convention of Chamber of
Commerce managers in Seattle in 1950. A new senator in the heyday of
McCarthyism, Nixon that day fanned flames of mistrust for suspected commie sympathizers. He openly questioned the presumption of innocence for

anyone taking the Fifth Amendment. "How can such a person expect to be believed?" he asked.

Nixon carved out a career with verbal knives sharpened on the Red scare. I had not admired the appeals to hysteria, which, filtered through press reports and enlarged by outbursts of Democratic indignation, seemed to characterize his California campaigns against Jerry Voorhies and Helen Gahagan Douglas. ("Pink down to her underwear," Nixon was reported to have said of her.) Still, I told myself that he may have changed, matured in the crucible of two defeats. Some observers were saying they saw signs of a "new Nixon." Now, he was our president, and I wanted to believe that he had changed. I wanted him to succeed.

Richard Nixon never lacked political courage, I told myself. Nor were his convictions mere figments of convenience. I studied several of his old speeches and found a lot of publicly stated positions, particularly in the international arena, with which I agreed. As I analyzed them now, I was happily surprised. His discourses echoed the teachings of Woodrow Wilson, whose speeches I devoured as a student and whose philosophy I heartily embraced. Nixon played political hardball and had an instinct for the jugular in the domestic political arena, true enough. During his presidency I was to oppose him vigorously on several economic and even constitutional issues. Yet we became friends. He did not smile easily, joke freely, or laugh often. To fight hard was part of his character. So was hard work and homework, inseparable parts of the Quaker heritage absorbed in his mother's home. But he also knew when to subordinate partisanship to patriotism. After the 1960 election, a razor-thin margin in each of several states tilting the balance barely to John F. Kennedy, there were several reports of vote fraud and pleas by prominent Republicans that Nixon, the GOP standard bearer, demand a recount. Nixon refused. Earl Mazo of the *New York Herald Tribune* began a series of articles questioning the results. Nixon personally persuaded the writer to desist. "Our country can't afford the agony of a constitutional crisis," Nixon told him, "and I damn well will not be a party to creating one."

Now, in the wake of the 1968 election, Nixon the victor by a similarly narrow margin, I remembered that. Seated on the steps of the Capitol's east front listening to Nixon's inaugural speech, I thought of it again when he said: "The greatest honor history can bestow is the title of peacemaker. This honor now beckons America—the chance to help lead the world at last out of the valley of turmoil and onto that high ground of peace that man has dreamed of since the dawn of civilization." If this is what he really wants to do, I decided, I'll damn well try to help.

Perhaps no other president, except for Lincoln, had a harder task holding the nation together in the face of internally combustible divisions. Widening domestic polarization over our involvement in Vietnam rocked the White House repeatedly, shattering all hope of the new president's success in his first announced goal: "to bring the American people together." President Nixon's "Vietnamization plan," vaguely alluded to in the campaign and elaborated upon during his first months in office, was to extricate American forces from Southeast Asia while preserving South Vietnam's right to political independence. He wanted a gradual disengagement, training South Vietnamese to assume responsibility for their self-defense while appealing to the North for a negotiated settlement. But try as he might, he never could persuade antiwar protesters at home to give his plan a chance.

On February 23, the North Vietnamese launched a major offensive in one hundred cities of South Vietnam. They seemed to gather strength and encouragement from each new headlined report of protests on the home front. My old friend, Senator George McGovern, with whom I had traveled the roads of South Dakota during his first House reelection campaign in 1958, now joined Arkansas Senator Bill Fulbright and a growing number of other congressional Democrats in outspoken opposition to our involvement in Southeast Asia. Once, near desperation, the president pleaded at the White House with hard-line congressional opponents to give him "just one month" without publicly criticizing his Vietnam policy, "so that I can speak to Hanoi without being drowned out."

In late February of that first year in office, Nixon made a quick trip to Europe. In a week of whirlwind visits, he consulted with heads of state and other leaders in Belgium, Great Britain, Germany, Italy, and France. In public speeches and private conversations, he tried to assure our western European allies that, despite appearances to the contrary, the American people were united in support of American foreign policy.

On May 14, the president delivered a comprehensive speech via television to the American people. The entire message dealt with his administration's goals in Vietnam and the so far unavailing efforts to negotiate peace with the North. Our one indispensable objective, he stressed, was the opportunity for the South Vietnamese "to determine their own political future without outside interference." Nixon was on solid philosophical ground, hewing to the Wilsonian principle of self-determination so deeply embedded in the American character. He made a personal appeal to Americans who had been opposing the country's efforts in Vietnam:

> *Tonight, all I ask is that you consider these facts, and, whatever our differences, that you support a program which can lead to a peace we*

*can live with and a peace we can be proud of. Nothing could have a
greater effect in convincing the enemy that he should negotiate in
good faith than to see the American people united behind a generous
and reasonable peace offer.*

In Baltimore on June 6, the so-called Catonsville Nine were convicted in a
state court of charges that stemmed from their willful destruction of Selective
Service records. The group, which included two Catholic priests, Daniel and
Philip Berrigan, had broken into the Catonsville, Maryland, draft board
offices and burned the files in protest of the war. A federal court also found
them guilty, but neither verdicts by the courts nor appeals from the president
did anything to stanch the flow of protest.

The monody of disparagement was broken briefly on July 20 by the landing of astronauts Neil Armstrong and Edwin "Buzz" Aldrin on the moon.
Americans everywhere were riveted to television screens as Armstrong
bounced and glided over the powdery lunar surface. His words, through the
vast nothingness of space, were faint but audible: "One small step for man,
one giant leap for mankind." Nixon, genuinely moved by the planting of the
American flag on the stark lunar landscape, sent word to the astronauts that
"For one priceless moment in the whole history of man the people of this
earth are truly one."

But the president's joy was short-lived. In less than a month, a gigantic rag-
tag and heterogeneous group of mostly youthful and determinedly
nonviolent protestors came together on a six-hundred-acre farm outside
Woodstock, New York, for what sponsors of "the happening" called an
Aquarian Exposition. It attracted an assortment of rock bands and perform-
ers and approximately four hundred thousand celebrants for an entire
weekend in mid-August. Musical ensembles with names like Jefferson
Airplane and The Who, along with singers Jimi Hendrix and Janis Joplin,
celebrities of the growing antiwar cult, entertained to the amplified
accompaniment of electric guitars. Some horrified observers reported incidents of nudism, hedonistic sex orgies, endless traffic jams, rampant use of
marijuana, and at least one death from an overdose of LSD. In fact, for the
most part, peaceful revelers slept and cavorted for three days under the stars,
shelterless in a peppering rain.

It was hard for any middle-aged member of the so-called
"Establishment"—I was forty-six—to comprehend their exact message, but
they obviously had a message. "Make love, not war," may have summed it up.
A growing number of young people were trying, by the extravagant display of
deliberately unconventional behavior, to express their disgust with the war in
Vietnam and to disengage themselves from the society they believed had

created it. There was growing up across our land a sort of amorphous collection of social protestors loosely banded together as the New Left. Someone dubbed them the Hippies.

A writer named Theodore Roszak wrote a fairly scholarly treatise, *The Making of a Counterculture*, which preached deliberate estrangement from the disciplines of formal society. Jerry Rubin, one of the so-called Chicago Seven defendants, published a tract called *Do It*, in which he advocated arming students, longhaired youths, workers, and "peasants" to create a bloody "Youth International Revolution." Among the objectives of his proposed revolt: Replace the Pentagon with an "LSD experimental farm," and the White House with "One Big Commune."

Easy enough, perhaps, to laugh off Rubin's ramblings as the works of a lunatic fringe, but children of army officer friends in McLean, Virginia, invited me to address their high school commencement and spent all of one Sunday afternoon trying to convince me that we should simply abandon our commitment to South Vietnam. "The Vietnamese are all corrupt," one of them insisted. Another said, "Ho Chi Minh is the only honest one of the bunch!"

Each war protest was given generous media coverage. President Nixon felt painfully what he saw as disproportionate news attention to every domestic anti-Vietnam expression. It bothered him that what he called "sensible" or "responsible" commentary by elected officials was routinely ignored. He had a point. Not only kids, but some members of Congress, eager for attention, were learning that they could evoke a fuller and often much more flattering story in some of the nation's best-read journals by assailing the war effort. Vice President Spiro Agnew became the White House point man in a deliberately orchestrated counter-attack. Agnew went on a speaking tour across the nation, spicing his assaults on news media and antiwar activists with colorful and alliterative language. He attacked what he called "an effete corps of impudent snobs," said they were encouraging "a spirit of national masochism." He characterized the growing band of antiwar journalists as "nattering nabobs of negativism," declared that they and "self-styled intellectuals" leading the antiwar movement were spewing forth a "cacophony of seditious drivel." Agnew's foray, by the sheer premeditated extravagance of language, did succeed in getting some press coverage for his and the president's position.

I never really knew Spiro Agnew. I met him a few times at ceremonial occasions, but never had an opportunity for any sort of philosophical discussion with him. My first impressions of the man, when he ran for governor of Maryland, had been negative. His campaign commercials, appealing via Washington stations for suburban Maryland votes, had seemed shallower than a saucer. "Ted Agnew is your kind of man," chanted a singing commercial. I remember thinking, "Not quite. If he were *my* kind of man, he'd tell us something he stands for." On that, his commercials were as mute as a statue of Calvin Coolidge. I recall wondering in 1968 why Nixon had chosen Agnew as his running mate. Conventional wisdom holds that a vice presidential nominee never gains any votes for the ticket. At best, by displaying acceptable manners and managing not to look stupid, he may avoid losing any votes. There are a few exceptions. Johnson, I thought, added a reassuring dimension to the Kennedy ticket, particularly for Southerners in 1960, but, for the most part, nobody votes for or against the vice president. Once installed in office, it is assumed that he says and does what the president wants him to. So, everyone concluded—rightly, I think—that Dick Nixon approved of his vice president's slashing rhetoric.

Agnew's blistering counterattacks upon the media sowed the seeds of his own downfall, attracting hostility among newsmen. Stories began appearing holding Agnew up to public ridicule. One featured a maladroit swing with a tennis racket, which sent the ball soaring into the stands. Another told of an Agnew golf stroke, which beaned an unfortunate bystander. The image was being crafted of a reckless man. Within four years, of course, Agnew would be hounded out of office and later convicted of accepting a bribe while governor of Maryland.

Now, in the fall of 1969, public opinion polls and the daily mail of most congressmen showed that a majority of Americans still supported the Vietnam effort. But the majority position was getting less and less news attention. This fact became increasingly evident to members of Congress. Several of us in the House grew concerned that the surfeit of media coverage highlighting dissident expressions from a minority in House and Senate was being misread in Hanoi.

One day I discussed with a group of colleagues what we might do to help stimulate productive movement at the peace table. It was ever more obvious that the military leaders in charge of North Vietnam following Ho Chi Minh's death believed American public opinion had deserted the president entirely. Fellow Democrats Ed Edmondson of Oklahoma and Sam Stratton of New York were certain that the vocal and highly publicized protests, including prominent statements by Senators like McGovern and Eugene McCarthy of Minnesota, had convinced Hanoi that it didn't have to come to terms with the United States. Communist policy makers apparently were persuaded that a majority in Congress opposed Nixon's peace initiatives and would very soon demand abandonment of all effort in Vietnam. Democrat Wayne Hays of Ohio and Republican Ross Adair of Indiana, both members of the House Foreign Affairs Committee, told us they had read transcripts of statements by Hanoi's Paris negotiators that clearly confirmed this impression.

"They openly sneer at our negotiations," said Hays. "They flaunt head-lines in the Paris newspapers, wave them in the faces of State Department representatives, and taunt them with daily claims that the American public is against Nixon on Vietnam."

That same day, I received a letter from a Fort Worth constituent named "Mac" Laughbaum. Manager of a local J. C. Penney outlet, Laughbaum asked why Congress could not make some visible demonstration of unity to show Hanoi that the lawmaking branch of our government supported the president. The idea made sense to me. I sat down at my typewriter that after-noon and began drafting a resolution of support for President Nixon's peace initiative:

> **Resolved**, *That the House of Representatives affirms its support for the president in his efforts to negotiate a just peace in Vietnam, expresses the earnest hope of the people of the United States for such a peace, calls attention to the numerous peaceful overtures which the United States has made in good faith toward the Government of North Vietnam, approves and supports the principles enunciated by the president that the people of South Vietnam are entitled to choose their own government by means of free elections open to all South Vietnamese and supervised by an impartial international body, and that the United States is willing to abide by the results of such elec-tions, and supports the president in his call upon the Government of North Vietnam to announce its willingness to honor such elections and to abide by such results and to allow the issues in controversy to be peacefully so resolved in order that the war may be ended and peace may be restored at last in Southeast Asia.*

The most important thing, in my opinion, was to embrace without reser-vation the idea of free elections. If the South Vietnamese people wanted reunification with the North, for example, they were entitled to have it. If they didn't, it shouldn't be forced upon them. That position, I believed, would put us on high moral ground. It bothered me that, after Vietnam's war for independence from French colonial rule, American policy makers report-edly had thwarted an early attempt to determine the nascent state's future through a national election. Eisenhower's State Department and intelligence people under John Foster and Allen Dulles were said to have feared that vot-ers, given a choice, would have installed Ho Chi Minh as president, whom they believed to be a Marxist. Whether Ho was a classic communist or merely a zealous nationalist intent on a government liberated from all foreign influ-ence, was unclear to me. Anyway, it was now a moot point. What *was* apparent was that we couldn't expect to promote democracy by suppressing elections, nor favor them only where it was preordained that our side would win.

Having drafted this statement, I ran off copies for those with whom I had been discussing our government's dilemma. I prepared a copy also for Speaker McCormack, one for House Minority Leader Gerald Ford, another for Tom Morgan, Chairman of the House Foreign Affairs Committee. House Minority Leader Jerry Ford told me he was making a copy for President Nixon. I said we'd be amenable to any suggestions the White House might have.

The next morning, I got a personal call from the President. Nixon thanked me enthusiastically. He said that he, Henry Kissinger, and Secretary of State William P. Rogers had gone over my suggested text carefully and could not recommend any changes whatever. "It's fine just like it is," said the president.

Edmondson, Hays, Stratton, Jim Kee of West Virginia, and I immediately began circulating the text among our Democratic colleagues, seeking cosponsors. Adair and Ohio Republican Sam Devine recruited others in their party. It came at a propitious moment, well-timed with a new White House initiative. On the evening of November 3, President Nixon made another televised address to the nation. He appealed to America's "silent majority" for a show of support. President Nixon read aloud the full text of his conciliatory August letter to Ho Chi Minh, reported a new plan adopted in cooperation with the South Vietnamese for the phased withdrawal of all U.S. combat ground forces to be replaced in stages by newly trained South Vietnamese forces. "And so tonight—to you, the great silent majority of my fellow Americans," he pleaded, "I ask for your support."

In the House, our campaign to sign up joint sponsors for our resolution of unity was succeeding beyond our fondest hopes. Within three days of its drafting, a broadly representative group of fifty Democrats and fifty Republicans jointly introduced the resolution. News of our initiative was carried by the wire services. The *Fort Worth Star-Telegram* bannered the story, and it was given decent treatment in a few "middle America" newspapers— but not a word in the *Washington Post* or *The New York Times*. The *Post* was carrying a story about an adverse resolution introduced by a lone Republican, Paul Findley of Illinois.

Three days later, the House Foreign Affairs Committee held a hearing and quickly voted our resolution out by affirmative bipartisan vote of 21 to 8. The action of the committee was not reported at all in the next day's *Washington Post*, but ungrudging, even enthusiastic support spread quickly across the House. By November 12, just ten days after the circulation of the first draft and nine days after President Nixon's "silent majority" appeal, three hundred members, more than two-thirds the entire House membership, had signed on as formal cosponsors. Among them were 181 Republicans and 119 Democrats. On that day, President Nixon called and asked if I would assemble eight or ten of the leading sponsors, about half from each political party, and meet him at the White House that evening. He wanted us to call and tell the good news by trans-Atlantic telephone to Ambassador Henry Cabot Lodge Jr., who was in Paris with the U.S. negotiating team. In the Senate, Republican Gordon Allott of Colorado had been circulating a letter to Ambassador Lodge expressing similar support for the president's position. He had already acquired 58 signatures—37 Republicans and 21 Democrats, a clear majority of the Senate.

The usually reserved Nixon was awaiting us eagerly when our group arrived. He thanked us profusely. "This is just exactly what we have been needing!" he exclaimed. "Now the news media can no longer ignore the unity of this country and of this government!" The president talked briefly with Lodge, who had been alerted to expect his call. Then he put each of us on the line, starting with me, for a brief personal conversation with our ambassador. Lodge was elated. He said he would put the good news of our joint declaration to effective use immediately.

Next, Ron Ziegler accompanied our bipartisan vanguard into the press room. We threw it open to questions from the press corps. None of us was prepared for the negative, highly suspicious tone that pervaded the queries. What had motivated us to launch this initiative, someone asked.

"We wanted to strengthen Ambassador Lodge's hand," replied Senate sponsor Gordon Allott. "We wanted him to know that someone in this country was behind him, that the voices of discord were not the only ones in this country."

Why did senators circulate a letter rather than introducing a resolution as the three hundred House sponsors had done, someone else demanded.

The senator pointed to the desirability of orchestrating some finished product in synch with the House action. He explained that Senate rules, providing for unlimited debate, might have produced a filibuster. Surely they would have bogged the action down by long premeditated delays.

Another newsman asserted that "some of the prominent members of the Senate Foreign Relations Committee did not sign this, I would gather." Allott acknowledged that to be the case. "What do you think that does to your unity?" the questioner triumphantly demanded.

"None of us has claimed that our position enjoys unanimity," I said. "Hardly any position ever does. When the resolution comes to a vote in the House, there will be at least a four-to-one margin in favor of it."

Wayne Hays emphasized that so great a number in Congress coalescing in support of the president's position surely indicated widespread popular support. Les Arends, the Republican Whip, stressed that our resolution was "a bipartisan effort in the fullest extent of the word."

Another newsman returned to the question of our motivation. "Would it be fair to characterize the timing of this announcement as an attempt to defuse the events that are coming up the end of this week?" The questioner had reference to antiwar protests (called a "moratorium") scheduled for the coming weekend in Washington.

Allot said no. Hays said no, pointing out that the resolution could not possibly come up for a vote in the House until some days after the scheduled demonstration.

"Wasn't it proposed after the fact was known that this moratorium was going to be held?"

The line of questioning puzzled me. It was clearly off the subject. I had not even been aware of any upcoming public protests at the time I drafted the resolution.

"I don't think the moratorium had anything to do with the resolution," said Hays.

"Then why should you feel you had to demonstrate this broad-scale congressional support?" Some in the White House corps were obviously fixated on this tangent.

"I think it is high time to get it on the record that there is a great majority of members of the Congress who are behind the president, any president, this president—he is the only one we have at the moment—in his search for peace." Hays was getting warm under the collar.

Then came a personal zinger, obviously addressed to me. "Mr. Congressman, I understand you are somewhat unhappy with the remarks of the Attorney General concerning the Johnson Administration."

I should have expected this. Earlier that very day I had spoken briefly on the House floor in response to a comment attributed in a news story to Attorney General John Mitchell. The cabinet officer had said something to the effect that former President Lyndon Johnson set in motion an "epidemic of cynicism" throughout America. As a friend of Johnson's, I had resented the statement and had said so. It seemed to me an unworthy attempt to blame the present administration's problems on its predecessor.

Taking a deep breath, I replied, "I made a statement about that on the floor today, and I will stand on that statement. I hope that the paraphrase attributed to the Attorney General was an inaccuracy. I would like to believe that the Attorney General did not characterize the Johnson administration in just that way. I think it would be unhelpful and counterproductive in the broader and far more important effort in which we are engaged."

The question provoked me. It had nothing to do with Vietnam. It was an obvious attempt to start a fight, to drive a wedge between the Democratic Congress and the Republican Administration.

"Now, look, I am a Democrat," I said. "I don't make any bones about that. I was cochairman of the Humphrey campaign in Texas last fall. We did pretty well down there. I am a Johnson Democrat. He is a friend of mine. I believe in him. I think he was a great American. I don't think that he contributed to any disease of cynicism in this country, and I don't believe that the Attorney General really feels that either.

"I am not here today to appear in the interest of being a Democrat, however. I am here primarily to appear in the interest of being an American and supporting the president of the United States."

At the end of about thirty minutes, we walked out of the press conference and returned for a final few words with President Nixon. Ed Edmonson caught my eye and grinned. "You're going to have harmony if you have to fight for it, aren't you?"

"Don't worry," said Nixon. "They'll have to address the policy question in their stories. They have the copy of the resolution, and it speaks for itself." But if we expected prominent news play, we were courting disappointment. The evening network news largely ignored our entire effort. The *Washington Post* and *The New York Times* gave us short shrift. They were mostly preoccupied with anticipation of a colorful protest rally promised for the coming weekend.

Nixon, surprised and disappointed, now got personally involved. On the morning of the next day, November 13, he called Speaker Albert and Senate Majority Leader Mansfield to arrange personal appearances in the House and Senate chambers that very afternoon. The president called to tell me what he was going to do. "You will see, Jim, that I do not give up easily. We are going to *force* the media to take note of this great thing you have set in motion. I will make it impossible for them to ignore. I am coming up there today, and I'll publicly thank all those of you who have introduced that resolution. They *can't* ignore *that*!"

My own hopes soared. Word of the president's impending visit spread throughout the Hill that morning like dust before a West Texas windstorm. Soon after the House convened at noon, the big chamber, usually three-fourths empty at that hour, began filling. I looked up to the press gallery. The long balcony above the Speaker's podium by 12:30 was crowded with members of the Capitol press corps. The galleries were jammed.

President Nixon's talk began at 12:53: "I have come here today for an unusual purpose, perhaps an unprecedented purpose . . . to express appreciation to the members of this House, the members on both sides of this aisle, for their support of a just peace in Vietnam." He spoke of our resolution, expressed his gratification that over three hundred members had joined in

sponsoring it. "As I saw that resolution," he said, "I realized its great signifi-
cance . . . the effect it might—and I believe could—have in hastening the day
that this just peace may come."

A couple of hours later, after lunch with members of the leadership, the
embattled chief executive took his message to the Senate. Harking back to his
own days as a senator, he addressed his audience as "my colleagues in the
Senate." His message was distinct from that he had spoken in the House. He
talked of the constitutional doctrine of "advice and consent," pledging that he
earnestly sought not just the consent but the honest advice of the lawmakers.
The president was being conciliatory. He was trying his best to create the basis
of a friendlier dialogue with his critics in Congress. Most to all, he wanted to
focus national attention upon our resolution of support.

That night and the next morning, the television networks and the prestigious eastern media paid little heed to the president's central message. Two
days later, on November 15, twin antiwar demonstrations unfolded simultaneously. As a quarter of a million organized protestors descended on
Washington, a crowd almost as large besieged San Francisco.

For the next two weeks, our bipartisan group in the House firmed up support
among our cosponsors. We quietly encouraged others to join in our call upon
the North Vietnamese to accept President Nixon's terms, and let the future of
their country be settled by elections.

The only active resistance I encountered was among some members of the
Democratic Study Group. As two of the founding members of that organization, Edmondson and I had good credentials. A decade earlier, we had joined
with John Blatnik of Minnesota, James Roosevelt of California, and Frank
Thompson of New Jersey to bring together this group of generally progressive younger members. Now some of them, avid anti-Nixonites, balked at
our effort. They didn't oppose the substance. Settling matters by elections was
not abhorrent to them. Calling on North Vietnam to be forthcoming at the
peace table did not exactly offend them. They wanted Nixon simply to withdraw U.S. forces unilaterally.

Our resolution came to the House floor on December 2. During the
debate, I tried to steer proponents from any comments which could be interpreted as questioning the patriotism of those who just sincerely thought we
were on the wrong side in Vietnam. We had the votes. No use to rub it in.
Our goal, after all, was unity. When the vote did come, we chalked up an
astounding display of support. The resolution carried by 333 to 55.

I am not really sure how much good we achieved, given all that was to follow. We clarified the issue. We staked out a claim most Americans could
support. North Vietnamese leaders could no longer indulge the delusion that

Congress had abandoned the American president. The mail I received from throughout the country was overwhelmingly favorable. Maybe, for the moment at least, my action had helped to "bring us together." But, as I would see, the tidal flow of events kept splitting us apart.

CHAPTER FIFTEEN

PLAYING
TO
WIN

"The trouble with him is that he doesn't play to win. He plays not to lose," complained Richard Nixon. He referred to a professional tennis competitor who played the back court skillfully, returning shots well and waiting for his opponent to make a mistake, but seldom rushing the net. Then, as if for emphasis, Nixon declared: "I don't believe in playing not to lose. You gotta play to win!"

Listening to that comment, I felt an unexpected jolt of insight, a flash on one facet of President Nixon's character.

We were visiting in the presidential plane en route to Little Rock. It was December 5, 1969. The president had invited me to accompany him to the Texas-Arkansas football game. Sportscasters were saying the winner would assume the number one national ranking among that year's collegiate teams. Riding with us was Bud Wilkinson, former coach of a string of winning University of Oklahoma teams. Wilkinson and I had been talking of my friend Darrell Royal, then University of Texas coach, whom Wilkinson brought to college stardom as a quarterback under his tutelage at O.U. Conversation over most of the trip centered on sports and sports figures. Nixon was a sports fan, had played some football during his undergraduate years at Whittier College. He admired successful competitors. His tastes, I saw, ran with the power players, the aggressors who kept their opponents on the defensive. Nixon even considered himself something of a sports strategist. Admiring the big Texas team, the president had done an uncharacteristic thing. He publicly predicted a Texas victory. He even drew up a secret play and sent it to Coach Royal for his consideration—not that he had anything against the Arkansas Razorbacks, so far as I could tell; he just liked the Longhorn team.

When we arrived outside the stadium in Little Rock, hearing the loud throb of drums from a college band mounting a staccato rhythm through the cacophony of human voices, the first thing I noticed was a huge peace sign painted on the hillside that overlooked the stands. In glaring white paint, the big circle with the vertical line ending in a three pronged base glistened against its dull grassy background in the bright early afternoon sunlight. Nixon pretended not to notice it. Nobody in our party mentioned it to him. No newsmen were situated anywhere near the presidential seats; therefore, none could importune Nixon for comment on the prominent protest symbol. I was told later that television cameras with zoom lenses from remote locations in the stadium homed in on Nixon and followed our party from the moment we entered the stadium.

It was a close game. Several explosive long plays by Arkansas kept it exciting. At the half, Texas trailed. The president left with a local escort to visit the Texas dressing room. He may also have stopped by for a few words with the Arkansas team. Some from the press intercepted him briefly. He gave a quick interview, predicting the Longhorns would recapture the lead and win. Someone asked him why.

"Texas has the superior power," said Nixon. "I always go with the power."

As things turned out, the president was right on target with his prophecy. The Texas team persisted with its punishing ground attack, controlling possession of the ball as it inched down the field with just enough yardage for first downs. Mixing handoffs and laterals from the wishbone formation, the Texas Longhorns' weight and strength gradually wore down the Arkansas defenders. Texas won, 15 to 14. President Nixon's face, so often dour and immobile, wreathed in a big smile.

Nixon went out of his way to show me courtesies. He obviously wanted to demonstrate his appreciation for my support of his foreign policy initiatives. Certainly I wasn't one of the House leaders. In the formal hierarchy, I was nothing more than a zone whip. There were twenty others like me, each representing a geographical slice of Americana. Yet the president seemed to single me out for special treatment. In the week before Christmas that year, he asked me to come by the White House for a little private visit. He opened a drawer to his desk and brought out a piece of jewelry. It was an exquisite little pendant of sapphire and small pearls.

"Pat and I would like for Mrs. Wright to have this as a little holiday remembrance," the president said—even then, a bit reserved and formal. He referred to my wife as "Mrs. Wright."

I was sure Mab would appreciate the little gift, with the presidential seal on the small velvet box. For the past several years, since shortly after the assassination of President Kennedy, we had grown slowly, almost imperceptibly apart. She no longer cared to go back to Texas with me for weekend trips, had to be coaxed to attend Texas State Society meetings and dinners with colleagues. And I had been increasingly absorbed with the all-consuming business of the Hill. I was glad to take her the personal token from the president.

Within a year, my wife of twenty-seven years would ask for a no-fault divorce. My college classmate, wed to me short days after I received my Army Air Corps wings and second lieutenant's commission, had never been as happy since those early days. Mab never really liked Washington, none of the tinsel and trappings of political life. There were the constant pressures of time, the uncertainties of schedule, the changes of plans. There was the financial drain of maintaining two homes, the needs of two children in college, and now the Senate campaign debt, still suffocating us for payments nine years after that race. We had never suffered privation, never been in real financial need. In those eight postwar years before I ran for Congress, I had made more money than someone in his twenties should ever expect—enough personally to finance half my initial House race. I raised the other half in individual contributions of one hundred dollars and less. But now, the gradual maturation of reality told us we'd never know that degree of affluence again—not so long as I stayed in Congress. And Congress was my chosen career, perhaps my selfish obsession. Congressional life, with all its demands and occasional phoniness, can be extremely hard on any woman relegated to a supportive role, expected to be constantly on stage, cheerful and gregarious on demand, available at the whim of president, constituent, and uninvited guest from home or from abroad. All this and full-time mother, too.

For the moment now, she seemed to take a fleeting joy in the new level of presidential attention. Invitations to the White House began to come more frequently. When Bob Hope and his wife, Dolores, were overnight guests, Mab and I were asked to a dinner party. Twice in the next year we were on the guest list for official dinners honoring foreign leaders, and President and Mrs. Nixon began inviting us to Sunday morning worship services in the East Room of the White House.

This weekly White House religious service was an innovation. Most of Nixon's predecessors had gone to church at one or another of Washington's formal places of worship. Johnson sometimes spent weekends in Texas, where he showed up unannounced at small hill country churches. In Washington, he regularly attended services at the National City Christian Church. In fact, Johnson was quite ecumenical and enjoyed sermon-sampling. On one Sunday in Texas, after attending early mass at a nearby Catholic church accompanied by longtime aide Harry Middleton and the Secret Service contingent, Lyndon surprised his escort group by announcing he now wanted to hear the local Lutheran minister at the eleven o'clock service. Seated in pews at the picturesque little gray frame Lutheran church within sight of the LBJ ranch house across the Pedernales River and the Fredericksburg road, the Johnson entourage was in for a surprise. The minister, making a point on the dangers of jumping to judgmental conclusions about others, suddenly pulled a long-barreled pistol from behind the pulpit, pointed it toward the congregation and shouted "BANG!" Secret Servicemen panicked and scrambled to their feet, uncertain just what was happening. Then, everyone noticed a large pennant dangling from the gun barrel. It bore the printed word, "LOVE."

"You see," smiled the clergyman, "things are not always what they seem."

Nixon had a different approach. He told friends that he was loath to attach himself to any regular Washington congregation and afflict its members with the weekly retinue of newsmen and gawky tourists. He created a new practice, inviting selected guests and a varied menu of noted clergy for regular services in the East Room. A few predictable critics muttered about the separation of church and state. But every president since Eisenhower had presided annually at an enormous Presidential Prayer Breakfast, and none since William Howard Taft had thought it necessary to refuse any public discussion of his religious faith. Presidents and Congress, in face of the Supreme Court's ruling against prayer in the public schools, persistently refused to be deterred in any way from their long-standing institutional practices. Both House and Senate opened daily sessions with prayer by a chaplain paid from appropriated funds. In the Court itself, a bailiff daily intoned: "God save the United States and this honorable court." Every Thursday morning, a bipartisan group of House members attended a private prayer breakfast session to which any member was invited. A similar practice existed in the Senate. President Nixon followed that same pattern in his White House religious services. A succession of outstanding clergy from various denominations brought sermons. I recall hearing Billy Graham, Norman Vincent Peale, and Bishop Fulton J. Sheen. Once, the splendid New York Avenue Presbyterian Church choir sang a medley of hymns.

Given Nixon's personal instincts about playing to win, the long night of anguish in Vietnam must have been every bit as frustrating to him as it was to Lyndon Johnson. Former Defense Secretary Robert McNamara now says it should have been obvious to a perceptive observer as early as 1966 that the war was unwinnable. I knew something, but not much, of McNamara's personal torment and remember when he resigned the defense secretary's post to become president of the World Bank. He tells eloquently of his agonized awakening in his 1995 memoir, *In Retrospect.* Such insights as he now reveals, however, were rare, and even more rarely expressed in public, among the nation's top policymakers, but there was no shortage of voices crying out for an end to the conflict. Gathering volume as frustration mounted, critics grew ever more shrill when their arguments seemed to fall unheard on official ears. It was as though neither side could hear what the other was trying to say.

Never in my lifetime has any other controversy so sharply split Americans into hostile camps. To a very large extent the division was generational. Growing numbers among the college generation, despising the war, denounced the whole set of values held dear by their parents. They saw my age group, children of the Depression, as being motivated by materialism. "You can't trust anyone over thirty" became a common wisdom. My daughter Ginger and her best friend Jean Vandervanter, sophomores at the University of Tennessee, were reprimanded by school administrators for waving signs and chanting during an address by a guest speaker on campus. The speaker? Not Nixon or any of his cabinet. The object of their hostile demonstration was former Vice President Hubert Humphrey, with whom Ginger had proudly posed for a picture two years earlier. Nothing against Humphrey, my daughter assured me. She thought he was great. It was just a chance, she explained, to "speak out for peace."

Most of us who were adults during World War II clung tenaciously to the domino theory. We had seen a failure to recognize it draw our generation inexorably into war. Hitler's unresisted militarization of the Rhineland, Japan's unencumbered assault on Manchuria, Mussolini's unchallenged invasion of Ethiopia without question had emboldened the aggressors. Many in my father's generation felt moral guilt that somebody hadn't stood in the breach earlier. Military aggression permitted was more aggression encouraged, we reasoned from observed experience.

It is useful to recall the events that influenced so many of my generation. Having finally won World War II at such unprecedented cost in human life and treasure, we were horrified to see Joseph Stalin's expansive domineering grip tightening over countries of Eastern Europe, a reflex of Stalin's own paranoia. We recoiled when China's indigenous Red Army first forced Premier Chiang Kai-shek to accept a coalition government and then in 1949 pushed Chiang and his followers off the Chinese mainland into exile on Taiwan. It seemed, in the late 1940s and early 1950s, that a new Communist menace had seized both the military and psychological offensive and threatened, unless resolutely resisted, to steal from us the fruits of our World War II victory. It was in large part a fear of the military spread of Communism throughout Asia that dictated our armed resistance to the North Korean dictatorship and now to the North Vietnamese.

Our arguments, so logical to us, were often lost upon our offspring. My son, now back from Vietnam, in deference to my convictions avoided public disputation—but he told me privately that he just didn't think all this applied in Vietnam. When my usually gentle-mannered niece and some of her contemporaries excoriated President Nixon in shockingly harsh terms for not simply calling off the war and getting out, I turned to her husband, Army Warrant Officer David Simpson, for confirmation of the views I had been expressing. I was sure that he, a helicopter pilot returning from service in Southeast Asia, would embrace my philosophy. He, to my surprise, agreed with the others.

This was, to me, a new phenomenon—bewildering and disturbing. Twenty-six years earlier, flying combat missions in the South Pacific during World War II, I had known hundreds of uniformed servicemen. We could be frank, unguarded, our inner thoughts nakedly exposed in private gab sessions. But in those years, I hadn't known a single person in uniform who didn't unequivocally identify with our country's mission.

On December 22, 1941, two weeks after Pearl Harbor, five college contemporaries and I had dinner at my family's old Victorian home in Weatherford in celebration of my nineteenth birthday. We had been classmates at Weatherford College. Now Glen and Albert and I were at the University of Texas, Joe at North Texas State Teachers College, Harold still at Weatherford and Bob at Cumberland law school in Tennessee. We all were eager to volunteer for early induction into the armed services. Within nine days, I was a private in the Army Air Corps. In four months, all six were in the military service. We all saw combat duty overseas. Harold and Glen did not return. Ten days before my twentieth birthday, I received my flier's wings and a second lieutenant's commission. God, how proud we were! And how young.

But that was another time. And this was another war. Now, I learned to my growing dismay, a privately felt alienation from U.S. policies in Vietnam was almost common among military personnel on duty there, nor was it confined to enlisted ranks.

Why didn't the South Vietnamese have a greater *will* for their own defense? That question haunted me. With a numerically larger army, more wealth and resources at their command, massive financial and technical help from the most powerful nation on earth, why were they constantly on the defensive, incapable of their own unassisted survival? Part of the problem lay with their leadership. General Nguyen Cao Ky had been an embarrassment, a strutting martinet who told newsmen that he admired Adolf Hitler. His U.S.-sponsored successor, Nguyen Van Thieu, was not a great deal better—less abrasive but not very inspiring.

How did we manage so often to get tangled up in close alliance with unpopular, undemocratic, or ineffective local leaders? Juan Fulgencio Batista in Cuba? Rafael Trujillo in the Dominican Republic? François "Papa Doc" Duvalier in Haiti? The Somoza dynasty in Nicaragua? Soon, we'd be widely seen as covert sponsors of General Augusto Pinochet, the grim, unsmiling military dictator who banished constitutional rights in Chile for the better part of two decades. We had stood by Chiang Kai-shek in China until the ground of popular support crumbled beneath him. As in the present case, the *will* of his followers in the final showdown was not equal to that of his Communist adversaries. Why was that? And, now in Vietnam, why was the North able to sustain such massive losses and keep coming, while southern resistance was melting like butter in the hot sun? Was nationalism that much more magnetic an appeal than the claims of liberty? Or did the South Vietnamese even associate their own defense with liberty? Sometimes we Americans make a powerful presumption in assuming we know what is best for other people, or what they really want.

My mind went back to a day three or four years earlier at the Center for East-West Studies in Hawaii. The State Department gave study scholarships to promising students from the U.S. and Asian countries. The idea, inspired by Lyndon Johnson, was to provide an environment in which these young people could mix and learn to appreciate one another's cultures. Tip O'Neill and I each took a daughter with us on a trip to inspect this educational bridge located at the University of Hawaii. Tip took Rosemary, and I brought Kay, then a junior in Arlington's Yorktown High School. Kay had a notion she might like to study there someday. My middle daughter has always been an easygoing, kindhearted kid. Neither as idealistically opinionated as her brother nor ambitious and hard-driving as her older sister, Kay was well liked by contemporaries and comfortable with herself. So it was no surprise to me when Kay, left to explore part of the campus while Tip and I talked with Hawaii's Governor John Burns, returned with a bevy of Asian students. They had been sounding off about why America should get out of Vietnam. "Come and meet my dad," Kay invited. "He'd love to hear your ideas." Kay was always volunteering me for things.

The encounter proved both disquieting and enlightening. Principal spokesman for the little group was a young woman, maybe nineteen. I'm not sure, but I think she was Burmese—not Vietnamese, but she did presume to speak for them. Other students in the group were from Indochina. One was Laotian, as I recall.

"Please tell Congress that America must get out and let us arrange our own affairs. It is wrong to come and bring more war to us," she began. She was very earnest, almost tearful.

"But we didn't begin the war," I insisted. "We were requested by the South Vietnamese government to come and help defend their country against an invasion. We had an obligation by treaty to help them. It is called the South East Asia Treaty Organization. Haven't you read or heard about that?"

Some of the other Asian students began talking with their spokeswoman in a language I didn't understand. After a few brief exchanges with them, she resumed.

"We know only a little about that," she responded. "Those are legal things, perhaps. Our Asian people know only from our own experience. Foreigners, the French and the British, have ruled over our countries too long. Our fathers and mothers thought Americans would be different. But now we see you doing the same as they did, and our people wish to be free."

This exasperated me a bit. I began trying to explain that America was different, that we were not a colonial power. I told her we had helped Cuba and the Philippines free themselves from Spain. I reminded her that, just a few years earlier, we had ended Hawaii's territorial status and welcomed Hawaiians as a state, with all the freedoms and equality the rest of us enjoyed.

She said Asians knew all that. "Those are the reasons we thought you would understand our wish to govern ourselves without foreign armies. Sir, we do not wish to be rude, but we wish for all the light-skinned people with uniforms and weapons to return to their homes and leave us in peace." Her voice trembled.

I was beginning to understand her first premise. "Light-skinned people with uniforms and weapons." Prejudice can run both ways. It always has. The best of intentions cannot exterminate it, nor subdue it totally. It lies there in the smoldering embers. Then an appearance of arrogance, of presumed superiority (with uniforms and weapons) is a breeze that blows the dry leaves of nationalistic aspiration across the embers, and a flame erupts. That flame had consumed the French at Dien Bien Phu.

I asked if these students had no concerns about the invasion from North Vietnam or the spread of world communism. But, of course, the Vietcong did not evoke the visual phobia of light-skinned people with uniforms and weapons. As for communism, "that is but a word to us," said the young Asian. "We know it governs Russia, and hear it said that it is bad, but we've never seen any Russian soldiers in our countries. We do not wish to be like them, nor like the Americans, either."

At this, a few of the others began to speak up. Their attitudes were not a great deal different from ones I had often encountered in Central and South America. Being seen as Yankee surrogates was more liability than asset politically.

Reflecting back later upon that conversation with the Asian students at the University of Hawaii, I thought I had a glimmer of the lack of zeal, or "will," among South Vietnam's armed forces. We'd been so sure we knew what was best for these people. We had told ourselves we were acting, God knew, in *their* interest as well as our own. Self-congratulatory paternalism can be culturally blind and blind to its own blindness, zealous, well-meaning, and cruel. There was also the matter of our own national pride, of course. This weighed heavily in the White House. Lyndon Johnson once said he didn't want to be the first American president to lose a war. Neither did Richard Nixon. If South Vietnam's army troops were lacking in will, Nixon was not. Frustrated by lack of progress in the peace talks, he resolved to bring his adversary to terms. Presidential speech writer William Safire, in his book *Before the Fall*, recalls the president's regaling his military and political advisors at about this time, "Don't worry about divisiveness. Having drawn the sword, don't take it out—stick it in hard. . . . Hit 'em in the gut. No defensiveness."

On April 30, 1970, the president sent forty thousand U.S. cavalry and paratroop forces into Cambodia. Their limited mission, he explained, was to clean out a nest of secret bases and supply depots just across the South Vietnam border, where Vietcong rebels had been finding sanctuaries. To fail to act, the president insisted, would render us, the world's most powerful nation, no more than a "pitiful, helpless giant."

The decision precipitated an explosive storm of protest. Critics saw it as a willful and unauthorized extension of the war into yet another country. On the following day, at a middle-America college in Ohio named Kent State, students began throwing bottles at police. Somebody tossed a firebomb into the ROTC building. Ohio's Governor James Rhodes, blaming the violence on what he called a "communist element," dispatched the National Guard to the campus to maintain order. For two days there was an uneasy standoff. On the morning of May 4, according to eyewitness accounts, a few of the students began throwing rocks and other objects at the phalanx of Guardsmen deployed on a campus ridge overlooking a student parking lot. As other students poured out of their classes at noon, a large entourage assembled and, spurred on by activists, began taunting the Guard. One group, ignoring a tear gas volley and warnings to disperse amplified over a National Guard bullhorn, began advancing on the Guardsmen. Nobody is certain what happened next, or just who, if anyone, gave an order to open fire.

But at 12:24 P.M., members of the Guard began firing. Some Guardsmen said they were trying to aim over the heads of the students, then about twenty-five yards away. For thirteen frenzied seconds the rifles sounded. When they stopped, four unarmed students lay dead. Nine others were wounded. Students and Guardsmen were weeping in stunned disbelief.

"My God!" someone swore in the cloak room off the House chamber. A news announcer had just broken in to tell of the tragedy. Others gaped in uncomprehending silence. I listened briefly. Then I walked out the rear door, down the hall, outside, and around the building to the Capitol's west balcony. I stared briefly at the city skyline, then walked down a long flight of stairs and slowly across the southwest lawn to a little park where flowers nurtured in the botanical greenhouse had recently been planted. I stood there for a long time.

The Kent State massacre, as it came to be called, set off a sudden chain reaction. Campuses across the country exploded. The student strike center at Brandeis University, a sort of clearing house for antiwar campus protesters, reported within a few days that 451 universities and colleges throughout America had conducted sympathy strikes. Classes were boycotted and shut down, some for days.

Violence begat violence. On Wall Street, student protesters clashed with a group of building trades laborers who supported the war. Seventy people were injured. At Mississippi's Jackson State College, two students were killed by police.

On Capitol Hill, more Democrats and at least some Republicans became increasingly outspoken in opposition to the conflict. Democratic Whip Thomas P. O'Neill, whose Massachusetts district housed a higher percentage of university students than any other in the nation, had spoken out early against the war, while Johnson was president. Now a widening stream of others joined. Hugh Carey and Ben Rosenthal of New York, with whom I'd made common cause on a variety of domestic issues, now hinted openly that the Wright Resolution of the previous year should be repealed. In the Senate, several of my good friends became open advocates of immediate withdrawal. Alaska's senator Ernest Gruening, with whom I'd worked closely on the statehood issue, cornered me at a Father's Day picnic and tried to persuade me to denounce Nixon's Cambodia maneuver. My old ally, George McGovern, broke openly with South Vietnam's leaders. I respected George's sincerity, but his vocal criticism of the South Vietnam government, highly publicized during a McGovern trip to the Far East, seemed likely in my mind to reinforce Hanoi's resistance to our peace overtures. Ed Muskie, whom I admired and planned to support for the Democratic presidential nomination, began separating himself from those who continued to back the president.

Public support for Nixon's policy plunged sharply in the wake of the Kent State disaster. Polls showed approval, at 65 percent in January, falling to 48 percent by midyear. But if Kent State gave antiwar activists fodder for bitterness, other events fed the mounting resentment of those whom Nixon described as "the silent majority." At 1:32 in the early morning of March 1, a bomb exploded in a bathroom on the Senate side of the Capitol, shattering windows, splitting walls, and inflicting damages estimated at $300,000. Americans were horrified on learning that an anonymous caller, shortly in advance of the explosion, had given notice to an operator on the Capitol switchboard, taking credit in name of the "Weather Underground." On May 3, the day before the Kent State debacle, a huge cadre of war protestors surrounded the Capitol, cramming the outer stairways and blocking entrances in an effort to close off access and shut down the building. When demonstrators refused orders by the Capitol police to leave avenues open for public ingress and egress, more than seven thousand were arrested by Washington, D.C. police and military units. After the jails were filled, they were detained in the football stadium and the city coliseum.

Every step in the escalating contest of overreaction provoked its own indignant backlash. As the nation grew increasingly polarized, resentments ran in as many directions as the spider web cracks that emanate outward from the blow of a hailstone on a window. To prescribe for the president any one step to contain the simmering anger would be like trying to carry a watermelon in a teaspoon. Baffled by the mounting wave of protests, but believing that most Americans were on his side, Richard Nixon was a contrast in sunlight and shadow. John Connally, who served Nixon for eighteen months as Secretary of the Treasury, more than twenty years later would write of the "unmarked side of him, a hunger to please that was at war with a lifetime of shyness."

This side of the Nixon personality blossomed briefly on May 22, 1971, when the president invited a group of us to join him on a flight to Austin. We celebrated the official opening of the Lyndon B. Johnson Library on the University of Texas campus. Nixon accompanied former President Johnson on a private guided tour of the magnificent facility with its sweeping expanses and its state-of-the-art modernity. It was a joyous moment, a time of pleasant reverie for some and happy revelry for others. Just as the two presidents completed their private walk-through and prepared to commence the short dedicatory program, someone turned on the mechanism that activated the newly installed upward-arcing fountain in the center of the pond. The fountain, empowered, suddenly went berserk, generously spraying the assembled throng and soaking some to the skin.

Everyone had a good laugh. Nobody minded. The day was dry and the Texas sun was warm. It toasted us dry in no time. Someone made a clever remark about the rain falling indiscriminately on Democrats and Republicans alike.

On the return flight, I told President Nixon I thought he had scored a coup. Taking part in that dedication, exhibiting such goodwill for his predecessor must have won him some friends, I said.

"Former presidents have the smallest club on earth," Nixon replied. "A lot of people can offer advice, and they all mean well. But there are precious few who can begin to understand the decisions a president has to make." After a pause, he added, "Another thing, Jim. Lyndon Johnson is one of the wisest men I've ever met. I observed him closely when he ran the Senate. Anybody would be a fool to sell him short."

He was singing from my hymn book. We exchanged a couple of Johnson anecdotes. Finally, I said something to the effect that a serious search for bipartisanship and a real effort to understand what's troubling one another just might help us find a way through the division and turmoil of Vietnam, if that could be done.

"It *has* to be done," said the president.

Nixon still saw the war as a contest of will, a question of standing by our word and our national honor. "The Vietcong cannot defeat or humiliate the United States. Only Americans can do that," he insisted.

Soon, a series of new battles broke out on the domestic economic front. The president urged Congress to join him in "a new American revolution." The heart of his plan was a concept he called "revenue sharing." We should distribute the power of the federal government "back to the people," he said. Nixon called for taking money earmarked for specific federal programs such as highways, health, environmental improvements, and education, lumping it all together in a package, and dividing it among the states and cities. Let local governments take the federal money and decide their own priorities, he argued.

This plan, offered in Nixon's State of the Union address in January of 1971, met barricades of resistance in House and Senate committees. My own instinctive reaction was negative. I wanted the hand of federal authority to leave cities unhampered in the discretionary, even experimental expenditure of their own local taxes. But I felt that where our central government provides cash raised from taxpayers throughout the entire country, it has a responsibility to monitor that money's prudent usage.

"If these programs were not urgent priorities that served a national purpose," said Wilbur Mills, " Congress should not have authorized them in the first place." The opposition of Mills, Chairman of the House Ways and Means Committee, was crucial. Revenue sharing didn't move.

In a more successful effort at partial federal dismantling, Nixon called for the abolition of the Post Office Department. Delivering the mail was our central government's oldest function. From the republic's inception, that duty had been closely monitored by Congress. The nation's lawmakers had exercised control even over the selection of village postmasters and rural letter carriers. If the local official responsible for so personal a service as the delivery of a citizen's mail were inattentive, lazy or arrogant, people felt they had a right to hold their congressman responsible. Congress approved all postal rates. It had doggedly maintained the penny post card and the three-cent stamp as guarantors that access to daily mail delivery would stay forever available to the poorest and humblest. Now, bowing to the claims of businesslike modernization, legislators voted to relinquish their time-honored role. Most did not foresee that, under a new Postal Corporation, rates would double, triple, multiply by ten, frequency of deliveries would shrink, such services as mail forwarding would be restricted, and Congress would be powerless to alter those unpopular trends.

This was the forerunner of a succession of moves over the coming decades to "deregulate," disestablish, and devolve the machinery and control of federal government. Nixon's Postal Corporation unleashed a chain of actions—airline, motor carrier, savings and loan and banking deregulation, to name a few—which Speaker Newt Gingrich in 1995 would hail as "devolution." If Nixon didn't set in motion a "new American revolution," he started a movement toward dismembering government that Ronald Reagan's people ten years later would mold into an art form.

The biggest and most unexpected domestic bombshell was Nixon's wage and price freeze. Actually, it was John Connally's freeze. The president, who had looked around for a prominent Democrat to bring into his cabinet, called Connally, as 1970 was ending, and offered the Treasury secretary's job to the former Texas governor.

Nixon and Connally were alike in some respects, totally different in others. John Connally had a swashbuckling, debonair manner. Handsome as a matinee idol, gallant as a knight, he seemed supremely self-confident in everything he did. In contrast to the image I sometimes had of Richard Nixon, John Connally seemed absolutely self-assured, comfortable with who he was. Connally and I were friends. Not intimates, but associates who respected one another. He was a bit more conservative than I. Some thought of us as rivals within the party. We weren't, really. We both were devoted to Lyndon Johnson. Connally was closer to him, had known him longer. In 1956, Connally and I both worked hard for Johnson delegates to take over the State Democratic Convention. We were out to wrest control of the party from Governor Alan Shivers who had bolted in 1952 and backed Eisenhower. We wanted to send a slate of party loyalists, under Lyndon Johnson's leadership, to the national convention in Chicago. Our team triumphed in precinct and county conventions across the state by putting together a broad coalition of liberal and moderate Democrats. Now it was up to us to hold them together. When the nominating committee at the state convention in Dallas picked its list of delegates for the trip to Chicago, it chose two from my Fort Worth district—myself and a longtime local party leader named Margaret Carter. Connally, then a resident of my district, was not included. I knew he would want to go, and Johnson would want him; and Margaret Carter, for her long years of faithful service, deserved to be a delegate.

Some of Connally's friends, considering Margaret too liberal for their taste, wanted to take the issue to the convention floor. When the delegate list was read, they would move to substitute John's name for that of Margaret Carter. Margaret's friends, including most of the people from organized labor, began to rally in her defense. John Connally, they insisted, had never worked in the precincts and didn't know the rank and file Democrats. A destructive fight was brewing. Whichever side won, it would leave scars. At this, I asked the nominating committee to reopen the matter, remove my name from the delegate list, and substitute that of John Connally. The committee did as I requested. The fight was aborted. Both John and Margaret went as delegates, I as an alternate. Throughout my career, I helped hold the party together.

As a self-appointed peacemaker among the factions, I came to know John Connally well. In late 1961, John told me he wanted to be governor. In asking my support for his gubernatorial bid, John promised he would stand aside in any future Senate race in which I was interested. That's the kind of relationship we had.

During Connally's governorship, he and Senator Ralph Yarborough developed a long-running, well-advertised feud. Neither bothered to deny it. Both were proud men. Neither trusted the other. Yarborough thought Connally too conservative; Connally regarded Yarborough as too liberal. Each suspected the other of trying to stir up intra-party opponents for him at election time. In 1968, during the presidential campaign between Humphrey and Nixon, I brokered a détente between the two. Both came at my invitation to a Fort Worth luncheon honoring Humphrey. By mutually agreed prearrangement, they sat side by side. Each managed to say something nice about the other. That little exercise healed a gaping breach in the party and helped Hubert Humphrey carry Texas.

When Nixon announced Connally's appointment to the Treasury post, rumor mills started churning. Some irresponsible tales circulated with concocted scenarios of an imaginary payoff. Connally, according to the fanciful account, gave Nixon surreptitious support while publicly endorsing Humphrey in the presidential race. One or two suspicious newsmen hinted darkly that Connally had secretly raised money from Texas oilmen for the Nixon campaign. There was no truth in any of these canards. When John Connally endorsed Hubert Humphrey, he put his own prestige on the line. For one thing, it became a matter of pride to him. John had an abundance of personal pride. To lose Texas would have been a blow to his ego. Another consideration was that he didn't want Lyndon Johnson embarrassed, as he would have been if his home state had turned down Hubert Humphrey. There's another reason, too. Whatever John's faults—pride, ego, or a hint of arrogance with which his enemies sometimes charged him—John Connally was never two-faced.

For better than a year, he and President Nixon got along well. Their relationship was symbiotic. Nixon admired John's charismatic style. He liked the idea of having a Democrat in his cabinet. John enjoyed the spotlight. He relished being in the cabinet as long as the president and his White House aides gave him a free hand. Both liked power. "State has the glamour, Defense has the toys," Connally wrote in his memoir, "but Treasury is and always has been the most powerful job in the cabinet."

In 1971, the nation suffered a momentary financial crisis. European trading partners were demanding that the dollar be devalued against their currencies. We were importing more than we sold abroad in American-made goods. U.S. unemployment had begun to rise. Inflation was at 4 percent and moving upward. On August 15, in a meeting at Camp David, Assistant Treasury Secretary Paul Volcker, OBM Director George Shultz, Connally, and Nixon groped for a solution. Connally was the most persistent—also, from accounts, the most decisive. What emerged from that meeting was a 10 percent surcharge on all items imported into this country, an end to the practice of redeeming U.S. currency in the hands of foreign governments for gold, and the only peacetime wage and price controls in American history. Beginning immediately, all wages and prices would be frozen for ninety days. Thereafter, commencing in November, a Wage and Price Administration, advised by a Cost of Living Council, would apply a set of rules permitting gradual price increases to accommodate provable rises in manufacturing and distribution costs. The total wage freeze gave way to a guideline limiting wage increases to no more than 6.6 percent per year.

The controls may have averted a crisis. Connally believed that they had. But they were widely unpopular. In May of 1972, not quite eighteen months after taking over as Treasury secretary, John Connally resigned.

Disagreeing with items on Nixon's domestic agenda, I found several things in which to take comfort. On July 25, 1971, the 26th Amendment to the Constitution was ratified, granting eighteen-year-olds the right to vote in all elections. This was the fruition of Lyndon Johnson's 1968 proposal at the Texas Christian University commencement. It was poetic justice for young Americans fighting in Vietnam. And that year an amendment guaranteeing equal rights for women was working its way through the Houses of Congress. To the surprise of some who regarded Texas as the last bastion of *machismo*, my state would move in the vanguard, one of the very first to ratify the new amendment.

Democracy was working. The slow, inexorable widening of the franchise, the broadening of the electorate, which began with Thomas Jefferson's assault on laws that limited voting to propertied squires, continued its liberating procession. In the generation since World War II, a revolution had taken place, but I could not even imagine the dramatic changes in world events that lay just over the horizon as the calendar turned to welcome 1972.

CHAPTER SIXTEEN

MAKING
PEACE

I f Richard Nixon had been a Democrat, he probably could not have brought off the spectacular thaw in the Cold War, which he made happen during his presidency. A Democratic president would have been pilloried, scalded by conservative Republican zealots as a gullible dupe who'd gone "soft on Communism." The détentes with China and the Soviet Union would have been branded as shameful "sell outs" to sinister red forces committed to our destruction. Some super-patriots were still insisting in 1972 that President Franklin D. Roosevelt had knowingly sold out Eastern Europe at Yalta. The illogic of some Cold War blame placers—ignoring the Marshall Plan, the Berlin Airlift, the Greek and Turkish aid programs—even held that President Harry Truman had collaborated with Stalin at Potsdam to betray Europe to the Communists. In actuality, Truman probably did more than any other American president to halt Communism's spread.

Only someone with Nixon's unassailably outspoken anti-Communist reputation could have pulled off the peace overtures, relatively immune to such mindless attacks. Americans intensely mistrusted both Chinese and Russian leaders. Most people in our country still tended to think of them as in cahoots, plotting with one another to do us in. The reality was that each feared and distrusted the other more than either distrusted us. China and Russia, mutually suspicious, each tended to see an improved relationship with us as a form of self-protection against the other.

Another ace in the hole for Nixon was the nature and disposition of his political opposition. Those of us who had supported his efforts to negotiate from strength with Vietnam believed in the basic principle of bipartisan foreign policy. We couldn't advocate that and desert the president in initiatives as crucial as his proposed agreements with Russia and mainland China. In 1967, when Johnson was our chief executive, I had said in a speech on the House floor, quoted approvingly in a *New York Times* editorial: "The very least we owe to any president is a modicum of understanding and an assumption of his good faith. . . . In the counsels of the world, he is our spokesman. If we cannot uphold him, surely we should not undermine him."

If I believed that then—and I did—how could I not believe it in 1972? As for those in my party who disagreed with Nixon's Vietnam policy, believing we should just get out and let North Vietnam have its way, how could they argue for a harder-nosed attitude toward Beijing and Moscow than they advocated for Hanoi?

Bipartisanship had not always been the guiding star of American foreign policy. It owed its post–World War II genesis to a celebrated 1947 meeting between President Harry Truman and Republican Senator Arthur Vandenberg of Michigan. The 1946 elections had just given Congress over to Republican leadership. Vandenberg was the new chairman of the Senate Foreign Relations Committee. Truman appealed to the Republican leader for his party to close ranks and join hands with the administration "at the water's edge" and face the world as a people united. Vandenberg agreed, with this one caveat: "If you expect us with you on the landing, Mr. President, you need us with you on the takeoff."

In other words, tell us *before* you're up to your eyeballs in some adventure we knew nothing about. Invading Cambodia, for example, Nixon gave his opposition party insufficient notice. Caught totally by surprise, many Democrats were irate. Some clamored to curb the chief executive's unilateral war powers. But in the president's détente with Red China, nobody could make this complaint. Nixon had been moving incrementally ever since his election with changes, first small and then major, in our China policy.

In 1971, the third year of his presidency, Nixon made a series of dramatic changes. On June 10, he brought an end to the trade embargo we had enforced against mainland China ever since December 1950. He secretly diverted Henry A. Kissinger, his National Security Advisor, from the announced route of a worldwide fact-finding mission to meet covertly with Chinese Premier Chou En-lai in Peking. It was during this meeting that Chou sent an invitation to the president to visit China. Less than a week later, on July 15, Nixon announced that he would go to Peking "to seek normalization of relations."

Several top Congressional Democrats, told in advance of Nixon's announcement, spoke out immediately in hearty approval. House Majority

Leader Hale Boggs told a weekly whip meeting: "To demagogue on this one would be like playing Russian roulette with humanity's future."

Finally, on August 2, Secretary of State William P. Rogers announced a stunning change in our longstanding policy of opposing Red China's admission to the United Nations. After a second visit by Kissinger and a highly advertised invitation from the Chinese to the United States' top amateur ping pong teams, in which Chinese hosts showered their guests with extravagant hospitality while beating them consistently at table tennis, the stage was set for Nixon's visit.

The world watched, transfixed, on February 21, 1972, as satellite television beamed the images of President Richard Nixon and China's premier, Chou En-lai, toasting one another's countries from China's grandiloquent Great Hall of the People in Peking. It was the first time in history that any American president had visited China, the world's largest country and home to one-fourth of the earth's total population.

Nixon arose in China's Great Hall to answer the toast to the American people given by Premier Chou En-lai, the general who had commanded Chinese forces against U.S. and U.N. troops in Korea.

"What legacy shall we leave our children?" the president asked. "Are they destined to die for the hatreds which have plagued the old world, or are they destined to live because we had the vision to build a new world?"

On that day, Nixon spoke for me. Like most of the world's people, I was ready for the more hopeful answer. Our generation had lived too long under a nuclear cloud. It was the right cause, and the right time. And Nixon, the cold warrior, was the right man to promote it.

Upon the president's return, he briefed the Congressional leadership. The Chinese had promised not to intervene with military force in Vietnam, something military leaders with a memory of Korea had apprehended. They dropped objections they'd earlier had to our defense alliance with Japan, in which we served as guarantors against Japan's being attacked from any source. The Chinese now viewed that arrangement, they told the president, as a good thing. It obviated any reason for Japan, China's old enemy, to rearm unilaterally.

The only major issue upon which a disagreement persisted was the status of Taiwan. Chinese leaders considered it an inseparable part of China. We respected its claim to autonomy. But the mainlanders, in a country noted for its patience, were in no hurry for a resolution of that problem. China would not be represented, for the foreseeable future, by an embassy with formal diplomatic representation in Washington. They were content with that.

Barely three months later, in late May, Nixon signed ground-breaking arms agreements with Soviet General Secretary Leonid Brezhnev in Moscow.

No president before him had visited the Soviet capital. On his return June 1, the American chief executive traveled directly by helicopter from Andrews Air Force Base in nearby Maryland to the U.S. Capitol, where he addressed a joint session of Congress.

I had read a scientific treatise by an aerospace doctor at Brooks General Hospital in San Antonio, cautioning policy makers against scheduling important public appearances immediately after crossing so many time zones. I remember worrying vaguely whether the president should have postponed the appearance by twenty-four hours and opted for a good night's sleep. I needn't have been concerned. Nixon's was a boffo performance. He had requested that special joint session, he told us, to give Congress a first-hand report on agreements reached, to seek our approval and the funding necessary to carry out commitments he had made. "Agreements as important as these" can only be carried out if there is a "full partnership between the executive and legislative branches of our government," he said.

He stressed the world's first successful Strategic Arms Limitation Agreement. Freer trade between the two superpowers, a joint orbital mission of Russian and American spacecraft, cooperation in scientific and technological research, in the environment, in medicine and public health, joint agreements between our navies to reduce any chance of accidental conflict— all these rounded out what the president credibly described as a foundation of "concrete results, not atmospherics." Nixon was at the top of his form. I believe this moment, midway through his fourth year in office, was Richard Nixon's finest—the high point of his presidency.

Fred Friendly of ABC told a funny story in those days. It involved an articulate, gifted young woman who responded to a network invitation to college journalism students to submit scripts for possible use on television. The script she wrote showed sufficient talent and imagination that studio executives invited the young woman in for an interview. They told her they thought she had great promise and they'd like to consider offering her an internship with a good potential for a full-time script-writing job upon her graduation. "But, of course," they said, "we couldn't use this particular script, as you would understand."

"Why not?" demanded the girl.

Well, they explained rather stiffly, it contained too many double entendres, racy phrases, and suggestive allusions.

The young woman angrily denounced their prudishness. "That's the trouble with all you middle-aged people," she exploded. "You don't understand the first thing of what we're saying. You don't know the difference between making love and making out!"

With that, she stormed out of the studio.

Fred Friendly was relating this episode to Walter Lippmann, the venerable dean of Washington pundits. Lippmann shook his head in puzzlement. "She may have a point of some kind, Fred," said the sage. "It's true enough that we just can't seem to communicate across the generational lines any more. What on earth could that child have meant, for example, by 'making out'?"

A day or so later, Fred recited both conversations to his fifteen-year-old son. "The man's right, Dad," commented the boy. "We really don't communicate. But who is this Walter Lippmann?"

That episode seemed to me a metaphor of the time. It illustrated how easily intelligent, educated, even highly caring people, like the inheritors of the tower of Babel, could lose the one thing that sets humankind above the beasts—the capacity to communicate with one another.

Oh, we spoke words. But the words did not always convey the intended meaning. Most of us were too intent on being heard to make the effort necessary to hear and understand others whose vantage point was different than our own. The angrier and more frustrated we grew, the more incomprehensible became our messages. How ironic, I thought, and how infinitely sad that at this moment in history when the executive heads of our country and the Soviet Union, yes and even China, had made contact, the arteries of expression were hardening in our own country.

And while Nixon could talk and make sense with Brezhnev, and even Mao Tse-tung, he and the rulers in Hanoi kept simply talking, and shouting, past one another's heads. Both sending and nobody receiving.

Here at home, it was as though the avenues of verbal expression were closing, leaving us increasingly unable to communicate thought between the generations, between the races, between the haves and have-nots, and even between the sexes.

Me, for example. I thought I knew how to communicate. Some colleague was always calling me the best orator in the House. Words were the tools of my trade, my weapons and my shield. But I had lost the capacity to communicate with my own wife. Now divorced, after twenty-seven years of marriage and twenty-one months of separation, we were cordial, civilized, mutually respectful. But neither of us knew what was in the other's heart.

Increasingly, I was being sought out to serve as a peacemaker between factions in the Congress. I was becoming intermediary between big city northerners and the "boll weevil" conservative southern House Democrats. Carl Albert asked me twice to help referee disputes between turf-jealous members of different committees. It came to me in a quiet moment on the evening of December 30, 1971, that I was spending all this energy making peace between others when I needed to make peace with myself. I had just turned forty-nine. Beginning my fiftieth year, I really had to come to terms with where I was and where I was heading. I wrote that night in my diary:

> *My fiftieth year—a good time for stock taking. No longer do the fires of ambition burn with such hot intensity. A person begins to accept himself, to be content with lesser gain, to moderate his demands upon himself. Maybe just in the past year have I really acknowledged that I won't ever be president. Conceivably I've know it subconsciously for several years but only in this year have said it to myself. It's a relief!*

Some fights just aren't worth making. Probably I could win the Senate seat against John Tower in the upcoming year, I decided. A lot of people were encouraging me, as they had in 1966. But it would cost a mint of money, and I was still slowly paying off the debt accumulated from the 1961 try. Such a race would absorb my total energies for the entire year, win or lose. I'd have to absent myself from all the action in Congress. I was becoming ever more involved in the decision-making process, and I liked that. To run, I'd have to give that up.

That night I faced the truth. My marriage was down the drain. Irretrievable. I still could save a good relationship with my former wife and cultivate my children's love and well-being. I didn't need to chase that elusive butterfly of political upward mobility. There was plenty for me to do right where I was. If roles of greater service demanded my future attentions, they would find me. I was in debt, but with perseverance I could pay that off. I felt a burden of self-imposed demands slip from my shoulders. Making peace with my own reality, I found increasing fulfillment in the House, where I realized with a start that I had invested one-third of my entire life. During 1972, I carried the ball for our committee on the $2 billion water pollution control bill, leading the fight for its passage on the floor and defending its provisions to Senators in Conference Committee. I was chairman of an ever more active and visible subcommittee.

I also finished a manuscript updating my book *You and Your Congressman* for republication that year by Coward-McCann, made numerous election-year trips for colleagues, worked actively alongside Governor Nelson Rockefeller on the National Water Quality Commission, and at year's end represented Congress in an official fact-gathering trip to the Soviet Union. This was real! The work I had come to Congress to do.

The event that crowned the year with joy, however, came in the eleventh month. On November 12, just a little over two years after the divorce, I was married in the Calvary Methodist Church of Arlington, Virginia, to Betty Jean Hay. Our reception, featuring big band music, strawberries and champagne, was held at Carl Albert's invitation in the ornate Cannon caucus room.

Betty, eleven months younger than I, had been a pillar of strength to me for the past seven years. Quiet, productive, levelheaded, and always cheerful, she had done yeoman's duty on my congressional staff in Washington and in Fort Worth. In the 1968 election, she headed up the successful advance office for Vice President Hubert Humphrey in Texas. In 1971, when I became chairman of a major Public Works subcommittee, she took over management of its staff. I had grown increasingly reliant upon her good judgment. She was beautiful, sensible, and warmhearted. Her smile would melt Alaska's northern slope. My sometimes volatile temper found counterpoint in her never-failing calm, my occasional gloom in her sense of humor.

Sometime in early 1972 I realized that I was in love with Betty. Because of the glacial slowness with which I was paying off the 1961 campaign debt, I hesitated. That—along with my continuing responsibility to my children and the permanent financial commitment I had unbegrudgingly given to Mab—made me hesitant to ask Betty to share my limited fortunes. When I did, she readily assented. Earlier married, she had been single for fifteen years and had no children of her own. For the rest of my life, her abiding love would be my greatest asset.

That year I made a useful contribution to better relations with Mexico. Working with our Mexican neighbors had been a major satisfaction throughout my years in Congress. Ever since 1963, when appointed by Speaker McCormack to the inter-parliamentary delegation, I looked forward every year to the annual discussions of bilateral issues with Mexican lawmakers. To contribute more effectively, I had taken early morning Spanish classes at the Foreign Service Institute.

In odd-numbered years, we'd meet in Mexico. Even-numbered years brought the Mexicans to Washington. Invariably, in Mexico, our group was received by the Mexican president. In 1971, we were guests for lunch under the trees at Los Piños, Mexico's presidential residence, with President Luis Echeverria. Planning the 1972 visit of the Mexicans, I asked President Nixon to schedule a ceremony in their honor at the White House. He readily complied. He welcomed our guests cordially, stressing the importance he attached to the relations between our countries. He told them of his and Pat's honeymoon trip to Mexico. The president was surprised at the aggressiveness and specificity with which the spokesman for the Mexican delegation addressed one particular issue—salinity in the Colorado River. Observing the president's apparent unfamiliarity with the question, and knowing of its deadly seriousness to our neighbors, I asked for a private appointment after the Mexicans had left. I needed to brief Nixon on this matter. It was important to win his help to cure a grievance that threatened to rupture good relations with our southern neighbors.

By terms of a treaty signed in 1944, the United States was obligated to deliver to Mexico 1.5 million acre-feet of water every year through the Colorado River. That stream rises in the Rocky Mountains and travels about 1,200 miles through seven states before entering Mexican territory. On its way, the water is used and reused many times. It irrigates crop lands, powers industry, and provides drinking water for many American municipalities. Scores of our communities discharge effluent into the Colorado. Through the years, the quality of the water delivered to Mexico had deteriorated. Americans, without thinking about it, had been dumping crop-destructive salt for years on more than a million acres of Mexico's very best irrigated farmlands. The effect of what we were doing was not much different than that of pouring garbage into a neighbor's well.

When I told this to President Nixon, he was horrified. "Why didn't I know about the seriousness of this?" he immediately asked. "I don't know, Mr. President. Most folks in the United States are ignorant of the problem. Most people in Congress have never heard of it. Our State Department probably gives Mexico a low priority. But Mo Udall and I have been talking about it. We're trying to find a way to correct this injustice."

"What does the treaty say about our obligation to give them good water?" the president asked.

"The treaty is silent, Mr. President, on the question of purity," I replied, "but the presumption has to be that what we deliver will be usable water. What we're dumping on these people now is truly not usable. It's harmful," I stressed.

"Well, we must do something about that," declared President Nixon.

"That's what I thought you'd say, Mr. President," I replied. "Mo and I have been working on a bill to clean up that water before it reaches Mexico. We need your help. And I know the Mexican people will appreciate it greatly if the president of the United States shows a personal interest in this problem."

Congressman Morris Udall of Arizona was a member of the House Interior Committee. He also was a friend of mine and one of the most colorful, best liked, and most effective members of Congress. Having lost one eye as result of a youthful accident, Mo wore a glass replacement. This had not kept him from playing professional basketball for the Denver Nuggets. Mo once advertised himself as the only "triple minority" in Congress: a one-eyed, Navajo Mormon. (The Navajo part I secretly doubted.)

Udall's Interior Committee panel had jurisdiction over irrigation projects in the Colorado River basin. He and I jointly appeared before that committee. We pressed the claim of fairness for our neighbors. My Arizona friend and I also talked with State Department officials. We asked their support for our bill to correct the flagrant injury. We also suggested the need for a treaty amendment to clarify our intent to deliver *pure* water. These corrections took a couple of years to wend their way through the labyrinthine processes of government, but the result was worth the wait. On August 30, 1973, Presidents Nixon and Echeverria approved a new agreement on water quality. It set a specific limit of no more than 115 parts of salt per million parts of water poured into Mexico. To achieve this goal, our bill authorized $280 million to build a desalting plant near the Mexican-American border, to reduce water loss by lining about forty-nine miles of the main canal, and to construct four control units upstream in the states of Colorado, Utah, and Nevada, designed to eliminate 520 tons of salt a year. These works redeemed our national honor. They amounted to simple justice. They silenced a lot of vocal anti–U.S. agitators in Mexico, restored hope to a lot of Mexican people and revived confidence in the good faith of their neighbor to the north. All this gave me enormous satisfaction.

Speaker Carl Albert has received too little credit for his bold initiatives to democratize House procedure. Under his leadership in the early 1970s, Congress became more open and operationally more democratic. In January of 1969, at the start of McCormack's last term, Albert—then Majority Leader—seized an initiative long demanded by junior members and back benchers. He called for more frequent meetings of the Democratic Caucus. Rayburn and McCormack both had been content with one meeting of this caucus every two years. Its business was confined to nominating the Speaker, electing the Majority Leader and house functionaries and perfunctorily readopting rules for each new Congress. Any more meetings than that, the old leaders felt, would be inviting trouble.

Carl Albert, responding to importunings by younger members for greater opportunities to exchange views in a public forum and bounce their own ideas off the membership, introduced a resolution in 1969 calling for monthly meetings of the caucus. The effect as revolutionary. House leadership ceased to be monolithic. The atmosphere became more contentious at first, as lawmakers scurried to vent their pet peeves. But the long-term effect was settling.

Soon the caucus voted to create a Committee on Organization, Study and Review, to which members could bring their ideas for sweeping out the musty cobwebs of entrenched practice and examining the established order of things. That committee was chaired by Julia Butler Hansen, a businesslike, gray-haired woman from Washington who reminded me of a genial but not-too-permissive high school principal. Once the dam broke, members flooded Julia's Committee with hundreds of ideas. Some of them were impractical, unworkable, figments of individual member's frustrations. But some of them resulted in lasting and beneficial change.

The best of these were incorporated into the Reorganization Act of 1970. Its primary author was Dick Bolling of Missouri, a senior member of the Rules Committee. Bolling was intellectually gifted, generally respected by the press, ambitious for advancement, but a bit standoffish from rank-and-file members. When Rayburn died, Dick had run unsuccessfully against Carl Albert for Majority Leader. Now, Carl showed he could rise above that old rivalry by anointing Dick to head up the reformation.

One of the sweeping new reforms did away with an antiquated procedure known as the teller vote. Most amendments to important House bills had been adopted by members lining up and being counted as they were herded down two separate aisles like lines of cattle. One line was counted for, the other against. Only the numerical tally on each amendment was recorded. There was no listing of who voted for and who against. The public was left wholly in the dark as to positions taken by individual members. Under the 1970 reform, as few as 20 percent of lawmakers present in the Committee of the Whole, which is the name for the House during its amending process, now could demand a recorded vote.

As a further democratizing effort aimed at spreading the base of participation in decision-making, the new Speaker decreed that the Steering and Policy Committee, which makes committee assignments for Democrats, would contain two new members, at least two women, and at least two of racial minorities. Cleverly, Carl managed to fulfill exactly one-half of all three requirements in the appointment of Barbara Jordan, newly elected black representative from Houston.

An important part of the reorganization was a systematic realignment of committee jurisdictions. This was the first effort at reconfiguring committee turf since 1947, when Albert was a first-term member. From my point of view, it was great. The Public Works Committee, redesignated Public Works *and Transportation*, took on broader responsibilities covering the nation's aviation industry and inner-city mass transit operations. The subcommittee I chaired was given a much wider mandate and a new, all-inclusive title. It had been known as the Highway Investigating Subcommittee. Now it became the Public Works Subcommittee on Investigations and Review. Ours was the duty to keep a watchful eye on the actual operation of every government construction and economic stimulus program.

Fate plays tricks on all of us. An unexpected event can touch and alter careers in unwanted and wholly unforeseeable ways. Such an occurrence, on a still unidentified mountainside or snowy gulch in Alaska in October of 1972, gave an ironic turn to my own future.

As a relatively senior member now of the Public Works Committee, I

expected to be called upon by younger colleagues for help. I was not surprised, therefore, when first-termer Nick Begich of Alaska came, quite
apologetically, with a somewhat unusual request.

"Jim, I don't know how to put this, but you're the only one I know well
enough to ask a thing like I'm about to ask," he began.

"Sounds great, Nick," I laughed, trying to put him at ease. "How many
unemployed dogsled operators do I have to find jobs for?"

"Well, its not that bad. But some folks wouldn't understand what I'm
about to—" He was obviously ill at ease.

"I'll understand, Nick, whatever it is. Go ahead. Shoot the works!"

"Well, Hale Boggs has agreed to make two speeches for me in Alaska next
weekend, except that there may be a problem. He said he'd go with me unless
there was a Ways and Means Conference Committee meeting that weekend.
He thinks he'd have to stay here if there was one."

"So you're wondering if I could be his stand-in in case he has to cancel? Is
that it?"

"Yeah. Yeah, that's about the size of it. It's embarrassing to ask that way, but
I figured you'd understand what I was up against—"

"Sure, Nick. Sure I do, " I reassured him. I looked at the little calendar
notebook on which I entered future commitments. The dates were clear. "I
hope Hale is able to go, Nick. He is the best public speaker we have. He'll
make a big hit with your people. Besides, there's prestige in bringing the
Majority Leader into town! But if he can't go for some reason, I'll go up there
with you and pinch hit for him."

Majority Leader Hale Boggs, was just what I had said. He was, in my
book, the most convincing debater in the House, knowledgeable and helpful,
a born leader. I remembered still the first time I had heard him on the House
floor, early in my first year. Boggs responded extemporaneously that day to a
scornful attack on the United Nations. The preceding speaker was heaping
ridicule on what he called "one-worlders" and "do-gooders." Hale Boggs
smiled beguilingly as he twisted the verbal screw: "Just how many worlds does
my colleague suppose there ought to be? If he's not content with a 'one world'
view, how many would he like? And how many would we have if there were
no United Nations? Two? Six? None?"

Letting that rhetorical question sink in with its unavoidable implication,
Boggs turned to the other pejorative label. "And my colleague seems to have a
special fear of what he calls 'do-gooders.' Would he prefer 'do-badders?' I
seem to recall a scripture about a Nazarene carpenter who 'went about doing
good.' Must we apologize when we try, with all our imperfections, to emulate
that example?" It was vintage Hale Boggs. As deftly as a skilled fencer wield-
ing a rapier, he had done his adversary in.

Over the intervening years, I developed both admiration and affection for my Louisiana colleague. His wife, Lindy, the essence of southern graciousness, was universally respected. She often brought large homemade coffee cakes to the Thursday morning Whip meetings. Once, soon after my mother was killed in a 1959 automobile accident, my dad, wanting to get away from Weatherford and its familiar scenes for a few days, scheduled a trip to New Orleans. He was booked at the Hotel Monteleone. Worried about my father's grief-stricken mental state, I went to Hale. "I'm glad you came, Jim," he said, "because I would like to do something for you. I know the manager of that hotel. He owes me some favors. I'll see to it that he and his people keep an eye out for your dad and take real good care of him. You can count on that." This is the way things were done in our little fraternity.

Now, these years later, I considered Hale not only a good friend but an ideal Majority Leader. He probably had done a hundred such favors for colleagues at one time and another. It was hard for most of us to turn him down when he needed our help on a bill. I thought our young protégé, Nick Begich, lucky to have landed him. As it turned out, the conference committee that might have kept Hale in Washington did not meet. I would learn, more than a decade afterward, that Speaker Albert had called committee chairman Wilbur Mills and asked him to postpone a scheduled session expressly so that Hale could accompany young Begich to Alaska.

None of us anticipates the vagabond twists of destiny. The commercial airliner on which I would have replaced Hale landed in Anchorage per schedule. There Hale and Nick boarded a small chartered plane for the long northern flight over trackless snow-covered mountains to Juneau for the first of two scheduled appearances. The weather was bad. The pilot encountered high, unreported winds of blizzard force. The small aircraft's radio transmission was weak. Somewhere in the Alaskan wilderness, the little plane went down. It was October 16.

After more than two months of searching, a presumptive death certificate was recorded in the state of Alaska on December 29. On January 3, 1973, in its first official act, the 93rd Congress adopted House Resolution 1, presuming Thomas Hale Boggs and Nicholas Joseph Begich to be dead.

The office of Majority Leader now vacant, the Democratic caucus unanimously elected Thomas P. O'Neill to fill the void. Tip had been Democratic Whip under Hale for the past two years and was the natural successor. O'Neill appointed John McFall of California as his whip. Then, he selected four others to serve as regional deputies. He chose John Brademas of Indiana, Dick Fulton of Tennessee, Spark Matsunaga of Hawaii, and me. Now, instead of having responsibility just for the Texas delegation, I would be responsible for approximately one fourth of the country.

President Richard Nixon was reelected that November, to nobody's surprise. Texas, which had gone for Hubert Humphrey in 1968, now joined the national landslide for Nixon. George McGovern, as decent and honorably intentioned an individual as Congress had produced, simply could not get the Democratic campaign off the ground. Poor organization was compounded by the odd gyrations of sour luck. Bad break followed bad break.

Not even the unbelievable folly of the Watergate break-in could turn the course of the well-oiled Republican campaign juggernaut. Even John Connally broke with the Democrats that year. In April he invited a big crowd of well-heeled Texas oilmen, publishers, bankers and others to a party for Nixon at Connally's south Texas ranch. They raised a bundle of cash. Several of my Fort Worth friends and supporters, including Amon Carter, Jr., and Perry Bass, bolted the Democratic ranks with John to support Nixon that year. I stayed with the Democrats.

To tell the truth, people just weren't ready to turn against a sitting president on a matter of foreign policy. McGovern openly called for pulling out of Vietnam. Nixon himself—and Gerald Ford—would heed that call, but each in his own time. For the moment, the American people felt it was up to the president, not his political challenger, to say when it was quitting time.

What I hated worst was that the Nixon landslide took several of my closest friends and congressional allies down the tube of defeat. These included my Texas neighbor, Graham Purcell, and Ed Edmondson who resigned his House seat to run for the Senate in Oklahoma. Billboards across that state glared with the simplistic message: "ED IS LIKE TED, IS LIKE FRED, IS LIKE GEORGE." Senators Ted Kennedy and Fred Harris, outspoken foes of our presence in Vietnam, were simply thrown in for good measure, like blobs of meringue on a piece of rhubarb pie.

In December, I went to the Soviet Union as part of a bipartisan group from Public Works and Transportation. Our mission was twofold. We went in part to fulfill one of Nixon's international commitments. Point five of a twelve-point formal joint Statement of Principles, signed in Moscow on May 29, called for "productive contacts between representatives of the legislative bodies" of the two countries. Beyond that, we wanted to see, compare and learn anything we could from Russia's transportation system—its airline, rail and inner-city transit network.

We flew into Leningrad from Helsinki, Finland, aboard a commercial Aeroflot liner. From there we went by overnight train to Moscow. In both places top-level officials welcomed us warmly. Leningrad was to me the more interesting of the two cities. There were no more than five hours of real daylight in the winter season. The sun was rarely visible during those December days of our visit. A constant cold drizzle chilled the spirit. Even so, Leningrad life was rich by Soviet standards. I saw no evidence of real poverty. Our Intourist guide insisted to me that these street sweepers were paid as well as the average doctor.

"Why would anyone undergo the years of study to become a doctor," I asked, "if graduate doctors are paid no more than a street sweeper? Her reply: "The challenge of the work, of course. If you had your choice, and the pay were the same, which would you choose to be, a physician or a street sweeper?"

She had a point. There was no shortage of doctors, high pay or low. There were 147 hospitals and neighborhood clinics scattered throughout the city of Leningrad, I learned. People on the streets seemed well enough dressed. A man's suit, I discovered, cost the equivalent of a month's pay. To buy an automobile would swallow up the average breadwinner's total salary for almost two years. Hence, there were few private cars.

Leningrad's City Manager, with whom we had an interesting hour's visit, had been a general in World War II, a hero of the siege of Leningrad. He had a lively interest in American cities. We told him of the efforts to revive mass transportation in our bigger inner cities. He seemed surprised that we had ever done away with our street cars. Only 2 percent of Leningrad's citizens drove private vehicles into the downtown area, he said. There was an outstanding system of public transportation. The typical Leningrader might walk for six or seven minutes in the biting cold to catch the tram or bus or subway, but the fare was only five kopecks (about seven cents), and most riders were deposited close to their places of work.

It is in the metro at rush hour that you can sense a flavor of Russian city life. In underground tunnels people wait to board a car. An escalator plunges like a waterfall to a level 180 feet below the city's streets. There arriving subway cars are quickly jammed to capacity. It seems incongruous to recall that the wide streets above, now at the end of the work day, are not crowded with autos. Everyone is in a great hurry when work is over. It almost reminds you of an American crowd pouring into a football stadium, rushing to make the kick-off. There is one immediately recognizable difference, however. The people are not laughing. Most are not even talking to one another. They neither smile nor scowl.

The next morning I saw an entirely different facet of the Soviet character. Accompanied by U.S. Deputy Consul Franz Misch, who spoke fluent Russian, I slipped out at about five-thirty in the morning, avoiding the official guides, to visit a farmers' market where vendors sold fresh produce to the public from the surrounding farm lands. We arrived at the large, indoor farmer's market more than an hour before daylight. There I rubbed elbows with a much more relaxed and expressive crowd. This was the nearest thing I would see to a "free enterprise" operation. Almost every commodity, I noticed, was sold by weight. People brought their own shopping bags or fish net containers. Although it was still dark, the stalls already were doing a brisk business.

There I got to talk, unguardedly, with plain people. Both buyers and sellers were intensely curious when I was introduced as an American congressman. I sensed absolutely no hostility. Quite the reverse, in fact. One grinning fellow refused to let me pay for some cabbage salad I wanted to sample. I bought some cheese, a few apples, and for one ruble ($1.20 on the local exchange) a large white chrysanthemum to bring back to the hotel for Betty. Great bundles of flowers had been flown up on the day before by swarthy tradesmen from Georgia, a distance of several thousand miles. I wondered at the economic feasibility of such an operation, but apparently it paid off. Misch said the average Russian worker, making only about $150 a month at that time, would cheerfully buy a few flowers to relieve the winter's drabness.

The average Soviet citizen could not be very well informed about the outside world, given the limits upon his access to information. Russians were told in their newspapers that summer, for example, about the devastating drought that parched the plains of their wheat belt. But not one word was printed in any journal of public circulation about the huge purchase of wheat from the United States, probably the biggest grain transaction since the days of the pharaohs.

Nina Petrova, our Intourist guide, was highly intelligent, her English was good, her manner charming, her facts well rehearsed. Only, there were some questions she couldn't or wouldn't answer. There seemed incapacity to extemporize. Anything outside the established program flustered the Intourist people. Any detour on the route, a request to look inside a store, even a desire to walk around the block was upsetting to them. The official Soviet position, Nina insisted, was that there no longer existed any prohibition against the exercise of religious worship. She acknowledged, however, that no person was permitted to be a member of both the Communist Party and a religious organization. Considering the small percentage of Soviet citizens formally affiliated with the Party, this might seem inconsequential. Yet the official frown had obviously diminished the ranks of public worshipers. The old cathedrals, nonetheless, were prime points of tourist attraction. Intourist guides showed us through those within the Kremlin walls, pointing to the ancient paintings depicting in their words "the myth of Daniel and the lions" or the "folk belief" of the Angel Gabriel.

During my five days in Russia, an inchoate thought kept nagging at the subconscious level. Something was missing from the whole scene. Betty and I couldn't figure out just what it was. Suddenly we realized. It was December, and there was no sign of Christmas.

CHAPTER SEVENTEEN

THE WATERGATE
SYNDROME

W here did Richard Nixon go wrong? A conventional answer
is summed up in the catchall term, "Watergate." That word
has come to encompass an array of abuses stemming from a
self-permissive official attitude, a contempt for rules, and a
desire to use the powers of government to punish political opponents. What
most people mean by *Watergate* includes the whole frame of mind that
invaded, pervaded, and eventually doomed the Nixon administration. The
word itself derives from the architecturally daring upscale office and apartment complex, then new, that curls like a concrete caterpillar alongside the
rectangular Kennedy Center for the Performing Arts on the Potomac.

Richard Nixon came out of the 1972 election feeling bulletproof and ten
feet tall. He won an astounding 60.7 percent of the total vote, the highest percentage any Republican presidential candidate ever enjoyed. Higher than
Eisenhower, even. It should take nothing from the president's overwhelming
victory to note that his triumph owed less than might be supposed to Nixon's
personal popularity. There is some indication that Nixon, however, congeni-
tally hungry for approval, may have interpreted it wishfully as a blanket
personal endorsement. That is an easy but dangerous temptation for any
politician. Truth is that most folks considered the president competent but
not compassionate. They trusted him not to take risky chances with the
country's future or make foolish mistakes. They were ready to settle for that. It
didn't mean they agreed with all of Nixon's policies.

While most voters still considered themselves Democrats, returning a
solidly Democratic House and Senate, a great many were turned off by my

party's presidential campaign. Through a series of gaffes and amateurish ineptitudes, the Democrats in 1972 ham-handedly demolished any chance they might have had to win the presidency.

First came presidential candidate George McGovern's early abandonment of his vice presidential nominee, Missouri Senator Tom Eagleton. A thoroughly decent man, Eagleton was thrown overboard after it was discovered that, years earlier, he had been treated by a psychiatrist. McGovern first vowed firmly that he stood by his running mate "a thousand percent." Days later, yielding to a clamor from some of his advisors, he kicked Eagleton off the ticket and replaced him with Sargent Shriver. The public, watching the national Democratic convention and its aftermath, found little to cheer. Blue collar Democrats might be forgiven if they associated the party's presidential campaign, in Michigan Democratic Congressman Jim O'Hara's words, with "gay liberation and welfare rights and pot smoking and black militants and women's lib and wise college kids." I liked McGovern personally but entertained no illusion about his electability.

Twelve days before the election, on October 26, Henry Kissinger suddenly announced that "peace is at hand" in Vietnam. Next day, President Nixon halted the bombing of Hanoi and Haiphong. Millions of voters, no doubt relieved, rejoiced at the prospect of an end to American's longest-running war and decided it was no time to jump ship on the sitting president.

In December, however, the election past and the peace treaty still not signed, the president peremptorily ordered the bombing resumed and its pace dramatically intensified. According to inside reports, the president told the chairman of his Joint Chiefs of Staff, "This is your chance to use military power to win this war, and if you don't, I'll consider you responsible." Nixon aide Chuck Colson said both the president and his staff knew they were "racing the clock" to force North Vietnamese negotiators back to the table in Paris before Congress could reconvene in January and force a stop to the bombing.

During the previous year, recurrent efforts by an ever more insistent group of antiwar Senators had repeatedly come close to narrowing the president's military options, even shutting them down. On July 24, 1972, Republican Senator Edward Brooke of Massachusetts moved to cut off all funds for military operations in Indochina in four months, subject only to the requirement that North Vietnam release all U.S. prisoners of war. That amendment to the military assistance bill passed by a surprising 62 to 33. After many years of close calls, this was the first successful effort of the Senate doves to shut off monies and thus force a withdrawal of American troops. The next day, the Senate voted by 48 to 42 to doom the entire military assistance measure, which included about $300 million for Cambodian operations. Nixon's forces later managed to revive it, but this was an unmistakable warning sign. Time was running out.

Toward the end of December, the North Vietnamese agreed to return to the Paris peace talks, and Nixon ended the massive storm of saturation bombing as suddenly as it had begun. Antiwar legislators, furious that the president had acted in the first place without consulting Congress, knew they had been one-upped. Complaints now would be futile. The Christmas bombing spree, though unauthorized, apparently had achieved its purpose.

On January 27, in Paris, Kissinger and North Vietnamese negotiator Le Duc Tho announced an official ceasefire agreement, effective immediately. North Vietnam promised to release all American prisoners of war. The United States agreed to remove all American troops from South Vietnam. President Nixon ordered cessation of air and naval operations against North Vietnam.

I do not believe that President Nixon gave consent to, or had any prior knowledge of, the crude and clumsy break-in at the headquarters offices of my political party. Aside from its total immorality, it was stupid. And Nixon was not a stupid man. Paranoid? Probably. Frustrated over the Vietnam issue? Definitely. Driven slightly mad by persistent domestic criticism of his efforts to end the war through negotiations? Perhaps. Disappointed and distracted by his treatment at the hands of some in the media? Decidedly. Maybe all of these things. But stupid—never.

It had to be clear to Nixon in June of 1972 that his reelection campaign could ride the cresting wave of popular support right up onto the beach of a second term so long as he didn't foolishly rock the boat. Democrats, internally divided over Vietnam, were destroying themselves. The blatant illegality of sending burglars to break and enter the private property of the rival political party was as desperate and foolhardy a deed as any sensible person might imagine. Nixon, no fool, had no reason for desperation, but he did have a penchant for secretiveness. He indulged an intense private loathing for many who had opposed him and a powerful disinclination ever to admit that they were right, or he and his friends in error. He tended to interpret domestic antiwar sentiment as a threat to national security. It was these traits that wove an encircling and ultimately self-defeating web of deception around himself and the White House.

It could be said, I suppose, that Nixon's eventual downfall sprang from a resoluteness of purpose carried to a villainous extreme. Richard Nixon, and most of the men who worked closely with him—Bob Haldeman, John Erlichman, Ron Zeigler, Chuck Colson—were unquestionably patriotic, and essentially moralistic. It is an anomaly of the entire set of misdeeds of which they were guilty that none ever seemed to be motivated by self-enrichment. It was their very self-righteousness and self-assumed purity of purpose which led to the abuses of power that became known for all time as "Watergate." There is a terrible temptation to confuse ends with means, to excuse egregious mistreatment of foes, and to justify saprogenous departures from the rules on the ground that they will serve the greater good. It has to do with hubris, and with self-righteousness.

Emboldened by his dizzying electoral win and the intoxicating plaudits of well-wishers and sycophantic hangers-on, Nixon began to assert powers not contained in the Constitution nor in most commonly accepted codes of conduct. He began to assume as president an air of detached exemption from the legal and moral restraints which applied to others.

For the office itself, Nixon began to demand a new form of homage. He discussed with me one evening his program to install reflective night lighting around all the grand public buildings that line Pennsylvania, Constitution and Independence Avenues. This would impart a sense of majesty to our government, he explained, and exalt private citizens' and foreign visitors' sentiments of pride and grandeur for the Capital city. As a practical by-product, Nixon pointed out, it also would illumine vegetation and cornice-shadowed areas, making the streets of downtown Washington measurably safer.

Listening to this, I found myself nodding in agreement. Each time I return to Washington even now, I am pleased as a citizen that Nixon inspired the lighting of our federal buildings. Even if it costs me as a taxpayer about ten cents every eight years, it's worth it. We citizens are entitled to look upon the institutions of our common government with pride.

But pride carried to an extreme becomes a vanity. I was negatively impressed, as were most of my colleagues, when President Nixon decided to costume the White House police in ceremonial French uniforms. It smacked of affectation, a delusion of nobility. These were the visual warning signs, the iceberg's tip.

Nixon, even before the 1972 election, began to chafe at congressional and court restraints which had bound other presidents and to search for ways to circumvent them. He became singularly defensive of the rights of the Presidency and boldly assertive in claiming powers never before assumed by previous presidents. His expansionary views of presidential authority precipitated a head-on confrontation with both Congress and the courts. The president frontally challenged the other two branches of government through his deliberate actions involving three distinct constitutional issues. First, he claimed the unilateral right to rearrange spending priorities by personally impounding funds appropriated by Congress, and thus killing programs that Congress directed to be carried out. Second, he began to consider himself legally immune from any constitutional restraints upon his power to make war. Finally, as the noose of the Watergate inquiry tightened, Nixon frostily asserted that "executive privilege" protected him from responding to congressional or court subpoenas.

Nixon's view of presidential power revealed itself nakedly in one of his interviews with David Frost. He argued that wiretaps, nocturnal invasions of private property and theft of private records—all patently illegal—ceased to be illegal when authorized by the president or his duly constituted agent.

"So what in a sense you are saying is that there are certain situations where the president can decide that it's in the best interests of the nation or something and do something illegal?"

"Well," replied Nixon, "when the president does it, that means it is not illegal."

This comes close to the heart of the matter. The final, fatal flaw of the Nixon White House was Nixon's tendency to insist that executive power is almost anything the president wants to make it in a given case and immune from legislative and judicial restraint. The issue of impoundment was a prime case. President Nixon outrageously incurred the wrath of Congress by assuming authority simply to dismantle congressionally created programs. This encounter quickly rose to a constitutional dimension that transcended the normal circus atmosphere of partisan political strife. Nixon ripped whole chunks out of antipoverty and public construction projects by simply refusing to carry out laws passed by Congress. The argument was not over the total level of spending (Congress each year on average was appropriating slightly less in all than presidential budgets contained), but which branch of government, the president or the Congress, had the right to determine spending *priorities*. From our republic's inception, control of the purse was the one great constitutional power reserved exclusively to the legislative branch. Now, even that was threatened.

Nixon in 1972 vetoed the water pollution abatement bill in which I, along with Congressman Bob Jones of Alabama and Senator Ed Muskie of Maine, had invested countless hours of tedious work. We were proud of our product. The comprehensive, carefully drafted bill passed both houses by virtually unanimous votes. The president, however, called the bill "excessive."

Excessive? My committee recoiled in disbelief. Republicans included. We're spending more every week in Vietnam, I calculated, than we'll invest in a whole year through our clean water bill to purify the nation's increasingly contaminated water supplies. Intent on establishing a higher level of commitment to cleaning up the nation's polluted streams, Congress promptly moved to override the veto, not by just the required two-thirds, but by an astounding ten to one! Notwithstanding, the chief executive on his own simply withheld more than half the funds. Nixon stubbornly refused to carry out the program.

In effect, Nixon claimed the right to a line-item veto, a power repeatedly sought by presidents and repeatedly denied.

In similar actions, President Nixon arbitrarily withheld funds intended for highway improvements, public housing, help for traffic-congested cities to build public transit systems, and Job Corps training for disadvantaged youth.

Congressman Jake Pickle of Austin, the district once represented by LBJ, asked my help in rescuing the Job Corps, just beginning to show impressive results, from being strangled in its cradle. Critics within the Nixon administration were consigning that experiment in practical vocational training to the ash heap of lost causes. They pointed out disparagingly that thirty percent of the Job Corps inductees dropped out before finishing their course and mastering a marketable trade. But this meant that seventy percent *were* finishing! What's more, ninety percent of those who did were being placed in productive jobs. Paying jobs. Instead of drawing welfare they were drawing paychecks in the private economy. And paying taxes.

Jake and I invited a bipartisan cross section of colleagues for a weekend trip to the San Marcos Job Corps Center between Austin and San Antonio. We talked to instructors, and to some of the kids. Many of the youngsters were from crowded single-parent homes. Some had no parents. A few were refugees from abusive home environments. Several, needing money, had flirted with trouble and barely escaped jail sentences. It would have cost society a lot more to keep them in prison, and yielded nothing in return, than to equip them with job skills.

Jake's and my recruits went back and told our colleagues what we'd seen. Congress salvaged enough money to keep the program fully operational. Then the president just decided to ignore the level of funding Congress had mandated.

Never before in American history had a chief executive employed the impoundment technique in a deliberate effort to change by fiat the legally established policies of the country.

As the controversy over impoundment reached a head, Professor Alexander Bickel of Yale University Law School said, "The power of Congress to appropriate money and ultimately to control how that money will be spent is the foundation of all legislative powers."

That position was quickly upheld in two federal court cases—a Missouri case involving the president's impoundment of highway trust funds, and a District of Columbia case disallowing Nixon's unilateral dismantling of the Office of Economic Opportunity. In restraining the Administration from summarily dismembering the poverty program, the court cited Article II, Section 3, of the Constitution. It directs the president to "take care that the laws be faithfully executed."

Tempers in Congress reached a boiling point. Several House members rose at one Thursday morning whip meeting to demand retaliatory action against the president. "He isn't spending money we appropriate," insisted one, "well, he damn sure can't spend money we *don't* appropriate. Let's give him a taste of his own medicine!" What he and a couple of others proposed was a cutoff of funds for White House operations until the president came to his senses. Wiser counsel prevailed. Speaker Carl Albert stressed how petty retaliation, tit for tat, could paralyze the government. Instead, he convened two task forces to address the problems of impoundment and war powers. The resulting legislation amounted to a legislative counterrevolution, the resolute reassertion of congressional powers threatened by presidential usurpation.

In 1973 and 1974, Congress took three critical stands. It restricted the president's war making power, allowing the president as Commander in Chief to dispatch American troops in emergency situations for up to sixty days, but requiring the express consent of Congress to keep them longer than that in any potential war zone. It also gave Congress power to remand such an action and recall American forces if it chose to do so. Congress also outlawed executive impoundments and created the machinery to restore effective congressional control over the federal budget. And, with help from federal courts, it severely limited the doctrine of "Executive Privilege," under which President Nixon increasingly tried to withhold information from congressional committees.

Perhaps the most significant of the three, in the long run, was the budget bill. Faced with so defiant a challenge as President Nixon had posed to the very root of its authority, Congress responded with a sweeping procedural revision known as The Budget Control and Impoundment Act of 1974. It not only outlawed impoundments; it established the House and Senate Budget Committees, a Congressional Budget Office, and the specific machinery for across-the-board budgetary control.

Senator Sam Ervin called this the most significant law on which he had worked during his twenty years in the Senate. Previously, departmental appropriations had come through Congress in thirteen different packages, at different points throughout the year, and with no clear relation to one another. In effect, Congress had been like a team of thirteen carpenters each building a separate room for a common house, but with no overall blueprint or building design prescribing the dimensions of each room. No longer, after passage of this bill, could a president simply reorder national priorities to his own liking without the lawmaking body's consent. If he wishes to reduce or withhold spending for a given purpose, he now must submit a message to Congress. He may defer a given item for a specific time unless the Congress acts within sixty days to deny the deferral. But he may not simply rescind an appropriation, as President Nixon had been doing, without first getting formal legislative consent.

The War Powers Resolution limited the president's dispatch of military units in any new emergency to sixty days unless accompanied by specific Congressional authorization. Opposing this measure as an intrusion upon his constitutional rights, Nixon vetoed the resolution. On November 7, 1973, Congress voted to override.

Throughout our history, most American presidents have considered it their duty to defend presidential powers against encroachment. And congressional leaders, myself included, have felt responsible to see that the rights of the legislative branch are not eroded. To a considerable degree this tug of war is healthy. But our system can thrive only when there is a mutual respect for the rational and constitutional limits upon our respective powers—even those of the presidency.

Scores of books have been written concerning the sordid procession of events which began with an unbelievably clumsy attempted burglary at the Democratic National Committee, and ended with the resignation of an American president. A single thread runs through all of the eyewitness accounts: that Nixon did not *believe* he had done anything wrong. Influential men in the White House—and Nixon chief among them—suffered primarily from a surfeit of zeal. They believed so unquestioningly in their cause and their right to impose it that anyone who resisted or obstructed it was not only catalogued as a personal enemy, and a misguided fool, but became in their eyes an enemy of the people.

While campaigning in Montana in the fall of 1972, Senate Majority Leader Mike Mansfield pledged to get to the bottom of widely reported rumors of electoral abuses, including who was responsible for the Watergate break-in, and to investigate certain reports of unsavory practices involving campaign financing.

The lean, soft-spoken Senate leader came as near as anybody in Congress to being liked by everyone. If he had an enemy, I never knew of it. A former teacher and one-time copper miner, Mike Mansfield was a man without pretense. Almost uniquely among his Senate peers, he seemed wholly unaffected by titles and honors.

Nobody ever accused the Montana senator of overstatement. Sucking on his ubiquitous pipe, his spare frame relaxed, a faint smile at the corners of his mouth and a reflective, faraway look in his squinty blue eyes, Mansfield may have been the most monosyllabic political personality since Calvin Coolidge.

This very trait made him the constant despair of interviewers. Several times I watched, amused, as television inquisitors pried at him with convoluted questions which Mike would manage almost invariably to answer with a simple "yes," "no," "sometimes," or "not necessarily."

One interviewer, trying to provoke a public quarrel, quoted at some length from an adversarial statement by a critic of something Mansfield had supported. "Would you agree with that comment?" the newsman teased.

"No," Mansfield quietly responded.

"Would you care to elaborate on your reasons for disagreeing with that statement?"

"No."

"Well, in other words, you feel that he was mistaken?"

"That's right," said Mansfield.

"Well, just how far off mark do you feel that he was in arriving at that conclusion?"

"Considerably."

Betty and I came to know Mike Mansfield and his gracious wife, Maureen, quite well through the years when he and I would accompany our respective House and Senate delegations to the inter-parliamentary meetings with Mexico. Mike never tried to learn Spanish. He didn't have to. He spoke a kind of universal language of genuine respect and transparent sincerity. Mansfield's easygoing personality stood in stark contrast to those of two recent predecessors in Senate leadership. He exhibited neither the furious hyperactivity of Lyndon Johnson nor the impelling eloquence of Hubert Humphrey. But his laid-back, laconic style tended to make people listen when he did offer an opinion. And in the matters involved in the upcoming Watergate investigation, he had some pronounced convictions. He was deeply disturbed by the burglary of the Watergate office building, and he bitterly resented Nixon's attacks on Hubert Humphrey and Ed Muskie.

The logical vehicle for the investigation was the Senate Judiciary Committee, headed by James Eastland of Mississippi, an old-style southern conservative Democrat and passionate pro-Nixon partisan on Vietnam. Seeing the inner conflict this could produce if Eastland were to preside over the inquiry, and in some part as a courtesy to his colleague, Mansfield asked Eastland to turn the proposed investigation over to a Select Committee headed by Sam Ervin of North Carolina, a stickler for individual liberties. Eastland consented.

In his initial discussions with Sam Ervin, in which Mansfield described the resolution they would eventually cosponsor, the Senate leader made it clear that he wanted no Democratic presidential candidates or hopefuls involved in the process. He was adamant that the Select Committee should not become a political bully pulpit, nor a forum for partisan campaign posturing.

Ervin, self-described "country lawyer" with a reverence for the Constitution, wholeheartedly agreed. When the resolution reached the Senate floor, Republicans clamored to expand the investigation to cover the elections of '64 and '68—which they steadfastly maintained had been permeated by widespread wiretapping, fraud, eavesdropping and similar illegal activities. Their amendment was overwhelmingly rejected as an obvious distraction. In the end even these ardent Republican partisans supported the resolution, the Senate voting 77–0 on February 7, 1973 for a Select Committee whose prime purpose was to conduct an investigation of illegal, improper, or unethical activities during the recent 1972 election.

Patiently and methodically, preparations began for the hearings. The careful atmosphere of judicious calm, so studiously maintained at Mansfield's insistence, was repeatedly broken by a series of stunning developments. A pattern of flagrant abuses began to emerge, at first slowly, like a thread unraveling in the sleeve of a sweater. It soon became apparent that unauthorized wiretaps and other forms of electronic surveillance against various political opponents of the administration were not uncommon.

The trial of the seven Watergate burglars in January 1973 produced no new information. The seven pleaded guilty but clammed up, denying knowledge of any connection to their crime by administration higher-ups. At the trial's end on January 30, Judge John J. Sirica expressed dissatisfaction. The actual motive of the break-in still remained a mystery. Sirica, feeling certain that his court had not heard the whole truth, said he hoped the Senate hearings could get to the bottom of it.

Seven weeks later, on March 23, the judge announced he had received a letter from one of the burglars, James W. McCord Jr., in which he confessed perjury, declaring that "there was political pressure applied to the defendants to plead guilty and remain silent." It developed that the burglars had been hired and paid by funds from the Committee to Reelect the President, appropriately—if astoundingly—acronymed CREEP.

McCord, according to news leaks that would later be confirmed, identified Jeb Stuart Magruder, Deputy Director of CREEP, and White House Counsel John Dean as having prior knowledge of the break-in and implicated them in the cover-up. As this shocking disclosure reverberated through downtown press rooms and Capitol Hill cloakrooms, President Nixon on April 17 reversed an earlier position. Up to that time, he had claimed that executive privilege protected presidential assistants from testifying to Congress even if subpoenaed. Now Nixon told a press conference that all White House staff members would be available to the Senate committee if called.

On April 30, the president announced to a nationwide television audience the resignations of his top assistants, Erlichman, Haldeman and Dean, and that of Attorney General Richard Kleindienst. He revealed that he was moving Secretary of Defense Elliot L. Richardson, a man generally respected by the press, into the Attorney General's post.

A real blockbuster fell on May 10, just one week before the Senate hearings were scheduled to commence. A New York grand jury indicted former Attorney General John N. Mitchell, who had served as chairman of CREEP, and former Secretary of Commerce Maurice Stans. They were charged with having provided official government favors to a shadowy financier, Robert L. Vesco, in exchange for secret and illegal campaign contributions delivered in cash. This brought things closer than ever to the president. Mitchell had been Nixon's law partner in New York before the 1968 election. He was generally considered a presidential confidante. I felt a surge of anger. Mitchell knew better! My God, he had been Attorney General of the United States! There was no excuse for this, if it were true.

Still not wanting to believe the president personally involved in the rancid pile of garbage which began to reek so nauseously, I felt a sharp pain of resentment that someone who had been given the honor to serve as our nation's chief legal officer would embarrass the country, and his president, by so sordid a deed. Sleazy cash campaign contributions for official favors!

More cruel and pettily corrupt than any of the rest, perhaps, was the revelation from Los Angeles on the following day, May 11. Judge W. Matthew Byrne, presiding over the conspiracy trial of Daniel Ellsberg, dropped charges and released damning evidence of conspiratorial White House involvement in the systematic and mean-spirited abuse of the defendant's rights. So eager had been administration officials to prosecute Ellsberg for leaking the Pentagon papers to *The New York Times* that they not only put illegal taps on his telephone but hired burglars to break into the private office of Ellsberg's psychiatrist. Obviously they were seeking something personal with which to smear the defendant. This gave me a sick feeling at the pit of my stomach. For all our pious pronouncements about protecting the free world from Communist tyranny, I saw, people high in our own government were copying the most detestable abuses of the tyrants we deplored.

I think most Democrats as well as Republicans on the Senate committee wanted, as I did, to believe that the president himself had been personally unaware of such flagrant invasions of citizens' rights. But then it developed that there existed a White House "Enemies List," containing names of private citizens to be subjected to harassment by government agencies. Could this have occurred without the president's knowledge?

By mid-May, when the Ervin committee's public hearings were ready to commence, what began as an almost comically bungled burglary had already attained the proportions of an international scandal. The committee's examination of the Watergate-related abuses exhibited a remarkably businesslike atmosphere, considering the sensational nature of the subject matter. Formal open hearings began on May 17, amid historic print and video coverage. Each evening, PBS reran videotapes of the day's sessions to the largest audience in its history. Relatively obscure White House personnel became household names throughout America, as bits of the drama unfolded from a procession of witnesses.

News of Watergate appeared on the front page of *The New York Times* every day during May, June, and July of 1973. Not since World War II had a single story so long sustained the fixation of the mass media. Newspapers across America routinely featured headlines, spurred by leaks and perhaps even magnified to some degree motivated by the press's subjective fear of Richard Nixon.

It began to come out that the president had rashly, illegally, and dumbfoundingly placed wiretaps on selected reporters, while having other media personnel subjected to audits by the IRS! Some Democratic financial contributors had been similarly targeted. The only excuse offered by apologists evoked a flimsy claim of "national security." In the end, it was just such abuses of power that would remove Richard Nixon from the White House.

The question posed one day by Senator Howard Baker pierced like a laser to the core of the issue: "How much did the president know, and when did he know it?"

On the afternoon of July 16—more than a year after the original break-in at the DNC—a man named Alexander Butterfield, previously unheard of by most Americans, revealed the existence of the infamous White House tapes. Butterfield, then head of the Federal Aviation Administration, had served formerly as aide to Bob Haldeman in the White House. Unbeknown to oval office visitors and even to many on the White House payroll, according to Butterfield's testimony, the president for many months had kept oral recordings of everything said in that room. Those tapes surely would hold the answer to Howard Baker's question.

But Nixon, confronted with the fact, quickly declared that the tapes were his confidential property. He'd share them with future historians, he said. Lyndon Johnson had once suggested to him that such a record could be historically valuable. It would violate executive privilege, Nixon asserted, to let others hear them now. From that date until Labor Day, while the president doggedly refused to release or allow committee access to the audio tapes, an immense volume of mail cascaded into the Capitol, addressed to the Senate Select Committee. The number rose to nine thousand letters a day. In the month of November, it topped one million.

In the polls, Richard Nixon—who'd enjoyed an impressive 68 percent approval as recently as February—had slipped to 40 percent by July. Caspar Weinberger, known as "Cap the Knife" for his budget-cutting propensities as Nixon's chairman of the Office of Management and Budget, later commented, "I don't think Nixon began to take the matter seriously until the polls went down." Throughout those months of his ordeal, President Nixon seems to have viewed the entire matter as a public relations problem; one that could be solved only by standing firm and not yielding to demands of the press: "stonewalling."

Meanwhile, the administration had other legal problems. Both Maryland and federal prosecutors were on the trail of Vice President Spiro Agnew. Criminal investigations into charges of bribery, involving contributions Agnew had received both as Governor of Maryland and as vice president, surfaced publicly on August 7. Meeting with the president that day, Spiro Agnew vowed that the charges were "just a pack of lies."

But on September 25, Attorney General Elliot Richardson privately told Nixon that there were some forty charges against the vice president which he thought legally sustainable. Later that day, the president had a private meeting with Agnew, in which the vice president contended that, if he had done anything wrong, he should be impeached by Congress rather than tried in a court of law.

Nixon called House Minority Leader Gerald Ford, and Agnew paid a personal call on Speaker Carl Albert to discuss that alternative. In the end, everyone decided that an impeachment proceeding would be pointless in the vice president's case, since, regardless of its outcome, a grand jury still could indict and a court try the vice president on such charges as it might seek to pursue.

Speaker Carl Albert told Majority Leader Tip O'Neill, Whip John McFall and the four regional whips confidentially that he had received a personal call from President Nixon, warning him privately of the seriousness of the charges against Agnew. Albert felt the call was motivated by a decent intent, that of protecting him and other leaders from the embarrassment of possibly speaking out in public defense of the vice president, not aware of the gravity of the counts against him.

For Richard Nixon, October 1973 must have seemed a month made in hell. On the international scene, where he would eternally have preferred to concentrate his attention, the Arabs attacked Israel, launching the Yom Kippur War.

On October 10, Spiro Agnew resigned as vice president, amid awful accusations of financial misconduct, after pleading "no contest" to charges of income tax evasion.

The very next day, October 11, I was seated on the House floor when a page came and told me that the White House was holding on a line in one of the private booths just off the floor in the House cloak room. When I answered, to my surprise the president himself came on the line.

Nixon was anxious to move with dispatch in naming a successor to Agnew, he told me. Under the new procedure adopted at Lyndon Johnson's insistence, the president could nominate and the Congress confirm a vice president whenever that office became vacant. Speaker Carl Albert, in fact, had urged the president to act speedily. Albert, next in line and successor to the president in absence of a vice president, wanted the vacancy filled promptly.

"I am considering two men, and you know them both," the president informed me. "I am anxious to have your evaluation of Jerry Ford and John Connally."

I was greatly surprised that President Nixon had called me regarding this matter. Surely I was not the only one. He must have called a number of others as well.

"Yes, Mr. President, I do know them both," I responded. "Either man in my opinion is well-qualified to be vice president of the United States."

"Which of the two would you choose if you were I?"

"Mr. President, both are my friends. Each has different qualities. I think it may depend upon what you feel you most need in that office at this particular time."

"In just what way do you mean that?" the president asked. "Would you be a bit more specific?"

"As I see it, Mr. President, you have two sets of problems. You have some serious problems with the Congress, and a slightly different set of problems with the press. I think it depends on where you feel you are likely to need help the most. In my opinion, John Connally could help you more with the press; while Jerry Ford can help you more with Congress. The media tend to like Connally. Jerry Ford has more friends on the hill. That's where their strengths lie, as I see it."

The president asked which place I thought he needed help more.

"I don't know, Mr. President," I told him. "That is a choice only you can make. I hope I've been of some help."

"You have." He thanked me, and our conversation was ended.

But President Nixon's troubles had only begun. The next day, he announced his nomination of House Minority Leader Gerald R. Ford to be vice president. Congress quickly confirmed him. Ford was liked by Democrats as well as Republicans. Nixon needed someone to help calm the troubled waters in Congress.

Only a week later, as we shall see, the Saturday Night Massacre would set the president's sea of troubles to roiling and splattering and boiling over like a bowl of soup left too long in a microwave oven.

CHAPTER EIGHTEEN

SATURDAY
NIGHT
AFTERMATH

The Saturday Night Massacre was what finally doomed Richard Nixon. It was a colossal miscalculation, after which all efforts of the president to recoup were like running to retrieve a stream of water that kept gushing from a hose.

To appreciate its finality, we need to go back and refocus on the week of swiftly moving events that preceded it.

On Friday, October 12, the Court of Appeals upheld a district court's order commanding the president to surrender nine specific tapes that were being sought by a Special Prosecutor, Archibald Cox, whom Attorney General Richardson had appointed with the president's compliance to monitor legal aspects of the whole Watergate matter. Nixon had refused the tapes to Cox, just as he had to the Senate, on grounds of executive privilege. This court ruling had to be a major disappointment to Nixon.

From a strictly Machiavellian point of view, questions of principle entirely aside, Nixon would have been better off if one of the White House "plumbers" had made a bonfire of those tapes when their existence was first disclosed by Alexander Butterfield—just as thirteen years later, in 1986, Lt. Col. Oliver North would stealthily destroy all written records of the unlawful Iran-Contra transactions before Congress or court could subpoena them.

As though there weren't troubles enough, a new international crisis had arisen. Egyptian and Syrian forces attacked Israel. At the Pentagon and the State Department, Israeli representatives spent that entire day of October 12 pleading for American aid in defense of their country. Armed with the most sophisticated Russian weapons, the Arab aggressors had left Israel reeling: a loss of 20 percent of the Israeli air force, and one-third of their armored forces within the first five days of conflict. Without resupply, the Israelis were doomed—and they believed only the United States could help. Prime Minister Golda Meir sent a message saying just that.

The Pentagon and the State Department were in abject disagreement with one another concerning what should be done about Israel. Secretary of State Henry Kissinger strongly felt America must act promptly, or see the Arabs sweep the Middle East into the Soviet sphere. Defense Secretary James Schlesinger saw the matter less urgently. The Pentagon argued that any U.S. transport planes involved should be disguised as Israeli aircraft.

After a brief mandatory appearance at a private White House ceremony for Gerald Ford, whom he had chosen to nominate for vice president, Nixon left his guests and closeted himself with Henry Kissinger until 1 A.M., discussing and reviewing the various options in the Middle East and weighing their consequences. By 10 A.M. the following morning, the president had made his decision. He ordered the Pentagon to resupply the Israelis, beginning that very day. This would represent Richard Nixon's last grand presidential action.

On October 16, District Judge John Sirica denied bail to five of the original Watergate defendants. These five, headed by E. Howard Hunt Jr., were directly involved in the break-in. All of them had originally pleaded guilty back in January, but later asked to change their pleas after John McCord disclosed White House pressure. They now were wanting out of jail until their sentencing, but Sirica declined. On the following day, three major U.S. corporations—American Airlines, Goodyear Tire and Rubber Company, and Minnesota Mining and Manufacturing Company— pleaded guilty to making illegal corporate campaign contributions to Nixon's 1972 reelection effort.

The president, on October 19, offered a compromise to the surrender of the nine tapes called for by the U.S. circuit court of appeals. He said he would not appeal the case to the Supreme Court if his conditions were accepted. He would give to Judge Sirica and the Senate investigating committee not the tapes themselves but a summary statement of their contents.

Nixon also offered to grant to Democratic Senator John C. Stennis of Mississippi full exclusive access to the tapes. Stennis could listen to them, under the president's plan, and verify the validity of the written summary. In exchange for this, special prosecutor Archibald Cox would have to agree to make no further attempt to subpoena any additional tapes or presidential papers.

I remember wondering at the time why Nixon supposed anyone would have faith in such an arrangement.

Cox quickly responded in a written statement, saying that he simply could not comply with that proposal. It would be inconsistent with his re-sponsibilities as special prosecutor, he said, and would defeat the cause of justice.

The next day was Saturday, October 20 — the date of what came to be called the Saturday Night Massacre. The day the sky fell in. In a very frank press conference that afternoon, Archibald Cox told the media why he had refused to comply with the president's proposal. Any such agreement would destroy his independence, he said. The prosecutor went on to talk of what he called "repeated frustration" in his efforts to gain information from the White House.

That Saturday night, I was back in Fort Worth, billed as principal speaker at the annual banquet of the North Texas Homebuilders Association. The banquet was at Hotel Texas, in the very room where President John F. Kennedy had made his last speech. During the meal preceding the program, an assistant manager of the hotel came to me at the head table. He said I had an emergency call from Marshall Lynam, my principal assistant who headed my Washington office. Marshall had just received stunning news and was anxious that I have it before anyone from the press could reach me for comment. Nixon, at the end of his rope with Cox, had ordered Attorney General Elliot Richardson to dismiss the Special Prosecutor. Richardson flatly refused and resigned.

Deputy Attorney General William D. Ruckelshaus, then told by the president to carry out the order, also refused. Nixon fired him on the spot. White House Press Secretary Ron Ziegler announced that Solicitor General Robert C. Bork had become acting attorney general and had fired Cox.

My first reaction was disbelief. Returning to the banquet, my head reeling from the bizarre events so recently transpired, I recounted them at the beginning of my speech—factually and without editorial comment. Several in the audience gasped audibly. These were business people. Most of them, I knew, had voted for Nixon in the 1972 election. They were stunned.

Within two days, the AFL–CIO, meeting in biennial convention at Bal Harbor, Florida, passed a resolution calling for the president's resignation and petitioning Congress to take up impeachment proceedings against him if he did not resign. Labor was not alone in this demand. A chorus of calls for impeachment arose in academic and professional circles.

On Monday morning following the Saturday Night Massacre, Speaker Carl Albert called Majority Leader O'Neill and a small group of advisors to his office to discuss possible grounds of impeachment. He told the four deputy whips of his decision prior to his 11:45 A.M. daily press conference which we routinely attended. House Judiciary Chairman Peter Rodino of New Jersey would initiate an official impeachment inquiry.

I dug out an ancient set of books my mother had given me one Christmas years earlier. They contained the official papers and public statements of presidents from George Washington to Theodore Roosevelt. I turned to the period of Andrew Johnson and spent several days studying all available material that touched on his impeachment. I was in for several surprises. Some of the articles voted by Congress against Andrew Johnson had been ludicrously flimsy. They included two counts asserting President Johnson impeachable because of public speeches in which he "did in a loud voice" criticize Congress. I read the statements attributed to the former president. They were pussy-cat tame compared with charges Harry Truman made in 1948 against "that terrible, know-nothing, do-nothing 80th Congress!" The Andrew Johnson impeachment, I concluded, had been a disgraceful exercise in congressional bullying.

Apparently, the constitutional provision describing impeachable offenses simply as "high crimes and misdemeanors," never before nor since invoked against any president, was subject to whatever definition Congress had the votes to impose at a given moment. I began to worry that partisan fevers and angry public pressures now growing rife against Nixon might move eager members of the House Judiciary Committee to extravagant charges or imprudent language which history would scorn. I wrote a memorandum and discussed these apprehensions with Speaker Albert at the next meeting of the regional whips.

I needn't have worried. Several of my friends on Judiciary—including Jack Brooks, Walter Flowers and Barbara Jordan—told me of Chairman Peter Rodino's insistent emphasis upon the very restraint I was advocating. On October 30, Rodino convened the Judiciary Committee for the first of what would become the most carefully watched and generally applauded set of hearings held by any committee of Congress during my thirty-four years in the House.

For the next nine months President Nixon struggled to refocus public attention on other problems. He tried valiantly to be presidential. He celebrated passage of his bill to add automatic cost-of-living adjustments to Social Security monthly benefits. He commented at length on proposals to free our country from the gasoline crisis, brought on by the Arab oil embargo of late 1973 and early 1974. But every press conference Nixon called to make some major policy announcement quickly degenerated into a fresh media inquisition devoted exclusively to Watergate-related topics. The president, gasping for any help he could find in the vain pursuit of renewed public favor, chose attorney Leon Jaworski of Houston to take the role of special prosecutor from which he had fired Archibald Cox. Jaworski's reputation was spotless. He had served as a prosecutor at the Nuremberg War Crimes Trials. Barbara Jordan, who represented Jaworski's home city in Congress, asked me at the next whip meeting if I thought Nixon knew what he had done.

"One of two things, Barbara. Either President Nixon honestly believes in his innocence; or else he doesn't know Leon Jaworski."

"I think it's the latter, Jim," she said.

Observing the president's slow slide from grace was like watching a classic Greek tragedy. Events built inexorably upon one another, leading to the inevitable climax. Nothing Nixon could do from this point forward would alter the outcome.

The president, on October 23, publicly relented, agreeing to release the tapes to the U.S. District Court as ordered by the appellate court's ruling. Excerpts would be played by the congressional committees, and the public would hear audio broadcasts of long snatches of inner White House conversations. Transcripts would appear in the newspapers with frequent notations of "expletives deleted." At first, the public's impassioned indignation seemed to center less upon the substance revealed within the tapes and more upon the profanity employed by President Nixon in these sometimes frantic private conversations. The greatest fury I heard expressed by most people, incomprehensibly, focused on this vulgarity of language—the scatological terms with which a frightened and beleaguered president had seasoned his unguarded comments, believing himself to be speaking within the privacy of his own home and office.

As these tapes reeled out their secrets to inquiring lawmakers and a voyeuristic public, it became apparent that the first, and inescapable, personal misdeed of Richard Nixon's had occurred on June 23, 1972, shortly after the burglary. The president, apparently fearing negative campaign fallout, had cavalierly authorized use of the CIA to obstruct, or to halt, the FBI investigation of the Watergate burglary.

It was this one action, so carelessly undertaken, which more than any subsequent event doomed Richard Nixon's presidency. It is tempting, but no doubt idle, to speculate what might have happened if Nixon, upon learning of the burglary, had immediately revealed it, condemned it, and let the chips fall where they may. I strongly suspect that the public would have held him blameless, talked about the bizarre occurrence for two or three days, and moved on to other, bigger things, dropping the burglary from their consciousness.

But as Francesca Johnson says to Robert Kincaid in *The Bridges of Madison County*, we are the choices we make. And Richard Milhous Nixon, at that moment of his career, amid the haste and passion of a gathering presidential campaign, had chosen to try to hush it up. That choice, and the other maladroit and unfortunate ones that flowed forth as a consequence of it, were paving stones in the road to President Nixon's downfall.

I was busy with a gathering host of jobs that year. As Chairman of the Public Works Subcommittee on Investigations and Review, I was increasingly involved in the drafting and oversight of legislative programs. The Clean Water bill had created a National Water Quality Commission to oversee the cleanup. Appointed to that commission, I worked closely with New York Governor Nelson Rockefeller. As one of four regional whips, I enjoyed increasing responsibility for rounding up the votes to pass of Speaker Albert's major legislative objectives.

Even as life went on for the rest of us, it must have been a bleeding nightmare for President Nixon and his family. More people began calling for his resignation. Senator Barry Goldwater, "Mr. Republican" to the conservative wing of the GOP, issued a statement saying that the president's credibility was at an all-time low "from which he may never be able to recover." Senator Edward W. Brooke of Massachusetts, considered a moderate-to-liberal Republican, called on Nixon to resign. Across the country, newspapers were in full cry. Like hounds in pursuit of a fox, *The New York Times*, the *Denver Post*, and the *Detroit News* were baying for the president's resignation. *Time* magazine, printing an editorial for the first time in its fifty-year history, echoed the call that now was becoming a clamor.

Combative by nature, always a believer in playing aggressively, the president at first resorted to bombast. In news conferences, he attacked the press and assorted political opponents. Blasting back at news coverage of the Saturday Night Massacre, he declaimed that it had been the most "outrageous, vicious, distorted reporting" in his twenty-seven years of public life.

But people weren't buying this line.

For the first time in his political career, Richard Nixon now was reduced to playing "not to lose." Friends and advisors arranged humanizing events that might recapture a sense of public identification with the beleaguered president. On March 16, 1974, Nixon flew out to Nashville to greet his wife, Pat, who was just returning from a six-day trip to South America. It was Mrs. Nixon's birthday, and it seemed a wonderfully endearing thing for the president and First Lady to celebrate it together at Nashville's Grand Ole Opry. But not even in this picture-perfect middle America setting, surrounded by lovers of country music, would Nixon be spared criticism. With the president accompanying on the piano, the entire audience rose to its feet and sang a lusty Happy Birthday to the First Lady. In a rare spontaneous gesture, Pat got up from her seat and walked over to her husband with her arms open to hug him. Maybe Nixon didn't see her, but everyone in the audience did. Just as she approached, the president arose from the piano stool and walked in the opposite direction, toward the center of the stage. Women reporters used the unfortunate episode to pan President Nixon for coldness, rudeness, and insensitivity.

Daughter Julie Eisenhower explained that her father was unaware of her mother's endearing gesture and was simply trying to indicate modestly that they both were ready to leave the stage and let the show resume. Julie also took that occasion to explain a fundamental characteristic of her family. They had a strong, innate aversion to demonstrating their affection for one another in public. Their private feelings, Julie very politely stressed, were just that—private. This particular key to Richard Nixon's personality helps explain his inability to display his emotions in public. Doing so would be, in his view, a sign of weakness, and weakness was despicable.

This turn of temperament separated Nixon from other political types. A James Michael Curley could be a lovable rogue. Knowing him guilty of sundry sins, constituents were attracted by his human warmth and showered him with their affection. Edward Kennedy, grandson of Curley's nemesis, could survive Chappaquiddick and other more conventional transgressions for much the same reason. Agree with him or not, you had to love him. Ronald Reagan could commit egregious factual misstatements, shrug them off with a joke when they were called to his attention, and get by with it because of his personality.

Nixon was not like that. He was a private person. There was in him, as there was in me, a mixture of the dour Scot and the gregarious Irish. In Nixon, the Scot predominated. He once applied to himself a Dean Acheson anecdote about Lyndon Johnson. The former secretary of State, to whom Johnson was complaining of unfair press treatment, is supposed to have told the president, "You want the press to love you. And they won't—because you're not very lovable." Nixon, in a rare moment of self-deprecating humor, said it applied more to him than it did to Lyndon.

A comparison between the two former presidents is inescapable. Each had a certain brilliance. Both Johnson and Nixon suffered what they considered ill-treatment at the hands of the media. Both had great dreams for their presidencies; neither found whole fulfillment. Both were frustrated, each by a different aspect of the chief executive's increasingly dual function of foreign and domestic leadership.

Johnson dreamed of improving and enriching the domestic life of his native land to the betterment of its humblest citizen. He did arguably more than any predecessor to achieve broader fields of opportunity and a more abundant life for America's deprived, but he was partially cheated of his place in history by the intractable quagmire of Vietnam. Nixon, by contrast, had a passion for foreign policy. His grand goal was to make a lasting contribution to world peace. This he achieved, but the fruits of recognition for that achievement were snatched from him by a flawed and impatient approach to domestic government.

The personalities of the two were altogether different. While both could be manipulative and each had a strain of secretiveness, some would say deviousness, their methods had very little in common. Lyndon was garrulous, intensely personal, his arm around your shoulder and his face four inches from your own. He loved handshaking and intimate palaver, "pressing the flesh" as he called it. Johnson was a *people* man. Richard Nixon, by almost total contrast, never seemed comfortable when anyone got too close. He wasn't wont to confide, as Lyndon was, his personal feelings or anecdotes of his childhood. Johnson would gush on about his family and brag of their achievements. Nixon considered that a part of his privacy. Lyndon Johnson really didn't give a horned toad's hide about privacy. Could anyone imagine Richard Nixon opening his shirt to show strangers the scar from his abdominal operation?

As the impeachment hearings proceeded deliberately toward their perhaps foreordained destination, Nixon tried to build a sort of Maginot Line of friends and supporters in the House. Nixon sought out the moderate and conservative Democrats. He invited me to come one evening in July, along with a number of other moderates, mostly southerners and midwesterners. I went for cocktails, dinner, and an unstructured session of informal conversation following the meal. I noticed that the president carried a glass of scotch in his hand and nursed it through the whole predinner reception. It was a very soft sell. Nixon seemed to prefer talking about anything and everything *except* the impeachment hearings. When a question alluded to their threat, Nixon would briefly disavow any alleged wrongdoing, as though all present were fully aware of his innocence, and turn to another subject.

As I sat there that evening, silently studying President Nixon, I was overcome by a deep sorrow for him. I got the idea that he didn't come right out and ask for support that evening for fear of the hurt of being turned down.

The president was counting on a Louisiana Democrat named Joe Waggonner to round up as many conservatives and southerners as possible to stand by his side against impeachment. Joe, after counting, told Nixon following the 4th of July recess that he probably could rely on "about fifty" Democrats to stay with him. But then, as testimony piled up, positions began to solidify, one by one, among Judiciary Committee members who had been struggling internally to maintain an open-minded attitude. Some wouldn't even tell their spouses how they were leaning.

On July 12, a jarring court verdict delivered a vital blow. John D. Erlichman, Nixon's top White House domestic advisor, was convicted of conspiring with others to break unlawfully into the office of Daniel Ellsberg's former psychiatrist. A jury of six men and six women found Erlichman personally involved in the planning, guilty along with three members of the so-called White House "plumbers unit." This was the same group that staged the Watergate break-in.

Joe Waggonner called the president on July 23 with some dismal news. He sadly told Nixon that he had lost the committee's three southern Democrats. Walter Flowers of Alabama, James Mann of South Carolina, and Ray Thornton of Arkansas—for whose support the president was hoping—had all reached their agonizing decisions. All three would support impeachment. Replacing the telephone receiver, Nixon reportedly turned to his Chief of Staff, General Alexander Haig. "Well, Al," Nixon is supposed to have said, "there goes the presidency."

Most Americans who were adults at the time remember something of the televised deliberations of the House Judiciary Committee. It was the abuse of power issues that formed the impelling nub of the second Article of Impeachment. Nobody alleged, even at this point, that Nixon knew in advance of the Watergate burglary. But members had seen evidence that convinced them he did know, and consent to, other abuses just as onerous—the use of the IRS, the CIA, and other agencies of the government to spy upon, threaten, harass and intimidate private citizens whose only sin was opposing the president. And he did permit use of the powers of his office to conceal those covert activities. In his determination to have his way, the president of the United States had ignored the will of Congress and violated the Constitution. That's really what it came down to.

Most people remember the painful ordeal of Mr. Nixon's August 8 resignation speech. "I would have preferred to carry through to the finish, whatever the personal agony," the president said, but "the interest of the nation" impelled him to step aside. "America needs a full time president," he asserted. Continuing the fight for his own vindication would absorb his total energies and rob us of the leadership to which the country was entitled.

He pleaded that his successor, Gerald Ford, be granted the "understanding, the patience, the cooperation he will need" to put the bitterness and divisiveness of the recent past behind and "to begin healing the wounds of this nation." It was the essential Richard Nixon—controlled, reserved, not giving in to emotion even as his heart ached within him.

More poignant yet, surely more personal and probably more revealing of the inner man, were the informal words he spoke the next morning, August 9, prior to his departure by helicopter from the spacious lawn south of the White House. He spoke of the White House itself ("This house has a great heart"); of his father and mother, their tribulations and business failures ("He was a great man . . . she was a saint"). He quoted a sentimental passage from Theodore Roosevelt.

And then, preparing to leave the White House for the last time, Nixon addressed these words of parting advice to his cabinet, personal staff and friends who had stood with him during the good and bad years: "Always give your best, never get discouraged, never be petty; always remember, others may hate you, but those who hate you don't win unless you hate them, and then you destroy yourself." Tears rolled silently down his cheek.

I would see Richard Nixon again, several times and in pleasanter circumstances. Years later, during the Reagan presidency, I would spend several days with him and our other two living former presidents in the official party attending the funeral of Anwar Sadat in Cairo. He was a different Nixon, more relaxed and less intense, more at peace with himself, I believe.

But as I watched him wave goodbye that sultry August morning in 1974, I thought whimsically of a happier moment, an evening at the Washington Press Club in the mid-1950s. With the curtain drawn, the announcer intoned, "Our mystery guest tonight once served as vice president of the United States, and one of his hobbies is playing the piano." From behind the screen came the unmistakable strains of *The Missouri Waltz.* Everyone was certain it was Harry Truman.

Then the curtains opened to reveal Vice President Richard Nixon stroking the keys, playing the piece quite well. He had fun that night.

Personally, I hope Dick Nixon had a lot more fun in life than most of us saw him having. He deserved to. Beneath the conscious dignity that guarded his emotions, I believe that Richard Nixon loved America. From the time he served in the Navy in World War II, he gave fifty years of his life to it. And that fact deserves to have some of the good times remembered, along with the bad.

Now there was a new president—a likable, decent, uncomplicated man named Jerry Ford. For the transient moment, everyone in America wished him well.

CHAPTER NINETEEN

FORD'S ERA OF GOOD FEELINGS

G erald Ford has always been what people call, in simple parlance, "a good man." Trusting and trustworthy. Not a mean bone in his body. Being instinctively honest, Ford lacked any habitual suspicion of others' motives. It is trite to say that a public official, like Caesar's wife, should be "above suspicion." It is equally true, in my personal scale of values, that a public servant should be above casting unwarranted suspicion on fallible fellow creatures, including competitors. Jerry Ford qualified on all these counts.

Ever since he became Minority Leader in 1965, replacing Charles Halleck of Indiana, Ford had come to symbolize a new wave of House Republicans more conscious of social needs and public sentiment. I had been impressed by Jerry Ford's personal manner. He was every bit as conservative as his leadership predecessors on economic issues, but he was polite, honest, and personally considerate in his dealings with Democratic colleagues. So, on his assumption of the presidency, he enjoyed a big reservoir of good will.

In the summer of 1969, after graduating from high school and before starting college, my middle daughter, Kay, found a part-time job to earn some pocket money. Washington is a lot like a one company town. That "company," of course, is government. Kay asked if I knew of any summer jobs on the Hill.

"I'm sure there are lots of them, Honey, but the nepotism law doesn't let me recommend you for any, or even point you in the direction of one. I could recommend other folks, but not family. If you're interested in getting some experience working on the Hill, you'll have to find some job strictly on your own."

Somebody in my office told Kay how to put in an application at the non-partisan congressional placement office, a clearing house where lawmakers and committee staffs in need of temporary summer help, would list available jobs. Kay, after two or three hours, came cheerily into my office that afternoon to announce her landing of a summer job. "That's great!" I exclaimed, "Where is it?"

"I'm going to work in the House Minority Leader's office for Congressman Ford," she declared. My heart sank.

"I hate to tell you this, darlin', but Mr. Ford may not think that is a real good idea. Did you tell him who you are? I mean, did you tell him you are my daughter?"

"No, Dad, I didn't see Mr. Ford. I saw another man in his office. He just looked at my resume and said 'fine.' He told me I could start tomorrow."

"Did the folks in the placement office know that I am your father?"

"No, Dad. You said you couldn't recommend me, and they didn't ask me anything about who my father is. They asked if I had any preference to work for a Democrat or a Republican, and I said 'no.' I didn't think it would make any difference."

"Well, maybe it won't. But I have to tell Jerry Ford who his office has just hired. You see, He is the top Republican in the House. His Republican colleagues elected him to be their leader. Some of them are sure to have daughters who want summer jobs, and they might not look kindly on his hiring the daughter of a Democrat."

"Oh, I see," Kay sighed. "Have I done something wrong?"

I assured her to the contrary. But Jerry Ford did need to know about it right away in order to avoid any possible embarrassment.

When I told him, the next day on the House floor, Jerry said, "That's just fine, Jim. I don't have any problem with that. I've got to meet that girl! I know that no daughter of yours would think of being anything but trustworthy and loyal to whomever she works for. You tell her to come introduce herself, and I hope she enjoys the summer. We'll work the socks off her."

Following that, Kay and I had a long talk about loyalty. She must never tell me or any other Democrat of anything she might happen to learn about Republican political strategy—or anything else that happened in that office, for that matter.

For the summer, or as long as the job lasted, I insisted, her loyalty must be to Mr. Ford, for whom she worked. Twenty-six years later, she would tell me that our conversation about loyalty, and her errand-running job that summer had made a lifelong impression.

The episode made an impression on me, too. I thought it told a lot about the kind of guy who had now become our president. As he suddenly began to gain a saturation level of public exposure he'd never expected to attain, people all over the country started piecing him together. It would be awhile before the media started taking him apart.

In his first public statement after bidding a sympathetic farewell to President Nixon, whom he'd known since both were young House members together, immediately following his oath of office, President Gerald Ford said, "Our long national nightmare is over."

Ford's simile was apt. The big American family, heads spinning from the only presidential resignation in history, were as shaken—and as relieved—as a grateful survivor of a near-fatal automobile accident. A major constitutional collision had been averted. And the whole experience had been a nightmare.

There was something of the all-American boy in Jerry Ford. In 1932 and 1933, he had been a star on the University of Michigan's undefeated national championship football team. The following year, 1934, Ford was voted most valuable player on the Wolverine squad. Following graduation, he went to law school at Yale.

In 1947, after military service in World War II, the former football hero and now Grand Rapids lawyer met Elizabeth Bloomer, a model, dance teacher, and coordinator of fashion shows for a large Grand Rapids department store. The two were married in October of the following year, while Jerry was engaged in his first campaign for Congress. Both the campaign and the marriage were successes, portents of Jerry Ford's future.

Open, outspoken Betty Ford had easily as many friends as her likeable and hardworking husband. One of Jerry's family confided to her that she'd never have to worry about another woman. "Jerry's work will be the other woman." Popular with colleagues, Ford was much in demand among Republicans to speak at campaign fund solicitation dinners and Chamber of Commerce banquets. I understood the urge to do these things for colleagues, having by then made guest appearances in their home districts for at least fifty or sixty members. By the time he was appointed vice president, Ford had made easily three times that many.

There was something particularly refreshing about the couple. Part of it had to do with Betty's candor. Uncharacteristic for a political wife, Betty Ford was plainspoken on any issue on which she had a conviction, even if her husband had been voting the other way. White House press secretary Sheila Weidenfeld called the new first lady "the most up-front person I ever knew."

My Betty had a special affinity for Betty Ford, whom she'd known in the Congressional Wives Club. Both had been dancers in their youth; each had done some modeling; both had brief previous marriages; each said exactly what she thought. Once, when my wife answered a question with a frank, outspoken response, I interceded. "I'm not sure that's exactly what you want to say," I commented.

"But it is," said Betty. "It's exactly what I wanted to say."

So it was with the new First Lady. More than any presidential wife since Eleanor Roosevelt, Betty Ford was accessible any time the press sought an interview. More than once, her spontaneity, particularly on women's issues, surprised her interviewer.

On one occasion, following a televised statement by President Ford of his conservative views on abortion, the first lady sent him a handwritten message on a piece of paper: "Baloney!" Ford's press aide Ron Nessen told newsmen that Ford had "long ceased to be perturbed by his wife's remarks."

After Lyndon Johnson's persistent efforts to convince, cajole, and massage the press into agreement and Richard Nixon's defensive, often suspicious caution and avoidance, the new openness of both president and wife was like a cool, fresh breeze on a sultry August afternoon.

At his first nationally televised presidential news conference, on August 28, President Ford began by saying he had an important and very serious announcement. Both he and Mrs. Ford, each without consulting the other, had scheduled news conferences for that very same day. Hers, at the last minute, had been postponed.

"We worked this out between us in a calm and orderly way," Ford deadpanned. "She will postpone her press conference until next week—and until then I will be making my own breakfast, my own lunch and my own dinner."

Veteran Washington newswoman Sarah McClendon wrote that President Ford's calling on seven women at his first formal White House press conference "set a new record and inspired me to think that a new day of equal rights was dawning for women reporters." She also noted that the new president was "relaxed and natural" and wore absolutely no television makeup. The latter was, to her, a sign that he intended "to remain the same old Jerry Ford."

More impressive than any of this to me were Ford's candid answers in a session at the White House just a couple of days after he took office as president. Present were newsmen, members of Congress and wives. Someone asked the president if he'd had a chance to check on whether, in 1970 and 1971, there had been covert involvement by the CIA, dirty tricks in effect, in stirring up riots and financing other political opposition to the Salvador Allende regime in Chile, ending in the killing of the elected president.

Yes, Ford answered directly and without hesitating. He had checked up on that. And the CIA indeed had been involved, contrary to earlier official White House denials. Seated in the front row and looking directly into the new president's face, I felt as though someone had stabbed me with an electric cattle prod.

Stinging and infuriating was a hot surge of instant recall. I remembered that morning in 1971, after the stealthy military coup led by Augusto Pinochet resulted in the death of the elected president and the suspension of parliamentary democracy in that country where constitutional rule had long been respected. Members of Congress had been invited to an official State Department briefing on the coup in Chile. On that day three years earlier, it was I who asked the question point blank.

"Did the CIA or any other agency of the U.S. government have anything to do with these events, with attempts to rig the election last year, or with efforts to overthrow the Allende government?"

No, the State Department spokesman solemnly assured me. Not one solitary thing. In no way had we interfered with that country's electoral processes or its internal political affairs.

Believing these assurances, given to me in that private meeting of elected lawmakers, I several times had publicly denied persistent rumors that tied covert intervention by agents paid by U.S. taxpayers to the disgraceful events which had ended democratic rule in Chile. Added to this was the anger I now felt at having been categorically lied to by our State Department. And the shame I felt, having taken the word of our executive branch at face value, that I had unknowingly perpetuated this lie.

Had I not already felt kindly toward the new president, I would have been grateful for this candor which—coming belatedly though it did—represented a significant tactical change and a major step, so far as I was concerned, in redeeming the honor of our country.

Two other events of that late summer and early fall of 1974 strongly reaffirmed my existing conviction of Gerald Ford's political integrity. Ironically, the first of these brought Ford more unthinking personal criticism than any other act of his presidency.

On Sunday morning, September 8, President Ford unconditionally pardoned former President Richard M. Nixon of any punishable crimes that might have been committed arising from all the acrimonious and convoluted Watergate-related activities. As soon as the pardon was announced, a raucous noise of protest arose. Across the country, Ford became the object of an angry outcry. Some of Nixon's harshest critics, thirsting for personal retribution, seemed to feel they had been cheated. "The son of a bitch embarrassed the country, and we won't be even until we embarrass him," insisted one irate caller who rang me up that Sunday on my home telephone immediately upon hearing the news. "I say put Nixon behind bars! Don't let Ford get away with this cover-up!"

I explained that the president of the United States, under our constitution, has absolute and unrestrained authority to pardon any citizen of any federal crime. "Nobody can veto a presidential pardon," I told him, "and further-more I think President Ford did the right thing." I said the same to news reporters who called demanding to know my position.

Ford stated his reason clearly. The "tranquillity" to which the nation was carefully restored following his assuming the presidency, Ford believed, could be "irreparably lost" by dragging a former president and the American people through a high-visibility public trial.

Any such possible legal action would predictably dominate all other news for a year or more, preoccupy, distract and paralyze the government while the public chose mutually hostile sides and battered one another with invective. It was obvious to me that Gerald Ford had thought it through carefully with America's best interests at heart. He knew he would be criticized, his motives grossly misconstrued. A month earlier, on July 26, polls showed Nixon's pub-lic support at only 24 percent. And 66 percent of all Americans on August 2, according to pollster Louis Harris, favored impeachment.

Predictably, some accused Ford and Nixon of having made a secret agreement for such a pardon in exchange for Nixon's recommendation of Ford to become vice president. This, I am certain, was not the case. It would not square with Jerry Ford's character, for one thing. Furthermore, Nixon still believed at the time he chose Ford that the House Judiciary Committee would reject impeachment. Both men, in my estimation, were too proud to be parties to any such crude, cheap deal. Nixon, after all, could have pardoned Agnew and did not.

Moreover, the former president, whose physicians worried privately at the time over a possible stroke or heart attack, was obviously moved by his succes-sor's action. Nixon surely sensed that it put the new president's own clean image and political credibility at considerable risk.

Ten minutes after receiving Ford's pardon, Nixon said, "No words can describe the depths of my regret and pain at the anguish my mistakes over Watergate have caused the nation and the presidency." In a rambling and unself-assured statement, he then went on to speak of those occurrences as "still in my mind a confusing maze of events, decisions, pressures and person-alities." All of it had grown, he said, "from a political scandal into a national tragedy."

Part of that tragedy, I believe, has been its lingering legacy of suspicion and doubt. Cynicism toward public officials in general has escalated to a point where young people who value their reputations are no longer attracted to careers in public office. That is, indeed, a tragedy.

In the wake of the unprecedented notoriety received by *Washington Post* reporters Bob Woodward and Carl Bernstein, a whole generation of "inves-tigative" reporters, whose careers constantly depend upon their finding some scandal to report, has created, and in turn feeds upon, a cannibalistic public tendency to mistrust its own government and to suspect nefarious conspiracies under every rug.

And many politicians themselves have become addicted to negative campaigning. People, it seems, are ready to believe the worst and impatient to hear it. In this climate, a candidate who is, in the sense of my own upbringing, a "gentlemen," or a "lady," assumes a large handicap. The advantage increasingly lies with the mudslinger. This, too, is a tragedy. But it was away from just such an atmosphere that Gerald Ford, in granting the pardon, endeavored to lead us.

The second incident that confirmed my faith in President Ford's integrity was unimportant nationally but impressive to me personally. For the past four elections since defeating my Democratic primary opponent nine-to-one in 1964, I had not had an opponent in either the Democratic primary or the general election. Now, in 1974, a successful Fort Worth businessman named James Garvey, owner of a chain of grain elevators in Texas, Oklahoma and Kansas, announced as a Republican candidate for the congressional seat I held.

Garvey had made a personal fortune and seemed willing to spend whatever sums might contribute to making his candidacy a serious threat. He hired a veteran Fort Worth newsman to write speeches, compose statements, issue press releases, and otherwise conduct the public relations end of his campaign. Garvey was unopposed for the Republican nomination.

On September 30, President Ford, responding to a request of the Republican Congressional Campaign Committee, scheduled a White House photo session for all candidates nominated in GOP primaries. Each had his picture taken, for whatever campaign use he might wish to make of it, shaking hands with the new president. Garvey attended the session. In transmitting the photo to Tarrant County newspapers, the campaign consultant could not resist accompanying it with an inventive press release in the candidate's name. Garvey's ghosted statement said: "The president told me that it was essential that Congressman Jim Wright, who has been a notorious voter for spending bills, be defeated." Claiming Ford had endorsed his candidacy on the grounds that I was a dangerous radical and big spender, the Garvey statement further asserted the president had told him that I represented "one of the major causes of inflation."

As soon as I read this, I knew the purported conversation with Ford was a phony. That was just not something Gerald Ford would have said. To make a personal attack on a Democratic friend was not something he would do. So I called Jerry Ford and read him the statement. "I know you didn't say anything like that, Mr. President," I chuckled, "but I just thought you'd like to see how we Texans got our reputation for tall tales."

"Well, of course I didn't say anything like that, Jim. In the first place, it doesn't represent my sentiments. In the second place, I didn't say it. In fact, I didn't have time for a personal visit with any of those fellows. They just lined up and came by and had their pictures taken shaking hands. What do you want me to do about it?"

"Well, Mr. President," I replied, "I don't think it's necessary to embarrass the Republican candidate by your issuing an outright statement on the matter. Certainly not at this point. I suspect the statement was written for Garvey by his PR man, and Garvey may not even have looked at it. Would it be all right if I simply said to the papers that you and I had talked, and that you authorized me to say that you had not made this statement?"

"Of course, that would be all right, Jim. By all means. You have my total authorization to say just that. If anyone should contradict you, which I doubt, you can refer the next inquiry directly to me." This is how we left it. I told the media exactly what I said I would. That was enough. President Ford surely would have been pleased with a Republican congress, but he was not willing to be used, or have words put in his mouth.

In all of my political campaigns, I took a great deal of pride in never making a personal attack upon an opponent. I wouldn't have felt that I'd accomplished anything worthwhile if the only reason people voted for me was because of their dislike for my competitor. From my first campaign to my last, I made it an almost unvarying practice never even to mention the name of my opponent. I talked instead of what I believed and what I was trying to achieve.

For this reason, I turned a deaf ear to several that year who came bearing tales of one kind and another about Jim Garvey's business practices. I suspect that most of the negative stories people offered me originated from disappointed business competitors in the grain business. So far as I was concerned, Jim Garvey was an honest person and a good businessman. He deserved credit, not calumny. He just didn't deserve to be congressman from the 12th district of Texas.

After twenty years in Congress, I was enjoying bipartisan popularity in my home area. At the beginning of that year, a group of civic leaders in Fort Worth and environs had thrown a big dinner in my honor. It was billed as an appreciation banquet. The theme was my two decades of service. The sponsoring committee included the elected mayors of all twenty-one municipalities in the county, current officers of Chambers of Commerce and Labor Unions alike.

Testimonials at the banquet came from a politically ecumenical cross section. Among those participating were Governor Nelson Rockefeller, Congressman John Anderson of Illinois who was chairman of the House

Republican Conference, and Bill Harsha of Ohio, ranking Republican on the House Public Works Committee.

Rockefeller presented me a beautiful Steubenware crystal representation titled The Trout Pond, a heavy round section featuring the internally etched outline of a sleek trout rising toward a tiny gold lure which intersected the surface of the stream. From that point outward emanated the effect of gentle concentric ripples. It was, Rockefeller said, a token of his appreciation of our work together on the Water Quality Commission.

About three thousand people attended the dinner. They included Democrats and Republicans, labor and management, rich and poor and neither, white and black and brown.

As confident of reelection as Muhammad Ali following his October 29 kayo of George Foreman in Zaire, I nevertheless was eager to win as big a victory as possible. The thought occurred to me that a top-heavy triumph, if I could bring it off, might discourage future opposition.

So thinking, I set about building a block-by-block political fortress. A friend named Carlos Moore and I conceived the pattern of recruiting a block captain for every residential block in the entire district. Telemarketing was not yet a word. The idea itself had not really been put to the test, let alone worn out its welcome. We pioneered in perfecting its political potential. With all the care of the Dallas Cowboys coaching staff, we trained a team of twenty men and women, armed with the precinct voting lists, to recruit a veritable army of volunteer block captains. Each captain's duty was to distribute literature, enlist active supporters and see that the committed ones got to the polls on election day. Our recruiters' first rule: we love everybody, argue with nobody, listen to what we hear, respect any who criticize, irritate none, and thank everyone.

In much less time than we supposed it would take, our team of telephone solicitors, identifying themselves in their opening sentence as representing my campaign, had enrolled 6,500 block captains. Someone had agreed to perform these unpaid tasks for us in every single identifiable residential block in our whole county. Our problem, we decided, was that it had been too easy. In too many cases, the first person called at random in a city block had agreed to play on the team. Fully five out of six of our county's households had not even been called by the time our team was in place. Those to whom we'd talked had been so pleased to be asked, that we started looking for reasons to call the others. In several fast-growing areas of our metroplex, whole neighborhoods had sprung up and many thousands of new constituents moved into the area since last I had been challenged for reelection. In these localities, we decided to have a series of big, informal coffees at which I'd shake hands, speak briefly and answer questions.

To fulfill this schedule, I was flying back and forth from Washington every week during September and October. Campaigning and legislating both, I was getting little sleep. The well of my physical resources didn't quite run dry, but the water table was low.

After twenty years in office, as the number of constituents with whom I had shaken hands at least once ran into tens of thousands, I was coming to appreciate the value of name tags. The print had not yet begun to shrink from the grasp of my slowing retreating eyesight. I had practiced glancing quickly and unobtrusively at the tag, then locking eyes in a friendly greeting. "Hi, Bill!" or "How are you, Sally?" Name tags, we had taught our volunteers, should be on the right lapel, not on the left, so they are quickly visible when shaking hands.

Even the most practiced eye, however, can sometimes betray its owner. During that 1974 campaign, I was invited to a 7 A.M. breakfast meeting of the realtors in Northeast Tarrant County. As usual, I got there early, about 6:30. Not fully awake, I was trying my best to exude cheerfulness. Approaches a man with hand outstretched. I look quickly at the name tag. "Hi there, Red!" A second comes forward. A quick glance and a glad greeting. "Nice to see you today, Red!" Strange, I thought, this fellow's hair is coal-black. I cheerily greeted another "Red." Next came a middle-aged woman. With a swift visual sweep at the name tag, I chirruped, "How are things going for you, Mrs. Carpet?"

Finally, it dawned on me. They all belonged to the same agency: RED CARPET. When I realized my error, I expect my face was as red as their carpet.

My gaffes notwithstanding, that election brought a personally gratifying result. There was a huge turnout, exceptionally big for an off-presidential year. The ballots tallied, I'd won right at eighty percent of all votes cast! We carried every one of the big county's 153 precincts. In two of them, I'd won a clean sweep—every single vote. Indeed, across the nation, Democrats had carried the day with a surprisingly big string of victories. A lot of voters, disenchanted by Watergate, took out their vengeance against Republican incumbents. In their place, the election installed a gaggle of new Democrats—bright, moralistic, contemptuous of political tradition, and for the most part totally inexperienced at any level of government.

That mixture, in the days ahead, would make for unusually colorful pyrotechnics.

CHAPTER TWENTY

A YEAR
OF CONFLICT
AND CRISIS

ongress in early 1975 took on an ambitious challenge. In an effort to improve the nation's sagging economy, we originated a broad range of major national economic initiatives. This produced a clash of wills with President Ford, to which I had a ringside seat as a member of the newly created House Budget Committee and chairman of Speaker Carl Albert's economics task force. As 1974 was winding to a close, a mix of hostile economic forces suddenly struck with hurricane force. Some in Congress and at least a few in the administration had tried during the summer to warn of tripled energy prices in a slowly stagnating economy. But the nation was focused on Watergate. From late 1973 through the summer of 1974, the distracted Nixon administration had put the nation's economy on automatic pilot and left it to drift untended. At the urging of congressional leaders, Ford shortly after taking office agreed to convene a "domestic summit" for a closer look at America's economic situation. But the summit produced no clear consensus.

A two-day conference in Washington, held September 27–28, brought together spokesmen for labor, business, farming, and consumer interests. They presented their respective views, each from his own vantage point. Several economists spoke. Some saw inflation as the problem; others feared recession. In truth, it was both: a new phenomenon tagged "stagflation." Like standing in mud up to your ankles and having sand blow in your face.

Ford, on October 8, made a televised address to the nation. His top priority, he promised listeners, would be to "Whip Inflation Now." But the speech was more like a coach's pep talk in the locker room between halves of a football game, exhorting his team to greater efforts. Ford asked for a five percent "surcharge" on income taxes to dampen the deficit. And he pleaded with people to use less energy by turning off lights and avoiding unnecessary automobile trips. The president also displayed a round campaign-type button bearing the letters WIN. He offered to send one to any citizen who'd wear it on dress or jacket lapel as a testimonial to Ford's "Whip Inflation Now" theme.

In a faintly disturbing echo of Presidents Coolidge and Hoover, Ford admonished Congress—without specifics—to hold down spending and called for tighter monetary policy. The trouble was that most of the rise in the cost of living could be traced to high interest rates and rapidly rising oil and energy costs. The public was not overconsuming, and Congress already had been pursuing serious efforts at reducing the deficit projected in President Nixon's budget the previous January. In the very week prior to Ford's address, it had taken two big slices. In view of the winding down of the Vietnam conflict, Congress reduced Nixon's military spending request for the year by $4.9 billion. And the House voted to cut $9 billion from the six-year mass transit authorization.

A rapid slide in economic activity during October, November, and December of 1974 slashed the nation's total economic output by 9.1 percent. Gross national product for the year fell 2.2 percent below the 1973 level.

Unemployment, which had been holding at about 5 percent in midyear, shot up to 7.2 percent in December. It would climb to 8.3 percent in January. For every five Americans out of work in June 1974, there were eight in January 1975. Almost three million more bread-earners unemployed!

Even before these grim figures were reported, many of us in Congress had uneasy premonitions. Feedback from across the country convinced Albert the need for action was urgent. President Ford and his advisors—William Simon, William Seidman, Arthur Burns and Alan Greenspan—didn't see the problem. Their only concern seemed to be a fear of inflation.

On December 14, Speaker Albert appointed me chairman of a new ten-member special Task Force on the Economy and charged us with drafting a coherent program of action to stimulate economic recovery and put Americans back to work. The best we could hope to produce, Carl knew, was a general road map. A blueprint, a skeleton on which the committees of Congress would have to superimpose the flesh and muscle of actual legislation. Others serving on the task force with me were John Brademas of Indiana, Mel Price of Illinois, Richard Fulton of Tennessee, Morris Udall of Arizona, Henry Reuss of Wisconsin, Tom Bevill of Alabama, Philip Burton of California, Jonathan Bingham of New Hampshire, and Barbara Jordan of Texas.

"What I want," the Speaker told me, "is the kind of initiative Rayburn and Johnson put together in 1958. Remember that, Jim?"

The task force was not to write bills. This would have offended the sensitivities of individual committee chairmen, the "backbone of the House," Carl Albert called them. We were to point the direction. We worked through the Christmas holidays and put together a fourteen point program of major legislative action which the Speaker announced on January 14.

Our blueprint included tax relief for low- and middle-income families, and a 10 percent investment tax credit to revive job-creating business activity; additional funding for public service jobs; lower interest rates to stanch the hemorrhaging of small business and relieve American families of an increasingly oppressive drag on their buying power; an agriculture bill aimed at expanding food production; an emergency housing program, to stimulate the flow of mortgage money into new homebuilding; programs to assist the aged and needy to survive the inflation-recession; deferral of the president's proposed $3-a-barrel increase in oil tariffs, which would add about $7.6 billion to the cost of living in 1975.

For all our efforts, this ambitious plan got very little public notice. By either accident or design the president stole the spotlight from us. On that very night of January 14, President Ford went on nationwide television and announced an entirely different program with a different focus. His concentrated less on the economy, more on energy. Predictably, Ford's plan got the headlines and most of the public attention.

A lot of what the president proposed made sense. Some of it, we thought, didn't. Most Democrats opposed his central idea of boosting imported oil tariffs by $3 a barrel, figuring that would just add to the cost of fuel and thus to the cost of living, while doing nothing to enhance domestic production of energy. Ford planned to use existing presidential authority, contained in the Trade Expansion Act of 1962, to impose this additional tariff.

We did need to reduce our dependence on erratic foreign sources. Angry Arab leaders, intent on impressing the United States with their economic indispensability to our country, had inflicted punishing blows on the U.S. economy. They did this in sullen protest of our decisive intercession in Israel's behalf in the Yom Kippur war. For thirteen weeks they refused to sell any oil to our nation. This slowed down economic activity of all sorts. It stacked up U.S. motorists in long lines, waiting to buy scarce gasoline. That contrived shortage upped the price of fuel at the pump dramatically.

We in Congress didn't disagree with President Ford's goal of reducing America's reliance on foreign oil, but we had some ideas of our own for reaching that goal. Congressional leaders hoped we could find a consensus road on which Congress and White House could travel together toward greater energy independence. But we thought adding deliberately to the cost of fuel moved things in exactly the wrong direction.

One of Jerry Ford's admirable traits was his willingness to prescribe unpleasant medicine when he thought it needed regardless of political fallout. He was telling the American people in one breath that he wanted to add five percent to their income taxes and keep interest rates high to fight inflation. In the next breath, he vowed to add to the cost of their gasoline and heating oil as an energy-conservation strategy. None of this helped President Ford's personal popularity. He was spending his own political capital. It all reminded me of the story that made the rounds after President and Mrs. Ford's trip of a few months before to Vail, Colorado. The president's golden retriever got sick and made a mess on the floor. As an eager steward moved to clean it up, the president stopped him and mopped up the mess himself. "No man should ever have to clean up after another man's dog," Ford reportedly said. That seemed to represent his view of presidential responsibility.

While disagreeing fundamentally with the president on economic issues, most of us involved in the legislative initiatives liked him personally, honored him for his integrity, and hoped we could work with him on the energy front.

As one step toward energy conservation, Congress already had passed, and President Nixon had signed, a bill requiring states to limit vehicle speeds on the federal highways to no more than 55 miles per hour. Scientific data revealed a dramatic increase in fuel consumption at speeds above that level. Our elected leaders trusted the American public to accept that minimal inconvenience as part of the price for American energy independence.

One highly significant byproduct of that law was a sudden, measurable saving in human life. More Americans had been dying in highway accidents each year than were killed in ten whole years by the war in Vietnam. For decades, annual highway fatalities came to about fifty-six thousand. In the first full year after adoption of the fifty-five mile per hour limit, they fell dramatically, by almost eight thousand.

What a commentary on American life and political leadership! Elected officials were willing to support, and the public willing to accept, the inconvenience of a limit on how fast they might drive when it seemed to involve an element of national security. A few years later, however, the energy emphasis fading, politicians began coddling public favor by inventing reasons to oppose the speed limit. In late 1995, the limit was dropped altogether, and some states began permitting seventy and seventy-five miles per hour. Human life sometimes has surprisingly little sex appeal at the ballot box.

In proposing more taxes, higher energy costs, and a modicum of personal inconvenience, President Ford was doing his best to rise to the demands of his office. He wasn't an exciting speaker. His delivery was slow and deliberate, as though he were choosing each word with the care of a person arranging flowers in a vase.

This characteristic of speech, lacking the spark of spontaneity, led some critics to conclude that Ford was slow of wit. Lyndon Johnson, once despairing of Ford's ability to see the value of Great Society legislation, remarked in exasperation that Jerry couldn't walk and chew gum at the same time. Another time, Johnson said the Michigan congressman had played too much football without a helmet. Neither comic exaggeration, in my opinion, was ever intended by Johnson to be taken seriously. Even if Ford's imagination was a bit hidebound by the old-time religion of orthodox conservative political doctrine, he was nevertheless a man of obvious and certifiable intelligence. He'd finished in the top one-third of his class, after all, at both the University of Michigan and Yale Law School. Still, President Ford just wasn't coming to grips with the very immediate need to get things moving again on the home front. As he stalled, the recession deepened.

Undiscouraged, Speaker Albert in late January called a series of meetings with committee chairmen. It would be their responsibilities, he stressed, to bring forth the detailed legislation to carry out the task force mandates. Because of the severity of the prolonged and worsening economic downturn and the highest unemployment rate since the Great Depression, the task force called for House action within ninety days on its program. In February, with the shocking news that unemployment had risen to 8.3 percent— even worse than the gloomiest economists had predicted—Senate Majority Leader Mike Mansfield convened a similar task force in the Senate. The House and Senate programs, while not identical, were in basic harmony.

This effort to synthesize a clear legislative road map at the beginning of a year was an uncustomary exercise. In the past fifteen years or so, Congress had fallen into a habit of waiting passively for individual recommendations from the president and then reacting to each in a sort of leisurely, disjointed, piecemeal fashion. The role of policy enunciator has never been an easy one for Congress. Composed of 535 opinionated individualists, the legislative branch has trouble speaking with one voice. President Ford knew this when he twitted the lawmakers in early 1975 for having "no program" on energy. The problem was the exact reverse. We had *too many* programs, embodied in more than 240 separate and widely disparate energy bills already introduced. The task of leadership in 1975 was compounded by the heterogeneous character of its swollen Democratic majority. The sudden infusion of 86 bright, unpredictable and sometimes fractious new House members intent on having more than a perfunctory piece of the action sparked a series of minor rebellions against the elected leadership.

The class of new members that invaded the staid old institutions of Congress as result of the Watergate landslide of 1974 was different than any I'd seen. Insistent, assertive, suspicious of authority, and determined to change things in the name of *reform*, the group was like molasses in Carl Albert's hair. There was Berkley Bedell, a bespectacled manufacturer of fishing tackle from Iowa. There were cherub-faced Robert Cornell, a Catholic priest from Wisconsin, and Floyd Fithian, a prematurely balding college professor from Lafayette, Indiana. Martin Russo, thirty-year-old Illinois lawyer and scratch golfer, told me he never expected to be elected in his suburban Republican district but just agreed to the use of his name to fill out the Democratic ticket. Tom Downey of West Islip, New York, was only twenty-five when he took the oath of office. But, unlike some of his classmates, Downey had served as a Suffolk County legislator. Bill Hefner of Concord, North Carolina, had been president of a radio station, television performer in the Harvesters Quartet, and a promoter of gospel music. The nearest thing to a public office he'd held was president of the PTA.

There were several very bright new women members. Gladys Noon Spellman of Maryland had a mile-long list of credits in public service. She had been chairman of the Prince Georges County Board of Commissioners and was appointed in 1967 by President Johnson to the Advisory Commission on Intergovernmental Relations. Gladys was a leveling influence among the bumptious class. In private banter, I called her the "den mother." She seemed to like the designation. Marilyn Lloyd of Chattanooga, Tennessee, recently widowed, replaced her late husband as Democratic nominee for Congress when he, a radio executive, died of a heart attack. And new Congresswoman Helen Meyner's husband Robert had been Governor of New Jersey. Martha Keys of Kansas, elected to Congress without previous experience in public office, would become the wife of longtime Indiana Congressman Andy Jacobs. Another first!

Most of the big batch of new Democratic members had been elected as self-styled reformers. Appealing to public outrage over Watergate, they had promised change. The class of 1974 was like a combustible pile of dry timber awaiting a spark. And there was one smart, ambitious member with a torch in his hand, ready to show these neophytes how to use their combined strength to burn down the barricades of entrenched power. His name was Philip Burton.

Phil Burton, a seventh term member from San Francisco, was as clever a political strategist as Congress had in either house. Big, deep voiced, with an unruly shock of dark hair falling over his forehead, he was hard to ignore. A lifelong overachiever, Burton could be mercurial, impelling, at times domineering. He would never be ordinary.

A lawyer and veteran of both World War II and Korea (though barely twenty when World Ward II ended), Burton in 1956 was the youngest member of the California State Assembly. He was a national officer in the Young

Democrats and in 1959 was the youngest delegate to represent the United States at the Atlantic Treaty Association Conference in France. Once in Congress, he became active in the Democratic Study Group and swiftly moved up to its chairmanship.

Now, Burton wanted to be chairman of the House Democratic Caucus. That role in the past had been largely ceremonial. Nobody, so far as I knew, ever "ran" for it before. The current chairman, Olin E. (Tiger) Teague of Texas, had been drafted by colleagues, nominated without his permission, and hadn't even voted for himself. (I know he hadn't, because Tiger showed me his ballot before dropping it in the box.) Seeing the caucus chairmanship, however, as a tool of leadership and a forum of self-expression, Phil Burton, in mid-1974, announced his candidacy for the post. And how he did campaign! Phil ran a personal recruitment and financial support operation, concentrating on new Democratic candidates in seats held by vulnerable Republicans. He also formed a close attachment with Representative Wayne Hays of Ohio, Chairman of the Democratic Congressional Campaign Committee which raised and distributed political contributions to short-funded party candidates.

By private agreement, Hays would advise Burton in advance of mailing out these individual contributions. Phil would call the recipient, discuss the campaign, and tell the candidate he was recommending financial help. Thus did Burton cultivate a wide and friendly acquaintance with first-time candidates. Not only did he get some credit for the campaign checks. He called all hopefuls on the phone, offering encouragement, savvy advice, and other forms of campaign help. Phil was, to say the very least, resourceful.

When the sizable class arrived on the Washington scene, it was only natural that they turned to Phil Burton for leadership and inspiration. One of the newly elected, in fact, was Phil's younger brother, John. Another was big George Miller, a protégé of Burton's elected from the adjoining district. At Phil's urging, the group organized itself, elected class officers, and set out to change things. The first forum in which it could exercise its muscle was the organizing caucus in December. With enthusiastic support from the freshmen and no other serious aspirant, Phil Burton was elected Caucus Chairman.

But this was only the beginning. The next job of this caucus was to confirm committee chairmen. This was done, in each case, by secret ballot. Since the gavel was no longer the automatic property of the most senior committee member, it was possible to pass over a sitting chairman and simply replace him with another. In practice, this had been done only on extraordinary occasions.

Now, upon Phil's suggestion, the new members insisted on interviewing each committee chairman and trying to decide en masse whether to support his continuance in office. Nothing like this had ever happened before. Some crusty old chairmen regarded it as an impertinence, but most tolerantly accepted the invitation and spoke to the freshman group, answering their questions.

Edward Hebert of Louisiana, seventy-three-year old Chairman of Armed Services and a veteran of thirty-five years in Congress, fumed indignantly to me after his session with the class that its questions were like an inquisition.

Older members had no idea what was coming. I learned only on the day of that caucus that a group of the new members had sworn to show they were collectively serious about change by toppling at least three sitting committee chairs. That would be the litmus test of their commitment to *reform*. The twenty-one chairmanships, by standing custom, would be voted upon by the alphabetical listing of committees.

First up was Agriculture. Seventy-five-year-old Chairman W. R. (Bob) Poage of Texas would have seemed impervious. Though he was feisty and opinionated, I wasn't aware that anyone disliked Poage. But down he went. In his place, the caucus elected Tom Foley of Washington, the next in seniority. Foley wasn't even seeking, let alone expecting the chairmanship.

George Mahon, also of Texas, was chairman of Appropriations. Apparently George had charmed the newcomers with his witty, conversational, noncondescending appearance before their group. He even invited the newcomers on a tour of the Appropriations committee rooms. Though some votes were registered against him, Mahon easily escaped removal.

The next two chairmen in order for consideration were F. Edward Hebert of Louisiana, Armed Services chairman, and Wright Patman, a third Texan, head of Banking, Currency and Housing. Hebert bit the dust. One of the freshmen told me later that the Louisianian had irritated their group by his patronizing manner. Hebert had addressed them as "boys and girls." In his place, mild-mannered Melvin Price of Illinois was installed as chairman.

We knew in advance that Patman would be challenged. A committed populist and arch enemy of high interest rates, Wright Patman was always a controversial figure. Many of the nation's bankers despised him. They would breathe easier if he could be deposed from his perch as chairman of the Banking Committee. One well placed member of that committee, Henry Reuss of Wisconsin, had made known his intention to oppose Patman for the chairmanship in 1975.

Wright Patman at eighty-one seemed a likely target for the reform minded new members. Most of them had no recollection of what a reformer Patman himself had been throughout his long career. It was as a crusading district attorney that Patman, then still in his twenties, put Ku Klux Klansmen behind bars in East Texas. As a freshman member of Congress during the Hoover administration, the young Patman insistently demanded and finally succeeded in getting the resignation of Secretary of the Treasury Andrew W. Mellon.

Since that time, he had been a dedicated trust buster and an undeviating people's man. But most of these new members saw only that Wright Patman was an octogenarian.

I liked Henry Reuss personally. He was a congressional classmate of mine. Serving in the House together for twenty years, the two of us had supported most of the same things. Aside from his more flexible position on interest rates and less fire where it came to monopolies, Reuss was seen as more "liberal" than Patman, although that term has always been hard to quantify. It means different things to different people. A few of the older members who embraced it as a self-classification favored Reuss's candidacy.

Henry was articulate, erudite, good humored. He laughed at press accounts referring to his effort to replace Patman as a "revolt of the young Turks." Congress, Henry quipped, was probably the only place on earth where a sixty-two-year-old would be called a "young" Turk.

As a lifetime admirer of Mr. Patman, I tried to help rally some of his friends. Before the balloting on the Banking chairmanship, I spoke briefly, addressing my remarks mainly to the new members. I said:

> *I have nothing to say against Henry Reuss. I have much to say in behalf of Wright Patman. Some members feel this caucus will be unfulfilled unless it makes an example of some committee chairmen. But why in the name of sweet reason would we single out Wright Patman?*
>
> *What example would we give the nation summarily to depose the one man who has been our most inveterate, most persistent, most consistent and most outspoken foe of monopoly, exorbitant interest rates, and special privileges of all sorts?*

I reminded old timers and uninformed newcomers that, year after year, Patman had repeatedly sold more tickets to Democratic Party dinners and unselfishly raised more money for other Democrats than any member of either house. He it was who issued the very first public demand, in September of 1972, for a full investigation of the Watergate burglary.

Then I asked: "What indictment does he bear? With what sin has he been charged? Is there any criticism, except that he has grown old? Must we engage in patricide to prove that we are not a patriarchy?" My somewhat emotional appeal tilted the balance, but only temporarily. It saved the day for my old friend, but not the year. The caucus, having ousted two committee chairs, voted to put off the decision on Patman and Reuss for one week. In the ensuing votes on the remaining seventeen committees that day, the caucus did not turn down any other sitting chairman.

Perhaps sobered by the thoughts I had tried to express, and realizing that a number of their elders may have credentials of which they were unaware, some of the freshmen slowed down their demands for instant change. I would soon turn fifty-two. Even with my twenty years of seniority, I was almost exactly median age for the membership as a whole. Carl Albert, sensing that I could at least communicate with the younger crowd, gave me the task of helping to bring the freshmen around to support the Economic Task Force's legislative objectives.

That was a daunting challenge, but it was fun. One day, about midway into 1975, the class asked for an audience with Carl to vent grievances. The Speaker, unexpectedly called to the White House, asked me to sit in for him. The meeting that ensued was one of the funniest I've attended, and one of the most revealing.

It turned out there were two complaints. The first was that the freshman class had not been consulted in the scheduling of bills for the floor. The second was that the leadership wasn't doing anything to punish Democrats who voted against parts of our program.

"They wouldn't get by with that if Rayburn were around," exclaimed one freshman indignantly.

After listening for almost an hour, I could no longer restrain my sense of the ridiculous. It finally became obvious to some that I was trying to suppress laughter and keep a straight face. Finally, I said: "I think I understand. You want it like it was when Rayburn was around. And you also want the Speaker to consult you before he schedules a bill. Did it ever occur to you that what you want is an oxymoron?" A few of the members smiled, realizing the self-contradictory nature of their demands.

"Okay, I'll try to help," I offered. "I'll tell Carl Albert he's got to become one of two things—either a timid dictator or a tyrannical wimp." Several of them laughed. Soon, everybody was laughing.

As we talked it through, I tried to help them see how much more freedom and participation they enjoyed than any of my class had dreamed of. Carl Albert, I explained to them, had helped bring about many of the democratizing changes they now enjoyed. And if Carl was to have any clout in passing the agenda, he needed all the help he could get from these young members who basically agreed with him. In the end, most of them came around. Some of these "Watergate babies," as they were disparagingly called by a few old timers, would stick around to become fixtures themselves.

Democrats Paul Tsongas of Massachusetts, Tim Worth of Colorado, Chris Dodd of Connecticut, Max Baucus of Montana, Tom Harkin of Iowa, and Paul Simon of Illinois would go on to serve in the Senate, as would

Republicans Charles Grassley of Iowa, James Jeffords of Vermont, Robert Kasten of Wisconsin, and Larry Pressler of South Dakota. Bob Krueger of Texas would serve as ambassador in two administrations. Jim Blanchard of Michigan and Jim Florio of New Jersey, both Democrats, would be elected governor in their respective states.

Exactly twenty years later, in 1994, when another and quite different influx of self-styled reformers, these Republicans, swarmed into the Capitol demanding change and reestablishing Republican majorities in both houses for the first time in forty years, twenty of the Watergate class were still in Congress. Eighteen of them would be targeted for removal in 1994 by conservative GOP aspirants who called themselves "reformers."

It was apparent in 1975 that profound change was coming to the nation. A lot of what was happening to America would be quickly reflected in Congress which has always been the public's mirror, a distillate of its good and bad qualities. In the once-solid South, a phalanx of conservative Democrats no longer held sway. Because of the Voting Rights Act of 1965 and the Supreme Court's insistence upon numerically equal "one man one vote" alignment of congressional districts, blacks and other racial minorities were turning out to vote in places where they hadn't before, and cities everywhere were gaining representation at the expense of rural areas.

Even as racial minorities became more active and wielded increasing influence in Democratic primaries, more and more middle-income white families fled the old inner-city neighborhoods to establish homes in the suburbs. There it became a new status symbol to vote Republican.

Northern voting patterns, too, were undergoing transformation. Old city machines which once held sway in places like Jersey City, the Bronx, Philadelphia, and Chicago were losing power. Black migration from the rural south into northern cities, spurred by the mechanization of agriculture and industrial wages, now simply overwhelmed the old European immigrant coalitions which so long had sustained the urban machines.

Longer annual sessions of Congress made necessary by the growing complexity of issues combined with our rapid national growth in both population and mobility to force stunning changes also in the very mode of campaigning. There were more voters in each district. More of them were newcomers. Members of Congress had ever less time to cultivate their constituencies by personal contact. Enamored of television, people no longer found excitement in attending political rallies.

All of this meant that a new breed of campaigner had arrived. The sound bite, the clever slogan became more important than the reasoned comment. The way to reach people now was by television.

And that meant money! It would become increasingly difficult for any candidate without independent wealth or ready sums of campaign cash to launch a successful bid for a congressional seat.

As labor unions gradually lost power and corporate mergers began to combine a lot of small companies into fewer and larger ones, wages increasingly fell behind the upward pace of prices. Such jobs as were available in our increasingly white-collar society required more education. For the average working family, the old American standard of a steadily employed father and a full-time homemaker mother no longer sufficed. In a growing number of families both parents had to work to maintain the same standard of living. The family unit in too many cases was beginning a slow disintegration.

One other change warrants noting. Serving in Congress was becoming ever more intrusive on legislators' personal lives. More and more, following Watergate, young journalists were being tutored to regard their relationship with public officials as that of adversaries. During my early years in Congress, I'd enjoyed a friendly camaraderie with newsmen like "Tex" Easley of Associated Press, Seth Kantor of the Scripps Howard chain, Vernon Louvierre of the *Fort Worth Star-Telegram*, Les Carpenter of Carpenter News Bureau and Walter Hornaday of the *Dallas News*. My family knew their families. We were frequent guests in their homes, and they in ours. No more. Now reporters were being schooled to shun such friendships. I'll never forget my surprise the first time a young woman reporter, in the course of an interview, referred to herself as "the enemy."

The odds are that on any given day, some one of the 535 members of House and Senate will do something foolish or say something irresponsible. Increasingly these unrepresentative words and deeds became the stuff of headlines. In 1975, a congressional staffer named Elizabeth Ray created a national sensation when she told newspeople that she really didn't do any constructive work for the House Administration Committee but had been hired mainly to perform sexual favors for its Chairman Wayne Hays.

Very soon the press galleries were abuzz with rumors, as journalists strove to scoop one another with a juicy story implicating some other lawmaker. One hapless female cub reporter was sent by her editor at the *Washington Post* to query all women members of Congress to see if any had ever been subjected to improper amorous approaches by male colleagues. The poor young woman had the misfortune to choose Barbara Jordan of Texas for her first interview.

Approaching the Texas legend as she was preparing to enter the House chamber, the neophyte reporter put the question bluntly. Barbara Jordan pulled herself to full height as she stared at the young journalist in disbelief. Finally, in that full-throated contralto voice for which she would become famous, Barbara Jordan answered the query in one indignant word: "ABSURD!" With that, she turned scornfully on her heel and walked through the doors of the House chamber. The girl reporter was left trembling in terror. She left the building, caught a cab back to the *Post*, and turned in her press pass. It was her first interview and her last.

During the media's feeding frenzy for some other story of sexual harassment or improper private relationships, a big city newspaper in the district represented by a respected black congressman ran a story suggesting that he preferred the intimate company of white women. I asked Barbara facetiously if she thought that story removed him from the young journalist's list of those suspected of harassing her.

"That is not funny, Jim!" Barbara stated in her precise and emphatic enunciation. "If John's constituents should come to believe that story, it would be the end of his congressional career!"

From early in the life of our republic, there has been a market for scandalous stories involving prominent public officials. Thomas Jefferson and Andrew Jackson did not escape their painful wounds. Now, however, there really was a change, at least so far as congressmen would be concerned. In Sam Rayburn's day the fact of being elected as their spokesman by a half million fellow Americans carried with it an assumption of honor. With Watergate there began a steady disintegration, shifting the burden of proof and tarnishing public office with a growing assumption of dishonor.

As a member of the newly created House Budget Committee, I was getting a macroeconomic education in our nation's finances. We had set up the committee for a rotating membership, reflecting the ratio of the two parties in the House. A few members would be chosen from Ways and Means and a few from Appropriations. The Majority Leader would serve as the Speaker's representative. The Minority Leader could designate one person to represent him. The rest were to be elected every two years from the membership at large. The original rule forbade any elected member from serving more than two consecutive terms.

The first year, there were four times as many applicants for the open seats as there were slots. I was chosen in the caucus on the first ballot, drawing more votes than any other candidate. As a longtime believer in both an activist government and a balanced budget, I took to the task with the enthusiasm of a fly fisherman in a trout stream.

The basic difference, I saw, between the congressional and presidential approaches to the nation's problems was in our differing perceptions of the severity of the economic crisis. President Ford did not want a depression any more than Congress did. But his advisors (William Simon, Alan Greenspan, and Arthur Burns) kept telling him that if we'd all just merely sit tight the recession would eventually "bottom out."

Perhaps so. But this is exactly what they'd said in 1974 while the nation suffered four successive quarters of declining economic output and joblessness almost doubled. Then as now, these very ones were warning against "overstimulating" the economy. There were, I had to acknowledge, dangers in overstimulation. Too big a budget deficit could have an adverse effect on interest rates, then on their way back down from the astronomical heights of 1974. But we were a long way from overstimulation. President Ford submitted a budget which asked for a $52 billion deficit in fiscal '76 and promised no better result than another year of declining economic output. Congressional Democrats recoiled against another year of unemployment in the eight percent range.

A close examination of the administration budget request disclosed one sharp and alarming fact central to all of our considerations. The overwhelming *reason* for the Ford deficit was the recession itself. Exactly because of the recession, the White House anticipated a $40 billion shortfall in Treasury receipts. And because unemployment was above eight percent instead of about five percent, the White House expected to pay out some $12 billion *more* than we'd otherwise be paying in unemployment compensation. Add the two figures, and you had the clear cause of the $52 billion deficit. To me, the inescapable conclusion was that the only healthy, realistic hope to balance the budget for the coming year was to get rid of the recession, turn the economy around, and put Americans back to work. Figures we analyzed in the House Budget Committee indicated that each percentage point of unemployment exerted on the budget deficit an adverse impact of about $16 billion. If we could get back to the mid-1960s level of around four percent unemployment, I reasoned—not likely in the coming year, I knew, even with our proposed stimulation—we'd have a budget surplus!

It was for these reasons that most Democrats in Congress believed the greater danger lay in doing nothing, or in doing too little. Acting on these conclusions, Congress, awkward and cumbersome, sometimes vain and wrongheaded but still collectively closer than either of the other two branches to the 230 million people it represented, called upon muscles long unused, struggling in 1975 and 1976 to reemerge as a dynamic, creative force in shaping the government's major economic policies.

By the end of March, the House had made good on most of the Economic Task Force commitments. We had passed eleven of the fourteen promised bills, and six of them had already cleared the Senate in one form or another. President Ford, apparently resenting the legislative initiative and convinced we were going too fast and too far, unleashed a string of vetoes. By the end of the year, he'd vetoed seventeen major bills. He would veto twenty more in 1976, for an all-time two-year record. Congress would muster the votes to override some of these and reach compromises with the president on several others. But Gerald Ford's active use of the veto pen served as an effective brake upon our hopes for speedy economic recovery.

Ford's first veto came on March 4 and set the tone of the contest. After that, he and Congress kept struggling to define the limits of executive and legislative powers. The first veto struck down our bill suspending for ninety days the president's authority to increase tariffs on petroleum imports. To avoid further conflict on the issue, Ford agreed to suspend two dollars of the three-dollar tariff he already had ordered. On May 1, the president vetoed the Emergency Agriculture Act, aimed at expanding food production. Ford argued that such a bill would undermine a more "market-oriented" thrust which his administration hoped to attain. He admitted in his veto message that prices farmers had to pay for things they used and needed were eleven percent above the level of one year earlier while prices they got for their own products had declined by seven percent.

Ford argued, however, that a free market was the best answer. Unfortunately, that "free market" in which others set the prices on commodities farmers sold as well as the farm machinery they bought and the rates of interest they had to pay, was driving more and more family farmers into bankruptcy.

As quickly as we passed them, the president vetoed bills to control and regulate strip mining in the interest of soil conservation and environmental protection; a bill to promote tourism; our emergency jobs bill; and an emergency housing initiative. Nixing the $3.3 billion jobs bill, Ford, on May 28, insisted that it was excessive. "Economic recovery is expected to be well underway by the end of 1975," Ford contended, "and the accelerative influences of this bill would come much too late to give impetus to this recovery." His message totally ignored the fact that every single project on which the unemployed would be put to work was something needed by the public, selected from the nationwide backlog of deferred works.

Our emergency housing bill drew the same criticism. Ford acknowledged that hundreds of thousands of home owners recently thrown out of work by the recession, faced the eminent threat of foreclosure. Helping to save American families from the trauma of losing homes would be wrong, according to Ford's June 24 veto message, because it would "place the Federal government in the retail loan making business." Ford did agree, however, to expedite the release of $2 billion in funds already authorized for use by the Federal mortgage assistance program and to sign a more limited bill to prevent foreclosures on out-of-work home owners.

Ford vetoed the annual education appropriation on July 24. He objected that Congress had made money available to continue helping community schools impacted by large numbers of children from military families that lived on federal installations and paid no local school taxes. Beyond that, in trying to help youngsters from modest income families stay in college, Congress had voted to add $434 million to the figures suggested by the president for assistance to higher education.

On a number of these issues, we worked out compromises, but not enough to activate a robust recovery. Answering a question in an April 3 press conference, Ford told newsmen all his indications showed that "the recession is receding and that economic conditions will get better in the third quarter of 1975." As the year wore on, and conditions showed no strong improvement, Congress began overriding President Ford's vetoes.

On October 3, the president vetoed the School Lunch and Child Nutrition bill. Both houses of Congress promptly overrode by decisive votes. Asked at his October 9 news conference if he were surprised by the vote, Ford replied, "Not at all." He said "the facts were not sufficiently exposed to the public." We were trying to do too much, he contended.

Yet, on the following day, Fred Barnes of the *Washington Star*, noting increasing presidential criticism of Congress, asked if Ford planned to "make Congress the whipping boy in your (reelection) campaign?" Ford replied, "Well, I am just being objective about their record. And I casually said at our meeting this morning with Mr. Nessen (White House Press Secretary Ron Nessen)—we were tickling off the things that Congress hasn't done—and I casually said, 'That sounds like a *Can't Do* Congress.'"

The president, from our point of view, was flat wrong. Congress had performed efficiently and well on the antirecession front. It was the chief executive who dragged his feet. But Ford did have a point, I thought, where it came to domestic energy production and conservation. Throughout that year, he kept hammering away at the theme that Congress hadn't developed any really comprehensive plan to make our country energy independent so we'd never again be so economically vulnerable to an Arab oil embargo. Finally I discussed this with Carl Albert. We both came from oil-producing states. We understood the problems of the domestic oil industry in trying to increase domestic production. Both of us, likewise, had instinctive inclinations against monopoly and for protection of consumers. We understood the difference between the thousands of mostly small independent explorers and the "majors." The independents had taken the risks and discovered ninety percent of this country's oil and gas production. A handful of giant, integrated companies took few risks. They bought, pipelined, refined, and retailed the products to consumers. Many of these latter were multinationals with substantial financial interests abroad, particularly in the Middle East.

Carl asked me to head a new and separate task force to come up with a comprehensive energy plan. We drafted an action outline embodying incentives to recover more domestic oil and gas, to develop other power alternatives, to encourage automobile manufacturers to perfect more energy-efficient engines, and to help American householders and small businesses weatherize and insulate buildings to promote energy conservation.

Learning of our draft, Senator John Pastore called the Speaker and asked that my task force meet with his to develop a joint House-Senate approach. The trouble was that Rhode Island's Pastore, understandably concerned over the availability of foreign residual heating oil, on which New Englanders relied, was suspicious of the oil-producing states. Shying away from any incentives to enhance domestic production, he would agree only to conservation measures. To get the Senate task force's concurrence, we had to drop most of the production stimulus.

John Pastore and I presented our truncated joint effort to President Ford. Looking at its outlined provisions, Ford said, "Well, this is at least a program." Pastore smiled broadly behind his tinted glasses and generous mustache. "What you sought to achieve by the escalation of price, Mr. President, we have attained through the elimination of waste." I liked John Pastore, agreed with most of his approach to economic issues, admired his oratory. But I don't think he ever really understood much about energy. Anyway, after that meeting, the president quit saying Congress had no energy program. In sad truth, we had only an unambitious one.

Ford asked for the imposition of "energy conservation taxes" on oil and natural gas purchases to reduce consumption of those fuels. Neither Pastore nor I liked this. Ford requested authority to allocate scarce resources so that no geographic area, such as New England, would suffer shortages. He ran into stiff opposition from environmentalists when he asked Congress to grant a five year delay on automobile emission standards. That combination of measures along with his tariff on imports, the president argued, would reduce foreign oil intake by a million barrels a day at the end of the year. By 1985—ten years in the future—he believed his program could make our country totally "invulnerable to foreign energy disruption or embargoes such as we experienced last year." Both president and Congress, in my estimation, were aiming too low to hit that target. The worst part of it was that each of the nostrums requested by President Ford to cut energy use would have slowed down the economy and added to the recession.

If there were any remaining doubts that the national economic crisis had taken a terrible toll, those doubts vanished when the nation's largest city announced it could not pay its creditors. Many thousands of people who'd invested savings in New York City municipal bonds, believing them gilt-edged and risk-free, were nervously holding the sack along with countless businesses, big and little, that provided services to the nation's best known city. That news was paralyzing. Who among us had ever heard of a city going bankrupt? And New York City, of *all* places! The home of Wall Street. The nation's economic nerve center. How could this have happened?

Tip O'Neill and I had met Mayor Abe Beame when we went together to New York to see the second Ali-Frazier bout. Tip's love of boxing was almost as legendary as his benign addiction to golf. The Majority Leader's wife Millie never let him forget that he'd lured her while on their honeymoon to accompany him to the Joe Louis–Billy Conn championship fight. Now, watching Tip tower over the diminutive Mayor Beame like an amiable polar bear talking with a penguin, I was amused to think that the nation's biggest city just possibly might have the nation's shortest mayor.

I remembered joking with Abe Beame that evening. Boasting that I had been Mayor of Weatherford, Texas, I assured him in jest that if he ever encountered any troubles he couldn't handle in running New York, I'd be glad to give him the benefit of my extensive big city experience and sage advice. With a twinkle in his eye, Beame promised to call on me. Now, his city's finances falling to shreds, he did just that. Mayor Beam and New York's Governor Hugh Carey called one day and asked if they could see me. It must have been in early fall. Hugh had served with me in the House before becoming governor. Starkly, they laid out the city's plight. The two were not yet frantic. Their plea, however, was urgent.

President Ford, they explained, had not been encouraging. He'd sent word that they shouldn't look to the U.S. government for any help in extricating themselves from the economic quicksands. A lot of people throughout America resented New York's success and its pretensions. Senator Barry Goldwater once had said we ought to saw it off and let it float out to sea. My Texas colleague Abraham Kazen of Laredo, whose general voting record was almost parallel to my own, shook his head in disbelief when I suggested we ought to give our neighbors a hand. Not outright cash, maybe, but a loan guarantee.

"If I tried to tell my poor constituents in South Texas that New York City needed their help," Chick Kazen told me, "they'd think I had lost my mind."

There were three good reasons, I began telling my colleagues, why we shouldn't let New York City go down the drain. The first was the tradition of the big American family. One for all and all for one. In the days of the frontier, I reminded my fellow westerners, when a neighbor's field caught afire, everyone in the community pitched in and fought the flames. If a neighbor's barn burned down, others helped out—one with a weaned calf, another with six laying hens, some with carpentry to help rebuild. If we lost that sense of community, I felt, something very sad would have happened to America.

To those for whom this argument was too esoteric, I recalled that taxes from New York citizens had helped out other regions, and turnabout was fair play. One dollar out of every nine paid in income taxes had come from New York City.

If members weren't impressed by what we owed our fellow citizens in New York, I reminded them of what our constituents would pay as a penalty if we sat idly by and allowed American's biggest city to default on its bonds. Bonding rates would be severely affected. Every municipality financing a new local improvement—water plant, sewer plant, street extension—would have to pay higher premiums to bond holders, and that meant every homeowner would have to pay more in local property taxes.

It could cost us a lot to do nothing, I stressed. And it might not cost us anything to do something. A group of Democrats, headed by new Banking Committee chairman Henry Reuss, joined by a Republican group including Chalmers Wylie of Ohio and Stewart McKinney of Connecticut, were working on a plan that would extend loan guarantees as incentives to private financial institutions to underwrite the necessary loans for New York City to refinance, pay creditors and avoid bankruptcy. To qualify for the guarantees, New York's city government would have to undertake stringent belt-tightening measures and meet several harsh arbitrary austerity goals. It would have to reduce its city payroll, cancel or postpone certain scheduled building projects and reduce its operating budget by specific amounts within stipulated time periods.

Still, President Ford seemed negative. In a speech to the National Press Club on October 29—of all dates, the forty-sixth anniversary of the 1929 stock market collapse—Ford lectured New York City on its profligacy. "I can tell you now that I am prepared to veto any bill that has as its purpose a federal bailout of New York City to prevent a default." The president went on to propose a special amendment to the bankruptcy act to allow federal courts to "preside over an orderly reorganization of New York City's financial affairs."

Leery of any such arrangement, and probably not understanding just what the president had in mind, many of New York City's print and broadcast journalists went into orbit. The *New York Daily News*, widely read afternoon tabloid, covered its front page with this lurid headline printed in enormous type: FORD TO NY: DROP DEAD! The president, of course, had not said that—at least, not in those words

Economist Felix Rohatyn and New York real estate factor Lew Rudin invited me to fly up one night and speak the next morning at a downtown gathering of New York civic and business leaders called The Committee of

One Hundred. When I walked into the ballroom where the breakfast was set up, there were more like three hundred than one hundred. Most of those present wore a little gold lapel pin in the shape of an apple. They wanted to know how to convince Congress of their city's need and their sincerity.

"This is rich!" I told them. "Here in this room are the slickest salesmen, the best merchandisers, and the most renowned promoters in the world. And you're asking the former mayor of Weatherford, Texas, how to sell your wares!" I couldn't tell them anything they didn't already know about their city. Maybe I told them a few things they didn't know about Congress. It seemed to make them feel better to know that not everybody in Washington hated them.

In deference to several of President Ford's express concerns, the Banking Committees of House and Senate tightened up several provisions requiring New York's fiscal austerity. Congressional leaders assured the president we didn't consider the bill a "bailout," something he'd promised to veto. Involving no cash payment, it wasn't even a "handout." It was, we said, a "hand up."

The bill passed, and Gerald Ford signed it on December 9, exactly two days before New York City would have defaulted on its loans. The treasury was authorized to lend up to $2.3 billion a year until June 30, 1978. The loans would be due annually. The interest rate was pegged at one percentage point above the current rate paid by the U.S. Treasury on its own borrowings. As a postscript, it is useful to remind readers that these payments were made in full and on time. The city did pull itself out of the pit of bankruptcy. Its creditors were paid. The federal government didn't lose a dime. In fact, it cleared a few dollars on the whole transaction.

Meanwhile, the Public Works Committee had been hard at work on a bill to put almost a million of the nation's unemployed to work on an expedited schedule designed to produce quick results. We had been meeting with mayors and city officials across the nation and had designed a new, streamlined approach free of delays and unnecessary red tape. We thought it was veto proof. We soon would see.

CHAPTER TWENTY-ONE

BICENTENNIAL
YEAR

O ur bicentennial in 1976 invited a year-long celebration. With two hundred candles on our national birthday cake, we Americans indulged a forgivable share of self-congratulations for having made it, together, this far. As 1975 limped into history with its bruises, newspaper editorialists began looking forward to commemorating the turn of a calendar page on July 4 that would usher in a third century of nationhood. The old year, laden with frustrations and flawed by failures and half successes, gave us reason to hope we might do better. The twelve months of 1975 had seen unemployment rise to its highest level in more than a generation, president and Congress exchanging blame for unsolved problems. The Vietnam war, finally ended, brought a sense of relief but left little room for national pride.

Shocked by findings of an eight man commission headed by Vice President Nelson Rockefeller, many Americans in 1975 found their confidence severely shaken in one of the country's sacrosanct institutions. Lawmakers gasped in horror on learning from the Rockefeller Commission's report that our Central Intelligence Agency had systematically spied on literally thousands of American citizens. Strictly prohibited by law from engaging in any "internal security functions," the super-spy agency had illegally opened private mail, put wiretaps on private telephones, and accumulated thirteen thousand files on private U.S. citizens. Betty and I even wondered if our own names might be in someone's dossier. We had become acquainted with Vladimir Mucheleyev, political officer of the Soviet embassy and his wife. Twice we had invited them to backyard barbecues at our town house, along with such variegated company as Senator and Mrs. Lloyd Bentsen, Majority Leader Tip O'Neill, news couple Les and Liz Carpenter, a colorful Greek florist named Plato Sowlakis from Brooklyn, who was married to Betty's cousin, various colleagues, a smattering of Latin American diplomats and politicians, and once a black professional boxer from Washington named Calvin Woodland. Surely, someone in that assortment raised a curious eyebrow.

Some things were going right, however. The rancor and suspicion of the Nixon years were fading, and the economy began the new year on the upturn. President Ford and Congress had quarreled and compromised our way into a slightly rising growth rate and a slowly declining unemployment rate. Lower jobless numbers would hold for the first three months of 1976 before moving upward again in the year's third quarter. And Congress quickly passed an emergency jobs bill which lay on the president's desk as 1976 got under way.

President Ford began the new year as he'd closed the old, with a veto. On January 2, he rejected the common-situs picketing bill. It would have permitted a local union to picket a building location, even if its grievance were against only one of several contractors working at the site. Such picketing had been outlawed since enactment of the Taft-Hartley Act twenty-nine years earlier. Passage of the common-site bill that year was organized labor's top legislative priority. The veto set off the first skirmish of the presidential election year. Ford's Secretary of Labor John T. Dunlop favored the bill and thought he had convinced the president to sign it. Believing he had Ford's express approval, Dunlop had assured representatives of labor that the bill would not be vetoed. Personally embarrassed by the president's change of position, the Secretary, on January 14, announced his resignation.

A broader controversy arose when Ford, on February 13, vetoed the Public Works Employment Act. This was one on which I'd worked hard both as a member of the Public Works Committee and as chairman of the Speaker's task force. The president contended the major $6.1 billion antirecession measure "would do little to create jobs," would put "at most some 250,000" people to work, would not reach its "peak impact" until sometime in "late 1977 or early 1978," and amounted to "little more than an election year pork barrel." This touched off an angry reaction among proponents of the measure, including a number of active Republicans. A bipartisan group of House and Senate sponsors objected not only to the veto itself but to statements made in the disapproval message. On the following day, I drafted a "critical analysis" of Ford's contentions, a single spaced point-by-point set of refutations on two legal size pages, and circulated it among the membership. We had been cautious in our claims, careful in our draftsmanship. The bill, by every reasonable calculation, would have created some 655,000 productive jobs, not 250,000 as Ford claimed. Its effect was designed to begin immediately, not two years down the line. Every penny in the measure had been encompassed in the Congressional Budget Resolution. Its cost was less than one-third the amount we were spending that year ($19.4 billion) in unemployment compensation. It made economic sense, we felt, to move 650,000 Americans off the unemployment rolls and put them back onto the tax rolls through useful work.

President Ford argued in his veto message that the best way to improve the economy was to "encourage the growth of the private sector." We agreed. Fully two-thirds of the jobs activated by our program would be in the private sector, in the building trades where unemployment was still rampant. We came close to overriding that veto but barely failed. The Senate had a solid majority favoring the bill but was unable to muster the requisite two-thirds. So we went back to the drawing board, pulled in our Republican supporters for tighter consultation, and squeezed $2 billion out of the bill, bringing the total price tag to just under $4 billion.

My personal feelings toward President Ford at this point were—well, to say ambivalent is too glib. Bob Jones, with whom I visited on a daily basis in crafting the bill, enjoyed playing with words. He said my feelings toward Ford were not ambivalent, they were merely "ambidextrous." Frank Thompson of New Jersey, who sometimes dropped by Bob's office for afternoon banter, corrected our Alabama friend. The way I felt toward the president, Frank said, was not ambidextrous; it was "amphibious."

One side of me was fiercely defensive of Jerry Ford, the person and the president. I instinctively rebelled against a growing fad among newsmen and personal critics to portray our president as a klutz. Ever since the previous May, when Ford's shoe one day got caught on a protuberance as he was coming down the portable stairway from his plane and the president tumbled to the ground—fortunately, unhurt—cameramen vied to show the world each time the president bumped his head or fell in the snow. After one wholly gaffe-free trip to Oklahoma, a local reporter admitted his personal disappointment that the nation's chief executive had not at least "skinned his shins or suffered some small mishap" for the eager journalist to peg a story on. In truth, Ford was an unusually athletic and well-coordinated individual. He stayed in excellent physical condition, swam, skied, played golf and tennis, and did all these things well. But the obsession with portraying him as accident-prone was giving millions of Americans the idea that their president was a clumsy oaf.

Maybe I shouldn't have minded. Ford himself took it all in good humor. Television comedian Chevy Chase on *Saturday Night Live* did a comic routine imitating President Ford's slips and stumbles. In March at the Radio and Television Correspondents' annual banquet, Ford good-naturedly agreed to appear on the program with the comedian. Chase, to the strains of "Hail to the Chief," stumbled and fell across the ballroom and bumped his head on the rostrum. Ford, introduced next, pretended to get tangled up in the table-cloth, spilling dishes and silverware on the floor behind the head table and purposely dropped his speech on the rostrum, scattering papers in every direction. The audience howled.

Admiring the man greatly for his personal qualities and unfeigned humility, I still couldn't help being irritated—maybe a better word is frustrated—at his repeated and apparently determined misinterpretation of our legislative efforts. For one thing, the president persistently refused to recognize that we had gone to extraordinary ends to divest the jobs bill of bureaucratic red tape so that its stimulative effect could begin immediately. Presiding over the Public Works Investigations subcommittee, I had become something of an authority on how domestic programs often were slowed down by the corroding accretion of paperwork and reporting requirements. In 1971 and '72, my subcommittee, at the suggestion of New Hampshire Republican James Cleveland, had conducted Congress' most in-depth study of red tape and how it accumulates. As many programs matured, we saw the development of a tendency to proliferate paper work, to stretch out the processing phase, to require more and more "studies," and to add new forms. Little wonder, I decided, that so many members of the younger generation—the "action now" crowd—were beginning to conclude that the system just wasn't working.

In order to overcome wasteful and time-consuming bureaucracy, we authorized construction of only projects which had already been planned for some time in communities throughout the nation, ones simply awaiting the necessary funding to move forward to immediate construction. These were not big, grandiose projects for the most part. To be eligible, the community had to show that actual construction could get under way "within 90 days." Our bill also stipulated that local applications for project eligibility must be acted upon by administrative agencies "within 60 days."

Republicans on the Public Works Committee were as enthusiastic as the Democrats. Bill Harsha of Ohio, Don Clausen of California, Gene Snider of Kentucky and John Paul Hammerschmidt of Arkansas—ranking minority members on the committee—were among the bill's most forceful supporters.

Our second bill passed both houses, in June, by even bigger margins than the earlier effort had amassed. January and February appearances of an economic upturn had proved ephemeral. The building sector of the American economy was still stagnating. In spite of a majority in the Senate that looked big enough this time for an override, Ford again used the veto pen. On July 6, he disapproved our bill. Ford argued that it was unwise "to stimulate further" an economy which was "showing signs" of recovery. National joblessness had averaged 8.5 percent during 1975, he acknowledged. But he said it was in the process of dropping to 7.5 percent, and he seemed to feel that was good enough. This time, Congress overrode easily. The vote came late in July, after the Democratic National Convention. Senator Hubert Humphrey, former vice president and 1968 Democratic presidential nominee, declared, "This will be the acid test. If the American people find out that this party cannot keep its word, we do not deserve to win elections!"

Our two-century quest for the right balance between legislative and executive authority in foreign affairs arrived at a new milestone in 1976 with passage of a National Emergencies Act. Sponsored by Senate Democrat Frank Church of Idaho and Republican Charles W. (Mac) Mathias of Maryland, that bill closed a little-known trap door through which American freedoms could have vanished.

Deeply disturbed by President Nixon's unauthorized invasion of Cambodia and his invoking of emergency powers, Church in 1970 began an at first lonely investigation of the true extent of presidential power. What alarmed the Idaho senator was a claim by Secretary of Defense Melvin Laird that Nixon had all the authority he needed to keep U.S. troops in Cambodia, even absent congressional approval. Pressed to defend that conclusion, Laird had cited an obscure law written in 1861. Under the Feed and Forage Act of that Civil War year, the administration was authorized to acquire feed for Union cavalry horses by such means as might be necessary if it ever ran out of funds when Congress was out of session. Laird contended that Nixon, or any other president, could use that ancient statute to carry on battle operations in Cambodia with or without congressional consent.

This began an intensive three-year search on the part of Church to discover just what other arcane laws existed on the books that a present or future chief executive might construe as permission "to govern without leave of Congress." Along the way, Church enlisted the help of Mathias. The two persuaded Majority Leader Mike Mansfield to appoint a special committee, equally divided between the two parties, to make a thorough inventory of the statutes to learn how many old laws lay around like loaded guns, ceding emergency powers to some power-hungry president.

The committee's careful search turned up 470 special laws a president might invoke during any declared national emergency. Most of those statutes had been written in times of temporary crisis and never repealed. In fact, four declared states of emergency still remained legally in effect—one pronounced in 1933 by Franklin Roosevelt to manage the banking crisis, another declared by Harry Truman in 1950 for the Korean War, and two declared by Nixon—one to combat a post office strike in 1970, and the other dealing with foreign trade.

Church and Mathias discussed this problem with Gerald Ford shortly after he became president. He was as surprised as they had been. Never greedy for power, Ford seemed at first sympathetic to their aim of repealing all hold-over emergency powers obviously intended for expiration when the crises for which they'd been created had passed.

But Ford's White House advisors had some worries that from the Vietnam War and Watergate had grown a climate hostile to the exercise of even legiti-mate powers. Ford at one time referred to his office as "imperiled." In August of 1976, the Senate passed the National Emergencies Act, which already had cleared the House. Ford, under pressure from advisors to veto it, signed it instead—repealing scores of emergency provisions giving extraordinary pow-ers to any chief executive brazen enough to assert them. In so doing, Gerald Ford showed his willingness to be reasonable, even where it meant ceding presidential advantage.

Even as I supported the War Powers Resolution and other initiatives aimed at reclaiming congressional authority challenged by the Nixon administra-tion, I began to worry in 1976 that Congress was starting to tamper meddlesomely with President Ford's foreign policy options. One prime example was a hastily-considered House vote on June 26, 1975 to prohibit the president from any further negotiation with Panama over the future of the Panama Canal. A quickly approved floor amendment to the State Department appropriations bill caused great difficulties by throwing a crow-bar into delicate ongoing talks. An "aye" vote on the unexpected amendment appealed superficially to members' latent jingoism. It made them feel tough and look patriotic. It denied any use of funds to conduct any official discus-sions regarding "any U.S. rights in the Panama Canal Zone." At that very time, former Treasury Secretary Robert B. Anderson was engaged in quiet exploratory talks with Panamanian leaders which had to be abruptly termi-nated. This rash action by Congress utterly tied President Ford's hands in pursuing delicate discussions underway with a friendly neighbor.

Having traveled extensively in Panama on several missions involving the Inter-American Highway, I knew how Panamanians and other Latin Americans felt about Panamanian sovereignty. Panama's nominal president was Demetrio (Jimmy) Lakas, a personal friend of some year's standing. As a youth in the late 1940s, Lakas had attended Texas Wesleyan College in Fort Worth. Since becoming president of Panama (Omar Torrijos, head of the National Guard, was the real power) Jimmy Lakas had talked at length with me on several occasions about this issue which more and more lay at the heart of U.S. relations with Central America.

Left: *Marie Lyster Wright, my mother, was strong on sound learning, right math, correct English, and good manners.*

Below: *James Claude Wright, my father, made an enormous impression upon my life. Dad was an egalitarian, who believed in ambition and hard work and had boundless faith in America.*

Left: *Most of my genera-
tion sought active
involvement in World
War II. I enlisted in the
Army Air Corps, flew
combat missions in the
South Pacific, and by
age twenty-one was
training combat crews.*

Below: *In 1956, we
threw a big dinner in
Fort Worth honoring
Speaker Sam Rayburn,
who was my mentor
and, unconsciously, my
model.*

Right: *John F. Kennedy and Lyndon B. Johnson, with whom I campaigned actively in 1960, were a well-balanced team. It was exciting to be a part of the New Frontier.*

Above: *Early on the morning of November 22, 1963, the saddest day of my political career, President Kennedy addressed a large outdoor crowd in my hometown. With us on the stage were Forth Worth Chamber President Raymond Buck, State Committeewoman Marjorie Belew, Senator Ralph Yarborough, Governor John Connally, and Vice President Lyndon Johnson.*
(Photo courtesy of Gene Gordon, *Fort Worth Press.*)

Right: *That November day was for me an emotional roller coaster. It had started on a high note, with President Kennedy declaring, "I'm glad to be here in Jim Wright's city." I would have walked to the end of the earth for him.*

Right: *As a spear carrier in the Great Society, I came to appreciate the quiet graciousness of Lady Bird Johnson and the deep conviction behind our president's folksy, down-to-earth persuasiveness.*

Above: *In 1968, I managed Hubert Humphrey's presidential campaign in Texas. We carried the state by a whisker.*

Right: *During Richard Nixon's first term as president, I tried to help fashion a bipartisan approach to foreign policy issues. He deserves more credit than he got for his détentes with China and the Soviet Union.*

Left: *Latin America has been a special interest of mine. Here, in 1970, I led a congressional inspection of the proposed Inter-American Highway route through the Darien jungle that connects Central and South America.*

Right: *President Gerald Ford, my friend from days when we served in Congress together and as decent a person as ever served in the White House, wanted to heal the wounds left by Watergate. In 1975, I disagreed with some of his domestic principles but tried to help him work out a bipartisan approach to the nation's energy shortage.*

Above, left: *Egyptian President Anwar Sadat and I met in 1977, and I was with him during his celebrated speech to the Israeli Knesset, which began the movement toward peace in the Middle East.*

Above, right: *When Prime Minister Menachem Begin of Israel came to Washington in 1978 during the search for a firm Middle East agreement, I presented him to my colleagues in the House.*

Above: *President Jimmy Carter, visiting here with Congressman Henry Gonzalez and me aboard Air Force One, never dodged the hard ones. His dogged personal diplomacy in pursuing the Camp David Accords and his courage in settling the long-festering problems of the Panama Canal are unparalleled.*

Left: *Vice President George Bush and I exchange banter at the 1987 Washington Gridiron Club dinner.*

Right: *Betty and I hosted a dinner at the Capitol honoring Lady Bird Johnson on her seventy-fifth birthday in December of 1987.*

Left: *In 1987, my first year as Speaker, President Ronald Reagan and I jointly called for a peaceful settlement of the Central American wars. My perseverance in pursuit of that objective ultimately created a schism between us.*

Right: *Since leaving public office, I have worked with former President Jimmy Carter for free elections throughout our hemisphere. Here, in December 1990, we helped monitor Haiti's first real election in fifty years.*

Left: *President Bill Clinton occasionally calls on a few of the old "retreads" for consultation. Here, in 1992, we talked of U.S. relations with Mexico.*

Above: *Speaker Tip O'Neill was a big man with a big heart; more than colleagues, we were pals.*

Below: *In 1992, the four living Speakers had a little reunion. Here, from left to right in time-honored order of seniority, Carl Albert, Tip O'Neill, myself, and Tom Foley.*

Here's the way that House vote was read by our smaller neighbors: "We are bigger and stronger than you, so we won't even talk with you about any of those things which you regard as legitimate grievances." Nothing could be more destructive of the carefully nurtured friendly relationship which we had been cultivating with our neighbors to the south. So bitter had feelings grown that Panamanians rioted on several occasions, venting years of pent-up frustrations against what they saw as an unfeeling, unhearing Yankee goliath that uncompromisingly dominated the business and legal systems of their country.

The first time I met popular Panamanian nationalist Omar Torrijos, in 1970, he told me of a strong resentment felt by Panamanian farmers and poultry raisers. The canal corporation had refused to buy their fresh eggs. Instead it was importing cold storage eggs at a higher price for consumption by U.S. personnel within the zone. I had to admit it made no apparent sense.

"I assure you," Torrijos said with an ironic mixture of humor and pathos, "our hens are very virtuous."

Through the process of negotiation, some progress was being made to alleviate these feelings of oppression, suspicion and mistrust. U.S. leaders had been attempting to demonstrate through those talks that our country was willing to consider just grievances of the types described. The House acted foolishly. It was not only cranky, I said at the time, but absolutely wrong and contrary to our national interests to deny our president the right to continue discussions with a neighboring country.

In addition to the Panama fiasco, I saw that clumsy congressional handling of the Greece-Turkey issue not only embarrassed President Ford abroad but jeopardized vital U.S. installations in Turkey, gummed up an important intelligence network along the southern border of Russia, and threw the eastern flank of NATO into temporary disarray. It may even have foredoomed chances of peacefully settling the Cyprus dispute.

In 1974, when Turkey under its former administration launched an invasion of Cyprus using U.S.–supplied military hardware, I joined a majority of my colleagues in voting to cut off military supplies to Turkey. The clear provision that those wares were for defense and not aggression had been violated. Something had to be done. We shut off the flow of goods. We made our point.

In July of 1975, President Ford met with members of Congress and disclosed very frankly the results of recent talks with new Turkish leaders. The new president of Turkey, Mr. Ford believed, would like to have some face-saving opportunity to renew friendly relations with our country and Greece and to pursue a peaceful settlement on Cyprus, but to insure public support among his own people, he needed a friendly gesture from the United States.

So House leaders drafted a carefully worded bill permitting Turkey to take delivery on certain U.S. goods for which it had offered payment, with the proviso that none of these goods would be introduced into Cyprus, that the Cypriot cease-fire would not be broken, and that negotiations for a peaceful settlement would be actively resumed. Believing this could break the deadlock, thaw out frozen lines of communication, help mend the fractured alliance and revive peace possibilities, President Ford and Secretary of State Henry Kissinger pleaded with Congress to pass the bill.

But the House majority was adamant. It refused to budge. By a vote of 223–206, it rejected the olive branch and continued its embargo on goods to Turkey. That action shut down the talks.

Congress had every right to demand adherence to our agreements, but Congress, made up of 535 individuals, could not conduct sensitive negotiations with foreign powers. It could not be the secretary of state.

Charlie Wilson quipped that Congress was to Henry Kissinger what hiccups was to a glass blower. Shoving it to Panama appealed to popular chauvinism. Shoving it to Turkey appealed to Greek-Americans, more numerous in every constituency than Turkish-Americans. The temptation to use foreign policy votes to curry favor back home is a recurring phenomenon: Maybe it's just part of the price we pay for the privilege of living in the world's greatest democracy.

Two elections in 1976 would profoundly alter the course of my life and Betty's. In addition to the presidential election, from which Democrat Jimmy Carter emerged as victor over President Gerald Ford, the internal House elections resulting from Speaker Carl Albert's retirement set me on a new course. The role into which it cast me would absorb my total energies for the next thirteen years as a thirsty sponge absorbs a drop of water.

When Speaker Albert decided to end his thirty-year career in Congress, this opened an ascending path of stair-steps on the House leadership ladder. Thomas P. (Tip) O'Neill, the big, likable Irishman from Boston who had moved up from the Whip's post on the death of Hale Boggs, was the heir apparent. Nobody came forward to challenge him, but Tip took no chances. He assembled a coterie of friends whom he asked to circulate among their delegations and get pledges of support. After only two hours tracking down Texans on the House floor and by cloakroom telephones, I was able to assure Tip of every vote in our twenty-one-member Democratic delegation. In three days, O'Neill announced preemptive victory.

Tip's success was no surprise. Since the creation of the Majority Leader post in the days of John Nance Garner, every retiring Speaker had been succeeded by his Majority Leader so long as the party they represented maintained its House majority. Similarly, almost like ceremonial chairs in a fraternal order, it had become traditional for the Whip to accede to the Majority Leader's role. When Albert's right to follow that upward path from Whip to Majority Leader was challenged by Richard Bolling of Missouri following Sam Rayburn's death in 1961, the Oklahoman won handily.

This time things were different. The Whip, John McFall of California, had problems. A friendly, likeable man with hardly any enemies, McFall had three counts against him in his race for Majority Leader. Some critics, while finding no other fault, perceived him as too mild, not forceful enough to lead floor debates, a chore expected of the leader. In addition, the liberal wing of the party regarded John as too moderate. "Conservative," they called him— although that term would be applicable only relative to their own positions. Actually, McFall's ideology and voting patterns were quite close to the party's center. But a third factor spelled further trouble for John. Fellow Californian Phil Burton, having become caucus chairman, now wanted to be Majority Leader and began splitting the big state's delegation down the middle.

Seeing a likely Burton victory, Missouri's Dick Bolling, a ranking member of the Rules Committee, now announced his own candidacy. Bolling despised Phil Burton. He considered him crude and opportunistic. Ambitious and with scholarly pretensions—the author of two widely acclaimed books—Dick Bolling enjoyed excellent relations with the press. From early in his career, he had dreamed of someday being Speaker. Both he and Burton were classified as liberals. But they had hardly anything else in common, except intelligence and ambition. As much as he wanted to be Majority Leader, Richard Bolling thirsted almost as strongly to deny that office to Phillip Burton.

By early spring of 1976, that race was shaping up as a three-man contest. All three were spending every spare moment courting colleagues, lining up pledges of support. Each began making numerical claims of promised votes, hoping to create a bandwagon effect to impress the undecideds. After several weeks, it seemed clear nobody had a commanding lead.

A few members began coming to me, asking if I'd consider running for Majority Leader. Flattered by the suggestion, I thanked them but made no commitment. At this point, I was intrigued by the lure of leadership but knew such a race would be tough. The three announced candidates had already lined up a considerable number of commitments.

Then John McFall suffered an unexpected blow. The media discovered Tongsun Park. A well-heeled Korean businessman, Park was enshrouded with just enough mystery to make fascinating copy. He bought up several Washington-area businesses, including a posh Georgetown eatery, and began cultivating the city's power elite, including members of Congress.

The first time I saw Park's name it was on the host list of an invitation to a dinner honoring Majority Leader Tip O'Neill. Betty and I attended the dinner, at the Georgetown Inn, where we saw a lot of our colleagues. Park stood up and presented the honored guest a gift—a set of golf clubs, as I recall. Something, in any event, that Tip already had plenty of. It turned out that O'Neill had never previously met the gregarious, pushy Korean. Soon, however, Park was making himself ubiquitous on the Washington scene. It quickly developed that the moneyed foreigner was a contributor to several candidates for reelection of both parties, but mostly Democrats. He also seemed to be lobbying for a number of Korean causes. Nobody seemed to know the exact source of his money. The very fact that he was not a U.S. citizen made his contributions subject to legitimate challenge.

Just as all this was kicking up a storm of news speculation, McFall announced that Park had come into his Capitol Hill office one day, made himself known and offered a campaign contribution which McFall politely declined. Then Park offered two thousand dollars in cash to replenish an "office fund" that the congressman used to entertain visiting constituents. This was not illegal, and McFall accepted. He said now that he wished he hadn't but he wanted to get it out in the open in view of all the speculation about Park. Nobody who knew John McFall thought the incident had corrupted his honor, but it had damaged his political credibility.

Now more colleagues began soliciting me to seek the Majority Leader post. I took a quick count and authorized an exploratory committee. The Texas delegation, at its next weekly luncheon, was enthusiastic. Nineteen of the twenty-one said they'd work actively for my election. Two—Jack Brooks of Beaumont and Bob Eckhardt of Houston—had already committed to Phil Burton. Some Texans began razzing the two, but I put a quick stop to that. Since a member's word among colleagues is his stock in trade, I told Jack and Bob I understood and honored them for sticking with their pledge.

By week's end, I could count forty-four solid votes. That many had volunteered, and I hadn't solicited anyone yet. Depending on the size of our postelection majority, victory could take as many as a hundred more. But not on the first ballot. I had a start.

When Jimmy Carter's name first began to emerge as one of a fairly large field of Democratic presidential hopefuls, I paid little attention. I'd never met the former Georgia governor and was solidly committed by personal loyalty to my fellow Texan, Lloyd Bentsen. Even after Carter did better than expected in the New Hampshire primary, I tended to discount his chances at the nomination. Only a week or so following that primary, I heard almost identical assessments one day from three widely scattered sources. It was uncanny. All three were people whose political instincts I trusted. All three were women.

They even bore the same first name. One was Betty Harris, veteran political consultant then living in New York. The second was Bettye Grant, wife of a longtime personal friend who'd left private medical practice to serve as Dean of the University of Alabama medical school. Bettye Grant was a longtime Lyndon Johnson activist and an experienced political observer. The third—and most influential upon my judgment—was my wife.

"I think Jimmy Carter is going to win," Betty Wright told me as we prepared to watch a televised debate featuring the party's contestants.

"Why do you say that?" I asked.

"I just have a good feeling about him," Betty said. "He emits a sense of good will. He seems to be at peace with himself. He gives me a feeling of confidence. I believe he's sincere."

"All of that sounds more visceral than cerebral," I challenged her.

"Of course it is," Betty acknowledged. "How many people vote from cerebral impulses?"

From that moment forward, I expected Carter to win. I wasn't even surprised that May when, declining to campaign in the Texas preferential primary in deference to Senator Bentsen, Jimmy Carter carried our state by an impressive margin.

The Carter persona and message were like refreshing breezes in the turgid political atmosphere. Their appeal partly subliminal, they seemed to fit our centennial year mood. A friendly Georgia peanut farmer and Baptist Sunday school teacher, the candidate came across to most Americans as genuine and unthreatening to their own basic beliefs. His family appeared to be as wholesome as a poem by James Whitcomb Riley, as American as peach cobbler and homemade ice cream. Introducing himself with a broad smile, the happy campaigner would begin every speech: "My name is Jimmy Carter and I'm runnin' for president." He wanted America to have, he said, "a government as good as its people are." And who could disagree with that? I worried some about Carter's lack of experience dealing with national problems. Several of the things he said on the campaign trail revealed an honest unfamiliarity with the way things worked.

But then I met him and was captivated by his sincerity. "This is a *good* man," I thought, "and I'd like to help him be a good president." About the only thing Carter actually promised was his solemn assurance to the American people that he'd never lie to them. A president shouldn't *have* to promise this, I remember thinking. It ought to be taken for granted. But, in view of recent history, I was certain that Carter felt sincerely both the pledge itself and the need to make it.

Besides, it produced one of the really funny private incidents of the campaign. And one that revealed the genuineness of Carter's mother, Miss Lillian, a true American original if ever one existed. During the campaign, an aggressive newswoman got an interview with the candidate's mother at her home and immediately began boring in with demanding and intrusive personal questions. The journalist's manner became almost abusive.

"Your son insists he'll never lie," the newswoman thrust. "But tell me, Mrs. Carter, is that literally true?"

Well, yes, of course, Miss Lillian assured her nosey guest, Jimmy had always been a truthful person. That's the way he had been raised and he hadn't strayed from his early upbringing.

"No, no, Mrs. Carter," the abrasive journalist persisted. "You misunderstand my question. What I want to know is whether it is true that your son has never told a lie."

At this, the loyal mother, wanting to be truthful herself, allowed that she was sure her son would never knowingly or intentionally lie. Perhaps an innocent "white lie," but . . .

"Aha! A white lie!" Miss Lillian's self-appointed adversary insisted. "Would you please define for me, Mrs. Carter, just what is meant by the term 'white lie'?"

With a sigh of exasperation, the always polite Miss Lillian, despairing of the other's ever comprehending the niceties of Southern manners, proceeded to oblige with an example.

"Do you remember a few minutes ago when you came to my door? Do you remember how I greeted you? I said, 'I'm glad to see you.' That was a white lie."

By the time the Democratic National Convention in New York City rolled around on July 13, two things had happened—Jimmy Carter had cinched the Democratic nomination for president, and I had become a full-fledged candidate for House Majority Leader. I had picked up heartening support from Pennsylvania, the western mountain states, Tennessee, West Virginia and rural Illinois as well as upstate New York where Sam Stratton was helping. Danny Rostenkowski and Frank Annunzio, who liked neither Burton nor Bolling, had told me they were working to sew up the Chicago delegation for me.

Arriving two days early in New York with Betty and several members of my staff, I reserved a small hospitality room in the Essex House where the Texas delegation would be billeted for the convention. Marshall Lynam and Craig Raupe had been talking by telephone with new Democratic candidates seeking open seats or opposing Republican House incumbents in the 1976 election. They had made appointments for me to meet twenty-four of these for personal get-acquainted visits at my Essex House hospitality room. Individual appointments were arranged at half hour intervals.

We offered coffee, fresh fruit, cheese, rolls and coffee cake. No booze. Betty arranged to sit in with me whenever the candidate was accompanied by a spouse. Otherwise, I'd just visit personally with the Democratic hopeful, answering whatever questions I could about the House itself, the upcoming fall campaign, what to expect in Washington, and my hope to be Majority Leader. This program came off better than I'd dared to expect. Of the twenty-four with whom I conducted individual interviews, I judged that most of them had good shots at being elected in November. Among them, I had won sixteen vote commitments in my Majority Leader bid. Maybe I'd have support from some of the others, but I wasn't counting on it. Everyone had been friendly. But I discovered early on that there are a thousand ways to encourage a colleague without making a commitment that he could take to the bank.

Others before me, I knew, had been lulled into self-deceptive euphoria by pats on the back and fulsome compliments from colleagues. Dick Bolling thought he had twice as many votes as he actually had against Carl Albert. Morris Udall, after his Quixotic effort to unseat Speaker McCormack, said he knew he must be the world's poorest counter; otherwise, he'd have to conclude that his colleagues were the world's biggest liars, and he knew that couldn't be the case. Another Udall comment of that time is even better remembered. The difference between a cactus and a caucus, he said, was that with a cactus the thorns are on the outside. Only he didn't use the word "thorns."

I knew I was making progress when it first became apparent that other candidates were worrying about me. Some of Burton's enthusiasts began talking down the idea of a Texan as Majority Leader. If they have to resort to attacking my origins, I figured, they must be growing desperate. At the next meeting of the caucus, I decided to make a left-handed joke of it. Feigning indignation, I said a lot of people seemed to have the impression that all Texans were rich, uncouth, swaggering braggarts. "That is grossly misleading," I said. "We're *not* all rich!"

On another occasion, I hinted that at least I'd be able to communicate with President-to-be Jimmy Carter, since both of us obviously were free of any accent. The best way to handle frivolous concerns was by exposing them to humor. *Reductio ad absurdum.* Like when I was running for Congress the first time at age thirty and someone would suggest I was too young. No use being huffy about it. I'd always just say: "Give me a chance, and I promise I'll get over that in time!"

In a ploy to influence votes, a few House members, no doubt conscientious in their concern, tried to bait those of us wanting to be Majority Leader into a kind of informal bidding war soliciting our support for future congressional pay raises. This, I decided, was really improper. Even to discuss the

topic in that context would cheapen the entire process. But how to tell colleagues this without seeming starchy and judgmental, holier-than-thou? I
decided to make a joke of this also. "It is well known," I'd say whenever asked,
"that I voted last year for a cost of living raise for *all* government employees—
including Vice President Nelson Rockefeller. And that, my friend, is like
sending the King of Saudi Arabia a quart can of Quaker State oil!"

My biggest liability in the Majority Leader race was my late start. By the
time I announced, at least a third of the membership was already committed
to one of the other three. My principal asset was a substantial reservoir of personal good will. I got along with the various factions in our heterogeneous
party and was seen as a possible bridge between ideological extremes. From
those previously pledged to other candidates, I began collecting commitments of support on later ballots should their candidate be eliminated. This,
it turns out, was critical. It was like a football team's having a depth of fresh
talent on the bench for the final quarter.

Some of my good friends in Texas wanted to know what they might do as
private citizens to help. Thanking them, I said it really would be counterproductive for any outside individual to approach a member of Congress about
an internal decision as intimate to the institution itself as its choice of
Majority Leader. If fellow members didn't know me well enough after twenty
years to make their own judgement, then that was my fault.

After all, I had been in the home districts of more members, speaking in
their behalf, than had anyone else in Congress except for Carl Albert and
probably Tip O'Neill. As fall began, I was spending every ounce of spare
time I could squeeze from the calendar, doing just this sort of thing. On one
swing, I spoke at dinners and receptions for Don Pease in Ohio, John
Jenrette in South Carolina, Morris Udall in Arizona, Leo Ryan in California,
Floyd Fithian in Indiana, Austin Murphy in Pittsburgh and Nick Joe Rahall
in West Virginia.

All the while, I was trying not to neglect congressional business or duties to
my Texas district. On Sunday, October 3, I was invited to bring the Lay
Sunday sermon to Fort Worth's First Methodist Church. It was one of two
large churches in the metroplex whose services were carried live every Sunday
by television. The other was Dallas' First Baptist, whose longtime minister
was Dr. W. A. Criswell. For that same Sunday, the Dallas church invited
President Ford to speak.

Here is an ironic twist: While I would not under any circumstance have
abused that invitation by so much as alluding to a current political campaign—and most folks surely knew this, since I had appeared in that pulpit
on numerous occasions through the years—someone objected and the

television station canceled coverage of the Methodist service for fear of having to give equal time to another. Unbothered, I spoke to the congregation. No word nor hint of politics. (I didn't even have an opponent that year.) Nobody complained, apparently, about telecasting the Baptist church service from Dallas. Dr. Criswell not only introduced President Ford for the main presentation. He *endorsed* him. The preacher publicly called on his audience in the televised service for Ford's reelection!

Four Sundays later—on October 31, two days before the election—Candidate Jimmy Carter came to Fort Worth for a noon appearance in our convention center. As was his unvarying custom, Carter first attended Sunday morning church services. He expressly requested of Dr. James Harris, a friend of mine who was minister of the University Baptist Church, that he be permitted to slip in unobtrusively and not even be acknowledged from the pulpit. Carter wanted to worship, not politic. Dr. Harris told me this.

During the course of that campaign, I developed a closer relationship with Carter. Also a much deeper appreciation for the man himself. When he left the campaign trail to go back to Plains and reason with the deacons in his home church about racial desegregation, I sent a telegram applauding him. He was nineteen years ahead of the Southern Baptist Convention, his official congregation, which did not formally integrate until 1995.

And I called to commiserate with Jimmy Carter personally when comments of his in a lengthy, serious interview for *Playboy* magazine were taken out of context and sensationalized. What he said in answer to a question—that he had often "lusted in his heart"—was not only honest but absolutely correct theologically if not physiologically, however politically daring.

Carter, of course, won his race in November. He carried my district and my state. I accompanied him on a tour of five major appearances, ending in San Antonio one pleasantly cool night in front of the Alamo. In San Antonio the week before, President Ford had been offered a tamale and tried to eat it without taking off the cornhusk shuck. Carter assured his delighted audience—including thousands of Mexican-Americans—that, in spite of his lack of Washington experience, he knew how to eat a tamale.

One month and four days after Carter's victory—on Monday, December 6—I was elected Majority Leader by a one vote margin over Phil Burton on the fourth ballot. The caucus rule held that, when the result of each secret balloting was tabulated, the candidate with the lowest number of votes would drop off. On the first ballot, Burton had 106; Bolling, 81; Wright, 77; McFall, 31. McFall was out.

On the second ballot, I picked up most of McFall's votes, as I had expected to do. The results: Burton, 107; Bolling, 93; Wright, 95. I had bested Bolling by two votes. Bolling was out. Now it was between me and Phil Burton. I felt sure I'd get more of Bolling's partisans than Phil would. But would my gain be enough to overcome Burton's 12 vote lead?

Things were tense as tellers tallied the final ballot. All votes counted, the official tellers rushed back into the chamber. I saw my Texas colleague, Ray Roberts, leap for joy. Then I heard Bill Alexander's voice in my ear. "You did it, Jim. You won!" I had defeated Burton, 148 to 147.

My first congratulatory award was a big kiss from Betty who rushed down from the gallery where she had been sitting. My second was a magnum of Dom Perignon from Lloyd Bentsen. He must have been holding it, anticipating my victory. My third was a phone call from Jimmy Carter. He looked forward to working with me, said the president-elect.

From that point forward, for the next twelve and a half years, I'd know the raptures and the agonies of leadership, and I'd stay as busy as an army of ants.

CHAPTER TWENTY-TWO

A MAN FROM GEORGIA

I have met ten presidents, served with eight, respected all of them, liked most of them. I came to consider several, in the common vernacular, as friends. There are two whom I felt I knew at a deeper, personal level. Lyndon Johnson was one, Jimmy Carter the other.

It was natural that I would identify quickly and empathetically with the former Georgia governor. We were about the same age, both from small towns. We'd known the Depression. We shared certain values. Each of us was active in the church. Our family roots were southern. Both of us were involved in the effort to tear down the old walls of racial denial and awaken our common region to a more egalitarian attitude. There were other things in common, and a few pesky differences, of which I'd soon learn.

After the organizing caucus in early December, 1976, I was mentally and physically exhausted. The two campaigns—helping Carter carry Texas and winning the Majority Leader race—had left my generally ample reservoir of energy about as flat as my bank account. Betty and I wanted to get completely away from the world and its problems for five or six days and just slowly recharge our batteries. The place that came to mind was a bucolic hideaway in the cedar brakes of the Texas hill country near the quaint little town of Wimberley.

As we were leaving Washington for our five-day idyll, Marshall Lynam told me that the Carter transition team had asked for telephone numbers where they might locate me during the brief congressional recess. He had given my sister's number, he explained, supposing that we'd be at her house near Wimberley. We flew to Austin, where my sister Dr. Betty Lee Wright met us and drove us to the secluded valley lodge.

Early the next morning, Frank Moore tried to reach me for the president-elect. Calling from Plains, Georgia, Moore reached my sister's home and quickly discovered the pecking order of the hill country. Steeped in years of enforcing classroom discipline at Southwest Texas State, where she taught, my maiden sister responded to the call from the Georgia White House:

"I shall assume, Mr. Moore, that you are who you say you are; and upon that presumption, I shall give you a number where my brother may be reached. But you must promise that you will not call for one hour. He was quite tired last night, and he needs his rest. While it may be eight o'clock in Georgia, it is only seven o'clock in Texas, and it is possible that he is not even yet awake."

Moore dutifully waited a full hour before calling. Then, deferential and solicitous of my good health, he told me of Betty Lee's concern and wanted assurances that he hadn't awakened me. Then he put me through to the president-elect. I laughed aloud, imagining how many thousands of people were yearning for an opportunity to get Carter's ear, if only for a minute. I wondered if anyone else had expected the president of the United States to wait an hour for an appointment to talk.

As it turned out, our president-to-be was calling eight Democratic congressional leaders to a private preinaugural meeting with him outside the sleepy Georgia town of Plains, where Carter lived in a comfortable farm house. He greeted our arrival and we made sandwiches from ingredients displayed on a rectangular table in the dining room. Afterward, we all arranged chairs in a circle in the living room, where Carter and a small group of advisors discussed the new president's hopes for a program of legislative action. Dr. Charles Schultze, who had been chief White House economist on Lyndon Johnson's staff, laid out a rough outline of economic initiatives. Dr. James R. Schlesinger, whom I'd known as Secretary of Defense under Nixon and Ford, would advise the president on energy policy. Carter made clear that this would be a major thrust and sought our counsel.

During one break in the structured discussions that day, Carter asked me privately if I could intercede with Jack Brooks, then chairman of the House Government Operations Committee. The successful presidential candidate had promised several times during the campaign to ask Congress for what he called a "sunset" law. To be enacted, it would have to come through Jack's committee. And Jack was hostile. Carter's idea, as he explained it, would formally end all currently authorized government programs indiscriminately at periodic intervals. It was the president-elect's impression that all federal activities, once approved, just automatically continued indefinitely. Terminating all of them at once and forcing the legislative branch to re-authorize only those it wanted continued, he thought, would demand a closer examination and maybe even lapse a lot of meaningless efforts that Congress didn't even know were still in effect.

"It won't work," Brooks had said.

The new president asked if I could persuade Jack to change his mind.

Carter assumed that Congress, like the Georgia legislature, simply put programs in motion and let them run without review. As Governor, he had used the "sunset" provision to clear a lot of dead wood from the Georgia forest of archaic statutes. What he didn't realize was that, in Congress, most programs came up regularly for re-authorization, but they didn't all expire at once. To renew them all simultaneously would be totally unmanageable, Brooks believed.

One other thing the president-elect did not fully comprehend was the prideful independence of Jack Brooks. That spirited Texan guarded his jurisdictional turf with the proprietary passion of a mother grizzly protecting her pack of cubs. Carter mentioned that as governor he'd several times had to appeal to the public over the heads of hardheaded committee chairs to get his plans enacted. Tip looked as if our new friend had casually offered him a strychnine-on-the-rocks. "That would be the *worst* thing you could do, Mr. President, "O'Neill pleaded. "particularly with a fellow like Brooks! Jack doesn't get mad; he gets *even*—and you don't know your throat is cut until you try to turn your head."

"I believe I can help you, Mr. President," I said, "but not just the way you're thinking about. I've known Jack since we were kids in college. He's one of the sharpest guys on the hill. He can help you a lot, and you need him. But don't try to overpower him. Respect his opinions. Get his advice. Take him into your confidence. Make him a member of your team. Why not ask him to help you put together the kind of reorganization plan that will achieve the best of what you really want done without colliding frontally?"

Jimmy Carter agreed. He swiftly saw the possibilities of the course I had outlined. In matters of this kind, he was quick to learn. Throughout that day, I was repeatedly impressed, as I would be again and again during the next four years, by the speed with which President Carter could assimilate information. His was an absorptive, orderly engineer's mind. He had an amazing capacity to memorize and retain statistical data and to summon it back to his mind when needed.

Many people fail to appreciate Jimmy Carter's intellectual qualities precisely because of his friendly informality. He dislikes affectation, strives to express himself plainly. A friend of mine named Griffin Smith, who had written for the *Texas Monthly,* was hired for a time in Carter's first year as a presidential speech writer. Smith told me of his exasperation with the president's repeated use of the blue pencil on what Smith regarded as his best prose. Carter wanted no flowery language, no colorful figures of speech, no ringing affirmations with classically memorable phrases. What he did want, Smith said, reminded him of Sgt. Joe Friday in the television series, *Dragnet:* "Just the facts, Ma'am." I found this Carter trait endearing if slightly baffling. My instinct was too much the opposite. In writing and speaking, I had always reached for the colorful phrase like a warrior reaches for a weapon. My linguistic heroes were Franklin Roosevelt and Winston Churchill. Once at the National Archives I found the actual platform copy of Roosevelt's December 8, 1941, speech asking for a declaration of war against Japan. The one word that lingers in American memory was FDR's own last-minute addition. Roosevelt scratched through the typed word "history" in the opening sentence and in his own hand substituted "infamy." Like Kennedy, Roosevelt had that indefinable something called "flair."

Now, in Carter, we had a president whose goal was to take the puffery out of the presidency. On trips he carried his own luggage. ("I just don't want to lose them," he told me once.) He put a stop to instrumental renditions of *Ruffles and Flourishes* and *Hail to the Chief* that previously heralded presidential arrivals. "It just isn't necessary," Carter told me, grinning. "It makes me feel like some Oriental potentate." He ended the customary use of long White House limousines and substituted standard automobiles. Ordering all government executives to fly coach rather than first class, he said, "You get there just as soon." To top it off, he walked—rather than rode—in his inaugural parade almost all the way from the Capitol to the White House. Carter even sold the presidential yacht, *The Sequoia.* That move, I thought, was a mistake. I had seen that yacht used to enormous advantage by several presidents. They'd get key lawmakers and foreign leaders, and often their wives, away from telephones and other distractions long enough for unhurried conversations. Captives to the slowed-down pace of the boat as it cruised unhurriedly downstream on the Potomac, away from the slowly fading Washington lights, guests relaxed often into a comfortable rapport with their host—the president—on important issues.

A few days after Carter's inauguration came the national Presidential Prayer Breakfast, an annual observance begun in Eisenhower days and attended by every succeeding president. Approximately two thousand people overflowed the seated breakfast in a huge auditorium of the Washington Hilton hotel. For the 1977 observance, the bipartisan committee chose me as speaker.

I began solemnly, reading from the King James version the seventh verse from the first chapter of Paul's letter to the Philippians, wherein the second person plural is twice translated as "you all." Each time I drawled the term deliberately. Closing the Bible, I turned to President Carter and said, "Mr.

President, that verse has no particular relevance to what I want to say, but I thought it would be useful for all these people here to understand that St. Paul apparently came from our part of the country!" Carter, surprised, laughed spontaneously along with all the rest.

When the laughter subsided, I said, feigning sadness, "I must confess, however, that Paul surely was not a Texan. For he said in another of his letters, 'I have learned in whatsoever *state* I am to be content.'" The silly joke was a good icebreaker. It was not, incidentally, original with me. Many years earlier, I'd once heard Brooks Hayes of Arkansas make the same whimsical analysis. At the close of my remarks, I had everyone in the entire audience reach out and clasp hands with the persons on either side, while I made an appeal for world peace and good will for others who saw things differently, or worshipped differently, than ourselves.

Afterward, as I stopped to shake hands and pay my respects to President Carter, he said, "Jim, I'd like to be your good friend if you'll let me." I certainly did want to take him up on that offer. On Tuesday mornings the Democratic House and Senate leadership gathered for breakfast at the White House in a small meeting room just north of the large west ballroom where official state dinners occurred. Several times, the president invited me to drop by for lunch, just one-on-one. Sometimes, weather permitting, he'd have a small table set up outdoors in a shady alcove surrounded by huge trees off the southwest corner of the White House.

Carter didn't go in much for parties. He banished hard liquor from White House receptions, and that was just as well. He did serve wine. Early on in his presidency, Jimmy Carter wanted to amend the tax code so as to cut out, or at least put limits on, the deductibility of the business luncheon. President Carter began referring to extravagant lunchtime entertainment as "the three martini lunch." I remember thinking that if anybody actually drank three martinis at lunch, he'd surely fall asleep at his desk that afternoon.

An acquaintance of mine named Bob Juliano, who was president of the bartenders international union, told me the members of his craft were complaining to him about our president's repeated references to the martini as though it were something inherently evil. Bob wanted me to see if I couldn't get Carter to tone down the rhetoric a tad. I thought he was joking, but then several teetotalling lawmakers remarked privately that they thought press emphasis on the "three martini" theme was trivializing the serious effort to reform and tighten up the tax code.

At the next Tuesday morning breakfast, I told President Carter I had a scriptural question for him. "If the Lord hadn't intended man to have a three martini lunch," I asked, "then why do you suppose He put all those olive trees in the Holy Land?"

Carter was impatient with ceremony. He told me he thought government wasted too much time on formal dinners and receptions. Determined to reduce the number of once-obligatory social functions, he laid that law down early. He decided, for example, that the longstanding practice of entertaining a visiting head of state with a formal dinner at the White House and then attending a reception in his own honor the following night at the Embassy of the visitor was redundant. The first foreign president to visit Washington after Carter took office was José Lopez Portillo, of Mexico. It was unfortunate that the new rule had to be established with his visit, given the enormous emphasis placed by Mexico upon the equality of states. Our president hosted the usual state dinner for the Mexican leader. Then, pursuant to established practice, Mr. Carter received the customary invitation to a formal event in his honor at the Mexican Embassy. Carter declined with thanks. Our State Department begged him to change his mind. The Mexicans wouldn't understand, they insisted. But the president was adamant. The rule had to be established at the beginning, he felt. If he went to one, he'd be obliged to go to others. Lopez Portillo felt shunned.

Temperamentally, Carter was a lot different than Lyndon Johnson, the other president with whom I had frequent personal visits. By contrast to Johnson, Carter is quiet, low-keyed, his arguments usually understated. There is no bombast, no flattering, no cajolery, no big brotherly arm on your shoulder. Jimmy Carter keeps his temper in check. I almost never saw him lose composure. All this is part of the man's really remarkable self-discipline. And that, I think, is one of the keys to the Carter personality. Self-discipline. He manages his time well and does not neglect his health or personal growth. Bombarded by the world's biggest problems, Jimmy Carter nevertheless made time for continued self-growth. He listened to classical music, studied Spanish with Rosalyn, completed a speed-reading course—all after becoming president. He also read philosophy. Twice as I left a luncheon with him, he handed me a book he thought I'd enjoy reading.

President Carter told me one day that he still wore the waist size he wore when he was a cadet at the Naval Academy. It is thirty-two inches. "When my trousers begin to feel tight, Rosalyn tells me I ought to buy a larger size," he said. "I don't do it. I just eat a little less and get more exercise."

Another, and even more important, facet of Carter's character was his instinctive and absolute honesty. He didn't tell people what they wanted to hear but what he thought they *ought* to hear. Nor did Carter invent pleasant euphemisms with which to honey-coat unpleasant messages. He didn't take polls before deciding where he stood. He even lectured the public when he felt their apathy—or their "malaise"—warranted it. Jimmy Carter had the political courage to take positions of doubtful popularity—like amnesty for

Vietnam draft evaders, one of his first official acts, and the Panama Canal Treaty—simply because he believed them to be right. I agreed with him on both of those, and when I disagreed I had to admire the president's stubborn integrity.

I never really got settled in the Majority Leader's role. For ten years it soaked up my time and energies like a dry sponge. I began to feel like the hyperkinetic rabbit in the Walt Disney version of *Alice in Wonderland*. Remember the lines? Dashing in and out of successive scenes, the character chattered this refrain: "I'm late! I'm late! For a very important date! No time to say goodbye. Hello! I'm late, I'm late, I'm late."

Somehow, I relished it all.

It must have been the challenge of the thing that so totally fascinated me. I'd had a good mentor. Tip O'Neill, now Speaker, had made it all seem easy. Ambling through the halls of Congress like a big amiable polar bear, Tip must have had a head full of problems, but he hardly ever let them wear any grooves in his nervous system. O'Neill had an enviable ability to turn it all off at five o'clock every afternoon. He didn't like to discuss serious business, and absolutely refused to argue, after that hour.

Early in my tenure, I decided that the House Majority Leader had to be a tripartite person. He was part parish priest, part evangelist, and part prophet. An effective leader had to be a combination father-confessor and mother hen to the flock of Democratic members. Tip told me his biggest headaches came from refereeing turf disputes over committee jurisdiction. This task he gratefully turned over to his Majority Leader. But the bigger role was that of the evangelist, seeing to it that the leadership program got adopted on the House floor. This part of the job took constant salesmanship, cajoling members one-on-one or regaling them from the microphone in the well of the House. The Speaker selected John Brademas of Indiana as Whip and told me I could choose the Chief Deputy Whip. I picked Dan Rostenkowski of Chicago. So far as the prophet's role was concerned, the leader sometimes had to goad members into making hard choices for the country's long-range good, when some of those choices were not immediately popular.

With 289 Democratic members, I always had more speaking invitations than I could fill. There is hardly anything that cements the loyalties of individual colleagues like going with them to their home districts, speaking in their behalf, meeting their supporters and identifying with the problems distinct to their areas. And it broadened my perspective. In West Virginia, I once vocalized with Congressman Bob Mollohan in his rendition of *Country Roads* and played harmonica to Senator Robert Byrd's violin. In California, I saw a colleague presented a motel room key, all that was left of the structure where he'd spent the night two weeks earlier, now washed away by a devastating flood. In the Sangre de Cristo region of Northern New Mexico, I saw three brilliant rainbows adorning the sky at once. With Peter Kostmayer I would visit a township in Pennsylvania more than twice the age of my state. Its name, I discovered, was "New Town." I visited the sparkling new Baltimore Harbor project with Barbara Mikulski and heard the wails of unemployed steel workers in Youngstown, Ohio. I spoke at one small, parched desert town near El Paso where average rainfall is less than nine inches a year, and in Buffalo I drove down city streets cleared like canals between five-foot piles of snow on either side.

Early in 1977, Betty and I discussed the almost suffocating pile of invitations and tried to lay out a rough outline for budgeting our time. We would divide our weekends in threes. I'd spend the first with colleagues, trying to bunch two or three appearances together on a weekend. The second weekend we'd devote to the Fort Worth area, keeping in touch with my own constituency. On the third weekend, we'd try to get away together somewhere or just reserve two days of private time. In August, Betty reminded me we had been on that program for roughly eight months, and that third weekend had only come around four times.

When I assumed the post, one of the prerogatives of the office was a chauffeur-driven limousine. For as long as anyone could remember, there had been five long, stately, black vehicles that rolled imperiously into the Capitol grounds every morning to disgorge their official cargo, three under the broad stairway leading to the House chamber, and two under the identical stairway on the Senate side. These were for the House Speaker and the Majority and Minority Leaders of the two bodies. I inherited as my driver a marvelously resourceful gentleman my own approximate age named Irvin Nickens who had driven for Carl Albert during the six years Carl served as Speaker. Irvin knew the location of every place in Washington and the best and quickest route there at any given time of day. He was indefatigable. We became good friends.

When he first applied to me for the driver's position, I told Irvin that I was contemplating the possibility of not even having an official car. Betty and I each had a car, and I wasn't sure I would need a driver. Irvin knitted his brow, looked me straight in the eye, and said, "Mr. Wright, before you make that decision one way or the other, I think you ought to try it for two weeks with a driver and then form your opinion."

After fourteen days, I was convinced. It would have been next to impossible to attend half the functions I managed if I had to combat the traffic while sorting out my thoughts in preparation for each upcoming event and then search for a place to park once arriving. I learned to devour the essential news from the morning paper, make notes for the day's speeches and meetings, use the car phone to arrange or confirm appointments, and sometimes record memoranda on a hand Dictaphone—all on my way to work.

Sometimes in the early evenings, en route home from my office in the Capitol, I would flit quickly in and out of as many as four or even five receptions honoring colleagues. We had it down to an art. Irvin would deposit me at the site of the reception and wait. I'd hurry in, shake hands with guests, maybe execute a fast pass at the hors d'oeuvre table, be spotted by the host, and be quickly introduced. I'd speak for five minutes, ease my way through the crowd toward the door, and be back in the car on my way to the next reception—all within fifteen minutes at most.

A major emphasis of President Carter's administration was his effort to put together a national energy program. America's voracious consumption of energy was rapidly outpacing our domestic production capacity. Our nation-wide usage was growing by about 4.6 percent a year, and our purchases of foreign oil were growing by 29 percent. On April 18, President Carter made a televised broadcast. Appearing in a sweater, with the White House thermostats turned down to the sixties, the Chief Executive said our need to free ourselves from dependence on unpredictable foreign sources amounted to "the moral equivalent of war." Carter began his speech, "Tonight I want to have an unpleasant talk with you about a problem unprecedented in our history. With the exception of preventing war, this is the greatest challenge our country will face during our lifetimes." The president called upon the American people for a series of tough conservation measures including voluntary reduction by every citizen in unnecessary energy consumption. Otherwise, we'd soon be sending $80 billion abroad every year for energy.

With President Carter pleading for individual austerity, I felt both guilty and foolish riding around in a big, ostentatious, gas guzzling limousine. It just wasn't the kind of example the country's leaders ought to be setting, I decided. So I confided to Speaker O'Neill and Minority Leader John Rhodes, the other House officers for whom limousines were provided, that I was going to trade mine in immediately for a standard four-door car. After a short discussion, those two agreed to join in what we thought might be a decent joint example. The gesture attained hardly any media notice, and deserved little. It wasn't much of a sacrifice, but I felt good about it.

President Carter and Speaker O'Neill hit it off pretty well. Their cultural backgrounds were different. They had come to office by different roads. One was the product of ethnocentric big city wards, the other from Georgia's red clay hills and sandy lanes. They never fully learned to understand one another, but they came to like one another.

I was seated beside Tip when the waiter came by that first Tuesday morning with a big steaming platter of grits. Maneuvering the huge plate between us, he offered some first to the Speaker. "Would you care for some grits, Mr. Speaker?" he asked. I watched Tip look balefully at the white mound of uncertain substance. It is doubtful that Tip had previously been exposed to grits. "I'll try one," said O'Neill somewhat dubiously. One grit!

The president would begin each of these breakfasts by calling on one or another of us to offer an invocation. To those brought up in small town Protestant churches, there was nothing daunting nor unusual in being asked to say the blessing. Tip was reared in the Catholic tradition, in a time before Pope John XXIII, when mass was said in Latin and the laity were hardly ever expected to lead in formal prayer.

Vice President Walter Mondale, on the other hand, a preacher's kid from small town Minnesota, was as much at home as a catfish in a warm southern stream. Yet Fritz Mondale, known among friends for his sometimes impious sense of humor, had a finely developed flair for the ridiculous. Sometimes he and I would be seated next to one another at the weekly breakfast. Following some colleague's prayer, Fritz would whisper to me some such inanity as, "I can give that effort a B-plus, but I don't think it quite makes an A-minus. What do you think?"

Tip was impressed by the effortless aplomb with which some approached the assignment. "You Protestants surely do know how to pray!" he said to me one day. "Maybe we just need it more," I replied.

One day, the Speaker mentioned to President Carter following one of our regular breakfast meetings his admiration for the ability of Protestant colleagues to offer apparently extemporaneous supplications to deity.

"Tip, I really don't know which ones of the leadership are Protestant and which are Catholic," confessed Carter. "Are any of the fellows Jewish?"

The Speaker replied that none of the elected leaders who met regularly with the president were Jewish. "Danny Rostenkowski and I are the only Catholics. The rest are Protestants," he explained. The regulars included Senators Robert Byrd, Alan Cranston and Hubert Humphrey, as well as Brademas, Danny, Tip, and me.

Between that time and our next meeting, the thought came to Tip that he probably had put the president, quite unintentionally, in a position of feeling that he should call on either the Speaker or Danny for the next Tuesday's invocation. Not wanting Rostenkowski to be caught unaware, Tip called and told our Chicago compatriot to be prepared.

"You're kidding," was Danny's first reaction. But he got ready.

Sure enough, the president's first words at the next meeting were a request for Danny to ask the blessing. There issued forth a stream of eloquence that would have done justice to the Archbishop of Canterbury! Tip beamed. Mondale, eyebrows raised in surprise, exclaimed, "A-plus!"

Speaker O'Neill, for all his amiability, was an adroit and forceful leader. Early in his first year, he resolutely set out to protect the integrity of the House from stories and rumors swirling about the highly publicized antics of Tongsun Park and a handful of other Koreans representing various national and business interests. Tip appointed a special committee, with bipartisan input from Minority Leader John J. Rhodes, to oversee a swift and thorough investigation. A key ingredient to restoring public confidence in the institution he headed, O'Neill saw, was the selection of some universally respected outside counsel to conduct the actual investigation. Tip, Rhodes, Assistant Republican Leader Bob Michel, John Brademas and I decided on Leon Jaworski of Houston. He had conducted himself with dignity and honor in the Nixon investigation. In the public mind, the name Jaworski was synonymous with integrity. But would he do it? It would add no luster to his reputation. It would require his absenting himself from his own lucrative law practice to spend several months in Washington. Since I was the only one of the group who knew Jaworski personally, Tip asked me to make the call.

Leon Jaworski came on the line immediately. I laid it out plainly to him. I knew he didn't hunger for more public exposure and that he had more clients already than he could comfortably handle. I told him very simply that we all realized he had nothing whatever to gain from taking on the assignment but that it would be an important service to our country and we didn't think anyone else could do it as well as he.

"When you put it that way, Jim," said Jaworski, "you make it very difficult for me to say no."

As we ended the conversation and I replaced the receiver, I told Tip I felt certain that Jaworski would accept. In the meantime, Park fled the country, taking refuge in Korea and refusing to testify or be deposed for questioning under oath. At Jaworski's request, we passed a formal resolution holding Park in contempt of Congress. Our State Department sought extradition, but the South Korean government refused to grant it. Other than that, those hearings went well.

Speaker O'Neill also convened a special bipartisan panel, chaired by David Obey of Wisconsin, to draft a tight new set of internal rules. These rules among other things, regulated outside income for members of Congress and required strict public accounting. Serving in the House, we determined, was a full-time job requiring every member's full-time attention. No member henceforth would be allowed to accept outside income amounting to more than one-third of his or her congressional pay. Speaking fees, which most of us then were not in the habit of receiving, were limited to no more than two thousand dollars. The receipt of any money for any service rendered would have to be reported annually. Exempted from this rule were dividends from stocks and bonds, business investments, family trusts, and passive income for which no work was performed. Some members felt this tilted unfairly toward those with wealthy families and discriminated against folks of moderate income. To a degree, it did. But the purpose was to assure that no member neglected congressional duties to build a big bank account, and to let the public know who if anyone was paying lawmakers for outside services. On balance it was a good reform.

Also exempted from earned income limits, by deliberate design, were royalties from books written by members of Congress. Minority Leader John Rhodes, Republican Conference Chairman John Anderson, Morris Udall, Dick Bolling, and about twenty others including myself, had written published books. The committee in drafting the reform decided it didn't want to discourage these literary endeavors. They were, it stated, in the public interest. Still another piece of legislation dealt with campaign financing. New arbitrary limits denied any individual the right to contribute more than one thousand dollars to any candidate for Congress in a primary or general election. But political action committees, presumably composed of a lot of people belonging to the same union or business organization, were allowed to contribute up to five thousand dollars.

These new rules, compromises of conflicting ideas as all rules tend to be, did at least represent a good faith effort to improve things. Their general goals were to broaden the base of political giving, restrict the degree of influence that any single wealthy American or business interest could exert, and bring all such transactions into the daylight of public inspection. Nobody, of course, will ever be able to write a law that changes human character. Laws can improve behavior, however. Tip O'Neill was trying hard to help Congress live up to the high expectations to which people had every right to hold it. These very reforms, like most well-intentioned efforts to define acceptable behavior, would spawn their own abuses. In the wake of the 1977 law, political action committees sprouted and spread like Johnson grass after a rain. And the two-thousand-dollar speaking fee became not only a ceiling but a norm. Many Congressmen never had thought of charging a fee for a speech. Now they felt legally justified. But it would be a mistake to criticize the Speaker's motives, or those of the rest of us fallible mortals who make up the legislative branch of government, for failing to anticipate future problems.

Jimmy Carter didn't play politics in the traditional sense. For one thing, he had a kind of negative moralistic attitude toward patronage appointments.

There is nothing inherently wrong about appointing a trusted friend to a public position, assuming the friend is qualified. But Carter saw something tawdry in the process. In one of his last acts before leaving the White House, President Ford signed an executive order blanketing some three thousand political appointees of his and Nixon's under Civil Service. Ford's order, so long as it held, meant that Carter could not replace them with his own trusted allies or party faithful. Nice try, I thought. Jerry Ford must have supposed us stupid! It would be quite simple, of course, for President Carter to write a one-sentence executive order repealing that of his predecessor. But Carter was reluctant to perform the deed, which might look like a hunger for "patronage." I remembered something Sam Rayburn had said many years earlier and quoted it to President Carter: "You can write the most perfectly drafted law to carry out the most ideally conceived program; but put it in the hands of administrators inimical to its purpose or merely indifferent to it, and you'll have a very poor and ineffective law." Others in our group weighed in. They stressed how many able and dedicated people there were throughout the land who had supported Carter's presidential campaign with "money, marbles and chalk." Still, Carter hesitated. The very idea of appointing political friends was, in his mind, tainted. His was an idealized vision of meritocracy. A person's political leanings should not be brought into consideration in appointing government administrators. But whatever made him think, we asked, that Nixon and Ford had chosen without regard to politics?

Naive though I considered his views on questions of this kind, they were among the things that endeared him to me. He was so conscientious! There were many matters on which I agreed enthusiastically with Jimmy Carter, and a few on which we disagreed. But he was, I believed, as painfully honest a man as I'd ever met. I would come to appreciate him more the longer I knew him.

Once the president and I spent a half hour or so at lunch talking about our respective fathers, and of the towns where we grew up—Weatherford, Texas and Plains, Georgia. President Carter told me of the time when he decided to leave the Navy and return to the family business and the home of his youth. His father was suffering his terminal illness. Jimmy Carter was deeply impressed by how much the people of the little community cared.

"I decided that my father, who had never been many miles from that homestead, had done more good for humanity than I could achieve if I stayed in the Navy for an entire career and became Chief of Naval Operations," Carter said.

Another of his heroes was gruff old Admiral Hyman Rickover, a man demanding in his expectations of others and spare in his praise. In his 1976 campaign autobiography, Jimmy Carter told the story of their first meeting.

Rickover grilled him about his career at the Naval Academy, where Midshipman Carter had made good grades. Suddenly, Rickover asked, "Did you always do your best?" The young naval officer replied honestly that no, he really hadn't always. "Why not?" asked Rickover, abruptly signaling that the interview was ended.

The question seems to have haunted Jimmy Carter. It became the title of his first book, *Why Not the Best*. But that, I think, is exactly what Carter gave and is still giving—his best. Agree with him or not, one can't really ask for any more than that. He is at heart a peacemaker in a world that glorifies war makers. His presidency produced a few failures and some very splendid successes. Let me tell you of them.

CHAPTER TWENTY-THREE

ENERGY AND EXAMPLE

President Jimmy Carter is essentially a centrist, a combination of liberal and conservative instincts. He believes in the role of an activist government and its capacity to improve the human condition. Yet, he is frugal by nature, hates waste and is a devoted disciple of the work ethic. Carter combined idealism with a pragmatic recognition of limits. He was at heart a reformer. People in Congress sometimes thought he wanted to fix things that were not broken.

In May 1976, Bill Moyers interviewed Jimmy Carter on PBS. "I have a constant drive to do the best I can," Carter acknowledged, "and sometimes it's disconcerting to other people." Moyers asked what it was that drove him. Carter replied, "I don't know exactly how to express it. . . . I feel like I have one life to live—I feel that God wants me to do the best I can with it . . . and I enjoy tackling difficult problems, and finding solutions, and answering the difficult question, and the meticulous organization of a complicated effort."

Carter was, if nothing else, meticulous. He tried to know the details of every issue with which he dealt. Some thought he micro-managed to a fault. "It's nice to know the proprietor eats at his own restaurant," Charlie Wilson once mused, "but this guy Carter inspects every grain of salt that goes in the soup." Some insisted the president even kept the schedule for use of the White House tennis court. (Carter laughed about this years later. It wasn't so, he says.)

At one point, special presidential representative Alan Boyd was meeting with British envoys to work out a new bilateral set of airline flights. The British, having joined with European allies to build the supersonic Concorde, were anxious to introduce it into the United States. Braniff Airlines, domiciled in Dallas, was eager to get a toehold into Britain. Its executive officer, Harding Lawrence, told me his company would be glad to purchase one or more of the expensive needle-nosed planes for London-bound flights originating at the new Dallas–Fort Worth International Airport if Boyd could negotiate entry into the market for the Texas-based line. This sounded like a potentially good bargain to me. The English wanted to sell some Concordes and Braniff wanted a door to European markets. My interest was in promoting the then-new Dallas–Fort Worth airport as a direct international gateway for the citizens of North Texas. For years I had worked to get it built, and such an agreement with the British would be one small way to expand its usefulness. But it only involved two flights a week. It wasn't a decision of sufficient consequence to command the personal attention of the president.

I wrote a little one-page memo, outlining what Braniff would be prepared to do, and handed it to Frank Moore, Carter's legislative liaison. "If you're talking with Alan Boyd in the next two days," I said, "you might like to pass this on to him. As eager as the British are to sell Concordes, he might be able to use this as a bargaining chip."

On Tuesday morning, following the White House breakfast as I was preparing to leave, Frank stopped me at the elevator. "Did you want to talk with President Carter about that airline matter?" he asked. "Oh, heck no, Frank," I replied. "I wouldn't ask for any of the president's time to talk about a deal that size." With that, I got in the elevator and went down to the parking level.

Later that day, I got a call at my office from Moore. "Hold on, Mr. Leader," he began, "President Carter is right here and wants to talk to you." The president came on the line , told me he thought I had a good idea and was calling Alan Boyd to suggest that he implement it. No detail was too small for Jimmy Carter.

In this, Carter was the absolute antithesis of his successor, Ronald Reagan. The latter delegated almost all authority for day-to-day decisions. Even in matters which I thought demanded the president's personal judgment, Reagan deferred to his underlings. He was the front man. Reagan cut ribbons and made speeches. He did these things beautifully. But he never knew frijoles from pralines about the substantive facts of issues. Carter, by contrast, constantly impressed lawmakers with his mastery of factual detail and made most of the decisions, little as well as big, himself. Yet he didn't have Reagan's popularity with the people.

Carter's top policy priorities made up a family of E's—*energy, environment, education, efficiency.* To that list we could add *example.* Because they believed in the public schools and America's duty to support them, Jimmy and Rosalynn Carter sent their nine-year-old daughter, Amy, to the inner-city public school nearest the White House. Once, from a dentist's office in a nearby building, I watched the children at recess. Amy was one of a tiny minority of white children. The Carters believed in racial equality and integrated education; so they practiced it.

Because he believed in a lean, frugal federal establishment, Carter set the pace for what he hoped would be a shrinking of the government payroll. He announced soon after entering the White House that he would arbitrarily reduce the White House staff by one-third. Friends privately wondered at the advisability of so big a slash. Wasn't the work of his White House as big, as important, as demanding as that of his predecessors? Wouldn't this restrict his team's capacity to perform? What led him to suppose one-third fewer people could handle the load? These questions did not faze Carter. He wanted to establish the example.

The new president set a top priority on getting legislation to let him reorganize the whole executive branch. He thought he could increase government efficiency by whittling down the number of federal agencies. For as long as I can recall, most people have believed that government at all levels was bloated. As a freshman member of the Texas legislature thirty years earlier, I had proposed such a plan at the state level.

The historic difficulty is that the pledge to cut waste and duplication is easy. To perform the actual deed is toilsome and tedious. Carter's experience, granting his sincerity, was vaguely disappointing. Congress, urged on by my friend Jack Brooks whom Carter had now made an ally, gave our chief executive the power he requested. But lawmakers reserved a right to vote on each reorganization plan.

The president's first test of this new authority was a proposal he unveiled on March 1, 1977 to overhaul the federal energy bureaucracy. He saw it as a precursor to streamlining the entire federal government. Carter wanted to create a cabinet-level Department of Energy. Carter believed this would make a big difference. I hoped it would but had less faith in the efficacy of just moving agencies around like squares on an organization chart. The main changes we needed were in policy, not in the reshuffling of authority.

"All but two of the executive branch's cabinet departments now have some responsibility for energy policy, but no agency . . . has the broad authority to deal with our energy problems in a comprehensive way," Carter pointed out. He insisted that nowhere else in government was the need for reorganization and consolidation greater. Tip and I encouraged colleagues to support the president's proposal, and Congress went along with the plan. It gave new recognition to the emerging national importance of energy sufficiency.

We also followed President Carter's lead in establishing a Department of Education. If any domestic function deserved leadership at the federal level, it was the seminal role of education in strengthening our society. President Reagan would waste a lot of time and effort trying to undo the creation of these two new departments. I never understood why. It seemed petty, but the Californian throughout his eight years in office seemed obsessed with a desire to discredit Carter's achievements and scruff out all of his footprints. But he couldn't.

President Carter was earnest about reorganizing the administrative branch of government. Hardly any other goal, at first, seemed closer to his heart. During the 1976 campaign, Carter had promised to tighten up the structure of the sprawling federal establishment. Once he said he'd like to cut the number of agencies, bureaus, boards and commissions from approximately 1,800 down to maybe two hundred. This target defied the rational expectations of congressional leaders, but we did want to help him trim away the fat and make government work more effectively.

For several years on the Public Works and Transportation Committee, I had identified areas where the pruning shears could actually improve performance. It is trite and far too glib to say that government is out of control or just institutionally incapable of delivering services efficiently. It is altogether erroneous to contend, as Speaker Newt Gingrich would do in the 1990s, that Lyndon Johnson's Great Society failed. On the contrary it succeeded grandly. Because of its caring services, millions of illiterates were educated. Millions of hungry were fed. Millions of youth gained job skills that converted them into taxpayers. Millions are alive because of the Great Society's emphasis on health. And the golden years of a dignified retirement have become a reality for many millions more.

The problem was not in the programs but in their administration. Overzealous rulemakers and administrators with no sense of urgency had, however, corrupted sensible goals into bait for cruel jests. At several of our Tuesday morning leadership meetings, we discussed numerous examples of this tendency.

The country had awakened in the 1960s and early 1970s to the long-neglected needs of our environment. Clean air and clean water legislation has incontestably served the public interest, but in their zeal to exercise the police powers of the government, regulators had grossly magnified government paperwork. The environmental impact statement became an international joke, a synonym for fluff and needless delay.

I discovered this unpleasant fact on an official 1977 trip to Israel. I had been there ten years earlier, and now I saw a whole landscape of astounding progress. Marveling at the way in which that little country had in such a short time reforested its highlands, restored vegetative cover to its denuded pastures and transformed dismal swamps into productive orchards and gardens, I asked how so much had been accomplished so swiftly.

Our Israeli host replied, "Well, for one thing, we don't have to write environmental impact statements."

In my own Texas backyard, I had seen how the so-called EIS, too zealously and sometimes unrealistically pursued, became a tool not so much for protecting the environment as for slowing down development.

As a result of legislation I had sponsored, a circumferential highway was being built around Fort Worth, intersected by three major Interstate routes. At one point, the new highway had to cross a lake. Progress was delayed for six to eight months while local communities were expected to come up with lengthy written answers to a host of inapplicable questions, including one that asked for a separate study of what would happen if a large truck loaded with gasoline or chemicals should somehow crash through the protective concrete bridge railings and tumble into the lake. It was against just such contingencies that the bridge had been designed!

Another of the questions demanded a separate study on the feasibility of substituting a ferry boat operation for the bridge that crossed a half-mile of lake. When Mayor Sharkey Stovall told me of this requirement, I said, "Just write them a letter saying that Interstate traffic would be stacked up all the way to Memphis and Congressmen from five states would be demanding the head of whoever suggested the ferry boat." Apparently this sufficed.

Other worthwhile objectives also had been pursued on occasion with similar impracticalities. Protection of endangered species is a splendid ecological target. But the objective was sometimes unrealistically aimed at. My Texas colleague, Omar Burleson, told of a sheep rancher whose lamb crop was being systematically ravaged by wolves. Years earlier, before the wolf was designated for protection under the Endangered Species Act, the government had employed a trapper to help rid the region of wolves. Now, legally protected, the predatory creatures had returned in force. The rancher wanted to know what he could lawfully do to protect his flock.

An eager young man in the Agriculture Department office in Abilene thought he might have a solution. It was against the law to shoot or trap the beasts, even on private lands, he explained. But conceivably an application for an experimental program, if properly written and limited to a small geographic area where wolves were overpopulating, might be approved. The government agent had read that canines could be kept from reproducing by a variation of the irradiation treatment so successful with the fly that had spread hoof and mouth disease. This, he reasoned, could halt their proliferation.

The rancher could apply for a limited baiting of the wolves by treatment of meat samples, the government man reportedly proposed. The rancher, puzzled and uncomprehending, asked what good that would do. The agent explained that the treated meat would prevent the male wolves from sexually reproducing.

"Why, hell, man," the grizzled old rancher replied, "you don't understand a damn thing about wolves! *That's* not what they're doin' to the sheep! They're killin' and eatin' 'em."

Experiences of legislators, local public officials, businessmen and ordinary citizens seemed to coincide on one point: dealing with the departments and agencies of the federal government in recent years had become increasingly difficult, irritating and expensive. Meanwhile, departments and agencies had grown more lethargic, more burdened with time-consuming paperwork and hamstrung by regulations, more intrusive and more bumbling, ever less capable of acting swiftly and decisively.

One example: In 1972, Congress with my active help, had enacted a major clean water program. We mandated a three-year, $18 billion crash effort to help the communities of this country build badly-needed waste treatment plants. Nearly five years later, only $7 billion in projects had been put under construction. And it wasn't for lack of need. Six times that many applications were on file, gathering dust in the slow-moving bureaucracy.

Another: In 1968, Congress wrote a law to start construction on 600,000 new lowcost housing units each year. We hadn't even come close. There'd been only 41,000 construction starts in all of 1976. A maze of administrative regulations and red tape had contributed to frustrating delays in getting the job done for poor people in need of affordable living space.

Businessmen were having increasing problems with federal red tape. As result of well-meaning laws with meritorious goals, small businessmen now had to file a lot of additional reports dealing with equal employment, unemployment compensation, occupational health and safety, environmental protection and countless others. There were 4,000 separate safety rules, covering 800 pages, in the *Code of Federal Regulations*. The owner of a small drugstore estimated to me that he spent 15 percent of his time on paperwork relating to federal drug controls. The owner of a small foundry said he put in about an hour and a half every day filling out government forms.

A banker complained that his bank spent $8,000 printing forms to deal with real estate settlement procedures, only to have the government change the regulations once the forms were printed. One oil company said it had to use 636 miles of computer tape to store data required by the Federal Energy Administration, and thirty-four other agencies also demanded reports from that same company.

This sort of thing was happening all too generally. Each new regulation, perhaps not without merit when viewed in isolation, added to the overload. Most of this regulatory encumbrance was never even intended by Congress. During a two-year period in which Congress was passing some 500 laws, the unelected bureaucracy was writing almost 10,000 new regulations. There were about 75,000 full-time regulators on the federal payroll at an annual cost of about $3 billion.

What could a new president do to attack the problem of overregulation? It wasn't simple. One thing President Carter needed to realize was that greater efficiency and more simplicity would not be accomplished automatically through the "big tent" approach—simply lumping agencies into ever larger departments.

We had already seen some unintended results of this approach. At one time the Federal Housing Administration was a lean, efficient and effective agency. In one generation, it helped boost home ownership from about 30 percent of our population to nearly 70 percent. Then we folded FHA into the Department of Housing and Urban Development with its extra layers of regulations and extra tiers of second-guessers—and little had been heard from FHA since that time. Most builders didn't want to build under it any more. It had become too complicated.

There were situations, on the other hand, where combining functions under one heading could be helpful. Energy policy, I decided, was one good case in point. Some forty different agencies, scattered across the broad spectrum of government, made decisions relating directly to the nation's future energy outlook. President Carter's first reorganization plan, therefore, drew all these functions together into his new Department of Energy with James Schlesinger as Secretary.

On a practical everyday plane, President Carter told me he wanted to do a number of pragmatic things: (1) to eliminate boards and agencies that simply duplicated others, (2) to curtail very drastically the number of regulations written in the administration branch, (3) to see that those were written in plain English that the average citizen could understand, and (4) to get rid of a lot of deadwood in the executive branch of government. He also said he wanted to delegate broader authorities to his department heads instead of making all the real policy decisions in the White House via a kitchen cabinet.

One useful step in the dispersal of decision-making, I suggested, would be to let state and local officials simply certify that federal laws had been complied with instead of subjecting every application for a road, a school or a sewer plant to tiers upon tiers of second-guessers in Washington, far removed from the point of need. Another good move, I told him, would be to speed up the time-consuming process of interagency review. Sometimes it took as long as two years for all the other agencies to sign off on something one agency wanted to do.

The president's goals were admirable. They would run up against stubborn resistance in the entrenched bureaucracy, those of us in the Tuesday morning Congressional leadership meetings warned him, and some foreseeable opposition even in Congress. I didn't want to see President Carter disappointed. He deserved a chance, I thought, to try to make his program work.

A peacemaker at heart, Jimmy Carter on January 21, 1977, issued a presidential pardon to all those who had evaded the draft during the Vietnam War. Senator Barry Goldwater called this action "the craziest damn thing" he'd ever heard of. Other critics were just as vocal and even less charitable. But Carter had made no secret of his intention to do this. He insisted that he wasn't condoning the avoidance of military service; he was forgiving it. In August, before his election, he announced his plan to the American Legion at its annual convention. "I intend to grant a blanket pardon," he told the veterans' group. "Amnesty means what you did is right. Pardon means that what you did—right or wrong—is forgiven. . . . I think it is time for the damage, hatred and divisiveness of the Vietnam War to be over."

The symbolic move had its effect. A little of the lingering bitterness dissipated. The ugly wounds of division began to heal. It would be eighteen years, 1995, before diplomatic relations would be resumed with Vietnam, but Carter's bold pardon was the beginning of America's inner-healing process.

At the end of his first year in office, Jimmy Carter was proud of the fact that he had presided over the first full year in more than a generation in which not one single American serviceman died anywhere in the world from enemy action.

One might have guessed the direction of Carter's foreign policy initiatives by his nomination of Cyrus Vance for secretary of state and Paul Warnke to be director of the Arms Control and Disarmament Agency. Warnke also would be our negotiator in talks with the Soviet Union. Both Vance and Warnke were public servants with solid credentials. Both had served in the Defense Department. The service of each dated back to Kennedy-Johnson times, and both believed it possible to make real progress toward world peace.

Cy Vance began his government career in 1957 working as legal counsel to the Special Space and Astronautics Committee of the Senate. Lyndon Johnson chaired that committee which came into being after the Soviets beat us into space with Sputnik. Its mission was to gain superiority in space and in the missile race. A protege of Johnson's, Vance later served as general counsel of the Defense Department under Robert McNamara and those two developed a close rapport. One clue to Vance's more recent interests might be seen in his service on a four-man peace mission to Panama. The mission's purpose was to restore ruptured relations that followed bitter rioting in the mid-1960s over U.S. practices in the Canal Zone. The major recommendation the Vance peace team made was "an integral revision of the treaties that govern relations" between Panama and the United States. A series of subsequent diplomatic missions had fingered the fringes of that challenge ever since Vance's mission, but none had been daring enough to get a solid grip on the core problem. Carter would do so.

In the closing days of the Johnson administration, Vance was chosen to help start the process of negotiations with the North Vietnamese in Paris. He later became deeply concerned with the burgeoning international trade in weapons. The continuing growth in the arms race disturbed him. When President Ford vetoed a congressional effort in 1976 to reestablish some control over the unbridled proliferation in weapon sales, Vance, then out of government, wrote an op-ed column for *The New York Times* criticizing Ford's veto.

The Secretary-to-be of State said upon being designated, that moving the arms limitations talks into solid agreements would be his top priority. He also gave a preview of the new special thrust of Carter's foreign policy. "The undergirding principle," he declared, "must be a concern, and a deep concern, for human rights."

Warnke's nomination to carry on talks with the Soviet Union stirred up the right wing like a broomstick thrust into a nest of wasps. A partner in the law firm headed by longtime presidential advisor Clark Clifford, Warnke was an object of suspicion among those who did not think any agreement possible with the Russians. Carter himself made that point on the day of the vote to confirm the hotly contested nomination. The president stressed that he was committed to "a substantial reduction" in nuclear weapons. A lot of those who didn't want Warnke confirmed, Carter stated, "just don't want to see" any such reduction. The vote approving Warnke's appointment was 58 to 40.

Another clue to Carter's priorities was his selection of Walter Mondale as his vice presidential running mate. Mondale, a classic liberal of the Hubert Humphrey school, was mostly concerned with domestic issues. He felt the failure of America to live up to its promise as a land of universal opportunity and upward mobility for all was due in part to the huge amounts of money siphoned off every year for military weapons. It may be that Mondale's presence on the ticket marked one of the few occasions in American history when a vice presidential nominee made any notable difference in the outcome of the race. It takes nothing from Carter's personal performance in his victory over Ford to recall the televised Mondale-Dole debate during the 1976 campaign. I remember it vividly.

Dole went aggressively on the offensive in the first few minutes with a lightning series of barbed witticisms. Mondale, who knew his adversary from Senate debates, responded with equanimity, eschewing personal attack and contrasting his own pleasantness and fairness against Dole's acerbity. One result of that evening's performance was a reputation that dogged Bob Dole for years. People thought of him as mean spirited. Knowing Senator Dole, I think the reputation is exaggerated. He has an irrepressible sense of humor which, finding a victim, can sometimes sting, but I don't think Bob is essentially mean. Yet he has never erased from the public mind that image of a Doberman on the attack. For a lot of folks, it began that night with his debate against Mondale.

It was in the Humphrey campaign of 1968 that I first became acquainted with Fritz Mondale. He and Senator Fred Harris of Oklahoma were teamed as cochairmen of the preconvention delegate roundup. Jim O'Hara of Michigan and I headed a similar effort in the House. We all worked together closely through the tempestuous Chicago convention.

One of the popular knee-jerk shibboleths of the moment was a drive to outlaw the unit rule, which bound delegates to carry out the majority's wishes at national conventions. If a state's delegates split fifteen to five over a given issue, for example, all twenty votes from that state would be cast on the side of the fifteen. In the specific case of the 1968 Chicago convention struggle between Humphrey and his principal challenger, Senator Eugene McCarthy, the unit rule would have actually worked to Humphrey's benefit.

But a new emphasis on "reform" consigned this ancient and often honorable practice into the "smoke-filled room." To the unsullied palate of the reformer, the unit rule smacked of dirty politics. Better, it was thought, to require each state to poll its delegates on each issue and cast its votes proportionately.

Rather than seem like creaky relics of the political machine era, the Humphrey team got on the bandwagon. Fritz and the rest of us carried out our standard bearer's wishes by embracing a new rule, which arbitrarily outlawed enforcement of the unit rule. It became common at that convention for unit rule states, of which Texas was one, to poll their delegations carefully on each issue and then to report thirteen to four or seventeen to nine, or whatever the precise division might be. In the case of Texas, there was a matter of honor at stake. Governor John Connally, his pro-Humphrey forces having prevailed at our state convention, considerately allowed a number of McCarthy and Kennedy supporters to be included among the delegation. This was a nice gesture. It promoted harmony. McCarthy enthusiasts had agreed to the unit rule. They knew that, without it, they wouldn't have been permitted on the delegation, for Connally's troops at the state convention had the votes to exclude them.

Connally was irate when he heard of Humphrey's last-minute embrace of the reform. "It's stupid, Jim," he insisted to me. "Nothing less than self-destructive. The unit rule benefits Humphrey, and if he is too myopic to see this, then that fact casts some doubt on his capacity to be president!"

Not wanting a dangerous rift among Texans over this volatile issue and knowing how strongly our governor felt about it, I told John that I would take it upon myself to talk with the McCarthy delegates and others who had leaned toward the late Senator Robert Kennedy. I would persuade them if possible to swallow their instinctive wishes and voluntarily go along with the good faith agreement by which they had been included on the delegation. In other words, cast their votes on their own volition with the state's majority. Circulating among the delegation, I got almost all the dissidents to agree to this policy. Connally was pleased. Based on the code of the handshake, he had a legitimate grievance. Had Connally gone off the reservation at the last minute, it could have been quite hurtful to Humphrey's cause.

When the next roll call came, I was sitting with Fritz Mondale in the campaign suite, watching floor action via television. The unit rule had been outlawed. The current vote was over some other procedural issue. Mondale was astounded when we saw John Connally, his chin thrust upward in that characteristic mannerism of his, proudly announce that "Texas, *not* voting under the unit rule, casts all its votes for—"

Looking at me in disbelief, the senator asked, "What on earth has brought this about? *All* of you guys voting together?" I grinned. "Simple," I replied. "We just appealed to their sense of honor." Mondale thought for a moment. "Oh, that! I think we used to have that rule in Minnesota, but we reformed!" From that time on, the two of us have enjoyed a great relationship.

Mondale was an active supporter of the Legal Services Corporation and an advocate of better treatment for migratory farm workers. Staunch in behalf of civil rights, Mondale defended busing as a means to break down de facto school segregation. Outspoken advocacy of these causes would not have won election in Georgia, but Jimmy Carter did not find them abhorrent. In fact, Carter vowed from the beginning that his vice president would have a larger role in the administration than any previous occupant of the number two office. He moved the vice president's office from the next door Executive Office Building into the White House proper. The president sometimes referred to Mondale as his "chief of staff person" and to his actual participation in the decision process as "unprecedented." I believe Jimmy Carter actually considered Mondale in an almost coequal role.

The single most indispensable ingredient to an understanding of Jimmy Carter, however, is a recognition of his dependence on Rosalynn Carter. Most political leaders speak of closeness with their spouses, but in all my years I haven't observed a more genuine affinity nor a relationship more nearly based on true equality than that which exists between Carter and his wife.

Other first ladies have contributed to their husbands' success in office. Eleanor Roosevelt broke new ground in the 1930s as the first really outspoken first lady. Lady Bird Johnson influenced Lyndon's decisions so unobtrusively that hardly anyone knew the extent of her influence. She also exercised actual management of family business enterprises. Most observers, I think, recognize that Nancy Reagan had a highly developed protective instinct for her husband. Jacqueline Kennedy added her own stylistic dimension to the New Frontier. Hillary Clinton, brilliant and articulate in her own right, is distinctive in the independent assertion of her own perspective on issues of the day. Bess Truman and Barbara Bush, on the other hand, were publicly revered precisely for seeming more like wives and mothers than policy enthusiasts.

In my experience, no two White House occupants have ever been closer than Rosalynn and Jimmy Carter, nor any first lady more indispensable to the president. Jody Powell, Carter's press secretary, said it pretty well: "Her role is not just that of a *supportive* wife; they're doing it all *together*." Carter continually discussed things with his wife. They could disagree and often did so, without affecting their relationship. Rosalynn regularly sat in on cabinet meetings, something no other first lady has done, or probably even wanted to do. Since the Carters left the White House in 1980, I have been with the former president on several missions of peace. I've served alongside him monitoring elections in Nicaragua, Haiti and Panama. I've participated in four or five conferences and seminars at the Carter Center in Atlanta. Always, in every setting, at mealtime and at worktime, Rosalynn is at his side.

Just shortly after becoming president, Carter sent Rosalynn as his emissary to Central and South America. He wanted her to visit seven countries, meet the heads of state, and talk with them on his behalf. She was to stress his desires for a nuclear free zone in the hemisphere, his hopes for friendly relations based on equality, and his support of political democracy and human rights.

This was something new. Some Latins didn't know just how to take Rosalynn Carter. She had studied hard for the trip, and didn't it make sense that a president's wife could speak more freely and more personally for him than could any other diplomat?

Still, the cult of *machismo* is deeply rooted in the Latin persona. Many of our southern neighbors could see a president's wife as a polite symbolic emissary, but not as a policy spokesperson. One editor grumbled that Mrs. Carter had not been elected; her husband had. A Brazilian leader sniffed that it was ridiculous to expect Latin Americans to listen to the first lady speak on atom bombs. Reporters for U.S. journals asked her if she didn't feel "presumptuous."

Through this all, Rosalynn Carter kept her cool. It was not only her tactful charm, but her knowledge and efficiency, that ultimately prevailed. Unaccustomed though they were to such an ambassador, almost all the foreign officials Rosalynn encountered along the twelve-thousand-mile journey were impressed. One aspect of human rights, on President Carter's scales, was the doctrine of equal rights for women. *Avant-garde* for most of Latin America at the time, most certainly. But Carter believed in example.

The ultimate test of Jimmy Carter's political courage was the Panama Canal treaty. If he had been looking for votes, he would have dodged it. Previous presidents had done so. No issue in the previous two decades and probably longer was so intensely felt throughout Latin America. Nor was any so little understood initially in the United States. No other part of the world was as important to our country as Latin America, yet no other had been the subject of such continued neglect.

Too long had we taken Latin American friendship for granted. We hadn't bothered to learn the simplest things about the region, its people, and their priorities. Few North Americans realized the depth of emotion associated with the Canal not only in Panama but throughout the hemisphere. Panama had legitimate grievances, which, to our discredit, we had ignored. The problems surrounding our presumed sovereignty in the Canal had a fairly long history. Around the turn of the century, Colombia refused our proposal to dig a canal in their sovereign territory and take over its ownership and operation. U.S. interests encouraged the northern province to secede from Colombia. When it rebelled, a U.S. gunboat in the area prevented Colombian troops from landing to put down the rebellion. Thus was created the Republic of Panama, mainly to serve our convenience. In 1903, Washington lawyers wrote a treaty giving us what Colombia had refused us. Secretary of State John Hay, who signed that treaty, described it as "vastly advantageous to the United States and, we must confess, not so advantageous to Panama." Every politically aware person in Latin America knew this history. Few in our country remembered these salient details. The little country had been, for the most part, friendly to our interests. But, increasingly, Panamanians had come to resent the puppet relationship. As for the Canal, Panama contributed most of the labor; U.S. interests enjoyed the profits.

Having traveled many times in Latin America and talked personally with thousands of private citizens, hundreds of elected officials and at least eighteen heads of state, I was certain of one thing: our friends in the hemisphere wanted us to agree to a new treaty recognizing Panama's rightful sovereignty over its own country; our enemies did not. The U.S. exercised unilateral, exclusive authority in the Zone. The fifty-one-mile canal cut a wide swath through the Republic of Panama, from the Atlantic to the Pacific Ocean. Within the Zone, a ten mile wide strip of land, our country assumed in the words of our old unilaterally written treaty of 1903, "all the rights, power and authority . . . to the entire exclusion of the exercise by the Republic of Panama of any such sovereignty, power, or authority."

In 1964, bloody rioting had erupted when a few American students taunted the Panamanians by raising the Stars and Stripes on the Canal Zone campus. The anti–U.S. demonstrators were met with force by U.S. troops. The government of Panama immediately broke off diplomatic relations, accusing us of aggression. In three days of bloody turmoil, four American soldiers and twenty Panamanians were killed. Dozens more were injured. Panama's President Roberto Chiari told President Johnson that all existing treaties had to be completely revised in order to prevent further violence. Johnson's memoirs reveal his conviction that "it was indeed time for the United States and Panama to take a new look at our treaties."

Johnson in fact had come to an agreement with Panama's president in June of 1967 on three new treaties. Opposition in Congress was so intense, however, that the treaties were never sent up for Senate approval. This provoked an angry public reaction in Panama, whose people felt betrayed.

In the following year, as public hostility grew and new demonstrations flared up, thoughtful Panamanians became increasingly apprehensive over disruptions of the public order. In October 1968, the head of Panama's national guard, General Omar Torrijos, seized power and installed U.S.–educated Jimmy Lakas as president, announcing that he would maintain civil order, then gladly step aside and turn leadership over to elected civilian authority as soon as acceptable treaties were ratified with the United States. Ten years later, he would make good on that pledge.

Omar Torrijos was, by instinct and personality, the direct antithesis of Manuel Noriega, who replaced him years later as head of the National Guard, following the fatal crash of Torrijos' plane, caused by apparent engine failure. Noriega wanted power for power's sake, and had no intention of respecting civilian authority. Many Panamanians believed the crash that took Torrijos' life was no accident but the result of sabotage plotted by Noriega. On that subject I have no basis for an informed opinion. But I do believe Omar Torrijos was a man of honor. He kept every promise I ever knew him to make to our country. And he was enormously popular among the plain people in Panama.

Torrijos told me the first time I met him in 1970, and reiterated three years later when we met again, that his life's principal goal was to establish between his country and mine a fair and friendly relationship based on equality. The Panama Canal and the question of sovereignty were central to this. Treaty opponents in our country homed in on Torrijos, seeking to make him a scapegoat. Their usual descriptive reference was a "tin-horn dictator." But Carter wrote a poignant passage in his memoirs about the emotional reaction of Torrijos upon the formal signing of the treaties in September, 1977. The Panamanian general actually broke down and cried at this step in the fruition of his long efforts. "The more my colleagues and I learned about this man," President Carter wrote, "the greater the respect and affection we had for him."

Both Nixon and Ford struggled with the problem behind the scenes during their administrations, both were convinced that Panama's rights were indeed being violated. Both tried to find ways to get a new treaty affirmed by Congress, but the issue was too politically sensitive. Ronald Reagan, trying to wrest the Republican presidential nomination away from Ford, publicly accused the president of "mouselike silence" and succumbing to "blackmail" by a "dictator." Ford believed that simplistic attack had been decisive in his loss of several primaries to the California governor.

Against this background, it is easy to see why Carter so clearly recognized the political danger involved in seeking a solution. Nevertheless, he pursued the matter to a resolute conclusion. His negotiators, Ellsworth Bunker and Sol Linowitz, concluded a treaty draft, and Carter vowed to see it through, whatever the political fallout.

The struggle for public approval of the treaty was uphill all the way. The first polls indicated that people in our country opposed any change affecting the canal by about four-to-one. It was clear also that an even larger percentage had no idea what the proposed treaty would contain. Most saw it as a "give-away." Carter knew he was undertaking a monumental endeavor. He also knew that he would be bitterly criticized by opponents. The new draft treaty called for a nine-member board, five U.S. and four Panamanians, to manage and operate the canal for the next quarter of a century. After the year 2000, the canal would be operated by Panama. The treaty guaranteed that the passage would be kept open, as it had been, to shipping from all nations. It gave the U.S. a perpetual right to defend the Canal against any foreign threat. Our joint military Chiefs of Staff endorsed the plan. They said it would not only protect but improve our military position.

Still, it was an explosive issue politically. Opponents appealed jingoistically to themes of patriotism and American greatness. General Alexander Haig, then serving as commander of NATO forces in Europe, spoke to a gathering in Fort Worth. I attended the meeting and introduced the general. Haig and I had been nearby neighbors in Northern Virginia. The Canal Zone question arose, and Haig dodged it. I guessed then that he had ambitions either to run for president or to serve in some future Republican cabinet.

Why support a treaty such as this? Well, because it was right. No other reason was necessary. That's how President Carter felt, and that's exactly how I felt. The basic justification for recognizing Panama's rights was as simple as the Golden Rule. Speaking before dozens of groups—colleagues as well as constituents—I would simply hypothesize a situation in which our roles were reversed.

How would Americans like it, I'd ask, if France, having helped us win our independence from England, insisted on controlling a broad swath of territory running straight through the middle of the United States—let us say an area on both sides of the Mississippi River?

How would we like it if any American citizen desiring to travel from the western to the eastern half of our own country would have to apply to France for permission and depend upon a French decision whether to be permitted to cross? How would we react if our citizens were grilled and frisked and inspected—and often detained for considerable periods—before being allowed to cross that zone?

And if we should engage in some minor traffic infraction while crossing the zone, how would we like to be held there awaiting trial, then forced to stand trial in foreign military courts, with the trial conducted in a language foreign to us?

How would we like it if that foreign country preached "free enterprise," but refused to allow any American to do business in this foreign-controlled zone? Or how would we like it if Americans permitted to perform manual labor in the zone were paid only about half as much as French citizens for the same identical work?

The questions answer themselves.

Carter deserved enormous credit for taking on the issue and seeing it through, doggedly, to fruition. Richard Viguerie and other archconservatives were cranking out computer-printed letters by the hundreds of thousands. They called it a "sell out." Right-wing radio talk show hosts spewed a stream of venom. We were being *forced* to cave in to threats, they asserted, weakening America. In truth, we weren't being *forced* to do anything. Certainly we were strong enough militarily to prevail against any expression of Panamanian frustrations. But did might make right?

Public opinion, so one-sidedly negative in the beginning, slowly grew more favorable. For most of the fall of 1977, and through the spring of 1978, the president campaigned. He prevailed upon as many as thirty-eight members of the Senate to travel to Panama and see for themselves. He got Gerald Ford, Nelson Rockefeller and Henry Kissinger to call doubtful Republican senators. Carter called every senator, one by one, patiently making his case. He even visited Nashville, New Hampshire, with Senators Tom McIntyre and John Durkin, to address a televised townhall meeting. When he defended the treaty, the crowd interrupted with sustained applause. The tide was turning.

What five previous presidents had been unable to do because of its political sensitivity, Jimmy Carter pulled off. When the Senate voted approval, Carter recorded it in his diary as one of the greatest moments of his life. Now, it was up to the House to provide laws and funds to carry out the agreement. In May, the House passed implementing legislation. I counted votes, worked the floor intensely, spoke in debate and was proud of that supportive role.

Carter, in my view, got too little credit for the achievement. His open advocacy and persistent support of the Panama Canal treaties—laying his whole prestige and popularity on the line and never wavering—may have been the most politically courageous stance taken by any American president in the second half of the 20th century.

But the greatest deed Jimmy Carter performed while in office was the Camp David Accords, the first formal peace between Israel and Egypt in three thousand years. That agreement has been in force, as this book goes to press, for sixteen years. The final accord was largely the work of one man—Jimmy Carter. No American president—not even Woodrow Wilson at Versailles—has ever conducted a more personal bit of diplomacy, nor a more intensive hands-on negotiation. My own part in that drama was only a supporting one. But I've never felt better about any role I ever performed in my life.

CHAPTER TWENTY-FOUR

THE ROAD
TO
CAMP DAVID

I n November of 1977, Jimmy Carter's first year as president and my first as House majority leader, I was thrown by a sheer accident of timing into the vortex of world events. Few occurrences of my life have been more fatefully consequential, and few as emotionally satisfying. My part in the historic drama came about largely as result of a recommendation by Speaker Tip O'Neill.

Among his most effective leadership tools, the Speaker insisted, was an annual official trip with a few carefully selected colleagues and their wives. Each year while serving as majority leader, Tip explained, he had led a bipartisan House delegation on a formal working mission during the congressional recess to some critical area of the world. The Speaker insisted that this fulfilled three good purposes: It improved our relationships with other countries, let the Leader cultivate closer relations with traveling members and their spouses, and enhanced the capacity of Congress to deal with foreign problems. He strongly recommended that I follow that practice.

Looking across the horizon for potential trouble spots, I decided in the late summer of 1977 that Congress needed much better firsthand knowledge of the shifting political currents in the Middle East. There had been four wars in the past generation between Israel and its Arab neighbors, and the tentative peace prevailing since the 1973 conflict seemed in danger of shattering. Our country, committed to Israel's safety, could not help but be directly affected. Accordingly, I scheduled a trip for ten or twelve members and their wives to include official stops in Egypt and Israel during the latter half of November 1977, following that year's congressional adjournment. In preparation for the trip, I had some long talks with members of the American Jewish community and with Ashraf Ghorbal, Egypt's ambassador to the United States. A lot of the leading supporters of Israel in America had been disappointed at the election of Menachem Begin as prime minister. They saw him as a hardliner, who would resist any efforts to achieve a peace settlement, even a reasonable one, with Egypt. The two countries were technically still at war, observing only a nervous truce since the bloody clash of October, 1973.

Ambassador Ghorbal insisted, on the other hand, that Americans should get to know Egypt's President Anwar Sadat, who was much different than his predecessor, Gamel Abdul Nasser. Sadat was a thoughtful, creative man, Ambassador Ghorbal stressed, whom Congress should get to know.

On the eve of our departure, Sadat made a startling statement in a speech to the Egyptian parliament. Emphasizing his desire for peace, Sadat said he would go to the ends of the earth, "even to Jerusalem" if he thought doing so could achieve a lasting peace in the Middle East. Most people, knowing the history of the region and Sadat's personal background as a military leader, devout Muslim and Egyptian nationalist, considered the reference as a figure of speech, a hyperbole, like saying he'd be willing to go "to the gates of hell" to achieve his objective.

In a couple of interviews with American newspeople, however, Sadat in the past twenty-four hours had reaffirmed the statement. One veteran careerist at the State Department, when I asked on the day we were scheduled to leave if he thought the comment meant anything significant, snorted in disdain. "It'll be a cold day in hell when the president of Egypt ever gets to go to Jerusalem," he said. Both Sadat and Begin were seen as warriors, not peacemakers. A career military man, Sadat had been in his youth an admirer of Hitler. Begin, son and brother of Holocaust victims, was an early Zionist zealot, a terrorist who once led a small group that planted explosives, blowing up Jerusalem's King David Hotel and killing a number of people in an anti-British cabal. An unlikely pair for peacemaking!

We had been granted an appointment to talk with President Sadat on November 15. The Egyptian leader was staying at The Barrages, a sort of presidential retreat more than an hour's drive out of Cairo up the Nile River. Along the route as we moved through the streets of the sprawling ancient city, we saw families of homeless who had taken up residence on the roofs of office buildings and apartment complexes. The roadway beyond Cairo was lined that morning with loads of crops grown in the fertile Nile delta and handcrafts that vendors hoped to sell in Cairo. Larger carts were pulled by donkeys or oxen. Most, however, were pushed by hand. In all that sad procession, we saw literally no traveler who appeared affluent. Egypt had been economically devastated by its series of wars with Israel.

President Sadat greeted our party personally after we drove through the pillared passageway and into reserved parking spaces beside a garden that lay outside the presidential house. His welcome was hearty and enthusiastic. As others in the group were ushered into a room set aside for our meeting, the Egyptian leader asked me and James Quillen of Tennessee, our delegation's senior Republican, to have a few words with him in his private office. He toyed with a pipe but drew little smoke from it.

Sadat exuded a sense of vibrant energy. He asked first about President Carter, his health and personal well-being. The question, I saw, was not perfunctory. Anwar Sadat really cared how Jimmy Carter was doing, personally as well as professionally. It was clear to me that Carter had the Egyptian's admiration.

"People in my country trust your president," Sadat said to Quillen and me. "He is a man of the book, and a man of truth. I believe he is a man of God." There was neither hesitation nor embarrassment in Sadat's appraisal. I thought it absolutely and refreshingly sincere.

He wanted to warn us in advance, the Egyptian leader explained, that the room where we would meet was filled with newspeople. "I hope you don't mind," said the president, "but there is great interest in your visit and in what is going on." He continued, "We can talk very freely. There are no secrets. Please do not hesitate to ask me any questions whatever that are on your minds."

"About your comments to your parliament and your reference to being willing to go to Jerusalem," I began, "would you mind our asking for some public elaboration of just what you are thinking?"

"By all means," Sadat boomed out in his full baritone. "The whole world is interested in that! I hope that in Israel people are interested in that." I smiled. I thought I saw exactly what he intended this day to mean. His enthusiasm was contagious. All of a sudden, I felt exhilarated.

We entered the large room where others in our fifteen-member delegation were already seated in a semicircle around a low table. We took seats on a long couch behind the table, Sadat in the middle, Quillen and I on either side. On the table arose a battery of radio and television microphones. Beyond the tight circle of our group, facing the couch where we and the president sat, was a substantial assemblage of press. I counted nine television cameras.

The president began brief prefatory remarks with a welcome to our American delegation. He introduced me for comments.

I wasted no time in getting to what was on everyone's mind. Was he actually hoping for an invitation to Jerusalem, did he expect to receive such an invitation, and on what conditions would he accept?

There had been some indication of interest, Sadat replied, but he had received no formal invitation. He reaffirmed his willingness to go if invited. He said he would like to address the Knesset, Israel's parliament. This was new, something specific. Sadat said he would put no conditions on such a trip, assuming any invitation to be sincere.

"Whenever this invitation arrives, I shall be ready to go because we shouldn't lose time in procedural arguments," Sadat declared. It was becoming suddenly quite apparent to everyone that Sadat earnestly desired to undertake such a mission. He wanted to carry his message directly to the Israeli political leadership. He was making it, I reflected, very difficult for the Israelis to refuse.

Sadat drew a clear distinction between his personal appeal to the enemy, which he said required no advance preparation or agreement, and the actual negotiating process. "Without good preparation for Geneva," Sadat stated, "we shouldn't go, because we would not reach anything. We (would just) sit and differ and argue about this and that." But taking his message to Jerusalem was different. He was ready right now. And waiting would dissipate opportunity.

Pressing luck, I asked if Sadat thought there was a way to achieve Arab desires for fair treatment of the Palestinians while assuring Israelis against the creation of a hostile state "dedicated to the destruction of Israel." I thought this came to the heart of the controversy. Sadat replied that any such Palestinian state as might emerge should not pose any danger to Israel's safety. It could be linked in a confederation with Jordan, he suggested.

A reporter asked if the Egyptian president wouldn't be concerned about his personal safety on a trip to Jerusalem. Sadat responded in a firm voice, "I never take security into consideration." Asked if he had a time frame in mind, the president said "as early as possible."

Leaving the hour-long meeting, I couldn't think of anything remotely like this in modern history, any occasion in which the head of a state at war with another would carry his message personally into the enemy's camp. The nearest to a parallel that I could recall was the bizarre flight into England by Nazi General Rudolph Hess during World War II. Hess, apparently without sanction from Hitler, had boldly parachuted into the English countryside to plead for Britain's surrender. The poor man was arrested on the spot and never released. Sentenced to life imprisonment in the war crimes trials, he was held incommunicado in Spandau prison outside Berlin for the remainder of his life, finally dying in 1987 at ninety-three years of age. Not an example to inspire emulation. Several things, however, distinguished Sadat's open bid from the German's erratic solo flight.

Unlike Hess, Sadat was an elected head of state who presumably could speak for his nation. Further, he would not just show up unannounced.

Moreover, he wasn't asking for a surrender but a peace, which would have to be characterized by mutual concessions. I could think of no historic precedent.

Sadat's bold unilateral move caught the world's diplomatic community completely by surprise. It had not been discussed with any of his colleagues prior to its launching, he said. Nor had the advice of any other been sought. It was "a personal initiative," the charismatic Egyptian told CBS correspondent Walter Cronkite later that afternoon in a satellite broadcast. "My responsibility as president of Egypt is to try all means to reach a peace," he stressed. Asked why he wanted to address the Knesset, Sadat replied, "I want to put the cards before them and to discuss the alternative. Really, it would be horrible."

Cronkite also interviewed Israeli Prime Minister Menachem Begin, who said he would like to invite the Egyptian president, but first must present that plan to the Knesset. That night, the Israeli parliament overwhelmingly approved Begin's proposal, even though Lt. Gen. Mordechai Gur, Israeli chief of staff, warned the prime minister against it.

Talks of a peace mission, General Gur hypothesized, might be a guise for Egypt to launch war again after lulling Israelis into euphoric apathy. War Minister Ezer Weizman very quickly reprimanded the general, saying he had exceeded his authority. Indeed, most Israelis seemed to be for giving the peace mission a chance. Sadat's very boldness captured their imaginations. His pronouncements had the unmistakable ring of sincerity.

Ten minutes after the Knesset's meeting adjourned, Prime Minister Begin delivered to Sam Lewis, U.S. Ambassador in Israel, a formal written invitation addressed to President Sadat. Lewis personally carried the invitation to Hermann Eilts, our Ambassador to Egypt. Eilts handed it, late that night, to Sadat.

It was Friday, November 18, when our party arrived at Tel Aviv airport. We were greeted by a delegation from the Knesset and two or three members of the cabinet. Jerusalem Mayor Teddy Kollek and Foreign Minister Moshe Dayan, whom several of us had met, welcomed us. Prime Minister Menachem Begin would be expecting us for a little private dinner, we were told, to be followed by a press conference.

Sadat's bold move and Begin's invitation had upstaged all other world news in the three days since our meeting. The peace initiative had been warmly praised by most world leaders. But it met mixed reaction among the Arab spokesmen. Several hardliners—particularly in Syria, Libya, and Iraq— were angry, expressing fear that Sadat's unilateral move would drive a dividing wedge into Arab unity.

One significant development, I thought, was the negative reaction from the Soviet Union and Sadat's reply to that. In several conflicts with Israel, Russia had favored the Arab side, even furnishing arms to Syria. Sadat acknowledged that, in further peace talks at Geneva, Egypt's relations with the Soviet Union would be "tense," but he made clear his total independence from the Soviet position. "Let me tell you that I do not fear the Soviet Union or any other super power, for I feel we have right on our side, and if we reach an agreement in Geneva, neither the Soviet Union nor any other power can prevent us from carrying out the agreement." Some took this as a subtle warning to other Arab leaders not to interfere.

Prime Minister Begin welcomed us graciously. Then he sprang the news. Sadat had accepted his invitation, would fly into Jerusalem the following evening (Saturday after sundown in respectful deference to the Jewish Sabbath) and address the Knesset on Sunday afternoon.

Begin told us privately that a wave of vocal and possibly violent protest was arising throughout the Arab world. Fanatical anti-Israeli spokesmen were demonstrating in various capitals. Demonstrators harshly opposed Sadat's abandonment of prior Arab solidarity in anathematizing Israel. Some, of course, wanted no peace, only Israel's destruction.

The Prime Minister's press conference unleashed the exciting news of the arrangements for Sadat's trip. Afterward, our delegation returned to the King David Hotel. The lobby was a mob scene, and we learned that the official Sadat party would take over occupancy of the hotel on the following night. Other guests were being requested to leave—all except our delegation. The government wished us to stay, we were told.

I called a hasty meeting of our group. Several, including Danny Rostenkowski, felt that we'd do our hosts a favor by terminating our visit on Saturday so as to give a little breathing room to the suddenly crowded city. Sid Yates of Illinois, and his wife, Addie, wanted to stay. Republicans Quillen and Thad Cochran of Mississippi left it in my hands. Our meeting was interrupted by a personal call from the Prime Minister. There would be reserved seats in the balcony of the Knesset for our delegation, Begin told me, to witness Sadat's address. I tried to demur. "Mr. Prime Minister," I said, "we appreciate that more than you can possibly realize. This is a moment like none other in history. But it would be very selfish of us to deny your own citizens the privilege of those precious seats. I have seen the Knesset gallery, and I know its limited space. You have at least a hundred valid claims among Israelis, I am sure, for each available seat. Therefore, I really think we should decline with grateful thanks and arrange an early departure so as to relieve you of any additional security worries or . . ."

Begin interrupted me. "You don't understand, Mr. Leader. We very much *want* you and your group from the American Congress to be present with us for this event. If you will look outside you will see that three flags are being raised in front of the King David Hotel—ours, Egypt's, and that of the United States. We want you as parties to this historic moment!"

Now I understood. It wasn't just courtesy. Both the Israelis and the Egyptians, facing a spate of opposition to their peace overtures from the Soviet Union and several Middle Eastern sources, wanted a United States presence. There had not been another moment quite like this in the region's three-thousand-year history. Blind luck, or perhaps providence, had led us there at this particular time. Our presence, as emissaries of the world's greatest power, was fortuitous to the peace effort. We'd stay.

On Saturday evening, lines of military troops and civilian onlookers hugged the crowded apron of the Tel Aviv airport, awaiting the arrival of President Sadat's plane. At 7:58 a trumpet fanfare heralded the arrival of Prime Minister Begin and Israeli President Emphraim Katzir. The guard of honor dipped its flags and presented arms.

All heads turned suddenly at the appearance of three white lights on the runway. The presidential aircraft from Egypt, having landed, taxied slowly around and stopped in front of the red carpet.

A smiling Sadat disembarked, exchanging quips and embraces with his Israeli hosts. The huge crowd applauded vigorously as the guest passed down a receiving line, shaking hands with past and present Israeli leaders, many for the first time. He obviously relished the act of greeting, and being greeted by, old foes.

One of these was Ariel Sharon, now Agriculture Minister but years earlier the Israeli army commander who had led the counterattack across the Suez Canal in the Yom Kippur War.

"I wanted to catch you there," Sadat greeted his old foe. Sharon replied, "I'm glad to have you here!"

Happy, demonstrative crowds lined the road and streets into Jerusalem as the inbound motorcade moved by. Many Israelis carried hastily painted signs greeting the guest, praising his courage, proclaiming the hope for peace. The single word, PEACE, was a constant theme in the handmade banners. A lot of children were in the crowd of spectators. A father explained his two-year-old daughter's presence, "I want her here so she can tell her grandchildren someday." A group of youngsters sang a song titled "Sheyavo Shalom" (When Peace Comes).

About a thousand Israelis, held at a distance by police cordons, whistled and applauded from a distance as President Sadat and his party arrived at the King David Hotel about 9:35. The carillon in the tower of the YMCA building played "Getting to Know You." Recognizable in the entourage were ABC's Barbara Walters, along with Walter Cronkite and John Chancellor from CBS and NBC. They had flown in from Cairo as Sadat's guests on the Egyptian plane.

In Washington, President Carter watched the historic arrival by television and issued a statement that "the hopes and prayers of all Americans" were with Begin and Sadat. Our president sent personal messages to the leaders of Jordan, Syria, Saudi Arabia and other Arab states pleading with them to support Sadat in his mission for peace.

On Sunday morning, Sadat's party left the King David at about 6:30 for prayers at the al-Aksa Mosque, hallowed throughout Islam as the site from which Mohammed is believed to have ascended. For Sadat, a practicing Muslim, the journey was a sacred pilgrimage. People familiar with the city's history shuddered nervously in recalling that the grandfather of Jordan's King Hussein had been slain in that very mosque a full generation earlier by religious fanatics who considered the Jordanian ruler too friendly to the Jews.

After prayers at the mosque, Sadat and his party, in a demonstration of religious ecumenicity, visited the Dome of the Rock, the Christian Church of the Holy Sepulchre, and accompanied Prime Minister Begin on a visit to Yad Vashem, the memorial to victims of the Holocaust. Everywhere abounded signs of goodwill. I saw a uniformed Israeli soldier hugging an Arab girl on the streets. It was as though the millennium had arrived, the lamb and the lion embraced.

The long awaited speech crowned a three-hour-long presentation ceremony that began at four o'clock. The Sadat address was telecast worldwide. The Egyptian president's delivery was confident and forceful. Earphones in the visitor's gallery offered simultaneous translation of the two speeches in Hebrew, Arabic, and English. In Rome, Pope Paul VI said "we are dazzled with trust and joy," offering a prayer that the thirty-year war was coming to an end.

Everywhere was a euphoric sense that reminded me of the religious revivals of my youth. Sadat began his historic appeal with an invocation, "I wish to say peace and the mercy of God Almighty be upon you, and may peace be for us all, God willing." In his first paragraph he spoke of Gandhi, later quoted from Solomon's Proverbs and from one of David's psalms. "I have come to Jerusalem, the City of Peace, which will always remain as a living embodiment of coexistence among believers of the three religions." Instead of "awakening the prejudices of the Crusades," he said we should revive the "spirit of tolerance and respect for rights."

Sadat made an appeal for the "legitimate rights" of the Palestinian people, calling this "the core and essence of the conflict." Saying that he had "chosen to set aside all precedents and traditions known by warring countries," he alluded to the intermittent bloodshed that had stained the region for a generation and appealed for an end to it.

"To every man, woman and child in Israel, I say: encourage your leadership to struggle for peace, for peace . . . be heros to your sons. Tell them that past wars were the last of wars and the end of sorrows . . . you, bewailing mother; you, widowed wife; you, the son who lost a brother or a father; you, all victims of wars, fill the earth and space with recitals of peace." He ended with a quote from Zacharias of the Old Testament, another from the Koran, and a reference to Jesus—and these words: Peace be upon you.

As oratory, the speech was moving. As strategy, it was a blockbuster. Diplomatic opinion held that Egypt's president had painted his hardline Arab adversaries into a corner. Some of them, wanting no peace with Israel, called him a traitor. Syria's official Radio Damascus broadcast an appeal by a terrorist group urging the Egyptian army "to revolt against treason and to overthrow the traitor." Similar appeals were made in Libya and Baghdad.

But Prime Minister Begin, at the end of Sadat's speech, made overtures of reciprocity. He said Egypt and Israel should establish diplomatic relations and stated his own hope to go one day to Cairo and talk with Egypt's people. In a gesture of goodwill, he declared "I open our land for travel to the citizens of Egypt unconditionally." Begin also declared the desire to cooperation with Egypt economically, "to aid its development, to make its deserts bloom, to help fight poverty and hunger."

To other Arab neighbors who had expressed apprehension over the prospects of an Egypt-Israeli peace, Begin publicly invited President Hafez Assad of Syria and King Hussein of Jordan to come to Jerusalem in visits similar to Sadat's and receive a similar welcome. For his own part Begin said he would be glad to go to Damascus, Amman, or Beirut to talk peace if invited.

It wasn't the end of the region's agony. There wasn't any treaty for signature. But Begin and Sadat during the two days had talked twice privately. Each thought a beginning had been made. There still was a long road to travel, and there would be detours and many disappointments, but the two countries were on a new and different path at last.

On my return, I talked at length with President Carter. He was intensely interested in everything that had happened. I gave him my appraisal, my personal impressions of all the major players. From that point on, the progress toward peace would be a principal staple of our Tuesday morning leadership meetings.

The complete settlement between Egypt and Israel would not be formally signed until 1980. But without Sadat's courageous initiative in going to Jerusalem, the journey would not have begun. The next highpoint would come ten months later on another Sunday evening, September 17, 1978, with the late-night signing at the White House of the Camp David Accords.

This unprecedented peace, ending centuries of hostility between the two neighboring nations, had three heros—Sadat, Begin and Carter. Sadat was one of the most fearless men I ever met. Begin at the top of his career outgrew a life of harsh adversity steeped in centuries of prejudice. But the greatest of these, in my view, was Carter. He was the glue that held it all together, the patient, insistent friend who repeatedly kept the other two from flying apart by the centripetal force of rival nationalist ambitions and the political realities ingrained by history.

While I knew of President Carter's lifelong interest in the region, stemming from his study of the Bible, I did not realize until many years later how profoundly he had affected Sadat, and Begin to only a slightly lesser degree. In reading Carter's memoir, *Keeping Faith*, so generously interspersed with excerpts from his personal diary, I came to understand how frequently in the course of his four years in office our president interrupted his preoccupation with pressing domestic concerns to make a personal appeal to one or another of the protagonists.

It is clear that President Carter felt an unusual, even protective affinity for Anwar Sadat. Carter admired the man's remarkable political courage and simple honesty. Carter's admiration of Sadat's intrepidity was an inspiration to the bold Egyptian. Liking Carter immensely and coveting our president's approval, I believe, helped embolden Sadat to go all out, laying his whole prestige and personal credibility on the line for peace and braving the censure of more militant Arabs. Many of these began calling publicly for Sadat's assassination immediately following his trip to Jerusalem.

"I never take [personal] security into consideration," Sadat had replied to a question about his own physical safety that day at The Barrages. This was almost prophetic, I reflected at Sadat's funeral in 1981. He was killed by a terrorist junta in his own armed forces. Knowledge that this fate surely might confront him must have dwelt in his mind but never deterred him in the slightest.

Following the dramatic November, 1977 scene at the Knesset, both Sadat and Begin made several trips to the United States. Each time one of them would come, I was asked to host him on Capitol Hill and assemble colleagues for a discussion. Both craved the approval of our Congress. Our obvious bipartisan interest in an eventual settlement probably helped to keep either from straying completely off track. However, progress toward an agreement began to deteriorate shortly after Christmas, following a meeting of the two leaders in Ismailia. Begin had run into trouble with his cabinet and had to retract his offer to give more autonomy to Arab villages on the West Bank. Sadat was deeply embarrassed, having told other Arab leaders his understanding of Begin's earlier position. He thought the meeting a total failure.

Sadat explained to me, on his next Washington visit a traditional Arab belief that if a neighbor from whom you'd been estranged came to your home and there laid his grievance at your feet, you'd be obliged then to give him fair treatment. Failing to do so, you'd be dishonored in the village. "I humbled myself and went to the Israelis' home in Jerusalem to beg for fair treatment to our Palestinian kinsmen," Sadat said, "and it is as though the home owner threw slop on me from an upper window as I was departing. Throughout the whole Arab world now, they are saying I was a fool." I sympathized, tried to help Sadat understand the root of Israeli suspicion and even Begin's own problems, having his family torn from him and slaughtered in the Nazi gas chambers.

As for Begin and the Israelis, it was easy to see their reluctance to create a Palestinian state, particularly as the PLO grew more and more militant. "We have offered to give back almost all of the Sinai which we took from Egypt," Begin would say, "but you have seen the narrowness of our borders. It would be suicide to make ourselves so vulnerable again by giving away the whole West Bank, up to the gates of Jerusalem, to an organized group which refuses to recognize our right to exist!"

Territory was security, in the Israelis' eye. Sadat didn't insist on return of *all* the land taken by Israel in the 1967 war. But he felt sympathy for the subordinate status of Palestinian refugees forced from their homes and wanted Israel to treat them better.

And Sadat felt the incessant criticism of other Arabs, who accused him of selling out their territorial claims just to make a separate peace for Egypt. I was never sure that Begin fully understood the terrible pressures on Sadat to get some concessions for the Palestinians. Nor was Sadat able to comprehend the internal pressures of a besieged people, determined never to be persecuted again. But Jimmy Carter understood and sympathized with both.

On New Year's Eve, Carter flew to Tehran where he met with the Shah of Iran and King Hussein of Jordan. He persuaded these two moderate leaders to give Sadat's peace initiative support. They would approve some modification in the pre-1967 national boundaries if Israel would give self-determination in local matters, but not nationhood, to Palestinians in the West Bank and Gaza.

Through the next nine months, however, things kept unraveling faster than peacemakers could patch them together. Moderate Arab leaders were pilloried, eventually intimidated, by their radical neighbors. The PLO, egged on by Khadafi of Libya and Saddam Hussein of Iraq, became an infestuous thorn in Jordanian King Hussein's side, and virtually overran Lebanon. Jerusalem swiftly reacted, invaded Lebanon, wiping out PLO strongholds from which attacks had been launched on Israelis in the upper Galilee.

After a series of initiatives and false starts on both sides, all ending in setbacks, progress had reached a total stalemate. About the end of July, Carter decided to go "all out." He wrote long personal letters to Begin and Sadat. Secretary of State Cyrus Vance carried them personally in sealed envelopes and hand-delivered them to the two principals. Carter invited the two for private, three-way discussions at Camp David, the presidential retreat in the Cacoctin Mountains of Maryland. The meetings would take place in early September. Each would be prepared to stay until an agreement was worked out or it became apparent that none could be. There'd be no press, no intruders, and minimal staffing. The two agreed.

Nothing such as this had ever happened. Never had an American president simply shut off domestic alarms that constantly clamored for his attentions and spent two whole weeks in seclusion with the heads of two rival states. Carter was determined to find a formula for peace, unwilling to let the chance go by or a settlement be foregone for want of effort.

On September 6, 1978, as the fateful conclave began, they issued this joint statement: "As we meet here at Camp David we ask people of all faiths to pray with us that peace and justice may result from these deliberations." Some will reject the idea of a divine presence there in the cool morning breezes rustling the leaves of mountain trees in the early autumn of 1978. They will put it down to the eventual triumph of human reasoning among three reasonable people.

None of the three expected it to take fourteen full days. The sessions were intensely personal. The seclusion surely worked. The men worked, and talked, and retired to think and rethink. After fourteen days, they came down from the mountain together.

Carter was the catalyst, the go-between, the patient mediator. Never has an American president been so intimately engaged, hands-on, in such a tireless pilgrimage of personal diplomacy.

In the end, faith paid off. All three leaders took significant risk. Peace usually involves political hazard. Its practice often takes more courage than the practice of war.

It was the very success of the Camp David agreements that claimed the life of Anwar Sadat. Courageous, visionary, willing to strike out in a new direction and to swim upstream against the sullen tides of hatred, Sadat fell to the bullets of fanatics who did not want to be at peace with Israel.

So it was with Gandhi. And Lincoln. And Martin Luther King Jr. Blessed are the peacemakers. Humanity with all its folly is ever in their debt.

CHAPTER TWENTY-FIVE

COACH
AND THE
PEACEMAKERS

I t's funny, I was thinking, as I strategized and rounded up votes for one of President Carter's legislative initiatives: All those years ago, back in high school, I thought I wanted to be a football coach. I gave that up for an ambition to serve in Congress. Here, after almost twenty-five years in this august institution, I was calling plays, teaching rudiments of the legislative game to younger participants, cultivating their skills, praising good performance, coaxing a sense of team spirit, keeping score, trying to win. The majority leader, I decided, was a glorified football coach.

When Texas colleague John Young was defeated for reelection, I talked Speaker O'Neill in 1979 into appointing freshman Martin Frost to Young's vacated post on the Rules Committee. Tip was at first reluctant. That was the Speaker's personal committee, the one on which he depended to schedule his bills for the floor. But I had watched Martin Frost for several years and was convinced that he'd do an excellent job. I knew his family, had observed his work as a reporter for *Congressional Quarterly*, and had closely followed his campaign in a Dallas district adjacent to my own.

"I'll vouch for him, Mr. Speaker. He can stand the heat, he understands the loyalty that post requires, and he'll be dependable." Tip took a puff on his cigar and stabbed his finger at my chest. "Okay, Jim," he said, "but I'm holding *you* responsible." I never had occasion to regret that recommendation.

When Jim Corman of California left Congress in 1980, vacating chairmanship of the Democratic Congressional Campaign Committee, there was a scramble to find the right replacement. The success of that committee in raising funds was vital to the maintenance of the Democratic majority. I had been watching another Californian, a young fellow named Tony Coelho. He had ideas, character, and energy. A former seminarian, Tony actually enjoyed asking for money, a task I personally despised. I nominated him for the job.

Some of the older members balked: "There is no precedent for handing *this* job to a one-term member!"

"Oh, yes, there is," I corrected them. "There *is* a precedent! Back in the late thirties, House Democrats elected a young fellow with only one term. His name was Lyndon Johnson. And he raised twice as much money as any predecessor had!"

In an institution that puts a lot of weight on precedent, that argument sold. In subsequent years, I watched Tony modernize not only that committee's fundraising techniques but its services to members.

For years I had been picking protégés and helping them learn the ropes. There were few satisfactions like watching them blossom and grow in their effectiveness as lawmakers. Ten years earlier, I had taken a liking to a young New Jersey school teacher named Jim Howard. Now I saw him spreading his wings as chairman of the Water Resources Subcommittee. I took similar pride in the achievements of a couple of young Arkansans, David Pryor and Bill Alexander. Dave became governor of his state and then served admirably in the U.S. Senate. Bill would become my Chief Deputy Whip in the Reagan years.

Now I spotted talent in a young Tennessean, Albert Gore Jr., whose parents I knew and admired. My own advice was sometimes less than perfect, I discovered. Al, not yet twenty-nine, wanted to go for a spot on the Commerce Committee in his first term. I tried to dissuade him. "First termers are hardly ever considered for assignments to that committee," I told him. "To make a big run for it this year might irritate folks. They might think you too brash. Why not bide your time and get better known?"

The youngster thanked me for my advice but ignored it. He worked every member of the Steering Committee diligently and won the assignment he sought. He exceeded my expectations, and I was delighted. I've never again underestimated Al Gore.

Part of the joy came in coaching eager and gifted members in the achievement of legislative objectives. A big, personable lawyer from Cleveland named Jim Stanton had some very workable ideas about helping cities develop transportation alternatives. I helped him steer to passage a bill that allows a minor fraction of the highway trust funds for express bus lanes, high-occupancy vehicle lanes, and satellite parking lots to make the use of existing transit facilities more attractive to the public.

Bob Krueger of Texas, a Shakespeare scholar and college dean, somewhat surprisingly had enormously useful ideas about how to maximize recovery of the oil and gas potential from existing fields, going to waste at a time of our severe national energy shortage. With my help, Bob got a post on the Commerce Committee, where I watched him patiently and persuasively explain the realities of the "oil patch" (as Texans refer to the well-drilling end of the sprawling petroleum industry), one on one, to enough members to pass his bill.

My solicitude as Majority Leader was not confined to Democrats. I had occasion to weigh in several times in behalf of Republican members who needed help with useful projects. I assisted Don Young of Alaska in his attempt to plow through a maze of snarls to complete the Alaska pipeline. I helped Stewart McKinney of Connecticut pass a bill for synthetic fuels, and worked with Bill Young of Florida and Bill Dickinson of Alabama on Defense issues. Republicans Jim Collins and Tom Loeffler of Texas became not only occasional legislative allies but good personal friends.

A friendly, straightforward Republican named Joe Skeen was elected to represent southeastern New Mexico. Several times I had taken off from the dangerous old Ruidoso airport in private aircraft and knew the serious hazard of a takeoff pattern leading directly into a steep mountainside. I enlisted with Joe in his fight to get a new, safe airport for his citizens, even spending a day on an inspection of a high plateau several miles from town which ultimately became the site of a fine new facility. All of this, I figured, was part of being majority leader.

Relations between the two parties were a lot more relaxed in those days than they grew to be in the 1990s. The rivalry was much less intense, less angry and hostile. Nobody was out to destroy a colleague personally just because he or she belonged to the other party. Party discipline was never rigid among Democrats, anyway. We represented such a wide spectrum of opinion that we hardly ever voted monolithically. Even with large majorities in the House, we frequently needed some Republican votes to pass the president's legislative programs.

We had what might be called a floating majority for most of the Democratic program. New coalitions would have to be formed around each issue. The most difficult challenge each year was putting together a budget resolution that could command allegiance of half the membership plus one.

Twice we had to come back to the floor a second time with alterations in the package after the first resolution was rejected. Neither doctrinaire conservatives nor ultra liberals would be pleased with any spending plan that could command a majority of the votes. Henry Clay was right. It took the glue of compromise to hold the union together.

Speaker O'Neill and I worked to develop new variations of Carl Albert's

Task Force concept. As each major bill arose on the House agenda, we'd first assemble a group of active supporters. Some would be from the committee of jurisdiction, others from our Whip organization, a few from the Steering Committee, and always a few from the membership at large who just believed strongly in the bill. This group would undertake a multidisciplinary selling job, fanning out among different geographic and ideological factions in the House, trying to be sure of enough votes to pass the measure when it came up on the floor. On the day of the vote, we'd try to keep Task Force members present in the chamber during debate. They knew the intricacies of the legislation and the best arguments to deflect or defuse predictable assaults upon its various provisions. Before the critical vote, either Tip or I would make the final speech closing debate.

Once, on a national water conservation initiative, I got carried away in a rhapsodic flight of rhetoric. Picking up a glass of water, which always was set beside the podium from which members spoke, I held it aloft and extolled its contents:

> *There is no such thing as new water. Science tells us that this glass of water contains some tiny molecules that fell in the flood of Noah, some that floated fishing craft in the Sea of Galilee two thousand years ago, and some that washed blood from the beaches of Normandy on D-Day, 1944.*
>
> *An unending cosmic rotation steadily moves man's life-giving liquid by gravity through the incessant flow of streams to the great reservoirs of our oceans, then draws it skyward by the sun's attraction. There it is purified anew by nature's chemistry and returned by cloud and rain to refresh the thirsty earth and renew man's lease on life—ad infinitum. It is an ever-recurring miracle, the most wondrous natural marvel of a wondrous universe.*
>
> *Science can comprehend it but never duplicate it. Man cannot change it nor substitute a synthetic. He can locally and temporally befoul the process and bring death. Or we can form a sort of divine partnership with nature, help it along—and preserve life. This is our choice.*

The membership, more amused than impressed, arose in boisterous applause. We carried the vote, but thereafter, whenever I got tempted into a realm of poetic fancy over some other issue, a Democratic or Republican colleague was likely to seek recognition and ask with feigned earnestness, "Will the Majority Leader please tell us again about the glass of water?"

There was an easygoing camaraderie that is missing from Congress today.

Each time I have returned to Washington during the decade of the '90s, encountering former colleagues makes me feel like a psychiatrist listening to a patient recount the difficulties of his environment. The most frequent comment these days is, "It's just no fun anymore!"

From Tip O'Neill I learned a lot about the use of leadership to cultivate a spirit of conviviality. Tip and I both loved Irish songs and Irish stories. He always invited me to his annual St. Patrick's Day luncheon in the Speaker's private dining room for a toast or a tale. Twice the Prime Minister of Ireland attended. Other Irish-descended members of House and Senate would join for corned beef and cabbage. One year, Ben Rosenthal of New York sent us all some green bagels.

The issues with which we dealt those years of the Carter Administration were as serious as any the nation had ever experienced. We struggled with energy shortages, maddening hikes in the price of oil orchestrated by OPEC, resultant inflation, and misplaced attempts by the Federal Reserve to control it with exorbitant interest rates. Sometimes I grew too intense. Tip's ability to relax and roll with the punches was a leavening agent.

Politicians are mostly gregarious folks by nature, and Tip was a master at promoting an atmosphere of relaxed informality. There were a few times, however, when I had to be peacemaker between Tip and Jimmy Carter. One of those occasions came in 1977, the president's first year. Carter, unfamiliar with Washington custom and instinctively contemptuous of patronage, appointed two prominent Republicans from Tip's home state to high-level administrative posts without first checking with Tip. He named Elliot Richardson ambassador to the Law of the Sea conference and Mayor Evan Dobell of Pittsfield as chief of protocol. It was an unintended breach of courtesy, but the Speaker was furious. His sense of being slighted was magnified when the president, without so much as a word to Tip, relieved Bob Griffin, an O'Neill protégé and close ally, from the number-two position at General Services Administration. The Speaker was so hurt and angry that he refused to see Frank Moore and sent word to the White House that the president's legislative liaison was no longer welcome in his office. Tip told me privately that he didn't intend to darken the door of Carter's White House again.

"Mr. Speaker, I don't think the president realized what he was doing," I sympathized. "I'm sure that when he understands the personal offense he unintentionally inflicted, he'll want to make amends."

Immediately I called for an appointment and went that afternoon to see the president, explaining the personal sensitivity of the matter. I stressed how loyally Tip had labored to carry out each of the president's wishes in the House and how much store he put in personal loyalty.

Carter explained that he was unaware of the ties between O'Neill and Griffin. "I can't go back on my word," said the president, "and I wouldn't have offended Tip for anything on earth. What can I do to rectify matters?" I suggested that he send the Speaker a note of apology, or, better yet, call him. Maybe he also could invite Bob Griffin in for an audience and find another, equally useful role for him to perform in the administration.

Neither of the two men was ever known to hold grudges. The breach closed within a few days and the wound healed within a few weeks.

A constant inspiration at our Tuesday morning leadership breakfasts at the White House was Senator Hubert Humphrey. Stricken by terminal cancer, the former vice president was a happy warrior who often arrived directly from a physically debilitating chemotherapy session to cheer and encourage the rest of us. Even in his last days, Humphrey never lost heart or confidence in the triumph of his principles. Liberalism, for the eloquent Minnesotan, was not just a political posture but a compassionate way of life. He may have been the most forgiving man I knew. I never heard Hubert utter a personally disparaging word about his harshest critics or bitterest political opponent.

The coach's job was not confined to the male side of the family while I was majority leader. Betty sought out and cultivated other members' wives, taking some of the younger ones under her wing. She took an active role in the Congressional Wives Club. Among other events, that organization sponsored an annual chili cookoff. Lawmakers were the contestants. Between ten and twenty members would participate in a given year. Each would cook a large vat of chili. Three ambassadors from foreign countries would make up a judging panel. One year, Betty volunteered me as a contestant.

As the day approached, a series of crises in the legislative schedule had me by the lapels. I felt like a man juggling five balls already and being thrown another every few seconds to work into the cycle. I had no time for practicing culinary arts that week. Betty came to the rescue. She made the chili.

About fourteen contestants brought samples of their skills. The judges were ambassadors from Ireland, Iran, and some Far Eastern nation. None, by native custom, had any experience with chili. Jake Pickle displayed the carcass of a rattlesnake and vowed that he'd cooked the meat of that reptile in his chili. Pickle's and my offerings finished in a tie for first place. Embarrassed to accept credit for Betty's chili, I insisted that Pickle get the award. A *New York Times* reporter was doing a feature on the event. She wanted to know the ingredients in each of our two offerings. Having no clear idea, I rattled off the logical ingredients, then got carried away: "One tender leaf of the Mexican maguey plant, chopped fine; one pint of tequila; and a cup of mesquite leaves, sun dried on a tin roof and then crushed and powdered between the palms of your hands." I thought surely she would know I was kidding. The next day my recipe appeared, straightfaced, in the *Times*. I've often wondered if anybody tried it. And what happened to them.

President Carter had a lot of ideas. His fertile mind churned out a plethora of about eighty legislative proposals sent to Congress in his first year. Except for Lyndon Johnson in 1965 or Franklin Roosevelt in 1933, no other chief executive had issued so many specific recommendations for congressional action. At one of our Tuesday morning breakfast sessions, Speaker O'Neill and Senate Majority Leader Bob Byrd both asked Carter to shorten his list or at least give us a clear sense of his priorities. "Give us six or eight that you really want, Mr. President," said Tip, "and Jim and I will pass them in the House."

Carter's first energy package, for example, was drawn up largely without consulting congressional committee chairs on whom its passage would rely. As we neared the 1978 elections, embarrassingly few of the president's various energy proposals had progressed to final passage. In the next Congress, as the crisis deepened, Tip decided we should put together a comprehensive package and pass it as one big omnibus bill. To me he assigned the task of shepherding its various components through eight separate committees, combining them as titles of a single bill, and passing it on the House floor.

During the first two years of Carter's presidency, the energy outlook grew ever more foreboding. Our consumption grew faster than domestic energy production. We were consuming about 5 percent more than we had during the previous year, and crude oil imports soared by 29 percent. Making matters worse, OPEC kept raising the price per barrel.

Although I didn't agree with the president on everything, I was the nearest he had to a point man on the House floor. As 1978 business ground down to a close, I was determined to get as much of his package as possible through Congress before adjournment. During the hectic final two weeks of that session, I was constantly on the move, from one conference committee to another, cajoling, wheedling, begging for action in time to put bills on the president's desk before our adjournment. House sessions lasted late into the night, as they always do in the closing days of each Congress. I was on the telephone incessantly, pleading with dilatory committee chairs and recalcitrant conferees, then rushing in and out of the Rules Committee to get bills scheduled for final action. On the House floor late at night, I'd be talking the bills through to final passage. When we finally adjourned, my voice was shot.

But speechmaking demands were only heating up. As the election approached, I flew to Pittsburgh, Dayton, Atlantic City, St. Louis, Kansas City, Philadelphia, Minneapolis, Lincoln, Council Bluffs, Winston-Salem,

Cincinnati, Hartford, Toledo, then to Texas. In my home state that fall, I made appearances for colleagues in College Station, Seguin, Denton, San Angelo, Corpus Christi, Kerrville, and San Antonio. Then to Utah, and a final stop in Olney, Illinois, before returning home for election day.

Returning to Washington after that election, I was so hoarse I could hardly make myself heard. Prolonged hoarseness, I had read, is one danger signal of throat cancer. Concerned, I went to see a doctor who ascertained that I had been smoking cigarettes since my days in the Army Air Corps, thirty-five years earlier. Quit? Sure, I had quit lots of times!

Fortunately, the specialist saw no indication of cancer but told me I had badly damaged my vocal chords. He sent me to a voice therapist. This learned fellow, apparently knowing nothing of the job I held, looked at the medical data and then at my throat and began in his most soothing manner. "Hummmm. I see we have rather serious damage to the vocal chords, and they need more rest. Many people live happily with this condition. It just takes a few little adjustments in your life-style. Tell me, Mr. Wright, do you ever attend receptions—you know, where there are a lot of people in one room, and some of them smoking, and everyone having to raise his voice by several decibels in order to be heard?"

"Well, yes," I acknowledged, "I do sometimes attend receptions of that type." I didn't tell him I frequently went to four and five in an evening.

"I'd recommend that you discontinue that practice," he intoned blandly. "Just decline those invitations. And, tell me, are you ever sometimes called upon to make a speech in public?" I nodded my head in affirmation.

"I would recommend that you decline all such invitations and use your voice only for well-modulated personal communications in acoustically friendly environments."

Thanking him, I rose, shook hands, returned to my car, and started home. The choice was clear: I could either talk or smoke. Two blocks from the therapist's office, I reached into my pocket, pulled out my half-empty pack of cigarettes, and threw them out the car window into a culvert. I haven't had or wanted one since. Haven't even thought about it. That was Wednesday, November 15, 1978, at 4:18 P.M., Eastern Standard Time.

The new Congress that convened in January of 1979 brought seventy-five new House members, forty-one of them Democrats and thirty-four Republicans. Several among them were destined for prominence. There was Geraldine Ferraro, who would be nominated in 1984 as Democratic vice presidential standard bearer. Bill Nelson of Florida would become the first, and perhaps only, person to fly on a space mission while a member of Congress. Tom Daschle of South Dakota was to be chosen Senate majority leader in 1995. And, of course, there was Newt Gingrich of Georgia.

The first time I noticed Gingrich was only about an hour after his swearing in. The fledgling gadfly stood and offered a motion against the seating of Charles Diggs, a twenty-four-year member from Detroit and chairman of the Committee on the District of Columbia. Press accounts said Diggs was being charged by a federal prosecutor with having received unlawful kickbacks from members of his staff. The matter had not gone to a grand jury and there had been no indictment. Caucus rules specified that any member, upon indictment for a felony, would relinquish any House chairmanship while standing trial. This was not good enough for Gingrich. The Georgia freshman insisted that the veteran member should be kicked out of his post forthwith, without even waiting to see if there was evidence sufficient for a grand jury indictment. Lawmakers on both sides of the aisle were shocked by the newcomer's obvious thirst for attention. Diggs was black, and many suspected the thirty-six-year-old Gingrich of an opportunistic bid for favor among racially prejudiced constituents in his rural Georgia district.

Diggs ultimately was indicted, and convicted, leaving Congress as a result. But none of us could have known this at the time. We had examined no evidence. The precious presumption of innocence, essential not only to Congress but to the very fabric of American society, was openly flouted by the brash young Georgian.

When the vote was taken and the new member's ploy voted down, Gingrich made a point of looking me up on the House floor. As Majority Leader, I had explained the standing rule during the debate on Gingrich's motion. "One day, I'm going to be as good as you are," crowed Gingrich. I remember trying to make a polite reply, while thinking at the time that the young fellow was awfully full of himself and unusually greedy for attention.

Gingrich reminded Tip of a gadfly member from Yonkers, New York, named Bruce Caputo, defeated in the 1978 election after serving only one term. The Speaker did not mourn Caputo's departure. During his brief tenure, the New York freshman had earned O'Neill's contempt by repeated exhibitionistic attacks on the Speaker and other members. Caputo had managed to get himself appointed to the special committee investigating the Tongsun Park scandal. There he repeatedly took issue with professional counsel Jaworski, hired private investigators as members of his congressional staff, accused the Speaker of a cover-up, and made a general nuisance of himself with publicity-hungry behavior and outrageous attacks on the character of other people.

O'Neill had a firm conviction that any member who actively sought appointment to an investigating committee with the power to damage others' reputations with reckless charges should be shunned. A young fellow named John Cavanaugh from Nebraska was denied service on the highly publicized investigating panel precisely because his father had come personally to the Speaker and asked for the son's appointment. "If John can get on that committee," the father had pleaded, "he can get enough publicity to make him president of the United States."

On numerous occasions Tip made clear to me his disdain for "the greedy vultures" who like to prey on other people's reputations. I felt the same way. More than once we discussed the quirk of character that makes some people want positions in which they can defame the good name of others. Years earlier, a New Jersey Republican named J. Parnell Thomas had become chairman of the House Committee on UnAmerican Activities. "Mr. Patriotism!" Tip would snort. It turned out that Thomas was extorting kickbacks from staff members, for which he was convicted and served a prison term.

Before that, a Kentucky Democrat named Andrew Jackson May maneuvered himself during World War II onto a committee looking into profiteering by military procurement contractors. May, as things developed, was shamelessly trying to gouge responsible companies for contributions by private threats of bad publicity.

Two decades earlier, in the 1920s, a Texas demagogue named Tom Blanton had terrorized and disgusted the House until he was censured for repeated untrue attacks upon its character. Once he browbeat a clerk in the House stationery store into ordering for him a silver whiskey flask and then, dramatically displaying the object on the floor, excoriated the store for selling such wares to members. All such men, like Senator Joseph McCarthy, manufactured scapegoats for their own deification as they preyed upon the reputations of others. Fortunately, such examples had been rare and ultimately self-defeating.

Now, toward the end of the 1970s, we saw the gradual unfolding of a disturbing new phenomenon. Ever since Watergate, we had been observing a deterioration in respect for all institutions of government. Just as President Carter himself had run for office as an outsider, so candidates for Congress were finding it expedient to condemn, and once in office to continue condemning, the very institution in which they had sought membership. It became harder and harder to maintain the degree of company loyalty on which any common human endeavor must rely for its success.

Young members found they could always get a good ride in the newspapers if they scolded and scalded Congress. One day a group of first- and second-termers came to me, demanding that Speaker O'Neill answer press accounts charging Congress with institutional lethargy.

"Aren't you some of the very guys who've been *making* those charges?" I asked. Two or three admitted that they had been tempted into assailing the

House for imagined inaction. "It's about the only way you can get any public-ity," one of them asserted. Richard F. Fenno Jr., a political scientist, after traveling for several years with House and Senate members to their home dis-tricts, concluded that the most important preoccupation in the minds of many was reelection. "Members of Congress run for Congress by running *against* Congress," Fenno noted. "The strategy is ubiquitous, addictive, cost-free and foolproof . . . the institution bleeds from 435 separate cuts. In the long run, therefore, somebody must lose." To the extent the legislative arm of government is weakened by such activity, of course, everyone loses. We in the leadership simply had to inspire positive action and justifiable pride among our colleagues in their collective accomplishments. It wasn't easy.

President Carter, who entered office as Mr. Clean, soon felt the lash of the pervading cynicism. Throughout most of his term in the White House, he suffered from generally poor relations with the media. Carter did a number of very positive things for which he received little credit.

Carter's foreign-policy initiatives were often downplayed or upstaged by headlines given to some minor mishap. On his first trip abroad, a bad inter-preter in Poland stole the show from the president's positive message. I was with President Carter on his official state visit to Mexico, where I heard him address the Mexican Congress and the nation's leaders in Spanish. It was an historic first. Never before had any American president delivered an entire, formal speech to a foreign audience in its native language. Carter spoke for thirty minutes in good Spanish, and was well received. To my dismay, I dis-covered, upon returning from that trip, that hardly anyone in the United States even knew of the president's speech. But everyone knew, unfortunately, about a socially inappropriate bit of intended humor when Carter, the previ-ous day, had referred to "Montezuma's revenge," in a more private setting before proposing a toast.

Carter achieved a breakthrough in relations with the Chinese. He wel-comed China's leader, Deng Xiao Ping, in Washington and managed the delicate task of broadening diplomatic relationships with the mainland superpower without abandoning or alienating our longtime friends on Taiwan.

After a series of hard bargaining sessions between Secretary of State Cyrus Vance and Soviet Foreign Minister Andrei Gromyko, President Carter met Soviet Leader Leonid Brezhnev in Vienna in June 1979 and concluded a SALT II agreement, which would reduce Russian missile launchers and bombers by one-third. The accomplishment was sublimated six months later as relations with the Soviet Union soured following Russia's invasion of Afghanistan.

In domestic policy, Carter performed some noteworthy feats, even in the face of setbacks. His Labor Secretary Ray Marshall brought about a settlement in the crippling coal strike of 1978. When Chrysler Corporation faced bankruptcy that would have left the country with only two remaining automobile manufacturers and thrown at least two hundred thousand Americans out of work, Carter and Congress worked out a rescue plan of heroic proportions. The result was an unqualified success. Every penny was repaid—ahead of time—and the Treasury lost nothing.

The president's battle against red tape and overregulation brought some noteworthy but largely unnoted results. In one triumph of common sense, a Carter administrator wiped out almost a thousand silly regulations and saved American business and consumers as much as one hundred million dollars annually. Dr. Eula Bingham, Assistant Secretary of Labor, set out to reduce paperwork and harassment of small businessmen by Occupational Safety and Health (OSHA) administrators. Carter ordered radical pruning. Dr. Bingham's response reduced the written regulations from four hundred pages to just thirty-two, exempted places with fewer than ten employees from most record-keeping, and shrank standard forms from eighty entries to nineteen.

Under Carter's prodding, Congress in 1980 voted a balanced budget for the first time in twelve years. Negative economic developments robbed us of this elusive goal, but the four Carter years deficits combined came to a mere fraction of the annual deficit in any single year of his successor's administration. President Carter emphasized fiscal restraint. In fact, Agriculture Committee Chairman Tom Foley and I tried hard to convince our chief executive that some of his tightfisted economies were shortsighted. Since 1973, the average family farm had suffered a drop in net annual income from $9,950 to $5,300. Meanwhile, the cost of farm machinery, necessary fuel, and interest rates continued to rise. A bushel of wheat worth $2.70 on the market cost $5.06 to produce. A farmer himself, Carter insisted that family agriculture's plight was due to systemic conditions that could be relieved only by coming to grips with the nation's core problems: the energy crunch, resultant inflation, and suffocating interest rates.

Energy was the most intractable problem of all. Spurred by the Arab oil embargo of 1979, it confronted us with choking shortages, oppressive oil price increases, and a pervasive economic slowdown. The price of imported oil, which accounted for half our total domestic usage, spiraled suddenly from sixteen to thirty dollars a barrel. A gallon of gasoline was selling for three times its 1973 price. The U.S. bill for oil imports drained seventy billion dollars out of our economy in 1979. Aside from its economic impact, our growing dependence on foreign sources had alarming foreign policy implications.

This ominous threat to our country's future called for a response as big as the problem. We needed a carefully coordinated attack, consisting of long-term as well as short-term measures. Actually, America had been chalking up some modest gains on the conservation side. The set of initiatives Congress passed in 1978 were doing more than most of us realized—not nearly enough, but a start. By mandating better mileage performance in new automobiles, we were helping to realize savings that would come to almost one million barrels of oil daily. By encouraging home insulation and weatherization, through loans and tax incentives, we had set in motion improvements that collectively would save another million barrels a day. In the previous year, Congress had put in motion a phased decontrol of natural gas prices at the wellhead. This definitely had stimulated new exploration and new production. All in all, President Carter reported happily to congressional leaders at a breakfast in early September 1979, we had cut the total amount of energy consumption required for each percent of growth in the gross national product. In the past, a one percent growth in the economy had meant an inevitable one percent growth in the use of energy. Conservation initiatives we had put into effect were allowing us to achieve a one percent growth in the nation's economy at a cost of only about six-tenths of a percent of increase in energy consumption.

All this didn't mean we had whipped the problem. It meant things would be a lot worse if we hadn't begun the national energy conservation program. That included the fifty-five mile per hour speed limit. Imperfectly enforced and indifferently observed, it was saving at least five hundred thousand barrels of oil a day—and about eight thousand lives a year.

There was much more to be done, mostly on the supply side, and I was determined to see it through. By early September, under my constant prodding, the House had passed three of the major bills in our package: a synthetic fuels bill, a windfall profits tax, and standby rationing authority. The Senate had acted on the latter and had the first two scheduled for approval that month.

The real problem, very plainly, was that we'd been using more energy than we produced. Until the late 1940s, our country produced more oil and gas than we used. Since then, our consumption had grown enormously. Domestic discovery and production of oil had not kept pace, so imports had soared, until we were importing about half of all we consumed. In May 1979, President Carter called a group of congressional leaders together to discuss whether or not to decontrol domestic oil prices as an incentive to stimulate more domestic drilling. Senator Lloyd Bentsen and I were the only two of the dozen present who urged him to take that step. Other Democrats feared negative public reaction in the anticipation of price increases. But we were already paying substantially more for that half of our energy we imported than we were for American oil. That made no sense. While understanding the apprehension of my colleagues, I thought they were following a self-destructive urge. Focusing on price only, they were ignoring the problem of supply. Price, Bentsen and I stressed, is an inverse result of supply. The shorter the supply the higher the price, and the very best way to keep prices down in the long run was to increase domestic supplies.

Carter, in the end, agreed with us. Knowing his decision would evoke criticism, he made it boldly. For the next several years, exploration increased markedly. We found more oil and a lot more gas, and domestic oil prices never reached the level we were paying at that moment for overpriced Middle Eastern petroleum. Over the next several years, the new policy recovered billions of barrels that otherwise never would have been produced. And that recovery clearly benefited American consumers by making us less dependent on foreign products in an economy of scarcity.

To go with decontrol, President Carter proposed an excess profits tax. As the lid came off domestic prices, American producers would be getting more. Carter asked Congress to take half the difference between what oil producers were getting before decontrol and what they'd receive in a free market after decontrol, and put that half of the windfall into an "Energy Conservation Trust Fund." Out of that fund the president believed we should finance research into other long-range energy replacements, development of rail transit systems that would save energy by offering attractive alternatives to the use of private cars, and some way of indemnifying low-income Americans against high utility bills.

I supported this concept as well and helped steer the excess profits tax through the House. This irritated a number of my friends in the Texas oil fraternity. A few complained vigorously. Offered half a loaf, they were dissatisfied. They wanted it all, and that's human nature. When the election rolled around, most of them forgot that Carter used his discretionary power, at some cost to his popularity in northern states, to decontrol oil prices, from which they profited. But they all remembered that government, at Carter's request, took part of it back in the excess profits tax.

For several months, the energy package was my main preoccupation. I hounded committees, urging them to meet deadlines; held seminars for members to show them how it all fit together; tried to absorb all I could learn from researchers in various modes of synthetic oil production—ethanol, methanol, coal liquification, extraction of fuel from corn stalks and wood pulp, adaptations of solar and thermal energy. I visited a pioneering plant on the western Colorado slope of the Rockies where pure, clear oil was being squeezed at high compression from rocky shale. To demonstrate to colleagues the extents to which oil-poor societies had gone to find petroleum substitutes,

I led an official delegation to visit Sasol 1, the successful South African plant that was producing oil and gas from coal. We also saw two primitive old World War II vintage plants in the Ruhr Valley of Germany by which, long after they ran out of oil, the Nazis kept the Wehrmacht and Luftwaffe operating on high-octane fuel extracted from their soft brown coal.

Every workday morning for three weeks, I made a presentation to one or another group of colleagues, with charts, answering their questions, convincing them of the importance of supporting the whole energy package. At the Commerce committee I made a pest of myself, repeatedly appearing during their prolonged markup. The session had gone on for two weeks, and the deadline was approaching to have the bill on the floor. Crusty old John Dingell of Michigan, my contemporary from the class of 1955, finally became exasperated with my constant prodding.

"Now, Glorious Leader," he said, his voice dripping in mock homage, "you have made that same speech, or variations of it, to this group on three occasions. If you really are interested in expediting our deliberations, I recommend that we simply label that 'speech number one.' Then, whenever you feel impelled to exhort us to greater effort, you may simply stick your head in the doorway and hold up one finger. We'll know you have reference to the spirited comments you have just shared with us. We'll be inspired to greater effort and will save the time required to listen again to those thrilling words."
I figured I had done all the good I could with that crowd.

At last, our bills were packaged and passed. They went to the president in two large parcels and several smaller ones and were signed. One provision empowered the chief executive to invoke fast-track powers to reduce the regulatory time lag on major energy projects from a current average of five years down to possibly eighteen months. The whole legislative effort had been an exhausting process, but an immensely satisfying one.

A year later, some heartening progress was evident. During the first six months of 1980, we imported 14 percent less oil than during the first half of 1979. New American-made cars were getting an average of twenty-one miles to the gallon of gasoline, a 50 percent improvement over the average thirteen miles in 1974. American industry was producing at 16 percent less energy consumed per unit of production than it had been six years previously, following the first Arab embargo. Approximately 13 percent of America's families had fully insulated their homes. And there was more exploratory drilling for oil and gas in the United States than at any time since the mid-1950s.

A large part of our package, to my dismay, would be unraveled during the eight years of the next administration. The American people would lose their sense of urgency. Congress would weary of the long-term commitment and stop funding certain features of it. New leaders would succumb to a popular clamor for faster speeds and abandon the fifty-five mile per hour limit. By the time of the Gulf War in 1991, we had drifted back to once more importing 50 percent of our energy needs. But Jimmy Carter deserves credit for facing up squarely to the crisis, making the hard decisions, taking the political risks. If sincerity of purpose, political courage and resolute determination were all that holding public favor required, Carter would have been reelected in 1980. But other things entered in. Among them were the whims of oil rich Middle Eastern leaders, the winsome personal appeal of Ronald Reagan, and the angry religious zealotry of the Ayatollah Ruholla Khomeini of Iran.

CHAPTER TWENTY-SIX

ELECTIONS 1980: HATE, FATE, AND KHOMEINI

T he elections of 1980 marked a major turning point in our country's political direction. We saw the flowering of the National Conservative Political Action Committee (NCPAC) and the political emergence of the religious right, led by Reverend Jerry Falwell. Historians would compare the prevailing political sentiments of the next twelve years to those that reigned from 1920 to 1932. As in the 1920 election, voters in 1980 were angry about high prices and disillusioned by world events. With Thomas Carlyle, I had always felt history was given shape by the deeds and teachings of "great men," but I was beginning to see a near-inexorability to cyclic patterns, inevitable swings of the political pendulum, and to realize that, for all of man's faith and striving, extraneous events can upset our best-laid plans.

For Jimmy Carter, the 1979 Arab oil embargo was one such event. It profoundly disrupted our domestic economy. Another series of happenings, defying Carter's comprehension and control, was set in motion by the seizure and imprisonment of American hostages in Iran, egged on by the fanatical anti-American rantings of a hate-filled seventy-nine-year-old fundamentalist Islamic priest named Ruhollah Khomeini.

It should take nothing from the persuasive personal appeal of Carter's Republican challenger, Ronald Reagan, to recognize how exogenous occurrences in faraway Iran debilitated Carter's public image as a leader. Reagan was, unquestionably, a skillful and attractive campaigner. He was, in the judgment of many, the greatest television candidate in history. Reagan was to television, I decided, what Franklin Roosevelt had been to radio. But it was

Khomeini, and the year-long American hostage crisis, which angered and disgusted the American public. Ironically, it was exactly one year to the day before the 1980 election, November 4, 1979, that a band of "student" revolutionaries occupied the American Embassy in Tehran, taking the entire contingent of fifty-three Americans hostage and threatening to kill them if the terrorists' demands were not met. They wanted the recently deposed shah of Iran, Mohammed Reza Pahlavi, who had come to the United States for medical treatment following his overthrow in a Khomeini-led revolution, returned to Iran. The brazen event and President Carter's unyielding response first triggered an immediate rise in Carter's popularity. The president stood firm, let the Shah complete his treatment before leaving the country, froze Iranian assets in America, demanded immediate release of our citizens, and called on the United Nations to intervene. American lives at stake, the president attempted to walk a fine line between firmness and provocation. He didn't want to trigger a sudden, violent reaction, which could end in a mass public execution of our embassy personnel.

Americans, at first supportive of Carter's efforts, became increasingly dissatisfied as the months wore on. Thousands began wearing yellow ribbons in honor of the hostages. Carter tried everything. He sent Warren Christopher on a fruitless attempt to negotiate. He persuaded more moderate Islamic leaders to plead personally with Khomeini, reciting passages from the Koran, which forbade such ill treatment of visitors within one's country.

The mad Iranian leader remained adamant.

Frustrated American citizens began demanding a more forceful presidential response. "What exactly do you feel the president should do?" I asked all who came to me. "Lay an atomic bomb on 'em, like we did at Hiroshima," came one reply. Another said, "Bomb the whole country back into the stone age!"

"But wouldn't that kill the American hostages, too?" I'd ask.

The situation was maddening to Carter. He worried personally about the hostages. I watched new worry lines appear in his face as, week after week, he tried some new effort to persuade the implacable, self-righteous Khomeini to release our fellow citizens. Carter withdrew from all campaign and social appearances early in 1980, feeling they would detract from his efforts to obtain the hostages' freedom. At our Tuesday morning sessions, he sometimes let down his customary reserve, confessing his frustration. To use military force, the president saw, would not only pose serious risks to the hostages. It could set off convulsive anti–U.S. reactions throughout the Muslim world. It even might trigger a worldwide conflagration, if opportunistic Soviet leaders chose to intervene in Iran's behalf. We had stopped buying oil from Iran, and called for an international economic boycott. But to disrupt the flow of Iranian oil to other countries by force could be economically crippling to some of our allies and only make the Iranians more insular and hateful than ever.

Finally, on April 24, 1980, a secret rescue attempt led by Colonel Charles Beckwith ran aground after advancing undetected to the approximate center of Iran. The mission had been well planned, down to the last detail. From a dependable inside source, we knew the precise location of each hostage within the compound. We had satellite pictures confirming the stationing of each guard in the embassy grounds. Six large helicopters would fly suddenly into the center of Tehran, swiftly pick up the three Americans in the foreign ministry building and the forty-nine other hostages in the embassy, then carry them all to safety. Needing a minimum of six large craft, we laid on eight for safety.

The helicopters took off at dusk, on perfect schedule, from their prepositioned aircraft carrier base, headed for the overnight rendezvous point, code-named Desert One, in the sandy wastes of interior Iran. Then, one by one, things started going wrong. Defying official weather reports, a blinding sand storm in southern Iran downed one helicopter and forced another to return to base. This left only six, not a single one to spare, as they huddled at their secret desert rendezvous, refueled from a companion C-130, and awaited dawn. They monitored Iranian radio and were satisfied their presence had not been detected. President Carter followed the mission's progress personally, minute by minute, via radio reports.

Suddenly, bad luck. A busload of about forty Iranians unexpectedly drove by the secluded landing site and had to be physically detained lest they report what they'd seen. The passengers were unloaded and sent by C-130 to Egypt until the rescue mission was complete. Then, worse news! A helicopter smashed into a C-130 on takeoff. The transport was disabled and there were casualties. With injured personnel needing hospitalization, and now without enough aircraft to complete the rescue mission, it had to be aborted. Remaining planes and personnel, on Colonel Beckwith's recommendation and with the president's consent, were returned to base, clearing Iranian airspace in the early morning hours.

It was a little before two o'clock in the morning, Washington time, when I received a call from Secretary of State Cy Vance, awakening me to relate the whole sad episode. Vance asked me to come to the White House for a 7:30 A.M. briefing of congressional leaders. I stayed awake the rest of the night, worrying about the failed effort, its casualties, its likely aftermath.

When we sat down at a table in the West room for our briefing, the president asked if I would lead the group in prayer. Before I could finish, the doors opened and a rush of newsmen crowded noisily into the room, cameras recording. The first view Americans had of their president and congressional leaders on the morning news was with our heads bowed. That was well enough. It was a humbling moment. I learned within minutes that Vance had opposed the venture from the beginning and now was resigning as secretary of state. "We should do it right or not do it at all!" I had angrily insisted the night before. Now remorseful for my outburst, I tried to console the president and others engaged in the secret planning. "It is better to have tried and failed," I assured them, "than to have failed to try. Congress will understand that, and so will the American people."

Part of what I said that morning was wishful thinking. The president needed all the confidence, moral support, and self-assurance he could get. It would be a long day—a long year, in fact. From that moment on, President Carter's reelection chances were been doomed.

Soon I would have my hands full helping to steer Carter's legislative program through a Congress increasingly tuned to election year jitters. This, along with assisting colleagues in their reelection campaigns, would have been enough to occupy anyone's full time and more. In 1980, I also had to fight off a vigorous, well-financed, year-long effort to defeat my own reelection. It would be the hardest campaign of my thirty-four years in Congress.

Like other prominent House and Senate Democrats that year, I was targeted by NCPAC and Moral Majority. Their emergence was a new political phenomenon. It began the era of increasingly negative campaign tactics. NCPAC, Moral Majority, and other clandestinely organized fronts could receive contributions without revealing their source and spend undisclosed amounts attacking a candidate. His opponent, though beneficiary of the expenditures, did not have to report them, nor assume any responsibility for scurrilous assaults on his competitor's public record or personal integrity. Truth was no hindrance to a growing genre of furtive character assassins and poison-pen operatives. Several of Congress's most influential and respected members fell to the 1980 sneak attacks. These provided a pattern from which Newt Gingrich and others would develop the more sophisticated GOPAC and engineer a Republican takeover of the House in 1994. I sometimes wondered in those days whether men like Richard Viguerie and Terry Dolan, professionals in the iniquitous arts of verbal abuse, were motivated by ideology or simple greed, or if what they were doing would have any long-term effect on our political system. In 1980, however, the perspective from which I observed these developments became more personal than academic.

Just days after my 1978 reelection, I got a rude shock. One morning the *Fort Worth Star-Telegram* carried a full-page ad excoriating me for my support of Carter. The colorful diatribe was addressed to me personally and signed, "Your friend, Eddie." My self-appointed tormentor was a well-known local oilman named Eddie Chiles, head of a successful oilfield service organization called The Western Company. During the next two years, he would run no fewer than ten big display ads attacking me. It made him angry, for example, that I had voted to support loan guarantees for New York City, and that, having assisted in freeing domestic oil from price controls, I had supported the windfall profits tax. Eddie's theme was that I had outlived my usefulness to the Fort Worth district. One full-page appeal was headed, "COME HOME, JIM," in big bold type. It, too, like others in the series, was signed, "Your friend, Eddie."

Chiles had made a big pile of money in the oil patch. He enjoyed spending it now to promote his favorite right-wing political causes. When not rubbing verbal sandpaper on my nose, he bought and narrated a series of "I'M MAD" commercials on a network of radio stations and promoted bumper stickers reading "I'm Mad Too, Eddie." The dominating theme was from an Ayn Rand novel in which the central character, fed up with society's restrictions, asserted, "I'm mad, and I'm not going to take it anymore!"

Chiles and I had been friends, sort of. Each time he traveled to Washington, he'd come by to regale me with his homespun wisdom and exhort me to vote more conservatively. I valued his insight on matters affecting the oil industry but considered him less sagacious in the ever-growing universe of conservative philosophy that he increasingly espoused. Still, Eddie was a colorful character. The only trouble was his notion that you couldn't be his friend without letting him own you and control the way you thought. That I couldn't do. Every weekend that I was home in the district, I'd have a call from Eddie wanting me to come by and see him. I accommodated him several times, but finally grew weary with explaining on each occasion why several times in the past month I had voted differently than the U.S. Chamber of Commerce recommended in its bulletins. "You see, Eddie," I tried to explain, "I'm floor leader for the Democrats in the House. I can't simply pattern my voting record on the U.S. Chamber or any other lobby."

In October of 1979, a large cross-section of my friends threw a party in my honor at the Fort Worth Convention Center. Celebrating my twenty-five years in Congress, the group invited Speaker O'Neill and Lee Iacocca, among others. The sponsoring committee covered the whole broad spectrum of local life—business, labor, agriculture, the arts and professions, leaders of the town's various ethnic communities. One of the sponsors was Jim Nichols, a prominent local engineer, who had been elected president of the Fort Worth Chamber of Commerce.

On seeing Nichols's name on the list of sponsors, Eddie Chiles threw a tizzy. He publicly resigned from the local Chamber, saying that if its president was inviting people to come to a dinner in my honor, then the civic organization no longer represented his interests. It was a tempest in a teapot, but the tempest blew its way through the front pages of the *Star-Telegram* for several days. When more than five thousand people paid twenty-five dollars apiece to come to the dinner, Nichols and I both felt amply vindicated. If Chiles had been trying to spray cold rain on our parade, he had failed. I supposed he might see the handwriting on the wall and decide it was futile to spend more money trying to chip away at my local support. I also hoped would-be candidates, eager to milk Eddie for campaign money, might be dissuaded by the huge turnout. I was disappointed on both counts.

Eddie began actively soliciting someone to run against me. He hired the Finklestein Organization, a Republican polling firm in New York, to do a district-wide poll, probing my vulnerabilities. At least two locally prominent people confirmed to *Star-Telegram* reporters that they'd been approached by Chiles, and that he had promised to raise up to $500,000 for any credible candidate who would oppose me.

Soon, Chiles found a taker. James Bradshaw, a successful businessman and well-known member of the Fort Worth City Council, announced in December that he'd run for my congressional seat as a Republican. While councilman, Bradshaw had been apolitical. Some thought he was a Democrat, although not an active one. He was thirty-nine years old, nice looking, and articulate. His wife, Ouida, was personable and socially popular. Betty and I did not know the Bradshaws well, although once, some months earlier, we had joined them for dinner at a local country club. On that occasion, Bradshaw had been effusive in thanks for my help in getting approval for a City Council–sponsored grant to revitalize Fort Worth's downtown area. I thought Bradshaw likable, although something of a publicity hound—but, then, most politicians are. As Mayor Pro Tem, he had attended the October function in my honor and sat at the head table.

Now, in December, Bradshaw vowed he would work the next eleven months full time to unseat me. He said he expected to spend "whatever it takes" to win. He was financially comfortable, a self-acknowledged millionaire, partner in a family-owned auto-supply chain. And Chiles was boasting that he'd personally raise $500,000 for Bradshaw's campaign. The candidate, at Eddie's insistence, quickly enrolled in a school for Republican hopefuls conducted by NCPAC. That experience transformed Bradshaw's whole political approach. It schooled him to be aggressive, constantly on the attack, focused on tearing down my standing in the community. "Stay on the offense," NCPAC's political operatives indoctrinated, "keep him answering your charges, and you'll win."

Shortly after the first of the year, a friend accidently overheard a Washington conversation among Republican Campaign Committee staffers.

They were talking about raising money to help Bradshaw. With them, it seemed to be a matter of tying me down. Keeping me busy in my own backyard would leave me less time to help other Democratic candidates. The Republican campaign strategists talked of targeting all the most influential Democrats. *U.S. News and World Report* had just conducted an extensive survey of all members of Congress, Democrats and Republicans, asking what three members of House and Senate they most respected, and which three they considered most persuasive in debate. That poll, published January 14, 1980, showed me first among House members in both categories. In the Senate, Russell Long was named most persuasive and Howard Baker most respected. The GOP campaign people made reference to this poll, doubting they could beat me, but considering it a top priority to finance an active effort against me. "Scuff up his new shoes," one reportedly said.

It quickly became apparent that an enormous amount of money would be spent in Bradshaw's behalf. His campaign began running television spots in February. Never before had I seen TV ads that early for a November election. The commercials hardly mentioned Bradshaw. They were totally negative in character, their aim to tear away at my credibility.

One video appeal, repeatedly rebroadcast in prime time, began with footage of a riotous mob setting fire to a huge American flag. The voice-over ominously intoned: "Did you know that *your* congressman, Jim Wright, voted to give the Panama Canal away to a *Communist dictatorship?*" The video image changed to a big-city ghetto scene featuring sullen black faces and sinister-looking characters. "And did you know that *your* congressman, Jim Wright, voted to spend *your* tax dollars to bail out New York City?" Next, a scene of military aircraft in flight, blending to a May Day parade in Red Square. "And did you know that *your* Congressman, Jim Wright, consistently votes to *weaken* our country's defenses?" Finally, the audio message accused me of voting to raise my own pay, then ended, with a vocal inflection of incredulity, "And *he* thinks *we're* going to reelect *him?*

After viewing the commercial for about the third time, I remarked to Betty, "If I took all that at face value, I don't think *I'd* vote for that guy Wright." There were many factual holes in the presentation, of course. I hadn't voted to "give away" the Canal. Panama was not a "Communist dictatorship." We didn't "spend" any "tax dollars" to "bail out" New York City. We had guaranteed loans. They were repaid, and the Treasury lost nothing. I had not voted to weaken military defenses, and congressional pay was set now through a presidentially approved commission. But it was too early to spend money answering charges. We'd hear this kind of thing for the next nine months.

Local well-wishers began coming to me with negative stories about

Bradshaw, about some of his votes on the City Council, even about his family life. Some insisted he had a drinking problem. They wanted me to spend money besmirching *his* good name. That was not my style, I reminded them. If I had nothing better to recommend me than casting aspersions on my opponent's reputation, I didn't deserve to be reelected. I had never seen the man in any condition but sobriety, and his family life was, in my view, his own business.

A friend of mine named Jim Kitchens had earned a doctorate from Duke University in political communications. Recently Jim had made an in-depth study of NCPAC, its teachings and its tactics. He told a group of us one day in mid-spring exactly how Bradshaw's campaign would be configured, and exactly what things that organization would try to hang around my neck. Among other things, Bradshaw's wife would write a long letter by pen, Kitchens predicted, and NCPAC artisans would reproduce it and contrive salutations so as to make the copies appear as originals, for mailing to many thousands of women in the district. The letter, composed by professional political wordsmiths, would contain phrases and buzz words calculated to embrace wholesome family values and to hint indiscretions and aberrations of various sorts on the part of her husband's opponent. This, Kitchens said, was standard fare being promoted by NCPAC and the Republican Campaign Committee against Democratic incumbents throughout the country. Then, Kitchens said, NCPAC and Moral Majority, in their own or some other organizational name, would follow up with an "independent" attack phase, not attributed to the Bradshaw campaign nor reportable by it. This phase would charge me, as other individual Democrats were being charged, with such things as promoting abortions, favoring homosexuality, coddling criminals, and an assortment of other high-voltage forms of unpopular behavior. This, according to Kitchens, was boilerplate NCPAC technique.

We were at first incredulous, but, quickly enough, I witnessed exactly what Kitchens had predicted. A letter in Ouida Bradshaw's handwriting, printed on her modest feminine personal stationery, was mailed to a wide list. Kitchens showed us several samples, bearing identical passages, mailed to voters in other states on letterheads of other Republican candidates' wives. Then friends began bringing scurrilous circulars—not sent through the mails, but placed under windshield wipers of automobiles in the parking lots of fundamentalist churches while Sunday morning religious services were in progress. One particularly gruesome example featured art work portraying a garbage can full of dead babies. Its message was that I favored abortions and therefore was anti-Christian and should be defeated. In truth, I had never voted to favor abortions, except in cases of rape, incest, or to save the life of the mother.

Following the national lead of Reverend Jerry Falwell, a group of fundamentalist preachers, mostly but not exclusively Baptists, held a political
conclave in Dallas emphasizing "Christian" values in the election. They
roundly excoriated President Carter. One of them conducted a prayer meeting asking divine assistance in defeating me at the polls. One reference
described me as "led by the devil." Candidate Ronald Reagan attended the
group's concluding session. "I know you can't endorse me," he began his
speech, "but I can endorse you."

On witnessing this phenomenon, I was stunned by the brash presumptions of right-wing clergy and others who now presumed to speak for God in
the political arena. Watching the Republican National Convention by television that year, I was surprised on hearing an interview with Reverend Falwell.
He was asked if he didn't think it possible for a Christian to be a Democrat.
"Not a well-informed Christian," Falwell replied.

During the campaign, Falwell announced publicly that he had been to
the White House once for a conference in the Oval Office. President Carter,
Falwell asserted, had told him he believed homosexuals deserved representation in the White House and therefore had appointed several to his staff. The
truth, it developed, was that there had never been any such conversation.
Falwell had never even been inside the Oval Office. Confronted by
reporters, the man who pronounced himself head of the Moral Majority
admitted he had "fabricated" the tale. What I found disturbing was the
apparent lack of embarrassment or remorse. It was as though the commandment forbidding the bearing of false witness against one's neighbor had been
suspended for the political season. A "religious" TV commercial continued
to depict a mother counseling her child that Carter was a bad man who
encouraged homosexuals.

The Bradshaw campaign never wanted for money, nor for chutzpah. It
was, I would learn, a sort of flagship for other Republican campaigns across
America against other prominent House and Senate Democrats. Whatever
seemed to work in one place was replicated, with only minor adaptations,
elsewhere. Published charges circulated against several congressmen in widely
separated areas, were verbatim. The only substitutions were the names of candidates and opponents. I believe it is more than merely my imagination that
from that point, 1980, political campaigns have become observably more
negative. The malevolent attack on opposing candidates has not been confined by any means to Republicans. Democrats all too often have copied the
techniques used against them that year. During the fifteen years following the
1980 campaign, the politics of anger and personal disparagement have grown
commonplace, and gross exaggerations have come close to gaining social
acceptance in the political arena.

In my case, the charges didn't stick. I let others answer them. One Chiles-Bradshaw allegation was that I had "gone national," neglecting local interests. Some who had served on the city council and in business community groups with Bradshaw knew of my attentiveness to local concerns. They also knew Bradshaw was aware of it. They began publicly reciting a litany of refutation: I had, in recent months, acquired federal grants to help in the historic preservation of Fort Worth's old North Side; promoted attractive neighborhood civic centers for youth in hispanic and black neighborhoods; gone to bat for environmental enhancement with hiking and biking trails along the Trinity River floodway; won an urban high-density improvement, relieving a bad case of local traffic congestion; and helped arrange the move of American Airlines' national headquarters from New York City to Dallas–Fort Worth Regional Airport. This move, then in process of completion, meant about 10,000 more jobs for our area.

During the spring and summer, I held my fire. My old and close friend, Craig Raupe, opened a campaign office for me on a street called The Locke Block in western Fort Worth. A few doors down that block, Carlos Moore opened a boiler room for telephone banks. That operation began with twenty people, methodically calling everyone on the voter registration list. They discovered that my popularity was still high, people liked what I had been doing for the community, and wanted to help. By September, we had quietly amassed 6,000 block captains; 28,000 folks who said they wanted automobile window stickers; and 31,000 homes, whose occupants agreed to yard signs for the three weeks prior to election day.

In September, I made a thirty-minute television broadcast over Channel 5, the dominant local station. The first twelve minutes were a videotaped presentation of public initiatives, local and national, in which I'd been involved. Then I looked into the camera and talked about the problems facing American public policy and what I thought must be done. The whole message was positive. I didn't mention Bradshaw's name. Explaining that I'd been busy with the public's business in Washington, I asked for volunteers who would assist me in the campaign for reelection. During the final five minutes, we superimposed a telephone number, on which we had twenty rotary lines at campaign headquarters. All the lines stayed busy for the next hour, and some calls were coming in two hours later. In all, we had enrolled more than two thousand new campaign volunteers.

Nine times I met Bradshaw in debates, two of them televised. On one show, I answered telephoned questions for thirty minutes. I made three trips to other parts of the country for colleagues. But in mid-October, John Murtha of Pennsylvania called to tell me he and four other area candidates were cancelling a visit I had promised. They'd heard of the vigorous attack on my seat. "We think it's more important that you stay home and get reelected," Murtha said.

As the 1980 campaign developed nationally, it became a pattern for the standard Republican attack to include an assertion that any Democrat was "soft on defense" and to claim that America's armed forces had been dangerously eroded. Reagan himself charged Carter with "his vacillation, his weakness, his allowing our allies throughout the world to no longer respect us." In fact, the last budget proposed by Carter and adopted by Congress with the usual modifications, earmarked $148 billion for the country's military defenses, the largest amount ever appropriated in peacetime.

Reagan presented a consistent theme. Over and again, his campaign speeches resonated with three basic promises: to strengthen America's military defense, to cut taxes, and to balance the budget. Given that the first would cost money and the second reduce government income, it was mystifying to imagine how they, in tandem, could lead to the third. Reagan had a stock answer, appealing though illogical: cutting taxes would increase government revenue. This was the claim that George Bush, while a candidate for the presidential nomination, branded as "voodoo economics."

The Republican nominee was a skillful campaigner, a polished actor with a quick sense of humor and a practiced knack of getting off the hook. He never let a campaign gaffe or misstatement embarrass him. My earliest observation of the ease with which Reagan slipped in and out of the noose on the budget-balancing promise came on Sunday, March 16. Betty and I were in Pensacola, Florida, where I'd spoken the evening before to the local chamber of commerce, which was honoring Florida congressman Earl Hutto. We watched a Sunday television talk show on which candidate Reagan was interviewed. A reporter pointed out a factual inaccuracy in a recent Reagan claim concerning tax cuts and his assertion that they always brought the government more money. Reagan was wholly unruffled. Any inaccuracy, he replied in wide-eyed innocence, must have been an error on the part of his speechwriter.

Reagan even had a gift for good-humoredly turning misstatements to his own advantage. In one speech he said America was in the throes of a depression. Economists pointed out the inaccuracy of the term to describe the country's current condition. The old actor began delighting his audiences by saying, "I'm told I can't use the word 'depression.' Well, I'll tell you the definition. A recession is when your neighbor loses his job, and a depression is when you lose your job. (Wait for laugh) A recovery is when Jimmy Carter loses his!"

The GOP campaign was aided mightily by the rate of inflation set off by the oil embargo. When the price of oil went up, the price of almost everything rose. Moreover, Carter and the nation had been ill-served, in my judgment, by the president's appointee to head the Federal Reserve Board. Paul Volcker thought there was no way to fight inflation except through high interest rates. He didn't realize this inflation was different. People were not buying too much nor borrowing too much. They were simply paying too much. Each time Volcker arbitrarily raised the interest rate, as he did repeatedly over the anguished objections of people like Hubert Humphrey and myself, he raised the cost of living and doing business for all Americans. It was like medieval medicine—bleeding patients for whatever ailed them, even the anemic ones.

Candidate Reagan played upon rising prices and higher interest rates as on a set of bongo drums. In each speech, he would ask the crowd, "Are you better off than you were four years ago? Is it easier for you to go out and buy things in the stores than it was four years ago?" It became like a cabalistic incantation, to which the crowds would respond with a resounding "Nooooo!"

President Carter was frustrated by Reagan's popularity and the ease with which he slipped off some obvious bloopers like contending that trees and not automobiles were the causes of smog and air pollution. The chief executive began attacking his GOP rival. This probably was a mistake. It made Carter appear less than presidential to suggest that some of his opponent's statements sounded like those of a racist and others like those of a warmonger. Commentators began to suggest that the president's refutations had a mean edge to them.

Finally, on October 28, exactly one week before the election, the two candidates met in Cleveland for a nationally televised debate. From the beginning, Reagan seized the initiative. Entering the stage, with an actor's sense of timing, he strode across with a big smile and outstretched hand to greet Carter heartily. The president was momentarily, and visibly, taken aback by the unexpected gesture. "Round one for Reagan," I thought.

It rattled Carter to be so adroitly upstaged. His presentation in answer to questions was just a little ragged as result. Reagan, by contrast, was as poised as a palm tree swaying in the ocean breeze. At one point, when Carter, concentrating on factual substance, seemed too critical of one of Reagan's statements, the GOP standard bearer shook his head in pretended sadness. "There you go again," he said. The crowd roared in laughter. Round two for Reagan.

When time came for each contestant to sum up his case in a concluding statement, Carter tried too hard to cram too many facts into the brief remaining time. Reagan's memorized finale was worthy of an Academy Award. A grandly eloquent homily about the greatness of America and the goodness of its people was spoken with just the right touch of feeling and humility. Round three! And it was over.

On the Saturday before the election, we turned out an impressive crowd of the Democratic faithful on Fort Worth's historic old North Side for President

Carter. It was I who chose the location, in the heart of a working class neighborhood and reminiscent of Fort Worth's heritage. Carter spoke well and was
enthusiastically received. But I knew by then, while trying not to admit it to
myself, that his reelection was a hopeless cause. The main question at this
point was whether we'd be able to hold onto a congressional majority. Tip and
I discussed that question by telephone. The year had witnessed a revival of the
most negative sort of campaigning since the days of Joe McCarthy. The repe-
titious use of radio and television commercials, some with utterly no factual
foundation, met mixed reactions in different parts of the country. They
played upon public frustrations and prejudices. Left wholly unanswered, they
could be devastating. In other places, exposed for their barrenness of truth,
they were made to boomerang upon their perpetrators.

In my own case, I believe Bradshaw's advisors did him an unwitting dis-
service. The public did not know him nearly as well as it did me after
twenty-five years in Congress. His backers spent their entire bankroll on
anti-Wright advertising, some of which backfired. One example comes to
mind. The Bradshaw campaign bought ads on KNOK and other radio stations with wide listenership among black citizens. Two voices came on in jive
talk. That itself was degrading to many black listeners. One voice said, "Hey,
man, you know Congressman Jim Wright?" The other: "Yeh, I know that
cat. What about him?" The first: "You know, that cat has been in Congress
for twenty-five years—he hadn't never hired no black folks yet!" The second:
"What you mean, he hadn't never hired no black folks? He talk too friendly
for that." The first: "He don't *act* friendly. I got a phone number right here.
You call him and find out right now, how come in twenty-five years he hadn't
hired no black folks at all." The second: "If he ain't never hired no black
folks, he ain't goin' get my vote. I voted for him all my life, but I ain't goin'
vote for him no more."

The whole ad was premised on a lie. I quickly produced the names of
eleven black people whom I'd employed officially during the past decade.
Three of them were on my congressional staff at that moment. A number of
very reputable members of the local black community, aware of these facts,
cut tapes that were played on the same stations, pointing out the misrepresen-
tation. The amazing thing to me was that, the fraud exposed, the opposition
campaign did not withdraw it

Things of this type were going on across the country. The old rule of
thumb among many political professionals was not to dignify charges of this
type with an answer. Some consultants even believed that answering a fraudu-
lent charge gave it additional currency. Many Senators and House members
followed this time honored wisdom. The only trouble was that a lie, so often
repeated and unanswered, sometimes is believed. My own strategy was to run

a clean campaign and not answer charges of this type personally, but to enlist credible witnesses in the community to respond.

My campaign raised and spent $654,000—about three times the amount I'd ever spent in any previous election. Bradshaw's campaign listed $530,000 in contributions, including some lent by the candidate himself, but this figure excluded very substantial amounts spent by NCPAC and other so-called "independent" purchasers of ads, circulars, and media commercials. An analyst calculated that very close to $1 million was spent in the effort to defeat me.

On November 4, we had the largest voter turnout in the history of our county. I received 61.4 percent of the total vote to Bradshaw's 38.6 percent. At the same time, however, Ronald Reagan carried my district by a 56 percent majority and the nation by 51 percent to 41 percent for Carter and 7 percent for independent candidate John Anderson. Democrats lost the Senate and, while holding onto our House majority, suffered surprising losses among our senior and most influential members. NCPAC and the Moral Majority took a deadly toll of senior senators. In all, nine lost their seats to Republican challengers. Four of the six targeted by NCPAC were defeated, and five of the six marked for extinction by Reverend Jerry Falwell. Those five—former presidential nominee George McGovern of South Dakota, Frank Church of Idaho, John Culver of Iowa, Birch Bayh of Indiana, and Gaylord Nelson of Wisconsin—all had been considered favorites early in the year. In fact, Alan Cranston of California was the only Democratic senator publicly targeted by both organizations to survive.

In the House, we suffered surprising losses, while holding our majority. The GOP gained a net of thirty-three seats, winning thirty-seven victories in districts we had held, while Democrats picked up only four districts from Republican hands. This was the largest numerical increase for the Republicans since 1966. Among Democratic losses were John Brademas of Indiana, the Whip, and House Ways and Means Committee Chairman Al Ullman of Oregon. Harold Johnson of California, Chairman of Public Works and Transportation; Jim Corman of California, Chairman of the Democratic Congressional Campaign Committee; Lud Ashley of Ohio, Chairman of the Banking Subcommittee; and Lionel Van Deerlin of California, Communications Subcommittee Chair, rounded out the list.

Mo Udall of Arizona and I seemed to be the only House Democrats targeted for a full-court press who survived. Knowing we'd have a new president and a Republican Senate with which to contend, I had several long talks with Speaker O'Neill about how we'd handle the situation. The people had spoken, and we both felt it our responsibility to help the new president adjust to the Washington scene. We were determined to give him every bit of assistance we could short of sacrificing deeply held principles and convictions. There was much he didn't know about the federal government and its programs. Tip and I saw ourselves in similar roles to those of Rayburn and Johnson when Eisenhower became president. They helped him craft domestic as well as international policies. Were we in for a shock!

CHAPTER TWENTY-SEVEN

EMERGENCE OF
THE GREAT
COMMUNICATOR

onald Reagan dropped by the Capitol one early December day, maybe a month after his election. It was a courtesy call, he said, "just to get acquainted." His manner was relaxed and friendly, his amiable informality both charming and disarming. Tip and I sat for an hour or so in the Speaker's office with the president-elect, exchanging stories. Reagan was a gifted raconteur, and we let him lead the conversation in whatever direction he chose. He told stories about his days in the movies, and there was a long series of tales relating to his research into the life and times of the ill-starred Notre Dame football hero, George Gipp, the celebrated "Gipper," whose character Reagan played for the 1940 film *Knute Rockne: All American.*

Reagan was fun to be around, O'Neill and I would agree later, so long as the subject did not deal with public policy. Reagan was an entertainer, a super salesman, an enjoyable companion with a ready sense of humor, but his grasp of issues, and of history, was superficial. Tip sat behind a large desk which, he explained to the president, had once belonged to Grover Cleveland. "I played him once in a movie," Reagan said. "No, Mr. President," Tip gently corrected, "you played Grover Cleveland Alexander, the baseball player."

Just a year into Reagan's first term, the veteran newsman Lou Cannon, who had covered the Californian for years and would write a biography of him, sighed following a Reagan press conference of January 19, 1982: "More disquieting than Reagan's performance or prospects on any specific issue is a growing suspicion that the president has only a passing acquaintance with some of the most important issues of his administration." The Speaker and I

were at first appalled, as were others on Capitol Hill, with our new president's lack of information and surfeit of misinformation on matters so basic
his self-deceptions dumfounded us. But Tip O'Neill and I were victims of
wishful thinking to imagine we could show the popular chief executive that
some of his preconceptions were in error, or moderate his more extreme
views, or halt his crippling assaults upon popular and effective domestic programs. We may have qualified as skilled and practiced legislators. We knew
our way around the Capitol, to be sure. But the popular old thespian showed
us things we'd never dreamed about passing laws. To put it bluntly, we two
old pros got rolled.

Reagan was a superb showman. He had a feel for the dramatic, knew how
to play the lead role in a performance, and how to play upon his listeners'
emotions. Changing the time-honored location of presidential inaugurals,
he moved the 1981 event from the Capitol's east front to the more scenic
and grandiloquent west front, elevated high above the spacious Capitol
grounds and looking out upon the city, the great monuments and Arlington
National Cemetery visible on the gentle Virginia hillside beyond the
Lincoln Memorial.

The January 20 inaugural speech itself was schmaltzy, full of inspirational
homilies, but lacking in substance. Listening, I knew that a lot of people
would love it. I heard Reagan's voice soar aloft on wings of rhetoric, as he
spoke of heroes and decried the idea that there were no more. "They just don't
know where to look. You can see heroes every day going in and out of factory
gates . . . you meet heroes across the counter . . . their patriotism is quiet but
deep. Their values sustain our national life. . . . I am addressing the heroes of
whom I speak—you, the citizens of this blessed land." As a student of oratory,
I drank it in as opera fans must once have thrilled to hear Enrico Caruso. But
then came passages so trite that they made me cringe. "Government is not the
solution to our problem," Reagan intoned. "Government is the problem." I
had heard that hackneyed line for thirty years at small town Rotary Clubs.
Reagan must have used it often during his years on the carrots-and-green-
peas circuit. "We are a nation that has a government—not the other way
around," he now declaimed. It bothered me faintly to hear such banal phrases
among the polished prose of a presidential inaugural address. What purpose
could these glib dismissals serve other than to denigrate the very institutions
of American government, hallowed by heroes' blood, which Ronald Reagan
now took the oath to lead and direct?

One comment from the campaign trail returned to mind. "I used to fanta-
size," Reagan had said, "what it would be like if everyone in government
would quietly slip away and close the doors and disappear. See how long it
would take the people of this country to miss them. . . . We would get along a

lot better than we think." Did he really believe this? I wondered now. Had exhibiting contempt for our government somehow gotten confused with an act of patriotism?

Next came Reagan's standard theme on the national debt. "For decades we have piled deficit upon deficit, mortgaging our future and our children's future for the temporary pleasures of the present," Reagan was saying. "To continue this long trend is to guarantee tremendous social, cultural, political, and economic upheaval." I'd heard this, too, from childhood, in scores of stump speeches. I endorsed its basic truth, in fact had tried to set us on a course of making payments on the national debt. I wondered, listening now, if Reagan knew the last balanced budget was under Lyndon Johnson. I hoped he was actually serious about paying as we go, but I knew absolutely that it couldn't be done by cutting taxes while raising military spending.

The speech was followed by a luncheon in Statuary Hall, where, wanting desperately to like and respect our new president, I tried to shake the cobwebs of doubt from my brain. I was seated at a table with Mrs. Edith Davis, Nancy Reagan's mother, and found that dear lady a delightful respite from political platitudes. Mrs. Davis told how a young Secret Service agent assigned to her protection during the inaugural had walked accidentally into her bedroom just as she had stepped from her bath, totally nude, and was fanning herself with a towel. Observing the young agent's shock and embarrassment, she had said: "Now, young man, see what you have done! Until now, Dr. Davis was the only man ever to see me in the buff. And now, Sir, you will have to marry me!"

My faith was renewed. I could like a man with a mother-in-law like that. And what a phenomenal stroke of incredible good luck! As the luncheon was ending, we learned that the fifty-two American hostages so long held by the Iranian theocracy were free at last and on their way to Washington. It was not Reagan's doing, of course. He had hardly been president for an hour. Tedious negotiations had been under way for weeks. Khomeini, as a final parting indignity to President Carter, deliberately delayed the release until after Carter's successor was sworn in. Later, people would suggest the possibility that Reagan emissaries in some surreptitious preelection meeting with Khomeini, had conspired with the Iranian leader to prevent the hostages' freeing on Carter's watch. I never believed that. Khomeini simply despised Carter and didn't want any credit to inure to him. Now the country bathed in a wave of nonpartisan rejoicing.

On February 6, Reagan's seventieth birthday, Nancy Reagan invited a bipartisan group of House leaders to an impromptu surprise celebration in the White House. She had ordered an enormous, multitiered birthday cake, whose candle on the tallest tier was higher than she could reach. Someone suggested turning the job over to the tallest man in the room, but Nancy wanted to light the candle. I suggested that House Republican leader Bob Michel and I each kneel on one knee, and invited Mrs. Reagan to use our other knees as a step stool, giving her maybe two extra feet of height, enough to light the candle. With polite sputterings about "how gallant," she complied, and the candle took flame. "Who says we can't be bipartisan?" someone exclaimed.

I hoped that we could be—in the broader field of policy. On the previous day, February 5, Reagan had delivered a major economic policy address. It set forth the features of a program he said he was sending to Congress. He proposed budget cuts in virtually every department of government—all except the military, which he wanted to increase. He also proposed a 10 percent reduction in personal income tax rates for each of the next three years. Wow! That troubled me. A cut in *rates*, I reflected, would clearly benefit the wealthy most of all. And a 30 percent cut in three years! What would that do to deficits?

On February 15, on *Meet the Press*, a reporter asked me to evaluate the beginnings of the Reagan presidency. Hoping to influence our new chief executive into a more moderate direction, I consciously refrained from harsh criticism. Every new president deserves a honeymoon. "I very much want the president to succeed, because I want our country to succeed," I began.

"Will you be opposed to some of the president's proposed budget cuts?" the reporter pressed. He was tying to draw me into an early public fight with Reagan. It's too soon for that, I thought. I tried a conciliatory approach. If I was to influence this man, I owed him certain courtesies. Congress always made certain alterations in presidential proposals, I pointed out. "I don't want to see this become a bona fide confrontation," I said. "I'd much rather see a bipartisan effort by which Congress and those in the administration work together to find ways to make our system more efficient."

But on the day following this interview an article by David Montgomery appeared on the front page of the *Fort Worth Star-Telegram* promoting an open fight between me and the president. The headline read "Democrats 'Building Wall' to Guard Social Programs." Conflict makes news, I knew. I was beginning to realize it would be harder than I had thought to cultivate and keep a friendly relationship.

President Reagan addressed a joint session of Congress on February 18, delineating a four-point proposal. His plan called for cutting domestic government spending; reducing taxes so enormously as to outpace any possible cuts in domestic programs; reforming and eliminating the maze of government regulations; and encouraging a monetary policy, never quite clearly explained, to maintain the value of the currency. During this speech, Reagan criticized interest rates. "Interest rates have reached absurd levels of more than 20 percent, and over 15 percent for those who would borrow to buy a home," he said. The fact was that borrowing rates during the final few months of the Carter administration did rise briefly to double digits, due to policies followed by Federal Reserve Chairman Paul Volcker. We did not then know that average interest charges during the first four years of the Reagan administration would remain substantially higher than the average rates under Carter. Real interest rates (the difference between the prime rate and the rate of inflation) would elevate to the highest in history. I don't believe news commentators ever focused on this fact. I know the public did not.

In the most dramatic flair of his presentation, the president made reference to the national debt, which he said equated to a stack of one-thousand-dollar bills sixty-seven miles high. Nobody dreamed that Reagan's own policies would lead, by the same reckoning, to a stack two hundred miles high by the time he left office. The national debt stood at $940 billion on the day Ronald Reagan took office. That was the cumulative result of our almost two hundred-year history—thirty-nine presidential administrations, a civil war, two world wars, Korea and Vietnam, the Great Depression, and eight or more generations of periodic economic crises and alarms. In the next eight years, we would add more than twice and almost three times as much as had been amassed in the previous two centuries!

Following Reagan's February 15 speech, an NBC reporter asked me what I found missing in the president's program. I gave a brief summary of things missing: any credible plan beyond rhetoric to reduce the national debt, any dynamic approach to make America energy independent, any commitment to putting the unemployed to work, any definite plan to bring down exorbitant interest rates, any effort to improve education and job training, any specifics on his claimed "safety net" to protect the poor from future hurt.

Several of the president's public comments were making it harder for people who believed in a strong social commitment to find common ground with him. On February 20, a story in the Philadelphia *Evening Bulletin* cited Reagan as pondering a *voluntary* form of Social Security. "I've been wondering if you couldn't reform the system in such a way that, if you could prove you are providing for your retirement, you could *waive* participating in Social Security," the president was quoted. In other words, let the rich folks out, relieve them of paying into the trust fund. I couldn't imagine a more certain way to bankrupt the system.

A month had passed since the inaugural ceremony. I did not agree with major aspects of Reagan's program, but I liked our new president personally, assumed him educable in budgetary realities, took at face value his repeated entreaties to "bipartisan" cooperation, assumed him serious about the national debt, and supposed he could be brought around once we got him to focus on the drastic effect his combination of plans could have on that debt. I still looked forward to working *with* him.

Reagan had sailed in on a great wave of hope. For several weeks the mail that most of us in Congress received from our districts ran almost thirty to one in favor of doing what this gifted communicator wanted. But, slowly, in March, people began to see a few holes in the web of oversimplification. Most of those who found a promise of reduced taxes alluring didn't understand the exact nature of the so-called Kemp-Roth tax cut. Named for its sponsors, Representative Jack Kemp of New York and Senator William Roth of Delaware, it now was being backed by Reagan. Unrecognized by the public, that plan portended a substantial increase in the deficit, due to the huge losses of revenue that would occur if Congress should adopt it. Publications such as *Business Week* dubbed Kemp-Roth highly deficit prone as well as unfair. The plan would shower tax benefits upon those at the top of the economic ladder, giving little by way of a tax cut to working people on the lower wage-earning rungs. Supporters argued that the wealthiest would invest their windfalls in job-creating endeavors, while people lacking wealth wouldn't. This was the heart of the "trickle down" theory: If lawmakers pile up enough benefits for the few at the top, some of it will naturally "trickle down" to those at the bottom. It put me in mind of the biblical story of Dives and Lazarus, in which the beggar received permission to sit at the foot of the table and sustain himself on the crumbs that fell from the lavish banquet above.

During March, the bipartisan leadership of Congress met twice at the White House with President Reagan. Senate Minority Leader Robert Byrd, Speaker O'Neill, and I each had additional occasion for private discussion with the president. What we heard disturbed us. When we presented data that conflicted with his preconception, the president would simply suspend belief. He quoted sometimes from *Human Events* bulletins—homiletic reinforcements of right-wing ideology published in limited-circulation newsletters—as though they were infallible truth. Once Reagan insisted that more than half the money appropriated by government for worthy causes never even reached its intended beneficiaries. Most of it, he contended, was siphoned off through "waste, fraud, and abuse." We were dumbfounded. "Where do you get an idea like that, Mr. President?" Tip asked incredulously. The president smiled, "You forget, Tip, I've been dealing with these figures for years on the lecture circuit."

Reagan was a positive thinker and a true believer. These traits, which could be endearing in a companion, might be dangerous in a president. They closed his mind to any possibility of conceptual error. Reagan actually thought any act of cutting upper-income-bracket taxes would automatically result in greater revenues for the treasury. This was a theory faddish at the time among some conservatives theorists and known as the Laffer Curve, for its principal proponent, an economist named George Laffer. Reagan bought it hook, line, and sinker. Once he said, "the additional revenues gained from the tax cut will help us finance our military buildup." It boggled the mind.

The House Budget Committee had to deal with realities, not theories. Under the chairmanship of Oklahoma Congressman Jim Jones, and with my input from the leadership, we worked diligently through March to find just the right combination of reasonable budget cuts to move credibly in the direction of Reagan's frequently repeated pledge of a balanced budget by 1983. This could not be done, we saw, if we granted all of the chief executive's rather grandiose requests for a huge buildup in military spending.

Reagan's budget submission, in harmony with the president's personality, was characterized by dangerously wishful positive thinking. Professional economists in the Congressional Budget Office (CBO) were horrified. The White House forecasts projected such unrealistically low levels of unemployment, inflation, and probable interest rates that they skewed the deficit likely to result from the sum of the president's requests downward by $20 billion to $25 billion, according to CBO. When we showed the study to the president, he angrily labeled it as "phony." And in a public meeting with women members of Congress, who expressed their concern over the effects of Reagan's proposed budget cuts on the poor, the president blamed "bureaucrats" for "distorting" his intention.

The president believed, among other things, that most food stamp recipients were cheating on the program. He told stories about people driving up to grocery stores in "big Cadillac cars," filling up grocery baskets with food-stamp purchases, and driving away. One anecdote involved a woman who, he said, had bought a lime with a five-dollar food stamp, taken the change in cash, and used the cash to buy a bottle of gin. Tom Foley, who had served as Chairman of the Agriculture Committee, the group that drafted and oversaw the food-stamp law, explained that such a scenario could not lawfully occur. The merchant would have been in legal violation to have permitted it. Reagan gave no sign of being reassured, or of questioning his acceptance of the anecdote. He continued telling it.

On March 18, the Gallup Poll showed Reagan, two months after his inauguration, had a disapproval rating of 24 percent. That was at least fifteen points higher than the number of people expressing outright disapproval of any of his four immediate predecessors at the same point in their first terms. Fifty-nine percent, however, approved of the president's overall record.

Twelve days later, public perceptions and American political reality would undergo a cataclysmic change. On March 30, 1981, a mentally unbalanced young man named John Hinckley, carrying a concealed handgun, lay in wait outside the Washington Hilton hotel and shot President Reagan in the upper chest.

On Monday morning, March 30, following a busy weekend in Texas, I was hoping to catch a noon plane back to Washington. I'd promised first to stop off in downtown Fort Worth for a ceremony dedicating a new city park and a historic marker to commemorate the site of President John F. Kennedy's speech to an outdoor crowd on November 22, 1963. Vice President George Bush and I spoke at the dedication.

The vice president asked if I'd like a ride back to Washington with him on the presidential plane. I happily accepted. Bush and I, friends from the days he served in the House, hadn't had many recent opportunities to visit privately. We heard the news of the assassination attempt on Reagan en route to Austin. The vice president had been scheduled to address the Texas legislature before returning to the nation's capital. Dazed by the news and not certain from early accounts how critically the president was wounded, Bush made an immediate decision to scrub the Austin appearance and return with minimum delay to Washington. Since Governor Bill Clements was awaiting our arrival at the Austin airport, however, the vice president gave orders to land the plane, stop it on a remote runway, and send word for the Governor to drive by car to board the aircraft and accept our apologies for the sudden change in plans.

Following the first startling shock, Bush quickly gained composure and calmly took command. I was impressed with his steadiness and decisiveness. We were receiving continuous radio updates from the White House. We knew soon that the president had not been mortally wounded, was undergoing surgery for removal of the bullet, and was diagnosed to recover without any physical impairment. (We would learn later that the location of the bullet posed a greater potential danger to Reagan's life than originally reported.) Word also came to us of a minor brouhaha over Secretary of State Alexander Haig's assertion of command at the White House. At 4:15 eastern time, the former general had declared, "I am in control here at the White House." Bush and I discussed it. Knowing Haig personally, we both put it down to his military training. By announcing he was in charge in the vice president's absence and had things well in hand, Al was trying to reassure the public that all was well and there was no reason to panic. Unfortunately for Haig, his statement had the reverse effect. It alarmed people. Folks who didn't know Al Haig thought him brash, presumptuous, possibly even dangerous. He may not, even today, have lived down that unfortunate impression. In point of fact, Haig was not constitutionally third in command, as he seemed to believe. Speaker O'Neill would have been. Bush made what I considered a very wise decision. Instead of going directly to the White House, which might have raised alarms about the president's condition or have been misinterpreted as petty resentment of Haig's overstatement, the vice president decided to be driven to his official residence on Massachusetts Avenue.

Reagan demonstrated an abundance of grace under fire. His conduct befit a president. The seventy-year-old Reagan walked into the hospital under his own power, engaging in friendly, humorous banter. He joked to his wife that he "forgot to duck." In the operating room, the president quipped to his surgeons, "please tell me you're Republicans." Thus a wounded president reassured the American people. His countrymen saw his conduct under stress as that of an essentially good and decent man—a person of overriding good humor and instinctive goodwill. Reagan's popularity immediately rose eleven percentage points.

Ronald Reagan was, as has been noted by others, the quintessential actor. Wholly unlike Jimmy Carter, he didn't even try to master details of programs. Factual data bored him. He didn't like to discuss it. He wanted his cabinet people and aides to work up position papers. A gifted wordsmith named Peggy Noonan would weave them into a beguiling speech. Then, when readied with a script, a smiling Ronald Reagan appeared on television to perform a masterful job of salesmanship.

David Stockman was Reagan's first Budget Director. He was the administration's Svengali of supply-side economics. He was thin, wiry, ascetic-looking, with prematurely graying hair, and teeth that did not quite join one another. He seldom smiled. It was Stockman's arithmetic that encouraged Reagan in his boldest economic ventures. Stockman would say later, in an interview with William Greider of *Atlantic Monthly*, that the arithmetic was carved to fit Reagan's answers. I had known David when he served in the House as a doctrinaire conservative, always glib and sure of himself, never admitting to the possibility of error. He had tried, unsuccessfully, to disrupt elements of President Carter's energy program. Stockman had undergone several metamorphoses in his personal loyalties and ideological attachments. As a college student in Michigan, he opposed the war in Vietnam. He avoided service by becoming a divinity student and gaining admission to Harvard. While there, Stockman admired the politics of Pat Moynihan, the New York Democrat. Pat took Stockman under his wing, making him a protege of sorts. Once in Washington, Stockman allied himself with John Anderson, the moderately liberal Republican. Anderson employed Stockman to serve as an aide to the Republican Conference of which

Anderson was chairman. But when his benefactor ran for president in 1980, Stockman found it convenient to abandon him, attaching himself instead to the Reagan bandwagon. He personally helped Reagan prepare for his debate against Anderson.

Stockman seemed to me a bright fellow, self-centered, extremely Machiavellian, and willing to switch loyalties wherever it best served him. Once in the Reagan White House, he lectured the nation's college students that they could manage, given enough spirit and determination, to attend college without depending on low-interest government loans. His and Reagan's budget featured sharp cuts in all such loans and grants, reinforced by harsh rhetoric about student loan defaults. It developed, however, that Stockman himself had depended on just such a low-interest government loan to graduate from college, a loan he made no effort to pay back for thirteen years.

On April 9 the House Budget Committee, after weeks of careful work, endorsed an alternative to Reagan's proposed budget. I felt we had done an excellent job. We scaled back the president's proposed tax cut and reprieved from the hangman's noose some of the programs we believed vital to the future of America—things like job training, student loans, and nutritional services for infants and elderly. We approved important increases in defense spending, but not as much as Reagan had wanted. Significantly, we came out with a bottom line deficit substantially lower than the Reagan-Stockman deficit. Their's came to $47 billion in new debt for the coming year, ours to $19 billion.

To the surprise of some and disappointment of many, President Reagan, recovering nicely ten days after his operation, flatly refused to compromise. Even some Republicans were dismayed. Senator Bob Dole, among others, had expressed reservations about the Kemp-Roth tax cuts. It was my surmise that Stockman had told the president to hold out and insist on having his way on the entire budget in a manner no previous chief executive—neither Roosevelt nor Johnson—had ever employed. I would learn to my chagrin and deep personal sorrow that another also had encouraged Reagan to pursue an all-or-nothing course. He was a beneficiary of my help and recipient of my naive faith. His name was Phil Gramm.

Gramm was a second-term member from College Station, Texas. Two years earlier, he had won a hair-thin primary victory to fill the House vacancy opened by Olin Teague's retirement. Prior to that he once had run, quite unsuccessfully, against U.S. Senator Lloyd Bentsen. A college professor at Texas A & M, Phil was interested academically in the budget process. During his first term, he and I had discussed ways to ensure an annual balance, including an adaptation of the automatic budget board system employed by the State of Texas. Half way into each fiscal year, a midterm analysis would determine whether income and outgo would come out even, under current spending and taxing levels, at year's end. If spending exceeded income, then the president at that point would be ordered by law to curtail every discretionary expenditure in the budget by the same fixed percent necessary to guarantee a balanced budget at year's end.

As 1981 began, Phil made known his desire to serve on the House Budget Committee. But he was not popular with members of the Democratic Steering and Policy Committee, whose job it was to make committee nominations. Peering owlishly through bifocaled glasses, Phil had a tendency to lecture colleagues as though they were errant or slow-witted students. He and Kent Hance, another second-termer from Texas, were repeatedly passed over on successive balloting rounds, Gramm in his bid to serve on the Budget Committee and Hance in his request for assignment to Ways and Means. Each had flaked off on several tough votes in the previous congress, Steering Committee members felt, and they didn't consider either very dependable.

Both came to me pleading for my help. I explained to each that these particular assignments were choice plums reserved for colleagues on whom the Democratic caucus could count when the chips were down. Both promised earnestly to be team players. They vowed to stick with the leadership on major issues involving those committees. Both authorized me to convey that pledge to the Steering and Policy Committee.

Hance said his West Texas constituency was accustomed to being represented by a responsible team member. Hance's longtime predecessor, George Mahon, had been chairman of the House Appropriations Committee. "People understood why Mr. Mahon had to stick with the leadership," Hance acknowledged, "If I can just show them I have an important committee, too, they'll be proud enough to back me up, even if I have to make some tough, hard votes. You can count on it, Mr. Leader. If I can get on Ways and Means, I'll be your most loyal member." Phil Gramm promised me, and others, in January that, if he were favored by a Budget Committee assignment, he would make his arguments within the committee and then would close ranks and back whatever budget resolution the committee majority approved. That sounded fair enough. I hoped he could contribute something. A relic of the old Texas school that values a handshake over a gilt-edged bond, I took each at his word.

I would feel absolutely betrayed when they became the only two Democratic members of either committee to desert on the two big battles that so dominantly set the nation's budgetary course for the next fifteen years.

While Speaker O'Neill was on an overseas trip during the Easter congressional recess, President Reagan reached him by telephone with a special request. He was almost fully recovered, the president said, and would like to make a personal appearance before Congress to thank all of America for its prayers and good wishes. He also might like to say a word or two about economic matters. O'Neill, never suspecting a frontal assault on the leadership's budget resolution, readily assented to Reagan's request. The nation would rejoice, Tip knew, to see their president looking hale and hearty. Thus it was that on April 28, the virtual eve of the scheduled House debate on the budget resolution for the coming fiscal year, Reagan spoke to Congress in a dramatic prime time session.

Reagan, cloaked in a mantle of heroism, thanked people heartily for their support during his hospitalization. Then he moved rapidly to the heart of his subject:

> The House will soon be choosing between two different versions or measures to deal with the economy. One is the measure offered by the House Budget Committee. The other is a bipartisan measure, a substitute introduced by Congressman Phil Gramm of Texas and Del Latta of Ohio.
>
> On behalf of the Administration, let me say that we embrace and fully support that bipartisan substitute . . .
>
> These policies will make our economy stronger and the stronger economy will balance the budget which we are committed to do by 1984.

I'd had a warning some days before. As Budget Committee Democrats met for a final skull session prior to going to the floor with the resolution, there was real enthusiasm. It was like a final football drill before the big game. Everyone felt we had an excellent package to present, well, almost everyone. I made the usual appeal for all committeemen to stay on the floor during debate to answer questions from others, then looked around the group for assent. All but one agreed with alacrity. Finally, Phil Gramm said, "Well, I don't want you to think that you can necessarily have my support on the House floor."

I was nonplussed. Flabbergasted!

"But, Phil, that's exactly what you *promised* to give. You said you'd make your arguments inside the committee and then support the bill produced by the committee majority!"

"Oh, you misunderstood me, Jim," replied Phil. "I meant I would support whatever was produced by a majority in the Committee of the Whole."

Everybody in the room groaned. That pledge meant nothing. To support what the whole House finally agreed upon would be empty. It would be like trying to defeat your own team, but promising to wish it well after the game and rejoin it if it won. Then I learned that Phil had been slipping out regularly following budget committee sessions for clandestine meetings with David Stockman. Gramm and Stockman had strategized about how to counter and defeat the Democratic budget. There even were meetings with the president, in which Phil had bargained for a bigger role in upsetting committee plans. Secretly he had agreed to lend his name as cosponsor of an alternate budget. If Reagan could name one Democrat, he could advertise a new option as a *bipartisan* plan. So it happened that the single, junior-most Democrat among eighteen on the House Budget Committee became the lone deserter and linked up with the ranking Republican, Delbert Latta of Ohio, as putative cosponsors of a yet-to-be written substitute to be backed by Reagan. Gramm insisted his name be first. So it was called *Gramm-Latta*. Nobody knew just what would be in it.

Now, listening to the president's April 28 speech for clues, I heard nothing definitive about Gramm-Latta. But I heard the committee budget, our careful work of the past several weeks, downgraded and denounced.

Our committee budget, the president told America, would cut $14 billion in "essential" defense spending. Not so. Truth was that our budget contained proposed *increases* in defense appropriations of approximately 22 percent above the previous year's—the biggest peacetime increase in the country's history.

Astounded at the brazen claims coming from the president's lips, I seethed with increasing outrage as I listened to our chief executive address the nation that night. Our budget, Reagan brashly asserted, "projects spending $141 billion more" than the administration-favored plan. Absurd! Who possibly could have so grossly misinformed the president? The House committee budget projected total spending at a level slightly *under* that of the Reagan budget proposal sent earlier to Congress.

The winsome, pleasant-featured chief executive warned his listeners that the Democratic plan favored by the committee "would increase tax payments by over a third, adding up to a staggering quarter of a trillion dollars." American taxpayers, he said, would be "paying a larger share of their income" to the government in 1984 than at present, if our budget were adopted. Federal taxes, he claimed, "would increase 12 percent each year." Preposterous!

Ignoring the simple fact that our committee budget reduced the projected deficit to less than half that which would result from the original Reagan-Stockman submission, the president threw in an offhand comment about current polling which showed that most Americans, "with the common sense that characterizes the people of this country," would prefer a balanced budget to a tax cut. Yet the plan Reagan had been proposing featured a whopping 30 percent income tax rate cut over the next three years. His apparent explanation: "The answer to a government that is too big is to stop feeding its growth."

There he stood, in the House chamber at the Speaker's invitation, supposedly there to thank the nation for its moral support during his physical crisis, grotesquely misrepresenting the plans of the House leadership to an adoring American public. After verbally ripping apart our product and holding it up to scorn, he smiled sweetly and in saccharin voice implored, "Tonight I renew my call for us to work as a team, to join in cooperation so that we can find answers. . . . I think the bipartisan substitute bill has achieved that purpose."

Nobody knew exactly what would be in the so-called *bipartisan* plan. But the people were sold on it. Telegrams and long distance calls began pouring in over the Capitol switchboard.

Immediately, I sent telegrams to each of the networks, asking that Democratic leaders of Congress have a chance to present our side of this issue, including facts that had been so grossly distorted. I asked, in the interest of fairness and equity, that networks let us appear at the same hour the following night. Not one complied. It is not surprising, therefore, that the American people responded in overwhelming numbers. They didn't know our deficit would be smaller under the committee's bill. They didn't know we actually would increase military spending, not decrease it. They didn't know we hadn't proposed to raise their taxes or that the president's Kemp-Roth plan would largely favor the very wealthy. They couldn't know David Stockman would later write in his memoir, "It was the Democratic budget, in fact, that should have won. . . . It included no deep tax cut like Kemp-Roth."

And so, as happens in a democratic society, the Gramm-Latta budget substitute prevailed. I would learn later that a highly sophisticated network of conservative public relations professionals across the country was helping to manufacture a grass-roots letter writing campaign in behalf of the Gramm-Latta budget. A man named Joseph Baroody and his firm, Wagner & Baroody, had been privately hired to orchestrate a nationwide deluge of mail to Congress. But that takes nothing from the articulate salesmanship of Ronald Reagan. He convinced the American people, and they convinced Congress.

The substitute called for reductions in spending of some $35 billion in all and targeted those cuts among social programs of several sorts. In a speech on the floor, Gramm had said, "Make no mistake about it, we are shooting real bullets." I had replied, "The question is: At whom are we shooting? Who are our targets?"

The basic Reagan-Stockman plan aimed its gun at those least able to get out of the way—the most needy in our society. Funds for the school lunch program suffered such a big cut, in fact, that administrators had to come up with new nutritional criteria. Instead of eight ounces of milk a day, a child would receive four ounces. Catsup was counted as a vegetable, tofu classified as meat. When a public outcry arose among parents, Stockman argued that these results had not been intended. The decisions were, he said, a bureaucratic snafu.

The Republican-dominated Senate, predictably, followed suit, passing Reagan's budget resolution. Defeated in our first clash with the popular president, Democratic leaders regrouped. We determined to make the best of a bad situation, hoping we could sew enough patches on Reagan's promised "safety net" to make it less shreddable than our own ranks had been. We needed patches on them too. There'd be other battles ahead.

CHAPTER TWENTY-EIGHT

REAGAN'S REVOLUTION

T he Gramm-Latta budget was only the first of three major losses the Democratic leadership would suffer at the hands of President Reagan and his eager followers in 1981. Before that crucial year ended, significant portions of the American social agenda would be set back to pre-Johnson, some would say pre-Roosevelt, days. New taxing and spending policies, sold as part of an "economic recovery" plan, began a dramatic widening of the gap between the richest and poorest segments of American society. President Reagan's unquestioning faith in the efficacy of huge tax cuts for America's economic elite while doubling military spending would set up history's most dramatic deficits and the swift, apparently irreversible tripling of our national debt. Events of that year would cast long shadows into America's future.

For the two months following adoption of Gramm-Latta, House committees worked diligently to fulfill the dollar mandates of that budget. Prevailing law required the standing legislative committees, after the adoption of a budget resolution, to make specific adjustments in programs under their respective jurisdictions sufficient to reach the bottom line figures mandated by that budget document. All these amendatory changes were then gathered into a common package known as the Reconciliation Bill. The budget was only a skeleton; the Reconciliation Bill was flesh and blood.

Short days after our dismal defeat on the budget resolution, Speaker O'Neill called a meeting of House committee chairs. To each he gave a deadline, with a clear instruction to make the cuts called for in Gramm-Latta. For some senior committee members, making these painful choices—cutting programs they believed in—was almost like amputating their own toes. But the House Committees faithfully fulfilled the duties assigned to them. The composite of their work, joined together in the Reconciliation Bill that June, reduced expenditures not just by the $35.5 billion commanded by the Gramm-Latta budget resolution, but by $37 billion. In at least half the cases, decisions were bipartisan. Republican leader Bob Michel and I discussed the general degree of bipartisanship we saw going into the Reconciliation Bill. Neither of us knew at that time that David Stockman and a small group in the White House were working with Phil Gramm to undo the entire package.

We should have suspected that another secret plan was being hatched. Gramm and other Democrats who had joined him in upsetting the leadership's budget were meeting regularly and issuing press releases boasting of their devotion to Reagan's "economic recovery plan." They regularly attacked governmental "waste, fraud and abuse" and vowed to root it out. The most vocal leaders of the cabal were Gramm and Charles Stenholm, another second termer from Texas. It seemed passingly strange to me that these two in particular would be as hostile as they seemed toward government activity in general. Stenholm before his election to Congress had been manager of a Rural Electrification cooperative. That program was a success story, a fine example of government activism. Prior to the REA, fewer than 10 percent of America's farm families had the benefit of electric power. Now, because of that program, more than 90 percent of all farms enjoyed its labor saving boon. Gramm, throughout his entire life, had been a consistent personal beneficiary of taxpayer-supported programs. Born in a military hospital, Phil had grown up on military bases, sustained by his father's pay as a master sergeant, attended a military high school on his father's government insurance, gone through college on federal grants and loans while less favored ones of his generation were serving in Vietnam, and, in his only career prior to Congress, had received his salary from Texas A & M University, a taxpayer-supported federal land-grant institution. Now, Phil became the self-appointed nemesis of "big government."

Reagan worked diligently during May and June, aided by Gramm, Stenholm and others, to woo as many Democratic members into his economic tent as possible. On June 4 he held a closed-door meeting with maverick Democrats, pleading with them to desert the Democratic leadership and join him on the tax bill and other undisclosed initiatives. He promised that neither he nor the national Republican apparatus would campaign against the reelection of any Democrat who voted with him. "I could not oppose someone who supported my principles," he pledged. "I could not look myself in the mirror."

On Sunday, June 7, Speaker O'Neill, answering questions on ABC's *Issues and Answers,* assailed the president's tax cut proposal. It favored the wealthy, O'Neill explained. Emphasizing his own working-class background, the Speaker said that Reagan simply "doesn't understand the working class, middle America . . . and what they go through. . . . He doesn't associate himself with that type of people." A few days later, in a June 16 press conference, the president lashed out at the Speaker, accusing O'Neill of "sheer demagoguery." The next day, June 17, Reagan called the Speaker and invited him to the White House for a personal tête-à-tête. Without apologizing for his outburst of the day before, the president schmoozed and exchanged stories with the Speaker. Afterward, he told the press that the two had "a good relationship." O'Neill said, "We may disagree during the day, but six P.M., we become friends."

On June 19, the Friday before the Tuesday on which the reconciliation bill was scheduled for debate in the House, Speaker O'Neill received a surprise call from the president. Reagan asked if the Speaker would allow his—Reagan's—amendment to our reconciliation bill to be considered in whole on a single up or down vote.

O'Neill was mystified. "Why, Mr. President," he stammered, "I was not aware that you *had* an amendment. This is very uncustomary. Tell me what your amendment is—what is in it?"

"Well, I am not just sure," replied the president. "You can get that from David Stockman."

The Speaker was becoming irritated. No previous president had ever called about a matter so internal to the House as the rule for dividing or uniting an amendment for voting purposes. And Reagan seemed to have no idea what his amendment contained.

"I don't really know David Stockman," the Speaker told Reagan. "I haven't heard a word from Bob Michel about any Republican substitute. He's your House Republican leader. He is the one I usually deal with on matters of this kind. Just basically, what is in your proposal?"

"Well, Tip, I'll tell you what you can do," the president said. "You can get it from Jim Jones, because David Stockman gave it to him today."

President Reagan obviously had something new up his sleeve, but he didn't appear to have the faintest notion, or want to tell us, on the Friday before the vote, just what his amendment would contain.

So the Speaker called me, Budget Committee Chairman Jim Jones, and Bob Michel into his office to discuss this development. Michel, the House Republican leader responsible for legislative consultations with the Speaker, was as bewildered as the rest of us. He was wholly unaware of the existence of any such amendment, let alone what it might consist of. What Stockman had handed Jones that day was not an amendment, it turned out, but a one page summary of new ideas favored by the president's budget director. Those ideas included cutting food stamps by several billion dollars over a three-year period; reducing Social Security payments by $7 billion in the next three years; slashing Medicare and Medicaid payments by $8.8 billion; reductions amounting to $2 billion in childcare and nutrition, summer feeding, and school lunches; and cutting $2.5 billion out of the guaranteed student loan program. None of these items was necessary as an amendment to carry out the Gramm-Latta budget mandate.

All of us in the meeting agreed that members deserved the right to vote up or down on each such proposal separately. It would be ridiculous to lump so many different and far reaching propositions into one vote. If the president wanted these separate matters considered, we would make them in order, but vote on each as a free-standing proposition. At the Speaker's request, I went to the Rules Committee, asking it to make amendments on these particular subjects in order, and to allow the Republican minority to offer any of them it might desire. The Rules Committee agreed.

But this did not suit Gramm, Stockman, and others of the conservative legislative junta. They had been secretly planning far more radical surgery than indicated in Stockman's one-page memo. Over the weekend, they began a loud hew and cry, accusing the leadership of heavy-handed tactics. By calling for separate votes on individual amendments, they asserted, we were throttling the president's right to have his "economic recovery program" considered in context. We were using "storm trooper" methods. We were denying President Reagan and the American people the right of a vote on "Reagan's plan." After receiving a call from the president, Bob Michel let us know he was under enormous pressures. To keep peace in the Republican family, he would have to join in the demand for a single up-or-down vote on the whole package, to be known as Gramm-Latta II. Michel acknowledged that he hadn't seen the amendment, but said it would be in the nature of a substitute for the entire Reconciliation Bill. To consider a matter of such sweep and gravity without knowing its contents was very nearly unprecedented.

To my utter amazement, the president's forces, with the help of southern Democrats, narrowly defeated the rule proposed by the Rules Committee. They insisted on considering the ill-defined package all together, in one up-or-down, all-or-nothing vote. That vote, in open defiance of the House leadership, also defied long-standing tradition and common sense. It amounted to legislative anarchy. An overnight blitz of telegrams and long distance calls had once again stampeded the membership. We would have one vote on an entire substitute identified only as Gramm-Latta II. Nobody had seen a copy. What, and how much of what, it would contain was anyone's guess.

Congress and the nation would ultimately learn the astounding extent and far-reaching contents of Gramm-Latta II, but not until after it was voted on and passed. Gramm didn't really know what was in it, and neither did Latta. When the huge substitute was seen on the House floor on June 26, the one page memo had grown to a fat book consisting of approximately one thousand pages. Nobody could know its precise length, because the pages were not numbered sequentially. After 209 pages in one sequence, numbers began again at 1 and went through 26 before commencing numerically anew. Many pages were not numbered at all. One compendium of thirty-nine pages appeared twice, at widely separated intervals, in the lengthy tome. The copy, patched together overnight by several separate staffs working in clandestine Capitol Hill rooms and in the White House under Stockman's general direction, was published by offset printing from typed sheets. It contained numerous handwritten annotations and various sizes of type.

This Gramm-Latta substitute was the sloppiest piece of draftsmanship I ever saw offered for a serious vote on the House floor in thirty-four years. I still have a dogeared copy I have kept for its enduring value as a curiosity and as a warning against a legislative body's being stampeded into a vote its members do not understand and know they don't understand. As first offered for members' viewing on the day of the vote, this protracted document contained numerous pen scratchings through initially typed material, addended by many handwritten annotations, in the penmanship of different authors. At the bottom of one page, the substitute offered a telephone number for someone named Rita Seymour. The manuscript contained many legal references proposing to strike out whole sections of existing laws, citing those laws only by title and section numbers. But the laws to which the amendatory language and drastic omissions and alterations were being proposed were not readily available for our inspection. Nobody could have intelligently guessed at the real effect of most such provisions. It was this entire, hastily assembled one thousand-page sheaf of papers that the president had implored the House to accept or reject in one up-or-down vote.

At one point in that day's debate, I asked cosponsor Del Latta if he realized that one of the provisions in his substitute would repeal the entire Randolph-Sheppard Act, which permitted blind people to operate concession stands in federal buildings. No, he didn't know that, said Latta. "If it does, I would have no objection to deleting that language." So I asked unanimous consent that the offending provision be removed, and everyone agreed. We would discover afterwards to our dismay that the same two lines appeared at another place, on a page numbered 26, about four hundred pages deeper into the rambling manuscript.

During the floor debate, we discovered numerous other palpable errors—one faulty referencing, which had the effect of striking out twenty pages of law that the authors did not intend to obliterate. That inadvertent error would have abolished the entire National Science Foundation, all of the nation's weather stations, and all civil defense activities.

The shoddy manuscript contained four pages of print repeated twice in two separate titles of the bill and one undisclosed provision that dangerously enhanced the powers of the Office of Management and Budget, the very office that Stockman headed. Through this incredible hidden stipulation, buried deep within the lengthy tome, Stockman would achieve powers never before granted to an OMB director. They would empower him virtually to supplant Congress in important areas of economic policy. Stockman would, among other things, be given the power to define poverty and, from time to time, to change the legal definition of the word. His unilateral determination, consequently, could radically change the meaning and application of laws of many sorts. By simply decreeing a lower income ceiling as the new parameter defining "poverty," he could single-handedly disqualify hundreds of thousands of families from eligibility to government help previously authorized by Congress.

Both Gramm and Latta firmly denied on the floor that their substitute adversely affected Social Security payments. They probably didn't realize the drastic changes someone had written into the long manuscript. Among other things, it would abolish death and burial benefits, reduce eligibility for juvenile survivor benefits, and totally do away with the "minimum benefit," a provision by which existing law guaranteed a floor of $122 monthly for the very poorest of the poor.

Members did not discover this latter provision, in fact, until after the entire monstrosity had passed. More than three weeks later, on July 21, I offered a motion on the floor vitiating this particular change and restoring the $122 monthly minimum benefit. My motion passed by 405 to 13. Many other hurtful consequences buried away in the gigantic pile of hastily assembled papers known as Gramm-Latta II would have been rejected just as resoundingly if members had insisted on considering them one at a time and knowing what they were voting upon.

We almost beat Gramm-Latta II in the House. A change of four votes would have done it. Tip and I, and the rest of the elected leadership, did everything within our power to get members to listen, to stop and think of the consequences before making that final, irrevocable vote. The vote was 217 to 211.

Surveying the wreckage after our unavailing efforts to slow down the juggernaut of Reagan's powerful appeal, I thought ruefully of a comment once made by the late County Judge Woodrow Bean of El Paso. "I've been on the steamroller, and I've been under the steamroller," Bean averred. "I can tell you from experience that on is better."

What it came to was a triumph of perception over reality. The public perception of Reagan, and the congressional perception of public opinion were both critically involved. "People don't *want* to hear what's in the bill," Kent Hance reported. "They just want us to back Reagan. The only question they ask me is this: Are you for him, or agin' him?"

Congressmen who supported Gramm-Latta II on that simple premise, however, may have sold the public short. A Harris Survey of the previous day, June 25, indicated that approval of the president's handling of the economy had fallen from 58–36 five weeks earlier, to a current 51–47. The poll indicated further that Reagan had a 68–30 percent *negative* public rating on "caring for the poor, the elderly, and the handicapped."

Several unintended provisions, drafted by some unnamed staff person and hidden within the gargantuan opus, were discovered in time to be removed in the conference committee. The Republican Senate had passed a similar measure on the day before our vote by a lopsided margin of 80 to 15. A number of responsible Republican Senators were almost as offended as House leaders had been by the haphazard collection of sweeping changes, but the House-Senate conferees closed action on the bill with most of the severely radical changes intact. On July 31, the omnibus reconciliation bill cleared Congress, and Reagan signed it into law on August 13.

Before the vote, on Monday, July 27, President Reagan addressed the American people. In his book, *The Triumph of Politics*, David Stockman would write the following of Reagan's speech:

> *[Reagan] delivered a masterpiece of propaganda. . . . There was not a hint, not one scintilla, about what all this fabulous "giving" actually meant. The tens of millions of Social Security recipients, students, farmers, government pensioners . . . watching that night received no warning that their benefits would have to be deeply and suddenly slashed in order to keep the budget equation whole.*

It was becoming increasingly clear that President Reagan and I were simply never going to agree on fundamental domestic economic policies. David Stockman, in his 1986 book, wrote of me that I was "as misguided as O'Neill, and had more energy. He [Wright] practiced the politics of envy, pure and simple: The deliberate inciting of middle and lower class resentment against the rich." Stockman seemed to cast me among those adversaries whom he described as "hard-core redistributionist liberals." Never having had much faith in political labels—a given term can mean such widely differing things to different people—I was amused to recall how a considerable number in my party had thought of me as "too conservative" only five years earlier when I became majority leader. I had never consciously tried to sow the seeds of envy, but I had frequently pointed out the unfairness of policies that actually hurt the poor and tax cuts that gave their greatest benefits to those in the very top income brackets while placing ever greater reliance on regressive taxation such as sales and excise taxes. That had been my consistent position through-out my whole public career. President Reagan's philosophy may have been described accurately as "trickle down." Reagan's economic policies mimicked those of the 1890s and 1920s. I, by contrast, might be described as a devotee of the "percolate up" theory. I believed that buying power, widely distributed among millions of wage earners, was the oil that lubricated the machinery of national prosperity. Perhaps that made me, in Stockman's eyes, a "redistribu-tionist liberal." Whatever it made me, I could see many of my most cherished public ideals being systematically ravaged by the Reagan Revolution of 1981.

Reagan had one hurdle left, and it was a big one. The Reagan White House, flushed with the heady wine of two victories, next demanded its Kemp-Roth tax cuts. With typical Reaganesque salesmanship, the bill would be labeled by its sponsors the "Economic Recovery" tax cut of 1981. Again, White House lobbyists scoured the parent committee—in this case Ways and Means—searching for at least one Democrat to cross over and give a bipartisan illusion to their list of sponsors. Chairman Dan Rostenkowski was determined other-wise. He growled to fellow Democrats on the committee that he would tolerate no defectors. Kent Hance came by to tell me one day that he had been invited to have a personal conference with the president. "I know what he wants, Mr. Leader. He wants me to be his Phil Gramm on the tax bill. I'd like to go over to the White House and see him. I've never talked to a presi-dent just one on one. But I'm going to tell him I can't do it. I won't leave you, Mr. Leader," he promised.

Kent caved. A day in the sun as nationally advertised coauthor of a major bill to be called Hance-Conable was just too alluring. At least, unlike Gramm, Kent had a sense of humor about his defection. He came by my office, grinned, and said, "You have one consolation, Mr. Leader. Just remem-ber that time wounds all heels."

Any way you sliced it, a 30 percent rate cut over a three-year period would amount to at least $300 billion in revenue lost. Reagan's argument, of course, was that most of this would be used to start new businesses or invest in plant improvements that eventually would generate economic growth. At that, such a huge tax cut would have been history's most expensive act of govern-ment pump-priming. Knowing the president probably considered himself in a position where he didn't have to deal with the Democratic leaders, I had nevertheless prepared a memorandum outlining a more cautious and much less costly approach. In a "bipartisan" oval office meeting, I handed a copy of the memorandum first to President Reagan. Then, passing copies around the room to colleagues and presidential advisors, I began explaining how we might test the theory of economically stimulative tax cuts without committing ourselves irretrievably to what Senator Howard Baker would call "a riverboat gamble." My memorandum recommended a more modest cut of 5 percent a year, with a ceiling on eligibility. I would limit individual income tax cuts to people earning $100,000 a year or less, and I would make corporate tax cuts available only for such nationally productive purposes as capital improvements that gave promise of raising productivity, and for worker training and retraining. Thus, I argued, we could guarantee at least a strong likelihood that the money would actually stimulate economic growth and improve our competitiveness in world markets.

As I talked, I was watching President Reagan's face. He looked at the points on the memo, his lips pursed. He seemed to be considering them. Then, he glanced toward Ed Meese, who was seated across the room from him to his right. I saw Meese shake his head negatively. Reagan folded up the paper and laid it in his lap. "I don't think that's quite what we had in mind, Jim."

Tip made the argument of retrogressive taxation. "The lion's share of these cuts will go to people who don't need them," he said. "And the people who *could* use a tax cut will get little or nothing." Senate Majority Leader Bob Byrd pleaded with the president to try it for one year and see whether it worked or not. "If this kind of tax reduction really does stimulate the economy in the way you hope, Mr. President," said Byrd, "there'll be plenty of time next year to ladle out a second helping. If it doesn't work, we won't have bet our whole grubstake on an unproven theory."

As we left, most of us were disappointed in Reagan's apparent lack of understanding, and his reliance on Meese and Regan. O'Neill, who had known Regan in Boston when both were young, felt the financier had systematically wiped out the memory of where he came from, a cardinal sin in Tip's eyes. I wondered what Meese knew about national deficits or the way taxes affected plain people. Jim Baker followed us as we left the White House and whispered in my ear, "keep trying." I wondered what he meant by that.

The only result I could attribute, even indirectly, to that meeting was a decision to reduce the first year's cut to 5 percent. The rate cuts finally proposed by the president would be five percent in 1982, 10 percent more in 1983, and a final 10 percent in 1984. The cumulative three-year reduction would be 25 percent. Apparently there was apprehension of too big a treasury loss in the first year.

Dan Rostenkowski of Illinois had faced a big choice at the beginning of that Congress. The defeat of Indiana's John Brademas had opened up the job of House Democratic whip. Danny was in line for that post, if he wanted it. At that time, the whip was appointed by the Speaker and Majority Leader. But the Oregon voters' rejection of House Ways and Means Chairman Al Ullman in 1980 created an equally interesting opportunity. Rostenkowski was next in line of seniority and could have that chairmanship. What he couldn't have was both. After much soul searching, the big, broad-shouldered, blunt-talking Chicagoan opted for chairmanship of the tax writing committee. O'Neill, with my enthusiastic concurrence, picked Tom Foley of Washington for Whip. I chose Bill Alexander of Arkansas to be Deputy Whip.

One thought burned inside Rostenkowski's breast: he didn't like to lose. It was one of Danny's strongest characteristics. Rather than face Reagan frontally on his costly tax cut and base our main argument on its certainty to produce monstrous deficits, Dan tried to cobble together a more alluring set of alternate tax reductions. "You can't beat something with nothing," he said. As his fellow Chicagoan Frank Annunzio would put it, "All that counts is the votes; everything else is bullshit."

Little by little, it became a bidding war between Rostenkowski and Reagan. I thought both bills were excessive in their capacity to bleed the treasury, but Dan's on balance was a lot fairer. Reagan scheduled a nationally televised address for Monday evening, July 27. Initially, he planned to talk about both taxes and ways to reduce the cost of Social Security, another goal to which he was privately committed. But Senate Majority Leader Howard Baker and House Minority Leader Bob Michel wrote a joint appeal to the president, imploring him not to mention Social Security. It was too politically sensitive, they told him.

Earlier that year, Reagan had terrified GOP congressional leaders by reading to them a speech he had personally composed, advocating that Social Security be made voluntary. Staff members of the Department of Health and Human Services had even sent a proposal calling for sudden and potentially frightening benefit reductions. Senator Pat Moynihan, on May 20, had maneuvered to get a Senate vote on that proposal. The Republican dominated Senate, at Democrat Moynihan's prodding, voted 96–0 to reject it out of hand. Still, Reagan had persisted, apparently believing he could sell the idea. On July 25, two days before the televised appeal, White House spokesman David Gergen announced to the press corps that Reagan had backed off and would devote his July 27 address to his tax proposal. Reagan applauded the public for supporting his earlier initiatives "with your telegrams, your letters, your phone calls and, yes, personal visits to talk to your elected representatives." He called on them for a repeat performance in behalf of his tax cuts. He even quoted Kent Hance's line, telling of a mythical farmer who listened to his congressman explain the details of the bill and then replied, "Don't give me an essay. What I want to know is are you for him or agin' him?"

"With our program in place," Reagan promised, deficits would get smaller, "and we hope we can begin whittling at that almost $1 trillion debt that hangs over the future of our children." Just how he squared that with the loss to the treasury of several hundred billion dollars through his proposed tax cuts he did not make clear.

This time, the networks did allow Speaker O'Neill and Chairman Rostenkowski to reply. In a broadcast immediately following the president's, they strove to draw the distinctions between the House committee-proposed cuts and those contained in the president's package. Their most telling point was that more than one-third of the total benefit would go, under Reagan's plan, to people in the top 5 percent of the annual income brackets while average and lower income taxpayer's would receive proportionately less.

By now, the Reagan program's lobbying team had perfected the manufacture of simulated "grass roots" demand to the level of a new political art form. Representative Les AuCoin of Oregon discovered one particularly flagrant example. A large Portland real estate management company known as CTL, operator of some eighty apartment buildings, held a drawing in which the hundreds of tenants in its properties could participate by writing and mailing letters to congressmen demanding they vote for Reagan's "economic recovery" program. Prizes included a fancy cocktail and dinner boat cruise. Tenants, to be eligible, had merely to write to a member of Congress and send a blind copy to the landlord company. Each writer was urged to submit multiple letters. A notice posted on apartment doors, blatantly appealed: "The more letters, the better. . . . Use different stationery—change the words— and mail one every few days."

On the day of the vote, July 29, an indignant woman arrived in my northeast Tarrant County office. She had rushed there from a local upscale beauty shop, her hair still wet. She told my local office manager, Paul Driskell, that she'd overheard several beauticians—when not engaged with customers—calling people by telephone, asking permission to use their names to help bludgeon lawmakers into voting for the president's tax cut. The beauticians, then posing as these other women, would each call the Washington offices of three area congressmen. They had a pat, written message, which they read in scores of telephone calls that day: "I've been a Democrat all my life. But I want the congressman to know that unless he votes for President Reagan's tax cut, I'm not going to vote for him anymore." The owner of the chain of shops that employed them, the hairdressers told our friend, had promised them an extra paid day off that week in exchange for at least twenty-five completed calls to lawmakers' offices. Variations of this kind of thing were inundating congressional switchboards. Reports surfaced after the House vote of a number of large national corporations—Exxon, Philip Morris, McDonnell Douglas, Monsanto, PaineWebber, and others—importuning corporate employees to write members of Congress and in some cases to call acquaintances, asking permission to use their names in behalf of President Reagan's tax plan.

It seemed to me that men and women in Congress should be smart enough to distinguish between spontaneous public reaction and an orchestrated deluge. Many could. Easy, too, to say a lawmaker should be above bowing to intimidation. But Richard A. Viguerie of Falls Church, Virginia, a leading professional practitioner of mass mailings, saw it another way. Viguerie, whose computer banks generated sixty to seventy million pieces of mail for conservative causes that year, put it in these words: "If an official tells you he got forty thousand pieces of mail from his district on a particular issue and he's going to ignore them, you know one of two things. He's lying to you, or he's not going to be around very long."

On the key vote, Reagan's plan beat the Ways and Means substitute by 238 to 195. The manipulative skill I'd seen appalled me. I worried about public gullibility for the president's pleasant over-simplifications, and what I saw as the weakness of my colleagues. What bothered me equally as much had been my inability to turn it around. I was supposed to be a good communicator. Wow! In Ronald Reagan I'd met my master.

The bill as finally passed contained one particularly egregious invitation to abuse, quietly sneaked into the measure in conference committee. None but a handful would know until months later that the new law invited big individual and corporate taxpayers to barter and trade among themselves in loopholes. It actually set up a private market in tax dodges!

Here is how that worked: If one private corporation had already deducted enough from its reportable income to render itself tax free for the year but still found additional deductions or tax credits it could have claimed but didn't need because it now owed no taxes—get this!—that company now, under the new law, would be allowed to *sell* that tax benefit privately to some *other* corporation. Having *bought* a tax credit it had done nothing to earn, and paid the first company less than the amount it now would claim as its own in tax *savings*, corporation number two would acquire a windfall at the public's expense. Both companies would make money on the transaction. Only the government—which is to say, the public—would lose. This brought such cries of indignation once it was publicly discovered, that even the White House, which had initially favored the provision, finally agreed to its removal from the law the following year.

One simple equation shed light on where the country was heading. Under the Hance-Conable tax bill, a full 10 percent of all individual tax cuts—amounting to some $7 billion in the first two years—would go to the wealthiest two-tenths of one percent of the American people, folks who made $200,000 a year and above in reportable annual income. Meanwhile, Stockman and Gramm conspired to cut $7 billion from Social Security recipients in the coming five years. Taken together, the two actions would constitute a purposeful redistribution of wealth upward, from the poorest to the wealthiest. Reagan's tax cut set into motion a reduction over the next three years of $285 billion in government revenues. If we were to avoid galloping deficits, we'd have to make this up somewhere. Lawmakers had experienced agony in trying to find some $36 billion in domestic cuts. Now, if we just outright *abolished* all of discretionary domestic government—courts, law enforcement, highways, schools, pollution abatement, the whole thing—it still wouldn't be enough to offset the losses. Only Social Security, Medicare and defense remained as big ticket items. If one did not touch these, then the deficit would automatically rise out of control.

To compensate for its revenue loss, the pressure would intensify in the next few years to find more income from regressive taxes like sales or property taxes. Reagan would recommend "service fees" and "user fees," along with excise and payroll tax increases. Only he wouldn't call them taxes. He'd call them "revenue enhancers."

Even though some became disenchanted with President Reagan, he still remained popular throughout his first year, partly because he undertook popular, forceful-appearing positions. In early August he took a macho stance with the air traffic controllers, firing all who had gone on strike and replacing them with recruits. Legally, the president was right. Never mind that the traffic controllers had some legitimate points, including the need to install new, more sophisticated equipment; they had taken an oath not to strike against the government. It may have been a gift of phenomenal good luck that Reagan's abrupt permanent dismissal of the trained controllers did not result in some terrible mid-air calamity.

Reagan's decisive action built a he-man image for the president, and the public revelled in it. Later that same month, U.S. military aircraft one night shot down two Libyan jets that had made menacing moves toward American shipping in the Gulf of Sidra. The Libyan planes were shot out of the sky while Reagan slept. Naval commanders made the decision, and Navy pilots did the job, but Reagan got the credit. Americans felt there was a decisive hand at the helm.

In the wake of Reagan's three big victories over the House leadership, however, the economy began a downhill slide. Kent Hance, who'd allowed his name to be used as nominal cosponsor of the Kemp-Roth tax cut (known as Hance-Conable), acknowledged at least partial error. Hance now advocated postponing the second and third layers of the individual income tax cut.

With all the setbacks Democrats incurred that year, we claimed a few modest victories. On October 5 we won a notable skirmish in the House on the Voting Rights Act extension. Considered the nation's most effective civil rights legislation, the Voting Rights Act of 1965 had brought about a marked increase in the number of blacks and Hispanics voting in state, local and federal elections. Unless Congress acted again, its key provisions would expire on August 6, 1982. Although implored by civil rights groups to support extension, President Reagan took no public position. After the House passed the bill by a vote of 389–24, however, he announced he favored extension of the act. We also chalked up a victory October 6 on the Health and Human Services Appropriations bill. This measure provided funds for job training programs, health block grants, low income energy assistance, community services, and education. By an eighty-one-vote margin the House rejected efforts by the Republican leadership to force harsh Reagan-backed cuts on this selection of programs. We achieved another win of sorts on the Agriculture bill. It provided monies for farm programs, school lunches, food stamps, and nutrition.

By November, the economy was worsening. America had suffered two successive quarters of negative economic growth, meaning recession was closing its grip on the country. Leading economic indicators all showed negative prospects. Manufacturing industries would not hire new people, allowing their employment level to go down through attrition. So, unemployment figures rose. The housing industry suffered, the number of housing units constructed during the latter half of 1981 falling to an all-time low, putting 839,000 home-building craftsmen out of work. This began a ripple effect that spread out in concentric circles. During October, General Electric announced a layoff of fifteen thousand people in Louisville. If new homes weren't built, new home appliances wouldn't be ordered. In the automobile industry, new car sales plummeted to 35 percent below the fall of 1980. Consequently, General Motors announced in October that it would cancel plans for expansion by scrapping a new plant in Kansas City.

A *Washington Post/ABC News* poll released on November 25 demonstrated growing dissatisfaction with the president's economic program. People now disapproved his handling of unemployment by 57 to 34 percent. And, by 54 to 29 percent, they said new domestic budget cuts proposed by the White House would hurt needed programs, not eliminate waste. But Reagan's faith in his experiment was unfazed, and his personal popularity was high. There'd be lots of other battles ahead.

CHAPTER TWENTY-NINE

RECESSION, DEFICITS, AND IDEOLOGY

After Ronald Reagan's breathtaking *tour de force* of 1981, it took the rest of America a while to find its voice. It would be 1984, for example, before Dr. Joseph M. Giordano, the brilliant head of the trauma team that saved Reagan's life that day of the assassination attempt, would speak out. What moved the prominent surgeon to response was a poignantly personal reference the president made to him in a speech before the National Italian-American Foundation. Reagan told the story, à la Horatio Alger, of Giordano's Italian ancestry, of his milkman father who worked hard, persevered, and "put his son through medical school." In the president's words, "All of their money went to the education of their children." It was "because of their diligence," Reagan proclaimed, that the son had become a great surgeon. Then, in a dramatic flourish, the president announced: "One day that surgeon—that son of a milkman—saved the life of a president. . . . I know this story because I was the patient."

At this, Giordano felt he had to tell "another part of the story." In an op-ed article for *Los Angeles Times,* the doctor explained that, in addition to his father's help and fine example, he owed his education also to "low-interest government loans," without which he couldn't have made it through medical school. Giordano explained something few doctors write much about: how his profession, "stimulated by generous federal funding for biomedical research," had made the unprecedented progress. "The government social programs enacted over the last fifty years—and so frequently criticized by this president and his administration—have played a vital role" in America's progress, of which Reagan had been speaking. The surgeon continued: "In contrast to the president, who feels that government programs make people so dependent that they lose initiative, I feel that these programs have enabled people with little resources to reach their full potential. . . . They range from Headstart to housing for the elderly."

To some in Congress who had voted for parts or all of the president's three-part 1981 blitz, the need to speak out would come much sooner. The battles of Reagan's second and later years in the White House were quite different from those of his first. Alarmed by the state of the economy and aided by slowly growing public awareness, the Democratic House began in 1982 to patch together its tattered unity and reassert its strength.

On February 8, 1982, as recession fears mounted, President Reagan asked Congress to "persevere, to stay the course, to shun defeat." He proposed a fiscal 1983 blueprint featuring unprecedented deficits—$91.5 billion for the current year, which would end on September 30, and $98.6 billion for the coming year. The deficits, by his own official accounting, would rise to these alarming levels despite major new cuts he was recommending for domestic programs, and, in face of history's biggest bath in red ink, Reagan called for another boost in military spending.

The president invited a bipartisan group of leaders to the White House for a private briefing prior to presenting his budget to the press. I was there, along with Speaker O'Neill, Senate Minority Leader Bob Byrd, Republican leaders Bob Michel and Howard Baker, Whip Tom Foley, Senator Strom Thurmond, and a number of others. For ten or twelve minutes, President Reagan theorized as we listened in silence. Finally, he said: "I hope we can approach this on a bipartisan basis."

"Mr. President, I hear you say you'd like a bipartisan approach," I answered. "We tried that on the tax bill last year, you'll recall, and it didn't work. You didn't find any of our suggestions worthwhile. But let's see if there are things on which we *can* agree *this* year. Maybe we can both agree that the deficit is too high."

"Well, yes. Anything we can do to bring the deficit down; of course, we don't like high deficits," the president said.

"What about the possibility of curtailing or simply postponing some of the tax cut we gave last year?" I offered.

"Oh, well, I don't know about that," Reagan said. "I think all of that is necessary. You see, we are looking to that tax cut to stimulate the revival of the economy."

I started to point out that the president's own Commerce Department, rather than predicting an increase in economic business investment for the year ahead, was forecasting a decrease. But something stayed my tongue. There is a point at which respect and good manners keep most of us from speaking as bluntly to the president as we might to someone else.

Someone mentioned student loans, pointing out that President Reagan's budget cuts were making it much harder for young people to obtain a college education. "I don't know," said the president. "I've been told of instances where young people take low interest rate loans and, instead of going to college, they put that money into CDs and make money on it," the president said.

How pathetic! So *that* constituted his reason for doing away with student loans? Because some kid he heard about had taken the money and put it into a certificate of deposit?

Next, Speaker O'Neill discussed school lunches, pointing out that many schoolchildren could no longer eat lunch because cuts had cramped eligibility. Reagan responded: "A friend of mine in New York tells me that in one neighborhood where everybody makes from seventy-five to one hundred thousand dollars a year, schoolchildren are getting free lunches!"

"Mr. President, your friend is misinformed," said the Speaker. "He can't be correct about that, unless these are the children of the domestic servants in that neighborhood." O'Neill went on to report that in several school districts over the past weekend, lunch prices rose from thirty-five to seventy-five cents. The Speaker gave a figure on how many thousands of needy children had been knocked out of receiving lunches by the new, stricter eligibility standards. Reagan remained unimpressed.

Senate Republican leader Howard Baker next asked the president if we couldn't find some savings in military spending to help reduce the deficit. "Well, no, I don't think so. Cap Weinberger tells me they have made all the savings they can in the military budget."

"We must keep the heat on these people," Reagan insisted, referring to Communist interests. "What I want is to bring them to their knees so they will disarm and let us disarm; but we have got to do it by keeping the heat on, and we can do it. We have them on the ropes economically," he said. "I understand they're selling rat meat in the markets of Russia today!"

One sits there stunned when the president of the United States says something like that. Selling rat meat in the markets? You know within reason that can't be true. You wonder what possesses the president to believe a story like that—selling rat meat in the markets of Russia?

This deep suspicion of the Soviet Union and his intense dedication to continuously raising the ante in Cold War military spending were articles of faith to President Reagan. He believed it part of his mission to goad Russia, make it spend more and more on military hardware. Indeed, a good argument can be made that Reagan and his advisors foresaw that forcing the USSR to spend more than it could afford trying to keep up with us might ultimately cause the internal collapse of that wicked system. If this was the specific intent, then subsequent events surely seem to validate that vision. One problem, of course, is that the pace of spending and the level of debt it incurred put strains on our own economy from which we have not recovered a decade later.

What is clear is that each country was trying to outdo the other in military spending, to its own economic detriment. Both tacitly accepted the doctrine of *mutual assured destruction.* Critics pointed wryly to the acronym, MAD. Things long since had reached the point where aggression by either would have predictably resulted in the military destruction of both countries. The president sometimes spoke of Armageddon.

Ultimately, in 1985, Reagan would come around to encouraging negotiations to lessen the mutual arms burden, but for several years he pursued a course of relentless criticism, justifying almost any addition—cost-effective or not—to our military arsenal. His occasional rhetorical references to Russia as "the evil empire" and the "focus of evil" raised suspicions among Soviet leaders that almost matched his of them. And here is the bizarre part: Reagan actually managed to convince himself that military spending didn't really add anything to the deficit.

I did not realize that the president truly believed this illusion until, one day at the White House in the autumn of 1985, we were discussing the appropriation bills for the year. They had passed the House and been reported from the Senate committee. As became customary in the Reagan years, Congress was preparing to lump all the appropriations together into one Continuing Resolution. This was a device the legislative branch had perfected to prevent the president from simply signing the military appropriation and one or two others of his choice and vetoing domestic bills which Congress considered important. The procedure was supported by Republican as well as Democratic lawmakers. That 1985 White House meeting, around the long table in the Cabinet Room, was attended by Democratic and Republican leaders from the House and Senate. It included chairmen and ranking minority members of the appropriations committees. In all, there probably were twenty or more present, including several presidential advisors and legislative leaders equally divided between the two parties. I sat to Reagan's right, O'Neill to his left.

The president began, reading a statement typed on five-by-eight cards. It consisted of a lecture to lawmakers and a warning that Reagan intended to "hold Congress to the same standards of fiscal responsibility" as he would if individual appropriations bills were disjoined. When he finished, Senate Appropriations chairman Mark Hatfield, the respected Oregon Republican, spoke up.

"I'm surprised to hear you say that, Mr. President," said Hatfield. "Surely, you're aware that the bills have already passed the House and have been marked up ready for the Senate floor. I assume you are aware that our total level of spending is slightly *less* than the total amount you recommended in your own budget—just as it has been for each of the past five years."

At this point, Speaker O'Neill interceded. "Senator, I wish you would repeat that last statement. Each time I say something like that to the president, he acts as though he doesn't believe it."

"I *don't* believe it," asserted Reagan.

"Well, Mr. President, the facts are quite unequivocal," said Hatfield, obviously surprised at the president's denial. Then the Oregon Republican patiently recited the figures. He had with him a table of annual appropriation totals for every year beginning with 1981, alongside the totals of presidential spending requests.

"That's not what I mean," Reagan insisted. "You've spent all this money on wasteful social programs and ignored the defenses of our country." With Reagan, the three words *wasteful-social-programs* had become like one word.

Senator Hatfield took a deep breath and began again, with studied patience. "The fact is quite the contrary, Mr. President," he explained. "During these five years, we have almost exactly doubled annual military spending—from $148 billion in 1980 to right at $300 billion this year—while reducing total appropriations for all discretionary domestic activities by approximately 22 percent on a current services basis."

"That still isn't what I mean," Reagan persisted, with visible impatience. "You've spent less than I *requested* on the military expense of our country, and *more* than I requested on these wasteful-social-programs."

"I'm sorry, Mr. President," said Hatfield, "I seem to have misunderstood. I thought you were talking about the *budgetary* impact. We'd have to agree, of course, that one dollar spent on a school book or one dollar spent on a bomb would have the same impact on the year's deficit."

"Well, no, I wouldn't agree with that at all," Reagan responded. "It makes an enormous amount of difference! It *isn't* the same. I'd like for Cap Weinberger to address that."

At this, Weinberger rose from his seat and began a surprising dissertation, the conclusion of which was that military spending actually didn't add anything to the deficit. We spent most of the military budget with private procurement companies, Weinberger said, and those companies pay taxes. They hire employees who pay taxes. Those employees buy groceries and clothes and other things from businesses that pay taxes. So, you see, Weinberger was saying, it all comes back to the government eventually, and, therefore, military spending does not increase the deficit.

The rest of us in the room were flabbergasted! Weinberger knew better than that! This same argument could be made for almost any kind of spending. In fact, it would have more validity if applied to relatively more labor-intensive activities than military weapons procurement, which was increasingly capital-intensive. Only one person in that room could really have believed that spending money on weapons does not add to the deficit. Weinberger didn't believe that. He certainly hadn't espoused any such notion when he was chairman of OMB under Nixon. No Republican or Democratic leader of House or Senate could possibly believe it. But Ronald Reagan did believe it. He *wanted* to believe it.

In the end, that particular fantasy—the idea that military spending actually didn't matter for purposes of deficit calculation—may have been the most dangerous self-deception of all. Coupled with the president's obsessive insistence that upper bracket tax cuts would actually add money to the treasury, it set us on an almost irreversible path of rapidly mounting debt. During the eight years of Reagan's presidency the United States put almost exactly $2 trillion into our dramatic military buildup. That is just a bit more than the total amount by which our national debt grew during those same years. This, in turn, more than tripled what we had to cough up annually in interest payments on that debt. By the time Reagan left office, the taxpayers were being bled by some $180 billion every year in carrying charges.

Reagan, I am convinced, did not consciously or intentionally mislead the American people. There were three infallible creeds in his ideological catechism. He wouldn't even question them. They were, in his mind, absolute and inerrant. Reagan believed that most domestic spending was inherently wasteful and the only serious cause of government deficits. He believed that military spending, on the other hand, did not add to deficits. And he believed that "supply side" tax cuts, aimed at relieving the tax burden for people of wealth, would automatically result in more money for the treasury. So similar were the president's economic theories to those that prevailed in official circles during the 1920s, that I rummaged through my library shelves in 1982 and reread Frederick Lewis Allen's book, *It Was Only Yesterday,* which dealt with that dizzy decade. I also found a couple of relevant old economics texts and some lecture notes from my college days. Reading these in light of Reagan's economic rhetoric, I was intrigued. A succession of upper scale tax cuts in the 1920s, similar to those now being described as "supply side," indeed had apparently generated some worthwhile expansionary business investments. There were great improvements in workplace productivity. But wages across the board increased by only a very small percent during that decade, and because of rising prices, real *buying power* did not expand to absorb the new goods. People couldn't buy the products business was putting on the shelves. Ultimately, the result was that Black Tuesday of 1929. A child of the Depression, I was determined that we avoid repeating those mistakes or making similar ones.

But now, we were heading precisely in that direction. In March of 1982, our leading economic indicators continuing to point downward, a lot of us in Congress grew even more troubled about the economy. All that year, things got worse. Unemployment reached its highest pinnacle since the Great Depression. Business failures for 1982 were twice as high as two years before. We saw a rash of farm foreclosures.

The mail now consisted of exclamations from worried citizens: railroaders troubled by losses in the Railroad Retirement System; educators and students frightened by threats to college loans, Pell Grants, work-study grants and job training dollars; newly unemployed people wanting to know where to look for work; older Americans expressing concern about what could happen to their pensions. Other mail announced alarm at the rising national debt.

A vicious cycle had set in: high unemployment created higher deficits; rising deficits provided excuse to Federal Reserve Chairman Paul Volcker to keep interest rates high; the unaffordable rates choked off investment; this in turn created more unemployment, giving rise to still higher deficits. A number of us struggled to come up with workable ideas to interrupt that cycle. Recalling 1958, I suggested to other Democratic leaders that we ought to try to help the president find a way out, just as Rayburn and Johnson had helped Eisenhower out of that earlier recession. I talked with Tip and other fellow Democrats about ways to jump-start the economy. A few, to my surprise, were opposed. "Let Reagan wallow in his own juice," they insisted. "When things get bad enough, people will see what the Republicans have done."

That logic didn't appeal to me. They wanted issues; I wanted solutions. Recession and joblessness weren't partisan problems; they were national problems. Rather than announcing some program as a Democratic initiative, of which Reagan would be instinctively suspicious, we ought to offer it to him privately first as a plan we could jointly announce. I came with a package which I put into the form of a memorandum. It was bold, if nothing else. The two biggest generators of jobs in our economy were the automobile and homebuilding industries. Let's start with them, I proposed—set off a spark, and let the fire spread outward.

We could stimulate automobile production, I reasoned, and energize our biggest potential employment dynamo by offering a one thousand-dollar tax credit to any family purchasing a new energy-efficient American-made automobile. If 150,000 new car sales resulted in the next few months, that would cost the government approximately $150 million. But if that plan put 250,000 people back to work, as Lee Iacocca said it would, the Treasury could recover money from taxes paid on these workers' salaries and from government savings on not having to pay them any more unemployment compensation.

Some additional taxes would certainly come from the nation's car dealers on their revived sales. This plan would cost something, without doubt, but it might recover a substantial part of its cost. And surely it would help jump-start a vital American industry. Similarly, I reasoned, with the housing industry. Some variation of this initiative could reinvigorate the idled homebuilding crafts. Maybe we could grant a tax credit to young couples buying homes.

Of course, none of this would work over the long pull, or be of any lasting good to the economy, unless interest rates came down. Things had reached the point where a couple buying a home on a thirty-year mortgage would actually pay *more than three times* the advertised value of the property during the period of amortization. Worse yet, a gimmick known as the Adjustable Rate Mortgage was luring thousands of unsuspecting young couples into low monthly payments at the beginning of the seductive note, only to paralyze them with outrageously unaffordable increases in interest charges after a couple of years. This was forcing young families by the literal thousands to give up their homes and all they'd put into them, forsaking the American Dream.

So I suggested something quite unorthodox as part of the total package. Not since the early 1950s—when Harry Truman decisively ordered the Federal Reserve Board to regurgitate a one-half percent increase in the prime rate—had an American president forcefully asserted the public interest in the question of allowable lending charges. I suggested President Reagan might earn well deserved appreciation from the American people by taking a similar stance. He had stood up to "big labor" in the Air Traffic Controllers' strike. Now let him prove his *bone fides*, I suggested, by standing up to big lenders.

After discussing all of this with Speaker O'Neill, I put it in a private memo and sent copies to James Baker in the White House and Republican leader Howard Baker in the Senate. I got no immediate response. The next thing I heard was that Jim Baker had approached House Budget Committee Chairman Jim Jones of Oklahoma with an alternate scenario. On March 25, Baker began private negotiations, aimed almost exclusively at finding new ways to cut domestic expenditures. He held out to Jones the prospect of finding "common ground" sufficient to avoid a budget stalemate between House and Senate, or—just as bad—another train wreck between House and White House of the kind that had occurred the year before. For a full month, from March 25 to April 28, a sort of mating dance went on. Jones, eager to explore any opportunity to find a truly bipartisan approach, patiently attended a series of meetings with White House representatives, listening to proposals, offering counter proposals, finding small patches of common ground, but not enough to resolve the big deficit dilemma.

Finally, at Jim Jones's request, Speaker O'Neill agreed to a personal meeting with President Reagan in an ornate little ceremonial room behind the Senate chamber. Each of the two principals, by prior arrangement, would bring two or three associates of his choice. O'Neill asked me and Rules Committee Chairman Dick Bolling to accompany him. He also brought along a trusted administrative aide. The president brought Jim Baker, Senator Howard Baker, Senator Paul Laxalt, and Ed Meese.

No sooner had we entered the room than fireworks began. Reagan, pointing to O'Neill's assistant, demanded, "Who is this?"

"He is our aide, our historian," the Speaker replied. "He will record these events for us and help us keep an accurate record of whatever we agree to."

"I thought there was an agreement already," the president complained. "We didn't want any staff here."

"Mr. President," said O'Neill, nodding in the direction of Jim Baker and Ed Meese, "since you have staff present, I thought we should be entitled to have staff also."

With this, the president, Baker and Meese insisted on the presence of David Stockman and Donald Regan to enhance their representation. Reagan next demanded a specific seating arrangement. He wanted Speaker O'Neill to sit beside him; then a Republican of his choice would sit between Speaker O'Neill and Mr. Bolling. Another would separate Bolling from me; while a third would be placed between me and O'Neill. I could not be sure of the president's purpose. Either he didn't want House leaders to sit together and compare notes; or perhaps he had in mind staging the outward appearance of bipartisan unity. It could have been the latter. Soon the door to the little room was ordered opened, and a bevy of news photographers was admitted for pictures before the actual conference began. Photos taken, the room was swiftly cleared of all but participants.

O'Neill immediately made clear that the president did not intimidate him. He announced to Reagan that he intended to sit on the other side of the table, where he and the president could look one another straight in the face and exchange views freely. We all shifted to new positions, now resembling two opposing teams at the line of scrimmage—not a happy augury for what was to follow.

Reagan was testy, defensive, unwilling to consider any compromise in his basic plan. At one point, Reagan said sharply to me, "Jim, put down that pencil. Stop thinking about what you're going to say, and listen to what I'm trying to tell you."

This group talked for three and a half hours without resolving anything. We did agree to a set of goals for deficit reductions, but disagreed on the way to achieve them. Trying to help, I suggested we could cut deficits through an "equality of sacrifice." Let each side give a little. Let various segments share in the necessary pruning. I called my approach "five/five/five." Since Reagan's people had expressed concern about the growth of entitlements, including automatic cost-of-living increases for public servants and retirees, I suggested that we declare a five-month moratorium in which there would be no increases. "Those of us who work for the government would set the example," I said. "We could even establish an arbitrary 5 percent ceiling on any increase for the coming year."

But military and other government retirees, I pointed out, were certainly not wealthy. If we should expect them to sacrifice to help reach a balanced budget, I insisted, then other, considerably more wealthy segments of society should match their contribution. The least we should expect of the tax cut's major beneficiaries, I said, should be to give up a part of their windfall in order to advance the cause of a balanced budget. Let's reduce that 10 percent annual tax cut to a 5 percent cut, I proposed.

Reagan objected. "Don't you realize that the tax cut barely compensates for the tax increases that these poor working people will have to pay for in their payroll taxes?" he asked.

"All right, Mr. President," I responded. "If that is what you're truly concerned about, then we're on the same wavelength. Let us protect all of those poor *working people* about whom you have just expressed concern." I suggested that we place a ceiling of seven hundred dollars on the third-year tax cut. This way, every working person earning forty-five thousand dollars a year and under would receive all that he or she would get under Reagan's plan, but there'd be no third-year boondoggle for big business and the really wealthy.

President Reagan seemed exasperated. "Don't you see, Jim? That would simply exacerbate the progressivity of the income tax, and that is what has gotten us into all the terrible trouble we are suffering today!"

The president made it clear that he was satisfied with his "supply side" program, even in spite of its enormous deficit projections. When O'Neill reminded Reagan of rising unemployment figures—a million more thrown out of work in the past six months—the president stoutly defended his policies.

"Tip, you just don't understand," Reagan persisted. "I have read all that newspaper crap about people being hurt, but nobody is being hurt by my economic program. Let me tell you something, Tip. We have created 300,000 new jobs in this economy since I took office!"

"Mr. President," the Speaker replied, "three hundred thousand new jobs in fifteen months are not nearly enough!" We need to create between two million and three million new jobs a year, O'Neill pointed out, in order merely to stand still.

President Reagan was unable to acknowledge that fundamental precept. Even though it had been embraced by conservative and liberal economists alike for the past twenty years, Reagan rejected it. Some of the Republicans, tiring of ideological jousting and abstract sermonizing, began looking for practical ways to salvage something out of the meeting so that we could at least claim to have reached a bipartisan agreement. Senator Baker suggested that maybe we could agree to postpone application of the third year's 10 percent tax cut by three months and leave everything else as we'd structured it at year's end, making up whatever we could through more reductions in domestic social programs. Bolling scornfully likened this to the mythical story of a woodsman who claimed to have made a "horse and rabbit stew." When asked how he mixed his horses and rabbits, the woodsman said, "Well, it's fifty-fifty —half and half—one horse and one rabbit."

In the ultimate analysis, our discussion broke apart on the shoals of philosophical disagreement. The president did not see a need for any change in his tax program. Yet, Reagan did realize the breadth and gravity of public concern. In a nationally televised speech the following night, April 29, he began with a nod to current economic conditions. The speech started thusly: "Good evening. My fellow Americans, you know the most important goal that all of us share tonight is economic recovery—to see our factories reopening their gates, to see the unemployed returned to their jobs and every American enjoy the fruits of prosperity." Then he began to excoriate Democratic congressional leaders for failing to succumb to his budget blandishments of the day before. Portraying us as partisan and indifferent to the country's problems, Reagan made no mention of our suggestions to stimulate an economic recovery. He characterized us as intransigent and unwilling to compromise.

The House on June 23 agreed to a budget resolution for fiscal '83. Democrats pushed hard for repeal or delay of the July 1983 installment of Reagan's tax cut, but congressional Republicans and the administration refused to budge. By July, many of us were convinced that an economic depression was setting in.

Stockman and others, awakening to the treasury drain caused by the tax cut and military spending increases, approached Ways and Means Chairman Dan Rostenkowski that summer, asking his help in raising excise taxes to fill the gap. After talking with O'Neill and me, Rostenkowski agreed to work with the White House on such a bill, but only if President Reagan himself would go on television and publicly endorse the effort. What emerged was somewhat euphemistically labeled the *Tax Equity and Fiscal Responsibility Act.* It raised certain sales taxes and user fees, paid mostly by consumers. It did repeal several of the more onerous business tax breaks enacted in the 1981 bill. To that extent, it might have been called a compromise. I thought it basically regressive in nature, but supported it as the only available means to hold down the rising deficits. Reagan, in his televised speech endorsing the bill, was careful to refer to the excise levies not as "taxes" but as "revenue enhancers."

On August 13 the House and Senate completed action on a supplemental appropriations bill. Congress, exercising its prerogative, added some $917 million in educational programs and services for the elderly which the president had not wanted. At the same time, however, we reduced other programs by some $2.8 billion below his official asking. Almost $2 billion of this was shaved off Reagan's military spending request, although the bill still contained a substantial increase in defense spending over the year before. At Stockman's urging, Reagan vetoed the bill on August 28, claiming it would "bust the budget." That assertion seemed absurd, even to most Republican members. The bill rearranged Reagan's priorities, but it certainly didn't bust the budget. It spent less, by approximately $2 billion, than the president's official asking.

Senate Republican leader Howard Baker, accompanied by Appropriations Chairman Mark Hatfield and Senate Budget Committee Chairman Pete Domenici, implored the president to sign the bill. They thought they had his agreement. But his political operatives, those to whom Reagan seemed most prone to listen, told him otherwise. Republican leaders in both House and Senate were deeply embarrassed by that veto. Reagan's repeated successes of the previous year may have given him a delusion of invincibility.

On September 9, the House voted to override the veto. It was the first major turning point in the eight year tug of war between Reagan and the Democratic House over domestic policy. This was Reagan's first significant budget defeat. It would not be his last. Neither was it a knockout. The old thespian was clever. He was magnificent with a script. He would be, throughout his presidency, a formidable adversary.

In the November 2 election that year, Democrats captured twenty-six new seats in the House—six more than I had privately predicted and enough, I thought, to assure us a working majority in the next Congress. The outcome was, for me, a gratifying personal victory. Almost all the candidates for whom I had campaigned in a whirlwind tour across the country during the brief October recess were elected. In Texas, we had very nearly a clean sweep. We captured the governorship and won all contested statewide seats. All five newly elected members of the Texas congressional delegation were members of my party, for whose election I had worked. Democratic gubernatorial candidates won seven additional statehouses. But the Senate balance, almost incongruously, remained unchanged.

By December, a third of the nation's industrial capacity lay idle. The jobless rate continued to grow. "The economy is probably in the worst shape that it has been in nearly half a century," said Otto Eckstein, a Harvard economist. A few days after the election, I went early one morning to the streets outside the local Texas Employment office in Fort Worth and visited with the jobless who stood there every day hopefully awaiting the arrival of someone with day labor needing to be done. One man told me he landed a day's work perhaps one day in three. Another said he'd had two days' work in the past week. Another sadly explained he really couldn't take a regular, continuing job if one should be offered that day—unless he could get some advance on wages instead of waiting the customary two weeks for his pay. He was that close to the ragged edge.

Shades of the 1930s. It had been a sad year—the year that saw the reemergence of soup lines and of thousands of homeless, dispossessed, and with no place to go.

On December 23, the last day of the session, Congress produced a highway bill to support long overdue rehabilitation, improvements, repairs, and restoration of the nation's highways and bridges. To pay for this work, we voted an additional five-cent gasoline tax, obliging those using the roads to pay for the maintenance and resurfacing. We wondered if the president would sign it.

In a September news conference, a reporter had asked Reagan about this bill. "What about a five-cent tax on gasoline to pay for roads? Would you support that?"

"Well, possibly, if there were a palace coup," Reagan had quipped.

Something happened between then and December. Now, chafing from criticism for doing nothing to stimulate jobs, Reagan signed the bill. He said, with a straight face, "What I am suggesting here is not a tax increase. This is a five-cent *user fee.*" His semantic agility was amazing.

Bob Michel and I made the ceremonial call to the president, advising him that Congress had finished its work and stood ready to adjourn. Bob and I, on different telephone extensions, even sang Reagan a lusty chorus of "We Wish You a Merry Christmas."

And, as a matter of fact, I did. In spite of our repeated conflicts over domestic policy, which would continue throughout his whole time in office, frequently more exasperating than amusing, I liked the eloquent old scrapper personally. More than once, Tip and I would come willingly to his aid on matters of foreign affairs. He was our president. We owed him that.

CHAPTER THIRTY

GLIMPSES OF
THE WORLD

P resident Ronald Reagan and I had a sort of on-again, off-again relationship that lasted through his entire eight years in the White
House. It was utterly unlike my association with any other president.
Neither Reagan nor I willed it so. We just saw different glimpses of
our changing world and nation. Neither of us had the whole truth. We may
have been like two blind men inspecting an elephant. One grabs the trunk and
compares the elephant to a huge fire hose. The other touches the tail and sup-
poses the beast to be like a rope. Our views on the domestic role of American
government were poles apart. I wanted to make government responsive to our
national problems. He wanted to make government get out of the way.

Reagan knew he could almost always call on me as majority leader to help
him in a foreign policy crisis. But that didn't blunt the hard edge of his frequent and often unpredictable rhetorical blasts—sometimes quite
personal—at Tip O'Neill, me, and Democrats in general, sometimes within
hours of his appealing to us privately for help on foreign policy. And Tip,
Senate leader Bob Byrd, and I were often exasperated by what we saw as
Reagan's oversimplifications. We kept trying to nudge him toward a more
activistic view of America, a less bellicose one of the world.

For almost thirty years, ever since coming to Congress in 1954, I had been
a devotee of the basic premise of a bipartisan approach to foreign policy.
What had awakened me as a high school student to want a career in public
service was my perception that partisans in the U.S. Senate, led by Senator
Henry Cabot Lodge, had wrecked Woodrow Wilson's dream of a League of
Nations and made World War II inevitable.

During President Eisenhower's tenure, I had supported each of his world initiatives, helped personally to salvage his plan for a Pan American Health Organization headquartered in Washington, and worked eagerly to advance the Pan American Highway. Kennedy had inspired my active championing of the Alliance for Progress. I had gone to the Dominican Republic and Costa Rica on missions for President Johnson and been constant in my support of his foreign policy efforts, including those in Vietnam.

While Nixon was president, I incurred the resentment of some fellow Democrats by promoting bipartisan support for his call to the North Vietnamese to come to the peace table. I also persuaded Democratic colleagues to close ranks with him on other foreign policy matters. Later I discovered to my deep sorrow our covert involvement in the internal political affairs of Chile, which resulted in the death of Chile's president and the armed overthrow of its elected government.

Some of the happiest and most exhilarating moments of my career were in those months when I worked closely with Jimmy Carter to advance the cause of peace between Egypt and Israel. Carter called on me more than once to serve as a personal emissary for him to leaders in Latin American countries. After the overthrow of Somoza by revolution in Nicaragua, he asked me to lead a small group to that country to talk with members of the revolutionary junta and probe their intentions. We pressed them hard to respect individual rights and to hold free elections.

It was quite natural, given this background, that I would want to help Ronald Reagan in his role as chief executor of our foreign policy. During the hectic first year of his administration, while on domestic matters Reagan ripped our defensive line to shreds like a pro quarterback against a small town high school team, I never wavered in my support of his foreign policy objectives. My first serious doubts arose in August of 1982. They involved a resolution to put the United States officially on record endorsing a bilateral freeze in the production and deployment of nuclear weapons. Through Reagan's inaction, the SALT agreements negotiated with the Soviet Union had languished, unratified, for almost two years. Doubts plagued me. In the early predawn hours of August 5, I wrote the following in my journal:

> It is 3:50 A.M. I slept for three hours or so, then awakened. I've been tossing and turning, trying to lull my mind to let loose the question that troubles it . . .
>
> Today we must vote on a nuclear freeze resolution. . . . Several weeks ago, Chairman Clem Zablocki said he had a responsible position worked out—one which avoided the hysteria and stated our country's willingness to enter a mutual, not unilateral freeze on

nuclear weapons with Russia—one that would be both verifiable and enforceable. It seemed . . . a sensible position between that of the unilateral peaceniks who would leave us at the mercy of the Soviet Union and that of the Cold War hawks who would perpetuate the nuclear rivalry and its steely-nerved balance of terror out of sheer hatred for the Russians. Clem wanted to use my name as a cosponsor. I said alright. The bill was reported, with near unanimity. We scheduled it for the floor.

Then, out of the blue, the president came forth with a scathing attack on this resolution. He says it would undermine his efforts to negotiate a START agreement (his acronym) with the Soviet rulers. Yesterday he pleaded for support to block its adoption characterizing it as a "vote of no confidence" in his leadership.

All of this puts a new light on things. Frankly, I don't know just where it leaves me—and I have precious little time in which to decide. On the one hand, I think Reagan played cheap partisan politics with the SALT treaty. His cabinet people (Cap Weinberger and Shultz, at least) know now that he was wrong on that one—we've not breached its terms, nor have the Russians, even though it has gone unratified. It should have been approved two years ago. Pure politics defeated it, and self-serving stubbornness and pride have kept it in its limbo. Reagan was wrong then.

On the other hand, I don't want to be guilty of his errors. I don't want to pull the rug out from under him as he did his predecessor. In all the years I've been in Congress, I have tried to respect the right of every president of whichever party to speak for us in the councils of the world. If unable in conscience to uphold the president in a matter of international consequence, at least I've had the grace not to undermine him. . . . I do not want to be a party to making his task more difficult.

That decision was excruciating for me. Torn between conviction and habit, I agonized through most of the debate in Hamlet-like indecision. Unaccustomed to vacillating, I was intensely uncomfortable. I didn't speak on the bill. Finally, as debate ended, I had to choose: loyalty or conscience? I knew finally that I had to be for the nuclear freeze resolution. I believed in it. Reagan, I saw all too clearly, really didn't *want* a halt to the arms race. We *had* to move toward a sensible agreement with the Russians. I voted for it.

The president's side prevailed that day by two votes, 204–202. I felt certain I could have changed that outcome if I had spoken up. My vacillation and my silence had given the president a victory and an extension of time to come around to the inevitable rational choice. I knew now that I had a responsibility to *help Reagan reach that choice.*

The Caribbean Basin Initiative was a converse situation, in which I swallowed a dose of wounded pride and bucked strong segments of my own party to help Reagan with his plan. For too many generations the islands of the Caribbean and the countries of Latin America, which abutted its western shores, had languished, their economies stagnant. The short-lived Alliance for Progress had raised hopes and sparked some salutary results. Now, commodity prices for coffee, sugar, cocoa, hemp, and other products of the area were falling as interest rates rose, putting the historic debtor region in a vise-like squeeze.

Reagan's State and Commerce Departments, not eager to encourage government loans or grants, came up with an idea to stimulate private investments in new business enterprises that would provide useful jobs for people in the economically stricken region. The principal incentive would allow profits earned by American companies opening new plants in these countries to enjoy duty-free treatment and a special tax break. The president, knowing of my interest in Latin America, asked for my support. I liked the idea and agreed to help. Just as the bill was scheduled to come before Congress, Reagan vetoed the Supplemental Appropriation Bill, resuming his intermittent war against the legislative branch and blaming us for "budget busting." Infuriated at the patently phony charge, a great many Democrats were unwilling to give their tormentor a victory of any kind, certainly not one to help unemployed people outside our own country. The president's plan was in deep trouble.

Speaking to the House on the day of the vote, July 14, 1983, I said, directly addressing my colleagues on the Democratic side:

> *If ever you have found occasion to rise above partisanship . . . please do so on this occasion. There is far too much at stake for us to allow anything to interfere with our fulfilling the pledge that has been made in behalf of the United States by the president . . . to our closest neighbors in the world. There is no other region on Earth which is as vital to the security of the United States as Latin America and, specifically, the Caribbean Basin. . . .*
>
> *Now, if we abandon this latest promise of a Caribbean Basin plan . . . we shall undermine and embarrass not only the president, not only the State Department, but the very credibility of the United States in everything we want to do in the future throughout Latin America . . .*

The bill passed, narrowly. If we were keeping score, Reagan owed me one. A week or two after that, he pleaded with me personally to intervene with members of the Appropriations Committee to restore some funds they had cut from the State Department appropriation. Looking for relatively painless ways to reduce deficits, the committee had slashed monies for embassies, consulates, Voice of America broadcasts, and several other parts of our diplomatic mission abroad. The president complained that this reduced our presence and weakened our message to a dangerous degree. It is always easier politically to cut foreign programs, however praiseworthy, than things at home. After my personal appeal to three members of the Appropriations subcommittee, the funds were restored. Now Reagan owed me two. But *he* wasn't counting.

About ten days later, the president made a campaign appearance in Irving, Texas, between Fort Worth and Dallas, for North Texas Republican candidates. He took that occasion to blame me personally for failure of the House to pass his proposed constitutional amendment to decree a balanced budget. It would have been, I thought, a pretty poor substitute for real action to balance the budget. Reagan had sent Congress the most unbalanced budgets in history. If he really wanted a balanced budget, he easily could have proposed a budget that did balance.

An effort had been made to bring this proposal directly to the floor by "discharge petition," lifting it from the jurisdiction of the Judiciary Committee. That effort had failed. If one-half plus one of the House members sign a formal petition to "discharge" a committee from jurisdiction over a bill, it comes immediately to the full membership for a vote. Reagan seemed to hold me personally accountable that a majority of House members had not signed that petition. It is true enough that I'd discouraged any who asked me about signing it. So had Speaker O'Neill. The president, answering questions from newsmen representing papers in my district, said I was hypocritical. Pretty strong stuff.

The *Fort Worth Star-Telegram* bannered a headline, front page: REAGAN RIPS JIM WRIGHT FOR "HYPOCRISY." It was not as though I had ever made any pretense of favoring such an amendment. I'd stated my opposition publicly. The way to balance the budget, I had said, was to balance it, not to posture.

Reagan and the Democratic leaders engaged, throughout his administration, in a private, unacknowledged game of one-upmanship. He was an accomplished practitioner, an old scene-stealer from 'way back.' His favorite role was Preacher to the Nation on State of the Union occasions. Most people, watching that annual television spectacular, are wholly unaware of the two large transparent glass panels located diagonally, at the president's eye level, one about four feet to his front left, the other to his front right. Standing behind the podium, he can turn alternately in either direction, toward his seated audience in the chamber, and read the script of his speech without appearing to be reading. So gifted an actor was Reagan, so comfortable with a script, so natural and seemingly spontaneous his flow of rhetoric, so appropriate and sincere his facial expressions, that it seemed to most viewers that those polished phrases were springing extemporaneously, that very moment, from his fertile brain.

In 1982, the old thespian established a new tradition. He paused dramatically in his speech finale, devoted as it had been to the continuing phenomenon of modern American heroism, to introduce a young man named Lennie Skutnik. Lennie's story was known to all in the chamber. A short time earlier, on a bitterly cold evening, he had been driving near the Potomac and watched an Air Florida plane, floundering on takeoff from Washington's National Airport, crash into the Potomac with its cargo of passengers. Skutnik stopped his car and dove into the icy river, saving one shivering victim of the fatal crash.

Recounting the heroic feat, Reagan suddenly pointed to the president's gallery above the west wall of the House chamber, where Skutnik sat, in the front row, beside Nancy Reagan. When the young man rose, somewhat bashfully, to acknowledge the plaudits of the standing throng, Reagan looked his way and executed, for the television cameras, a snappy salute. It was high drama, good theater. Never mind that it violated House rules to refer to anyone in the gallery. Who was going to bang the gavel and call the president of the United States out of order? He had one-upped us! After that, it became an annual guessing game among members who the president's mystery guest would be on State of the Union night.

A year later, some of us undertook to upstage Reagan. By practice, the contents of a State of the Union message were embargoed until thirty minutes before delivery. At that time, copies would be available in the press gallery and to the members. On January 25, 1983, reading one of these advance copies of Reagan's speech, I spotted one line that echoed exactly what Democrats had been trying to emphasize. That line stated that we in government had a responsibility to take the steps necessary to reverse the recession. For most of the previous year, the president had been in official denial that there actually was a recession, and had only begrudgingly acquiesced to any degree of government activism to reverse it.

Hoping to call attention to that one line, about as obscure as lean pork in a can of pork and beans, I hastily gathered a dozen or so Democrats in the cloak room to the rear of the chamber. Each of them agreed to prompt ten or more other members to our plan. As soon as the president read that line, buried in a paragraph and far prefatory to any intended punch line, we would rise to our feet and cheer lustily.

Our gambit went off just as planned—well, almost just as planned. The incidental line spoken, a roar of instantaneous applause arose from the Democratic side as the entire section sprang to its feet, clapping our hands in approval. Republicans, supposing they had missed an important pronounce-ment, jumped up to join us, applauding just as vigorously, though somewhat mystified at what had sparked the demonstration. The president was taken by total surprise. I was watching his face. For a moment he stared in bewilder-ment. But only for a moment. Reagan figured out quickly that he'd been had. No doubt, as he delivered the speech, some part of his subconscious mind must have been wondering why so many were so intently following the printed script. The old actor, quickly recovering, grinned. "And all that while," he ad libbed, "I thought you fellows were reading the newspapers!" He had the last laugh.

But we had scored. Reagan had been put on notice, made aware of the gravity of feeling in Congress that unemployed Americans must not be ignored while we poured more and more of our resources into the arms race. A few days later, on January 31, Speaker O'Neill in a small budget gathering at the White House gave President Reagan the sternest face-to-face lecture I've ever heard a president subjected to. Asked by Reagan to support more cuts in domestic programs in order to allow a 14 percent increase in military spending above the previous year, Tip came unglued. He told the president very plainly that Democrats could not acquiesce in good conscience to Reagan's passive acceptance of high unemployment and its attendant evils. "We must make every effort at our disposal to change the course of this reces-sion!" Tip proclaimed.

Reagan's face grew red. "God damn it, Tip," he retorted, "we *do care* about those people." The Speaker was not assuaged. "It's easy to say that you care," he replied, "but you aren't willing to *do* anything about it." For the first ten minutes of the forty-minute session, nobody spoke but O'Neill and Reagan. Finally, I tried to break the tension by offering as calmly as I could the possi-bilities of some mid-course corrections to stimulate jobs. Others joined in. A brief discussion ranged over various options, but nobody really yielded. Reagan obviously was uncomfortable and anxious to adjourn this small group seated in the Oval Office, to get to a larger group, including most of the press corps, that was awaiting the president's briefing in the West Room. There, after making his brief presentation and turning explanations over to Treasury Secretary Don Regan, the president did an uncharacteristic thing. Quite unexpectedly, he walked around the side of the seated crowd toward the back of the room as though to exit, then turned and came quietly up the center aisle to a chair where Tip sat, toward the rear. He whispered to the Speaker. "Dave tells me we're really not that far apart on the jobs thing," said the president. "I'm going to ask him to come up and visit with you about it." Clearly O'Neill had scored. He'd gotten under the president's skin. Reagan was on the defensive.

Stockman and two aides came to the Hill on the following day. O'Neill, Tom Foley, and I worked out a $5 billion stimulus package to which they assented. The president would sign it, they promised. Before that month was ended, we acted on an Emergency Supplemental Appropriation that included nutrition for women, infants, and children; low income weatherization help for leaky homes; and summer youth jobs. In addition to this bill, we passed in the following two days an authorization for a Youth Conservation Corps, and a bill providing incentives for the education of teachers in math and sciences.

As spring approached, I was feeling better about everything. Washington springtimes are therapeutic. I watched tiny tendrils push forth at the tips of bare branches, promising leaves for the naked trees. Green shards emerged in fat clusters along our brick wall, assuring me that in a few weeks tall stems would sprout bright tulips. Soon, Forsythia, yellow as butter, would spring forth to cover the hedge rows. Just so, I felt that Congress had planted the seeds in fall and winter that should bring economic recovery by summertime.

The Federal Reserve Board, in desperation, had just lowered interest rates. This move, for which we had been clamoring, could help more than anything. By year's end, progress was observable. The next year, President Reagan would ride comfortably back into office on the soothing theme that it was "morning in America."

But critical new problems were emerging. Our increasingly high-tech society was leaving too many people behind. Real wages were not keeping up. A diminishing number of workers were covered by union contracts. Blue-collar people, when employed, were finding it harder to make ends meet. Antitrust was a forgotten tool. The growing rash of mergers resulted in fewer and bigger companies. Each new conglomerate resulted in layoffs. Homelessness grew. For the first time since the 1930s, it now was a common sight in Washington and other big cities to see people sleeping in doorways and on steam grates for warmth.

President Reagan's rhetorical Cold War with the Russians intensified abruptly as September of 1983 began. A tragic error by a Soviet air commander in the bleak sky over Siberia launched the president into orbits of verbal abuse and a month-long round of angry denunciation theretofore unmatched in Reagan's continuing crusade to discredit, embarrass and punish our Cold War rival.

One dark night, a Korean Air Lines passenger jet with 269 people aboard, strayed far off course and wandered a considerable distance into Soviet territory. It flew over a missile test site. Russian fighter planes scrambled to intercept it, signaling for it to land. The Korean Air Lines pilot ignored the warning. A Soviet fighter pilot shot down the big jet, which crashed, killing all those aboard, including one member of the U.S. Congress.

The Soviet pilots, unable to get a radio response, apparently thought the aircraft part of a U.S. aerial spying operation. An American RC-135 spy plane a short while earlier had flown to the edge of Soviet air space and been detected.

Reagan, immediately on learning of the incident, denounced it publicly as a deliberate act of "barbarism," directed "against the world and the moral precepts which guide human relations among people everywhere." He insisted that cruel Soviet officials had deliberately and callously destroyed a civilian aircraft without warning. By the time bipartisan congressional leaders could be assembled for a briefing by White House military spokesmen that next afternoon, American Air Force specialists suspected the tragic shootdown probably was a case of mistaken identity rather than premeditated murder. Admitting no such possibility, President Reagan and other top officials insisted on their conclusion that it was an open-and-shut case of premeditated murder of unarmed civilians.

On September 26, at President Reagan's request, I flew to New York and sat with the U.S. delegation at the United Nations while Reagan addressed the opening session. The speech was well crafted and delivered, vintage Reagan, even down to the little inspirational homily at the end of a series of blistering attacks upon the Russians. At the end, after scalding them with harsh condemnations, he appealed to the Soviet leaders to join him in his version of nuclear reduction.

That speech, all of us present recognized, was aimed not at the U.N. but at the American television audience. The U.N. delegations from other countries reacted tepidly at best. How could he be both confrontational and conciliatory at the same time, they must have wondered? Reagan surely knew that he could not successfully appeal to the Russian leaders for reasonableness immediately after having accused them of outright murder. He obviously enjoyed having them as a punching bag.

In much the same way, President Reagan and his most vociferous partisans ran the gamut in their treatment of Democratic colleagues. They alternated between calls for conciliatory "bipartisanship" and scalding attacks, sometimes over the same issue. One example: At the request of Treasury Secretary Regan, Speaker O'Neill and I both weighed in to persuade Democratic colleagues to support contributions which our administration had pledged to the International Monetary Fund (IMF), from which loans were made to developing countries. At our urging, Democrats supplied most of the votes for passage, while many in the president's own party ran for cover, denouncing the president's initiative as "money down foreign ratholes." After Democrats had heeded Regan's plea and come to the president's rescue, the GOP campaign committee sent press releases to newspapers in the districts of ten Democratic members accusing them of "supporting Communism with public tax dollars." Increasingly discouraged over the likelihood of achieving an enlightened consensus on foreign policy, I kept trying. Designated as congressional delegate to the Kissinger Commission in late 1983, I joined that group on its five-day, five-country hearings in Central America. That commission, broadly bipartisan in its makeup, concentrated principally on long-range issues. In several late night visits with Henry Kissinger, I came to appreciate anew his diligence and his capacity for the assimilation of facts. Kissinger acknowledged his unfamiliarity with Latin America and asked me for assistance. Bob Strauss, another member of the group, sometimes joined us in these brainstorming discussions.

Kissinger, Strauss, and I quickly developed an affinity. One day, arriving at the Guatemala City airport, we were greeted by a large contingent of government troops in military formation. Just as Kissinger started to walk across the tarmac toward the welcoming party, the troops executed a sudden maneuver, raising their rifles in salute. Startled, Kissinger called to Strauss and me in his heavy German accent: "Jim! Bob! Come and valk vith me. If *anyvone* is going to be shot, ve *all* are going to be shot!" That's what I called real bipartisanship!

In twenty-five years of studying and visiting Central America, I had acquired a deep awareness of its problems, an affinity for its people, and a sad acceptance of the difficulty and slowness of solutions. The principal recommendations of that bipartisan commission were constructive ones, which Reagan publicly welcomed but selectively ignored. They called for a five-year, $8 billion aid package aimed at reducing malnutrition, lowering the infant mortality rate, and eliminating illiteracy. That commission also endorsed an increase in both military and economic aid for the beleaguered new democracy in El Salvador. President Reagan and I joined forces on that one.

By the end of 1983, Congress had supported most of Reagan's foreign policy initiatives while decisively rejecting two of them. One of these was deployment of the MX missile. The other was a covert war to overthrow the Sandinista government of Nicaragua. Still, on every occasion where American troops were involved abroad, Democratic leaders closed ranks. Where disagreement existed, we managed to keep it private. The cases of Lebanon and Grenada come particularly to mind.

All the centuries of pent-up anger in the Middle East came to a boil during 1983 in tiny Lebanon, for years a shining example of public tolerance and civil accommodation among Christian, Muslim and Jewish factions. By unwritten agreement, the presidency alternated between Muslims and Maronite Christians. Suddenly nudged out of Jordan and Syria by President Assad and King Hussein, Palestinian Liberation Organization (PLO) forces under Yasser Arafat swarmed into Lebanon, agitating for a radical facedown with Israel over Palestine. They soon dominated the little country. Its long-peaceful landscape became a theater of terrorist attacks and constant strife.

The American University, to which our State Department had often pointed as an illustration of our country's capacity to help spread civilizing democratic values through an exercise in academic freedom, became a hotbed of political intrigue and fundamentalist propaganda as Muslim extremists took over the campus, harassing moderate professors and intimidating many with physical threats. On April 18, the United States Embassy in Beirut was demolished by a car bomb containing three hundred pounds of TNT. More than one hundred were wounded and dozens of American Embassy staff and Lebanese employees were killed. Responsibility for the car bombing, a suicide mission, was claimed by a group naming itself Islamic Jihad (or Holy War).

As moderate Islamic leaders struggled to preserve order and suppress acts of terror by the militant Shiite faction, a series of violent incidents led to an official call for U.S. help. President Reagan responded, sending a Marine Corps contingent to protect U.S. interests and help the elected government in its efforts to maintain order. The House, at Speaker O'Neill's instruction, quietly sent a delegation to inspect the situation and report to the House leadership. The group was headed by Representative John Murtha of Pennsylvania, a decorated military veteran and a ranking member of the Defense Appropriations subcommittee. Murtha reported to the Joint Chiefs of Staff as well as to House leaders. He privately described what he saw as a dangerous vulnerability of the Marine detachment, which was bivouacked together in a building at one edge of the international airport. Sitting beneath a range of mountains from which artillery shells could be fired without warning, that Marine base seemed an invitation to terrorist attacks. Murtha argued for physical dispersal of the troops over a wider area.

Shortly after dawn on October 23, a few weeks after Murtha's private report, a large Mercedes truck laden with twenty-five thousand pounds of TNT ripped through a barbed wire fence, smashed into the Marine head-quarters building, and exploded. More than two hundred marines were killed in their sleep. President Reagan expressed horror and indignation at the "vicious, cowardly, and ruthless" attack and vowed that the United States would remain in Lebanon.

This was the worst foreign policy debacle in the eight years of Reagan's presidency, but nobody sought to make political capital of the tragedy. None of us who had heard Murtha's warning went running to the press, piously demanding to know why Reagan's team had not heeded Murtha's advice. There still was in those days a sense of decent restraint, which, in the decade that followed, has suffered deep erosion.

About four o'clock in the afternoon of the day following the tragedy in Lebanon, I had a call from Speaker O'Neill. Could I come to his office immediately, he asked. When I arrived, Tip told me privately to walk down the hall to H-201, the little hideaway office at the north end of the long Speaker's hallway in the Capitol's east front. "Mike Deaver's waiting there," said Tip. "He wants to talk to you privately." Intrigued by the mystery, I went silently to the designated room. Presidential aide Deaver was the only person there.

"This is a matter of highest national security," Deaver said. "The president wants to see you at the White House at eight o'clock tonight. You must tell nobody of this conversation." I reached for the telephone to call Betty and advise her I wouldn't be home for dinner. Deaver stopped me before I could dial the number.

"Please don't even allude to this over the telephone," he insisted. "We'd prefer you go home exactly as usual. At seven-thirty tonight, there'll be a black, unmarked vehicle parked in your driveway and heading outward. Just get in the back seat, and the driver will bring you to the White House. When our meeting is ended, he'll take you home."

At 7:50 that evening, the unobtrusive-looking automobile, with me aboard, drove into the 17th Street entrance of the crannied old Executive Office Building just west and across a little protected alleyway from the basement entrance to the White House. I got out, walked briskly across the darkened alleyway, and entered the president's mansion undetected. At the door I was met, and from there escorted to the family quarters on the second floor. O'Neill, House Minority Leader Bob Michel, Senate leaders Howard Baker and Robert Byrd joined us, each individually conveyed to the meeting in a similar fashion.

The tiny island of Grenada, we were advised, had become a threat to the lives of several hundred U.S. medical students attending university there. Ruled for several years by an avowed Marxist, Maurice Bishop, it had been more a splinter than a thorn in our side. Now, following an even more left-leaning military junta, which overthrew and killed Bishop, Reagan insisted that Grenada was dominated by Castro and about to become a launching pad for communist subversion in the hemisphere. Cuban work cadres were helping to build a new airport with a long runway.

Reagan told us he had been asked formally by the Organization of

Eastern Caribbean States to intervene and restore order in the region. The little island states of Antigua, Barbados, Dominica, Jamaica, St. Lucia, and St. Vincent apparently felt their security threatened and feared a Cuban invasion from Grenada. Cubans, Reagan said, had stockpiled thousands of weapons on the island. The medical students had been ordered repatriated immediately, but approximately 1,100 U.S. citizens were believed to be on the island, and in the climate of wild anarchy that prevailed, he felt their lives were in danger.

"Unless you gentlemen strongly object," the president declared, it was his intention to land a Marine and Ranger force on the island beginning at 5 A.M. and thus establish order, protect free governments in the region, and secure the safety of American citizens.

All of us were aware of Bishop's overthrow some two weeks earlier. This was the first we knew, however, of the other developments. None of us was prepared to dispute the State Department findings. We had no knowledge to the contrary on which to base an objection.

"Be sure to send a sufficient force to mop it up quickly and secure the island within the first twenty-four hours," I suggested. "We certainly couldn't afford another Bay of Pigs."

Before we left, President Reagan seemed buoyant. "The people there don't want to be taken over by Cuba," he vowed. It would be wonderful, he speculated, to see the local citizens once again standing on the sidewalks, waving little American flags as our liberating troops marched into the city.

On our way downstairs, Tip asked me if I knew where Reagan had come by the precedent of local citizens with American flags. I thought for a minute, said I had a vague recollection that something like that may have happened, possibly somewhere in Italy, in World War II. "You and the president are both wrong," a hushed voice responded. "It happened in the movie *A Bell for Adano*."

The invasion was swift and decisive. A much smaller contingent of Cuban troops resisted, but were quickly overcome. Sixteen Americans were killed, many more Cubans died, and 630 were taken prisoner. It was all over in a matter of hours. The popular military victory and its immediate aftermath of rejoicing in Grenada dominated all news for the following several days. The chilling tragedy in Lebanon, which snuffed out the lives of more than 200 marines less than forty-eight hours earlier, was swept entirely off the front pages and out of the nightly news. It was as though it had never happened. A few days later, President Reagan ordered our troops out of Beirut.

During 1984, I became painfully aware of a steady erosion of American industrial strength. This stood in stark contrast to our military prowess. We needed, I felt, a conscious industrial policy based on modernizing our plants, our machinery, our processes, and techniques. With a young congressman named Lane Evans, I spoke one night in Peoria, Illinois. The next day we drove to the small town of Canton, in Lane's district. There we met with municipal, civic, and business leaders of that little city ravaged by unemployment and determined not to die. We visited the ghost of a once vibrant factory. Families leaving town for jobs, I learned, had been unable to sell their houses except at painfully sacrificial prices. Vacant rooms stared sightlessly out of undraped windows as through the eye sockets of a skull. The memory haunted me. It had been a *plowshare* factory. Military procurement plants, several in my own district, were thriving. So long as our country had need for more sophisticated weapons systems, I was eager for our Texas firms to design and build them, but I was witnessing a grotesque reversal of Isaiah's prophecy. All over America, forty years after World War II and ten years after the official end of hostilities in Vietnam, we were beating plowshares into swords.

At a series of weekly dinners at our house in northern Virginia, Betty and I discussed these things with colleagues. We invited both Democrats and Republicans, along with their wives, for open, freewheeling discussions. On one weekend we invited five younger congressional couples to join us for a two day retreat in the mountains above nearby Berkeley Springs, West Virginia. It gave us an opportunity to get better acquainted, on a personal level, with Dick and Jane Gephardt, Steny and Judy Hoyer, Robin and Susan Britt, Mike and Ann Andrews, Ron and Tami Coleman.

In a speech to the Washington Press Club, I tried to put it all in some sensible context. Every minute of that year, I pointed out, thirty children somewhere in the world died for want of food or relatively inexpensive vaccines. And every minute, the world's military budget absorbed $1.3 million for new implements of terror. It was tragic, I said, that we had cut education when our schools were deteriorating. We had cut nutrition while hunger was increasing. We had cut job training when millions were out of work. Perhaps the saddest phenomenon of all, I observed, was a poll that showed that most adult Americans, for the first time in our history, did not believe their children would have as high a standard of living as they themselves had enjoyed. The single most impelling world problem was that the United States and the Soviet Union, leapfrogging one another in the development of ever more awesome weaponry, were spending more than half a trillion dollars that year on the implements of devastation.

"Someone must take the initiative," I said. "I would like for that someone to be the president of the United States."

In the next four years, I would say these things directly to President Reagan. We would see the beginning of a historic turnaround. I'd work with the president for peace with the Soviet Union and work both with him and against him to promote peace in our own hemisphere. There would be arguments and clashes of will. And some of them would lead to peace.

CHAPTER THIRTY-ONE

BUMPY ROAD
TO PEACE

O ne day, following my retirement from Congress, a student at Texas Christian University asked what had been the three greatest satisfactions of my thirty-four years in office. After a moment's thought, I said the Camp David peace agreement, the achievement of peace in Central America, and the end of the Cold War. The student seemed a bit surprised that I hadn't named some of the domestic victories we'd won in legislative battles, or local projects that loomed large on the Fort Worth horizon. On reflection, I, too, was surprised. After all, I took more than a little parochial pride in things I'd sponsored to help our city, and a lot of proprietary pleasure flowed from several national legislative landmarks in which I'd played a part—things like Interstate highways, the clean water program, civil rights reforms, and several contributions to upgrading America's educational system. There were others, many, in which I had participated with gusto to revel in hard won victories. But in my first instinctive reaction to the question, I listed the three which led to peace. They were not my personal accomplishments. My role had been mainly a supportive one. Yet they gave me great satisfaction.

During Ronald Reagan's second term, I spent an unusual amount of time and effort pursuing peace and freedom among the strife-torn republics of Central America and the elusive grail of an end to our frightening and economically debilitating Cold War with the Soviet Union. But before I could make any major contribution to either cause, there was one piece of necessary homework that I needed to get behind me. Beginning the 1985 session, Speaker O'Neill announced that he would retire at the end of that term. He would have served for ten years, the longest consecutive tenure of any

Speaker in history. (Henry Clay's and Sam Rayburn's total years in the chair were longer but interrupted by electoral hiatuses, two in Rayburn's case.) Immediately upon Tip's announcement, news writers began speculating about his successor. Inventing imaginary intrigues and feuds, several wrote that I would surely have at least one major Democratic opponent for the speakership.

One commentator opined that the caucus vote to substitute forty-six-year-old Les Aspin for aging and ailing Mel Price, eighty, as Chairman of the Armed Services Committee foreboded trouble for me. At sixty-four, the logic went, I'd be victim of a generation gap in the House that would open a fissure as traumatic as an earthquake. Never mind that I was ten years younger than Tip. There was speculation that my old friend Dan Rostenkowski might seek the job. Other news people began looking for other nominees. I knew I had to put a decisive end to all this idle conjecture before I could concentrate effectively on the substantive tasks ahead.

On February 5, 1985, almost two full years before the formal election of Tip's successor, I assembled a steering committee of about thirty members. It included several Texans and a cross section of other good friends like Jack Murtha of Pennsylvania, Bill Alexander of Arkansas, Tony Coelho of California, and Brian Donnelly of Massachusetts. They agreed to conduct a whirlwind canvass of colleagues, that very day, to get solid pledges supporting my candidacy from a substantial majority of all House Democrats. It was to be done within forty-eight hours if possible. My longtime Texas friend, Jack Brooks, was picked as chairman of the informal group.

The work went more swiftly and much more smoothly than I had dared to expect. By the afternoon of February 7, we had 184 firm pledges out of approximately 250 members who expected to return. Calling a press conference, we announced our list of names. And that was the end of that. For the next two years, I was free to concentrate on legislative matters without having to look over my shoulder to see if anyone was gaining on me.

On February 20, British Prime Minister Margaret Thatcher spoke to a joint meeting of congress. The first half of her speech sounded like a reelection appeal for Ronald Reagan; the second half like one for Margaret Thatcher. She was articulate, doctrinaire, and unsurprising. That evening at the British embassy we celebrated two hundred years of diplomatic relations between our two countries. At the dinner, Betty sat at the table with the visiting head of government. I was seated between Barbara Bush and Mr. Thatcher. What a stereotypical Tory!

At one point, the Prime Minister's husband began fulminating about "the inordinate attention" given by the media to the famine in Africa. "One would think," exclaimed Mr. Thatcher, "that there'd never been a famine before, that nobody had ever starved to death before. Why!" he exclaimed, "it's been going on, you know, since the very beginning. People have *always* starved to death. There's nothing new in that!"

That evening, Betty and I sat in a small theater arrangement along with President Reagan and Mrs. Thatcher, listening to James Symington, a former colleague who had traveled and studied in Britain, play a ukelele and croon tunes dear to both countries. In this relaxed setting, the president asked me if I would undertake a mission for him.

"Next month," Reagan told me, "we'll be sending negotiators to meet with the Russians in Geneva. They'll be exploring possibilities for a treaty to reduce the burden of nuclear weapons. We don't know if it will work, but we're going to see how serious they are. Max Kampelman will be chairman of our group, and your old friend John Tower will be a member of our negotiating team."

"Wonderful!" I exclaimed. "Sounds like you're sending in the first string. I'm glad to hear we've arrived at this point, and I certainly do wish you well. *All* of us do—Democrats and Republicans alike. This is one that really transcends party lines."

"Well, that's just what I wanted to talk to you about," said the president. "We want to impress the Russians with the fact that our whole nation is united on this question. We would like for a bipartisan delegation from Congress to be present for the opening of the talks. We think it would give our negotiators some credibility and leverage if the Russians could see such a group there, showing that Congress is backing up our negotiators."

"Mr. President, you *know* I will do it," I said.

Reagan said the State Department people would be in touch with me. They would make one of the large presidential planes available for our group. The next day, Secretary Shultz called. State Department planners said it would be nice if we could have eight or more Democrats and a like number of Republicans, and that we should be accompanied for protocol purposes by our spouses.

On Friday March 1, the Evans and Novak column in the *Washington Post* took a cheap shot at House Democrats over the upcoming trip. Well-known as a Cold War hawk and GOP apologist, Bob Novak was one of those with whom administration hatchet men often planted stories to embarrass Democrats individually and collectively. Quoting unnamed administration "sources," Novak and Evans accused us of shameless junketeering, of creating a "circus" atmosphere for the peace talks, of planning to consume the valuable time of negotiators to give us "dog and pony shows" at Geneva. The column named and blamed me personally. At one point, Evans and Novak attributed to their unidentified source the statement that I had "invited half the members and their wives."

The claim, of course, was preposterous and malicious. Members of Congress were furious. Those few whom Michel and I had approached to go began backing out. An unnamed mischief-maker in the State Department and a couple of sensation-hungry journalists had just about torpedoed the president's hope for an impressive demonstration of unity at Geneva.

Others, too, seemed determined to break up any show of bipartisanship. On the following Monday, March 4—a day on which it had been announced the previous Thursday that there'd be no vote on any substantive matter so as to permit members to arrive late on flights from their home districts—a band of Republican House members tried to pull a fast one. They had been busy over the weekend, calling and quietly encouraging GOP members to be in attendance for an unadvertised insurgency immediately upon convening of the House. It all involved a hairline-close vote in Indiana's 8th district, where incumbent Frank McCloskey, a Democrat, was challenged by a Republican contender named Richard McIntyre in the November general election. On the basis of recounts and official certification by the state of Indiana, McCloskey had been declared winner and would be tentatively seated pending further legal action. Taking the Speaker wholly by surprise, a Republican spokesman moved suddenly to unseat McCloskey and replace him with McIntyre. This, coming as it did without notice, was an unprecedented maneuver.

Many members, mostly Democrats, were absent. O'Neill, Foley, Coelho, and I were barely able to muster enough, by frantic telephoning, to sustain the Leadership's counter-motion. Caught by surprise, we had moved to refer the unexpected proposal to the House Administration Committee for a hearing on its substance. After a quick, well-organized telephone effort, we prevailed by one vote. Thereupon, Republican Whip Trent Lott led a large number of GOP members in a noisy walkout, staged for the benefit of the press.

The next day, Tuesday, I received two calls from President Reagan. He asked me to reconsider and agree to accompanying a delegation to Geneva for the peace talks. I explained that it wasn't I personally but my colleagues who felt they were being used. They wouldn't mind going if it would achieve a purpose. But they were unwilling to make themselves vulnerable to sneak attacks from White House or State Department "moles" and headline-thirsty journalists. The only repair I could see would be for him, the president, to repudiate the Evans and Novak story.

"Well, you know I don't agree with that story, Jim," Reagan said. "I wouldn't have asked you to go if I hadn't really thought it would do some good."

We left it this way: I'd talk again with our group and see if I could persuade them to reconsider, and he would ease the pain by making a public statement declaring that it was he who had asked us to undertake the supportive assignment and that he believed it would be highly useful. Later that afternoon, I got a second call from the president. He had authorized the statement to the press, he said. No journalist chose to play the president's clarifying statement in any news account that I saw.

On Wednesday, March 6, I think I discovered a facet of Ronald Reagan's character that I had long suspected but never before plumbed. In the process, I thought maybe, just maybe, I had found a better way to deal with him than I had been pursuing. Previous entreaties, based on appeals to logic, always had fallen on deaf ears. So full was the president's head of ideologically reassuring half-facts and anecdotes of dubious actuality, that he instinctively called up from his repertoire some appealing or appalling non sequiturs. But in that particular meeting with the bipartisan Congressional leadership in the Cabinet room, I appealed directly to Reagan's raw emotions.

The president, after a brief summation, turned directly to me and personalized his appeal for a top congressional presence at the opening of the peace talks in Geneva. It was almost as though he thought I had exaggerated the disinclination of my colleagues to participate. Looking him directly in the eye, I made my response just as personal as he had made his appeal. "I'll go with you, Mr. President. I'll go to the gates of hell with you, if it will serve the cause of peace. I feel sure Bob Michel will go. But we don't need a big delegation, and we won't want to be wined and dined. We won't bring our wives, and we won't go to any big dinners or parties."

Then I told him how important I considered the historic opportunity. I recalled the great contribution of Richard Nixon in opening the long-closed gates to normalized relations with China and the Soviet Union. I said a Democrat might not have been able to do what Mr. Nixon had done, for fear of being blasted as soft on communism. "That never could be said of Nixon," I added, "and nobody can ever say that of *you*, Mr. President! There've been a lot of domestic things on which I've disagreed with you, Mr. President, but there is nothing on earth I would like better than to help Ronald Reagan go down in history and in the hearts of people everywhere on earth as the American president who made the step that ended the arms race and lifted from our lives the level of terror that tyrannizes people everywhere and burdens us with the terrible cost of weaponry we can't afford!"

Watching the president's face closely, I sensed that he was moved. In this effort to nudge Ronald Reagan toward a more active role in peacemaking that could end the Cold War, I was told by Bob Strauss, I had a quiet but powerful ally: Nancy Reagan.

In the kaleidoscope of life are infinite refractions of divine light, and we never can be sure if another sees the exact same image that comes into our range of sight. But I believe this moment in history may have brought an opening, however tentative, out of the sterile, landlocked desert of Cold War thinking onto an open sea of new possibilities. By either plan or fate, I had been working for some days during this same time with State Department representatives, who wanted me to host a high-ranking group of fifteen official visitors from the Soviet Union. That delegation was being led by Vladimir V. Shcherbitskiy, a member of the Politburo and Chairman of the Central Committee for the Ukraine, the broad equivalent of governor for that huge state.

Shcherbitskiy was a large man, sixty-seven years of age, with expressive eyes, dramatic countenance, and an almost leonine crop of gray hair, which flowed backward from his temples. A World War II veteran, he had served with the Red Army on the Caucasian front. For the first time in the American-Soviet relationship, a Politburo member heading a delegation had expressly asked to visit other parts of the United States outside Washington and the New York area. It was probably natural that Shcherbitskiy, from Kiev (the USSR's approximate equivalent of Chicago) and the grain fields of the sprawling breadbasket Republic of the Ukraine, would want to see other sections of America. We thought it important to show the group what we could of our country and its people, its underlying strength. The delegation included individuals of substantial power and accomplishment in the Soviet Union. Someone, perhaps Soviet Ambassador Anatoly Dobrynin, had recommended that the visiting team see Texas and California. Colleagues Martin Frost, Jake Pickle and I were approached by the State Department to host events in Austin, Dallas, and Fort Worth.

Following a series of planning sessions, we had an itinerary worked out. We would hold a series of talk sessions. They'd be at the Woodrow Wilson International Center for Scholars, part of the Smithsonian complex only a few blocks from the Capitol. That center's director, James H. Billington, was a serious scholar of Russian life, history and government. One of the discussants would be George F. Kennan, former ambassador to the Soviet Union.

On the second day of the Soviets' U.S. visit, we hosted a luncheon on the Hill for the Russian delegation. Seated in the stately old Cannon Caucus Room between Shcherbitskiy and Dobrynin, the latter acting as our interpreter, I answered our guests' questions about the trip to Texas. We wanted to show them a good cross section of Southwestern American life and regional history. One of several events laid on in Fort Worth was a visit to Billy Bob's Texas arena on the old North Side where cowboys nightly rode bucking bulls. As this particular feature was being recited in Russian by Ambassador Dobrynin, I saw Shcherbitskiy wince, frown and shake his head. He obviously found something distasteful in the idea. Dobrynin laughed and began explaining, along with appropriate gestures, that our visitor had misunderstood. Instead of bull *riding,* a sport with which he had never been acquainted, Shcherbitskiy thought we proposed taking him to a bull*fight.*

We planned an itinerary to show the delegation an American factory, at least one high-tech enterprise operated by computers, a ranch, some farms, and a small business or two. Also plans were made for a breakfast, two luncheons, and a dinner, where each Soviet guest would be seated beside some successful American with similar professional or cultural interests, with a bilingual person in an adjoining seat to translate. On the morning of their visit in Dallas, the Soviet visitors were entertained at breakfast in the upscale private home of Dr. Richard S. Fisher, a prominent citizen and personal friend of Congressman Frost. With the unguarded candor of youth, the host's seven-year-old son blurted out in high-pitched voice, "Daddy, why are you having our *enemies* here in our house?" A sudden hush fell over the room, like nightfall at midday. The translator's comment to Shcherbitskiy was muted, almost whispered. Everyone suddenly looked his way. The father frowned, put a protective arm around his son, and began trying to apologize for the boy's thoughtless inhospitality.

To everyone's relief, Shcherbitskiy smiled. Then he spoke. His words, translated, went like this: "Please don't feel unkindly toward the boy. He meant no harm. Our children are not to be blamed for the ill feeling we've allowed to grow up between us. They know only what they hear and are but mirrors of the cultures in which they are raised, so full of fear and misunderstanding. It is the same with us. Before I left, I talked with my eight-year-old granddaughter about our trip. She said, 'But, Grandfather, why are you going to Dallas, where they kill people?'"

The reference, of course, was to the assassination of President Kennedy, which school children throughout the world know occurred in Dallas. Shcherbitskiy continued: "We all should know many better things of Dallas than that one unfortunate event," he said, "and these things we are learning. This is why it is important for each of our countries to get to know the other better."

In Austin, we took the Soviet delegation on a tour of the Lyndon B. Johnson Library and the State Capitol. The visitors were interested in the library's display showing Johnson's visit with Soviet Premier Aleksey Kosygin at Glassboro, New Jersey. At a luncheon in our guests' honor, attended by university and state officials, Jake Pickle presented to each of our visitors a pair of Texas-made cowboy boots. They beamed with pleasure. The too brief era of the cowboy, memorialized in so many movies, is a subject of popular legend and mythology all over Europe, I had learned. We had the hat and boot sizes of each of our guests. In Fort Worth the next evening, I would present to each a high quality broad-brimmed western hat, a wide western belt with a large silver buckle, and a colorful bandanna.

At the state capitol we visited informally with Governor Mark White. Shcherbitskiy and two or three of the others were particularly interested in the topography, climatology, and geology of our region and how it had contributed to our industrialization. They also showed a lively curiosity about Texas agriculture and animal husbandry. They wanted to know how much acreage would be required to sustain a given number of livestock, and in what regions irrigation was required. Governor White and I both told stories of Texas' periodic droughts and the reliance of the land upon sufficient rainfall. Shcherbitskiy made a comment which came as a big surprise to me. Spreading his hands palms upward, he said, "There's no getting around it. Sometimes we just have to depend on God."

A few other occasional comments of this general type told me that a subtle but significant change had occurred in the years since my 1972 visit to Russia. At that time, it would have been altogether politically incorrect for a Soviet official to make any public reference to deity. I saw that other attitudes, too, had softened measurably.

There was one final phase of the visit about which I had been vaguely apprehensive. I had wondered how the assorted cowhands and good ol' boys and gals guzzling beer in the stands at Billy Bob's rodeo arena would greet a group of visiting public officials from communist Russia.

I needn't have worried. As the group of visitors entered to take seats reserved for them in the stands, the Texas crowd stood in perfect hospitality, applauding and raising beer cans in a visual toast to our guests. I glowed with pride, ashamed that I had ever doubted my fellow townsmen's instinctive good manners.

En route to Geneva three days later with Republican leader Bob Michel and a delegation of six, I was certain that ingredients existed for a major change in our relations with the Soviet Union. Geneva—where hopes of world peace blossomed briefly at the end of the first world war, where peacemakers returned again and again like migratory waterfowl. Adjacent to our hotel was the original League of Nations building, with a plaque dedicated to the memory of Woodrow Wilson. In the courtyard stood a rusted World War I artillery piece, its long barrel literally tied into a knot, a symbol of all that men of good will had tried over those sixty-five years and more to do. What intensities of heat had been required to make the metal malleable enough for that disabling transformation? And what extremes of pressure must humankind endure to subdue the folly of its recurrent temptation to violence?

George Kennan, who knew as much about the Soviet Union as any American, had told me a week earlier that the Soviets were, in his opinion, ready to negotiate in good faith. But Kennan held out only limited optimism for the success of these talks. He feared Reagan and those who advised him might lack the flexibility to let their Cold War rivals agree to a settlement that would not be humiliating to their pride. Max Kampelman, head of our negotiating team, however, impressed me as a levelheaded person who knew his business. "Sometimes it takes months during which you think you are getting absolutely nowhere," Kampelman explained. I was glad he had the job. I knew I'd never have the patience for that kind of work.

Two weeks later, President Reagan called and ask me to vote for a new appropriation to build twenty-one MX missiles. I explained the difficulty of supporting more credit card debt for weapons, particularly in light of a recent Reagan veto and other veto threats. "I have trouble voting to add more new weapons to the deficit, Mr. President, when you're vetoing loan guarantees for family farmers, help for low income students wanting to attend college and unemployment compensation for the jobless." I continued: "You'll prevail this time Mr. President," I told him, "but only by a narrow margin, and only because of the peace talks."

It turned out I was right. He won the twenty-one missiles by a six-vote margin on the following day. It is hard to deny any president a weapon that he describes as a necessary bargaining chip while we're trying to negotiate genuine weapons reductions with the Soviet Union. Ironic, wasn't it? It had taken a *peace initiative* to get weapons approved. I decided we were better off to have the administration's position prevail at the moment. Otherwise, those among Reagan's advisors who really didn't want the peace talks in the first place might have seized upon the congressional refusal of the MX as an excuse to sabotage those talks and blame their failure upon Congress.

There was deep skepticism among many in Congress over the seriousness of Reagan's intent at Geneva. Some suggested cynically that, rather than the MX being a "bargaining chip" for peace talks, the president had merely agreed to the talks as a bargaining chip to get more weapons from Congress. I did not share that view. I believed Reagan would like for the peace talks to succeed, but I wondered if he possessed the traits of character to negotiate peace. His repeated public assessments of his adversaries' motives had been so uniformly uncharitable to make it difficult now for him to accept the possibility that they were acting in good faith.

In November of that year, Reagan met Gorbachev in Geneva. It had to be an eye-opener for both men. Prior to his departure Reagan and his staff had warned congressional leaders against over-expectation. "If we have to come back empty handed," the president cautioned, "that's better than accepting a bad agreement." On November 16, the day Reagan left Washington for the summit, *The New York Times* surprisingly published a letter to Reagan written by Defense Secretary Caspar Weinberger. That letter disparaged the value of any arms control agreement and warned Reagan against accepting any limits on SDI research. Weinberger obviously hoped the summit would come to naught.

Gorbachev both surprised and intrigued Reagan. At fifty-four, the USSR's new General Secretary was much younger than any recent predecessor. Well educated, well traveled, urbane, and personable, Gorbachev obviously was taking charge, throwing open windows, and letting the fresh air of free thought clear out the cobwebs and stale cigar smoke of moribund ideology. The Geneva summit of November 1985 achieved little of substantive agreement, but it vastly improved the *atmospherics* of superpower relations. In spite of his well cultivated doubts, Reagan liked the young leader with the easy smile and sparkling eyes.

Gorbachev admitted candidly that the Soviet Union, in its preoccupation with expensive weaponry, had suffered a twenty-year "period of stagnation." His country, he stated openly, had fallen far behind the economic and technological progress of the United States and other modern societies. The old methods of authoritarian control had stifled innovation, he said. He would like for his country to embark upon revolutionary economic restructuring (*perestroika*) and democratizing political reforms (*glasnost*). What may really have opened the door to trust on a personal basis, however, was the series of increasingly relaxed private talks between the two leaders on subjects far less political. Gorbachev and his wife, Raisa, it turned out, were movie enthusiasts. They told Reagan how much they had admired his performance in *Kings Row*. They pumped him for anecdotes of his days in the movies, "stories involving James Stewart, John Wayne and Humphrey Bogart," according to Treasury Secretary Don Regan, who accompanied the president. In the briefing on Reagan's return from that Geneva meeting, it was clear that his basic attitude toward the prospects of peace had changed.

Almost a year later, in October of 1986, just as final touches were being put on the annual Armed Services authorization bill in conference committee, President Reagan called by long distance from Reykjavík, Iceland. It was the eve of his second summit meeting with Gorbachev. Conferees from both House and Senate had agreed tentatively to the elimination of several items of military hardware. Reagan pleaded with Tip and me to intercede.

"You guys are giving away several of the things I intended to yield up as inducements to Gorbachev for concessions on his side," Reagan complained. O'Neill and I at length agreed. I addressed my Democratic colleagues in

Congress. "Look, guys," I said. "You've made these choices to save money and serve peace. For Pete's sake, let's let the president take credit for it. We'll all get something damn good in return!" Somewhat begrudgingly, they agreed.

That Reykjavík summit got off to a fast start. It almost achieved a complete termination of the Cold War's forty-year mutual buildup of nuclear arms. Gorbachev seized the initiative with a stunningly bold proposal. Both countries, he suggested, should immediately eliminate half their long-range ballistic missiles and work out a timetable for the mutual elimination of the rest of them. In return, the anti-missile treaty would have to be observed for ten more years, consigning strategic defense initiative (SDI)—the still undeveloped Star Wars concept—to laboratory experimentation only.

Many American scientists had expressed public doubt that the missile shield ever could actually be made to work, but it was an idea close to Reagan's heart. One scientist had quipped that there were only two men in either country who took the concept seriously—Reagan and Gorbachev. This was not quite correct. Ambassador Dobrynin tells in his 1995 book, *In Confidence*, how Gorbachev came close to conceding the SDI issue. "Let them have it," he reportedly said at one point, "what harm is it to us? We don't intend to attack them." But Gorbachev's generals convinced him the SDI might give America, under some trigger-happy president, a first-strike capability.

In the recess that followed Gorbachev's dramatic offer, Reagan advisors worried that the Russian leader had stolen the initiative. The world would hail his boldness. Reagan needed a counter proposal, one just as bold to show that he was serious about peace; but one, preferably in their view, that Gorbachev would have to reject. This ploy of offering something we really didn't want accepted seemed to me, as the entire process was reconstructed at our debriefing a few days later in the White House, like a high-stakes game of chicken. Secretary George Shultz and Cold War hawk Richard Perle, a former staffer for Senator Henry Jackson whom Weinberger had installed in the Defense Department, came up with the counter offer. President Reagan, on their advice, boldly proposed to eliminate *all* ballistic missiles (presumably including NATO missiles in Europe) over a ten-year period. At the end of that time, however, the United States would be free, under Reagan's plan, to install the SDI anti-missiles system to guard against cheating or some missile threat by a third country.

To the consternation of all, the Russian leader called President Reagan and raised him. He counter-proposed that both sides agree to eliminate not just the delivery systems, but *all* the world's *existing* nuclear weapons. In exchange for this, Reagan would have to agree to give up the idea of the still-unbuilt SDI. That was too much! The president sternly replied that the SDI was not on the table and would not be a bargaining chip in any negotiation. This ended it; there was no agreement—but the two *had* talked, offered boldly, and come close. The process was irreversible. An end to the Cold War would come, eventually.

While all of this was happening, thoughtful Americans were awakening to an underlying economic crisis of a type wholly unfamiliar to our country's recent experience. During the previous year, seventy-nine banks had failed, more than in any other year since 1938. The Federal Deposit Insurance Corporation listed a record number of 817 others as "problem cases." In September, Commerce Department figures would reveal that ours had become, for the first time since 1914, a debtor nation. As cold weather began to stretch its chilling fingers into the urban North, legions of homeless faced the renewed challenge of survival. Throughout America there were only ninety-one thousand shelter beds operated by public and charitable institutions. Estimates of homeless individuals hit three million. The administration had again slashed spending on low-income housing.

In Congress, the troops grew restless, clamoring for a resolute approach. I took up the cudgel, persuading Tip to appoint a blue-ribbon leadership task force on trade. Next, I discussed the effort with Bob Michel. This had to be bipartisan, I insisted. Ultimately, we chose a nineteen-member group, consisting of the heads and ranking minority members of House subcommittees with jurisdiction over remedies that might contribute to solutions. Don Bonker of Washington was made chairman, and Sam Gibbons of Florida vice chairman. Our task force held a press conference to describe a bipartisan approach. We said we needed to find incentives for investments to modernize America's industrial base; to enlist the help of labor unions to improve productivity; and to expand and update job training to equip workers for new tasks. We needed also to insist that other nations impose no greater restrictions on American products than we required of theirs in our markets.

Alas, the nightly network news shows portrayed our effort in the now familiar adversarial terms that characterized most news stories. There had to be opposing teams, good guys and bad guys. Nothing more complicated, please. The abbreviated snippets that evening represented our effort as confrontational and aimed expressly at Japan.

The fact was, of course, that Japan for forty years, ever since the end of World War II, had spent absolutely nothing on its military defense. Unburdened of that economic responsibility—in fact, prohibited by treaty from all military activity—the Japanese had been free to devote all their efforts to the pursuit of social betterment and economic competitiveness. Not only had they made enormous inroads into our heavy industries like autos and steel, they now were outperforming us in electronics and sophisticated items like computer chips. And they were buying up ever bigger slices of America—American banks, hotels, and real estate of all sorts. They even owned a growing percentage of U.S. government bonds. As we sank deeper into debt, our taxpayers were paying several billion dollars in interest each year to Japanese bondholders. Spending relatively a lot more on higher education, they were reaping a harvest. In 1985, with only half our population, Japanese universities were graduating half again more scientists, engineers, and high-quality technical planners than our American universities were.

No use blaming the Japanese. Maybe we could learn some things from their example. If we were wise enough to bring off with the Russians a mutual, enforceable long-term reduction in our levels of military spending, we could work wonders. Just a small portion of our $300 billion annual military bill could perform miracles for higher education, for civilian research, for industrial retooling, and skills-retraining to convert our American productive genius from its preoccupation with weapons to new, better, more marketable civilian goods that enrich people's lives.

Throughout the first two years of Reagan's second term, I strove to broaden the base of bipartisan civility in the House. But this was an uphill struggle. During the August 1985 congressional recess, I scheduled a ten day inspection for interested members to probe the possibilities of peace with the negotiators in Geneva. While in Europe, we pursued other meetings to learn what we could of chances for peace in Northern Ireland and to respond to a request by U.S. Ambassador John Scanlan for a high-level congressional visit to Yugoslavia, just emerging from the forty-year cocoon of Tito's dictatorship.

In Ireland, en route to Dublin from Deerfield, the American ambassadorial residence, I observed a valuable lesson. Betty and I were seated in the rear of an Irish touring car, I on the left and she on the right. The entourage was following a motorcycle escort as it wove its way through traffic. I've always been uncomfortable with a motorcycle escort, thinking it an affectation of self-importance. But we were in the hands of our hosts, and I did not complain. I decided to sit back and enjoy it.

While the Irish had taken to driving on the right side of their roads and streets, as Americans do, the automobile in which we rode, like other British-made products, had the steering wheel on the right. Seated as I was in the left rear, the steering mechanism was clearly visible to me. Betty, sitting directly behind the actual driver, could not see the wheel. She imagined the vehicle to be driven by the large man in the left front seat. I was engaging this man in spirited conversation. For most of the route he turned his body, so as to look back over his right shoulder at me while we conversed.

Whenever the driver put on the brake to slow down, my conversation partner would turn his view instinctively frontward, just long enough to see what was happening, and then look back at me again as the car resumed speed, and we resumed our conversation. Betty, supposing him to be the driver, was as apprehensive as a rabbit chased by a pack of fierce dogs. How, she wondered wildly, could he keep the vehicle in the road while looking intently into the back seat? And how, pray tell, did he know to turn frontward just in time to apply the brakes? As the motorcade slowed suddenly to a near stop and my helpful host turned his gaze once again forward, Betty clutched my arm and demanded, "PLEASE don't ask him any more questions! You're going to get us KILLED!"

That episode, I decided, was a metaphor for most of our problems—our mistaken assumptions about the motives of people in foreign countries, with different steering mechanisms; and our failures to understand what's in the minds of our colleagues of the other political party, who sit in different seats and see from a different perspective. With what fears do they view our conduct, though it be wholly understandable to us, as Betty quite rationally felt terror in the guide's inattention to the road ahead?

My hopes for cultivating a higher degree of bipartisan civility and cooperation on the House floor were destined, however, for disappointment. A group of young GOP firebrands was emerging, impatient for attention and contemptuous of the old rules of legislative courtesy. They were as irritating as a swarm of gnats. Intent on divisiveness and disruptions, their members despised efforts at conciliation. They constantly pressured fair and gentlemanly Bob Michel to be more confrontational. Some of them were not above McCarthyite tactics. And the growing, bubbling controversy over Central America was grist for their mills. It would lead our country, in 1986, to the brink of the most serious constitutional crisis since Watergate.

CHAPTER THIRTY-TWO

CENTRAL AMERICAN QUAGMIRE

N o foreign policy issue since the Vietnam war has been so politically polarizing as the Reagan administration's efforts to
overthrow Nicaragua's Sandinista government using an armed
group called *Contras* as a proxy force. The American people
split, and Congress fractured into two near-irreconcilable camps, each side
claiming moral superiority. One was determined to avoid another Cuba,
the other to avoid another Vietnam. Taunts such as "Communist!" and
"Warmonger!" shattered the calm of reasoned debate. There was little room
in the middle for creative solutions or constructive maneuvering.

Civil wars in El Salvador and Nicaragua claimed more than 100,000 lives
during the 1980s. The Reagan administration wanted to help the Salvadoran
government defeat its indigenous guerilla insurgency, but at the same time to
sponsor and finance another group of armed insurgents to overthrow the
Nicaraguan government. Congress ultimately united behind the president in
the former task, but balked at the latter. Former Secretary of State James A.
Baker, in his 1995 book *The Politics of Diplomacy*, would call the
U.S.–funded war in Nicaragua "our country's Vietnam of the 1980s."

On several occasions, I personally provided the extra push necessary to sustain the administration's position in the House in support of El Salvador's
fledgling democracy. Like many others, however, I became disenchanted
with what our government was trying to do in Nicaragua. As I learned to my
dismay and described more fully in a 1993 book, *Worth It All: My War for
Peace*, a small secret cabal in the executive branch of government, operating
behind closed doors, began directing a systematic invasion of Nicaragua in

direct defiance of Congress. This group, privately led by Lt. Col. Oliver North, stealthily planned and conducted acts of military aggression, which were at the time legally prohibited. Its covert activities led ultimately to the disastrous Iran-Contra scandal that blemished the Reagan presidency as nothing else had done. Those bizarre events violated no fewer than six separate laws, enraging Congress and putting the country on the brink of a constitutional crisis.

Our involvement began innocently enough. Upon the fall of Anastasio Somoza in July 1979, the newly installed Nicaraguan government—a coalition of priests, publishers, small businessmen, and students—inherited an economy devastated by civil war and a decade of corruption. Fleeing into exile, the Somoza regime took with it much of the nation's remaining wealth. It left a national debt of $1.64 billion and only $3.5 million in the national treasury—slightly more than a dollar per person for the entire population of that war-ravaged land. Five years of intensive civil war had destroyed a billion dollars' worth of industrial facilities. The little country was in desperate need of foreign assistance if it was to rebuild its shattered economy. President Carter moved swiftly to transfer small amounts of emergency aid, including food and medicine. Secretary of State Cyrus Vance said, "We cannot guarantee that democracy will take hold there. But if we turn our backs on Nicaragua, we can almost surely guarantee that democracy will fail." Carter requested swift passage of a $75 million economic aid bill. Many conservative congressmen, however, bridled at the revolutionary rhetoric of the new regime. They came to suspect the victors in the civil war as communists and wanted no part in helping the devastated country.

Two hardline members of the junta probably were Marxists, I would come to believe; but most, including the Ortega brothers, were homegrown nationalists, inexperienced in governing, suspicious of imperialism, and groping for the best path to economic development. Some of them instinctively associated our country with the Somoza dynasty, with which we had maintained a long supportive relationship. Fears of Cuban or Soviet intervention in Central America began to emerge in the U.S. public dialogue. These doubts intensified in March 1980 when several Sandinista leaders traveled to the Soviet Union. There they publicly decried the U.S. "imperialist policy of interference" in Latin America. As a result, final passage of the $75 million aid package requested by Carter was delayed until the summer of 1980. Meanwhile, Cuban cadres of teachers and health workers, armed with medicine and vaccines, began to flock into the smitten country. It was almost as though, fearing the intrusion of leftist influence, we were paralyzed into a failure to compete against it for leverage in the emerging country.

My first personal encounter with the Sandinistas came in June of 1980. At the request of President Carter, I took a small delegation to Nicaragua to see what was going on, to ask questions, to appraise our chance of influencing the rapidly moving events, and to report our findings back to the president.

On the eve of our delegation's departure, Representative Robert Bauman of Maryland proposed an amendment to strip away all the money earmarked in the supplemental appropriation bill for emergency Nicaraguan aid. I offered a substitute to allow the aid, but to require that the president report to Congress every ninety days on that government's progress in the observance of human rights. By a ninety-nine vote margin, the House adopted my substitute, retaining $25 million in emergency aid. This would be the widest margin of any vote on aid to a Central American country during the entire decade of the 1980s.

The little delegation had to be assembled in a hurry. We arranged for a highly respected Nicaraguan banker, Arturo Cruz, to fly to Managua with us. We met with people from all sides—Enrique Dreyfus, spokesman for local business interests; Frank Bandana, head of the coffee growers; Pedro Joaquín Chamorro of *La Prensa*, the major privately owned newspaper; and his younger brother Carlos Chamorro, who edited *Barricada*, the official Sandinista newspaper. The brothers were sons of *La Prensa*'s crusading publisher, Pedro Joaquín Chamorro Cardenal, whose murder in 1978 had galvanized the Somoza opposition, precipitating a general strike and hastening the end of Somoza's regime. The victim's widow, Violeta Chamorro, was part of the original governing junta that took power upon the fall of Somoza. So was Alfonso Robelo, a moderate businessman who had left the regime and spoke now of running for president as soon as elections could be held. We talked with both.

Everyone with whom we talked believed the United States should work with the new regime. They all felt a show of friendship by our country would influence political developments for the better. Nobody we consulted wanted Cuba to be the principal source of assistance to the needy country.

Meeting with Daniel Ortega and five members of the governing junta, we pressed hard for assurances. "Will your government respect private property?" asked Kent Hance.

"Everyone's rights will be respected," replied Ortega. The thirty-six-year-old *commandante* said an enormous amount of land "already belongs to the nation," having been held apart by Somoza and never used for anything except his "personal profit and enjoyment." Ortega hoped this could be distributed in family plots to landless peasants and "legal titles" awarded.

"Can we assure our president and our Congress that Nicaragua will protect civil liberties?" Bill Alexander persisted. Upon Ortega's affirmative response, Bill demanded specifics. Free speech? Free press? Freedom of assembly? Even for the political opposition?

"All of these things are being guaranteed in our new constitution," insisted Ortega. "None of them existed under Somoza, and that is why our people revolted!"

Steve Neal of North Carolina wanted some elaboration on the "mixed economy" and "pluralistic society" about which the new leaders had spoken. Were these code words for a form of socialism?

"We are looking at many models," Ortega said. "The banks and public utilities could be owned by the people. The same as in many other democracies," he declared. "Beyond this, we want private business in private hands. We want them to be successful. We want private citizens to own land. We want *more* of them to own land, and own businesses. We want *more* of our people to be capitalists."

"When will you have elections?" I asked.

"Just as soon as possible. Just as soon as we can get enough tranquility to have *real* elections. Our country has never had a real election. One time Somoza pretended to have an election but nobody paid any attention, nobody voted. We want *real* elections. We want *everybody* to participate," Ortega said.

U.S. Ambassador Lawrence Pezzullo seemed pleased by the meetings and by the answers we received. "Extremely positive," he said. "The most positive responses we've had to date."

Our group reported to President Carter that the economic aid had taken on symbolic importance. Everyone with whom we talked considered it potentially decisive in shaping the future of U.S.–Nicaraguan relations. I told the House that, from all we had learned, the direction of the new government in Nicaragua was still to be determined.

Three months later, I had a surprise visit from Ambassador Pezzullo. He was disturbed. Daniel Ortega's brother, Humberto, who served the fledgling junta as minister of defense, had made a public statement that Nicaraguan elections would not be held until 1985. This contradicted the junta's assurances to our group in June. The ambassador thought it would be useful for us who had heard those promises to lodge a strongly worded complaint. I dictated a letter. Alexander, Neal, and Hance all joined in signing. Humberto's public statement, we wrote, came as "a major disappointment to those of us in Congress who have held out hope that Nicaragua, with our understanding and help, could move swiftly toward a truly democratic society."

The campaign of 1980 raised the decibel level of the debate over Central America, making a bipartisan consensus more difficult. Throughout that election year, Ronald Reagan's campaign rhetoric scathingly attacked

President Carter's policies. Reagan inveighed against our "Marxist" neighbors in the Caribbean. He repeatedly charged that the Nicaraguan leaders were "Cuban-trained, Cuban-armed, and dedicated to creating another Communist country in the Hemisphere." On February 17, 1981, after new Secretary of State Alexander M. Haig Jr., told House and Senate leaders he had "evidence" that leftist insurgents in El Salvador were receiving weapons from "Soviet-bloc nations," I moved to close ranks in the face of what was perceived and represented to us as a threat to the independence of El Salvador. I had spent time in El Salvador, knew its people and something of its problems, sympathized deeply with its heroic effort now to create a real democracy. I didn't want to see that process frustrated.

"Central America is probably more vitally important to us than any other part of the world," I told the press following that briefing at the White House. "Our response to what is happening there requires a bipartisan, unified approach, and I fully expect that is what the president and the secretary of state will receive."

The Reagan camp was not content, however, with protecting the territorial integrity of El Salvador. Emboldened by the president's electoral victory, Reaganites construed this as proof that the public supported using U.S. power to control other governments in the hemisphere. Reagan's new ambassador to the United Nations, Jeane Kirkpatrick, made a public policy distinction between "authoritarian" and "totalitarian" governments. Some now wanted to make a policy distinction between "rightist" and "leftist" leadership. Military dictator Augusto Pinochet of Chile was acceptable; the new group in Managua was not. Reagan quickly suspended the sale of American wheat to Nicaragua and terminated economic aid. He attributed these actions to Nicaragua's alleged encouragement of rebel forces in El Salvador. Those U.S. actions greatly distressed Ambassador Pezzullo, who felt it left him no bargaining room. Nicaraguan leaders viewed the embargo on wheat sales as an act of economic "aggression." Even Nicaraguans who opposed the Sandinistas expressed dismay.

Ambassador Pezzullo met with CIA Director Casey, arguing that the Sandinista revolution was still popular inside Nicaragua. Any open attack on it by the United States would only strengthen its hold on the population, Pezzullo warned. He expressed deep concern that the United States was destroying its own position, forfeiting its chance to influence events for the better. The Sandinistas wanted a friendly relationship with the United States, he insisted. Making an open break, as the administration was doing, undermined his efforts to improve relations. Casey and others in the administration were not moved by our emissary's warnings. They disagreed. Instead of trying to win the Nicaraguans over, Casey wanted to whip them into line by punitive measures. Casey had the president's favor. Ultimately, Pezzullo was replaced as ambassador.

The administration's rhetoric grew harsher. In November of 1981, the CIA proposed a $19-million covert-action program. The president signed a "finding," as required by law, stating that a covert action was in the "national interest." William Casey came to Capitol Hill to inform the House and Senate intelligence committees of plans for political and paramilitary operations in the area. I listened carefully to his presentation. These activities would be limited, Casey assured us, to thwarting Nicaragua's "support of subversion" in neighboring El Salvador. The sole purpose would be interdiction of arms intended for Salvadoran guerrillas.

Arturo Cruz, the pro–U.S. banker who had been appointed Nicaraguan ambassador to the United States in the spring of that year, now resigned his post. It was Cruz who had accompanied me to his country the previous year, introducing my group to people on all sides of the political spectrum. "What the United States does not realize," Cruz wrote in his resignation statement, "is that its continuing mistrust of the revolution might be pushing the Sandinista government to the left and forcing it, in spite of itself, to use the kind of measures that the United States finds so troubling. . . . Washington's hard line continues to encourage the armed aggression of the counterrevolution."

Assistant Secretary of State Thomas Enders had been privately negotiating with the Sandinista government for an end to Nicaraguan support of insurgent movements in Central America and for a lessening of security ties between the Sandinistas and the Eastern bloc. In exchange, the United States would cease punitive actions against the Sandinista government. Now, Enders was ordered by higher-ups to terminate the talks. Administration officials continued to escalate their anti-Nicaragua rhetoric. They arranged closed-door briefings where they presented secret aerial photographs to bolster their claim of a dramatic Nicaraguan arms buildup. I examined the photos, could not make out most of the images, but accepted uncritically the briefers' interpretation. Later, the House Intelligence Subcommittee on Oversight and Evaluation would write that the briefing was "flawed by several instances of overstatement and overinterpretation."

On March 12 the State Department presented to the news media an account of a nineteen-year-old Nicaraguan supposedly trained in Cuba and captured in El Salvador and sent by his government to fight with the Salvadoran rebels. The publicity stunt backfired badly when the youngster, whose name was Orlando José Tardencillas Espinosa, confronted the press and repudiated the entire account. He reported that he had been tortured by military captors in El Salvador and threatened into conspiring with

Salvadoran and U.S. officials to fabricate the story. During that same month, details of a CIA-sponsored secret war in Nicaragua began to appear on the front pages of major newspapers. The reported activity was far more extensive than the interdiction of weapons into El Salvador. Anti-Sandinista guerrillas badly damaged two major bridges along the Nicaraguan-Honduran border. Land mines were laid around the perimeters of several villages in northern Nicaragua, spurring the government to declare a state of emergency.

In April of 1982, a crisis of a new sort arose in El Salvador. Partly in response to that crisis, and partly to prevail upon the Sandinistas to leave their neighbors alone, a House delegation was sent to Central America. The first Constituent Assembly elections held under El Salvador's new constitution resulted in a three-way split. President José Napoleon Duarte's Christian Democrat party won a plurality, but not a majority, of the Assembly seats. The more conservative ARENA party, headed by charismatic firebrand Major Roberto D'Aubuisson, was a close second. Now D'Aubuisson was maneuvering behind the scenes, meeting with leaders of other parties, conspiring to form a coalition to freeze out the moderate-to-liberal Christian Democrats. D'Aubuisson's plan would deny any chairmanships, any seat in the cabinet, or any representation in government agencies to any Christian Democrat.

The fledgling democracy, so patiently nursed through its first real elections by Duarte, seemed doomed to the politics of polarization and disintegration. Many in the United States feared D'Aubuisson's close ties to the military and his outspoken extremism. Death squads had terrorized the Salvadoran countryside for years. The United States had invested heavily in the Salvadoran experiment in democracy. Two years earlier I had visited Duarte in El Salvador and had been impressed by his dedication. For the first time in the little nation's whole violent history, someone was making an effort to subdue the military and make its officers amenable to civil law. Now, U.S. observers feared, all of this could be in jeopardy.

U.S. Ambassador Deane Hinton briefed our delegation on the internal dangers inherent in a right-wing military cabal. The military establishment was deeply dependent on U.S. aid, he pointed out. Hinton asked me, as House majority leader, to talk personally with D'Aubuisson, to stress the apprehensions in Congress over death-squad activity, and to tell him that aid could be terminated entirely if it appeared extremists were silencing voices of moderation and reason in the government.

Seated beside the vigorous young militarist at dinner in the ambassador's residence, I sensed the tension. D'Aubuisson's body was like a tightly coiled spring. He drummed his fingers on the tablecloth and tapped his feet beneath the table in an incessant venting of nervous energy. When he spoke it was in staccato bursts that reminded me of machine-gun fire. He talked too rapidly for my poor Spanish to follow, and I had to call upon a State Department translator to sit between us and help. But I made my point. By the time dinner was over, I was sure Roberto D'Aubuisson had received the message. He knew that the U.S. Congress would not back a reign of terror.

On leaving that violence-prone little country, our delegation traveled to Managua. There I confronted the Sandinistas with the demand that they respect their neighbor's border. Sergio Ramirez and Jaime Wheelock, arguably the two most pro–U.S. members of the ruling junta, insisted they had no territorial designs whatever, but that *we* were threatening *their* sovereignty. "Damn it, Sergio," I finally exploded, "the United States is *not* going to invade your country! We're *not* trying to overthrow your government!"

I thought I was speaking gospel truth. We were only trying to interdict weapons bound for El Salvadoran guerrillas and dry up the arms flow. I had the personal assurance of Bill Casey. Like most of my colleagues on the congressional intelligence committees, I had taken CIA Director Casey's testimony at face value. "Please understand," Chairman Edward Boland had admonished Casey that day, "this committee is *not* authorizing a war against Nicaragua's government." Casey said he understood that.

"Your nation's weapons are killing our people," Sergio Ramirez answered coolly. "Your mines are blowing up our bridges. Your bombs destroy watertanks and leave our villages without water—"

"Yes," interrupted Jaime Wheelock, "and the former Somoza guardsmen who now carry your guns are boasting that they'll be in Managua in six months to put their old crowd back in power! The United States is paying them. Your country is paying in dollars and the Nicaraguan people are paying in blood."

"Look, gentlemen, "I said, "if you're honestly worried about an invasion of your country, there is one clear way you can avoid it. Respect the territorial boundaries of El Salvador, and we'll respect yours. Just leave your neighbors alone and we'll leave you alone. You have my word for that."

What an awesome presumption.

After that visit to Nicaragua, my uncritical acceptance of the CIA's description of events between the two countries and of our purpose in financing the paramilitary intrusion began to be shaken by events. Try as I would to justify the administration's official story, it just wouldn't wash. Others in Congress, including several members of the House and Senate Intelligence committees, were having the same problem. It became increasingly apparent that the real purpose of the covert operation was to overthrow the Sandinista government. During the months ahead the CIA-supported insurgent force continued to grow. Contra leaders, including former Somoza National Guardsmen, began openly expressing their central goal: the violent overthrow of the governing junta.

Speaker Thomas P. O'Neill became adamantly opposed to Contra aid in any form. The Speaker's ninety-one-year-old aunt, who died in 1981, had been a Maryknoll nun, and Tip felt a close kinship to Maryknollers. A Maryknoll missionary named Peggy Healy, based in Nicaragua, strongly opposed the CIA's support of the Contras. I met with her at the Speaker's request. She outspokenly denounced the terror, bullying, and needless violence perpetrated by the growing bands of U.S.–armed insurgents. As opposition to the Contra war mounted, increasing numbers of CIA-trained contra forces based in Honduras, were making hit-and-run attacks on northern Nicaraguan villages, then fleeing to sanctuaries across the Honduran border. Finally, on December 8, 1982, Intelligence Committee Chairman Edward Boland moved on the House floor to prohibit the use of any U.S. funds to overthrow the Nicaraguan government or to provoke a military exchange between Nicaragua and Honduras. His amendment carried by a big vote. The very next day, CIA Director Casey met with the Senate Intelligence Committee. He argued that arms interdiction remained the principal goal of the Reagan administration's efforts. But he acknowledged that the CIA was hoping also to "harass" and pressure the Nicaraguan government into becoming more "democratic." Senator Patrick Moynihan raised a question: Just how and where did the United States draw the line between deliberate harassment and an effort to overthrow? What about the U.S.–financed Contras? Regardless of *our* intentions, weren't *they* fighting to overthrow the government and gain power for themselves? Moynihan subsequently introduced the Boland Amendment in the Senate, where it passed. Reagan signed it into law on December 21, 1982, prohibiting the use of any U.S. funds to attempt an overthrow of the Nicaraguan government.

Immediately following passage of the Boland prohibition, Casey's CIA counsel, Stan Sporkin, assembled a task force composed of the agency's best lawyers. As noted in Bob Woodward's book, *Veil—The Secret Wars of the CIA, 1981 to 1987*, Sporkin told the task force, "This thing [the Boland Amendment] is going to come back and bite us in the ass like nothing you've ever seen." The agency decided, however, that it could continue its operation unchanged, simply *asserting* that nothing was done for the ostensible "purpose" of overthrowing the Sandinista government.

Senator Patrick Leahy of Vermont, a member of the Senate Intelligence Committee, visited Central America for a firsthand look. Leahy took with him Rob Simmons of Senator Goldwater's staff, three other Senate staffers, and a CIA legislative liaison officer. In Honduras, Leahy's party was briefed on Contra training and projected combat-unit movements. Although they saw Casey's cable on the Boland prohibition tacked to a bulletin board, Leahy concluded that the information he was receiving confirmed an active effort to overthrow the Sandinista government.

Honduran armed forces chief General Gustavo Alvarez told Leahy, "We'll have our soldiers in Managua by Christmas." Per Woodward's account in *Veil*, when the senator pointed out that U.S. policy specifically forbade supporting activities to overthrow the Sandinistas, General Alvarez replied, "Oh, yeah, but wouldn't it be great to do anyway?"

On Leahy's next stop, in Panama, the senator asked for specific information on the Nicaraguan program. The CIA station chief said he had orders from his division chief, Dewey Clarridge, not to respond. Eventually Clarridge came to Leahy's hotel where he informed the senator of a top secret undertaking to train Contra rebels in Panama. Clarridge revealed that the strongman leader of Panama, General Manuel Noriega, was an undercover provider of information for the CIA and was helping the CIA build a secret Contra training center in Panama. Leahy was irate. This clearly had nothing to do with interdicting arms. He and the Senate staffers put together a top secret report, concluding that the CIA operation in sponsoring and financing the Contra army was bigger in every respect than it had been officially described as being.

During 1983, the administration launched a massive campaign to win Congress over to its agenda. Increasingly the issue was stated in anticommunist terms. President Reagan emphasized his vision of a Marxist threat in the Western Hemisphere. His style became more confrontational, and an effort to bar all funding for the Contras gained momentum in the House. During April of 1983, thirty-seven House members wrote to President Reagan stating that continued financial support for so large an anti-Sandinista force bivouacked in Honduras was a "violation of the Boland Amendment." Eddie Boland, denouncing the administration's noncompliance, now joined House Foreign Affairs Committee Chairman Clement Zablocki in introducing H.R. 2760, a bill "to prohibit United States' support for military or paramilitary operations in Nicaragua."

On the same day President Reagan addressed a joint session of Congress. He raised the rhetorical stakes, insisting that, "the national security of all the Americas is at stake in Central America. If we cannot defend ourselves there . . . the safety of our homeland would be put in jeopardy . . . Who among us would wish to bear responsibility for failing to meet our shared obligation?" By stressing the national security aspects of Central America and hinting that he would blame Congress for failure, Reagan hoped to line up congressional support for his Nicaraguan agenda. Six days later, the House Intelligence Committee voted nine to five along straight party lines to support the Boland-Zablocki bill and halt all U.S. support for the military operation.

Assistant Secretary of State Enders devised a last-minute proposal that would limit the number of Contra troops and reform the Contra leadership. Enders thought the right policy would be to remove the Soviets and Cubans from Nicaragua by renewing a dialogue with the Sandinistas, but Reagan and Casey questioned the personal loyalty of anyone wanting to carry on a dialogue. The Nicaraguan government, they had decided, was the enemy. On May 27, Enders was transferred away from the Latin American desk. He chose to resign in July, replaced by an administration hardliner contemptuous of the congressional role in foreign policy.

This drove another wedge between the branches of government. By early May 1983 objections to the president's Nicaragua policy spread to the Senate. There, the Intelligence Committee voted thirteen to two not to authorize funds for covert operations in Nicaragua until the president submitted a new finding delineating the purposes of such operations. In the House, Speaker O'Neill strongly censured the president's efforts to sell his Central American war on national security grounds. O'Neill put the issue plainly and harshly: "The president of the United States broke the law and then laughed to the American people that he broke the law."

As the domestic debate escalated, it became more partisan. The polarizing debate and hardening positions, I felt, needed a new focus. It really wasn't a question of pro- or anti-communism. The fundamental question was whether we had a unilateral right to dictate the violent overthrow of another country's government. I offered an amendment calling for a regional approach:

> *The question is this: Do we go it alone? Do we postulate ourselves as a sort of Lone Ranger riding throughout the hemisphere shooting silver bullets at people who misbehave from our point of view? Or do we call on that organization (the OAS) which has been created for that express purpose? . . . I believe we should do the latter.*

My amendment directed the president to seek intervention by the OAS to resolve the conflicts in Central America. It also prohibited direct or indirect support by U.S. intelligence agencies for military or paramilitary operations in Nicaragua. The Boland-Zablocki bill, with my amendment attached, passed the House on July 28. The vote was 228 to 195.

While this measure was pending in the Senate, the administration suddenly ordered two large military exercises off the Honduran coast, involving 16,000 sailors and 5,000 U.S. ground troops, apparently designed to intimidate Nicaragua. Secretary of State Shultz, according to reports, had not been informed of the decision of the National Security Council (NSC) to deploy a battle group. House Speaker O'Neill and Senate Minority Leader Robert Byrd were alarmed. In a joint letter to President Reagan on July 28 they expressed dismay that his administration had not consulted with the Congress "prior to initiating such serious action."

These military maneuvers in Honduras marked the rise of the NSC, which would later orchestrate the Iran-Contra affair. But at this stage in 1983, the CIA still directed anti-Nicaraguan activity. With congressional support eroding, things were getting out of hand. The administration needed to regain the initiative. Casey told Clarridge, his CIA division chief in Latin America, to "get something." He needed "news" to establish credibility for the Contras within Nicaragua. Two U.S. senators would soon experience that news firsthand.

Senator William S. Cohen, a Republican from Maine, wanted to support the administration on Nicaragua and had told the president he would. But Cohen had apprehensions. Casey suggested that Cohen visit Nicaragua. Thus, in September, he and Democratic Senator Gary Hart of Colorado departed Washington on a C-140 bound for Managua. One hour outside Managua, the pilots received word that the Augusto César Sandino Airport was closed due to an air attack. A twin-engine Cessna with a five-hundred-pound bomb strapped under each wing had been shot down over the airport.

Eventually arriving in Managua, Hart and Cohen found vast destruction. The crash had wiped out part of the terminal, hurling oil and glass over the surrounding area. Both the pilot and copilot were killed. The Nicaraguan news media arrived, and one reporter attributed the bombing attack to a CIA sponsored Contra raid.

"The CIA is not that dumb," Cohen retorted.

Nicaraguan officials, however, produced a briefcase retrieved from the plane. Cohen and Hart, looking through its contents, found the pilot's Florida driver's license and American credit cards, along with code identifications for the operation: authentic CIA paperwork.

The Senators were dumbfounded. How could the CIA think it would achieve anything by bombing a civilian airport? The CIA station chief responded that the operation was meant to show that the Contras were serious and could strike the capital. Furthermore, he dissembled, the Contras were free agents and the CIA could not control their targets. Hart asked what "free agent" would carry his CIA paperwork in a briefcase on a covert bombing raid?

The House voted twice more before the end of 1983 to stop all covert operations against Nicaragua. President Reagan put his prestige on the line with personal telephone calls to individual senators. That effort paid off. The Senate continued to support the administration, and while the two houses debated, the Boland amendment expired with the end of the fiscal year on September 30, 1983.

During this agonizing legislative battle, the NSC approved an increase in the authorized strength of the Contra rebels, up to a force of eighteen thousand. On October 11, 1983, CIA-trained speedboat teams conducted a predawn raid against Nicaraguan fuel storage at the port of Corinto. Five storage tanks, supposedly housing most of Nicaragua's oil reserves, were blown up. Some 20,000 residents of the city were forced to evacuate because of fires. Three days later the CIA-sponsored teams hit Puerto Sandino, another major Nicaraguan port. Next came the sabotage of a Nicaraguan pipeline. Evidence began to surface that CIA employees not only helped plan these attacks but actually executed them. This was something new. If true, it violated assurances given to Congress that no U.S. personnel would take part in covert attacks against Nicaragua.

There also was a new team directing the war. Anthony Motley had replaced Tom Enders as assistant secretary of state for inter-American affairs. Motley had convened a working group on the Contra operation called the RIG (Restricted Interagency Group). Motley, Clarridge of the CIA, and Lieutenant Colonel Oliver North of the NSC formed the core. It was at a private meeting of this group, Congress would learn, that Clarridge proposed mining the Nicaraguan harbors. Casey presented the reckless and illegal plan to the president, who approved. A determined cabal had the bit in its teeth.

From early 1984 through late 1986, this Restricted Interagency Group became a secret government within our government. It privately conducted a secret war against Nicaragua making decisions behind closed doors and carrying them out in stealth. Congress was not informed of its activities as the law required; it was, in fact, deliberately lied to. Ironically, this closed cabal was plotting its first fateful ventures at the very time the National Bipartisan Commission on Central America (dubbed the Kissinger Commission) was publicly seeking a basis for national consensus. After weeks of study and nine days in the region listening to heads of state and opposition leaders, that high-level commission submitted a 132-page report to President Reagan on January 10, 1984. A majority of the members felt that the United States should support continued assistance to El Salvador, "conditioned on terminating death squads" and establishing "the rule of law," as well as continued "incentive and pressures for the regime in Managua to negotiate seriously." Both Democrats and Republicans on the panel urged the U.S. government to support a "comprehensive regional settlement" and to "commit itself to respect results of elections within countries" that observe "pluralism at home and restraint abroad." The report ended with a ringing call for consensus: "The people of Central America are neither Republicans nor Democrats. The crisis is nonpartisan, and it calls for a nonpartisan response."

As if responding to the Kissinger Commission's call for the United States to respect democratic elections, the Managua government announced that national elections would be held that November (1984). Ortega ordered the lifting of press censorship imposed under the emergency law. He also proclaimed freedom for political parties to organize and hold rallies.

Alfonso Robelo, the U.S. educated business leader whom I had met first in 1980 on the mission for President Carter, told a group of congressional leaders in March that he believed there was a chance for an upset in the elections. Robelo was trying to persuade Edén Pastora, a popular hero of the 1979 anti-Somoza revolution, to run for president against Ortega, but his principal goal, Robelo told us, was to remove the root cause of hostility between our two countries. Robelo asked if several of us would write to Ortega commending him on the decision to hold elections and appealing to him to make a reality of his promise that all parties would be allowed to participate equally. Ten of us signed such a letter on March 20 and mailed it to Daniel Ortega. We wrote, "with the hope that the initial steps you have taken will be followed by others designed to guarantee a fully open and democratic electoral process." The letter continued:

> We note that some who have become exiles from Nicaragua have expressed a willingness to return to participate in the elections, if assurances are provided that their security will be protected, and their political rights recognized. Among these exiles are some who have taken up arms against your government, and who have stated their willingness to lay down those arms to participate in a truly democratic process. If this were to occur, the prospects for peace and stability throughout Central America would be dramatically enhanced. . . . A decision on your part to provide these reasonable assurances and conduct truly free and open elections would significantly improve the prospect of better relations between our two countries.

Signatories joining me in this appeal were Chairman Edward Boland of the House Intelligence Committee; three subcommittee chairmen of the House Foreign Affairs Committee—Mike Barnes of Maryland, Stephen Solarz of New York, and Lee Hamilton of Indiana; three members of the House Appropriations Committee—David Obey of Wisconsin, Matt McHugh of New York, and Bill Alexander of Arkansas; as well as Bob Torricelli of New

Jersey and Robert Garcia of New York, both members of the House Foreign Affairs Committee.

Scarcely did we dream, even in the emotionally charged atmosphere of the day, that our letter, with what we considered its reasonable appeal, would subject us to personal attack. We supposed almost everyone wanted the very result for which we pleaded: truly free elections. Our disillusionment came swiftly. A small band of militant conservative Republicans in early April began a series of long, hostile speeches on the House floor. The principal spokesman for the group, Newt Gingrich of Georgia, boasted to me that he had mailed copies of the speeches to newspapers in the home districts of signatories to the Ortega letter, asking for editorial condemnation of our efforts. In a case of classic overstatement, Gingrich fulminated, "There is no modern example of so blatant an effort by one faction of American politicians. . . . This letter is almost certainly illegal and unconstitutional . . . a clear violation by legislators of the executive's right to deal with foreign governments. . . . These ten congressmen clearly undercut the efforts of their own government to apply pressure to the Nicaraguan regime."

His hyperbole rendered the attacks ludicrous and ineffectual. Letters from members of Congress to foreign heads of state were not uncommon. Only recently, some of those now objecting had petitioned the head of the Soviet Union on behalf of a more permissive Jewish emigration policy. On April 12 I responded briefly in the House: "The Nicaraguan government has announced at last that it will have elections. We are trying to gain assurances that those elections be truly open, free and fair. That is what we were asking in the letter, and I do not apologize for that. That is what I think most of us in Congress are for."

President Reagan's instinct was to discount the Nicaraguan elections as unworthy of notice. In a March 29 *New York Times* interview, he told a reporter that covert attacks would stop when the Sandinista leaders "keep their promises and restore the democratic rule and have elections." Reminded that elections had been scheduled for November, Reagan dismissed them as "the kind of rubber-stamp election that we see in any totalitarian government."

Reagan *did* take seriously the presidential elections that spring of 1984 in El Salvador, appointing me chairman of a team of official observers. Leftist guerrilla insurgents tried hard to disrupt and discourage the process. On election morning they blew up a transformer, causing a power outage in San Salvador. I shaved in the dark. The previous evening, as one group of our American delegation ate dinner at a restaurant described by our embassy as "safe," a carload of unidentified men drove by, threw open a rear door, dumped a freshly slain victim on the sidewalk in front of the restaurant, and sped away. Nevertheless, voters responded in massive numbers. In San Miguel, the nation's second largest city, I saw long lines of voters waiting patiently—and cheerfully—for an hour and more to cast their ballots. An estimated 87 percent of all Salvadorans of eligible age participated that day. When the votes were counted, President José Napoleon Duarte had won reelection, soundly defeating Roberto D'Aubuisson.

Back in Washington on May 10, I helped salvage the president's proposed aid package for the embattled government. Many of my fellow Democrats, including notably Speaker O'Neill, wanted to cut the proposed figure, give only a third, and wait to see how the government fared. At the risk of alienating them, I spoke against that effort on the floor. The Salvadoran elections had proven that democracy could take root in barren soil, where it had never grown before. Duarte was the first elected leader in El Salvador's four-hundred year history to complete his term of office without being overthrown and ousted by a military clique. That was worth preserving and encouraging, I said.

By autumn it would be apparent, nevertheless, that those now calling the shots in administration policy had no interest whatever in pursuing either elections or any effort to find a policy consensus on Nicaragua as called for in the Kissinger report. Their singleminded goal was to bring so much misery on Nicaragua's three and a half million people that its government would just collapse. If Congress passed laws forbidding U.S. participation in efforts to overthrow that government, the secret interagency group would find ways to achieve that goal and make it appear that someone else had done it.

One night in late February 1984, the deadly business began. Trained frogmen started stringing underwater mines in Nicaragua's three busiest harbors. It would be almost six weeks before the fingerprints of the U.S. government would surface.

On Thursday night, April 5, Barry Goldwater stood on the Senate floor attempting to salvage the extra $21 million requested by the administration for Contra aid. He castigated his colleagues for "congressional meddling with the efforts by the president to defend the national security." As Goldwater spoke, Senator Joseph Biden sat at his desk poring over a classified memo, which stated that the CIA had played a direct role in mining three Nicaraguan harbors. He delivered the memo to a fellow Intelligence Committee member, Republican Bill Cohen. After reading the startling revelation, Cohen carried it over to Goldwater, now through with his speech, and demanded an explanation.

Goldwater was stunned. He gained permission to speak again and began reading the classified memo to his Senate colleagues. His staff director, Rob

Simmons, rushed over abruptly, interrupting Goldwater's delivery. This was highly classified material! Simmons and Goldwater stared at one another in dismay. This was the first either had heard of the minings.

Simmons later had Goldwater's reading of the secret memo excised from the *Congressional Record*. Few senators had been on the floor when he was reading it. Some may not have grasped its full import. However, Dave Rogers, a reporter for the *Wall Street Journal*, heard it. He wrote a story about the episode that was published in the next morning's edition. The headline read: "U.S. Role in Mining Nicaraguan Harbors Reportedly is Larger Than First Thought." Now the lid was off.

Senator Edward Kennedy branded administration policy in Nicaragua "illegal" and "indefensible." On the previous day, Kennedy had sponsored an amendment to slash all of the $21 million from the bill. Just prior to the vote on the Kennedy amendment, Majority Leader Howard Baker had read a letter from Reagan to Senate members. Reagan pledged in the letter, "The United States does not seek to destabilize or overthrow the government of Nicaragua; nor to impose or compel any particular form of government there." The Senate, thus formally reassured, passed the bill, including the $21 million. Now, one day later, doubt cast an ominous shadow over the president's solemn assurance. Did Reagan not know of the illegal mining, or had he deliberately deceived the Senate?

News of the real scope and dimension of the minings trickled in slowly to members of congressional committees. Approximately seventy-five mines had been laid on the bottom of three Nicaraguan harbors. Some of the mines had up to three hundred pounds of C-4 explosive, enough for a gigantic explosion. On February 25 two fishing boats had hit mines and sunk at the Caribbean port of El Bluff. Two more vessels suffered damage. Two crew members were killed and seven were wounded. On March 1 a Dutch dredging ship hit a mine at the Pacific port of Corinto. Five people were injured and damages were assessed at $1 million. On March 7 a mine explosion at Corinto cracked up a Panamanian freighter. On March 20 a Soviet oil tanker was seriously crippled when it ran over a mine at the Pacific port of Sandino. Five crewmen suffered injuries.

Goldwater was incensed. He fired off a scathing letter to CIA Director Casey condemning the mining. This was a flagrant violation of international law. The United States itself had once gone to war when its own harbors were mined! Who could have put the country in so untenable a position?

On April 10 the Senate voted 84 to 12 for a forcefully worded resolution condemning the mining. On April 12 the House followed in a 281 to 111 vote. Nicaragua formally protested the mining before the World Court at The Hague, which, on May 10, 1984, officially condemned the CIA's action as a violation of international law and called on the United States to "immediately cease and refrain" from all such mining operations in Nicaraguan territory. As a matter of fact, the United States already had ceased. The dangerous adventure had been highly counterproductive. It had cost our country respect in the world community, had solidified public support in Nicaragua for the Sandinistas, and was costing the administration support in Congress.

That weekend President Reagan joked about the controversy. At the White House Correspondents Association annual black-tie dinner, the president quipped, "How come nobody told me? Well, I've laid down the law to everyone from now on about anything that happens, that no matter what time it is, *wake me*, even if it's in the middle of a Cabinet meeting."

But the displeasure in Congress was not to be laughed off. On May 9, Reagan went on the offensive in a nationally televised address, trying to portray Nicaragua as a threat to the entire Western Hemisphere. He called it "a communist reign of terror." On May 24, despite his forensic efforts, the House voted 241 to 177 against further military involvement in Nicaragua. Still, the secret government had not given up. Casey wrote a highly classified letter to Robert McFarlane asking him to explore funding alternatives with the Saudis, Israelis, and others. McFarlane met with the Saudi ambassador to the United States, Prince Bandar, a man with access to great wealth. The two men conspired in a scheme whereby the Saudis would contribute eight to ten million dollars to the Contras at the rate of one million per month. The contributions, they realized, would have to be handled with the greatest secrecy.

According to Bob Woodward's *Veil* and Cynthia Arnson's *Crossroads: Congress, the Reagan Administration and Central America,* here is how they worked it: Bandar obtained a Saudi government check for eight million dollars. McFarlane acquired a secret bank account number from the BAC International Bank in the Cayman Islands. Bandar, given the account number, traveled to Geneva, Switzerland, handed the eight million to an official from the Swiss Bank Corporation, and privately directed that one million dollars a month be transferred to the Cayman Islands account. This way the money's origin could not be traced. Thus, in mid-1984, Arabs were persuaded to do clandestinely what our government was forbidden to do legally. The Saudis were funding the Contras. McFarlane informed the president, who expressed his appreciation. Congress and the public would not learn of this until a year and a half later.

Toward the end of that year, House and Senate conferees agreed on a compromise. Reagan could get fourteen million dollars for Contra aid during fiscal 1985, but not for military use inside Nicaragua, and only if the president could certify after February 28 that the money was needed to fight

Sandinista *expansionism*. The measure passed the House 294 to 118. It became known as the Second Boland Amendment.

As Nicaraguan elections approached, Arturo Cruz, the international banker who had accompanied me on my 1980 trip and who had served briefly as Nicaragua's ambassador, told me that he wanted to run for the presidency of his country. Two weeks later he told me that the U.S. State Department and the White House had dissuaded him from running. As it turned out, Daniel Ortega won the 1984 election in Nicaragua, leading the Sandinista Party to victory with slightly over 60 percent of the popular vote. Ortega was no longer just the leader of a junta. He was the elected president of Nicaragua.

Our government had officially ignored the Nicaraguan election and declined to send observers. *Newsday* reporter Roy Gutman maintained that certain people in the Nicaraguan opposition and the Reagan administration collaborated to keep Cruz from participating in the election, so that it would attract less international attention and could be more easily discredited.

Ronald Reagan was himself reelected in November, winning an enormous electoral plurality—every state but Minnesota—over Democratic nominee Walter Mondale. The House remained in Democratic hands, while Republicans held a slim majority in the Senate. Domestic issues dominated the campaigns, and no serious analyst claimed that a mandate had emerged, one way or the other, concerning Central America. But the size of Reagan's victory seemed to inspire his followers. Funds from third countries for Contra military aid continued to grow in 1985. The Saudis doubled their contribution from the 1984 pledge of one million dollars per month. During February, Lieutenant Colonel Oliver North (under the name "Steelhammer") wrote to Contra leader Adolfo Calero ("Friend"), asking him to keep the expanded Saudi donation quiet.

On April 17, *The New York Times* published sections of a leaked document in which the president asserted that "direct application of U.S. military force . . . must realistically be recognized as an eventual option . . . if other policy alternatives fail." Some lawmakers now decided the president was actually considering sending U.S. troops into Nicaragua. President Reagan, sensing the blacklash, dropped his request for military aid and agreed to provide assistance to the Contras only for food, medicine, clothing, and general survival. Of course, he knew, though Congress did not, that Saudi arms money could keep the war going. The Senate, thus mollified, voted 53 to 46 to approve the president's altered request, but the House defeated even that Contra aid proposal by a 248 to 180 vote.

The men who formed the secret government were not deterred. Determined to defy Congress, North and his collaborators went further underground, and during May 1985, William Casey reviewed a memo from Graham Fuller, his national intelligence officer for the Near East and south Asia, who argued that denying arms to Iran because of Iranian-sponsored terrorism had become counterproductive. He advocated a more daring policy: Work *with* Iran.

Sell Iran weapons? But Congress had outlawed that. Draw up a new national security decision directive, for the president's signature, saying such sales were necessary in the national interest? Shultz disagreed with that suggestion. Weinberger wrote the word "absurd" on his copy and returned it.

The objections of these two senior department heads would ultimately be overruled.

President Reagan's crusade approach to Contra aid had kindled a harsh accusatory debate on Capitol Hill. Republican Representative Dan Burton said during the House debate in June 1985, "My friends, don't be soft on Communism!" Representative Newt Gingrich called a vote restricting military aid to the Contras a "vote for the unilateral disarmament of the side that favors freedom in Central America." On the House floor, I described these assaults as "to some degree" reminiscent of McCarthyism. That was understatement.

The use of personal invective and poisonous innuendo was reaching a level I had never previously witnessed. A band of mostly youngish GOP House members had been attacking Speaker O'Neill, branding him a tyrant, and worse. Their campaign committee had even run a demeaning television commercial parodying the Speaker with a look-alike actor. An acid-tongued young firebrand from New York, John LeBoutillier, had gone yet further. O'Neill, he said, was "big, fat, and out of control, just like the federal government." Language of this type began to proliferate, poisoning the well of civil discourse.

Beginning in 1984, a handful of confrontation-minded Republicans began using the free television time provided by C-SPAN, after all legislative business had ended and other members had left the chamber, to spew forth negative propaganda against their Democratic colleagues. A Republican aide named Frank Gregorsky wrote a treatise criticizing the Democratic record on communism and national security. Gingrich and Bob Walker of Pennsylvania read this report aloud, the chamber empty of other members, staining the reputations of several colleagues with the general charge of being "soft on communism." Nothing quite this flagrant had occurred since the heyday of Senator Joseph McCarthy.

One of those wantonly tarred by the brush was Representative Edward Boland of Massachusetts, Chairman of the House Intelligence Committee and author of the amendment that restricted the CIA. Unaware that he would be the target of a sneak attack, Boland was not present to answer the gratuitous slurs. Neither were others attacked by similar innuendos.

Many members, including a number of Republicans, were shocked by the brazen ploy. Speaker O'Neill was livid. One day, finally goaded to the point of utter disgust, he stepped down from the rostrum, leaving a colleague to preside in his stead, and addressed Gingrich directly. "You deliberately stood in that well before an empty House and challenged these people," said O'Neill, "and you challenged their Americanism, and it is the lowest thing that I have ever seen in my thirty-two years in Congress!" Republican Whip Trent Lott objected to this characterization and made a point of order that the Speaker's comments were unparliamentary. Nobody had been present, of course, to make such a point of order against the firebrands when they were making late-night personal attacks on their Democratic colleagues.

The young turks of the GOP, far from being chastened, seemed to enjoy stirring things up. They thrived on the personal attention it got them. Reagan finally realized, however, that all this was costing him credibility. On the eve of the vote on the fiscal 1986 authorization, he sent a letter promising to "pursue political, not military solutions in Central America." This letter assured the president at least a down payment on the long-denied victory he was looking for. On June 12, 1985, the House reversed itself and voted, 248 to 184, for $27 million in *humanitarian*—not military—aid for the Contra forces. We owed them this, it was argued. After all, the U.S. had recruited them. Some thought this meant the war was winding down. They were mistaken.

With increased Contra funds in pocket, William Casey concentrated on the plan to exchange arms with Iran for American hostages. A plan evolved for Israel to ship TOW antitank missiles to Iran, the United States to replenish Israeli stocks, and Iran to obtain the release of American hostages held in Lebanon. The CIA would not conduct this operation, it was decided. Lieutenant Colonel Oliver North would be the operational commander.

Two months later, North arranged for a CIA-supplied aircraft to fly eighteen Hawk missiles (claimed by U.S. officials to be oil-drilling parts) from Israel to Iran. That plane had been scheduled the same day as the flight to Iran to carry a load of ammunition to the Contras. John McMahon, CIA deputy director, learned that the CIA aircraft had flown arms to Iran without his approval. He instructed that no additional CIA activity supporting the NSC operation be undertaken in absence of a presidential finding to authorize covert action. The next day, November 26, 1985, CIA General Counsel Stanley Sporkin drafted the finding, which provided *retroactive* approval of all preceding covert missions involving the Iran undertaking.

Reagan met with Shultz, Weinberger, McFarlane, Poindexter, and McMahon on December 7 to discuss the Iran program. He signed the finding, certifying the covert deal to be in the national interest and authorizing the CIA to participate. Poindexter put the only copy in his safe, sending word to the CIA that the finding had been signed. Congress was *not advised.* It would not be told for almost a year, and this was an absolute breach of the National Security Act. The heads of "*all* departments, agencies, and *other entities*" of the United States must report "fully and currently" to House and Senate intelligence committees on "*all* intelligence activities" and any significant "anticipated" activities. In the event of circumstances so "extraordinary" that *prior* notice could not be given to those committees, then the *president himself* is required to give prior notice to a bipartisan group of eight specified people, including the elected leaders of both parties in each House.

No notice came.

Between February 15 and 18, another one thousand TOW missiles were shipped to Israel. Half of them went on to Iran. However, no hostages were released. Ghorbanifar, the international arms merchant chosen by North as the go-between, explained the distressing discrepancy by claiming that Iran no longer wanted the TOWs, so they did not count. Doubts already had begun to arise about Ghorbanifar's veracity. At this point Poindexter, according to some reports, wanted to halt the whole operation, but North persisted.

As the arms for hostages effort moved forward in secret, President Reagan initiated a new request for increased Contra arms aid. In February 1986, he went public via television in a speech billed as a report on national defense. In it he asked for one hundred million dollars in Contra military assistance: "You can't fight attack helicopters piloted by Cubans with Band-Aids and mosquito nets," he said. Reagan evoked images of terrorists and revolutionaries "just two days' driving time from Harlingen, Texas."

A few days before the president's scheduled February 26 televised appeal, Tip and Bob Byrd asked if I would respond for the Democrats in Congress. The networks had offered eight minutes immediately following the president's speech. In my response, I tried to put it all in perspective, stressing that national defense should not be a partisan issue. I pointed out how dramatically we had already increased defense spending, and how the national debt had grown as much in the five years of the current administration as our ancestors had added "in the entire 192 years of our previous history—from George Washington through Jimmy Carter." Then I turned to the question of our nation's priorities:

The American people know, too, that real national security depends on certain other things equally as important to this country's future as armaments and weapons. It depends first of all on education—the brain power of our citizenry.

Three years ago, the President's Commission on Education reported on what it called A Nation at Risk. it said, "If an unfriendly foreign power had attempted to impose on America the mediocre education performance that exists today, we might well have viewed it as an act of war."

And yet, three years later, the president's budget asks that we zero out the G.I. Bill for our Vietnam veterans, and that we cut student loans and work-study grants which make it possible for young Americans of modest means to get an education. We think that is a misplaced priority.

Last year, Japan with only half our population graduated half again more scientists and engineers than we did. And people wonder why we're losing out in trade.

As for Latin America, I said this:

Most certainly our relations with the other nations of this hemisphere constitute an indispensable element in our national security.

We worry about communism, but we don't seem to worry about the conditions that breed communism.

Oh, surely, we are big enough and powerful enough that we could physically overthrow the government in Managua, or the one in Havana, if that should be necessary. It would cost a lot more than one hundred million dollars and a precious lot of bloodshed, but we could do it.

Yes, but what then? The problems of Latin America would still be with us—problems of illiteracy, and malnutrition, and disease, the problems of joblessness and a bondage of debt that amounts almost to servitude and a growing sense of hopeless disillusionment with society. This is the stuff of which revolutions are made.

Finally, I reached for a word of inspiration:

In the last century, patriots like Bolívar and San Martin patterned their popular people's movements after us. We were the inspiration and the example, and we have a residue of good will if we'll build upon it.

> *Throughout Latin America, plain people cherish the memory of three American presidents:*
> *Abraham Lincoln who freed the slaves;*
> *Franklin Delano Roosevelt who withdrew U.S. troops from Latin America and declared a "Good Neighbor Policy"; and*
> *John F. Kennedy who inspired hopes of economic betterment for the average people through his short-lived Alliance for Progress.*
> *If we would reap the respect of our neighbors to the south, we'll have to cultivate a sustained interest in them and their very real problems, not just that of a fire engine which rushes in to put out a fire and departs as swiftly to ignore the combustibles that lie everywhere upon the tattered landscape of a civilization cruelly battered by a history of neglect.*
> *They have a saying south of the border: "La mejor manera de conseguir una amistad es ser amigo"... the way to have a friend is to be a friend. In seeking a policy for Latin America, that may be the best place to start.*

Those comments were widely well received. At the whip meeting the next morning, colleagues gave me a standing ovation. Larry Grossman of NBC sent an emissary to convey his personal compliments. Our telephones in Fort Worth and Washington were jammed with gratifying calls. People had hungered for a reasonable, hopeful perspective to counter the flamboyant and too often exaggerated rhetoric that had reverberated around the Capitol over Central American issues. But White House Communications Director Patrick Buchanan wrote in the March 5 *Washington Post* that, by obstructing Contra aid, "the National Democratic Party has now become, with Moscow, co-guarantor of the Brezhnev doctrine in Central America.... With the vote on Contra aid, the Democratic Party will reveal whether it stands with Ronald Reagan and the resistance—or Daniel Ortega and the communists."

In spite of, or perhaps partly because of, such verbal overkill, Reagan's new request for one hundred million dollars to buy weapons for the Contras was rejected by the House on March 20, 1986. Reagan branded the action "a dark day for freedom." The Senate on March 27 approved the $100 million to arm the Contras, but withheld the bipartisan victory Reagan wanted.

By April 1986, Oliver North had begun integrating the Iran and Contra operations. In an internal memo, he wrote that a major portion of the fifteen million dollars expected to be paid by Iran for the arms could be diverted to the Contras. Poindexter apparently approved the diversion. From this point until November, the two operations moved closer and closer until they fused.

In August, Assistant Secretary of State Elliott Abrams obtained an additional ten million dollars in assistance to the Contras from the government of Brunei. Oliver North's private network was directing regular airdrops of military equipment and supplies to Contra field locations. Congress still had not been informed.

On October 5, the Sandinistas shot down an airplane loaded with ammunition and supplies for the Contra forces in northern Nicaragua. Three crew members were killed. Another, a U.S. citizen named Eugene Hasenfus, parachuted to safety and was captured. Hasenfus carried Salvadoran Air Force identification indicating that he was an "adviser." One of the dead passengers bore an ID card issued by Southern Air Transport, formerly operated by the CIA. President Reagan denied any U.S. connection with the flight. (Later, Oliver North would testify, "I was the U.S. Government connection.") Following the Hasenfus incident, North undertook a major housecleaning, trying in vain to shred all written memos that referred to the Contra diversion.

On October 7, a New York businessman named Roy M. Furmark informed Casey that two Canadians who helped finance the arms sales had not been repaid and were threatening to reveal the affair. On November 2, David P. Jacobsen was released from Lebanon following seventeen months in captivity. The next day, a Lebanese magazine, *Al-Shiraa*, reported that the United States had secretly been supplying arms to Iran and that McFarlane had secretly visited Tehran. When Reagan met with the former hostage at the White House on November 7, he told reporters that this story had no foundation. But now no amount of dissembling could cover the trail. Discovery was inevitable.

My wife and I were enjoying a rare afternoon of leisure together at our home in suburban Virginia when the call came from the White House. Would I come right away to the southwest gate and enter on the lower level across from the Executive Office Building?

Senator Robert Byrd was just arriving as I disembarked in the narrow alleyway between the White House and the ornate old executive mansion that once served as home for the State Department. Byrd and I congratulated one another. In the elections just a few days earlier, Democrats had reclaimed the Senate and improved our position in the House. I would be Speaker of the House, and Bob would resume his interrupted role as Senate majority leader.

"Know what this is all about?" I asked, as we walked toward the door.

"No," Bob said. "I was just going to ask you."

We soon found out.

Admiral Poindexter conducted the solemn briefing. Present were Vice

President Bush, Senator Dole, House Minority Leader Michel, Byrd, and I. The president was not there; neither was Tip O'Neill. The meeting had been hastily put together. We listened as the story unfolded. TOW missiles had been delivered to Iran. The presidential finding authorizing the adventure almost a year earlier had not been reported to Congress, as the law required. We would not be told until a day later, in a second briefing by Attorney General Meese, that funds from the missile sales had been diverted to buy weapons for the Contras, but immediately we could see that several provisions of law had been violated: the National Security Act, the Anti-Terrorism Act, the Arms Export Control Act, and the Defense Department Appropriations Act.

In a nationally televised speech on November 13, 1986, President Reagan described the arms shipments to Iran as good-faith gestures to establish contact with Iranian "moderates." He strongly denied that he ever had engaged in an arms-for-hostages trade. Then, during a November 19 press conference he denied four times that he had "condoned" the Israeli shipments. Immediately following the press conference, however, Reagan issued a correction, stating that he *had* condoned a shipment by another country. On November 21, Congress began investigations into the Iran arms program with closed hearings by the House and Senate intelligence committees. That same day, Attorney General Meese contacted NSC head Poindexter asking that he gather all relevant documents. When Poindexter came upon the December 5, 1985, finding (now almost a year old) that portrayed the Iran operation as a straight arms-for-hostage deal, he tore it up and put it in a bag to be burned. Later that evening, North entered his office and directed his secretary, Fawn Hall, to assist him in shredding documents, memos, and messages from his safe and files.

Reagan announced the resignation of Poindexter and the dismissal of North on November 25. He cited evidence discovered by Meese that funds from the Iran arms sales had been diverted to the Contras as the reason for North's firing. In the announcement, Reagan denied knowledge of the Contra diversion, saying he had not been "fully informed" about the Iran arms project.

Now I had a new worry. Within six weeks I would be Speaker. Several committees in each house of Congress were clamoring to get into the act. This was the juiciest thing since Watergate. So many interests were involved that it would be hard to deny a right to hearings by the Senate Foreign Affairs and House Foreign Relations committees, the Armed Services committees, and the Judiciary Committees, which had responsibility for constitutional relations between the two branches of government.

Bob Byrd and I met with Dole and Michel. The others were as concerned as I. Headline-hungry members of several of these committees might be tempted to make "Irangate" into a year-long feeding frenzy. Hearings could degenerate to partisan name calling and exhibitionism. The matter was too grave, I thought, to be handled as a three-ring circus, each committee vying with the others for sensation and attention. I told the other leaders of my desire to appoint a special blue-ribbon committee for developing the facts in a dignified public way. They agreed.

My hope was to lay it all out with decorum, to avoid rancor wherever possible, and to discourage any future escapades in secret government. I had high hopes. But, then, I was new at being Speaker.

CHAPTER THIRTY-THREE

SPEAKER!
FOUR BIG
CHALLENGES

To be Speaker of the U.S. House of Representatives provides as much challenge as any person is prepared to accept. Ordained by the Constitution as a spokesman for the legislative branch of government and second in line of succession to the presidency, the Speakership has been what changing times and individual occupants have made of it. Some, like Henry Clay and Sam Rayburn, have been catalysts of major change. A few, like Joseph Cannon and Thomas Reed, have thoroughly dominated the House. Others have seen their function essentially as presiding with fairness and decorum.

Sam Rayburn was Speaker when I entered the House in 1955. No doubt I formed my basic concept of the Speaker's function from his example. Rayburn saw national needs and made things happen. Under his guidance, the legislative branch fulfilled a role more creative than passive. It initiated much of the domestic agenda during the Eisenhower presidency, when one party held the White House and the other led in Congress. From this, and from my personal admiration of Speakers McCormack, Albert, and O'Neill, I had an exalted view of the Speaker's role. Maybe mine was an impossibly demanding conception of what a Speaker should be able to achieve for the country, but my notion of the job's blend of duty and opportunity went far beyond the ceremonial niceties of Washington social rank. If I couldn't make a significant difference in public policy, there'd be no point in being Speaker.

On the occasion of my first swearing in, set by my wish on January 6, 1987, the 105th anniversary of Speaker Rayburn's birth, I called the office "a treasure more precious than any material possession and an honor more sublime than royalty." To be Speaker, I said, was "the highest responsibility that can come to a lawmaker anywhere in the world." That's exactly how I felt.

The Capitol swarmed with Texans that day. At the swearing-in, the galleries were jammed. All seats taken, people were sitting on the steps. My sister Betty Lee, up from the Texas hill country, saw Ethel Kennedy standing in an aisle in the members' gallery and offered Ethel her seat. Ethel's and Robert's son Joe was being sworn in for the first time as a member. Afterward, more than eight hundred Texans crowded into the Cannon Caucus room. My distant successor as mayor of Weatherford, a personable young woman named Sherry Watson, presented me an original woodcarving of rugged comic portraiture by local artist Chris Hammack. Back in Fort Worth, thousands filled the exhibition hall at Will Rogers Memorial Coliseum to watch via a special satellite hookup. It was a gala sendoff. I'd need, as things turned out, all the good wishes I could get.

Aside from the institutional problems inherent in the office, every Speaker faces a peculiar set of challenges that arise with his particular moment in history. Carl Albert, Tip O'Neill, and I each would comment on this ever shifting focus of priorities in chapters written for a 1994 book, *The Speaker* (published by Congressional Quarterly, Inc.). As I assumed the Speaker's office in January 1987, our government faced four problems of critical proportion: a *budget deficit,* a *trade deficit,* a growing *social deficit* consisting of unmet domestic needs, and a threatened constitutional *crisis arising from the Iran-Contra revelations.* I had watched the first three grow menacingly during the years of the Reagan administration, and I worried that they were reaching a point where, absent a serious effort to arrest or at least slow them down, their economic momentum would become enormously difficult to reverse. Inextricably connected, the deficits fed on one another. The fourth, the Iran-Contra scandal, had erupted suddenly on the public consciousness only six weeks prior to my election as Speaker. These four realities of the historic moment would shape my two-and-a-half years as Speaker.

It was difficult, I quickly learned, to strategize effectively on these broad problems, for smaller crises kept jumping out from the bushes to grab me by the lapel, demanding my immediate attention. I sometimes felt like a boxer kept off balance by repetitive left jabs in the face, or a quarterback repeatedly forced to dodge onrushing tacklers before he could spot an open receiver. Being Speaker, I once told political scientist Ron Peters, was like trying to play chess and table tennis simultaneously. But sometimes the distractions turned into unexpected opportunities.

My first immediate challenge was to head off a train wreck: a major constitutional crisis brewing over the newly revealed Iran-Contra scandal. Only then could I hope to help settle the bitterly divisive issues of our covert involvements in Central American wars. The nation was traumatized by the November 1986 discovery of the illegal Iran-Contra scheme. That was the most alarming revelation since the Watergate burglary. A volcanic lava of anger began boiling inside the Congress. First whispers, then quite audible demands for impeachment proceedings growled in private conversations wherever Democratic members met. Fortunately for President Reagan, Congress was out of session when the shocking news broke, but subsequent activities in the White House did little to abate the outrage. Tempers flared when it was discovered that Colonel Oliver North was shredding all written evidence before Congress could reconvene and subpoena the documents. The situation had explosive potential. Six committee and subcommittee chairs contacted me during December, each wanting to schedule hearings on some facet of the big story that dominated Washington news that month. Without a clear sense of direction, the new Congress could degenerate into a nine-ring circus as committees vied with one another for sensational confrontations with officials of the executive branch.

The last thing our country needed, I felt, was an impeachment outcry or a frontal challenge to the president's personal integrity. While disagreeing with Reagan's policy and appalled at the glaring illegalities committed by his underlings, I wanted to believe that Reagan, as he vowed, had not personally condoned the elaborate flouting of law. I knew his habit of running things with a very loose rein and his dislike of detail. Along with others in our country, I had agonized through the long weeks in 1974 that led to the resignation of President Nixon. America needed no repeat of that bitter scenario.

Determined that all the pertinent facts must be disclosed with dignity, preserving the congressional authority without precipitating a full-scale constitutional confrontation, Senate Majority Leader Byrd and I began meeting regularly weeks prior to convening of the 100th Congress, before either of us was technically empowered to act. After discussing our plan with Republican leaders, we announced that there would be one congressional hearing on the subject, not several. Byrd and I would appoint Democratic members; minority leaders Michel and Dole would select Republican panelists. Eager to protect the credibility and prestige of the Special Select Committees, I very carefully chose the most respected authorities I could find: Chairs Peter Rodino of Judiciary, Jack Brooks of Government Operations, Dante Fascell of Foreign Affairs, Les Aspin of Armed Services, and Louis Stokes of Intelligence. To signal the importance I attached to this mission, I asked new House Majority Leader Tom Foley to serve as my personal representative and appointed Edward P. Boland, principal author of several of the laws that had been violated.

I thought a long while before choosing a chair for the whole group and finally settled on Lee Hamilton of Indiana, ranking member of the Foreign Affairs Committee and former chair of the House Intelligence Committee. I picked Hamilton because of his reputation for objectivity and his judicious, noninflammatory manner. The worst thing would be for these hearings to degenerate into a partisan witch hunt. As much as I disagreed with Reagan on domestic priorities and disliked his inflammatory rhetoric on the Contra affair, I did not want anyone on the committee with a private agenda of personally embarrassing the president. To complete my list of appointees, I named Ed Jenkins of Georgia, a good country lawyer.

Senator Byrd also chose a responsible panel. He and I agreed that, to the extent of our ability to influence it, the hearing must not smack of political partisanship. It would be open to the media and nationally televised. Byrd's chair, Senator Daniel Inouye (D-Hawaii), was ideally suited by temperament and conviction for his role. His demeanor was calm and rational. He and Hamilton, I felt sure, would do their best to be impartial and scrupulously fair to Republican colleagues appointed by Dole and Michel and to hold down temptations to inflammatory rhetoric.

Determined to have our team in place to hit the ground running as soon as Congress convened, Majority Leader Tom Foley and I began daily skull sessions with those who'd be helping us. The caucus's choice for Democratic whip, which Foley and I welcomed, was Tony Coelho, the energetic Californian who had modernized and transformed our Democratic Congressional Campaign Committee. Tony was as hyper as a hummingbird and as tireless in the pursuit of votes on House issues as he'd been in his quest for campaign contributors. Dick Gephardt of Missouri, who would win the Iowa caucuses before running out of money in a respectable run for the 1988 presidential nomination, was elected caucus chairman. In a further nod of encouragement to younger members, I selected as Chief Deputy Whip forty-one-year-old David Bonior of Michigan. It was a results-oriented team.

The holiday season brought its own crisis. Social activist Mitch Snyder and a group of advocates for the homeless, one night in early January in the season of Epiphany, quietly moved a nativity scene onto the Capitol grounds across the parking lot northeast of the Senate chamber and set up an around-the-clock vigil, identifying the plight of the city's homeless with the holy family that sought refuge in the manger of Bethlehem. The statuary figures were lifesize, artfully sculpted, and rendered in plastic for weight and easier mobility. However sympathetic their intent, however evocative their point about the indisputable needs of the homeless, their bold maneuver was clearly a violation of the law expressly forbidding erection of any statue, monument, or other appurtenance on the Capitol grounds except as expressly authorized by Congress.

My first knowledge of the problem came the next day as I was trying to move some of my furniture into the Speaker's office in the Capitol's east front. Jack Russ, House Sergeant at Arms, who, in that capacity directed the 175 member Capitol police, burst into the half-vacant Speaker's office. I had only become Speaker the day before and was unprepared for the sudden mini-crisis with which this situation confronted me. Yet, as the constitutional authority figure, I'd have to make the call.

"They're determined to break the law, Mr. Speaker," said Jack, "and I'm sworn to uphold it. I've been over there twice and warned them politely that they're in violation. I don't like the idea of sending the police force over to remove them physically, but I know of nothing else to do. I can't allow them to keep breaking the law when it's my responsibility to carry it out!"

"What did they say to you?" I asked.

Jack flushed. "They don't say anything. They just smile. I think they *want* us to carry them and their statue off the Capitol grounds! They'll probably just sit there like Gandhi between us and the display and make us move them away physically while the television cameras grind away. If they resist, of course, we'll have to subdue them."

"We don't want this, Jack." I said. "It's embarrassing enough that Congress hasn't done anything to *help* the homeless. We surely don't want the police using force against these unfortunate people when they're not doing anything to hurt anybody."

"But do you want an open defiance of the law? Do you want me not to carry out my sworn duty?"

"No, Jack, I don't want that. I understand your position, and I appreciate your diligence. There's just got to be a better way."

"Well, what do you want me to do?"

I looked out the Speaker's office window toward the scene, maybe 150 yards away. It appeared that about twenty-five people were gathered near the manger display. It was about five o'clock in the afternoon. A number of tourists were strolling by, stopping to look at the nativity figures in the pale January sunlight.

"Don't do anything, Jack," I said. "This is one I'm going to have to handle myself." I called in Steve Charnovitz, a Yale graduate and labor law specialist whom I'd just brought onto my official staff. "Steve," I said, "please walk over there and find Mitch Snyder. Tell him I surely would love to see him here in my office, if he wouldn't mind."

Ten minutes later, Mitch appeared. He and I had never met, but I knew his reputation. As I opened the door from the Speaker's inner office to the reception room where he and a woman associate, Carol Fennelly, were waiting, I could tell that Mitch was slightly wary, uncertain what to expect.

"Hey, Mitch!" I smiled. "Thanks for coming so soon! I've been wanting to meet you for a long time. You and the young lady, please come in and sit down. How do you like your coffee? You're bound to need some; it's getting a little chilly outside!"

After steaming mugs of coffee were poured, I looked straight into Mitch's eyes and said: "What can we do to help you?"

He seemed both taken aback and relieved by my question. He knew he was in violation of the law. He knew I knew it and that I knew he knew it.

"Well, its just that nobody in any official capacity seems to care. Nobody—at least, not until right now—has even asked what they could do to help. I'm trying to give shelter to about three hundred people in quarters that are not really big enough for half that many. But nobody else is doing anything! If somebody in authority would just come and *look* at what we are trying to do, and see how hard these people are having it, we'd be glad to move our crypt to another location. We don't want to embarrass you. We just want *somebody* to be interested in these poor people's problems."

"That's fair enough," I said. "*I'll* darn well go with you. I'd *like* to see your shelter and find out what you think our government should be doing that we aren't doing."

"Will you?" Snyder was as pleased as a child. "I'll give you a personal tour. You can see for yourself how we are trying to help as many of these folks as possible—and how we are keeping them off drugs and with enough food not to go hungry."

Reaching for a topcoat that hung in a little closet, I said "Let's go before it gets completely dark. I want to see it all!"

"Oh, not yet!" said Snyder. "In about fifteen minutes, it'll be too dark to see anything. Besides, I've got to get things ready and notify the press. Could you go with me tomorrow morning?"

So, that was it. I should have known he'd want a press accompaniment, so it wouldn't appear that he and his little group, bundled up against the weather, had been ignominiously removed. My going with him to see the shelter for which he had worked so hard would dignify his efforts. Fine! It just might help us both get something done for the homeless all over America.

Before he left my office that evening, Mitch Snyder promised to have the display removed by noon on the following day. Later, Tony Coelho and about a dozen younger members and staffers, along with Connecticut Congressman Steward McKinney, ranking Republican on the House Banking Committee, brought sleeping bags and spent a chill wintery night with the homeless contingent around the new place where the nativity scene now rested. That was Tony's idea. I wish it had been mine. Their presence helped change the whole focus. It wasn't a confrontation anymore, and it wasn't civil disobedience. It was an exercise in brotherhood.

At eight o'clock the next morning, I met Snyder as arranged. We toured his sparsely furnished facility in the city's northeast quadrant. Homeless people were getting shelter in crowded dormitory-style rooms. Women and children were housed in rooms separate from the men. Extreme care was taken, Mitch insisted, to keep the environment drug free. Accompanied now by a retinue of newspeople, including several with television cameras, we walked through a bay where mostly children were being fed a breakfast of hot cereal, cafeteria style.

A few of the occupants were in family groups, but most were singles. Some of these tenants, by my casual appraisal, probably were unqualified for any but the most menial or low-skilled tasks. A few appeared emotionally unbalanced. They averted their eyes when I greeted them, but that might have been shyness or apprehension at seeing me, so unexpectedly, dressed as I was. Newspeople pressed me for my reactions. I told them the statistics on the growing national phenomenon of homelessness, described as well as I could the human aspects of the problem I had witnessed that morning. "This is one manifestation, and perhaps the saddest one, of the social deficit we have allowed to develop in our country during the past few years."

We could not be content with it, I said. I didn't know the whole solution but saw it in two main parts. The first was immediate: relief, help. We should by all means encourage private charities and local governments, but there were ways in which the federal government could help, too—by sharing food surpluses, for example, and assisting in their nationwide distribution to local food banks manned by volunteers. The second phase of government's response, I told the media that day, was in providing a climate where there'd be useful jobs for all who could work, job training for those without marketable skill, medical help for those with disabling physical or mental handicaps, and a consistent government policy to encourage affordable housing. "Work for all who can work," I summed it up, "and help for the few who can't work."

Back at the Capitol, I called Fred St. Germain, Chairman of the Banking, Finance and Urban Affairs Committee. In the first week after the new Congress convened, I told Fred I would appreciate the opportunity to appear before his committee and begin putting together a creative approach to the homeless problem. I had reserved, I promised, a low bill number for a leadership initiative on housing and would actively support quick passage of a separate initiative on the growing problem of homelessness. Fred was enthusiastic, as were Henry Gonzalez, Frank Annunzio, and Walter Fauntroy, delegate from the District of Columbia who served on that committee. Another willing booster with creative ideas was ranking committee Republican Stewart B. McKinney, then terminally ill, although most of us did not realize it. The homeless bill ultimately would be named for him.

This became a pattern of my first year in the speakership, and a deliberate policy. By prearrangement with the House parliamentarian, Bill Brown, I reserved the first ten bill numbers—H.R. 1 through H.R. 10—for major leadership initiatives. Several of these, spelled out on television immediately following President Reagan's State of the Union message on January 27, would address our efforts to reverse the nation's growing deficit of social and public services.

For the better part of a decade, America had ignored its public infrastructure: that vital network of roads and bridges, rivers and harbors, school buildings, public transportation facilities and underground water pipes upon which our citizens all must rely. One third of the bridges in Ohio were so old they were declared unsafe for school buses. In some of our older eastern cities, leaky water mains were wasting more than 30 percent of the public water supply. We reserved the first two bill numbers—H.R. 1 and H.R. 2—for a revitalized clean water program and a five-year $88 billion highway–mass transit commitment. H.R. 3 would be a landmark trade bill, the most sweeping in twenty-five years. The next two, H.R. 4 and H.R. 5, would deal with affordable housing and a $7.5 billion school-aid authorization, reasserting the neglected federal interest in public elementary, secondary, and vocational education.

Each of these bills would pass the House that year by impressive margins, each attracting some Republican support. We had a specific agenda, for which we established a specific time table. Calling all the committee chairmen together in the Speaker's private dining room, we allocated a definite date on the House calendar—with the appropriate committee head's concurrence—for each major leadership bill, a specific time for it to be marked up, reported out of committee, and on the House floor for passage. Instead of autonomous feudal barons each pursuing a leisurely independent course, most members of the hierarchy once described by O'Neill as his "College of Cardinals" now felt part of a purposeful team.

Our very first order of legislative business was the clean water initiative. The House moved with lightning speed. Public Works chairman Jim Howard of New Jersey already had the bill drafted and formally approved by his committee. We moved it onto the House floor in the very first week of our session. This was a ten-year commitment of federal matching funds to state and local governments to help them keep America's streams free of pollution by building modern wastewater disposal plants. On the second day of business in January 1987, the House passed the initiative and sent it to the Senate, which promptly followed suit. Our speedy action on this bill revived a long running disagreement with President Reagan over environmental priorities. He had wanted to end the federal role in promoting clean water. Reagan, in fact, had pocket-vetoed a similar bill after our adjournment the previous year. Now, in spite of top heavy votes in both houses, Reagan vetoed the new bill, beginning what would be a year of confrontation on domestic issues. On February 3, the House overrode the chief executive's veto by 401 to 26. Obviously, this environmental imperative had heavy bipartisan support. The next day, the Senate overrode by 86 to 14. Most Republicans in both houses had defied the president on the issue. H.R. 1 was law.

Next, we moved on H.R. 2. The highway bill's fate followed a similar pattern. Reagan had been stinting on road building in spite of a growing backlog of deferred needs, and he stoutly resisted the idea that government had any interest in promoting public transportation. Several billion dollars of road-user taxes were piling up, unused, in the highway trust fund. They couldn't legally be spent on anything else. Our bill sailed through the House and Senate. Word came that the president was considering a second veto. Realizing his relations with Congress were getting out of hand, Reagan prevailed on former Senate Majority Leader Howard Baker—freshly retired from his years of public service—to return and help restore the president's effectiveness in dealing with the legislative branch. Baker agreed to serve, at least for a time, as White House Chief of Staff.

Howard came by to talk with me about how the president might establish a better dialogue. "Howard," I said, "try to explain that Congress has a *responsibility* to initiate legislation of this type. He seems to take it as a personal affront. He should have known we'd have the votes to override his veto of the clean water bill. Don't you think he might have made a gesture of reasonableness by going along on that?"

"Yes, I do, Jim, and I've already told the president that. I have also tried to show him that he'd be wise to sign the highway bill. But some of his other advisers are telling him to veto it. They think he could be sustained and insist he has to reassert his mastery. I'm hoping calmer heads will prevail."

Reagan vetoed the highway bill on March 27, criticizing it as a "pork barrel" measure. The House overrode quickly, and on April 2 the Senate followed suit. H.R. 2 was law.

Problems of an entirely different kind would face me in my efforts to come to grips with the budget and trade deficits, and to reconcile a policy on Central

America. I knew from the beginning that we'd face starchy resistance, even open confrontation on our domestic social priorities. But I had strong hopes of building a bridge across the partisan aisle and finding consensus on an effort to redress the trade imbalance and its costly outflow of dollars. Of ever-increasing urgency, I thought, was the need to do something constructive about the galloping budget deficits.

To make any serious progress against those huge annual budget shortfalls which had begun in 1981, I knew, would require an abrupt reversal of direction. America would have to start paying as we went. Those accumulating budget deficits, unattended, could doom any serious effort to come to grips with our growing deficiencies in trade and public investment. The alarming rise in public debt was the inevitable result, I believed, of the colossal economic misjudgments indulged by President Reagan in 1981, of the Democrats' lack of a cohesive resistance, and of the public's gleeful gullibility when winsomely promised something for nothing.

The figures were clear. We had tripled the national debt. In these six years of peace and relative plenty, it had skyrocketed from slightly under $1 trillion to almost $3 trillion when I took the Speaker's chair.

President Truman had presided over the whole Korean War effort without increasing the national debt. We paid it down a bit, in fact. During President Johnson's last year in office, while the Vietnam War was at its height and we were conducting a massive effort to eradicate poverty, Congress actually produced a slight budget *surplus* through taxes adequate to sustain all of our government's current activities. Now, in peacetime, and having largely abandoned the war on poverty, the nation was plunging deeply into debt.

I'd never doubted that Mr. Reagan actually believed we could double military spending, drastically reduce taxes for the rich, and still balance the budget by 1983. He seemed to suppose this possible simply through cutting out "waste, fraud, and abuse." When the mathematics proved unworkable, Reagan steadfastly refused to admit error or alter course. If a change in direction was to come, Congress would have to take the initiative. To *reduce* the deficit substantially would require *more taxes*, among other things, and taxes have never been popular.

That was the stickiest of the four big challenges that confronted congressional leadership. I considered it unavoidable. If the essential immorality of indulging whims on a credit card and sending the bills to grandchildren were not enough to concern us, we desperately needed to consider how much this profligacy was beginning to cost the *current* generation simply for the *privilege of owing* such unprecedented sums. Interest payments on the debt were the fastest-growing item in our federal budget. They would drag $169 billion away from more productive uses in 1987, and this was fully three times the burden they posed in 1980. Clearly, this frightening growth in the budget deficit demanded resolute action. I was convinced that it could not be arrested except by a combination of three things: more revenues (translate *taxes*), cuts in military spending, and cuts in domestic expenditures. No one of these three actions alone could attain the result. Most members of Congress realized this truth, but to convince them that the *public* understood and would applaud heroic action on the budgetary front was a major challenge.

A large part of the difficulty arose from what many members perceived as a public aversion to the very mention of the forbidden word, "taxes." Walter Mondale, the Democratic presidential nominee in 1984, had told the nation candidly that we obviously must have more taxes if we ever expect to balance the budget. The only question, Mondale posited, was who would pay the taxes. The Reagan campaign spoke of "Morning in America" and pooh-poohed the notion of additional taxes. Reagan won. Members, therefore, were inclined to be as fractious at the mere whisper of the word as a flighty young colt confronted by a rattlesnake in the path.

What is a Speaker to do? He sees the treasury hemorrhaging, but is aware of his colleagues' nervousness about applying the only tourniquet that will stop the bleeding. My duty, I felt, was to find a way to demonstrate that Congress could face the crisis, swallow the bitter medicine, and survive. I had faith the public would respond to an honest, straightforward appeal for fairly distributed sacrifices *now* in the interest of the *future*.

Thirty years earlier, as a first-term Congressman, I'd been part of a group that persuaded President Eisenhower that the way to finance the Interstate Highway program was by pay-as-we-go taxes rather than by adding to the nation's debt. For three decades, people had willingly paid these taxes, driven the highways, and not grumbled. Now someone had to lead by example.

In my first press conference after the Democratic caucus nominated me for Speaker, in December of 1986, I proposed that we freeze tax breaks for people in the upper income brackets at the rates they were paying, and repeal the huge prospective rate cuts for high-income taxpayers scheduled to take effect in the so-called Tax Reform Act of 1986. That suggestion did not seem excessively brave. I was not even proposing a *hike* in taxes, merely opposing additional tax *cuts* scheduled for the wealthiest Americans.

That proposal was a lightning rod, and it drew immediate reaction. Treasury Secretary James Baker called my suggestion "nothing more than a general tax increase," and other administration spokesmen denounced it heartily. But several privately commissioned polls revealed a substantial majority of the people in support of the plan, once they understood it. The specific suggestion I offered that day was never enacted, but it served its purpose. It broke the ice and tended to demonstrate that Congress could raise revenues for deficit-reduction without being crucified.

I knew how hard it was to patch together any budget resolution that would pass the House, let alone one with real teeth in it. Not only did we need to make a genuine reduction in the deficit, we needed to do it in a *balanced* way while allowing some needed increases in several domestic programs. Bill Gray of Pennsylvania was the chairman of the Budget Committee and a gifted ally. He led the committee with skill and understanding, as its members worked their way toward a realistic plan. The budget resolution that emerged in mid-spring called for $36 billion in actual deficit reduction, half of this in new taxes and half in spending cuts. The $18 billion in reduced expenditures was divided evenly between defense spending and domestic programs. This budget package passed the House by a comfortable margin. Congress still was a long way from achieving the goal, but we had made a beginning. Ultimately, I would learn just how hard it was to pass any revenue increasing tax bill with the White House adamantly opposed.

The trade deficit in late 1986 was only starting to command serious public attention, but it already had reached its fingers deeply into American pockets. Six years earlier, as the 1980s began, we were the world's biggest creditor nation. By the time I assumed the speakership, our country had become the world's largest debtor. A growing number of American business, labor, and academic leaders, alarmed by the trends they saw, were asking for a concerted national effort to stem the tide. We were borrowing from other countries not only to finance our purchases from them but to finance our national debt. More and more of our government bonds were held by foreigners. Private owners had begun selling off an increasing share of America's important domestic assets: land, banks, factories, hotels, newspapers.

The Democratic Leadership Council—a gathering of mostly politically moderate elected Democratic officials, including such figures as Georgia's Senator Sam Nunn, Louisiana's John Breaux, and Governor Bill Clinton of Arkansas—held its annual conference in Williamsburg, Virginia, on December 12, 1986. Invited to speak there, I addressed the trade issue. Afterward, I had a long conversation with Lloyd Hand, former Johnson aide and White House Chief of protocol, now a prominent Washington lawyer. Hand made an appointment for me to meet with John Young and other business leaders, who, in the past year, had conducted an intensive study of the trade problem at President Reagan's request. The group issued a formal report filled with recommendations, which they felt both the White House and Congress had generally ignored. At the encouragement of these people, I began to explore the possibility of a national *Conference on Competitiveness* to be attended by distinguished specialists in trade from the fields of business, labor, and academia.

Anxious that our efforts should be bipartisan, I talked personally with House Republican Leader Bob Michel and Senate Minority Leader Bob Dole before taking any definite action, as well as with Senate Democratic Leader Robert Byrd. All readily acknowledged the importance of the problem. They agreed on the worth of such a meeting and on a broad list of invitees. Each of them quickly assented that invitations to the blue ribbon list go out jointly in our four names. That conference, a solicitation by Congress of the best advice available on the subject of trade, was scheduled for January 21 in the Caucus Room of the Cannon House Office Building. I talked with Treasury Secretary Jim Baker and U.S. Trade Representative Clayton Yuetter, inviting their participation. A week after the invitations went out to the selected cross section of experts, I discovered how difficult it would be to perfect a truly bipartisan approach to the trade issue. Both Republican leaders, Bob Michel and Bob Dole, called in some embarrassment to tell me they had been under pressure from Reagan administration officials to withdraw from formal sponsorship of the event. Nevertheless, the conference took place as scheduled. It was attended by many Republican as well as Democratic members of each house. The panel of distinguished authorities included corporate executives, union leaders, university presidents, and academic specialists, who made a probing analysis of the problems. They gave many constructive suggestions, ranging from improved job training for America's work force to a renewal of business incentives for modernizing America's aging industrial plants, to anti-trust enforcement, to renegotiation of copyright and intellectual property rights agreements.

I knew the proposed legislation would require the active cooperation of at least twelve House committees. On the next day, January 22, I hosted a luncheon for the chairmen of those specific committees in the Speaker's private dining room. In the first two weeks of the session, the House had already passed the clean water bill and the highway bill by votes easily big enough to override vetoes, and a spirit of ebullience prevailed. We had discussed the agenda for the year, the big bills that would comprise our effort to surmount the three deficits. We talked now of the trade bill, an important centerpiece of the agenda. I promised to respect each committee's turf by assigning separate titles of a composite work to the committees that had jurisdiction over the varied segments. Chairmen Dan Rostenkowski of Ways and Means, John Dingell of Commerce, Jack Brooks of Judiciary and Kika de la Garza of Agriculture each promised to give top priority to their segments of the trade legislation.

Five days later, following President Reagan's State of the Union message,

Senate Majority Leader Robert Byrd and I divided the thirty minutes allotted by the television networks for the Democratic response. By our prearrangement, Byrd addressed foreign and military affairs and I the domestic policy agenda. From the cascade of mail and telephoned calls that ensued, I knew I had struck a sensitive nerve with the public when I revealed that in the previous year, from the largest ports in the East Coast, the two top U.S. exports, by tonnage, had been scrap metal, mainly from junked cars, and waste paper. I explained that the latter, shipped mostly to the Far East, was reprocessed into cardboard boxes to carry television sets, toys, computers and shoe imports back to America. An avalanche of response assured me that the American public was enthusiastically supportive, whether or not the administration chose to cooperate in seeking solutions.

Still, I wanted very much to promote a bipartisan approach. In mid-afternoon on January 28, I invited leading Democrats and Republicans from twelve House committees to sit together around the tables in the Speaker's dining room and discuss ways to improve our nation's trade balance. We agreed to incorporate the best ideas from our several sources into an omnibus bill and to schedule it for action in the House on April 28. By request of Chairmen Dingell and Rostenkowski, I appeared personally before their committees in the first part of February to emphasize the importance of the bill. Cabinet spokesmen were invited to testify. Many members of both parties, in spite of a lukewarm White House attitude, were enthusiastic. Every committee met its time schedule. We all agreed that the bill's main thrust would be stimulative rather than protectionist.

In early March, I got a shocker. Japan's ambassador came by my office to tell me that his country's prime minister Yasuhiro Nakasone would like to be invited to address a joint meeting of Congress on April 28. This was disconcerting. Requests of this kind normally came from the White House. The April 28 date could hardly be coincidental, since I had announced that very date publicly as the day set for the trade bill vote. I suggested to the Japanese Ambassador that it would be much more fortuitous, and less potentially embarrassing, for his leader to speak on any other day—a week earlier or a week later, perhaps—since on April 28 we would be considering the omnibus trade bill.

"Could you not postpone that bill?" the emissary asked.

"No, Mr. Ambassador, I'm afraid we cannot."

I called Secretary of State George Shultz's office and suggested that it might save embarrassment all around to invite the Prime Minister to our country on some other week. I gave assurances that the House would cooperate in issuing an invitation at any other date the White House might desire. I never heard further. Nakasone came to our country during the last week in April, but no request was made for his appearance before Congress. I never knew whether the date of his visit was chosen by him or by our administration, nor what effect it was calculated to have upon our trade deliberations.

The bill, HR 3, was almost nine hundred pages long. Most of it had the active support of both Republicans and Democrats in Congress. It offered a fresh synergistic approach to our trade and competitiveness problems. One section authorized funding for new educational programs in science, math, engineering and foreign language training. Another included a $980 million fund for retraining and readjustment to help American workers losing their jobs as result of foreign imports. Another provision extended help in research and development to stimulate a domestic semiconductor industry. The bill also contained significant initiatives to promote American exports.

This measure passed the House by the preponderant vote of 290 to 137. It represented the most important trade legislation since President Kennedy's time. The Senate would hold the bill under consideration for more than a year, altering and fine-tuning several of its provisions, finally passing it largely intact in the summer of 1988. One Senate provision, requiring advance notification of the workers before summarily shutting down an American plant, drew the ire of President Reagan. He vetoed the big bill, protesting that such a requirement had no place in trade legislation. We simply removed that provision, made it into a separate bill, then reenacted both bills simultaneously without changing so much as a comma. President Reagan signed the trade bill and allowed the plant closing bill to become law without his signature, after we made it an issue of the 1988 Presidential campaign.

During the Easter recess in April of 1987, at the formal invitation of the Soviet government and upon the encouragement of President Reagan and our State Department, I headed a bipartisan delegation to the U.S.S.R. Richard Cheney, chairman of the House Republican conference, served as cochairman. Spouses accompanied the members. During that same week, nuclear arms reduction talks were being shifted temporarily from Geneva to Moscow. Secretary of State George Shultz chose to join us in the Soviet capitol that week. For three days our group of twenty Democrats and Republicans had talks with top Soviet government officials. It became quickly apparent to Betty and me, as to others who had visited that country in previous years, that official attitudes were undergoing a major, surprisingly swift metamorphosis under Gorbachev's leadership. For one entire day our group was invited to engage in long, serious discussions with Mikhail Gorbachev and his principal advisors. No subject was taboo. The charismatic leader seemed receptive to our suggestions, openly friendly to our country and frank in the admission of previous Soviet errors. At one point, I handed him a copy of my twenty-eight-year-old "Letter to Ivan," written during Christmas week 1959. That letter had suggested that both superpowers jointly begin reducing our respective military budgets by 10 percent annually. Gorbachev smiled. His eyes widened.

"That was 1959," he mused. "Twenty-eight years ago! Have you calculated how many billions of dollars and rubles—well, perhaps *trillions*—we both might have saved by now if we had done that then?"

Later that afternoon, back at the hotel, I received a call from our American embassy. "This is one for the books!" I was told. "Chairman Gorbachev invites you, if you're interested, to speak to the people of the Soviet Union by national television. He says you can have thirty minutes—or longer if you want—and say anything you'd like to say to the people of his country on behalf of the delegation from the U.S. Congress."

"No censorship?" I asked. "Absolutely none!" came the reply.

Later that evening, I got further elucidation. Fewer Soviet families owned television sets, of course, but, for market share, the deal I was offered was a lot better than any network could have provided in our country. The hookup and time slot, the Ambassador told me, were precisely what Gorbachev himself chose when making a major public statement. That evening, as I worked on my speech late into the night, my mind returned to an event early that morning, when our delegation had laid a wreath at the tomb of the Unknown Soviet Soldier. Twenty million of Russia's young gave up their lives in World War II, I reflected, just as friends and classmates of mine had done. I remembered the faces of the young Russian military guards, not much older than my eldest grandson, who kept early morning vigil at that national shrine, and thought what a tragic loss of opportunity if my generation should fail to find a sensible path away from the mindless hostility that plagued our two peoples.

The next day, in my simultaneously translated remarks via television, I said there was a sense in which we all were "fellow citizens."

> *We are citizens of the world. And the world is becoming a much smaller place. Science and technology have shrunk the planet Earth. It took Christopher Columbus 56 days to cross the Atlantic Ocean. I covered the same distance last week in six hours. To express this fact in the most dangerous way, my home town in Texas is only 40 minutes away from Vladivostok by Soviet intercontinental missiles. And so, in that sense, you and I do live in the same neighborhood.*
>
> *We can make it a less dangerous neighborhood. If combustible explosives were stored near our houses, yours and mine, or if ravening wolves were let loose in our children's playground, or if deadly poisons were left lying around within the reach of our infants—you and I would want to do something about it, wouldn't we? We'd get together*

*and insist, for the benefit of our families that those hazards be
removed and safety precautions be taken.*

*Well, that in a way is what your government and our government
are trying to do in our nuclear arms reduction talks which have been
underway in Moscow this past week . . .*

Next, I told the Soviet audience a bit about our American Congress, that
we are the ones who must levy the taxes and appropriate the money for everything our government does. Then:

*This year the United States will spend almost $300 billion—that's
equal to about 200 billion rubles—on machines of destruction and
unproductive implements of military power. Your country will spend
a similar amount on the same things. What waste that is for both of
us—when human wants go unmet and legitimate needs unfulfilled
. . .*

To listeners who often had to wait years for assignment to improved family
housing, I pointed out that the cost of one modern Russian nuclear submarine
would build comfortable living quarters for an entire city of 125,000 families.

By prearrangement, for the final four minutes of my comments the program
director superimposed at the bottom of the screen a logo bearing this simplified
address: JIM WRIGHT, THE CAPITOL, WASHINGTON, D.C., U.S.A. I
removed from my lapel a small emblem handed to each of us on our arrival by
our State Department. It contained small enameled replicas of the flags of the
U.S. and U.S.S.R., joined at the base. I offered one to each listener who would
write to me and tell me his or her feelings about the peace initiative:

*As a token of our friendship, I'd like to send you a little personal gift. It
has no great material value, but I would like to send you a little
remembrance as a sentimental expression of our will to work together
. . .*

*If you will write a note to me at this address, I'll be glad to send you
this little emblem with my personal best wishes.*

*I know that you of my generation love your children just as I love
mine. You of both older and younger generations love your country
just as I love mine. And so I offer this wish for your children and for
my children—and for their children: may they live in peace.*

The response was astounding. Shortly after I returned, a deluge of mail began
pouring in. Letters and cards, bearing exotic stamps and postmarks, arrived

from many parts of the sprawling Soviet Union. There were more than two thousand in all. From old people and young. From folks who remembered World War II and students who had only read of it. From young couples. From teachers, and from numerous classes of students, many of the younger ones sending original art work. Almost one-third of the letters were in some form of readable English. A few were grammatically perfect, some barely decipherable, but all clear in their meaning. The majority, written in Russian, I sent for translation to the Library of Congress. Each was distinct, individual. All, however—all of them—were supportive of the idea of peace.

One nine-year-old child sent drawings paneled like an American comic strip. The first panel portrayed a Soviet bomber; the second, a remarkably recognizable depiction of Manhattan Island's skyscrapers; in the third, bomb bay doors opened. The final panel showed the bomb load falling from the sky—candy, toys, flowers. "This is what we wish for American people," the inscription read.

"You're speech on Soviet TV make on me a great impression," wrote one viewer from his home in Gori, the town in Soviet Georgia where Josef Stalin had been born. "You are right. If we learn more about each other, we'll more trust each feelings. I'll wish you success in your business."

Each time I emerged from an hour's reading of these cards and letters, so genuine, from plain people in that faraway country from whom we had been so long estranged, I was buoyed anew with the conviction that peace was inevitable—if neither side did something stupid to gum it up.

Now, halfway into 1987, I felt we had made a good start on many fronts. Some domestic social and economic gains had emerged in spite of White House opposition. In foreign affairs, I thought we'd found one spot of common ground. Reagan had asked me for a briefing on my observations following our return from Moscow. Now I shared with him the contents of some of these letters from humble Soviet citizens. The Iran-Contra investigation was about to end its set of formal hearings. Even stranger things lay ahead.

CHAPTER THIRTY-FOUR

GIVING PEACE
A CHANCE

A career in public office is one long rollercoaster ride, lifting the emotions of any but the most phlegmatic to heights of enormous gratification and plunging them to depths of galling disappointment. If the emotional nadir of my thirty-four public years was the day of President Kennedy's assassination, their zenith was the ultimate success of the Central American peace plan. The pivotal role I played was more thrust upon me than sought. I was invited by President Reagan to join him in seeking a solution, and I took him at his word. Later, he wanted me to bug out and let the effort fail. I refused. That endeavor brought moments of pain and unquestionably hastened the end of my political career. But no other experience in my public life has given me quite the level of satisfying fulfillment as helping to end the wars in Central America and seeing democracy take root in El Salvador and Nicaragua where it had never before flourished.

By midsummer 1987, the highly publicized "Irangate" hearings had reached their climax. Lee Hamilton and Danny Inouye had done their best to be impartial and scrupulously fair to Republican colleagues. The latter, in turn, fought fiercely to exonerate President Reagan of personal culpability for the misdeeds unearthed. Several witnesses, including Assistant Secretary of State Elliott Abrams, admitted having deliberately lied to Congress about the whole affair. Abrams showed no remorse. He had not been "authorized" to tell the truth, he said.

Back in January, Lee Hamilton had agreed in advance to an arbitrary date to terminate the proceedings. Otherwise, he felt, they could go on indefinitely, to the detriment of other important legislative business. Hamilton also proposed granting limited immunity from prosecution to induce testimony from Lieutenant Colonel Oliver North, the individual most involved in the details of several covert transactions that broke the law. As it turned out, this may have compromised the efforts of Independent Counsel Lawrence E. Walsh, but our overriding interest in the congressional leadership was not to humiliate the administration and send people to jail, but to get at the truth, maintain the nation's equilibrium, emphasize the rule of law, and avoid a bloody constitutional confrontation.

Of equal importance now, I felt, was to heal the wound that had festered for five years over our country's secret, and sometimes illegal, sponsorship of the gory efforts to overthrow the Nicaraguan government by force. At least 30,000 people had died in Nicaragua, along with an estimated 70,000 in El Salvador, and the U.S.–backed Contras were no closer to their goal than when they'd started. Following the sensational revelations of the administration's bizarre schemes to fund them, it seemed quite unlikely to me that Congress would renew the flow of arms. That's what I had told Howard Baker earlier that spring. The people are disillusioned and Congress won't vote for it, I said. I'd suggested to Baker that Reagan would be wise to initiate talks aimed at a peaceful settlement while the Contras still had some money in the pipeline, rather than wait for it to run out in the forlorn expectation that Congress would renew it. "If Reagan took the initiative now and called for talks aimed at ending the war, he could seize the high ground—like Eisenhower in 1952. Remember the electricity when Ike said, 'I will go to Korea?'" Baker said it sounded like good advice.

In mid-July 1987, a Republican former colleague, Tom Loeffler, came by my office with a startling proposition. Tom had left Congress the year before to run unsuccessfully for governor of Texas. I liked and trusted Loeffler. Tom told me President Reagan had appointed him to help unravel the funding problem for the Nicaraguan rebels. Tom told me that he had a much better idea than renewing the fight for military funding.

"If the president and the Speaker could make a joint call for a peace settlement, that would make a huge impact in Central America," Loeffler offered. "I'd like to know if you would be willing to join Ronald Reagan in a bipartisan initiative aimed at settling the whole thing once and for all? People know you down there. They trust you. Everybody in Central America would pay heed if the president and Congress were united in a call for peace."

The idea was intriguing, but I was skeptical. Would the president's pro-Contra advisors be cynical enough to float a phony peace initiative, expecting it to fail, and then use the preordained failure as an excuse for renewing the war? I told Tom some Democrats were sure to be suspicious. "Mr. Speaker, I know there's a lot of suspicion on both sides," Loeffler said. "I came to you because you are the only one who can make this happen. I am convinced that the president is sincere in wanting a peaceful settlement. I wouldn't have come to you unless I felt that."

During the previous November, I had spoken at former President Carter's request to a conference of elected Latin American leaders at the Carter Center in Atlanta. That night at dinner, Carter had asked me to join him in a spirited conversation he was having with Nicaraguan Vice President Sergio Ramírez. I put the question straight to the Sandinista leader: "What would it take for you to expel the Cuban and Russian military, live in peace with your neighbors, stop giving aid to those who want to subvert the government of El Salvador, and restore the constitutional rights of free speech and press and assembly that you suspended in your emergency law?"

Ramírez replied evenly, "We are not intervening in El Salvador. For the rest, it would take one thing only—for your government to stop financing the invasion of our country. When that is done, there will be no need for an emergency law, and we will be glad to do everything you have mentioned." The Ramírez statement could not necessarily be taken at face value, but maybe it had to be tested—and maybe this was the time.

My visits to Nicaragua had convinced me that, much as their economy was hurting, the left wing would retain control just as long as it could credibly blame its failures and the people's misery on a U.S. "imperialistic" effort to break and dominate them. *Nationalism was a more powerful force in Latin America than Marxism.* Of this I was certain. The time might be right for a package of major concession from the Sandinistas, but I knew we would not wring it from them at the end of a rifle barrel.

Finally, I said to Loeffler, "Go back and check your sources again, Tom. Tell them I don't want any part in setting up a halfhearted effort doomed to fail. But tell them that if they are absolutely sincere in wanting to negotiate a peaceful settlement, I'll do everything within my power to help."

A midsummer haze shimmered over the lush green of the east Capitol lawn, softening the outlines of the Library of Congress beyond. Gazing out the window after Tom left, I thought back over the long panorama of my lifelong involvement with Latin America. Could I help end the agony and bloodshed that afflicted those people and kept splitting our own government into hostile camps?

The president and I had often clashed over domestic issues and spending priorities. He had resented it, I felt, when Congress asserted its own initiatives, as we were doing increasingly now on the economic front. Would this inhibit his and my ability to unite in an appeal for peace in Central America?

If things were handled correctly, I decided, that history might even add credibility to such a joint appeal. But I wondered if President Reagan was prepared for the shift that would have to be made in our policy toward Nicaragua. I thought of the long, sad history of our involvement in the affairs of that bedraggled country—of the Tennessee freebooter William Walker, who invaded with a private army and declared himself Nicaragua's emperor in the nineteenth century; of our later stationing U.S. Marines there for twenty-one years as a virtual army of occupation on the thin pretext of protecting Americans; of the forty-three years of the U.S.–backed Somoza dynasty; of the Sandinista revolution in 1979 and our ill-concealed efforts to overthrow it. All of this had fed fires of nationalistic resentment toward us.

Even more than most Latin Americans, Nicaraguans indulged a love-hate relationship with the United States. They secretly wanted to be like us, but they were not going to let us tell them how to run their country. We just might seize this moment to get them to change directions, but we'd have to change some of our attitudes also. I wondered if Ronald Reagan was prepared for that.

Two questions needed to be answered: was Tom Loeffler reading President Reagan correctly? And would a joint appeal make a decisive difference to Latin Americans? I probed my sources in the White House and in Central America. Chief of Staff Howard Baker assured me that Reagan was aware of Tom Loeffler's overture and would be supportive. Bob Strauss, who maintained close relations with cabinet and White House officials, called me back to say he believed there had been a change in Reagan's view. "I think he really would like to make peace," Bob reported, "and principally because Nancy would like for him to go out of office as a peacemaker."

The Arias plan, announced a few weeks earlier by the Costa Rican president, seemed broadly acceptable in substance. Nobody was willing to predict that it would produce results, however, without at least a nod or a nudge from the United States. If we indicated real interest in supporting a regional settlement drawn up by Latin Americans themselves, that might just get it off the ground.

There was, however, a sense of urgency. The five Central American presidents were to meet on August 6 and 7 in Guatemala at a place called Esquipulas. If they failed to make real progress or broke up in a vocal disagreement, that rare opportunity would be wasted. Nobody knew if another such chance would come. If a bipartisan U.S. pronouncement was to have significant effect, it would have to precede that summit. But there was precious little time. That meeting was only two weeks away.

My biggest job would be to make peace in Congress. I needed to line up support of the bipartisan leadership quietly in advance of any joint public appeal.

Then I would work diligently to solidify my fellow Democrats. It was very important to enlist a supportive response from Senate leaders, often touchy about their foreign policy prerogatives, making them parties to our initiative before the president and I issued any public statement. This would not be easy.

The Contra issue had polarized the House. Outraged by the secret plotting in the White House basement, anti-Contra lawmakers were aggressively insisting on an immediate end to all U.S.–sponsored involvement in Nicaragua. Militant conservatives, emboldened by Lieutenant Colonel North's six days of televised testimony in the recent hearings, were mobilizing for a legislative counteroffensive. We asked Republican Leader Bob Michel, House Foreign Affairs Chairman Dante Fascell, and ranking Republican Bill Broomfield to meet us for a discussion of what was being proposed. That meeting produced an agreement that Bob Michel and I would call the Nicaraguan Ambassador, Carlos Tünnermann, and ask him to come for a private visit in H-201, the "hideaway" office just off the Capitol rotunda. It was extremely important, I felt, for Republican leaders to be on board *before* the takeoff. The Ambassador's opening comment to us came as a surprise: "I've been in Washington as Nicaragua's ambassador for three years," he said, "and this is the very first time anyone in the U.S. government has asked to see me or talk with me about anything whatever."

Bob Michel and I pressed hard for a definitive commitment that Nicaragua would get rid of any weapons that threatened the United States, patch up its relations with its neighbors, and restore constitutional rights to its own citizens if U.S. military aid to the Contras were terminated. Tünnermann gave essentially the answer I had received in November from Ramírez in Atlanta. After that meeting, Michel and I agreed it was possible the Sandinistas might be ready to change their policies. Bob said he'd bring the rest of his Republican leadership into the effort. Everyone in our core group (Majority Leader Tom Foley, Michel, Fascell, and Broomfield) believed we saw a window of opportunity.

Selling the idea of a joint statement with Reagan to our Democratic colleagues was the harder task. They did not trust Reagan. Rather than any bipartisan effort, many would have preferred simply to kill all Contra aid and let nature take its course. Foley, Coelho, and I carefully assembled a cross section of Democrats who had been active on various sides of the Contra issue. Dave Bonior of Michigan, trusted by liberals and younger members, was a key player. Also present were Lee Hamilton, Matt McHugh, Dave McCurdy, Wayne Owens, Mel Levine, and George Miller.

"This is very dangerous, Mr. Speaker," said George Miller of California, who had consistently opposed aid to the Contras and earlier even worked against Duarte in El Salvador. "It could be a trap. The administration would love to get us divided among ourselves." Bonior was cautiously supportive, saying we'd be irresponsible not to pursue the opening if there were any real chance it could lead to peace. Mel Levine said we were being asked to bring credibility to an administration that had lost credibility in the Iran-Contra scandal. "He's the only president we have right now, Mel," I replied. "Only he can speak for the country. If he is truly *serious* about wanting a peace effort, maybe we ought to *give* him the credibly he needs." In the end, everyone agreed we had a responsibility to provide encouragement to the peace-seekers at the Guatemala meeting.

Wayne Owens summed it up. "The stakes are important enough to take a chance," he said. "You recognize the personal risk you are taking, Mr. Speaker, but I admire you for being willing to take it." The one hundred thousand people who had died in El Salvador and Nicaragua in the past six years, Owens pointed out, would equate—considering comparative population—to as many as three million deaths in the United States, more than we had lost in all the wars in our history combined. Our group left that meeting united, pledging to fan out and enlist support from other Democrats.

On the previous Sunday I had called President Arias in Costa Rica. He would leave the following day on a tour of Central American countries, talking with each president preparatory to his Guatemala gathering. Encouraged by what I told him, Arias promised to give me a report at the end of his tour. I'd talked also with El Salvador's President José Napoleon Duarte, who was enthusiastic. "A lot depends on Daniel [Ortega] and whether he thinks the rest of us are serious. . . . If the United States is solidly behind us and the president and the Congress are speaking as one, that would be a big help."

Now, having completed his tour of the region, Arias called me. He believed the time was ripe for a serious effort. He told me of his meeting with Ortega. "Daniel is in trouble, and he knows it. The whole economy is in shambles. The junta which governs the country is divided. Tomás Borge and Bayardo Arce are ideologues. They follow the Marxist line. But the others are wavering. They are discouraged by the failure of their experiment. Ortega is probably not a Marxist. I think he is a pragmatist. Your country's trade embargo has hurt more than the Contras have. I believe he would be willing to make major concessions to bring the war to an end and open up trade."

"What chance is there to get democratizing reforms in case we can get a cease-fire?"

Arias said he thought, "if all the other presidents will stick together," that Ortega would disband the most oppressive restrictions immediately and allow a truly democratic society to develop. "*But he must not be seen as bowing to pressures from the United States. That would kill him in Nicaragua.* The terms of the settlement should not seem to be dictated by your country." Arias felt that Reagan and I could help most by expressing strong interest in their success at Esquipulas and a willingness to support and cooperate with a reasonable peace settlement by the Central American presidents.

Arias thought the first step should be a sixty-day cease-fire, during which the United States should suspend military aid to the Contras and Nicaragua would deny any use of its territory to the guerrillas making war against El Salvador, as well as take concrete steps to restore civil rights to all Nicaraguans.

Now things seemed on track in the House, and I had a general idea what kind of statement Reagan and I might issue for maximum effect. Next, I must bring the Senate leadership up to date on everything that was happening, then get congressional leaders together with top administration spokesmen for mutual reassurance. I called Senate Majority Leader Robert Byrd and made an appointment to go by his home that evening. Byrd was intrigued, promising to have a cross section of the Senate leadership together in his office to meet with me the next afternoon. He said he would call Bob Dole, Sam Nunn, Claiborne Pell, maybe others.

Earlier that day, Secretary Shultz had come by with President Reagan's new National Security Advisor Frank Carlucci, State Department liaison Will Ball, and Tom Loeffler. Loeffler made the opening comment, "We're all on the team!" Upon suggestion of the others, I agreed to dictate a proposed draft of the statement to be made by the president and myself. I told Shultz I'd have him a copy within twenty-four hours to review and suggest changes. When Michel and I told the Secretary of our talk with Nicaraguan Ambassador Tünnermann, his interest perked up. Finally he said, "You can count on me to help. We need a solution."

The next morning, before my meeting with the Senators, I got a preview of the determined efforts that would emerge to rip our tenuous coalition apart and prevent our uniting on a plan for peace. The *Washington Times*, a right-wing newspaper with staunch pro-Contra leanings, ran a major story quoting Frank Carlucci saying that President Reagan would make a major address to the nation pressing his case for more military assistance to the Contras "after Congress adjourns" for its August recess. This was alarming. I did not believe the story but saw its potential for disruption. It could panic Democrats, already suspicious of the president's motives. I called Carlucci. He assured me the *Times* story was without foundation. There'd be no call for renewed military intervention, Carlucci insisted, so long as there was hope that a peace effort might work.

Reassured, I dictated the first formal draft of what was to be the Reagan-Wright plan. Hand-delivered copies went to Shultz, Baker, Carlucci, Democratic and Republican leaders in the House and Senate. The statement proposed a six-point process of reconciliation, including an immediate cease-fire; U.S. suspension of military aid to the Contras; a simultaneous Nicaraguan halt of aid from Cuba and the Soviet Union; immediate restoration of "all civil rights and liberties"; and establishment of an "independent, multiparty electoral commission" in Nicaragua to prepare for elections "to be supervised and guaranteed by an international body such as the OAS." Secretary Shultz came by the next morning with a few notations recommending only minor changes in the language.

The meeting with the Senators in Bob Byrd's office went well. At their suggestion, we set up a broader meeting for Monday in the Speaker's dining room. Howard Baker, Frank Carlucci, and George Shultz came to consult with a larger cross section of key House and Senate legislators. There, things began to fall rapidly into place. "Mr. Secretary," I said, "we are proposing a moratorium on military activities in Central America. We'd like to propose also a moratorium on inflammatory rhetoric between the president and congressional leadership."

On Wednesday, August 5, I met with President Reagan at the White House. Along with Shultz, Howard Baker, and Will Ball, we talked of how to launch the joint statement for maximum effect. Afterward, Reagan and I went together to the White House press room, handed out copies of our declaration, and answered questions. The joint leadership of Congress and a large number of House and Senate colleagues later stood with me in the Cannon Caucus Room across the street from the Capitol and responded to a barrage of questions from the Capitol Hill press corps. Our effort was launched.

The telephone awakened me at 4:30 on Friday morning, August 7, 1987. It was Costa Rica's amiable ambassador, Guido Fernández. He was ebullient. "President Arias wanted you to be the first to know," he announced. "The five presidents have just signed off on an agreement in principle. It is being drafted now. They will review it in written form within a few hours, and I am confident that they all will sign it."

It was going to be a magnificent day.

Later that morning, Richard Peña called me at the office from the Guatemala airport. Peña, formerly a specialist on the House Foreign Affairs Committee staff, had attended the meeting as my emissary at the request of Fernández. Peña spelled out the details of the agreement. The presidents had proclaimed that none of them would supply aid or permit use of their territories to any rebellious group aimed at undermining the government of any neighbor. A process of reconciliation and amnesty would be declared in both El Salvador and Nicaragua. Under the direction of a reconciliation commission, democratization would take place, with specific standards of individual liberty to be guaranteed to all. The five foreign ministers would meet in fifteen days, and within ninety days there would be a simultaneous cease-fire. The Esquipulas agreement embraced fully three-fourths of all the points included in the Wright-Reagan plan.

At my daily press conference in the Capitol that day, I announced the outlines of the historic agreement. Someone asked if this meant the U.S. government was officially supportive. "You'll want to get a statement from the president, of course," I replied, "but it is absolutely inconceivable to me that our government could be anything but fully and enthusiastically supportive."

It was a great day, one of the finest in my life. That night I slept on a cloud of euphoria.

The next day I had a call from Adolfo Calero, acting chairman of the Nicaraguan Contra movement. A robust balding man, Calero had been a Coca-Cola executive in Nicaragua in the Somoza days. Calling now from the office of U.S. Ambassador Everett Briggs in Tegucigalpa, Honduras, Calero expressed pleasure and some surprise that Ortega had signed the Esquipulas accord and that he had agreed to abolish military law and restore the democratic process in Nicaragua. The resistance leader pledged that he and the Contras would abide by the terms of the agreement. Response from other nations in the hemisphere was uniformly good. Editorial comment was extremely positive. While the *Wall Street Journal* and the *Washington Times* threw cold water on the plan, most newspapers agreed with *The New York Times*, whose lead editorial was titled "Risks Worth Taking on Nicaragua."

Will Ball, State Department specialist in Congressional relations, called privately to tell me a few problems were arising within the administration. Secretary Weinberger, Ball said, was irate over the ninety-day time span allowed for compliance with the Esquipulas accords. We had suggested sixty days in our bipartisan plan. Weinberger now was insisting to people in the White House that the United States should summarily repudiate the whole agreement and refuse to go along with it. That objection seemed petty. I reminded Ball that we had promised to be supportive of any reasonable plan Central American presidents could develop.

Meanwhile, the Sandinistas began taking formal steps to implement the Esquipulas Accord. Ortega declared a total amnesty to be effective with the cease-fire. He agreed to sit down and negotiate with someone who would speak on behalf of the Contras. He flew to Cuba and talked with Fidel Castro about removing all Cuban military presence from Nicaragua. He then appointed a reconciliation commission to carry out and oversee domestic reforms. In El Salvador, President Duarte was appointing a similar commission and calling on the armed guerrillas of the FMLN (Farabundo Marti

National Liberation Front) to come and talk with him at a place of their choice anywhere in the country.

All of this seemed ample cause for optimism. We should have been expressing encouragement and approval, I felt. Instead, I began to discern a pattern of negative response from State Department press spokesmen. Phyllis Oakley, in her daily press briefings, disparaged each of these steps. Whatever Ortega agreed to do, the State Department's official reaction seemed to be that it was cosmetic, unimportant, and in any event "not nearly enough." Finally, I called George Shultz to ask why we weren't being more publicly supportive of the positive developments. He said his deputy for Latin American affairs, Elliott Abrams, wanted to "make it clear to them that we aren't going to be satisfied with anything less than real performance." As much as I respected George Shultz and admired his integrity, I profoundly disagreed with the psychology of consistent disparagement. "Those people are like people everywhere, George," I said. "They're like you and me. When they do something they think should merit our approval and we scoff at it, it simply makes them less willing to try to please us in the future." Shultz said he agreed in principle but wanted to see more good-faith performance.

Throughout Latin America, there was genuine excitement. President Oscar Arias was selected to receive the Nobel Peace Prize for his leadership in perfecting the plan. The Nicaraguan Contra leaders formally endorsed it. Frank Carlucci called to ask if I would receive and visit with members of the Contra Directorate on August 27 after they had talked with President Reagan. I agreed and arranged to receive them at the Dallas–Fort Worth airport. En route to their meeting with the president, the resistance spokesmen made a concession of their own. They suggested that Reagan suspend all military aid to them as an act of good faith during the negotiating period. On August 27 I met with Alfonso Robelo, Alfredo César, and Aristides Sánchez. I knew the first two rather well. César had once attended the University of Texas. The Contra leaders, I noted, seemed more optimistic about the peace process than some of the hardliners in our own country.

President Arias, on his way to Europe to accept the Nobel award, spoke on September 22 to an overflow crowd in the House chamber. His appearance was an unqualified success as he reiterated his recurring theme: *Give peace a chance.* "The Sandinistas are not popular with the people," he told us privately, "but the Contras are even more unpopular. Believe me, they are not the solution; their armed presence is the problem." His election appraisal would prove prophetic.

In El Salvador, President Duarte was moving energetically to carry out the agreements. Having pointed the way to democracy, he was trying by example to show a way to peace. He offered total amnesty to the armed marauders who had made unrelenting guerrilla war against his elected government and some of whom had recently kidnapped his daughter, Inez, holding her captive for several days. Duarte went unarmed to a jungle rendezvous with the rebel leaders.

Here's how Duarte described that meeting to me: "They asked me just what I meant by amnesty. I said, 'It means forgiveness. It means that what you have done against us in the past is forgotten. The slate is wiped clean.' Then I looked around the circle and told them I knew which of them were involved in kidnapping my daughter. And I said, 'Amnesty means that your crime is forgiven. Your government forgives you, and I forgive you personally.'"

As this unpretentious and uncomplicated man recounted to me that event so hauntingly personal, I wondered how few people of my acquaintance could summon such generosity of spirit. The problem was that not everyone wants to forgive. Perhaps not everyone can. Most Americans approved the peace effort, according to opinion polls, but a powerful remnant had invested enormous time, money, and prestige in the effort to win a military victory. Several of them felt cheated. Assistant Secretary of State Elliott Abrams, following the U.S. assault on Grenada in 1983, had even called for a military invasion of Nicaragua using U.S. troops. Some highly placed people, regardless of what President Reagan and I had pledged in our statement, simply did not want any negotiated peace settlement.

A major problem loomed. It involved both pride and principle. Reagan refused to meet or talk with anyone in the Nicaraguan government. Ortega had refused to negotiate directly with the Contras. Most Nicaraguans, on both sides of the fratricidal controversy, were eager for peace, but some bitterness lingered. Someone had to be a go-between, a mediator, an honest broker who could bring the two sides together, set the ground rules for negotiation, maybe even recommend some terms of settlement. Only one person came to my mind: Cardinal Miguel Obando y Bravo, the Catholic prelate of Nicaragua, who was universally respected by Sandinista and Contra sympathizers alike.

Several times in September and October 1987, I urged Contra and Sandinista leaders to agree to a mediation with Cardinal Obando. Those with whom I talked in the Contra Directorate were amenable. For some time, however, Ortega held out. He knew, I suspected, that nobody in his government could control the stocky little Cardinal. Most people in the Reagan administration implicitly respected the prelate's integrity. Phyllis Oakley once had said, while disparaging other appointees to the reconciliation commission, that Obando was the only one she trusted.

A few days in advance of an OAS meeting in Washington, I had a call from Miguel D'Escoto, the Sandinista foreign minister. He wanted to come and talk with me about getting some American to serve as mediator. I said, "Come ahead. I'll be glad to see you. But please understand I think any North American would be a mistake. There is one man on whom both sides could agree, and that is Cardinal Obando." D'Escoto then told me that Ortega would be in town for the OAS meeting. "Can President Ortega come up and talk with you?" I said he would be welcome if he wished to come. "But please explain to him that I cannot take part in any negotiating. I still think the Cardinal is your very best choice."

The next day, I got a happy surprise. Ortega announced in Managua that he was asking Cardinal Obando to mediate the cease-fire. Apparently, my entreaty had made an impact. *The New York Times* published the story on November 7, quoting "Reagan administration officials" to the effect that they were highly pleased by the development.

On November 12, I got a call from the papal nuncio Popio Laghi saying the Cardinal would be at the official residence on Massachusetts Avenue the following morning. He asked if I could come and discuss with him his pending decision on the mediator role. I accepted. Ortega would be there also, I learned.

Secretary Shultz came by my office, asking my intervention with the appropriations committee to help restore some funds cut from USIA libraries, student exchange programs, and money to operate chanceries and embassies. I made a note to talk with David Obey and Chairman Jamie Whitten. I told Shultz of my invitation to meet with Cardinal Obando. "I'm sure you agree that his taking on the responsibility of intermediary in the cease-fire is the best possible thing for all concerned," I said. "Yes, I think that would be fine," Shultz agreed. "But Americans are not participants in that negotiation." That is just what I had told D'Escoto.

The next morning, I met with Cardinal Obando. We sat around a long table, Ortega at one end and the Cardinal at the other. I sat beside Monsignor Laghi to Obando's right and Ortega's left. I began with a brief comment to the Cardinal about the importance of the moment and the unusual opportunity it provided for service. I said I hoped he would undertake the role being offered him.

The cardinal went immediately to the heart of the matter. He asked the nature of the role itself—whether he would be serving as an actual arbiter or simply as a messenger. Ortega's response was not definitive. I stepped in to suggest that, for this to work, the cardinal would have to be a mediator with the power of originating proposals. "If I were the cardinal, I would insist on that," I said. Ortega finally nodded assent.

Obando said he had some ideas about whom he would like to have assist him. Clearly, that was important to him, and he looked at me for a response.

Finally, I looked directly toward Ortega and said: "It seems to me that if the Cardinal is asked to take on this enormously important job, he must be invested with all the moral authority he needs to carry it out—to select sites for meetings and issue invitations. He surely should be accorded the right to choose those who assist him in the endeavor." This was essential. If Ortega agreed, he wouldn't be able to surround the cardinal with people of his or any other's choosing. After only brief discussion, Ortega agreed.

That was about all I could do, I decided. I had helped direct the conversation in such a way that Cardinal Obando's principal concerns were resolved in his favor. He said he would want a letter from the government, signed by Ortega, and another from the Contra directorate, formally asking him to serve as mediator.

It was a good time for me to take my leave. I thanked Monsignor Laghi for his hospitality, apologized to all present for my departure, and shook hands warmly with the Cardinal. "Blessed are the peacemakers," I said.

"Son los hijos del Dios," replied Cardinal Obando. They are the children of God.

We were all in high spirits as we boarded a plane for Texas later that day to help raise funds to assist colleagues in their 1988 reelection efforts. When we landed at Meacham Field in Fort Worth, people from my office ran up the boarding stairs to tell me they were being inundated by press requests. Apparently someone in the State Department had been harshly criticizing my presence at the meeting in the papal embassy. Tom Brokaw would be on the air in five minutes, and I could take his questions from an office in the terminal building.

Brokaw asked if I thought I should have permission from the State Department before talking with foreign leaders. I mentally tried to calculate how many dozens of heads of state I had met, how many scores of conversations I'd had with foreign leaders, always in the interest of U.S. policy as I understood it. Never had I criticized a U.S. president in the presence of foreigners. But did I need *permission?* The suggestion was demeaning. I said the legislative branch was not "subservient" to the executive and that I didn't need "permission" to talk with anyone. An interview with Dan Rather went more smoothly, as did the dinner that evening. Still, it upset me that someone in the White House had deliberately decided to attack me for my role in the Central American peace effort. White House spokesmen Charles Redman and Marlin Fitzwater led the assault. Their theme was that I was "interfering" in foreign policy. Other quoted comments from unidentified people were more personal. One unnamed source called me an "egomaniac" for presuming the right to work for peace.

Sunday morning's *New York Times* and *Washington Post* both featured stories of a "feud" between Reagan and me. In the *Times*, Steve Roberts wrote that our relationship had "deteriorated so badly that it is complicating efforts to arrange compromises on domestic and foreign policy." The story said I had "virtually ignored the White House while consulting President Daniel Ortega Saavedra of Nicaragua"—no reference to Cardinal Obando or the aim of my consultation. According to unnamed White House aides, the president regarded me as "an egotistical and untrustworthy congressional leader who sees himself incorrectly as a coequal with the president."

The *Post* carried an even more stinging story, top of page one. By John Goshko, it quoted "a senior administrative official" as saying my effort to help the peace process was an "exercise in guerrilla theater" that dealt "a serious setback" to the regional peace process. The story reported "anger building inside the administration over the Speaker's efforts to prod it into a more active role in Central America."

Quite obviously, key elements inside the administration were deeply angered by what was happening. They blamed me. In a vicious, highly coordinated attack, they meant to discredit me. Why? Only one answer made sense: They wanted the talks to founder, to fail. They wanted to resume the fighting.

The unnamed source of Goshko's story obviously was Assistant Secretary of State Elliott Abrams, who had demonstrated such vocal disdain for Congress in the Iran-Contra hearings. In my daily press conference on Monday, Goshko was present. Asked about the story, I pointed out that the anonymous source was "not proud enough of his opinions to identify himself with them." I said I would name him, however. "It was Elliott Abrams. The author of the article is present, and if he can deny the truth of what I have just said, I will apologize both to him and to Mr. Abrams." John Goshko stared at the floor and said nothing.

My first reaction to the Sunday stories was outrage. Shultz had known I was going to that meeting and exactly what I would propose. I had told him. He agreed Obando was the best man for the job. Why all this malice? I called Howard Baker and asked for an appointment Monday morning with the president and Secretary Shultz. Monday, on *Good Morning America* I tried to be conciliatory. Disagree though we might on policy, an open rift with the White House would serve no good purpose. I extended an olive branch. I hoped the president and George Shultz were listening. We would talk personally in a short while.

Arriving at the White House, I got out of the car and quickly entered the building. I didn't want to run the press gauntlet before talking directly with President Reagan. I felt certain that once Reagan and Shultz understood exactly what I had achieved, they would approve and appreciate my efforts.

The two were waiting for me in the Oval Office. Reagan was angrier than I had ever seen him, stiff and unbending. He castigated Ortega as a chronic liar and scathingly remarked that in place of the Wright-Reagan plan, "we now have the Wright-Ortega plan." That was a needless blow, I thought. I braced myself, swallowed hard. "Mr. President, I'd like to tell you about that meeting—what I did and why I did it."

Reagan was implacable. I made no headway, and soon he excused himself and left. So I turned to George Shultz. "We say that we want peace, and I believe I have moved events one small step in that direction." Shultz indicated he wasn't sure if it was progress or retreat. "Whether we agree on that or not," I said, "there is no justification for leaking vicious diatribes against one another. We both know it was Elliott Abrams who gave that story to John Goshko. If a member of my staff ever leaked a story like that about you, Mr. Secretary, I'd fire his ass!" Shultz did not respond.

Colin Powell and Frank Carlucci, who had joined us in the Oval Office, repeated the president's charge about Ortega. You couldn't count on anything he said or did, they insisted, unless you had him at the end of a bayonet. They said the Contras had need for an additional thirty million dollars in military aid. They wanted to know if I could help them get it. It was an astounding request. I told them I was having a hard enough time getting approval for *humanitarian* aid—food, clothing, and medicine. Democratic liberals were criticizing me for trying to get even that! We were making progress on peace, and, no, I didn't think a majority would vote to renew the fighting.

After appearances that night as a guest on *MacNeil-Lehrer NewsHour* and the following night on *Larry King Live*, I was convinced that most people identified with my position. They thought we ought to assist the peace movement, not sabotage it.

But it was evident now that those calling the shots in the White House had abandoned the peace effort. They wanted me to do the same, and I would not. Those to whom Reagan was listening would not be happy unless they could renew the war. They had never expected the peace process to work. They'd seen it as a tactical ruse, doomed to fail, an excuse to say, "we tried," and promptly revive the fighting when it fizzled out. Now it was working, and they were angry.

On two occasions—in December 1987 and February 1988—the president's forces tried to forsake the peace process altogether and revive the war by providing fresh military aid for the Contras. On both occasions, a majority in Congress voted down the request. At my personal urging, Congress did appropriate funds for humanitarian assistance—food, clothing, shelter, and medical needs—for the Contra forces during the cease-fire.

Ronald Reagan was a patriot. His lyric calls to American pride dispelled the lingering Vietnam guilt syndrome and made his countrymen comfortable again with our nation's role as a world leader. Reagan's gift with a script and his inspirational homilies were of a piece with George M. Cohan, *The Grand Old Flag*, and *Yankee Doodle Dandy*—vintage America. I liked to think that it was others, less innocent of guile, who led him on occasion to invent demons that didn't exist, and to magnify a few that did.

Despite official platitudes endorsing the peace process, high-ranking people in the administration were determined to undo it. Perhaps truly fearing communism, they sought whatever excuses they might seize upon to reignite the war in hope of physically overthrowing the Sandinista regime, the goal that six years of bloodshed had failed to achieve. By their own lights they, too, were patriots. That they disagreed with me did not make them bad people. We had different views of the constitution, the balance of powers. Some, however, were not above demagoguery. Shortly before the February 1988 vote, the CIA produced a Major Roger Miranda, a military officer newly defected from the Sandinista regime. They paraded him before newsmen and groups of lawmakers. Miranda boldly claimed the Managua government was planning to raise an army of 600,000 men, obtain MiGs and other advanced weapons from the Soviet Union, and threaten the security of the United States.

These lurid claims were patently absurd. Nicaragua could not afford its present army, let alone one of six hundred thousand—ten times as large! Moreover, Gorbachev was clearly trying to conciliate the United States and had offered the previous December to withdraw all Soviet advisors from Nicaragua. In addition, Ortega had written Mr. Reagan a long personal letter, and another to *The New York Times*, agreeing to accept specific limits on Nicaragua's armed forces, to banish all foreign military advisors, and forbid any foreign military bases. Miranda, it turned out, had been given a $500,000 cash bonus, up front, by the CIA, plus a pledge of about $45,000 a year for five years and some $92,000 in moving expenses. This was three-quarters of a million in U.S. taxpayers' money, promised to Miranda to compensate him for coming to Washington and lobbying Congress for more Contra military aid.

On the eve of the February 3 vote, President Reagan made an emotional appeal over CNN. Accusing the Soviet Union of sending big shipments of military aid to Nicaragua for a communist takeover of Central America, he proclaimed, in a melodramatic paraphrase of Churchill, that he had not become president "to preside over the communization of Central America." To this I responded in the next day's floor debate. The important point, I said, was that "neither Mr. Reagan nor any of us came to Washington to *preside* over Central America in any sense."

The House defeated the administration's request for a renewal of military funding. Then, under my direction, a bipartisan task force produced a bill extending humanitarian aid to the Contra forces, so that they would not starve nor suffer medical privation until peace could come. That bill passed on March 30 with the preponderant margin of 345 to 70. The next day the Senate adopted it without change, 87 to 7. In Nicaragua, the Contras and Sandinistas met that month in the little town of Sapoa and entered into the historic agreement that finally ended the war. They proclaimed a sixty-day cease-fire. Contras would be free to receive humanitarian aid from the United States, including communications equipment. It was agreed that future meetings would ratify specific steps to internal democratic reform, the release of prisoners, and eventual elections. The two delegations, leaders of forces that until then had been killing one another, stood and smiled for photographs together. So standing, they joined in singing Nicaragua's national anthem.

A whole series of other efforts would be made to throw that tenuous peace off track, but they never succeeded. In early February of 1990, the promised elections occurred. Violetta Charmorro, widow of the martyred newspaper publisher slain by Somoza's national guard, won the presidency from Daniel Ortega by a comfortable margin. My faith in the process would be validated.

So bitter had the debate become, however, that I was never able fully to restore the sense of civility and mutual respect that is necessary for the healthy functioning of a legislative body in a free society. For those who actually feared a communist takeover of the hemisphere, I had become the enemy. During all my years in Congress, my patriotism had never been questioned, nor my personal honor. Now both came under bitter attack.

On February 6, 1988, three days after the last vote against a military solution, the *Fort Worth Star-Telegram* published an angry tirade by a new columnist named Bill Thompson. "Chalk up a victory for commie sympathizers, short-sighted pacifists, left-wing nitwits and Jim Wright's pal, Daniel Ortega." A Washington-based propaganda and fund-raising group calling itself the Council for Inter-American Security published a full-page ad attacking my efforts and urging my constituents to "Call Jim Wright today!" In big block letters, the advertisement asked "WHO DOES HE SPEAK FOR? Communist Dictator Daniel Ortega? Or the People of Texas and the United States?" News articles and editorials began appearing with stunning frequency in the *Wall Street Journal* and *Washington Times*, castigating me for my position on Contra aid and for a catalog of other real and imagined sins. A few questioned my patriotism.

House Republicans, in the minority for thirty-four years, had additional frustrations. Thus far in the one hundredth Congress they had not prevailed on a single significant vote. The old Dixiecrat coalition, so successfully mobilized in the early Reagan years, wasn't working for them now. From their point of view, it was my doing. In meetings of the Republican conference, according to reports brought to me by Republican friends, militant younger Republicans were advocating a strategy: "Discredit Wright! Sack the quarterback!"

Newt Gingrich of Georgia, who in the previous Congress had repeatedly attacked Speaker O'Neill as "corrupt," now went after me with a vengeance. After weeks of press conferences and verbal assaults, Gingrich filed formal charges accusing me of violating House rules in my personal finances. His specific charges, which relied on old newspaper stories going back eight and ten years, were ultimately dismissed. But I was now the target of a whole gaggle of right-wing groups.

Reverend Jerry Falwell's publication, *Moral Majority*, featured on its front page a hideous cartoon of me as Dracula, fangs dripping blood, as I trampled the forces of freedom underfoot. A man named Peter Flaherty, who ran a Washington-based operation called *Citizens for Reagan*, circularized national Republican mailing lists with a series of letters viciously upbraiding me for "open and repeated cooperation with the communists." One of his mailings solicited for letters to the House Ethics Committee: "HERE IS YOUR CHANCE TO HELP GET RID OF WRIGHT." Another accused me of having "Provided aid and comfort to the communist Sandinista regime" and pleaded, "HELP PUT JIM WRIGHT ON TRIAL!"—presumably for treason.

Throughout the latter half of 1988, I was preoccupied with the domestic agenda of Congress. My hands were full. We passed an education bill, reversing the years of decline in our commitment to the nation's schools. We overrode the president's veto of the civil rights bill and extended Medicare coverage for catastrophic illness. This was the first major expansion of Medicare since its inception in 1965. And, for the first time since 1948, we passed *all* appropriations bills *before* the start of the new fiscal year. We were on a roll, reversing the domestic priorities of the Reagan years.

This legislative agenda, added to what many critics saw as my "intrusion" into foreign affairs, had infuriated the political right wing. A hive of conservative Washington propagandists, journalists, and politicians began to swarm. I tried to shake them off, but they stung. Nobody likes to have his integrity impugned. Maybe I was too thin-skinned. I have often wondered how nature ever indulged such a profligate waste as to create the rhinoceros with a hide two feet thick and no apparent interest in politics.

It all started with an effort to build a *bipartisan* coalition to help President Reagan make peace.

CHAPTER THIRTY-FIVE

POWER:
ITS USE
AND LIMITS

P resident Franklin D. Roosevelt once said, "We are not developing the nation's wealth for its own sake. Wealth is the means; people are the ends." The same could be said for the cultivation of political power. Like wealth, it is coveted, collected, sometimes hoarded as though its enjoyment were simply in its possession. But to what end, power? And what are the proper limits of its exercise? These are the questions every practitioner of the political arts, sooner or later, must answer.

Why did I want to be Speaker? I saw things I thought needed doing, and I supposed that I could bring them about. During a full decade as House Majority Leader, I worked and waited, growing impatient for the chance. Why do people strive for decades to be president, sublimating all else to the pursuit, some trying multiple times—Adlai Stevenson, Richard Nixon, Hubert Humphrey, Ted Kennedy, Ronald Reagan, George Bush, Robert Dole—for the privilege of pouring health and wealth and energy upon the campaign altar until the quest soaks up all their vital juices? For the same reason, I imagine. They see the power of the office and want to test its limitations. All, without exception, believe they can do something good for our country. And all, at one time and another, run face first into rock-solid walls of resistance. Even presidents, particularly presidents.

The authors of the Constitution saw to that. Nobody gets his way all the time. Nobody's supposed to. The presidency is the man-killingest job on earth. Thomas Jefferson called it "a splendid misery." Harry Truman said, "The buck stops here." But the president is never really supreme, not even in foreign affairs. As presidents are restricted, and sometimes checkmated, so are speakers.

While some of the things that limit our power to perform are institutional, others are quite personal. They're inside us. Being human, we get carried away in our zeal to achieve great ends. Some politicians, concentrating on their destinies, judiciously husband their strength and jealously conserve their popularity, refusing to risk precious political capital on controversial causes—until time and tide pass them by, their brightest opportunities for leadership unseized. Others of us eagerly overreach, hastening to conquer every problem that we see, unmindful of the limits of our strength, the power of the forces we're offending, and the hazards to our popular credibility.

Most often, I erred on the side of activism—too sure of my rightness, too hard-driving, too intent. Maybe I tried to get too much done too quickly. I saw it my duty to help our government live up to its historic promise and the House fulfill its unique responsibilities. Like others before me and since, I never quite got it all done. In our system, with its elaborate checks and balances, nobody can. That, I have to believe, is a good thing.

All of us sometimes fall on our faces and look foolish trying to surmount big obstacles. When we do, there's no other antidote as effective as a sense of humor. We have to be careful that, in being serious about our goals and our roles, we don't begin to take *ourselves* too seriously. Public office can be awfully hard on humility. Try being humble as you edit a press release, carefully drafted to ensure that you get due credit. We try to recapture the fleeting ghost of erstwhile modesty. We strike poses. Finally, convinced that we are humble, we find it tempting to grow *proud* of our humility. But fake humility is worse than none at all, since it deceives not only others but ourselves. Then something always happens to bring us back to earth.

Once, unable to get the news media to focus on the serious proposals I was making, I fell to brooding. What could I do to get their attention? Soon I'd discover. I had made a whimsical private bet with Walter Fauntroy, delegate for the District of Columbia, on a football game between the Dallas Cowboys and the Washington Redskins. The loser, Walter and I had agreed, would push the winner in a wheelbarrow around the entire perimeter of the U.S. Capitol. Walter's Redskins won. As I hefted the handles of the homely conveyance—Fauntroy ensconced as in a royal coach, regally flaunting a maroon and gold redskins' toboggan like a crown—there, in full force, armed with cameras and notepads, were all the media mavens who had found my dry dissertations on public policy so supremely uninteresting! The problem was not that they were ignoring me; it was that I'd been boring them.

Other brakes upon the presumptions of political ambition occur almost accidentally. Ever since William Jennings Bryan stampeded the Democratic Convention of 1896 with his "Cross of Gold" oration and walked away with the presidential nomination, ambitious politicians have dreamed of being "discovered" at one of these conventions for the stellar quality of their brilliantly articulated philosophy. It happened to Adlai Stevenson at the 1952 convention in Chicago. But, of course, neither he nor Bryan ever became president. Like many others, when I was young I often dreamed of being tapped one day for a convention speaking role and rising like the morning mist to lofty heights of political stardom. When my chance finally came, it was one of the most humbling experiences of my life. It came for me, in fact, three times. I was hard to discourage.

At the New York convention in 1980, my speech had just begun to soar into heights of eloquence when a ripple of applause started in one of the galleries. Funny, I thought, they're not waiting for the punch lines. As I continued declaiming, the applause spread, gaining volume. Finally, many in the crowd began to stand. Looking up, I saw that Edmund Muskie and his wife Jane had entered the gallery from which the applause commenced. Oblivious that I was even making a speech, the audience was applauding *them!* Finally, I said somewhat lamely, "Ladies and gentlemen, please join me in welcoming a great American and his wife, former Senator and now Secretary of State and Mrs. Ed Muskie!"

On the next occasion, in San Francisco in 1984, I polished and practiced my message in advance. I was determined this time to have the mighty throng mesmerized into agreement and galvanized into action. I'd have them on their feet! They were on their feet, all right. Throughout my speech! Some were going east, some west, some to the snack counter, some to the bar, some to the restrooms, some just standing and gabbing. Or yawning.

I swore I would never attempt another formal speech to a Democratic National Convention. But when 1988 rolled around, as Speaker of the House, I was chairman of the Democratic National Convention. It fell my unpleasant lot to make another speech. This time I was so busy putting out fires and trying to keep the convention on schedule that I had scant time to prepare a speech and no time to think about its delivery. I hastily dictated a draft and sent it to the electronics room for printing on the TelePrompTer.

This time, I wouldn't worry about trying to stampede the convention with my oratory. I'd just read the words from the TelePrompTer and hope my hurriedly prepared remarks would make some sense. My time came. I stood for my brief moment in the now dreaded sunshine, ready to read my lines. The TelePrompTer began reeling out the text: "When I was but a small boy back in West Virginia. . . ."

WHAT?! *That's* not my speech!

The machine, in a grand comedic error, was rolling off Senate Majority Leader Robert Byrd's speech. Come to think of it, maybe that's why I've never been president.

With both of the last two presidents who served during my time in the House leadership, I had a very basic philosophical disagreement about our government's role in society. My view was basically that expressed by President Franklin D. Roosevelt in his 1938 message to Congress, when he said: "Government has a final responsibility for the welfare of its citizens. If private cooperative effort fails to provide work for willing hands and relief for the unfortunate, those suffering hardship through no fault of their own have a right to call upon the government for aid. And a government worthy of the name must make a fitting response."

President Reagan disagreed with those ideas. So did George Bush. It is natural that my efforts would come into conflict with theirs. Upon that basic Rooseveltian dictum, I had embroidered my own vision of the American dream. It was our distinct destiny, I believed, to keep broadening the base of participation in society, seeing that the good things of life—education, nutrition, affordable housing, job opportunities, and medical care—are made available to more and more of the American people in each succeeding generation. This, for me, was the business of government and the purpose of power. My fondest wish was to help some president move us farther in that direction. We had come a very long way in the first twenty-five years after World War II. Now, retrogression had set in.

Take higher education, for example. When I was a student at the University of Texas in 1941, only 4.5 percent of my age group were finishing four years of college. Under the G.I. Bill of Rights following World War II, and continuing through the time of Lyndon Johnson's determined leadership, we dramatically expanded that performance. Within just one generation, 21 percent—almost five times as many—were able to attain the goal of a bachelor's degree. Then, somehow, affordable learning for all young Americans regardless of their financial circumstances ceased to be an important presidential priority. Leaders now had begun to take for granted or even disparage public education. Reagan and Bush wanted to give tax credits for parents who could afford to send their offspring to *private* elementary and secondary schools. In fairness to those presidents, it must be said that they simply had a different vision. They thought government had taken on too much.

Each side could assert some claim to public approval. George Bush won the presidency in a landslide victory over Michael Dukakis in 1988, but in congressional elections throughout the country, we Democrats actually increased our House majority by four seats and our Senate majority by one. This was the first time in eighty years that one political party had captured the White House while the other was *increasing* its majority in House and Senate and in the ranks of the nation's governors. The electorate's message was ambivalent.

Congress, the institution for which I felt most responsible, had been gaining steadily in public esteem. Our positive agenda of identifiable legislative accomplishments had lifted approval ratings for Congress from around 45 percent to about 68 percent over a three-year period. I hoped to cement a better personal relationship with George Bush than I'd had with his predecessor. I had known Bush since before his first election to the House, but our relationship was never a close one.

Two days after the election, I was having breakfast with Bob Strauss in the hideaway office off the Capitol's rotunda when Bob asked, "Have you called to congratulate George Bush?"

"No, I haven't called. I sent a telegram yesterday morning."

"Why don't you call?" Bob insisted. "George Bush would love to hear from you. He needs your help and you need his. This is a critical time for getting things started in the right direction. I even have a number at which I think you could reach him."

I called. Bush came on the line immediately. "I'm awfully glad you called," said the president-elect. "I'd like to come up and talk with you. Could we have lunch together up there someday very soon?"

"Mr. Vice President, I'll be more than glad to. You just tell me where." I said I'd happily come any place and time that was convenient to him.

"No, I want to come up there, Jim," Bush answered. "Could we have lunch in your office? Just the two of us, with no staff or anybody else around?"

"You name the day," I said. "What would you like to eat?"

"I'd like a steak, if you won't tell Barbara."

On Friday, November 18, the two of us had steaks and salad and coffee on a small, round antique table in the Speaker's office. There was no broccoli. Bush insisted mainly on listening. He wanted to know where I saw areas of common agreement. I told him we were anxious to carry out his campaign call for a "kinder, gentler America." Frankly, I could not foresee how his pledges of major improvements in education, the environment, child care, and other areas could be accommodated within his resolute vow of "no new taxes," but I assured George Bush we were eager to hear his recommendations. We talked briefly of foreign policy. I brought up Central America. "This has been the most implacable issue of the last eight years," I declared. "Also the most politically polarizing and personally divisive. It's our only major foreign policy disagreement." Bush nodded his head. "I know," he said. "What do you think we might be able to agree upon?"

"The starting place is to substitute diplomacy for military action," I replied. "We're talking with Gorbachev and getting some good results. If we'd sit down and talk with the Nicaraguans, and Salvadorans, we might make more progress than we have."

"Would you be willing to work with Jim Baker in trying to search out the ingredients of a common policy?" Bush proposed.

"Of course I will," I assured him.

On the afternoon of March 2, 1989, new Secretary of State James A. Baker came by my office in the Capitol to explore prospects for a bipartisan approach to Central America. He had been working on some thoughts but had nothing in writing. "We want to wind this thing down," Baker stated. "But the president is getting some flak from the right-wing. They're already accusing him of *abandoning* the Contras. That's the one thing he promised in the campaign never to do."

In this exploratory conversation, Baker and I were alone. The Secretary had suggested that he and I could talk more candidly with nobody else in the room. I told him I understood his problem with the far right. I offered to help broaden humanitarian aid to assist the Contras reintegrate into civil life when peace was secured. Earlier that day I had been talking with President Marco Cerezo of Guatemala and shared some news with Baker. The Sandinistas, according to Cerezo, had told him they were willing to release all the prisoners they'd been holding for the past ten years. If Ortega actually announced such a plan, I remarked, "it ought to trigger a positive response on our side. We have to hold out some carrots, as well as sticks."

"You've given me an idea," said Baker. "Carrots as well as sticks! Maybe we could have a selective menu of carrots. A careful balance of carrots and sticks. A carrot for each good-faith performance on the part of the Sandinistas."

This was the first in a series of meetings in which Baker practiced shuttle diplomacy between Democratic and Republican leaders. The effort culminated in a bipartisan plan that marked a new beginning in our relations with Central America. The centerpiece of the agreement was an unequivocal commitment to the peace process, to "the bright promises of Esquipulas II and its successor agreements." Finally, Baker proposed that if the Nicaraguan elections scheduled for February 25, 1990, were conducted in a free and fair manner, regardless of the outcome, we would lift the trade embargo, restore the sugar quota, and make Nicaragua eligible for the benefits enjoyed by other countries in the Caribbean Basin Initiative.

Our agreement was ready for unveiling. In a formal ceremony at the White House on March 24, Good Friday, we released copies of the new bipartisan accord. This was, for me, a day of great relief. Whatever disagreements would erupt over the domestic agenda, the White House and Congress were singing from the same hymnal on Central America. For practical purposes, the U.S.–financed war in Nicaragua was over.

Through the first five months of 1989, I toiled and grappled to lead the House effectively. I appeared before the National Economics Commission to plead for an honest, forthright assault on the deficit; conferred with President Bush on the eve of his meeting with Gorbachev; consulted with Treasury Secretary Nicholas Brady concerning Third World debt; presented to the Senate Public Works Committee a plan for a *Build America Trust Fund* to finance needed rehabilitation of America's public infrastructure; negotiated a broad budget compromise with the president; and moved through the House a controversial bill to increase the minimum wage.

But my candle was burning out. The flame that had lighted my single-minded pursuit of political office for more than fifty years—since my junior year in high school—flickered now. I was tired. Congress wasn't fun anymore. After winning eighteen consecutive terms in Congress and making countless appearances in behalf of other candidates, I was weary to the bone with campaigning. The pursuit of elective office had grown increasingly venal. Throughout my forty years in public life, I had never waged a negative campaign. It was foreign to my instinct. But the rules of the game were changing. It was as though I had spent my years learning to handle a football well—to kick it, throw it, carry it—only now, in place of footballs, they were using hand grenades.

Another thing contributed to the decision taking shape in my mind. Attacks on my personal character intensified. Determined at first not to be distracted by the calculated harassments, I had ignored them. But they mounted. Every detail of my personal finances, to which I had paid so little attention, was now a subject of avid public scrutiny. Bad enough to have to divert precious time from important tasks to dig among old files and answer for first one and then another newsman questions with which I had dealt ten and twelve years before. Worse that a determined claque kept planting questions designed to impugn my motives for such things as helping to get federal grants for restoration projects on the historic old North Side of Fort Worth, and trying to intercede with regulators of lending institutions in an effort to avoid a rash of bankruptcies in my state. All of this—none of it ever secret— was now portrayed as sinister. For thirty-four years I had lived in the goldfish bowl that is the U.S. Congress. I knew my personal conduct was subject to constant inspection and had never minded. I expected my political judgments to be debated, disputed, disagreed with, and criticized vigorously. What I experienced now was entirely different. Now, people who disagreed with my political judgments were attacking my honor, trying to impeach my integrity and my patriotism. It made me burn with anger.

In the middle of the night I would wake up, tossing and turning, outraged by the indignities heaped on my name and frustrated by my inability, for the first time in my life, to cope effectively with a personal crisis. The harder I tried to satisfy the media, the more impossible that task seemed. My blood pressure went up and would not respond to medication. Capitol physicians William Narva and Robert Krasner changed the medications and remonstrated with me: "Get more exercise. Play golf. Take long walks. Get more rest."

Fine, but when? My schedule was jammed every waking hour.

"One more thing," Doctor Krasner admonished, a wicked twinkle in his eye. "Avoid stress!"

The people in my hometown, almost universally supportive, were increasingly puzzled and angered by the barrage of artfully planted negative stories suddenly appearing in the news media. My family and close friends began to be targeted. My wife, Betty, made it clear she would share whatever came, but more than once I saw tears of hurt in her eyes.

Before our marriage in 1972, Betty had enjoyed a career in business, employed at different times by a St. Louis publishing firm, a leading Fort Worth hotel, and a Texas manufacturing enterprise. When we married, she held a responsible job on the staff of the House Public Works Committee. When I was elected House majority leader in 1976, Betty voluntarily left her job to avoid any possible criticism of me for our both holding government jobs. Wanting to make some contribution to the family finances and to stay active, Betty helped organize a small family-owned investment corporation. I transferred to the corporation $58,000 worth of stocks, mostly in Texas-based corporations, that I had purchased little by little over the years. Also included was ten thousand dollars worth of stock in the First National Bank of Weatherford, inherited from my mother's estate. Our personal friends, George and Marlene Mallick, contributed an amount of cash equivalent to the market value of the stocks. Joining the names Mallick and Wright, we named the little corporation Mallightco. Since George was largely occupied with two apartment complexes and two office buildings he owned, Marlene was raising a family, and my time was totally devoted to Congress, Betty had assumed a principal role in the day-to-day management of our fledgling family business's investments.

Betty watched markets, studied opportunities for new investments, and decided when it was timely to recommend selling one of our holdings. On her suggestion we sold four of my original publicly traded stocks after a few years at the most propitious time, recouping for our little company about three times their appraised value as of the day we incorporated in 1979. Betty persuaded George and me against investing in the movie *Annie*, which turned out to be a financial loser. She also conducted a financial analysis that wisely kept us out of an investment in a proposed winery. These judgment calls, along with others she made, netted the two-family enterprise at least four times the token salary of eighteen thousand dollars a year that the corporation paid her as its only employee.

Now, however, charges leveled by my political opposition in Congress and fanned into the public dialogue by news accounts, alleged that Betty really didn't do anything for the corporation. The eighteen-thousand-dollar salary, a fraction of what she had earned before our marriage, was portrayed as a subterfuge by which our business partner Mallick funneled unearned money to me. I was pained by the presumption that my wife's time was not worth twelve hundred dollars a month. Never mind that half of whatever she received came from ourselves as equal owners of the corporation.

Newsmen began to hound George Mallick, as a consequence of which he had to spend days in Washington answering questions for the House Ethics Committee. "Just what are your legislative interests?" outside counsel Richard Phelan aggressively demanded. Phelan, politically ambitious to be governor of Illinois, apparently thought it would catapult him to stardom if he could somehow find a way to bring down the Speaker of the House. Truth was that George Mallick's business enterprises never depended upon the government in any way whatever. In all the years I had known him, never once had George asked me to vote for or against a piece of legislation or to intercede on his behalf with any federal agency. Of Lebanese ancestry, my friend now was being portrayed by Phelan as some sort of Mafia character. He was bound to be a lobbyist in some sense, Phelan argued, since he had business interests in real estate. If George could be presumptively classified as a lobbyist, someone pursuing an active financial interest in legislation, then by Phelan's argument Betty and I were in technical violation of a House rule for having accepted personal hospitality in our friends' home—as we had done on a number of occasions. By that tortured interpretation, a member of Congress could have no personal friends.

One of the few tangible assets of our little corporation was a 1979 car. The Mallicks and Betty alternated in driving the car and looking after its upkeep. Now the critics were in full voice, claiming that Mallick had given Betty an automobile. The implications were demeaning. In exasperation, I wrote a personal check to the corporation, buying the nine-year-old corporate car at its book value and giving it to Betty. What hurt was that my wife, through no error of her own, had been dragged so pointlessly and personally into the political debate. At one point things reached the absurd level in which *Star-Telegram* reporter David Montgomery insisted to my top aide Marshall Lynam that I must give Montgomery an interview to answer a charge that Betty actually was illiterate. "Tell him," I said, "that Betty is trilingual. She's fluent in three written languages—English, Spanish, and shorthand."

What frustrated me most, I think, was that, for the first time since becoming Speaker, I was having trouble communicating Democratic policy goals and our legislative program. Newsmen were more interested in asking questions about the Ethics Committee's investigation into my personal finances, an investigation which I had publicly invited, certain that I had done nothing for which to be criticized. Nobody was even suggesting that I had violated any law. But daily leaks orchestrated by Newt Gingrich and a few others artfully distracted the media from focusing on the congressional agenda for which I was responsible.

A Speaker must be symbol and spokesman of the institution itself. After President Bush, Secretary Baker and I presented the joint peace initiative, I sensed that my ability to provide a dynamic leadership was being compromised. That, no doubt, was what Gingrich and his clique had in mind. I was having trouble gaining attention to legislative programs and policy differences with the Bush administration for the cacophony of orchestrated aspersions on my character.

Another drama acted out in the glare of congressional spotlights that spring would have its own negative impact upon my ability to assert unifying leadership. On March 9, after several weeks of acrimonious debate, the Senate in a 53 to 47 vote rejected President Bush's nomination of former Senator John Tower to be his Secretary of Defense. The effect was explosive. It was the first time in history that a cabinet nominee had been turned down at the beginning of a president's first term and only the second time any former senator had been rejected for a cabinet post. Republicans were livid! Some Democratic senators had made damaging public allegations against the Texas Republican—that he had a drinking problem and that he was financially beholden to defense contractors.

I knew John Tower. Although we had been Texas political rivals and were on opposite sides of most domestic issues, I liked John personally and considered him totally trustworthy. I hated the attacks being made on his character. During the March 2 Texas Independence Day celebration at the Washington Press Club that year, I proposed a toast to my embattled fellow Texan. But the Senate vote one week later reflected party lines, with only one Republican deserting Tower and all but three Democrats voting to doom his confirmation. That loosed a torrent of anger among House GOP ranks. Two days after the Senate vote, a Republican colleague who was a longtime personal friend came by for a private visit. "You need to know, Mr. Speaker, that the John Tower rejection has hardened the ranks in my party against you," he told me. "A number of us have always believed in you, and some of us will support you come hell or high water, but we're under heavy pressure to make an example of you. The Gingrich crowd is putting Bob Michel and the moderates through a virtual inquisition. They want to make your personal downfall a litmus test of party loyalty. They want to go Hammurabi one better."

"You mean an eye for an eye and a tooth for a tooth?"

"It's an even more perfect symmetry," he said. "They want a Texan for a Texan!"

Ethics Committee Republican Charles Pashayan of California had said privately to a few congressional friends that he considered me innocent of wrongdoing. Suddenly, "Chip" Pashayan was bombarded by angry letters from right-wing constituents demanding he vote to oust me from the speakership. Conservatives in Pashayan's district were being actively mobilized by other Republican lawmakers on Capitol Hill to put pressure on Pashayan. For the first time since the Ethics Committee's creation, its internal workings were being politicized from outside the process. Many months later I would read in John Barry's *The Ambition and the Power: the Fall of Jim Wright* of the systematic orchestration by a busy conservative cabal of a series of attacks and harassments aimed at putting me on the defensive and keeping me off balance. Barry devotes most of the last six chapters of this book—177 printed pages—to a description of the scheme and its execution. For more than a year, a full-time staffer in Gingrich's office named Karen Van Brocklin had been spending her time on the public payroll calling people in my hometown and elsewhere seeking negative information, fact or rumor, of any sort concerning me that could be peddled to a newspaper or converted into some further inquiry by the House Ethics Committee. Gingrich and others in his group, according to Barry, would call newsmen repeatedly, importuning them to use these stories.

Almost daily now, from mid-March through April of 1989, a new story would appear in some news periodical. Anxious to beat the competition, some newsmen began running with stories before checking their veracity. One account said I had failed to report a supposed ride a year earlier in an aircraft owned by a Texas corporation. Before I could verify my innocence by contacting the chief executive of that company, who assured me that his business didn't even own an airplane, the news cycle had passed. The newspaper's disclaimer appeared toward the end of an unrelated story in the next day's edition. On another occasion, a Washington-based reporter quoted an unnamed "source" that the Internal Revenue Service had me under investigation for income tax fraud. It was not true, but by the time I got a declaration to this effect, the damage had been done.

Television networks now vied to find new angles. ABC ran with a primetime story about a $35,000 investment made by Mallightco a year or so earlier in a Florida housing development. There was nothing wrong with it, but the news hype made it sound sinister. In 1988 I had dissolved Betty's and my interest in Mallightco and put all of our financial holdings in a blind trust, prevailing on Thomas H. Law, one of Fort Worth's most respected attorneys, to serve as trustee. Law was not to discuss any investment or divestment with me. Now, suddenly, in April of 1989 all three networks reported an interest taken by my blind trust in an east Texas oil well and traded later for a profit. Other investors in the well were hauled before the Ethics Committee for questioning. There was nothing wrong, but exoneration never quite catches up with accusation.

Nor had my judgment been flawless. The Phelan law firm unearthed a few episodes that, while not illegal or immoral, reflected inattention and insensitivity on my part. In October of 1984, I had delivered the annual Lyndon B. Johnson lectures at Southwest Texas State University, where my sister, Dr. Betty Lee Wright, was a member of the faculty. At her request and that of university president Robert Hardisty, an old friend, I had accepted the invitation and expected no lecture fee. A few days after the event, my Fort Worth district director Phil Duncan called to tell me the university had sent a check for three thousand dollars. "Send it back with my thanks," I instructed.

"I have an idea," Phil said. "Why not give Dr. Hardisty an option? Let him use the check to buy copies of your book of essays to give political science and history students?" I liked it. "Fine idea, Phil, if Bob Hardisty wants to do that. Otherwise, just send it back." Hardisty agreed, and Phil ordered books for his students. That set a pattern. Other friends bought multiple copies for gifts. Insurance executive Bernard Rapoport and former Democratic National Chairman John White mailed copies to politically active people throughout the country. Dr. John Silber of Boston University sent copies to fellow academicians. While I did nothing to promote these sales, I approved heartily. I wanted everyone to read my book!

Political enthusiasts, including some members of my own staff, no doubt moved by my enthusiasm for the little volume, had suggested to several program chairmen before whose organizations I was scheduled to speak that listeners would enjoy having copies. I do not believe anyone ever represented a purchase of books as a fee, or a price for my speaking, or suggested that I expected it. I was in fact unaware of most of the purchases. But, learning now as this information dribbled out from the committee, I realized those sales could be subject to that interpretation. Although the sales violated no law and no House rule (book royalties were expressly exempted from the limits on speaking fees and outside earnings), they were being made to look like greedy efforts to skirt those very rules. Anybody smart enough to be Speaker should have had sufficient foresight to anticipate such criticism. In my preoccupation with other matters, I had failed to do so.

Phelan, who had lobbied ranking ethics committee Republican John

Myers for the role of outside counsel while stoutly disavowing any political ambitions, included a number of inaccuracies in his official report. One of these involved a prominent Fort Worth citizen named S. Gene Payte, who purchased bulk copies of the little book for gifts. Phelan alleged in his report that Payte had paid for more books than he got from the publisher. He claimed that Payte had so testified before the committee. That was false. Payte, upon reading Phelan's erroneous report, produced transcripts of his committee testimony, prepared a legal affidavit, and called a press conference in Fort Worth, where he reaffirmed that he had indeed received all the books he paid for. The businessman further demonstrated from the transcript that he had so testified, not once, but three separate times while Phelan and two committee Republicans persistently tried to get him to say otherwise.

Gene Payte was so indignant at having been lied about in Phelan's report that he sent copies of his sworn affidavit to members of the committee. On May 5, at Phelan's direction, the committee sent this private citizen an official notice ordering him to shut up, telling him his public statement was "in direct violation" of committee rules, and threatening to hold him in contempt of Congress if he spoke any further of the matter in public.

Now, in mid-May, I confronted a major legislative challenge. The minimum wage had not been addressed since 1981. H.R. 2, one of our top leadership priorities for the year, proposed to lift the legal minimum from $3.35 in three incremental annual steps to $4.55 by 1992. President Bush disagreed with our proposal, insisting the minimum should not go above $4.25 and that employers be allowed to pay an even lower "training wage" for newly hired workers.

The classic confrontation involved, in my mind, a matter of fundamental public policy. Bush was at the same time proposing a cut in the capital gains tax rate, from which the top one percent of America's income group would winnow on average some $30,000 each year. Yet he gagged at thirty cents an hour more for the working poor. If he was intending to veto the minimum wage bill, I reasoned, the only way we could dissuade him would be to pass it by two-thirds, enough to override a veto. I carefully directed the whip count and prepared a closing argument, which I would make personally on the House floor. This I saw as a test of my leadership—whether I still had the clout and following among my colleagues to provide the strength and inspiration the speakership needs.

I spoke last, just before the vote on May 11. On a table beside the microphone, I placed three large transparent bowls. "The difference between what we propose and what President Bush says he would accept is three dimes. That is it. Three thin dimes." I dropped three dimes into one bowl, identified for the *workers*. These were the people, I explained, "who look to us to repre-sent them. They have nobody else."

In 1981, I pointed out, the pay for three hours of work at minimum wages would purchase a ten-dollar sack of groceries. Now, that three hours of work would purchase the 1981 equivalent of only seven dollars worth of groceries.

The second bowl represented the *Vice President*. Under recommendations made by President Bush, I pointed out, the vice president's pay would be increased forty dollars an hour since its 1981 level. I dropped four hundred dimes into that bowl for visual contrast.

And what of the wealthiest one percent of Americans? As a result of tax cuts Congress had voted since 1981, I stressed, the average one in that bracket would keep about $36,000 more a year in income. Calculated on a forty-hour work week, I extrapolated, that would be an increase of $17.40 an hour. I dropped 174 dimes into the bowl representing the *top one percent*. Then, I stressed the practical effect of Bush's call for a new cut in the capital gains rate, estimating it at 144 dimes per hour, and deposited that many more in the transparent bowl.

I had done the best I could. We'd see. The vote was preponderant, but probably not enough. We'd held almost all the Democrats. I counted twenty-nine Republicans voting with us. The final tally was 247 to 172—an impressive majority, but clearly short of enough to override a veto. On May 18, Senate Majority Leader George Mitchell and I issued a joint plea, in the interest of "justice, fairness, and hope for millions of hardworking American families," to sign the bill. Bush vetoed it. By the end of that year, both presi-dent and Congress would be forced into a compromise—$4.35 an hour in two years. Maybe my effort helped some. For me, at the moment, it was a current measurement of my leadership.

Major national journals like *Time* magazine and the *Boston Globe*, joined by talk-show savants on nationwide television, some once supportive, were say-ing now that I should resign and relieve the Congress of a painful distraction. Meanwhile, each day's mail brought bushels of encouragement from individ-ual citizens all over the country. Polls taken in my constituency by the *Fort Worth Star-Telegram*, whose publisher by now was writing editorials pleading for me to quit, revealed that in April 78 percent of the local citizens—this would go up to 81 percent in June—were on my side.

The last six weeks of my tenure were agonizing. Throughout most of May, our home in McLean was surrounded morning and night by reporters, who shouted questions each time I opened the door. There were photographers who trained zoom lenses on me each time I entered my yard. I learned that in the news business they call this the "death watch."

Finally, toward the end of May, it became clear to me that all six of the Republicans on the Ethics Committee, half of its membership, were intent on dragging the inquiry out. All the initial charges were dropped, but now, in late May, it appeared that new complaints could make the inquiry last through most of 1989. Phelan boasted that he had the votes in his pocket—all six Republicans and Massachusetts Democrat Chet Atkins—to keep the investigation going. To date, Phelan's firm had reaped nearly $2 million from the government. The only way I could get a formal exoneration would be to pursue the process to its anguishing end—acquiring perhaps a million-dollar debt in legal fees, which I could not have paid—and then go to the House floor toward the end of the year and ask House members to override the committee if necessary.

Three weeks earlier, at the end of April, the votes were in hand to support my position if it came to the House floor. Ninety-five percent of the Democrats were pledged to back me, and several Republicans had told me privately that they would do so as well, in spite of internal party pressures.

That was before the sensationalized treatment in the *Washington Post* of an assault upon a young woman by a congressional aide of mine sixteen years earlier, when he was nineteen years of age. That happened before I even knew the young man. I had given him a job at the request of the Fairfax County sheriff and had never regretted having done so. He had rehabilitated himself and had become an exemplary employee and the father of two magnificent children. But this was not the thrust of the news treatment that was trumpeting his misdeed of so many years before. Now I was not certain how many of my colleagues could stand the heat.

I was tired, dog tired. Mentally and physically fatigued. My duty seemed clear. If I could not be an *effective* Speaker, providing moral leadership, I had no wish to be Speaker. The House deserved no less. And so, on May 31, 1989, I stood in the well of the House and explained that I had never knowingly violated any House rules. I spoke of the "mindless cannibalism" that had led us to prey on one another's reputations. I said, "Let me give you back this job . . . as a propitiation for this season of ill will." Perhaps foolishly, I offered: "Let that be a total payment for the anger and hostility we feel toward each other."

I loved my job. I loved the Congress. In the end, I loved it too much to stay. The House had changed insidiously since the days when Sam Rayburn insisted we could disagree without being disagreeable. It had hardened, elements within it grown cold and vicious, intent on destroying the mutual respect that was its vital fluid. Worse, from my point of view, this was happening on my watch. I had not been wise enough to prevent it.

Hoping to use my resignation to make a point worthy of what I was giving up, I pleaded, "Let us not try to get even with each other. Republicans, please do not get it in your heads you need to get somebody else because of John Tower. Democrats, please do not feel that you need to get somebody on the other side because of me. We ought to be more mature than that." Then, trying to imprint a lasting lesson, I said, very deliberately:

> *When vilification becomes an accepted form of political debate, when negative campaigning becomes a full-time occupation, when members of each party become self-appointed vigilantes carrying out personal vendettas against members of the other party, in God's name that is not what this institution is supposed to be about! When vengeance becomes more desirable than vindication, and harsh personal attacks upon one another's motives and one another's character drown out the quiet logic of serious debate on important issues . . . surely that is unworthy of our institution, unworthy of our American political process. All of us in both political parties must resolve to bring this period of mindless cannibalism to an end! There has been enough of it.*

At this, there was applause. They stood and applauded for a long while.

Tom Foley, my successor, inherited a thankless task and strove earnestly to restore a modicum of civility to the chamber. Thoughtful, friendly, patient, conciliatory, and a fine lawyer, Foley was uniquely well-suited to the effort. President Bush appointed House Republican Whip Richard Cheney as Secretary of Defense. Gingrich actively sought the Whip's job and won a narrow victory over moderate Ed Madigan of Illinois. Literally within days, Gingrich aide Karen Van Brocklin was caught trying to plant an utterly false story with newsmen that the new Speaker was a homosexual. The rotten smear attempt backfired. Gingrich publicly repudiated the story, but kept Van Brocklin on his payroll.

The symbiotic relationship between Gingrich and Phelan was a brief marriage of convenience. Gingrich wanted me out of the way to facilitate his personal ambition to be Speaker. Phelan gained personal notoriety that served his own political ambition. Though repeatedly disavowing any such ambitions while masterminding the investigation of my affairs, Phelan quickly put a good portion of his legal fee to use running for Cook County Board Chairman, to which he was elected. In 1994, he ran for Governor of Illinois, placing a poor fourth in a four-person Democratic primary. By 1995, he was publicly accusing Gingrich, now Speaker, of ethics violations and calling for appointment of an outside counsel, a job Phelan obviously would like to have. For the sake of the honor and decency of the system, I hope the

Chicago lawyer is never again paid money to blacken another human being's reputation.

As for me, I tell people that I'm not bitter. Honest to God, I *hope* I'm not. I shouldn't be. For thirty-four years, I got to do in life exactly what I'd wanted to do. Sure, I'd have preferred to stay on to the end of the 101st Congress and retire in 1990, under no pressure, as I had planned to do. But, then, I might have been flattered and cajoled by local well-wishers into running again. And again.

Often things happen for the best when we least realize it. At fifteen, a chipped cartilage in my knee turned my life's goal from being a football coach to being a congressman. In college, I wanted to be president of the student body. That honor eluded me. Almost as a consolation prize, I became editor of the college newspaper—the best and most rewarding experience of my college career.

Some of my greatest fulfillments have arisen from the tombs of ambitions denied. In 1961, overambitious and underfinanced, I barely lost a race for the U.S. Senate. That loss, though costly, was providential. Had I won, I never would have been Speaker of the U.S. House of Representatives. And—had I stayed on as Speaker? In 1991, I discovered a small lump, about the size of a buckshot, lodged at the base of my tongue. It was cancer. Surgically removed and treated by radiation, it seems wholly cured. Had I still been Speaker, I surely would have procrastinated, waiting for an unbusy moment to have it looked at, quite possibly waited too long.

On leaving Congress, I returned to Fort Worth, where Betty and I live among the people for whom I worked those thirty-four years. I've been writing, lecturing, and traveling, relearning the joys of private life. I teach a course at Texas Christian University and write a column for the *Fort Worth Star-Telegram*, sometimes picked up by other newspapers. I have accepted a lot of invitations to lecture at universities across the country and enjoy business relationships with American Income Life Insurance Company of Waco, Texas, and Arch Petroleum of Fort Worth.

While I do not lobby or serve on corporate boards, I've enjoyed serving on the boards of Texas Wesleyan University, the First United Methodist Church, and several charitable endeavors. Working with former President Jimmy Carter, I've monitored elections signaling the birth of Democracy in Nicaragua and Haiti, its rebirth in Panama, and its rejuvenation in Mexico.

From all of this, I have a few observations about how people of good will must stimulate a rebirth of the democratic spirit and a revived sense of community here in this blessed country of ours.

THE KIND OF AMERICA WE WANT

Politics is not a four letter word. It is not the name of a process inherently venal and corrupt. Politics is the art of living together, the science of operating a common country for the benefit of all. While *America* is essentially a geographic description, *the United States* is a political creation. To pretend to honor democracy while despising politics is to suppose we can love the product but hate the process that creates, nurtures, and defends it.

In *The Snows of Kilimanjaro*, Hemingway's character Harry Street concludes, "The fact that the airplane is faster than the horse does not necessarily mean the world is getting better." Progress always brings new problems. The planet earth, for purposes of transportation or communication, continues to shrink. Like the fact or not, we are a neighborhood. Its population grows exponentially, threatening to overwhelm its resources. The explosion of information and the speed of communication do not necessarily equate with the expansion of wisdom. Science speeds ahead at a blinding pace, threatening to outdistance the human arts of getting along together and governing our relationships intelligently. It is only through politics that we can hope to keep abreast, to make America what we want it to be, to be sculptors of the future and not its victims.

The Tyranny of Hate

The greatest danger facing America today is hate—unreasoning hate seeking targets to attack, someone or something to hurt. This is what I wrote in a recent column for the *Fort Worth Star-Telegram*. After a lifetime of observation,

I believe hate is a free society's mortal menace. It tears us apart, individually and collectively. It makes a mockery of our claim to be "one nation under God, indivisible." Deadly as an addictive drug, hate is cynically packaged and pushed by professionals, and ingested by well-meaning people. Some become addicts.

Americans need to be aware what genuine harm the merchants of hate are inflicting on ourselves and our political institutions. "Those whom God wishes to destroy, he first makes mad," wrote Euripides. Without blaming deity for our problems, most of us can recognize truth in that dictum. Nothing is more self-destructive than anger. It increases blood pressure, strains the heart and leads to rash acts that we later regret. This is true of nations as well as individuals.

That fact should be a warning. According to scientific samplings, Americans have let the manipulators of public opinion make us mad. In August of 1995, the *Dallas Morning News* published an extensive poll revealing public awareness of a rising tide of anger. Sixty-nine percent said people in general seem angrier today than a few years ago; 66 percent think people are less polite; 78 percent believe people are expressing their anger in more violent ways. According to the *News's* survey, half the people in the Dallas–Fort Worth metroplex acknowledge getting quite angry at least once a week!

When? While watching, reading, or listening to the news. Psychologists define anger as an emotional reaction to perceived injustice. Some radio talk show hosts, often spouting gross inaccuracies, pride themselves in the practiced ability to make gullible listeners jump like beads of water on a hot skillet. It seems illogical that the pernicious rise in the level of public anger, particularly as directed against our government, should reach such threatening heights at just this time. The national economy in 1995 was basically sound and had been improving. No international menace threatened us. Yet, the observable level of agitation with society in general, and against anyone who disagrees, was higher than I recall its ever before being. Almost everyone seemed angry at something. Permissiveness in others. Rules that inhibit our own actions. The cybernetic depersonalizing of society. Folks who don't accept our version of religion. Criminals. Drugs in school. We are outraged at drive-by shootings, themselves unreasoning expressions of indefinable hostilities, hate begetting hate.

Americans tend to take out their discontents at the ballot box. Victims of our anger, aside from public officialdom, often turn out to be the weakest and most defenseless people in our midst. Since time immemorial, demagogues have converted discontent into hate, scapegoating numerically or financially vulnerable groups of people. Today, the white American male, we learn from pollsters, is angrier and feels more frustrated than at any time in recent history. He feels victimized by corporate downsizing, by affirmative action plans to hire minorities, by the women's rights movement, by welfare recipients, and by immigrants who enter the work force. One expression of this simmering rage was Proposition 187, by which Californians voted in November 1994 to deny public benefits to undocumented workers, mostly Mexicans and other Latin Americans. That law could result in U.S. citizens of Hispanic extraction having to carry identification, constantly challenged to prove their citizenship. Now comes a proposal in Congress that, in its original form, would withhold public rights even from immigrants who've entered our country quite legally. Such responses to the current atmosphere of hostile anxiety fly in the face of deeply cherished American tenets of law.

The haste of politicians to identify quickly with the latest public angst does not usually make for good law. Like rushing to amend the Constitution just to express our righteous disapproval of the folly of a few sad fools who burn a U.S. flag! Eager to avoid popular wrath or the necessity of explaining, some officeholders go along with such popular quick fixes, even knowing that they can result in serious long-term problems.

One manifestation of the current level of anger, and its demands for retribution, is the increasing public clamor for more capital punishment and for mandatory sentences covering ever-wider categories of legal infractions. These arbitrary mandates remove all discretion from the judges who hear the cases. Justice is not promoted by such ventings of our national anger, nor is crime abated. Jurists and most legislators know this, but they're afraid to appear "soft on crime."

Public displeasure with the very institutions of society—fanned to a white-hot heat by hate-mongering talk-show hosts and "investigative" journalists—drives some politicians to introduce various nostrums weakening the very institutions of which they are a part. Arbitrary term limits for members of Congress, line-item veto power for presidents, together with other proposed restrictions upon congressional powers, would radically alter the carefully established constitutional balance among branches of our government to the detriment of Congress and the people. The irony is that many such efforts to weaken the legislative branch are being pushed by lawmakers themselves.

On Wednesday, January 19, 1995, the House erupted into an explosive orgy of partisan fury that was but a foretaste of an angry, disruptive year. The January argument involved Speaker Gingrich's proposed agreement to write two books for publisher Rupert Murdoch, whom critics contended had a large financial stake in certain pending government business. A young Republican, sitting in for Gingrich in the Speaker's chair, ruled that a Democratic member could not question the propriety of the arrangement in House debate. Pandemonium ensued! Throughout 1995, viewers of C-SPAN were repeatedly shocked at the rising level of anger on both sides.

Knowing nothing about the private transactions between Gingrich and Murdoch, I have no moral judgment to make. Absent evidence to the contrary, I assume their disputed book deal innocent of corrupt intent. It is deeply saddening, however, to see what has happened to Congress and to the once honored rules of civility among and between its members. Hate has bred an atmosphere of destructive attacks and counterattacks. The Speaker himself bears some responsibility for that.

Throughout his career, Gingrich has engaged in vicious assaults upon the patriotism and personal character of colleagues and political adversaries. He had sown the seeds of hate, whose weeds now threatened his own garden. In Dallas the previous fall, he had called Democratic representatives of Texas "traitors" and "enemies of normal Americans." The President and Mrs. Clinton were, in his lexicon of abuse, "counterculture McGovernicks." He charged that one-fourth of the White House staff used drugs. The Speaker even blamed Democrats that a South Carolina woman named Susan Smith deliberately drowned her two small sons. *Sick, nuts, traitors, corrupt, thugs, crooks*: these are words he uses publicly to describe President Clinton and members of the president's party. In one sad sense, Gingrich is like an arsonist who torches the building without supposing that the flames could consume his own bedroom.

A year later, in January 1996, the hate-charged atmosphere of intentional disruption and verbal overkill had twice shut down our government, and Gingrich's minions were gleefully threatening to shut it down a third time. On *Meet the Press* January 7, Republican Whip Tom DeLay boasted: "We're in charge. We don't have to negotiate with the Senate; we don't have to negotiate with the Democrats." And Gingrich's press aide, Tony Blankley, responded to news inquiries by calling House Democratic Whip David Bonior a "swine."

This growing decibel level of hate-mongering and negativity threatens democracy in four ways. It pollutes the atmosphere with self-destructive anger, it undermines faith in the system, it obscures any serious discussion of issues, and it keeps many good and decent people out of politics.

When young people ask my advice on whether to pursue a political career, I point out two things. First, they undoubtedly would make more money and have more job security in many other professions. Second, the higher they rise and the more successful they are in political life, the more likely they are to be targets of vicious personal abuse. If they understand these facts and still want to get into politics, good luck to them.

The late Lee Atwater, a specialist in negative campaigning, came to repent the personal damage his often politically successful tactics had inflicted on others. Stricken by a fatal brain tumor, Atwater asked forgiveness from those whom his campaign attacks had injured. His confession required courage and humility. Hateful words can produce hateful deeds, even violent ones. Two stunning events in 1995 shocked Americans to this realization. One was the senseless bombing of the federal office building in Oklahoma City that took 168 lives and left 500 more injured, apparently the work of an American who had been taught to hate his government. The other event was the slaying of Israeli Prime Minister Yitzhak Rabin, heroic survivor of four wars, at a peace rally. His confessed assassin, a fellow countryman crazed by hateful preachments, said he wanted to stop the peace process. Israelis must learn to be "cold hearted," he said.

We'd better sober up, Americans of both parties and of none, before the habituating narcotic of hate destroys all the good things that, together, we stand for. Some political practitioners are guilty of dealing in hate, others of cowering before it. Voters are equally guilty when they reward it.

What can we do to elevate the quality of public debate? To retain the services of decent people? To renew the participation of citizens in their country's public affairs? There are some things—one of which I'll describe now—but the ultimate solution lies with the people. When voters stop rewarding peddlers of hate with their ballots, they'll stop peddling hate.

Campaign Finance Reform

No phase of American life cries out more insistently for genuine reform than the dingy, gray areas of political campaigns and campaign financing. What ought to be our most wholesome public undertaking has been corrupted by two evils: the overweening power of money, and the sickening slide of campaign rhetoric into the gutters of trivia and slander. There are cures for both, but they aren't easy to get adopted.

In the impromptu televised debate during their 1995 chance encounter in New Hampshire, President Clinton pressed Speaker Gingrich for an agreement to pass a bill reforming campaign finances. The two shook hands in a mutual pledge of its being done. But don't bet the family mortgage on it. In 1967, I wrote an article for *Harper's* demanding campaign finance reform. It was well received, but nothing happened. Speaker Tom Foley pledged, as 1992 began, that Congress would pass a meaningful overhaul that year. He couldn't get his colleagues to follow.

The cost of campaigning has skyrocketed. I ought to know. in my first election to Congress in 1954, I ran successfully against an incumbent and spent less than $32,000. Half of that was money I had saved; half of it I raised—in individual contributions of $100 and less. That was my self-imposed limit. In 1980, I raised and spent the better part of a million dollars in my bid for reelection. My opponent and his supporters were spending a similar amount. Reality had forced me years earlier to abandon my idealistic

$100 ceiling on individual contributions, even though most of my backers still gave in that range and lower.

Look and shudder at how media costs have multiplied: In 1954, I could purchase thirty minutes in prime-time on the local NBC channel for $520. By 1980, that same slot on the same station cost me $8,000. In 1986, the station manager first refused to quote a figure, saying all stations in the metroplex were encouraging thirty-second spots instead of thirty-minute discussions. When pressed, he quoted a prohibitive $45,000.

The spiraling price tag is not confined to my city. Former Vice President Walter Mondale made a study, which concludes that the average successful contested campaign for Congress consumed about $100,000 in 1968. Twenty years later, the median figure had leaped to about $600,000. In 1996, it may be close to a million. Senate races, of course, cost more and vary with the size of the state. In the 1990 Texas governor's race, the losing candidate spent about $11 million, $8 million of which was his own money.

What's wrong with this? Lots of things. For one, politics is becoming a rich man's game. The gates to public service are being closed to people of average incomes. When a shrinking number of people can afford to seek public office, the public is cheated. Its choice is artificially narrowed. The people are cheated also by the extraordinary drain that money-raising imposes upon the time of their public servants. Almost any afternoon in Washington, there are fifteen or more money-raising "receptions" in the hotels and public eateries around the Capitol.

The insatiable demand for so much money in every election cycle unavoidably yields power and influence to those who contribute and raise money in large chunks, and it freezes out candidates, however qualified, who can't raise cash in the hundreds of thousands. When public offices are virtually auctioned off to the highest bidder like seats on the New York Stock Exchange, the public loses control. The average citizen is frozen out when office holders opt for $1,000-a-plate lunches and receptions (the present legal maximum for an individual to give one candidate in a given election cycle) as the preferred medium of fund raising. A political action committee can give up to $5,000.

Even more insidious is a loophole in the law so wide the *Queen Elizabeth II* could steam through without making a ripple. In one of the great euphemisms of our time, this is known as "soft money." So long as it isn't earmarked for any one candidate—but spent instead for party registration, or get-out-the-vote efforts—businesses and corporations with government contracts can legally contribute. And, if they can mask their political propaganda as "educational," they can avoid being identified in public reports and may even deduct their secret contributions, in unlimited amounts, for tax purposes. This subterfuge needs to be eliminated.

As late as 1987, I was holding fundraisers for six thousand people at $25 a couple. I liked it that way. Nobody owned me; I belonged to *everybody*. But, in bottom-line arithmetic, a candidate clears more money if he can lure thirty-five well-heeled contributors into a room for $1,000 apiece. Campaign costs being what they are, money is, in the words of James M. Curley, the mother's milk of politics. The cost-effective way of raising it, alas, is in big chunks!

As a mark of how things have changed, consider two events. In 1979, Vice President Walter Mondale came to Fort Worth. We served ranch-style beans and cornbread, charged five dollars, mainly to recover costs. Come as you are, we urged. Wear blue jeans. We called the event *Beans and Jeans.* Thousands attended. In 1995, Vice President Al Gore visited my town. I was ready to turn out another enthusiastic crowd of local citizens to meet and hear our vice president. A lady in Gore's office told me to forget it. What the Reelect Committee wanted, she said, was a *private* meeting limited to people who had contributed $1,000. Gore met with fewer than seventy of us. Good-bye, party of the people.

But this pales in comparison to the unapologetic effrontery with which both major political parties hold out private meetings with their top stars as lures to big financial contributors. In December 1995, Republican National Committee Chairman Haley Barbour promised lunch with the House Speaker and Senate Majority Leader and preferred seating at the party's national convention to any who would contribute $250,000. The Democrats have their own versions of financial elitism. The corrupting evil in all of this is the clear implication that big political contributions buy special access to law-makers and policymakers.

Washington Post writers David Maraniss and Michael Weisskopf, also in December 1995, wrote a study of the bold, calculating manner in which Republican House leaders have threatened Democratic contributors, leading corporations and industry PACs to infer that large gifts to the Republican Congressional Campaign Committee are expected from those who have business before Congress. The two report that 225 corporations and political action committees in a six-month period put up $5,000 apiece to join an elite group called the House Council, and 150 others enrolled at $15,000 to $20,000 each in an even more exclusive club named the Congressional Forum. Members are assured audiences with top lawmakers. Democratic fundraisers have cultivated similar groups. Both sides can make an argument that, given the intensely competitive campaign climate and the seemingly insatiable demand for campaign dollars, such schemes are necessary. Perhaps. But can anyone deny that they are wrong? Just fundamentally, diabolically antithetical to the basic precepts of democracy?

Clearly, the first requirement to revive democracy is to establish reasonable and enforceable *limits* on total campaign spending. Reform advocates agreed in 1991 on a figure: no more than $600,000 for any House seat. That seems fair. For Senate races, perhaps a sliding scale based on the state's population. But here's a major hitch: federal courts, notably in the case of *Buckley v. Valeo*, have invalidated the enforceablilty of any such limit, except through some form of public financing. What the public subsidizes, it may control, the court reasons.

Since it is the public, not big contributors, who *should* control, let's create a *Democracy Fund* to subsidize congressional elections and make them subject to a legal spending limit. Why not a voluntary checkoff as in the presidential elections? Each citizen, by checking a box on his or her income tax return, might authorize up to ten dollars of the tax payment to go into a fund to supplement congressional campaigns for both Democrat and Republican candidates—and any independents who might qualify by demonstrating a threshold level of public support. From this fund, the government could match a specified level of contributions raised by candidates who comply with the spending limits.

While we're at it, let's *broaden the base* of participation. Democratize political giving. Instead of a few big contributors, let's encourage a multitude of small contributors with no axes to grind except responsible government. First, we should restore the tax credit once allowed as an incentive for individuals to contribute up to $100. Any private citizen who gives $100 or less to the campaign of a favorite candidate should be able to take the amount off his or her income tax. But hold it to that level! What we want is a lot of common stock and no preferred stock.

Next, let's deliberately encourage *candidates* to rely on a multitude of small contributors. Provide that the *Democracy Fund* will match only individual contributions of $200 and less. Nobody expects special treatment for that amount. If the candidate can induce one thousand families in his district to come forward with $200 each, and will agree to abide by the established spending limit, then he or she would qualify for $200,000 from the fund. Or, better still, ten thousand contributors at $20 each! This would make it a lot easier for a person of average financial means and no big time sponsors to run for Congress. It also would go a long way to break the stranglehold of big money and give the electoral process back to the people.

One problem would remain—how to lift campaigns out of the gutters of trivia and onto a high road of sensible discourse, as befits a nation of intelligent people. If Ross Perot performed no other service by his Quixotic third party campaign for the presidency in 1992, his thirty-minute "infomercials" dispelled the popular myth that American voters have to be treated as children, spoon-fed in bite-sized morsels on the theory that they wouldn't listen longer than sixty seconds to a serious discussion of substance. In the arena where Lincoln and Douglas debated mighty issues, hucksters have been hawking candidates for high public office like soft drinks and shampoo. This trivialization of Democracy is the ultimate insult to the intelligence of the American public.

We have the tools with which to promote sensible discussion, if that's what we want. For the privilege of using the limited public airwaves frequencies, licensed broadcasters have been expected from the beginning—nay, required—to give certain amounts of broadcast time to public service. Most major democracies require the media to set aside time, free of charge, for candidates in the general elections to discuss the issues in a serious format. That time is not available for "quickie" commercials. The candidate may not send a film narrated by a smooth-talking professional. He or she must appear personally, look the camera straight in the eye, and talk about issues.

We might reasonably suggest that broadcasters, as part of their public responsibility, should give each local congressional candidate in the general election a total of one hour in prime time during the last ten days of the campaign. The candidate could use the hour in increments of 10, 15, 20, or 30 minutes. The appeal would have to be issue-oriented, not a personal diatribe attacking the private character of an opponent. This proposal is not a panacea. Clever manipulators would look for ways around it. But it could restore some public confidence in the most essential process of all—this thing we call political democracy.

America's Social Compact

The world is not fair, we are constantly reminded. Precisely. That is the principal business of government: to make it as fair as possible. If we were content with its unfairness, there'd be no need for government.

There is danger, I know, in fighting new wars with old weapons. My very age makes my ideas subject to that caution. But there is even greater danger, I submit, in forgetting what it is we're fighting for. My generation's prevailing vision of the human society we'd create has been, I firmly believe, a good one, even if our performance was flawed.

As one who cast his first vote for Franklin Roosevelt and joyously shared Lyndon Johnson's dream of a Great Society, I wrote one day in the *Fort Worth Star-Telegram* that I sometimes identify with an endangered timber wolf who watches warily from a hill as the habitat of his youth is systematically denuded by an alien culture. Trees, grasses and vegetative cover that meant provender and benign protection to the pack for which the old wolf shared responsibility now give way, mile by mile, to a hostile environment, slashed and burned and paved over with concrete. What the eager perpetrators of that landscape hail as progress is to the wolf desecration. In his view they are the predators.

From the time of my youth, the things that set our country apart from all others were our progress in building an upwardly mobile society without class distinctions, and a constantly expanding middle-income sector characterized by rising home ownership, rising educational standards, more family buying power and shrinking levels of unemployment. Through all this ran a strong strain of sympathy for the underdog, a desire to lift him up into the mainstream. This, we told ourselves, was America! To promote these ends was the business of government.

We said America didn't have, thank God, the hideous extremes of poverty and wealth that were to us so striking in most other countries we visited. No professional beggars, no homeless underclasses here. Ours was a democracy, after all!

Even if this self-image was distorted by rose-tinted glass, we knew at least where we wanted to go. Sure, blacks and Hispanics had been mistreated, but we were out to cure that. Where earlier generations had been economically shut out from college, we'd make that option universal. The Depression had left ugly scars, but our enlightened generation knew how to create here in this blessed country the bases for a self-perpetuating prosperity. That's what we told ourselves.

Today, a new band of Visigoths is at the gate with bulldozers and wrecking balls, gleefully preparing to tear down our temples and uproot the trees we planted. What gets me, I think, is not simply that they have a different vision of how to go where we were heading. They have an entirely different destination in mind. Their vision is not an egalitarian society but a predatory society, whose rewards are survival of the fittest. The devil take the hindmost. And the business of government: Stay out of the way.

The direction in which the new conservatives want to lead us portends an ever-wider spread between the richest and the poorest, with a steady diminution of the once-broad middle-income sector. The radical change in income distribution during the 1980s, so chillingly documented by Kevin Phillips in his book *The Politics of Rich and Poor*, provides merely a prelude to what is coming if Representatives Newt Gingrich, Dick Armey, and Bill Archer have their way. The rich will get richer; the poor will get poorer; there'll be fewer of us in the middle. These men do not think of that eventuality as either greedy or cruel. They see it as the dynamic fruition of the natural laws of economics. But if we follow this new leadership, entranced by its harsh rhetoric against welfare and its seductive promise of what it calls "middle-class" tax cuts (which mostly benefit the very wealthy), the income gap will grow. This is not the America most folks of my generation thought we were fighting for in World War II.

Admittedly, welfare programs are often inefficient and sometimes counterproductive. The whole system needs a careful overhauling. But anybody who tells you that the federal budget can be balanced just by cutting welfare is either uninformed or planning to reduce Social Security and Medicare much more drastically than others imagine. Outside those two programs—which most people don't consider "welfare"—eliminating all social spending entirely would hardly wipe out the annual deficit. House Majority Leader Dick Armey has been candid, at least. He advocates abolishing Social Security as we've known it and substituting a voluntary system.

And look carefully at who wins and who loses before going overboard for a seductive-sounding tax cut. Conservative tax theorists ascendant in the House following the 1994 elections describe their goal as taxing consumption rather than profits. This, they say, will lead to more savings. That may sound benign, but it really means more taxes from poor people, who have to spend their entire incomes on essential consumer goods, and less from those who make enough to set aside substantial savings. Some want to abolish the income tax and substitute a national sales tax. For years we preached that taxes should be based on ability to pay—but the new theory is based on inability to escape. Others talk of a "flat tax"—everyone paying the same fixed percentage of income. There is no way to configure such a result without increasing the burden on low and middle-income workers.

There's a sweet-sounding ring to the promise of "tax vouchers" to promote "freedom of choice" in education, but this means that people of modest income whose children go to our public schools will have some of their own taxes given to relatively more affluent families with children in private schools. This might help create an upper-caste educated elite—if that's our country's goal—but it won't do much for average American kids. The whole thing tilts away from equality and runs counter to our country's evolution of social principles. It will hurt rather than help hardworking, middle-income families.

Thoughts such as these might get you branded in some quarters as a "liberal," but don't let that make you afraid to think them. Our ancestors weren't. Among the first to translate these thoughts into political principle, in fact, were progressive Republicans of the Theodore Roosevelt school. Very early in this century, progressive thinkers were alarmed by the unrestrained power of huge corporate structures. That danger was recognized by some forward-looking leaders in the business community itself. George W. Perkins, who organized United States Steel and International Harvester, for example, urged upon his fellow industrialists an overriding social responsibility. "If this new order of things is better for capital and better for the consumer," Perkins warned, "then in order to succeed permanently it must demonstrate that it is also better for the laborer." Spurred by academicians, other visionary business leaders, and politicians like Theodore Roosevelt and Woodrow Wilson, there developed a sort of Social Compact to stabilize the new corporate order by granting conscious benefits to working people and protecting smaller businesses.

After World War I, the Russian Revolution set off a contagious Red scare in this country, which bred among some elements of America's business community an almost hysterical fear of unions and organized labor. This, together with the individualistic spirit of the Roaring Twenties and Calvin Coolidge's fascination for the philosophy of Adam Smith, put the Social Compact aside, only to see it revived by the Depression-era New Deal. Laborers' rights to organize unions, Social Security, full employment goals, and other reforms generated a sense of public responsibility, which continued as the prevailing American sentiment until the 1980s. It is time for a new Social Compact as we enter the twenty-first century.

America's Public Lifelines

The federal budget is not the only place where America is running troublesome deficits and running out of time. We are falling farther and farther behind in a critically important matter called by that awkward, esoteric-sounding name of *infrastructure*. What the word means is the nation's lifeline network of facilities on which we all depend every day: roads, pipes, wires, dams, rails, bridges, airports, and public buildings. This basic infrastructure is deteriorating much faster than we're repairing and replacing it. Unlike some of our other woes, however, this public works base so badly in need of renovation may be as much an opportunity as it is a problem. It offers a chance to put many thousands of unemployed people quickly to work doing highly useful things. Former Senator David Boren, now president of the University of Oklahoma, has pointed out that the WPA put 800,000 unemployed people to productive work in eight years. They built 650,000 miles of roads and sidewalks, 125,000 public buildings, 25,000 parks and playgrounds. Most of these facilities still serve the public today, more than fifty years later.

It need not add anything to the deficit. It won't if we have the gumption to follow our own example of the 1950s, when we launched the Interstate Highway program. I propose that we create a *Rebuild America Trust Fund* and pay as we go—just as we did then. Dedicate specific taxes to the fund, and keep it inviolate. It makes no more sense for a country to let its public facilities crumble than it does for a family to let its home go to rack and ruin for want of maintenance.

For a long time, we kept up with our country's needs. In the 1960s, federal investment in the infrastructure increased by 24 percent; during the 1970s, it increased by 46 percent; but in the 1980s, total government investment in our public works shrunk to less than half the level of a generation earlier. Federal aid to U.S. cities dropped from $45 billion in 1980 to $19.8 billion in 1990. The impact of this neglect is felt at all levels. In Pittsfield, Massachusetts, 8,000 people fell sick when a parasite invaded the town's inadequate water system. The water supply at Woodstock, New York, became undrinkable because of asbestos contamination. One-third of the bridges in the Pittsburgh area are either closed or under strict load limitations. Across the nation, 4,125 bridges have been closed to all traffic. Budget cuts in mass transit funding have been particularly cruel, since this is the one component of our transportation system that the poor rely upon most. Many U.S. water ports are obsolete and must be dredged if they are to handle world-class ships. A 1992 study at the Federal Reserve Bank of Chicago concluded that 80 percent of the decline in U.S. productivity since the 1970s results from the falloff of infrastructure investment.

By rising to the challenge, Americans can reassert their spirit and faith in our collective future, while putting a lot of willing people back to work. Or we can wallow in a self-imposed national paralysis. It was the six-hundred-mile Los Angeles aqueduct that transformed a sleepy town into the country's second-largest city. William Mullholland, the engineer who supervised its construction, was asked at the time what would happen if the aqueduct were never built. "If you don't build it, you'll never need it, because this place will become a desert populated only by lizards," he said. Surely that is not a fitting epitaph for our nation.

Our Best Investment: Education

The best investment America ever made was the G.I. Bill of Rights that followed World War II. It permitted an entire generation of Americans to finish college. Every dollar spent in student grants and assistance returned many dollars to the treasury in taxes paid on higher earnings made possible by learning. As we look to the twenty-first century, I can think of no single goal more vital to our future than renewing and building upon that example. It is an indispensable key to a new Social Compact.

President Bill Clinton offered a modest model in his proposed *Americorps*, which he has had enormous trouble getting Congress to fund. That program ought to be expanded at least ten times over. Clinton's plan would let students who can't afford rising college tuition rates *earn* their tuition by working on valid public projects. What could be more American?

And what could be more practical? Our biggest and most important investment deficiency has been our neglect to reinvest adequately in our national future through education. That neglect contributes perhaps more than any other factor to trade deficits. In a recent year, our universities graduated some 54,000 young Americans with advanced degrees in science, engineering, and mathematics. Japan, with half our population, graduated 77,000. An even bigger disparity exists in language skills, without which we can hardly expect to compete in global trading.

Americans should burn with shame to acknowledge how far behind that of several other countries we've allowed our education performance to fall. We should make ourselves this promise: In the first decade of the twenty-first century, we shall see to it that every American youth who wants to go to college gets that chance; that every secondary student who wants and can learn a job skill is taught one and actually placed in a job; and that a real effort is made to redeem every public school dropout.

While it grows harder to get in college, it grows easier to get in jail. The United States prison population grew in 1995 to an all-time high of more than 1.1 million. Our country locks up a bigger percentage of its citizens than any other nation does. And a year in prison costs the taxpayers more for each inmate than a year in one of America's best universities would cost. Meanwhile, our basic economic problem is a shortage of skilled workers and an oversupply of unskilled workers. Labor Secretary Robert Reich makes a good case that we could make money by subsidizing college loans for low-income students, providing work apprenticeships for noncollege-bound youngsters, and vouchers for the unemployed to spend on retraining.

There is nothing in American life more central to this nation's well-being than our public schools and institutions of higher learning. Education and democracy are inseparably linked. Absent public knowledge and understanding, democracy cannot endure. An unhappy constituent once complained to Senator Lloyd Bentsen that education is just too damned expensive! Yes, it is, agreed the senator. But not half as expensive as ignorance! A truly enlightened society will find ways to make sure that absolutely no youngster who really wants one is denied a higher education, since any nation that stints on its public schools cheats itself.

Against that background, let's reappraise our national attitude and ask just how well we are measuring up. Just where have we placed education in our national scale of priorities? Is it as important as recreation? Not if we measure it by what we spend on the two. Has our sense of values gotten slightly out of focus when the average big league ball player gets as much in a single season as a typical teacher in our public schools can make in a whole career? Isn't there something strangely amiss when a television comedian is paid more for a single performance than our best high school teacher with a doctor's degree will be paid all year? Should the reward be that much greater for making people laugh than it is for making people think?

In 1991, at age sixty-eight, I took on a brand new assignment. I agreed to teach a three-hour political science class one day a week at Texas Christian University. I had so much fun that I've signed up to do it again for four successive years. I hope my six hundred-plus students have enjoyed it half as much as I have. In election years, students in my class can earn a part of their term grade by voluntarily helping in some political campaign of their choice. Considering the socioeconomic status of most of their parents, I'd guess more of them have signed up with Republican campaigns than with Democratic ones. If so, that's fine with ol' Democrat me so long as it gives them a real taste of what our democracy is all about. As fine as this experience has been, I know I'm just a dilettante, not a bona fide teacher. I wouldn't want to teach five classes every day. But the challenge has heightened my admiration enormously for those who do. Whatever we're paying them, it is the best investment we can make.

Ol' Demon Guv'mint?

Throughout my adulthood, I've listened to a lot of well-meaning folks cuss the government. As one who has spent most of his career trying to make that government responsive to people's needs and responsible in its expenditure of their tax dollars, I sometimes cringe at popular stereotypes depicting public officials as pompous and government workers as lazy and inept. Some, of course, are; but not all, and not most. Some government money is wasted, some government programs don't work, but, on balance, our government is the best, freest, and fairest on earth.

Perhaps my best proof of this is in the lives of people I know. I'd like to tell you about one dear old friend of mine. Call him Bill. He's my age. We've known each other since grade-school days, still see each other once or twice a year. Like most of us, Bill's family scratched and scrambled to eke out a living in the Depression-ridden 1930s. An older brother worked briefly for the WPA. The family wanted Bill to go to college. He did, enrolling at a community junior college and then proudly at Texas A&M. Bill supplemented his pocket money by doing useful work, for which he received payment from the National Youth Administration. It helped him stay in school.

War came, and Bill enlisted, like most of us. He wondered aloud to me one night if he'd be able to finish college when the war was over. Fortunately for Bill and many thousands of our generation, the G.I. Bill of Rights gave him a passport back to the classroom. He got a bachelor's degree and, in the process, married a pretty girl named Jane. Back home, Bill found a job at the bomber plant. For a time he ran a trade school on the side. He and Jane bought a nice frame house with a 4 percent loan insured by the FHA. Later, with help from the Texas Veterans Land Board, they acquired a small piece of acreage south of town. Before long, the government built a new farm-to-market road along the front of Bill's property, and its value increased dramatically. It was already served by an REA electric power line. After several years, the Soil Conservation Service constructed an upstream soil retention dam in Bill's lower pasture that improved the land value further with a scenic little lake that doubled as a stock tank.

Times were good. Bill and Jane enjoyed a comfortable status as their kids went through school in the 1950s and 1960s. Bill, meanwhile, made a few fortunate investments in some West Texas oil and gas wells. The 27 percent depletion allowance helped some, and a bit of good luck didn't hurt. The couple invested in airline stock and computer stock, and I don't know for sure what else. The economic direction of the country was upward, and so were the family fortunes.

Things got so good, in fact, that one day Bill called his secretary into his office and dictated a letter to his congressman. That was I. What in the name of God, Bill wrote in high indignation, are you wasteful dunderheads doing with all of my tax dollars? That day when this old friend appealed to me for an end to all these "wasteful" government programs, I tried to suggest as gently as I could that his family, in fact, had done pretty well, at least partly as result of what other people assailed as wasteful government programs.

In his lifetime, Bill had been the recipient of fairly generous government help to finish school, a job with a federal contractor, subsidized home and business loans, a favorable tax climate for his business investments, and valuable enhancements to his property by at least three federally funded programs. He also benefited indirectly in the profits that accrue to most businessmen from a healthy economy, sustained by policies that enhance other people's buying power so they can buy cars that use gasoline, have home computers, and take airline trips—strongly reinforcing several of Bill's private investments.

Bill seemed a bit surprised that I would bring this up—almost offended. "You've known me since we were kids," he insisted. "I've worked for everything I ever got in life!" My friend had a point. He has worked hard, paid his taxes, been a good husband and father, but it also is true that, at critical points in his life and career, Bill and his family have been significant beneficiaries of federal government policies financed by other people's tax dollars. Nothing wrong in this. Certainly nothing dishonorable. It is a tradition as old as the American republic.

Among right-wing political practitioners, an assertive faction seems to believe that the only acceptable proof of patriotism is a contemptuous disdain for our government. Yet 75 percent of all government assistance goes to the nonpoor in the form of Medicare, housing subsidies, and tax breaks. In fact, the top 20 percent of the population gets four times the amount of assistance received by the bottom 40 percent, according to Professor Stephanie Coontz in her 1992 *The Way Things Never Were*. A popular fallacy holds that budget deficits would disappear if we'd just squeeze the fat out of domestic social programs. But the whole gamut of discretionary domestic spending is a very small part of the total budget. It has been cut by about 28 percent in constant dollars since 1980. And many who complain the loudest about domestic spending are among its most rewarded beneficiaries. Bill's numbers are legion. Thank God for them . . . and for their government.

Limits

There are limits, of course, to what government should be expected to do, or even try to do. The most precious thing about our constitutional system is its carefully drawn balance of limitations upon the power of government. Still, even with our elaborate set of protections, individuals in government sometimes get carried away with their own importance and overrun the levees erected to contain them. Throughout my years in office, I've seen this happen to some elected officials, but more often to appointed members of our government's enforcement bureaucracies, those given power over private citizens.

On the morning of September 1, 1994, sixty-four agents of the Internal Revenue Service, some carrying firearms, swarmed into the offices of the Moncrief Oil Company in downtown Fort Worth. They abruptly sealed off the building, banished its astonished owners to the lunchroom, and posted armed guards to keep them out of their own offices. This SWAT team, following a daylong search of the company's records, arbitrarily seized all its files and documents. These included private as well as business correspondence and the company's computers. The confiscated records, filling twenty file cabinets and about three hundred boxes, were taken from the property that very day, and the Moncrief family was denied any access to its own files for some two weeks.

This awesome and unannounced use of government force was thoroughly mystifying to a family that through sixty-five years and three generations has operated a successful independent exploration company, paid its taxes, and never had any serious problems with the IRS. Bereft of their records, the principals were severely handicapped for several weeks in trying to conduct necessary day-to-day business. The family-owned company operates in a number of states and is subject to numerous reporting requirements by various state agencies. These cannot be fulfilled without access to company files, which a federal court belatedly ordered returned. Meanwhile, the principals had no idea just what it was the government was looking for. If they knew, they said, they'd be glad to help the agents find it. Nothing in the background of this law-abiding American family would warrant the kind of treatment it received from an agency of its government.

After sixteen months of sifting, the Moncriefs paid some additional taxes, but no penalties were asked and no criminal violation even alleged. The same result could have been achieved without the pyrotechnics, and without exacerbating the growing mistrust and fear of government.

The IRS is a highly useful, necessary agency. But its agents and officers, armed with enormous power over private citizens, including the power to terrorize and intimidate, should be ever mindful of the need to exercise restraint in the use of this power. The complexities of the tax code are such that hardly anyone engaged in any business endeavor can be certain that his own most conscientious effort at calculating his obligation will be precisely the same as that of some IRS agent. Perhaps my own experience is fairly average. Through the years, I have been audited four times. The IRS concluded once that I had overpaid, once that I had underpaid, and twice that the accounting firm that helps with my return had done its job just right. Other citizens I know have not been so fortunate. One local woman, a widow in her forties who operated a small real-estate business, was hounded and personally harassed by an unusually aggressive agent for eighteen months. She went broke. Another woman I encountered while serving in Congress is convinced that hostile and persistent hounding by a team of IRS agents caused her father's death.

Abuse of power by other government enforcers, some in our Department of Justice, have been documented. We thought the compilation of "enemy lists" and official harassment of political opponents ended after the shocking disclosures of the Watergate era. Not so. Acting Secretary of State Lawrence Eagleburger, a respected professional and a decent man, was genuinely embarrassed to discover that political appointees of the Bush administration once grievously abused State Department powers in a blatant effort to discredit Governor Bill Clinton during the 1992 presidential election. Several times the Justice Department, during the regimes of Attorneys General Richard Thornburgh and William P. Barr, used public resources to injure elected officials and private citizens. One attempted prosecution, aimed at Democratic Representative Floyd Flake of New York, stands out. In that case, the federal prosecutors finally moved to dismiss their own groundless case after putting Flake through a three-year ordeal of highly publicized investigation and three weeks of trial. U.S. Judge Eugene H. Nickerson, after asking the jury to leave the room, told the prosecutors that every single bit of evidence had disproved their contention.

Just being innocent is not enough. Ambitious federal attorneys, with no case, sometimes can destroy a rival politician simply by planting news stories. Popular former Texas Agriculture Commissioner Jim Hightower is one example. Shortly after Hightower's speech to the 1988 Democratic Convention attracted national attention, stories began surfacing, leaked by government agents, that Hightower was under federal criminal investigation. These surely contributed to his narrow defeat in 1990. There was no case. Hightower was innocent. But his career was ruined.

The Justice Department had 85,000 employees in 1992 and an annual budget of $11 billion, five times as much as when Jimmy Carter left office in 1981. If it is determined to do so, it can break not only political careers but the financial stability of almost any private citizen. Wielding such power, it must be consciously restrained from engaging in vendettas against American citizens.

Perhaps what it comes down to is that in a free society, people who enjoy asserting power over others should not be entrusted with it. Many years ago, as mayor of Weatherford, I learned in hiring police officers to be alert to a particular personality trait. A latent bully, one who wants the job for the authority it gives him over others, who wants a license to pack a gun, is someone to be avoided at all costs. Just as a small town does not need an abusive cop, no civil society can thrive when those who have power over others—IRS agents, U.S. attorneys, sheriffs or G-men of any sort—forget that it is they who work for the private citizen and not the other way around.

A Sporting Proposition

Civility. The word is little used these days, the quality it describes too little practiced. We must rediscover and repopularize both the word and the virtue. Civility is the necessary lubricating oil for the machinery of a free society. In its absence, the gears of democracy grind in noisy dissonance to a screeching halt. *Webster's New Twentieth Century Dictionary* defines *civility* as the state of being civilized. Its marks, the dictionary notes, are politeness, consideration, courtesy. The modern term grew from a Latin word, *civilitas.* In its original form, it signified "the art of government."

The preservation of liberties—free speech, free press, free religious expression—has always exacted a price. Part of that price is the maintenance of civility, respect for the institutions of our government and fellow citizens with whom we disagree. Poking fun at Congress and at presidents is a longstanding American tradition, and a healthy one that keeps officials from getting inflated egos. Balloons invite pins.

Every now and then, I cringe when a self-appointed entertainer strains too hard for a laugh. When General Colin Powell announced in November 1995 that he would not be a candidate for president, a genial disc jockey on my favorite radio station offered: "Now we know why Colin Powell is not running for president. He has one handicap which is totally disabling—one which *disqualifies* him from being president—one which *no* president has *ever* had: sanity!"

Well, that was borderline—no malicious intent. But, having known each of the last nine presidents—four Democrats and five Republicans, Eisenhower through Clinton—I just shook my head. Whoever is president, he or she has the world's most responsible and demanding job. He or she deserves *something* from the rest of us. Just what? What assumption of honor? What privacy, if any? What allowance for human frailty, and the benefit of just what doubts? Certainly, we don't owe adulation, nor obedience, nor even agreement. Certainly, we can laugh at the person's human frailties.

What we owe, I think, is civility.

After the Iran-Contra scandal broke, I was at pains to protect President Reagan from a frontal assault on his personal integrity. Disagreeing with him strongly on matters of principle, I did not wish to see him humiliated nor his honor questioned. Maybe that's what I mean by civility. By the same token, I think President Bill Clinton's detractors have gone overboard in their personal attacks on him. They've several times breached the bounds of good taste, of civility, with hateful and unreasoning allegations brandished like weapons designed to inflict injury and mortal hurt. One week in October 1994, the mail brought astonished recipients a fund-raising appeal so rancid with hate as to offend the very garbage cans into which it should be forthrightly consigned. On an official-looking letterhead with a Washington address, the plea for contributions began with: "I have in my possession compelling evidence that proves beyond all shadow of a doubt that White House aid [sic] Vincent Foster was murdered . . . vital clues that lead right to the Oval Office." Begging for money to spew out more such bile, the writer promised to prosecute a case of impeachment against President Clinton, presumably for the murder of his lifelong friend. No president should have to contend with such unfounded libel. It is not enough that special counsel Robert B. Fiske, a Republican and no friend of Clinton's, looked carefully into this bizarre allegation concerning poor Foster's suicide and reported it to be just that.

Hate-Clinton solicitation letters have become a cottage industry. For some the goal is political power. For others, it's just a way to fill greedy coffers with contributions bilked from innocent, well-meaning Americans gullibly alarmed by the strident claims of right-wing media personalities such as Rush Limbaugh and the Reverend Jerry Falwell. Preachments of hate, prejudgments of guilt, and eagerness to repeat the vilest slanders are not new to American society, but they have reached preposterous proportions in the mid-1990s.

Sam Rayburn, who served as Speaker of the House longer than anyone else in history, was a gentleman. He believed in decorum, revered the democratic process, respected the majority will. Outspoken in his convictions and informally dubbed Mr. Democrat, the crusty old Texan never spoke a word of personal disparagement against any Republican president. He wouldn't even tolerate in his presence any degrading comment about House Republican Leader Joe Martin. The chief executive was special, Rayburn insisted. The president was the constitutional head of our government, chosen by the American people. As such, he was absolutely entitled to our respect—not our obedience, but our sympathetic consideration, and always our assumption and defense of his personal honor. That in Rayburn's view, was part of being an American.

What would Rayburn think? I gasped in instant disbelief one day in 1994, as I saw a bumper sticker on an expensive foreign car on a Fort Worth street. The message demanded not the impeachment but the *assassination* of President Clinton. My first impulse was to take the license number and report it to the Secret Service. But, no, I decided, that poor, foolish fellow is not a threat to the President's physical safety. He is merely an unwitting threat to the American system of government. And that, in our free society, is not a punishable offense.

In no other position is the decision of one human so fraught with potential for great good or ill, nor the task of deciding so lonely. Others can advise. All may criticize. But on some issues, only the president can decide. Now and again we all need to pause and think of the horrible weight that bears on one person's shoulders and one person's mind, and say a prayer for the well-being of the president of the United States.

President Clinton is at heart a warm and gracious person. Decent, kind, forgiving, tolerant of most criticism, patient with the misinformed, he is much nicer than his detractors recognize and infinitely kinder to them than most of them are to him. Clinton's dominant instincts are to make peace, to harmonize, to smooth over differences and work together, to spare the feelings of others, to conciliate, compromise and get things done. He has not only tolerated but even patronized congressional opponents. He has no taste for embarrassing adversaries personally. Clinton is not a saint—hasn't pretended to be. His appetites are human, his faults well advertised. But, as Ben Jonson said of William Shakespeare, he has redeemed his vices with his virtues, and there's more in him to be praised than to be pardoned. Politics, alas, is not a purist's game. Perfect solutions are unattainable. Do not despise compromise, wrote Henry Clay, it is the cement that holds the union together. Clinton understands this, and because he does, ideological absolutists despise him.

Being a nice guy, a conciliator, a peacemaker is not always the most effective self-protection. Nobody is afraid to attack Clinton. He isn't vindictive. He's not out to destroy his enemies by maligning their reputations, vetoing their projects, or using the government's enforcement machinery to harass them. This has encouraged detractors to make an art form and an industry of hazing him. Clinton has suffered more outrageous calumny in assaults upon his personal character than any other president of recent times. The attacks are deliberate, highly orchestrated, intensely personal, and quite often flagrantly untruthful. They are the work of a professional hate machine.

Americans expect a lot from our presidents. Sometimes our demands border on the ridiculous. We act as though the chief executive should be flawless, and we reserve the right to ridicule and belittle him when he isn't. We require that he be inspiring, commanding, right in judgment and victorious in battle, inexhaustible, entertaining, and humble to boot. We want a combination prophet, knight, court jester, and punching bag.

It was settled early in our national life that no president should equate his post with aristocracy. Our second president, John Adams, asked Congress to compose an appropriate title of office. Adams himself offered "His Excellency, the President and Protector of our Liberties." Congress reacted with ribald ridicule. One representative proposed in mock solemnity that the official presidential title be "His Rotundity." Adams, a chubby fellow, quickly dropped the whole idea. Nevertheless, the American presidency is surely the most demanding job on earth. Dr. William M. Narva, who served as Capitol physician and doctor to presidents, once estimated to me that eight years in the White House equates to fifteen years on the odometer of life.

And what of Congress? What respect do we owe to the legislative branch? What degree of civility? Congress, really, is a distillation of ourselves, a microcosm of the nation. It is not, alas, a convocation of saints and Olympian prophets. We owe to Congress what we owe to ourselves—a modicum of understanding. And civility. Moreover, we should hope its members have sense and backbone enough to resist emasculating the institution to appease popular whims—like term limits. Our ancestors tried that under the Articles of Confederation, and it didn't work. If the pop logic of its advocates should ever prevail, the legislative branch of our government will be vastly weakened, bereft of strong and experienced leaders, much more at the mercy of an authoritative executive branch. There will be no Sam Rayburns, no Robert A. Tafts, no Arthur Vandenbergs or Barry Goldwaters to curb the presidential appetite for power or to soften its occasional rashnesses with their wisdom—and civility.

We Americans really are a bit schizophrenic. We value our personal privacy and hate idle gossip about our loved ones, but we are titillated by juicy scandals about movie stars and public officials. When we hear one candidate for Congress making shrill and outrageous charges against another, we need to reflect that he or she has been told that's the kind of stuff we like: political pornography.

These abhorrent tactics are anything but new. In 1800, Thomas Jefferson, running for president against John Adams, was called a liar, a cheat, an atheist, a whoremonger, and a Francophile. In Andrew Jackson's 1828 campaign, even his wife, Rachel, was slandered as an adulteress and a bigamist. After reading of that calumny, from which vain efforts were made to shield her, Rachel Jackson suffered a fatal heart attack. If there is any redeeming grace in all this, it is that both Jefferson and Jackson were elected, and that the two make almost every historian's list of the top six American presidents. The public, even that early in our political history, had better sense and more sophistication than to be swayed by the libelous charges. There is in the veins of most Americans an abiding sense of fair play and an instinctive revulsion against unfair tactics.

Is the thirst for sportsmanship still being bred into us? Or are young Americans subjected to a different set of values today? It isn't that we won or lost—the unforgettable doggerel of my youth repeats to my subconscious mind—but how we played the game. Does that old poetry resonate in today's locker rooms? A cynical sportswear commercial ripped into my consciousness one evening from the television screen. An attractive young woman smirks into the camera: "Whoever said 'winning isn't everything' never won anything."

When I was thirteen, our coach told us the story of an amateur boxing champion whose name, I think, was Eddy Egan. His opponent in the national finals had incurred an ugly gash creasing one eyebrow in a preceding bout and was on the verge of being medically disqualified from competing. Egan, loath to accept the championship on the other's misfortune, approached his athletic rival with a sporting proposition. Tape a white bandage over the injury if you'd like to compete, Egan is said to have assured him, and neither glove of mine will touch the bandage. I cannot remember who won that bout or if it even was allowed to proceed. That really wasn't the point. But in sixty years I haven't forgotten what sportsmanship in those days was supposed to demand.

In the presidential election of 1912, which Paul Boller, in his fascinating *Presidential Campaigns*, regards as the most substantive, issue-oriented campaign in American history, three intelligent candidates vied for the presidency. Theodore Roosevelt was shot and wounded in the course of that campaign. A bullet lodged near his lung, the old Rough Rider nevertheless stood and delivered an eighty-minute speech to a large crowd in the Milwaukee auditorium. Immediately afterward, he was hospitalized and was obliged to recuperate before resuming the campaign trail. Roosevelt's opponents, President William Howard Taft and challenger Woodrow Wilson, in gentlemanly deference to their competitor, refrained from making any campaign appearances until Roosevelt recovered sufficiently to resume an active speaking schedule. Perhaps it is too much to expect the same level of sportsmanlike consideration for one's competitors in today's intensely competitive climate. Perhaps.

My dad gave me, when I was fifteen, a framed copy of Kipling's poem "If." I gave it a special place on the wall of my room. Now I bribe my grandsons to memorize it. Well, maybe *bribe* isn't the right word. *I coax them with appropriate financial incentive.* If any of them ever should get into politics—a prospect toward which I have highly mixed emotions—I want him to remember all the passages of that poem, and especially the one that says:

Or, being lied about, don't deal in lies
Or, being hated, don't give way to hating
And yet don't look too good, nor talk too wise.

INDEX

Coelho, Tony, 311, 399, 401, 442, 444, 461
Cohen, William S., 423, 427
Cold War, 64–66, 103, 180–83, 372–73, 390–91, 398, 402, 403
  see also defense spending; nuclear weapons; Soviet Union; *names of individual leaders*
Coleman, Ron, 396
Coleman, Tami, 396
Collins, Jim, 312
Colombia, 293
Colorado River, salinity of, 186–88
Colson, Chuck, 197, 198
Coming Water Famine, The (Wright), 130
Commerce Department, U.S., 15, 58, 371, 386, 409
  Office of International Trade and Tourism, 95
Committee to Reelect the President (CREEP), 205, 206
Commodity Credit Corporation, 59
Communications Act of 1934, 142
Conference on Competitiveness, 450, 451
Congress, U.S.:
  campaign finance reform, *see* Campaign finance reform
  limitations on presidential powers, 202–3, 256
  term limits, 494
  see also House of Representatives, U.S.; Senate, U.S.
Congressional Budget Office (CBO), 202, 347
Congressional Forum, 498
Congressional Quarterly, 310, 440
Congressional Record, 65, 140, 428
Congressional Wives Club, 223–24, 315
Connally, John, 88, 104, 106, 107, 115, 133, 150, 174, 176–78, 192, 209, 290, 291
Constitution, 201–2
Cooley, Harold, 44
Coolidge, Calvin, 503
Coontz, Stephanie, 507
Cooper, Jere, 44
Corman, Jim, 310, 339
Cornell, Robert, 236
Corps of Engineers, 47, 95, 126, 131–33
Costa Rica, 384
Cost of Living Council, 178
Council for Inter-American Security, 473
Cox, Archibald, 211, 212–13, 215
Cramer, Bill, 50, 140
Cranston, Alan, 276, 339
Criswell, Dr. W. A., 264, 265
Cronkite, Walter, 302, 304
Crouch, Doug, 90, 91
Cruz, Arturo, 414, 417, 430
Cuba, 66, 76, 170, 171, 413, 416, 465
  Grenada and, 394, 395
  missile crisis, 66, 96–98
Culver, John, 339
Curley, James Michael, 104, 217, 498
Curtis, Lawrence, 91
Cushing, Cardinal, 148
Cyprus, 257, 258

Dallas, Texas, assassination of John Kennedy in, 105, 107–9, 110, 115–16, 118, 404
Dallas–Fort Worth International Airport, 96, 282, 335
Dallas Morning News, 107, 493
Dallas News, 242
Daniel, Price, 17
Daschle, Tom, 317–18
D'Aubuisson, Roberto, 418–19, 427
Davis, Mrs. Edith, 343
Davis, Frank, 81, 82, 84
Davis, Will, 149
Dawson, Bill, 53
Dayan, Moshe, 302

Dean, John, 205
"Dear Ivan" letter (Wright), 65–66, 85, 453–54
Deaver, Mike, 394
Defense Department Appropriation Act, 437
Defense spending, 65–66, 77–85, 232
  B-58 bomber, 78–80, 83
  budget deficit and, 374–75, 406, 448
  under Johnson, 115
  mutual assured destruction (MAD), 373
  MX missiles, 406
  under Reagan, 344, 353, 368, 371, 372–75, 380, 381, 389, 406, 433
  social cost of, 396, 410, 434, 455
  TFX, 81–84, 121, 123
  see also Nuclear weapons
de la Garza, Kika, 451
Dellinger, David, 146
Democratic Congressional Campaign Committee, 31, 237, 442
Democratic Leadership Council, 450
Democratic National Convention of 1988, 477
Deng Xiao Ping, 320
Department of Agriculture, U.S., 59
Department of Defense, 211–12, 288, 289
Department of Education, 284
Department of Energy, 283, 287
Department of Health and Human Services, U.S., 365
Department of Housing and Urban Development, 146, 287
Department of Justice, 509
Department of Urban Affairs, U.S., 95
D'Escoto, Miguel, 468
Devine, Sam, 158
Dewey, Thomas E., 27
Dickinson, Bill, 312
Dielman, Fred, 123
Diggs, Charles, 318
Dingell, John, 324, 451
Dirksen, Everett, 14, 45
District of Columbia home rule, 132
Dobell, Evan, 314
Dobrynin, Anatoly, 97, 403, 404, 408
Dodd, Chris, 240
Dolan, Terry, 329
Dole, Bob, 290, 350, 437, 441, 442, 451, 475
Domenici, Pete, 381
Dominica, 395
Dominican Republic, 170, 384
Dondero, George, 36
Donnelly, Brian, 399
Donovan, George, 17, 18
Douglas, Helen Gahagan, 14, 152
Downey, Tom, 236
draft:
  amnesty for draft evaders, 273, 288
  protesters against the, 154
Dreyfus, Enrique, 414
Driskell, Paul, 366
Duarte, Inez, 466–67
Duarte, José Napoleon, 418, 427, 462, 464, 465, 466–67
Dukakis, Michael, 478
Dulles, Allen, 157
Dulles, John Foster, 34
Duncan, Phil, 486
Dunlop, John T., 252
Durkin, John, 297
Duvalier, François "Papa Doc," 170

Eagleburger, Lawrence, 509
Eagleton, Tom, 197
Easley, "Tex," 242

ACKNOWLEDGMENTS

Few things are so all-absorbing as writing a book. I owe an awful lot to a lot of people. Alan Axelrod of Turner Publishing gave me sound advice and constant encouragement. But for Norma Ritchson, the manuscript would never have been completed on time. My associate Larry Shannon kept my other affairs in order, no mean task, while I closeted myself in monklike seclusion during most of 1995, working my way through this long narrative journey. Steve Charnovitz, my sister Mary Connell, and my wife, Betty, made useful suggestions throughout, helping to keep this chronicle readable.

Beyond that, the story it tells owes so much more than I can ever say to so many more people than I can ever name. Outside my immediate family, let me list just a few: Craig Raupe, who was like a brother; John Mack, who was like a son; Kathy Mitchell and Marshall Lynam, who performed a myriad of services above the call of duty, picked up after me, and generally kept me on track for a generation; fellows like Bernard Rapoport, George Mallick, Ben Procter, Carlos Moore, George Nokes, and Johnny Vinson, who enlarge the meaning of the word "friend"; Joe Shosid, who has stuck with me through the years; Marge and Ed Youngblood; and finally James and Jimmie Lee Bodiford, whose love is beyond categorizing.

My appreciation to the *Fort Worth Star-Telegram* for permission to use copy from several of my weekly columns, to *Congressional Quarterly, Inc.*, for letting me repeat some thoughts from my chapter in their 1994 book, *The Speaker*, and to Brassey's (US) for use of information I first wrote in *Worth It All: My War for Peace*, published in 1993.

For preserving information in tens of thousands of documents that, once discarded could never be recovered, I am indebted to Dorothy Biard. Ora Beth McMullen contributed many hours of painstaking research. Volunteers, interns, and student employees of the Speaker Jim Wright Collection at Texas Christian University, headed by archivist Glenda Stevens, assisted in researching countless details covering the past forty years, helping me to assure factual and historical accuracy. To all of these, my thanks.

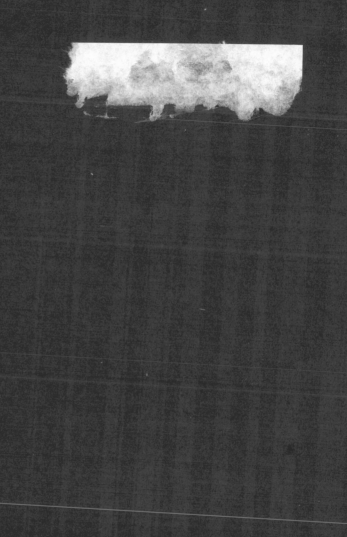